D1631189

60 MINUTES VERBATIM

WHO SAID WHAT TO WHOM
THE COMPLETE TEXT OF 114 STORIES WITH:

MIKE WALLACE
MORLEY SAFER
DAN RATHER
HARRY REASONER

AND

ANDY ROONEY

INTRODUCTION BY WILLIAM A. LEONARD
PRESIDENT, CBS NEWS

ARNO | CBS ⊙
PRESS | NEWS

805513

Library of Congress Cataloging in Publication Data

CBS Inc. CBS News.
  60 minutes verbatim.

  Transcripts of 60 minutes for the 1979 season.
  Includes index.
  1. History, Modern — 1945-   —Sources. 2. United
States — History — 1945-   —Sources. I 60 minutes
(Television program) II. Title.
D848.C23   1980   791.45'72   80-23836

ISBN 0-405-13723-0 hbk
     0-405-14020-7 pbk

Editor's Note: 60 Minutes / Verbatim contains stories aired during the 1979-80 television season. *Text* of stories repeated during the season appear in the book on the date of rebroadcast because they contain the most current information about the subject presented. However, the *titles* of those stories are listed in the table of contents in the order in which they appeared on the program. Stories that have been repeated from previous seasons or that have been revised in any way are so noted.

INTRODUCTION

The theory went something like this. Sooner or later plain folks would tire of watching all that junk on television. They would yearn for something better. And, sooner or later, the writers who turned out that junk would run out of ideas and start repeating themselves to the point of absurdity, because there just wouldn't be enough make-believe to go around. Not at the rate the networks chewed it up. When all of this happened — so the theory went — real life would take over. Reality would push pablum out of prime time.

Serious workers in the reality vineyards, documentarians, news people, and a few program executives, waited for what seemed like generations for the Great Day to arrive. Of course, it never did and probably never will. But something *did* happen. Not at the expense of but in the very midst of regular TV fare.

That something was "60 Minutes."

"60 Minutes" did not burst, but oozed into the prime time television schedule. It was not an overnight success, or even an "overyear" success. Rather, in a world dominated by "here–it–is–which–way–did–it–go" sensations, "60 Minutes" crept to the top over a period of nearly a decade, becoming more and more popular each year until, in the season of 1979–80, it became the most widely viewed (as for half a generation it had been the most widely praised) of all programs on all networks.

A number of people can legitimately claim credit for conceiving "60 Minutes," but one thing should be clearly understood. It was not an "idea" as such. Few series are. Certainly public affairs magazine broadcasts had been around for decades. They varied in success, in critical reaction, and in composition. Some carried more and some less cultural content. In general, the lively arts had a larger niche in early television multi-part broadcasts, such as the widely acclaimed "Omnibus," which played in the days when Sunday afternoon was a ghetto for the serious-minded viewer rather than for the football fan. The seminal "See It Now" often used the multi-part format, particularly in its early days. Gradually, as the 1950s passed into the 60s, the news divisions of the networks first absorbed, and eventually neglected, cultural affairs in favor of longer-form, harder-hitting investigative documentaries on a single subject. These were the broadcasts, like NBC's "The Tunnel" and several of the early "CBS Reports" that shook the nation. The hour form became the accepted expression of news department effort beyond the daily news broadcasts and the occasional "instant specials."

By the mid– to late 1960s, CBS News was producing documentaries at the rate of some 25 a year, mostly in the hour form under the "CBS Reports" rubric. At that time I remember feeling that there was something seriously missing from our coverage. We were doing a good job on the hard news of the day, but then we jumped over to a score or so of major undertakings, with nothing between. The hard news had the attention span of a day, the documentaries of perhaps a year. What about all the stories, problems, personalities, and, yes, scandals, that could not be developed for the evening news but did not merit a full hour or the hundreds of thousands of dollars that it cost to produce a major broadcast? This feeling that our line of products was incomplete — that we were, in effect, publishing *newspapers* and *books* but no *magazines* — was what really stimulated us to try something like "60 Minutes."

It took no stroke of genius to realize that the person best qualified to translate a vague executive itch to "do something" into the reality of a program was in the CBS News shop. That person was, of course, Don Hewitt. The project was put into his hands. The broadcast went on the air in the fall of 1968 at 10 PM every other Tuesday night, alternating with regular documentaries. Mike Wallace and Harry Reasoner were the hosts. Although it was an instant critical success, its ratings were not much higher than the documentaries — certainly nothing special by entertainment standards. A few years later "60 Minutes" was given a regular weekly time slot of its own at 6 PM on Sunday. It began to develop a larger and larger following, limited somewhat by the fact that in the autumn it was preempted by football.

What really put "60 Minutes" over the top in terms of audience was its move to 7 PM every single week . . . prime time. But prime time with a big plus; its competition was young people's family entertainment. This critical move took place in January 1975 against the advice of any number of network experts, but with the firm support of then Broadcast Group President Jack Schneider. It has been onward and upward ever since.

What makes us proudest at CBS News, though, is that "60 Minutes" has endured in quality and influence over the years. It has won countless awards. Hundreds of imitations have sprung up across the land, some of them excellent. Heaven only knows how many young journalists it has inspired, and that may be more important even than the number of wrongs it has righted or frauds it has exposed.

William A. Leonard
President, CBS News
New York, 1980

CONTENTS

INTRODUCTION   v
   William A. Leonard

PROGRAM STAFF, 1979-80   xiii

SEPTEMBER 16, 1979
   On Trial for Murder   1
   Palm Springs   7
   Jesse Jackson & Billy Graham   7
   A Few Minutes with Andy Rooney: on superstars   11

SEPTEMBER 23, 1979
   "Here's . . . Johnny"   12
   Oil in the Bank   12
   Judgment Day   17
   Letters   21

SEPTEMBER 30, 1979
   Castro   23
   Northern Ireland   27
   Getting High in School   33
   Letters   38

OCTOBER 7, 1979
   Who Killed Georgi Markov?   39
   The Luckiest Woman   39
   The $5 Bill   43
   A Few Minutes with Andy Rooney: on water faucets   47
   Letters   48

OCTOBER 14, 1979
   The Stolen Cezannes   49
   Wimpy   56
   The Grapes of Wealth   60
   A Few Minutes with Andy Rooney: on trees   66
   Letters   66

OCTOBER 21, 1979
   Edward Rubin, M.D.   68
   Deep in the Heart of Scotland   73
   By Design   77
   A Few Minutes with Andy Rooney: on candy bars   81
   Letters   82

OCTOBER 28, 1979
Holy Smoke   83
The Pink Panther   88
The Great Depression   93
A Few Minutes with Andy Rooney: on Sunday newspapers   95
Letters   96

NOVEMBER 4, 1979
Swine Flu   98
Pavarotti   104
"Give Me Your Tired . . ."   107
A Few Minutes with Andy Rooney: on names   112
Letters   113

NOVEMBER 11, 1979
Looking Back   115
Marva   115
It's a Doozie   121
A Few Minutes with Andy Rooney: on war and heroism   126
Letters   126

NOVEMBER 18, 1979
The Ayatollah   127
The Foreign Legion   131
Wellness   131
Letters   136

NOVEMBER 25, 1979
Roy Innis   137
Justifiable Homicide?   143
Who Pays? . . . You Do!   149
A Few Minutes with Andy Rooney: on electrical outlets   153
Update   154

DECEMBER 2, 1979
Equal Justice?   155
Safe Haven   160
The Brethren   165
A Few Minutes with Andy Rooney: on Type A and Type Z people   170
Letters   171

DECEMBER 9, 1979
It's No Accident   172
Helping   172
Garn Baum vs. the Mormons   177
Letters   181

DECEMBER 16, 1979
The Hooker Memos   183
Earn It!   189

Snake Venom   195
A Few Minutes with Andy Rooney: on sizes   199
Letters   199

DECEMBER 23, 1979
"Who Gives a Damn?"   200
The Sheik   200
Hypnosis   205
Letters   210
Update   210
Harry Reasoner: on Christmas   210

DECEMBER 30, 1979
Big John   212
Come Fly with Me   219
Roy Cohn   224
Letters   229

JANUARY 6, 1980
CCCP-TV in Moscow   230
B.M.O.C.   234
Native Sons   239
Letters   244

JANUARY 13, 1980
Deee-fense   245
Off the Books   251
George Who?   256
A Few Minutes with Andy Rooney: on saving   261
Letters   261

JANUARY 20, 1980
Bette Davis   263
The Thunderbirds   269
PDAP   271
A Few Minutes with Andy Rooney: on football   278
Letters   279

JANUARY 27, 1980
Russian Spies in the U.S.A.   280
All About Oral   284
The Frontrunner?   289
A Few Minutes with Andy Rooney: on following directions   294
Letters   294

FEBRUARY 3, 1980
Losers   296
Ezer   302
Wild to Regulate   308
Letters   313

FEBRUARY 10, 1980
Mr. "X"   314
"Lenny"   318
The Marketplace   323
A Few Minutes with Andy Rooney: on the draft   327
Letters   328

FEBRUARY 17, 1980
The Death of Edward Nevin   330
Anderson of Illinois   334
Yugoslavia   339
A Few Minutes with Andy Rooney: on hair   343
Update   344
Letters   344

FEBRUARY 24, 1980
Uncle Sam Wants Your Money   346
Where There's a Will   349
Citizen Loeb   354
A Few Minutes with Andy Rooney: on public art   359
Update   360
Letters   360

MARCH 2, 1980
The Iran File   362
Handcuffing the Cops?   371
Letters   371

MARCH 9, 1980
Oman   372
Bobby Knight   377
Barry Goldwater   382
A Few Minutes with Andy Rooney: on sales and coupons   386
Letters   386

MARCH 16, 1980
Remember Enewetak!   388
Blood Money   393
Cat Burglars   399
Letters   403

MARCH 23, 1980
The Riddle of DMSO   405
Jarrett vs. Jarrett   411
Libya's Qaddafi   415
A Few Minutes with Andy Rooney: on signs   418
Letters   419

MARCH 30, 1980
Looking Out for Mrs. Berwid   420

Strike Two!   426
One of Hitler's Favorites   430
A Few Minutes with Andy Rooney: on dogs   434
Letters   434

APRIL 6, 1980
Inside Afghanistan   436
High-Low Silver   445
A Few Minutes with Andy Rooney: on the costs of living   450
Letters   451
Update   452

APRIL 13, 1980
Scientology: The Clearwater Conspiracy   453
Gimme Shelter   459
Israeli Arms For Sale   465
Letters   469

APRIL 20, 1980
Omega 7   471
Anne Lindbergh   478
Dam   482
Letters   487

APRIL 27, 1980
Walking Small in Pitkin Country   488
"Here's . . . Johnny"   493
$200 a Week — Tax Free   500
A Few Minutes with Andy Rooney: on watches   505
Letters   505

MAY 4, 1980
The Kissinger-Shah Connection?   507
Palm Springs   513
"Not to My Kid, You Don't!"   517
A Few Minutes with Andy Rooney: on mail fantasies   521
Letters   522

MAY 11, 1980
Bonnie   524
Highway Robbery   529
Fellini   536
A Few Minutes with Andy Rooney: on cars   538
Letters   539

MAY 18, 1980
The Establishment vs. Dr. Burton   541
Who Killed Georgi Markov?   547
The Rock   552
Letters   554

MAY 25, 1980
Warning: Living Here May be Hazardous to Your Health!   555
Memory of Vietnam   560
Hired Gun   565
Letters   573

JUNE 1, 1980
A Nuclear Reaction   574
A Man Called L'Amour   579
This Year at Marienbad   584
A Few Minutes with Andy Rooney: on flowers   588

JUNE 8, 1980
Banking on Bahrain   589
God and Mammon   593
Cottage For Sale   600
Letters   605

JUNE 15, 1980
What Johnny Can't Read   606
The Foreign Legion   610
"Who Gives a Damn?"   615
A Few Minutes with Andy Rooney: on kitchen gadgets   619
Letters   620

JUNE 22, 1980
Canary   621
Handcuffing the Cops?   624
Rolls-Royce   631
Letters   635

INDEX   637

PROGRAM STAFF, 1979-80

Executive Producer
Don Hewitt

Managing Editor
Palmer Williams

Senior Producer
Philip Scheffler

Unit Producer
Merri Lieberthal

Director of Operations
Joe Illigasch

Director
Arthur Bloom

Graphics
Billy Sunshine

Producers

Joel Bernstein
Greg Cooke
Leslie Edwards
Steve Glauber
Marion Goldin
Norman Gorin
Jim Jackson

Barry Lando
Nancy Lea
Paul Loewenwarter
Allan Maraynes
William McClure
Igor Oganesoff

Drew Phillips
Martin Phillips
Jeanne Solomon
Suzanne St. Pierre
John Tiffin
Al Wasserman
Joe Wershba

Film Editors

Abid Ali
Ed Archer
Tony Baldo
Judy Benenson
Susan Braddon
Peter Callam

Antonietta Castro
Kenneth Dalglish
Hank Greenberg
Nick Harding
Stephen Milne
Joe Murania

Dick Sarna
Steve Sheppard
Hugh Thompson
Jim Trainor
David Turecamo
Alan Wegman

Vice President & Director of
Public Affairs Broadcasts

Robert Chandler

SEPTEMBER 16, 1979

On Trial for Murder

HARRY MOSES, PRODUCER

MIKE WALLACE: Does a doctor have the right to decide whether a new-born baby he judges to be brain-damaged, poisoned, dying, does he have the right to let that baby die without taking heroic measures to save its life? That was the issue last spring in Orange County, California, where Dr. William Waddill, a gynecologist and obstetrician, was on trial for murder. Dr. Waddill had been hired to perform a legal abortion — a legal abortion. But when the fetus unexpectedly emerged showing genuine life signs, the attending pediatrician accused Dr. Waddill of killing it by strangulation. Dr. Waddill denied that charge. But he did admit he had done nothing to help the infant survive, for he contends that, had it lived, it would have been severely brain-damaged.

Now, the State of California says there was little difference between Waddill's alleged act of commission, the alleged act of strangling the baby, and his admitted act of omission, of failing to take heroic measures to save the child. Either way, said the state, Dr. Waddill had committed murder. Assistant D.A. Bob Chatterton put that issue in the courtroom, where 60 MINUTES had been granted permission to bring its cameras.

ROBERT CHATTERTON (in court): We have the contention that there has been in this case no hint that Dr. Waddill didn't do everything he could. No hint? Have I

1

missed my point in three months? There's no hint that he didn't do everything he could? What did he do? What *did* he do? I submit to you he did everything he could to be sure that the baby didn't live.

WALLACE: Defending Dr. Waddill is attorney Charles Weedman.

CHARLES WEEDMAN (in court):   You haven't had a hint in this case that Dr. Waddill did not do everything that should have been done in this case — that *should* have been done in this case — and not a hint that he is anything but a capable, well-trained, responsible, caring physician.

WALLACE: Until two years ago, 43-year-old Bill Waddill had a half-million-dollar-a-year medical practice, administering gynecological care, delivering babies and performing legal abortions. He continues to work out of this elaborate suite of offices in Orange County, California, though his practice is severely diminished since he was caught up at the center of the murder trial.

The case against Dr. Waddill began back in 1977. He had agreed to perform an abortion on an 18-year-old unwed high school girl named Mary Weaver. She had told him she was 22 weeks pregnant. So the doctor used an abortion technique common with advanced pregnancies: the injection of a saline solution into her uterus. The saline fatally poisons the fetus by inducing hemorrhages in its circulatory system. And then, some 24 to 36 hours after the injection, the dead fetus is expelled from the mother's womb.

Over the years, Dr. Waddill had performed hundreds of saline abortions without incident, but there was a miscalculation on this one, for the three-pound fetus was older by several weeks than either the mother or Dr. Waddill had realized, and it was discharged from the womb not yet completely dead.

Dr. Waddill was reached immediately by phone, and his reaction was instantaneous. "Don't do a goddamn thing for that baby except give it oxygen until I get there," he said.

Dr. Cornelsen is the Chief of Pediatrics at the hospital where Dr. Waddill performed the Weaver abortion. When Dr. Waddill arrived in the hospital nursery to examine the Weaver baby, he cleared the room of all other personnel and asked that Cornelsen be called in. Cornelsen testified that he saw Waddill strangling the baby. But Waddill says, not true; what he did was feel the baby's neck for the infant's failing pulse.

You're on trial for murder because you are accused of strangling the baby. Did you?

DR. WILLIAM WADDILL: No, of course I didn't.

WALLACE: Are you convinced in your own mind that Bill Waddill murdered baby Weaver?

DR. RONALD CORNELSEN: Oh, there's no question in my mind as to what I saw and what took place, yes.

DR. WADDILL: Mike, you don't call in somebody to witness a murder.

WALLACE: If he is putting pressure on the neck, the throat of this baby, that's — and you're a chief of pediatrics — and it goes on for 15 minutes, and you watch and you don't say, "Hey, Bill, wait a minute!"

DR. CORNELSEN: I was frightened. I did not know what was taking place. It was a totally strange situation with only the obstetrician back there telling me that this baby came out a— alive from a saline abortion and it can't live, otherwise it's going to be a big mess, and there's going to be all sorts of lawsuits and — you know, these are all sorts of things that really at least panicked me to the point where I — I just — if you want to call it, I didn't have the guts to intervene.

WALLACE: This is the Orange County courthouse in Santa Ana, California, where Dr. Waddill has spent almost eight months of the last two years on trial for murder. The first trial ended in a hung jury. His second trial began in February of 1979 and wound up in June. We'll see the closing arguments and learn the verdict later on.

Dr. Waddill was prosecuted in both trials by Bob Chatterton, and the Waddill matter was more than just a case for Chatterton, it was a cause. For he believes that Waddill, having concluded that if the baby survived it would have suffered brain damage from the saline solution and would be in effect a vegetable, that Waddill took it upon himself to see that the baby died. And Chatterton says Waddill did not have the right to do that.

Suppose the strangulation issue did not exist, Mr. Chatterton, would you still prosecute Dr. Waddill for murder?

CHATTERTON: Absolutely.

WALLACE: Why?

CHATTERTON: Because he's still guilty of two other things that — that are just as responsible for that baby's death as the strangulation.

WALLACE: Number one?

CHATTERTON: He prevented the people from the hospital who wanted to help, who wanted to — to — to give medical care to the baby, he prevented them from doing it. He ordered them out of the room. And secondly, when he was there, he did nothing himself. He sat there and watched the baby dying.

DR. WADDILL: You know, there's a difference between resuscitation and resurrection, and there's nothing I could have done that would have made this baby survive. Had, by the wildest stretch of the imagination — and, of course, all things are possible — this baby survived, it would have been totally brain-damaged.

WALLACE: Is it not possible that the doctor has the right at that moment to say, "I'm not going to help this baby to survive?"

CHATTERTON: No, he doesn't have that right.

WALLACE: Who has the right?

CHATTERTON: You see, my belief is that the right to life is an individual right. You have it, I have it, little babies have it. And nobody has the right to take that individual right away from another.

WALLACE: Apparently you believe it was perfectly all right for Dr. Waddill, in effect, to kill that baby when it was in its mother's womb.

CHATTERTON: Legally it was.

WALLACE: Six inches away from the womb, it's murder.

CHATTERTON: That's right. And the reason for that is that, while a mother has a right not to be burdened by carrying a fetus that she doesn't want, she has no right to expect that, once it is separated from her, that that baby be killed, that that baby be terminated. That baby now becomes an individual and, just like you and I, it has its individual rights, it has its constitutional rights, it has the right to demand medical treatment.

WALLACE: It just doesn't know about it.

CHATTERTON: It hasn't learned yet.

WALLACE: You think that you have the right, in other words, to make that decision? In effect to say, "This child shall live, this child shall either die or be permitted to die" — that's your responsibility as a doctor?

DR. WADDILL: Yes, I do.

WALLACE: Well, what about it? What is the responsibility of a doctor in a life-or-death situation? Does he have the right to make a judgment call? This is the intensive-care unit for newborns at UCLA Hospital. And here at UCLA, Professor of Pediatrics Dr. Bernard Towers, a witness for the defense in the Waddill trial, directs a program in medicine, law and human values.

Had you been Dr. Waddill and you were ten minutes away, and you call the hospital and they say the baby is alive, or whatever was said to him, what would you have said?

DR. BERNARD TOWERS: I would have said, under those circumstances, that it was inappropriate to — to resuscitate, because that fetus — and I don't refer to it as a baby; it was fetus, developing in utero — had been subjected to a high level of saline, which it had ingested. Almost always those fetuses are dead when they are aborted, and the reason probably is that they have taken in what in effect is a poison.

WALLACE: You're saying that Dr. Waddill, or any doctor under similar circumstances, has the right to make a judgment, a judgment call, as to the viability of a given human life?

DR. TOWERS: I think so. I think we have to rely upon the clinical judgment of the physician to determine what the prognosis is.

WALLACE: You made a judgment call, if you will, through panic or whatever, not to do anything. He made a judgment call, through panic, to do something because he believed, apparently, that baby should not live. He may go to prison, and you're going to help him go there.

DR. CORNELSEN: Oh, don't say that. It's uncomfortable.

WALLACE: Well, it's uncomfortable, but it's the fact. You are the chief witness of the prosecution against your colleague.

DR. CORNELSEN: That's true.

WALLACE: One judgment call against the other.

DR. WADDILL: There was nothing that could be done. I made that decision, and I did not make the wrong decision.

WALLACE: You would perform heroic measures to keep that damaged, brain-damaged, baby alive?

DR. CORNELSEN: See, you're diagnosing brain damage. You don't know. I don't know. You know, I — I can't assume brain damage. I — I can tell you a — a horrendous story of a — a drowning: a five-year-old brought in by the paramedics, resuscitated at poolside with electroshock treatment to the heart three different times; took her into the intensive-care unit; had her full of tubes, everything you could think of. And I remember on two different occasions I came in and I stood at Tracy's bedside, and I said, "Tracy, die. Quit putting me through all this pressure." I said, "Just — just give up." And, you know, I knew darned well I was going to keep treating her; no way I was going to give up. So I sent her over to the Children's Hospital, where they have a more progressive rehabilitation department. From there they sent her to Rancho Los Amigos in Los Angeles.

And I more or less lose trace of what's happening over the next year, year and a half. And one day here in my office I come out of a room, and here comes Tracy. (Starts crying) It's — it's hard for me to talk about, but she says, "Hi, Dr. Cornelsen." Walking down the — the hallway, and it's — to this day I just — tears me up.

WALLACE: Are the cases of Tracy and of baby Weaver so similar that you think the same thing could have happened with baby Weaver?

DR. CORNELSEN: I really have no doubt in my mind. I think everybody that has a sign of life is entitled to at least an effort of either developing potential or at least preserving what potential is there. But I don't think as a physician I have any right to say — do harm to the patient.

WALLACE: The question is, Dr. Towers, suppose that there is a chance that this child could survive at 75 or 80 or 85 percent of what we regard as normal, does the doctor have the right to take away that chance?

DR. TOWERS: I think that a physician who judges that this fetus or this premature baby doesn't have a chance of survival, then I think he would be wrong to initiate resuscitative supports, because the first rule in medicine is, first, do no harm — do no harm to your patient. And the question is whether, by trying to preserve life, all you are doing is prolonging death. And if you prolong death, then everything that you do during the interval between initiating that and the death is an assault upon the person. You're doing harm to that per— every time you take a blood sample, every time you — every time you do anything. If the patient is dying, then you are harming that patient by not allowing them to die in peace and dignity.

WALLACE: And Dr. Waddill's attorney, Charles Weedman, argues that the physician has the responsibility to make tough judgment calls.

WEEDMAN: He has the responsibility to — to society and to that patient and to that patient's family and loved ones to make that medical judgment.

WALLACE: Who says so?

WEEDMAN: It has been — it — it has been that way. That is the way it is at the present time. Patients who are totally brain-damaged but who nonetheless still have some heart rate, some respiration, are allowed to die in hospital settings. It goes on every single day.

WALLACE: Do you have any doubt that a good deal of this goes on every day in hospitals from coast to coast?

CHATTERTON: I think it probably goes on a lot more than any of us even realize, and as long as the secrets of hospitals are kept behind hospital doors, without nurses talking, without other doctors talking, protecting each other, it will continue to go unprosecuted, unpunished.

WALLACE: You have said there's going to be a Bob Chatterton looking over the shoulder of every doctor in the country after this.

CHATTERTON: Not only do they have to watch out for me, but they're going to have to start watching out for people in the hospital —

WALLACE: Well, why is —

CHATTERTON: — the nurses, other doctors, who maybe will even look at this case as an example of what can happen; that prosecutors are interested, and the prosecutors will do something.

WEEDMAN: We're trying to avoid that. It would be a terrible thing for a physician to feel that every time he does what he feels he's ethically, morally obligated to do and in which he is supported by sound medical opinion, that he's risking a criminal prosecution.

DR. TOWERS: Are we then going to be guilty of homicide when the patient's heart stops and we don't start it up again? Or is it an appropriate clinical judgment to say that there comes a point in time when there is really no value for the patient, there's no advantage to the patient, to be resuscitated?

WALLACE: That's what this whole case is about.

DR. TOWERS: Yeah.

WALLACE: But the other side would say to you, Dr. Towers, how do we know that there's no value? How do we know that there isn't a life here? Maybe a mistake was made in the injection of the saline. Maybe this is an exceptionally strong baby. Maybe, maybe, maybe.

DR. TOWERS: Uh-hmm. Uh-hmm. Well, this is exactly the case. Can you trust Dr. Waddill's judgment or can't you? And the lawyers are trying to say, yes, we can or, no, we can't.

CHATTERTON (in court):   There was a baby so strong in its desire to live that it was able to survive for half an hour with no help, and despite the efforts of Dr. Waddill. We don't expect doctors to accomplish miracles, only that they try.

WEEDMAN (in court):   This is a murder case, a case where you're being asked to — to convict Dr. Waddill of the most serious of all crimes. And under the circumstances of this case, may I say that Dr. Waddill is not guilty, and you should not fear, any of you, to render that decision in this case.

WALLACE: The jury that heard the case in this courtroom deliberated over a period of nine days to no decision, and though they finally voted eleven to one for Dr. Waddill's acquittal, still it was a hung jury, and the judge finally dismissed all charges against the doctor.

And still the question nags: Who should have the right, the power, to determine that a human life will be meaningless, useless, and that it should be terminated? Should the state? The doctor? The family? The trial of Dr. Waddill raised those questions, but it settled nothing.

Palm Springs

See May 4, 1980, page 513

Jesse Jackson
& Billy Graham

LESLIE EDWARDS, PRODUCER

DAN RATHER: In the 1950's and sixties, America's blacks and America's Jews marched together in the struggle for black civil rights. In the seventies, as black objectives turned more to economic goals and affirmative-action programs, the alliance between black and Jewish leadership began to sour.

Blacks were incensed at Jewish opposition in the Bakke, DeFunis and Webber Supreme Court cases — cases dealing with college quotas and job quotas. And as the oil squeeze, with all that implies for blacks on the lower rung of the economic ladder, became an issue, the struggle between Israel and the Palestinians began to divide further America's blacks and America's Jews. And it all came to a head last month when the resignation of U.N. Ambassador Andrew Young over contact with Palestinians, touched off a new wave of hot words between black and Jewish leaders.

We asked two leading American clergymen, the Reverend Jesse Jackson, whose reaction to the Young resignation was a major factor in the current controversy, and long-time supporter of Israel, the Reverend Billy Graham — we asked them if the Young dispute and other issues dividing blacks and Jews is leading to a fresh outbreak of anti-Semitism in this country.

Reverend Graham, let me ask you, first of all, do you see a new wave of anti-Semitism building in this country?

THE REVEREND BILLY GRAHAM: I think anti-Semitism is always just under the surface, and I think we Christians especially, because of our past history, have to be on guard that there's not one slight blade of anti-Semitism grows in the Christian church.

RATHER: I'm thinking specifically, it seems to me that the further we go in support of Israel, the greater danger we run of touching off some new explosion of anti-Semitism here.

REVEREND GRAHAM: I don't see it at the moment, unless the oil crisis — you know, people sometimes will vote their pocketbooks more than their con— their moral convictions, and this could be a danger.

RATHER: But you see it as a possibility?

REVEREND GRAHAM: It is a possibility, I think, and — and could be a dangerous possibility.

RATHER: I'm thinking of the —

REVEREND GRAHAM: And people like me will — will — in the evangelical world that I represent would come out very strongly and — and denounce any type of anti-Semitism that we see appearing.

RATHER: Well, that was to be my next question. What are you prepared to do about that?

REVEREND GRAHAM: I'm prepared to take a full, all-out stand.

RATHER: I was thinking particularly of — many of your fellow Christian ministers who are black have recently been saying that if we continue to support Israel as a nation, then we're going to go through such things as oil shortages, and blacks, who are frequently low into the economic scale, will suffer. That is, a — when the price of heating oil goes up, it's tougher on someone at the low end of the economic scale.

REVEREND GRAHAM: Well, remember that more than — by far the majority of black people in America are church people. Some of the greatest Christians we have in the United States are black people. And most of your leadership in the civil rights movement were clergymen. And they know what they owe to the Jew. And I cannot see that — I can see that among some of the more secular or some people who perhaps don't know their Bibles, but when — when they realize how much we owe to the — to the Jewish people, I don't think you're going to see an uprising among blacks against Jewish people. Because they marched with them in the civil rights movement, and no group stood by them more than — than Jewish people during that period of the struggle through these years. And I think they owe a debt to them as well.

RATHER: So, how did relations between blacks and Jews deteriorate from those days when they marched together?

THE REVEREND JESSE JACKSON: The last ten years there has been a certain smoldering in the black and Jewish relations. We found ourselves together in the fifties and the sixties — indeed, before then — as we were fighting for decency. The Jews understand rejection. We were being rejected. There was identification there. But as we moved from sharing decency to sharing power, we found ourselves on different sides of the table.

RATHER: You said before — and I believe that you said a moment ago, if I heard you correctly — that as long as it was a matter of dealing with decency and trying to get decency, that you found Americans of Jewish heritage at your side; but when it came to trying to share power, that they wouldn't share it.

REVEREND JACKSON: Correct. In other words, with all of the talk of the black-Jewish alliance, we don't own radio stations together, we don't own TV stations together, we don't own banks together, we do not share in — in the ownership of the industries they have begun to get some hold on together. There is no economic substance in our relationship. There's tremendous identification with our — with our mutual rejection, with — with the Jewish Holocaust of World War II with the black slavery and the black holocaust. But once we beyon — move beyond our common heritage in suffering, there is no real economic substance, because our confrontations came over our drive for upward mobility. DeFunis and — and Bakke were drives for blacks to get equity and parity. And — and in many instances, when — when basic white America knew we were right and did not move, it — it was our confrontation with Jewish intellectuals and others who — because the real confrontation of the use of the word "quota." Because of institutional rejection, blacks see quotas as a way of — of locking us in, because we've always been locked out. Jews have a different experience with the concept quota. The quota was used to lock them out. We've tried to get locked in.

And so, there has been a heated confrontation over that issue, and — and the Andy Young situation simply blew the cap off the oil well. But the force has been building for — for at least ten years.

RATHER: All right, well, is it fair to say, then, that the explosion of black resentment against Jews in the wake of the Andy Young resignation was more about what the Jewish community had done or been perceived as doing in the court cases than it was having anything to do with the Middle East?

REVEREND JACKSON: Well, I think it would be fair to say that this was the end result of a long train of conflicts and it — and — and so it — it exploded.

RATHER: Let me ask you about what Jesse Jackson believes. Do you recognize the Palestinian Liberation Organization as the legitimate representative of the Palestinian people?

REVEREND JACKSON: Yes, I do. Some of their methods and techniques I abhor. I — I do not embrace the — their terrorism. And if we talk, we can begin to challenge PLO to — to accept Israel's right to exist. I think to accept PLO at — at a level with which we communicate with them is to be in a position to take out of their sting this real commitment to destroy Israel.

RATHER: How can a follower of Martin Luther King, who was the symbol of nonviolence in this country and to so much of the world, have anything to do with an organization such as the PLO, which is engaged in so much terrorism?

REVEREND JACKSON: Well, one could easily say that how could one identify with Israel with the continuous violations that — that they express in — in dropping their bombs on — on south Lebanon and using U.S. equipment?

RATHER: You know that they say that's different, that falls in a different category.

REVEREND JACKSON: Well, but that's not true. South Africa is — is consummate terrorism, a state of terrorism, and — and Israel has expanding relationship with South Africa. Israel sent military equipment to Somoza. This notion that — that Israel is — is innocent is not true. Israel has a right to exist, and I support Israel's right to exist. And I think America must do it for at least three reasons: morally, because our word is with Israel; secondly, because of our five-million-dollar-day investment that indicates some interest on the part of this country for Israel; and thirdly, because of the geopolitics, our military strategic position there. But at one and the same time, we cannot get bogged down into — into the agony of the last funeral. Somebody must rise above the acts of terrorism that are involved in daily war.

RATHER: Are you willing to meet with Yasir Arafat?

REVEREND JACKSON: Yes, I — I am willing to meet with Yasir Arafat.

RATHER: Why?

REVEREND JACKSON: I'm willing to meet with — with Menachem Begin. I'm willing to meet with — with Dayan. If Moshe Dayan can — can meet with PLO people — and I think that's valid — then Secretary Vance can meet with PLO people. I think that — that's also valid. I think if they — if — if — if Mr. Arafat is — is interested in a — a broader base of people in this country concerned about the — a sympathic understanding of — of Palestinian people, he must hear that which we have to say. And I think we must contend to him that — that we know

— we know and feel that Israel has a right to exist, and he should change that posture. And secondly, that his — that his threatening symbolism does not add substance to his position. It's a diversion in the real quest of the Palestinian people.

RATHER: You have to know, Reverend Jesse Jackson — one of, if perhaps not the, best-known black leader in this country at the moment — that if you meet with Yasir Arafat, you are, number one, going to scare the hell out of anyone who cares and cares deeply about Israel; and number two, that those who care and care deeply about Israel will never forgive you for that?

REVEREND JACKSON: I would hope that — that our Jewish brothers and sisters would — would appreciate this — this quest for freedom, and would — and would pull for us to be successful. I mean, they have not been able to do it. Perhaps we can do it. You see, if there is a — if there's a hot war in the Middle East, blacks will die first. We're 35 percent of the ground forces. If there's a cold war, we will starve first. We have a vested interest, and some identification, with the — with the plight of Palestinian people, because they are an oppressed people. We cannot be inconsistent in our concern for human rights. But thirdly, we have, as a people and as a nation, a vested interest in peace.

RATHER: Let me set the record straight on a few things. Are you or your organization currently getting money from Arab sources?

REVEREND JACKSON: No, we're not. We do not get money from any Arab sources, but — but Jews and Arabs do business together. Arabs have money in Jewish banks. I mean, why should we be cut off from access to the — to the economic flow of the world?

RATHER: Do I take that to mean that you're not opposed to accepting Arab money under certain circumstances?

REVEREND JACKSON: If it's valid.

RATHER: Reverend Jackson, I've talked to a number of Jewish leaders, and I can tell you, if you don't know already—and I suspect you do—that what they're most concerned about is a new wave of anti-Semitism. Aren't you running a real and present danger of unleashing anti-Semitism?

REVEREND JACKSON: Well, that's not true. It's unfortunate that — that the concern for opening up talks with PLO is not anti-Semitic; it's — it's pro-peace. So I think that the name-calling and the labeling is very cheap. But — but I sensed in — in no wise amongst black people any — any anti-Semitism. We simply have the right to speak on international issues, and we simply must be trusted to operate in the national interest and — and in our allies' interest.

RATHER: Billy Graham believes that a peace conference convened by the Pope could be the solution to problems that worry Jesse Jackson, the Jews and the Palestinians.

REVEREND JACKSON: I think Pope John Paul II has probably more moral influence in the world right at this moment than almost any other person in this century, and I would like to see him call a sort of a tremendous peace prayer conference about the Middle East. I think it would have a tremendous impact.

RATHER: Mr. Graham, have you been in touch with the Pope or anyone in the Vatican about this proposal?

REVEREND GRAHAM: I wouldn't be able to say at this time.

RATHER: I'll let that pass, but with a notation that indicates to me that you probably have.

No word about a date for the papal peace conference, or even if it will actually take place. But Jesse Jackson's meeting with Yasir Arafat will take place the latter part of this month in Beirut, Lebanon. En route to Lebanon, Jackson says he will visit Israel, and he has requested a meeting with Prime Minister Begin. And further, about Arab money, Jackson says he wants none of it for himself or his organization, but that he will urge the rich Arab nations to contribute to black education and economic development in Africa and America.

A Few Minutes with Andy Rooney

HARRY REASONER: Now that we're back for another season, can Andy Rooney be far behind?

ANDY ROONEY: I bought this book the other day called *Superstars*. It has 67 pictures of actors and actresses that the author thinks are superstars. It's fun to look through, but I think we ought to be more careful who we call superstars. I mean, look at the cover of this thing: Lauren Bacall and Humphrey Bogart. Are they both superstars? They're not. Bogart's a superstar. Lauren Bacall's a good actress.

Look at some of these. Katharine Hepburn — I agree with that. John Wayne — of course. Shirley Temple? Yes. Elizabeth Taylor? Afraid not. Barbra Streisand? Afraid so. Sean Connery? Of course not. Greta Garbo? Yes. Clark Gable? Yes. Dustin Hoffman? Good actor, but no superstar. Frank Sinatra? Yes. Sylvester Stallone? You're kidding!

It's so clear to me who the superstars are and who they aren't in various fields that I thought I'd tell you some of them. For instance, in the last 50 years we've had nine presidents. Only two of them were superstars: Franklin Delano Roosevelt, John F. Kennedy. You don't necessarily have to like someone to know they're superstars.

Baseball. Babe Ruth? Certainly a superstar. Roger Maris, broke Babe Ruth's home run record — not a superstar. The last superstars to play baseball were Willie Mays, Hank Aaron.

Boxing. Joe Louis? Superstar. Muhammad Ali? Superstar. Rocky Marciano, who retired undefeated — no.

Joe Namath was the last football superstar, even though he wasn't as good as Fran Tarkenton.

Okay, here's some more entertainers. I know you look to me for an answer in matters like this, so I thought I'd tell you some superstars. Farrah Fawcett-Majors? No. Jean Harlow? Yes. Marilyn Monroe? Yes. Brigitte Bardot? No. Elvis Presley? Superstar. Mick Jagger? Not a superstar. Wayne Newton? Not a superstar. Bob Hope? Sure.

A superstar is always a person who has something more than skill and talent that attracts the rest of us to him. In this business, Walter Cronkite's a superstar. Of the four correspondents on 60 MINUTES, two of them are and two of them aren't.

SEPTEMBER 23, 1979

"Here's . . . Johnny"

See April 27, 1980, page 493

Oil in the Bank

PHILIP SCHEFFLER, PRODUCER

DAN RATHER: What America needs is oil in the bank. That's what Congress said after the OPEC oil embargo six years ago. We'll put a billion barrels of oil into a strategic reserve, store that oil in salt caverns and abandoned salt mines against the day when foreign oil supplies again dry up or even slow down. But when long lines appeared at the gas pumps last spring, there wasn't enough oil in the bank to really make any difference. And what little there was couldn't have been taken out anyway. The pumps weren't ready. The price tag at the start? An estimated six billion dollars to buy the oil and store it. Now the best guess is 40 billion, if – *if* – the project ever gets finished.

I'm walking 750 feet beneath the surface of the Louisiana coast. It's dark and hot and eerie down here. One almost has the feeling of being on another planet. For

77 years this was a salt mine. This was the stuff — mostly rock salt, of the kind sent to the north for use on city streets during winter snowstorms. This is the old Morton Salt Mine at Weeks Island, Louisiana, one of five places in Louisiana and Texas the Department of Energy picked to store crude oil. Four years ago, the Ford Administration set a goal of 150 million barrels to be stored in the ground by the end of 1978. One hundred fifty million barrels is only about 17 days' worth of imported oil — just a drop in the pipeline, so to speak. But to reach even that goal in three years from a standing start was felt to be attainable only if everything worked perfectly. But before a single drop of oil was in the ground, the incoming Carter Administration upped the goal to 250 million barrels by the same December 1978 target date.

TOM NOEL: They were greatly impressed with the possibility of some Middle Eastern disturbance in the early years of the Administration, and they intended to do everything they knew how to do to minimize the impact of that on our country.

RATHER: Tom Noel was picked by the Ford Administration to head the oil reserve, and he was carried over into the Carter-James Schlesinger Department of Energy. He told us he felt there was an outside chance of meeting the Ford goal, but that the new Carter timetable put the project on a downhill slide from which it was impossible to recover.

NOEL: What they did not do is fully consider in a pragmatic, practical way what the impact of making — you know, scratching out 150 and writing 250 might have.

RATHER: Is that what the Carter Administration did, in your judgment?

NOEL: In my judgment, it did.

RATHER: Now, was this a case of over-optimism?

NOEL: On their part?

RATHER: On their part and, for that matter, on your part.

NOEL: I don't think I'd call it optimism. I would call it maybe idealism.

RATHER: Call it optimism or idealism, one impact of the Carter Administration decision to speed up the project can be seen here at the Weeks Island salt mine. It cost $120 million just to prepare this one abandoned mine to receive the oil. And according to the DOE timetable, the first of 75 million barrels of crude this mine can hold was supposed to have come pouring in September 15th. In fact, no oil was pumped in, and there will be no oil pumped in in the foreseeable future.

GOVERNOR EDWIN EDWARDS: They've rushed ahead and expended tremendous sums of money, but don't have the first barrel of oil to put in there.

RATHER: Louisiana's Governor Edwin Edwards is delighted the Department of Energy decided to spend all those millions at Weeks Island and the other storage sites in his state. Still, he has been and is the strategic oil reserve's leading critic.

GOVERNOR EDWARDS: Because the people who planned the program, I'm convinced, were trying to do too much too fast with too little, both in manpower, technology and the availability of oil. The only thing they had plenty of was money. And the money could have much been — better been spent in other areas trying to resolve the energy problems.

RATHER: I'm walking on 11 million barrels of oil stored in a salt dome. This facility could store up to 16 million barrels of oil, and therein lies the biggest current problem in this problem-plagued effort to give the United States a workable strategic oil reserve. A few years ago when the oil was available, the facilities were not ready. Now, when the facilities are ready, the oil is not available at anything near an acceptable price.

GOVERNOR EDWARDS: We should have been storing oil, if we were going to move into this program, at a time when it was possible to buy oil on the ready market at a reasonable price, and not when we were suffering from the shortages and scarcity which we have in America now. It is ill-advised, if it's for the expressed purpose of the Congress that it's there to take care of America's needs in the event of an embargo.

RATHER: What —

GOVERNOR EDWARDS: It just will not accomplish that purpose.

RATHER: That's what I was going to say. That's what Congress says this program is for.

GOVERNOR EDWARDS: Then — then it cannot and will not accomplish that purpose, except for a matter of 10 days, if you will look at what is now in the — in the ground; and 60 to 70 days, if you look at what they will have at a — at the ultimate stored in the ground under the program.

RATHER: Do you think it's too strong to say they're kidding themselves if they think it's going to serve that purpose?

GOVERNOR EDWARDS: Maybe so, but not us.

RATHER: They're not kidding you.

GOVERNOR EDWARDS: Not kidding me.

RATHER: The Department of Energy may not be kidding Governor Edwards, but they have been kidding almost everyone else — some would call it deceiving — about how much this mammoth project would cost, and in predicting how quickly the oil would be in the ground.

The project was in such shambles a year ago that retired Air Force Brigadier General Joseph DeLuca, a man with the reputation as one of the government's best management experts, was brought in to try to make some sense of the program.

JOSEPH DeLUCA: Vast construction job, underestimated. With the underest— personal opinion; my apologies to my predecessors — with the underestimation of the construction job, I subsequently believe, was the inadequacy of the management structure devoted to do that job.

RATHER: The first two years of the project were a case study in bureaucratic inefficiency, and everything that could go wrong did. In the first place, the project was run entirely out of Washington.

DeLUCA: We had too many differing contracts. In other words, we'd have contracts with pipeline engineers, contracts with dock engineers, contracts with cavern engineers, contracts with sustaining engineers or executive engineers; differing contracts for equipment, differing contracts for services, differing contracts for drilling. And all of these at different sites; and all of these then were umbrellaed in a Washington staff. And it just became, as the physical progress of the program came on line, it just became impossible to effectively manage so many differing contracts that had similar endeavors or missions.

RATHER: In order to speed up the process, existing caverns in natural salt domes were purchased at premium prices, and about one-quarter of those turned out to be unusable for one reason or another. Construction contracts were let and starting dates set before sites were acquired. And contractors had to be paid while waiting to start work. Oil tankers arrived before storage caverns were ready. Eight million dollars in overcharges for ships waiting to unload. Long after the project was first budgeted, they decided they didn't have a good way of getting the oil to the caverns, so a port and storage tanks and pipelines were added. Two hundred fifty million dollars extra there. At one site, a storage cavern exploded, spilling 72,000 barrels of oil and killing a workman. Inadequate safety precautions were blamed.

One of the biggest early problems was the acquisition of 200 miles of pipeline right-of-way; some 500 individual sections of land involved, several thousand individual owners. Among other things, the owners claimed that oil and gas companies traditionally had paid much more for right-of-way than the federal government was offering. Eventually, the Department of Energy went into court to seize the right-of-way through condemnation proceedings. They got rights to the land they needed, but they left behind a lot of hard feelings in Louisiana. Rightly or wrongly, the general feeling around here was that some insensitive Washington bureaucrats and bigwigs were crashing ahead with a program that hadn't been thought through; they were throwing their weight around, and hurting a lot of little people in the process.

GOVERNOR EDWARDS: They just showed up here one morning with bulldozers and equipment and contracts in their hand, and a — a public law that had been passed by the Congress, saying we're going to begin storing oil here. And they bored through levees in the marsh, rather than jacking over the levees, which is the environmentally acceptable way of doing it. That created some problems for us, and we had to go back and say, "Hey, hold on just a minute!" And so, we stopped them by using some of the very tools that the government sometimes uses, and that is environmental protection. And it took us some time to get them straightened out, but we finally did.

RATHER: Did they know what they were doing when they came down here?

GOVERNOR EDWARDS: I don't think so.

RATHER: These wells are creating new underground caverns for oil storage. Here's the way it works. They pump fresh water into salt below ground, and then pump it out as brine, creating new caverns for the oil storage. However, for every barrel of oil to be stored, about seven barrels of fresh water must be pumped underground and then pumped out with the waste brine. And nobody ever tried to dispose of such tremendous amounts of brine before. Originally, the Department of Energy believed it could simply build a pipeline five and a half miles out into the Gulf of Mexico and dump the brine there. But local residents, including fishermen and shrimpers, complained. So, the federal Environmental Protection Agency finally decided that the brine pipeline had to be built twelve and a half miles out into the Gulf of Mexico. That caused many months' delay, and cost an additional $20 million.

That's not the only problem with brine. The old existing salt caverns the Department of Energy purchased are full of brine, too; and when the oil is pumped in, the brine is forced out. It can't just be poured on the ground, so deep disposal wells had to be drilled — at twice the anticipated cost, by the way — but even that didn't work.

DeLUCA: We'd ordered the oil. It was coming in. We had a — a fleet of ships coming in with oil. But when we started to pour the brine that was in these caverns out to let the oil in, the brine did not dispose. The design rate for these disposal beds was 30,000 barrels a day. And we, along about October, started to hit ten to fifteen thousand a day. So immediately our disposal of brine was cut 50 percent, and that had to back up the oil. The pipelines were working, the pumps were working, the pressures were working, but we couldn't swallow the brine.

RATHER: Given all the problems with this project, it's no wonder the Carter Adminis-tration has finally scaled down its goal of 250 million barrels in the ground by the end of 1978. The newest target is 195 million barrels by the end of this year. But there's no way in the world even that can be met. They're 100 million barrels short at this moment and, given the world oil shortage, there seems to be no way to get more. And on top of that, even if nothing else goes wrong, it will cost twice as much just to store the oil as they projected only two years ago. So many things had gone wrong with the oil reserve that when we tried to ask the Department of Energy about it, top officials ducked. They referred all questions to the project manager, Don Mazur, who had been on the job only a year.

If you had to list three reasons — I know there are more than that — but if you had to list three reasons and only the three main reasons why the 250-million-barrels-in-the-ground-in-storage-by-the-end-of-1978 goal had not been met and has not been met, what would you list?

DON MAZUR: The over-optimistic schedule right from the start in terms of the complexity of the job, the underestimating of the size of the job and what it took to get it done; and then, in the early phases, the — the lack of having a dedicated project office that has only one mission in life and that is to get this job done, and versus trying to pull a number of agencies together to support the project.

RATHER: Don Mazur says that joining this project in the middle was like trying to jump aboard a runaway train.

MAZUR: We had to run to catch up the train — catch the train, and the train was picking up speed all the time. And our challenge was to — to at least gain the same increment of speed, if not greater, to catch that train. We've caught it, and our arms — we're on board now.

RATHER: You had a sense of jumping aboard a moving train?

MAZUR: Yes, sir. I — we've — terms like "we've turned the corner," "we can see light at the end of the tunnel." We've seen them and we've turned the corner and we're on board. Some have said that that light at the end of the tunnel is another train coming the other way. (Laughter) But we're on board, and we're there.

RATHER: You don't think that light at the end of the tunnel is a train coming the other way?

MAZUR: No, sir, that's the light. I'm sitting on part of it. I know that now. When you put your hand on some hardware and it vibrates from time to time, you're there. And we're there.

GOVERNOR EDWARDS: This is one of the many things that has — one that has been advanced as a facade to — to lull the people of America into believing that something is being done about their problem. And really, it's not doing any-thing about their problem. Storing oil which we do not have and can't get to store in expensive caverns that we have bored into doesn't help a poor fellow who's got to worry about where he's going to get fuel for his tractor or for his fishing boat or for his — heating his home.

We should have spent the money — for a billion dollars, which is one-sixth of what this cost — program was supposed to cost, we could have built a pipeline out of Mexico, which would have transported two billion cubic feet of gas every day to the south Texas border. And there's no telling how many barrels of oil we could have worked out on a purchase basis with the Mexicans had we gone there four years ago when they first got into the discovery of oil in Mexico. We could have used the money to build a pipeline from California to mid-America and the Northeast to transport the Alaskan oil, instead of shipping it all the way around the canal we used to own in the Panama Canal Zone.

RATHER: Furthermore, Governor Edwards believes the oil reserve fiasco indicates an even larger and more basic problem: the whole Department of Energy.

GOVERNOR EDWARDS: I think the whole DOE is the bad situation. That should be abolished.

RATHER: Should be abolished?

GOVERNOR EDWARDS: Absolutely. The country — the last thing we need in this whole thing is a Department of Energy spending $10 billion every year, hiring 20,000 people running around shuffling forms and sending out notices and making phone calls. That doesn't produce a bucket of coal, a cubic foot of gas or a barrel of oil. It has had nothing but an inhibiting factor on energy production in America since it was created. Let me say it again. It has had nothing but an inhibiting factor on the creation of energy or the production of energy since the day it was created.

RATHER: The plan to put oil in the bank is not only years behind schedule and billions over the projected cost, but it may turn out to be shot full of corruption too. One employee of a prime contractor already has pleaded guilty, and another has been indicted, in the theft of a half million dollars' worth of pipe, and more indictments are on the way.

Judgment Day

PAUL LOEWENWARTER, PRODUCER

HARRY REASONER: For most of America's history, many people would have considered it almost a sin to enjoy church. Church was more a penance and a punishment. You were a sinner, and boredom was your purgatory. Now that's not necessarily so. But if you are to be entertained in church and inspired and filled with exaltation, some of God's deputies have to make the arrangements. And if there are arrangers of churchly entertainment, surely as the day follows the night, there are now critics passing judgment on what goes on in church.

DR. WILLIAM MARTIN (mimicking preaching style):   We're not interested tonight in whitewashed, watered-down, soft-soaped, sugar-coated, bargain-counter religion. No, praise God! Tonight I'm going to preach to you an old-time, trail-blazin', hide-splittin', God-lovin', devil-hatin', soul-savin', sin-killin', 40-year-ago, black-back Bible, Holy Ghost-inspired and God-anointed sermon that will save everybody that believes and repents to the guttermost to the uttermost! (Takes a deep breath) Oh!

REASONER: That man is not a preacher, at least not any more. He is, instead, a fellow of impeccable academic background, a former evangelical preacher, giving a lecture audience an impression of one of the preaching styles that fascinate him. He is Dr. William Martin, graduate of Harvard Divinity School, now a professor at Rice University in Houston, enthralled but detached observer of many thousands of church services. But Dr. Martin is also one of a new breed — a reviewer of religious services. For *The Texas Monthly,* he writes a regular column, reporting on churches and ministers, as a movie critic reviews movies.

So, here is Bill Martin, looking at the state of God's church in Texas, and finding — what?

(Hymn singing in church)

For Texas Baptists, their Broadway, their Big Apple, their longest-running hit is the First Baptist Church of Dallas. There's a choir 170 strong, a 70-piece orchestra — all drawn from the 20,000 members of this largest Baptist congregation in America.

All this was prelude to the appearance in the pulpit of the man who has led this church for 35 years, The Reverend W. A. Criswell.

THE REVEREND W. A. CRISWELL: You see this pulpit desk? It's His. It's His. This belongs to the Blessed Jesus. This is His pulpit. And I just occupy it until He comes.

REASONER: Critic Martin watched Dr. Criswell, "Resplendent," he wrote, "punctuating his sermon with a hand drawn down in a controlled tremble, like slow lightning." And he wrote that Criswell looked like Nelson Rockefeller playing William Jennings Bryan in a fundamentalist pageant.

REVEREND CRISWELL: And finally, in the purpose and grace of God there shall be a new heaven and a new earth. God will purge His universe, and there'll be no more burned-out stars, and everything in the universe will be perfect and in order, just as God originally created it.

REASONER: This was old-fashioned stuff to Bill Martin. In a kind of left-handed compliment, he wrote that this was one of the more notable worship services this side of the 19th century, and that the sermon had little to do with today.

DR. MARTIN: I think that probably purposely he decides, rather than to try to deal with the kinds of questions that are raised by historical relativity, scientific questions, Biblical criticism, that he chooses to proclaim this basic message. And that's one way to go about it. But it does not speak so much to the kinds of questions that I'm interested in, and so I point that out as well.

REASONER: And what is Dr. Criswell's answer to Martin, who wrote that "times have changed but Criswell's message has not"?

REVEREND CRISWELL: I don't think they've changed. That's the point. I don't think there are any new attacks on the word of God. I don't think so.

REASONER: He thinks you're a little bit nineteenth century, doesn't he?

REVEREND CRISWELL: Yes.

REASONER: Are you?

REVEREND CRISWELL: I am. I am.

REASONER: Do you have any intention of changing it?

REVEREND CRISWELL: Not at all.

(Hymn singing in church)

REASONER: Old-fashioned or not, it is the evangelical fundamentalist churches like Criswell's that are today's fastest-growing congregations.

DR. MARTIN: I think that it — it has to do with the fact that the evangelical churches are saying, "This is the way, the truth, and the light. We have answers." And they also have a great deal of — of life and vitality. It's — it's part of being a — a going concern. They're not kind of drifting off. There is — there is real life there that — that has a great appeal. It has great appeal to me.

REASONER: Dr. Martin, what are you? Are you a Christian?

DR. MARTIN: I have been. I think that probably now it's fair to say that I am not a Christian in the sense that I have much respect for. I do attend church. I'm a lukewarm Christian, at best. I agree with I think it was William James, who said, "I believe everything I can. I would believe everything if only I could."

REASONER: But you're going into these churches where there are congregations and clergy who do support these bodies of belief and hold to these tenets and presumably live up to them, and you're criticizing them. Isn't that a – a little, in a dramatic exaggeration, a little bit like hiring Jane Fonda as Inspector General of the Army?

DR. MARTIN: Well, I prefer to think of my role less as that of a — a hostile critic than as an honest but friendly unauthorized consultant.

(Hymn singing in church)

REASONER: Bill Martin figures he has been to some 4,000 church services on one side of the pulpit or the other. But he wrote that he's never heard a congregation belt out four-part harmony gospel music the way they do at the Lakewood Assemblies of God Church near Dallas.

(Hymn singing in church)

DR. MARTIN: The congregational singing was just wonderful. I have seldom been in a service when the congregation seemed so caught up in it in an unqualified kind of way.

REASONER: Martin wrote that at a lot of Pentecostal churches you find plain Jane fashion, but not here. Martin found worldly worshippers, with lip rouge and frizzed hair and split skirts. And he wrote that some fundamentalists accuse the assemblies of God of dampening their religious enthusiasm – of having no more religion than the Methodists. But Martin said this assembly of God is hardly a valley of dry bones.

PASTOR E. M. FJORBAK: How many know what it is to be set free by the power of God? Amen? What it is for the Lord to come along and change your life.

REASONER: Of Pastor E. M. Fjorbak, Martin wrote that his rhetorical skills were adequate but unremarkable, with a countenance that could be intimidating if his eyes did not so quickly fill with tears and his chin so easily quiver with deep conviction and tender concern.

PASTOR FJORBAK: That's why we want to serve Him. That's why we want the whole world to know about Jesus. Amen. You may be seated, praise the Lord.

(Woman speaking unintelligibly)

REASONER: Several times the service simply stopped for a spontaneous chanting of unintelligible sounds called "speaking in tongues."

(Woman speaking unintelligibly)

Martin wrote that this speaking in tongues is a gift described in Scripture, often a part of a charismatic service. It was followed by another "gift" — a spontaneous interpretation of the tongues.

(Woman speaking)

PASTOR FJORBAK: Amen. (Applause) Hallelujah. Bless the Lord, bless the Lord . . .

(Hymn singing in church)

REASONER: The Pastor invited those who would to come forward to accept the Lord, and the trickle became a stream, until Bill Martin felt he and his wife were almost the only ones resisting the moving of the spirit. And though he was an outsider and no longer a devout Christian, he wrote that he was stirred by the openness of emotion, "to people who would hold you and rejoice with you and intercede on your behalf with the Lord of the universe."

(Hymn singing in church)

If the critic had any doubt that Vatican II reached Texas, it was quickly dispelled at St. Patrick's Roman Catholic Church in San Antonio. For the majority ethnic bloc in this parish, Martin wrote that here was the church reaching out with a happy mixture of Mexican culture and Catholicism.

(Singing . . . mariachi band playing in the church)

"If three or four mariachis can brighten a restaurant," wrote Bill Martin, "imagine the response when a full mariachi band strums down the aisle to serenade the Virgin" — for this is the Mass of the Virgin of Guadalupe. "This church," said Martin, "houses a joyful, if somewhat noisy, spirit that would be difficult not to share."

(Singing . . . mariachi band playing in the church)

The whole service is based on the claim that the Virgin Mary appeared in Mexico in the 1500's in the form of a peasant maiden. Bill Martin wonders whether that claim can stand careful historical scrutiny. But no matter, he felt, so long as it's celebrated in such a memorable form as this. Bill Martin's conclusion, which would have been a smash review in *Variety,* was "Viva La Iglesia de San Patricio" — "Long Live the Church of St. Patrick."

One thing Bill Martin never does is to criticize anyone's faith, no matter what he thinks of a service.

DR. MARTIN: Insofar as I try to make value judgments of these individuals and groups that I study, I try to do full — so for the most part in terms of the standards that they set for themselves. I don't expect Reverend Ike to be like Billy Graham, any more than I expect Baptists to be like Unitarians. I do expect them to make at least some effort to try to be pretty close to what they claim to be themselves.

THE REVEREND HAROLD O'CHESTER: I want you to know that the Lord Jesus Christ stands in the midst of the Allendale Baptist Church and says, "I know you. You phony, you hypocrite, I know you. I know you, preacher. Don't you try and put something on. I know you." God knows. Don't you ever forget it.

REASONER: Of all the ministers Martin has reviewed, his harshest verdict has fallen upon The Reverend Harold O'Chester of Austin. Martin called him a caricature of a Baptist preacher.

REVEREND O'CHESTER: We have adulterers standing in pulpits. We have homosexuals standing and preaching in pulpits. We have men and women teaching in Christian churches who don't even believe that the Word of God is the Word of God. And you expect God to bless that kind of a fellowship? Wow.

REASONER: When he said that you were a — a kind of a caricature of a Baptist minister —

REVEREND O'CHESTER: Uh-hmm.

REASONER: — what do you think he meant?

REVEREND O'CHESTER: I think that's — I think that's strange. Well, of course, I don't know what his caricature of a Baptist minister is. I'm a new breed today, Harry. I don't wear black suits and a string tie. I have a college and seminary education. But I believe with all my heart that what God has called me to do is to communicate truth.

DR. MARTIN: That particular church certainly represents an authentic slice of Texas culture, a slice that's represented by slogans and salesmanship and competition and boosterism and self-promotion.

I don't think it's necessarily a bad slice. I think it's a pretty thin slice. And I don't think it gets really at the — the deeper aspects of what I take to be the classic Christian tradition. Jesus didn't say, "Take up your sparkler and follow me."

REVEREND O'CHESTER: See, in effect he's saying, "You're a phony." Okay? I mean, that's what it means.

REASONER: Well, he's saying you're a lightweight, at least.

REVEREND O'CHESTER: Yeah, or a lightweight. And I may be a lightweight. I won't deny that I might be a lightweight. Because, you know, God's the one that's going to weigh everybody on the scales of life, and whether I weigh 16 ounces to a pound really doesn't depend upon whether Dr. Martin says so or not. It depends upon what He says.

REASONER: Have you ever had any intelligent criticism that made you stop and think about whether you were being fair or not?

DR. MARTIN: I got one letter. I had written of a church that it would likely be a continually satisfying source of living water only for those with small buckets. And I got a short letter which said I might find it more satisfying if I stood under the waterfall instead of above it. I thought that was well put. (Laughs) But I prefer to think of myself not so much as standing above as standing aside, and I hope not too far aside.

Letters

MORLEY SAFER: Our premiere broadcast last week brought lots of mail about the doctor who was charged with murder after he did nothing to prolong the life of a fetus that was delivered alive during an abortion. One viewer said: "The doctor . . . is no more guilty . . . of murder than his . . . colleagues across the nation (who practice abortion). Murder is murder whether it's inside the womb or outside the womb."

Another viewer asked: "If society, by legalizing an abortion, ends up half killing (a baby), doesn't society have a responsibility to finish the job? If I were (that baby) I would want them to finish the job."

About our interview with the Reverend Jesse Jackson, who talked about dissension between blacks and Jews, one viewer took exception to Jackson referring to Jewish-owned banks: "Which banks? (Rockefeller's) Chase Manhattan, (Walter Wriston's) Citibank, (Gabriel Hauge's) Manufacturers Hanover?"

There was also a letter that said: "Compassionate people, including Israelis, deplore the oppression of Palestinians, (but) they're oppressed because the Arab countries want them to be oppressed."

And finally, about our story on Palm Springs, California, a viewer from the East said the people who live there are guilty of: "A disgusting display of conspicuous consumption. I (only) wish I had the bread to (join them)."

SEPTEMBER 30, 1979

Castro

DON HEWITT, PRODUCER

MIKE WALLACE: Tomorrow night, President Carter talks to the nation about the issue of Soviet combat troops in Cuba. Last Friday, Fidel Castro said Jimmy Carter lied when he charged that there is a Soviet combat brigade there now. Well, this afternoon in the Palace of the Revolution in Havana, Dan Rather talked at length with the Cuban president. The tapes of their conversation arrived in Miami by plane only a short time ago. Here is an uninterrupted and unedited 20-minute portion of that interview.

To begin, Dan asked Castro to explain further his charge that Jimmy Carter lied.

DAN RATHER: Mister President, President Carter last Tuesday called you in Cuba a puppet of the Soviet Union. Then last Friday, you said that President Carter was dishonest. Less than two years ago, however, you said that President Carter was an ethical man. Now, what's happened in these recent weeks that made you change your mind?

PRESIDENT FIDEL CASTRO (through interpreter):   I did give my impression that Carter had a religious ethic, a Christian ethic. I believe that on this issue, in this concrete problem that we are discussing, Carter has not been honest. Carter has not been moral. He has not been sincere. That is what I am saying. I am not going to pass final judgment on his person, but I am referring specifically to this concrete fact. True, Carter made some recent statements. He called us puppets and things of that type. A bit strange, because he had not used that language concerning Cuba before. Because of an — an elemental feeling of dignity, I am not going to respond to this ridiculous charge. But I will ask a question. Why, if we are a satellite country, is so much attention paid to Cuba? And it is obvious that the U.S. government in the political field is practically paying more attention to Cuba than to the Soviet Union. So then, unquestionably, we are facing a strange case of a satellite.

RATHER: Mister President, regardless of who is right and who is wrong on the facts, when you describe a President of the United States as dishonest, and the headline reads "Castro Says Carter Is A Liar," regardless who —

PRESIDENT CASTRO: I did not want to use the word "liar." I said "dishonest."

23

RATHER: You said "dishonest," but the headline reads — you know the headline reads "Castro Calls Carter Liar."

PRESIDENT CASTRO: I did not want to use that word.

RATHER: Dishonest. But regardless of who's right or wrong on the facts, when you describe a President of the United States as dishonest, are you not contributing to world tension by taunting Mr. Carter that way?

PRESIDENT CASTRO: Actually, that is not my intention nor my wish, but how I am going to define the policy that he has followed concerning Cuba in — on this issue? I have a conception of things, and at least I follow a line, a line of principles in politics. So then, we are faced in a — with a situation in which a crisis has been artificially created, and dishonest procedures have been used. And this is what I say.

RATHER: Excuse me. You say that it has been artificially created?

PRESIDENT CASTRO: Yes.

RATHER: Now, President — President Carter's official spokesman said again within the past 24 hours this is not an artificial crisis. They say it's a real problem, that there's something new in Cuba — a Soviet combat brigade.

PRESIDENT CASTRO: Precisely in that, that is where falsehood precisely lies. I am not going to question — and I have already said this on Friday, that I will not go down low to give explanations to the United States concerning the nature of our military facilities. So, I will not even explain whether it is simply a question of advisors, or if these advisors can combat or not. That's not the question. That is not the essential problem. We are a sovereign country. The United States has no right whatsoever on Cuba, no privilege whatsoever, no jurisdiction over Cuba. Cuba is not a property of the United States. Latin America is not a property of the United States. And we consider ourselves to be a free country, and we have the right to think as a free country. If I go down low and give an explanation on the nature of these military facilities, I will be questioning Cuba's right to take the defensive measures it deems pertinent. And besides, we are not less than Japan nor England, nor are we less than the German Federal Republic, nor are we less than Spain, nor are we less than any other country who have considered themselves with the right to have even troops of another country for their defense. So therefore, I do not accept that Cuba — this right of Cuba be questioned. So therefore, I am not willing to give any explanations on that.

Now then, the problem is a different one. Actually it is a different one. Why has this crisis been created? So then, what I say is the following: that Soviet military personnel, which the U.S. government calls "brigade" and which we call Training Center Number 12, is a military facility which has been in Cuba for the past 17 years, 17 years, with a similar number and with a similar nature. That facility was established after the October crisis in conformity with the spirit of the October crisis and according to the status quo created at the October crisis. This — so this is nothing new.

RATHER: This is October, 1962.

PRESIDENT CASTRO: October, 1962 — 17 years ago.

RATHER: Has there been any change in the nature of the Soviet troops in that country since that time?

PRESIDENT CASTRO: There has been no change nor — neither in the nature nor the functions of the Soviet personnel in Cuba in the past 17 years. And that is the ess— essence of things. The existence of this facility was perfectly well known by Kennedy, was — was known by Johnson, by Nixon; it was known by Ford. It had to be known by Carter. It is impossible that they ignored this, a facility that has been in existence for 17 years in a country where they have had hundreds of flights, where they have used hundreds of agents for espionage, in a country where the United States has used all its electronic means to know what is happening. Whom are they going to make believe, after 17 years, that they ignored the existence of this facility? Whom are they going to make believe that?

RATHER: But when President —

PRESIDENT CASTRO: And that is why — that is why I challenge Carter to explain to the U.S. people and the world public opinion the truth, and to say since when was this supposed brigade been in Cuba. Since when? Whether it was set up during Carter's administration, whether it was set up during Ford's administration in 1976, whether it was set up during Nixon's administration in 1970, whether it was established during Johnson's administration in 1965, or if it existed or not in Cuba in October, 1962. I believe that this is the key thing, and this is the deceit that I am referring to — to try to make believe, and to try to make the world public opinion and the U.S. public opinion believe, that the Soviet Union and Cuba have taken new steps of a military nature to create a problem. That's exactly the crisis. That is the key.

RATHER: That — I agree that that's the key, and I — I can assure you I believe that President Carter on tomorrow night is going to say to the American people that this is — that the nature of the Soviet presence in Cuba has changed, that for the first time, to his knowledge, there is a Soviet combat brigade in Cuba, not training, combat brigade.

PRESIDENT CASTRO: Well, if President Carter tomorrow says that there has — there has been a change in the number or in the nature or in the functions of the Soviet military personnel in Cuba since 1962, the he will be telling a great lie to the U.S. public opinion and the world public opinion, because I maintain that neither in number nor in nature nor in functions has there been any change in the past 17 years.

RATHER: Mister President, we have only a limited amount of time, and I want to quickly move on. There are reports circulating in Washington tonight about possible American military movements: strengthening U.S. forces in Key West, Puerto Rico; even sending a contingent of U.S. Marines, a new contingent, to Guantanamo; and the possibility of sending a U.S. aircraft carrier towards the Caribbean — that this may be what President Carter announces tomorrow night. Now, do you have any intelligence information indicating that that's true?

PRESIDENT CASTRO: I have the news that have appeared in the papers, the cables, military moves. We have not detected any military moves —

RATHER: What's your attit—

PRESIDENT CASTRO: — in the past few time.

RATHER: What is your reaction to that kind of attitude, to that kind of talk?

PRESIDENT CASTRO: I believe, first of all, that what the United States should do and what Carter should do is not to create a crisis without any legal basis — without any legal basis, I repeat — and without any moral basis. I believe that the only thing that the U.S. government must do is not that — is not to do that, because that will mean to move into conflict, to move into crises. I believe that it would be much more constructive for Carter to announce the contrary, that is, the willingness of the United States government to respect Cuba's sovereign rights, to stop the economic blockade, which includes medicines, which has been maintained for the past 20 years, and the will to dismantle the Guantanamo Naval Base and withdraw their ships and troops from our waters and from our national territory.

RATHER: Mister President —

PRESIDENT CASTRO: Well, we are not frightened by any type of reaction. We are not intimidated by it. We have been suffering from this hostility on the part of the United States for the past 20 years. And to send soldiers to Puerto Rico, well, I believe that Puerto Ricans will not like it. That they are going to send soldiers to Key West, the tourists will not like that. That they are going to send soldiers to Guantanamo, that will mean more money for U.S. taxpayers, and it will not affect us at all, since we will not let ourselves be intimidated, nor are we going to become nervous because of that.

RATHER: Mister President, if President Carter should suggest a meeting with you, are you willing to agree?

PRESIDENT CASTRO: I will not propose it, but if he would propose it, I have no objection whatsoever to have a contact with President Carter or whomever he appoints, if he deems pertinent. We would not have an attitude of rejection.

RATHER: And the same thing would apply if Secretary of State Vance were willing to meet with your foreign minister?

PRESIDENT CASTRO: We have no objection either.

RATHER: Mister President, do you have —

PRESIDENT CASTRO: They have already met at another opportunity —

RATHER: But not on this subject.

PRESIDENT CASTRO: — with Vance.

RATHER: Not on this subject.

PRESIDENT CASTRO: No, not on this topic.

RATHER: Mister President, do you plan to go to the United Nations before the end of this year?

PRESIDENT CASTRO: It is a possibility, but no decis— no final decision has been made on this regard.

RATHER: Mister President, I want to make very clear. Are you flatly denying that there is not a Soviet combat brigade in Cuba?

PRESIDENT CASTRO: I'm not denying that there is Soviet military personnel in our country. I'm saying that it is exactly the same military personnel, organized in the same way, as 17 years ago. That is what I am saying, categorically saying so. And that you call the Soviet personnel, part of that Soviet personnel, you call it "brigade," and we call it Training Center Number 12.

RATHER: Now, Mister President, how is the situation right now different from the October crisis of 1962, if it is different?

PRESIDENT CASTRO: It is different in all ways. First, in the 1962 crisis there was a real, objective danger of nuclear conflict. And today, nothing similar exists. The October crisis was a real crisis. This is an invented crisis. The October crisis could have been a tragedy. This is a comedy.

Now then, during the October crisis there were dozens of nuclear missiles in Cuba; there were over 40,000 soldier — Soviet soldiers in Cuba; there were 28 bombing squads. At the present, none of that exists here, and this is why when a conclusion was reached in the October crisis, when an agreement was reached between the United States and the Soviet Union, an agreement in which we did not participate and which — which therefore we do not feel committed, when that agreement was reached that the Soviets decided to withdraw these weapons at the exchange of a guarantee of non-invasion to Cuba, the situation was different than that now.

Now none of these problems exist. When Kennedy reached those agreements with Khrushchev, he felt satisfied for the withdrawal of these weapons. It is not that he was right, it is not that he had the right. These are two different things. We did not agree. But they were different problems. From a real danger for peace at that time. And Kennedy was satisfied. Kennedy was not worried whether two or three thousand Soviet military wou— would remain here, you notice that? He simply did not pay any importance to that. So now, I ask myself, why does Carter is going to revive this whole problem and create a crisis? Why has Carter set up this comedy for the fact that there are two or three thousand Soviet military in Cuba? So, I want him to explain this. Why? And if he did not — if Kennedy did not do it, if Johnson did not do it, if Nixon did not do it, if Ford did not do it, why has Carter done this? How can he explain that? What is the reason behind his — what is his — his justification? He will not be able to make the people of the United States believe that no President of the United States knew about this. This is as if he were to admit that the CIA does not exist. It would be as if he would be admitting that the U.S. government is totally misinformed on all questions.

So then, there are two reasons. First, the attempt to sabotage this summit. Second, the attempt to raise Carter's image. The attempt to overcome the difficulties that Carter is facing for his re-election. That is, in my opinion, the only explanation for Carter to have created this artificial problem.

Northern Ireland

BARRY LANDO, PRODUCER

MIKE WALLACE: Over and over since he arrived yesterday in Ireland, Pope John Paul has beseeched, has pleaded with Catholics and Protestants alike to end the bloody violence in Northern Ireland. His most moving appeal came in Drogheda about 30 miles from the border with Northern Ireland. "On my knees," cried the Pope, "I beg you to turn away from violence." Originally, he had planned to travel to Northern Ireland himself during this pilgrimage, but the assassination of Lord Mountbatten and the slaughter of 18 British soldiers by the IRA Provos, the Provisionals, persuaded his advisers that it could be foolhardy for the Pope to go to the mainly Protestant North at this moment.

It was 10 years ago that British troops went to interpose themselves between Protestant and Catholic in Northern Ireland; but slowly, over the decade, those

British troops themselves have become the object of attack, not from the people they came to protect from one another, but instead from that same crowd of terrorists who assassinated Mountbatten, who want to drive the British out and unite all of Ireland, Ulster in the north with the Irish Republic to the south, and nowhere are those IRA Provos more effective than on the border between the two.

We had to go in by helicopter, because this is called "bandit country" by the British troops, this country down near the border. Its villages, they say, are havens for the Provos; the "Nasties," the British call them. And the roads below are vulnerable to Provo snipers and bombers. Most of the residents in these deceptively gentle and romantic-looking hills are Catholics, who would be happy to be united with the Republic to the south, and they are openly hostile to the troops based at our destination, the small army fort inside the town of Crossmaglen. It's not unlike an army outpost in our own Wild West a century ago. The 200 British troops stationed here leave the base only in heavily armed patrols, and with good reason, for just two days before their commander and 17 other British soldiers had been killed by the Provos.

Candidly, when you go out there on the street, are you a little afraid?

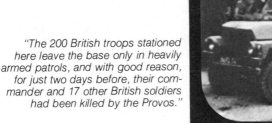

"The 200 British troops stationed here leave the base only in heavily armed patrols, and with good reason, for just two days before, their commander and 17 other British soldiers had been killed by the Provos."

BRITISH SOLDIER: Yeah, a little bit.

WALLACE: Afraid — Afraid of what?

SOLDIER: I'm afraid of everything. You know, getting shot, bombed, blown up. Yeah.

WALLACE: They don't like you.

SOLDIER: They don't seem to like us.

WALLACE: What do you think about when you're out there on the streets?

SOLDIER: Staying alive.

WALLACE: How are you ever going to lick them?

SOLIDER: I don't know the answer.

WALLACE: You don't believe you ever are.

SOLDIER: No.

WALLACE: Lieutenant, here are the three men that — who are going out on patrol with you in five minutes. You've heard what your men said. They confess, they're scared when they go out on patrol, and they're not sure that there's any point to all this.

LIEUTENANT: We lost 18 soldiers — two of which were Queens Own Highlanders, our own regiment — and our commanding officer.

WALLACE: Right.

LIEUTENANT: Now this is fresh in their minds, and then to go out with that in the back of their minds, it — obviously any normal human being is going to be upset, frightened, that it could happen to them.

WALLACE: That massacre took place here at Warren Point, just across this inlet from the Irish Republic. It was the bloody episode on this highway that stunned the British and demonstrated the ingenuity and the daring of the Provos.

Lest anyone doubt the canniness, the sophistication, the careful planning of the IRA Provisionals, listen to what happened here, near Warren Point, just two days ago. The IRA Provos had parked a large van piled high with hay by the roadside. Underneath the hay: 300 pounds of explosives. The Provos apparently had intelligence that a convoy of British troops would be coming along that route, and when the soldiers did indeed pass by, the Provos, evidently concealed on the other side of the river in the Irish Republic, detonated the charge, killing six men. That was only the beginning. The Provos had also calculated exactly where the rescue force, called in after the blast, exactly where they would set up their command post, at a gate a hundred yards down the road. That was where the second huge blast went off. It was the worst episode since the British troops arrived here in Northern Ireland 10 years ago, and it all happened just 15 miles away from that garrison at Crossmaglen. But if the massacre had shaken his men, it only seemed to reinforce the lieutenant's determination to persevere.

I heard your briefing, and what you were saying was very reminiscent of "We've got to win the minds and hearts of the people."

LIEUTENANT: Of course.

WALLACE: I — I heard that back in Vietnam.

LIEUTENANT: Exactly, but that is our job over here, isn't it? We are protecting the people. We consider — and it is — this part of the world is still part of the United Kingdom.

WALLACE: It may be the U.K. inside the walls, but outside on patrol it is hostile territory, and the first evidence of that is a monument under construction, a monument being built by the people of Crossmaglen to honor those who have been killed in the fight to drive the British out of Northern Ireland.

SOLDIER: Basically, you know, it appears to be a bloody monument to the IRA — appears to be.

WALLACE: They're thumbing in — their noses at you.

SOLDIER: Exactly. It's crazy, isn't it?

WALLACE: But everything looks so peaceful. I mean, face it, everything looks utterly peaceful. It looks almost as though you're play-acting.

SOLDIER: Believe me, it's far from play-acting. Now one of our men was killed within 48 hours of arriving in the province at that location there. In the past, a — a — an — a young officer was blown up just at that location there. A — a car bomb was placed outside it. He came along, and the bomb was set off, detonated, by radio control.

WALLACE: The troops on patrol constantly check cars coming into town for explosives, weapons, and the townspeople resent it. The morning we were there the first car that came under scrutiny belonged to Paddy Short, a local pub keeper and a vocal opponent of the British.

This is part of the U.K., no?

PADDY SHORT: No, not to us. This is part of Ireland. At least we think it's Ireland, anyhow.

WALLACE: And these soldiers?

SHORT: Well, to us, they're an army of occupation.

WALLACE: Really?

SHORT: Yeah.

WALLACE: You want them out?

SHORT: Yes. Yeah, they're here just to keep the flag flying, nothing more, nothing less.

WALLACE: But you know, the soldiers that I've talked to over here, they would not like to stand at your bar and drink —

SHORT: Yeah.

WALLACE: — for fear that they might not come out alive.

SHORT: That's true. That's true.

WALLACE: It would take you in that car how long to cross over into the Republic?

SHORT: Oh, five minutes.

WALLACE: You go over often?

SHORT: Oh, every — prac— practically every day. Some of us always go over across the border, yeah.

WALLACE: So a fella could come in, plant a bomb, go back —

SHORT: Uh-hmm.

WALLACE: — and even trigger it from the other side?

SHORT: Probably, yeah.

WALLACE: Brigadier General David Thorne commands the troops along most of the border, 300 miles of it.

As I understand it, there are about 35,000 security forces under arms here in Northern Ireland against perhaps five-, six-, eight hundred IRA keeping you immobilized, if you will; and when I say immobilized, they're beating you. Why?

BRIGADIER GENERAL DAVID THORNE: They are not beating us.

WALLACE: Ten years later they're beating you. They killed 20 of your men the other day.

GENERAL THORNE: That is not beating us. If you imagine that killing 20 men, however tragic, is going to beat the British Army, give us another song.

WALLACE: I spent some time this morning at Crossmaglen down here —

GENERAL THORNE: Yes.

WALLACE: — first-rate men who confess that they are frightened —

GENERAL THORNE: Uh-huh.

WALLACE: — that they want to get out —

GENERAL THORNE: Uh-huh.

WALLACE: — that they do not know, some of them said, what in the world they are fighting for.

GENERAL THORNE: Hmm. I will tell you that the ones you have spoken to are very rare indeed. I know I can communicate with my soldiers, and I know that they understand why they are there, and I know their officers know, and I know they do.

(Drums and band music)

WALLACE: A parade of Protestants near Belfast, a two-hour drive from the border. They are loyal to the Queen, determined to remain part of the United Kingdom. They outnumber the Catholics in Ulster by two to one, and the more militant among them vow to fight the Provo fire with their own fire. If the British troops can't do the job, they say, they'll do it for themselves; they'll go after the Provos.

And the Catholics of Belfast? They may not like the troops that constantly patrol their streets, but they realize that were they not there in force, the Catholic minority in Belfast might be prey to Protestant violence.

And probably no security forces anywhere are better equipped or trained to handle the possibility of urban violence or terrorism than are the British in Ulster. There are 70 members of the security forces for every one member of the Provos. Even shoppers in downtown Belfast must undergo a careful security check on their way to market. To hunt down the Provos, the security forces use methods which would provoke a violent outcry if they were used in the United States. From observation posts, soldiers using telescopes by day, electronic viewing equipment by night, keep a round-the-clock surveillance on the community below, plotting minute by minute the movements of targeted suspects. Remote-control TV cameras mounted on top of the army's base at Crossmaglen enable soldiers inside the base to monitor all activity in the main square of the town, zooming in on anything or anyone suspicious. The army also uses observation helicopters equipped with television cameras that can focus in on a suspect a thousand feet below and transmit that image back to an army command post.

SOLDIER: Your license, have you, sir?

WALLACE: Soldiers manning roadblocks in the north are able to read into a microphone the license number of any approaching car —

SOLDIER: Okay, sir.

WALLACE: — and within a couple of seconds, a computer signals whether or not that car, because of its owner or where it's been seen the past couple of weeks, whether or not that car should be stopped and checked. (Sound of beep) A beep means it's okay. (Sound of car) Those same computers are said to hold detailed information on more than half the adult population of Northern Ireland, everything from who lives in what house to the color of the paper on the walls inside. And yet, and yet, according to a secret army study, which wound up in the Provos' hands and which 60 MINUTES has obtained, the British Army, despite all its technology, the army has itself acknowledged that the Provos are not being defeated. The recent violence underscores that.

All together, 541 soldiers and police have been killed since 1969, and thousands more have been wounded by snipers and by car bombs and the like. And all the while, in the middle of Belfast, the political arm of the Provos sell their newspaper legally; in this issue boasting of their exploit in assassinating Lord Mountbatten and killing the 18 British soldiers.

The RUC, the Royal Ulster Constabulary, 90 percent Protestant, is the police force in Ulster, partners of the British Army. In fact, the British say their eventual aim is to withdraw their troops and let the RUC keep the peace, though no one expects that will happen for a long, long time. But the RUC has been undermanned and ineffective against the Provos, therefore, frustrated; and it is that frustration, say their critics, that has led some RUC investigators, operating in detention centers like this one at Castlereigh, to try to beat confessions out of, not just suspected Provos, but their sympathizers, as well.

Father Dennis Fall, a Catholic priest, was one of a number of critics of the RUC who told us of hundreds of allegations of brutality. Father Fall was going to bring three of those victims to talk to us.

FATHER DENNIS FALL: They would not come, becau— because they are afraid to come and go before your cameras, afraid of retaliation from the forces of law and order, security forces, in this community.

WALLACE: One man who did agree to appear on camera was Hugh Murphy, who drives a cab in Belfast. A Catholic, he says he was beaten up twice by the plainclothes investigators of the RUC.

HUGH MURPHY: They — they beat me for about an hour, an hour-and-a-half, never stopped; they just kept systematically punching me, and the one that had had me, he said that, "If you think you're sore now, wait until tomornin — wait until the morning."

WALLACE: A Briton, Sir Kenneth Newman, heads the RUC. We asked him about the torture charges.

SIR KENNETH NEWMAN: I don't rule out for one moment that in any — in a civilized country or any other country, there are people in any organization who will fall below the high standards set by that organization, of course. But —

WALLACE: What you're saying is that there is not a systematic —

NEWMAN: There is absolutely no sy— there is no systematic — any question of this. The whole system is against it.

WALLACE: What you are, in effect, saying —

FATHER FALL: Yes.

WALLACE: — is that Sir Kenneth Newman is a liar.

FATHER FALL: I'm not interested in Sir — Sir Kenneth Newman is an Englishman, a bird of passage, who comes here, like many other Englishmen from Oliver Cromwell on, and passes on. I give him neither credit nor blame. He's one of a long, long tribe of them.

WALLACE: Yes, but the British are generally regarded in the Western world as civilized people, and to hear you talk about the kind of —

FATHER FALL: Well, they're a very civilized people in their own country, but now the record in countries which they have colonized has not been good.

WALLACE: Sir Kenneth, the United States government suspended arms sales to police like yourself in Northern Ireland after Irish-American congressmen, among them the Speaker of the House of Representatives, Tip O'Neill, argued that the guns are used primarily against Catholics here.

NEWMAN: Hmm. That's a — that really is ludicrous, you know, because if you look at our record, we haven't shot anybody in the la— as a police force in the last four years. Utter rubbish. Utter rubbish.

WALLACE: Brigadier General David Thorne again:
You've been here for 10 years.

THORNE: Yep.

WALLACE: Another 10?

THORNE: Could be. Our resolve is total.

WALLACE: Not too big a price to pay for —

THORNE: For the democratic process to exist in Ulster. Never.

WALLACE: So, the British say they will not leave. And the leader of the Protestant Orange Order in Belfast said yesterday in a letter to Pope John Paul, "We can only conclude that your refusal to visit Northern Ireland stems from an unwillingness to recognize Northern Ireland as part of the United Kingdom."

Harry Reasoner is in Ireland covering the Pope's trip, and he reflects on the prospects for success in John Paul's call for an end to violence.

HARRY REASONER: The Pope may have an impossible task. There is, as we all know, something about the Irish, or at least about some of the Irish. G. K. Chesterton put it in a quatrain years before the present trouble:

The mighty gales of Ireland are the men whom God made mad,
For all of their wars are merry, and all of their songs are sad.

There's been something to that. Lord knows the fighters of Ireland have had enough to rebel about, but they have also somehow seemed to revel in their violence and martyrdom, unreachable by reason or by their mostly peaceful fellow men. Yesterday, the Pope appealed to them again.

POPE JOHN PAUL II: On my knees I beg you to turn away from the path of violence and to return to the ways of peace.

REASONER: Well, men and mothers and priests and saints have been on their knees to the wild men of passion for a long time now without much luck. It would be nice to think that this current visit would finally make a difference. It would be nice, but not realistic.

Getting High In School
RICHARD CLARK, PRODUCER

MIKE WALLACE: Last spring as school was coming to a close, Harry Reasoner looked into the growing use of marijuana among teenagers and pre-teenagers. He prepared the story to run now with the opening of another school year. Now Harry's story does not pretend to deal with the controversy over the legalization of marijuana, but rather with a simple message: that if parents think the problem is confined to the big cities, it might do them well to look at their own suburban playgrounds, even at their own tennis courts.

CARLA LOCKE: Some people get a high to do better in what they do. I think a high intensifies what you do.

DANNY: What do you do better when you're high than you would when you're not?

CARLA: Well, okay, I play tennis. When I get high I play —

DANNY: Yeah.

CARLA: — much better, because I want to play so well when I play that I just play even harder.

(sound of church carrillon)

HARRY REASONER: She lives in Moorestown, New Jersey, an upper-crust suburb of Philadelphia. Mostly professional people, mostly white, it's not the place where you would have looked for a drug problem in the past.

CARLA: It's everybody. It's not just sophomores.

REASONER: Uh-hmm.

CARLA: It's freshmen, it's every grade.

REASONER: Every grade.

CARLA: And it's becoming more and more.

REASONER: Her name is Carla Locke. Her mother is Kathy. Carla is 17 and has been smoking marijuana for two years.
How often do you use it? How often do you get high?

CARLA: Oh, God! It depends, it really does. I went through a stage where I probably — six times a day I was. But that was, you know, a stage I went through, and now I do it a lot, but I don't overdo it.

REASONER: Would it probably average every day?

CARLA: Oh, yeah, I'd say so. Yeah.

REASONER: We came to Moorestown, not because the drug problem is unusual here, but because it isn't. They have an excellent school system. Tonight the students are parents, and the lesson is difficult when you are being told that your child may be getting stoned on marijuana before class every day.

DR. MITCHELL ROSENTHAL (Child Psychiatrist, head of Phoenix House, N.Y.):   If my kid is sharing a joint, maybe it's — it's like having a martini before school. Hey, that's a lot of stuff! That's a lot of change of consciousness at 7:30 AM!

REASONER: That's Dr. Mitchell Rosenthal, a child psychiatrist and head of Phoenix House, a rehabilitation center based in New York. It's only recently that he has come to places like Moorestown to sound an alarm.

DR. ROSENTHAL: Today, nationally, 11 percent of high school seniors are getting high on marijuana every single day.

REASONER: The percentages may vary, but he isn't just talking about high school seniors.

DR. ROSENTHAL: We're talking about 12, 13, 14, 15, 16. I think it's that age group that is moving into maturity, that is developing sexually, that is trying to become adults very quickly and finding that difficult. That group is the group that's using a lot. The surveys that we've been doing in New York City and now in other parts of the country make me feel that anywhere from 50 to 70 percent of students in our high schools are getting high on marijuana three to five times a week.

WOMAN: Do you think children need more than — their general allowance to be able to buy these drugs?

DR. ROSENTHAL: If a kid decides that this week he or she is not going to buy a record album or is going to save on a — on a movie or save on — on something else, it doesn't take very much to, you know, buy a — a stick.

REASONER: There were a lot of questions and concern at that meeting, and a sense of "Maybe somebody else's kid, not mine." So a few days later, we visited a group of 28 Moorestown students.

But how many of this group have been offered a chance to smoke marijuana . . .?

We took an informal poll. Of any 28 Moorestown students, we were told, all would have been exposed to marijuana. They guessed that 20 of 28 would have tried it. About 18 of 28 would become regular users.

CARLA: We were reading *Hamlet* for school, and I studied for the test basically ve— very high, and I took the test, and I was pretty high, and I got 84, so we went — with — you study high, you take a test high, you get high grades better. (Laughs) It worked.

REASONER: Do you think she'd get maybe a 94 instead of an 84 if she wasn't using marijuana?

KATHY (Carla's mother):   That's very possible, because it kind of changes their life style a little bit, and it also changes their friends. It becomes a way of life.

DR. ROSENTHAL: We see kids that are using with regularity. We find that A-students become B-students, B-students become C-students, C-students flunk.

If an adult wants to make an informed decision about alcohol versus marijuana, that may be his decision to make. I'd certainly hope he or she had, you know, all of the facts and a lot of the new evidence that's coming out.

REASONER: The trouble is there isn't enough new evidence or old evidence, and much of both is contradictory. The federal government does have an ongoing research program into the effects of marijuana. This five-acre marijuana farm grows all the different types of the drug that make it to the streets of America, grows it for processing and shipment to scientists around the country. If you ask the scientists what they've found out, the first thing they'll say is, "Not nearly enough." There's been too little work done, especially on long-term effects.

Probably the scariest headline so far came from this UCLA laboratory. They compared the lungs of people who smoke about a joint of marijuana, but no cigarettes, with those of people who smoke a pack of cigarettes, but no marijuana. They found that the marijuana smokers developed blockages in their lungs that the cigarette smokers didn't. They don't know why. Further work is needed, but they're afraid that daily use over the years might mean chronic bronchitis, emphysema or lung cancer. Researchers have determined that driving while stoned can be hazardous to your health, and other people's, too. And in some parts of the country, marijuana dealers are lacing their product with foreign substances.

DR. ROSENTHAL: We find kids now who are using marijuana that has been sprayed with Raid or insect repellent, because they think when it (inhales to approxi-mate a drag) — they — they — they take a drag that the burning on their throat makes it stronger and makes it better. You have kids who are smoking pot laced with "Angel Dust" or PCP, and they're taking it — they don't even think it's a drug; they think it's a super joint or a — a — a — a — super high.

This looks like? (Inaudible response from group addressed) You're wrong. It isn't. This is a stash can in which one can put pills or pot. A sticker on the end allows you to — to put it on your dashboard — Well, it's not going to sti— it's not going to stick here, but the point is that you and your mate can smoke in the car as you roll down the highway. Some of you saw . . .

REASONER: Dr. Rosenthal thinks one of the major culprits that is spreading the problem is the burgeoning paraphernalia industry, now estimated to be worth about $400 million a year and, says Rosenthal, aimed straight at young people.

DR. ROSENTHAL: This cutey item of — or — or — or baby bottle is really a pipe, and one would in the — in the top put either pot or hashish, and then sucking through the nipple would tend to concentrate the smoke.

REASONER: Now there are 25,000 outlets, at least — they're called head shops — selling paraphernalia perfectly legally and with a clear appeal to the very young.

You could quite likely find a head shop in a mall like this one. We asked two 15-year-olds from Phoenix House to see how easy it would be to buy drug paraphernalia.

Let's see if I've gotten educated enough to see what that is. That's a double — a double-bubble bong.

YOUNG MAN: It is, sir.

REASONER: What did it cost?

YOUNG MAN: Twenty dollars.

REASONER: Twenty dollars. Did you have any trouble buying it?

YOUNG MAN: No.

REASONER: They didn't ask how old you were?

YOUNG MAN: No.

REASONER: Any conceivable use for this except to smoke marijuana —

YOUNG MAN: Nope.

REASONER: — that you could think of? You couldn't make an exhaust pipe out of it. Are they doing a pretty good business?

YOUNG MAN: Yeah. They got a lot — lot of nice pipes.

REASONER: Do they? A lot of other stuff, pipes?

YOUNG MAN: Yup.

REASONER: What do you call your shop here?

SHOP OWNER: Jolly Giant.

REASONER: Jolly — Jolly Giant or Jolly Joint?

SHOP OWNER: Jolly Joint. J-O-I-N-T.

REASONER: Yeah. Sounds more appropriate.

SHOP OWNER: Right.

REASONER: And I assume, except for the posters and stuff, that most of the equipment around here a suspicious person would associate with the use of controlled substances?

SHOP OWNER: Right.

REASONER: And no restrictions on the age of anybody who can come in here.

SHOP OWNER: Yes, we do, only on certain things, like I try to keep the youngsters out of here, like, what I mean, like up to a 16-year-old preferably.

REASONER: I don't mean to spring anything you — on you, but we sent a 15-year-old in a few minutes ago. He had no trouble buying a bong for twenty bucks.

SHOP OWNER: Uh (sighs) —

REASONER: That's what happened to you.

SHOP OWNER: Majority of people we see — majority of the people that come in I never ask for proof.

REASONER: Right.
We had planned to do half a dozen head shops in the area to see how many out of six would sell to the young people; but after three visits, the kids had made purchases in each store, so we decided to save a little money on bongs.

DR. ROSENTHAL: And I think the statement is clear to — to kids that this is part of the American way now, and drugs are here to stay, and "Come on, kid, try it; you'll like it. And we can help you get high, we can help you get high fast, we can help you get super high, and that's okay."

REASONER: There are no easy answers in Moorestown tonight, or in any other community watching the people of Moorestown. Dr. Rosenthal thinks the time is here for a firm parental no.

DR. ROSENTHAL: I think that parents have a responsibility to be parents, so that . . .

REASONER: Which is, of course, much easier to say than do.

KATHY: I do have the authority to stop it, naturally. I could make —

REASONER: What are you doing to stop her?

KATHY: I can say, "You can't do it anymore," and I could start following her around and causing havoc and make her stop it.

CARLA: And then we'd hate each other.

KATHY: And then we'd hate each other, and Carla would probably run away from home, because she's a very self-minded person, and what would I actually have accomplished? Nothing.

REASONER: And caught in the middle are the schools. They can have drug education programs for parents and young people; most don't. In the case of Moorestown, one thing they tried was closing down an outdoor area where the kids went to get stoned.

CARLA: The reason they closed it is they — they're trying to hide it from the general public, you know. They don't want the parents to know that their kids do, in fact, get high at school, so they took our outdoor area away, and now they're just getting high in the bathrooms.

Letters

MORLEY SAFER: And now the mail. It was pretty evenly divided among our stories on Johnny Carson, the preacher-critic and the salt mines.

On Carson, there was a letter that said: "Why don't (you guys) at 60 MINUTES give yourselves a break and do more stories like 'Here's Johnny' and fewer ones about problems. You'll live longer."

About our story on Dr. Martin, the reviewer of church services who says he's a lukewarm Christian, a viewer wrote: "Your review of the reviewer made it look like all Christians are evangelical and charismatic and scream a lot. Not so. I hope (Dr. Martin) gets to know some of the other breeds, so he can get off his fence and into a pew."

And there was this: "It's absurd that a meeting of people together for worship be given a performance rating."

And finally, about our story on the government fiasco surrounding a multibillion-dollar plan to store oil in caves and salt caverns, a viewer thought reporting that fiasco was hardly newsworthy. He wrote: "(If) a government project (ever) runs on time, runs smoothly within or near the projected cost and free of corruption, *that* will be news."

OCTOBER 7, 1979

Who Killed Georgi Markov?

See May 18, 1980, page 547

The Luckiest Woman

JOSEPH WERSHBA, PRODUCER

MORLEY SAFER: "The luckiest woman" is the way she describes herself. She is Clare Boothe Luce, and the reason we frame her in a cover of *Time* magazine is that her husband, Henry Luce, the editor and founder of *Time,* never did, though few would doubt that she'd achieved prominence enough in her lifetime to have been on half-a-dozen covers.

Clare Boothe Luce is 76 now, and in a kind of retirement in Hawaii. But she comes back to the mainland tomorrow to be the first woman ever to receive West Point's Alumni Award. If you're of a certain age, you'll remember that Clare Boothe Luce is a woman who went everywhere and did everything, achieved literary, political and diplomatic acclaim. Always a power in the Republican Party, and still is. People like Richard Nixon and Ronald Reagan still pay homage. But you'll most of all remember that she did not mince words. Every utterance was guaranteed to make an enemy.

CLARE BOOTHE LUCE: Oh, well, I'm so old now that I hardly have a warm, personal enemy left. (Laughter) And those I had I tend to miss, because they kept me in fighting form.

SAFER: Is she still in fighting form? We decided to test that by bringing up a sore subject. Why had the Luces and their powerful *Time* magazine been so strong in support of Nationalist China's Chiang Kai-shek at a time when others felt he was a loser and that supporting him was not in the best interests of the United States?

LUCE: There was no other leader. I mean, this passion that liberals in America have — which they do have — for getting rid of leaders on our side who aren't perfect has wound up in my lifetime with leaders who are then either Communist — bloody Communist dictators or atrocities.

Now, is you read the Washington press on the score of the Shah — not one of my favorite characters, but a friend of ours — the liberals could hardly get — wait to get rid of him. Who have they got now? Khomeini, a man who cuts people's hands off for the slightest moral infraction, who's shooting people. Is that what we want? Now we're going to do that — we'll probably do that in the Philippines. We did it in Cuba. We — we did it — we do this all the time. Chiang Kai-shek was all there was.

SAFER: You've had an uncanny knack, I must say, of — of backing an awful lot of losers over the last several years, beginning with Wendell Willkie, Tom Dewey, Richard Nixon, in a certain sense a loser, Madame Nhu—

LUCE: In a certain sense. (Laughs)

SAFER: — the war in Vietnam, Barry Goldwater.

LUCE: Well, when you see where things are, it might have been better if Goldwater had, for example, been elected. What was it Goldwater said? He said, "Let's win that war or get the hell out." That's what he said. Was he right? Was he wrong? I think he was right. We didn't. We fiddled and faddled along there, and finally left, deserting our friends and more or less with our honor and credibility seriously compromised. So, it's a pity Goldwater wasn't elected.

SAFER: Clare Boothe Luce has been a somebody all her grown-up life. As a teen-ager, she set her eye on the top: magazine writer, magazine editor, wife of the most powerful publisher in America, successful playwright, congresswoman, ambassador to Rome. And always the toast of the town, a glamor girl with a brain to match her looks and equal to any man with a shootin' iron. She was an Olympic-class swimmer, and still keeps in shape. When she was a girl, her mother filled her with ambition; told her that no matter how bad things got, a girl could get to the top so long as she had a string of big pearls and small hips. She comes from a fairly poor background. He father ran off when she was very small. She had very little formal education, but she was well-read, and she was hungry to excel.

It was not a lifetime of adulation. As one biographer put it, her enemies called her an ambitious phony, a conniving beauty, a designing, climbing woman without compassion or consideration. Her friends see her as brilliant, warm, someone who has marched through life the perpetual target of less talented, envious competitors.

LUCE: I—I found out as I've gone through life that there really are only two classes of people, only two. There are those who go along for the ride, who take things as they come, and they are the majority. And then there is that other minority that lays things on themselves, that discipline themselves.

And the Greeks had a word for that, for those kind of people: *aristoi*. The word means, as you know, aristocrats. And it means, in Greek, "the best." And all societies have really been saved and really have achieved whatever beauty or elegance or glory or fame they had because of this minority that strives for excellence and knows that it cannot be bought.

SAFER: Back in the thirties, the two most admired women in America were Eleanor Roosevelt and Clare Boothe Luce, two women who seemed to make a difference. As far as the Roosevelts were concerned, Clare loved her, hated him.

In very harsh language, you attacked President Roosevelt at the time. Do you have any regrets about that, about your own isolationist —

LUCE: Now, you know, what — I was never an isolationist. Never, never, never.

SAFER: You — you tweaked him — but you tweaked him constantly about the issue of sending American boys overseas.

LUCE: No, I did not. What I said at that convention was Roosevelt lied us into a war into which he should bravely have led us. That's what I said. I felt that Roosevelt wasn't telling the American people the truth.

SAFER: I would think that, to someone like Clare Boothe Luce, the present political situation in both parties have all the elements of really very good farce.

LUCE: Well, I'm not so sure that the people want another Presidency. I think what they seem to want — or at least if you believe the polls — is another series of episodes in the greatest soap opera in — in American history, the Kennedy story. Will David recover from his drug addiction and go into politics as an aide to his uncle? Will Jackie reappear in the White House and perhaps meet some great nobleman and marry them? We have come to see government even as entertainment, as fiction, as television serials. You have to believe that.

SAFER: Do you think that Democratic capitalism as you know it is finished?

LUCE: Oh, it's a long way from finished. I mean, if you just observe what's happening in the world, here are the Chinese trying to get into a market economy. Soviets shall most certainly go down the drain in — sooner or later. That's our great hope, that their system will wreck them. Unless —

SAFER: Just doesn't work, you're saying.

LUCE: Just doesn't work. It doesn't work. I think that if America, the United States of America, that most extraordinary area of the world, which has enjoyed more freedom than mankind has ever known in all previous history, if we hold on — if we hold on — if we try to restrain this ravenous government that would — is descending on everybody, a horde of locusts, if we do that, not only will we make the twenty-first century in good condition, but the whole rest of the world will be, however slowly, marching with us.

I really do believe that with all its weaknesses, with all the things that drive me and you and most people in this vast television audience right up the wall, this is nevertheless the best country and the best political form of government and the best economic system that has ever existed. The thing to do is to stay in there and make it better, not destroy it. And I don't think we will.

SAFER: When it came to women's rights, Clare Boothe Luce was light-years ahead of her time. She lobbied for women's rights — for ERA, in fact — back in 1924. Do women really want these rights that a minority of them worked so hard to achieve?

LUCE: Now, you see, I think — there's a funny little commercial on the air called "you can't fool Mother Nature," and I don't think you can. If — no one can go against their nature, neither male nor female. Nature — not men, nature — should decide what women can and can't do. Give nature a chance. If it is against their own nature to exercise power, to be in certain kinds of jobs, to undertake certain activities, they will gradually abandon those things, because it will not be in their nature to do so. And if it is, why should you sit on them? Why should men prevent them from doing it?

SAFER: In order to — to do it, though, does a woman have to be — and I don't mean to be unkind to her — but the kind of iron maiden, Margaret Thatcher sort of woman, all toughness and very little softness?

LUCE (laughs):   Well, you know, there's a word that they use for men who are overly masculine. Is that macho?

SAFER: Uh-hmm.

LUCE: Well, what about overly feminine women? "Facho?" Would you think that might do? Do women have to be facho? No, I think they don't have to be facho to achieve their end. Some of them like being that way. That's their — what's called personal life style. Let them alone. Let them do it.

SAFER: In 1936, she wrote a play called *The Women*. It was a hit. It was made into a movie that's still seen on the late show, and starred some of the sharpest tongues in Hollywood, and it gave a whole new meaning to the word "bitchiness." A lot of people thought it was autobiographical.

LUCE: Well, what made me write *The Women* was that I was so angry with bitchy women. That's why I wrote the play. I thought it unworthy of women to behave that way. And I had no sympathy for idle, bitchy women, and that's why I wrote *The Women*. (Laughs)

SAFER: And you still don't have any —

LUCE: And I still don't. And — and I'm very glad to see that there are fewer and fewer of them in America, that the more standard —

SAFER: I'm not sure you're right.

LUCE: Well, you may know more about it than I do. I don't see it in my life.

SAFER: I think that women, now that there are — more and more good jobs are open to them, are much bitchier about each other in those jobs than men —

LUCE: Oh, come off it! I have worked in the man's world all my life. And I would sit there with men in an embassy, on the floor of Congress, in an editorial office. What are the men doing? Yak, yak, yak, yak, yak, yak, yak, yak, yak.

SAFER: About each other.

LUCE: About everything, and each other. And then, the same man gets home at night, and there's the poor little woman, who hasn't been out of the house all day, and she opens her mouth, and he says, "Why do you women have to talk so much?"

SAFER: Are you disappointed in a way that — that if Clare Boothe Luce was in her twenties or thirties today, in 1980, call it, there would be a very good chance that she might be — one day be Vice President or President of this country? That in a sense you were born at the wrong time?

LUCE: I was born, it seems to me, at the very best moment in the history of the world into the very best country in the history of the world. I was born at the beginning of the really glorious twentieth century. And in my lifetime, I have witnessed more progress in the direction of human comfort, human health, human well-being, than has happened in all the previous years of mankind.

And if I may make one more observation, I was young and at my peak and serving my country when my country was at its peak in the 1950s. Now, how can you say I was born at the wrong time? I'm the luckiest of women in the time I was born!

The $5 Bill

DREW PHILLIPS, PRODUCER

HARRY REASONER: Does, as Gilbert and Sullivan once wrote in song, does the punishment fit the crime? The plain fact is that it doesn't always, and it varies from state to state, even from county to county. And that worries the American Bar Association, which feels some drastic reform toward uniformity of sentencing is long overdue.

Take the California case of Dan White, who killed the mayor of San Francisco. He got seven years eight months in jail. Now take the Florida case of Terry Jean Moore, who stole a five dollar bill and got seven years six months, and an additional five years for burning the mattress in her cell. Few people ever would have heard of Terry Jean Moore if she hadn't ended up pregnant by a prison guard and sharing her cell with her baby. How did such a petty theft get a 20-year-old a prison sentence of twelve and a half years, and a baby girl? It all started when Terry found a purse in a car that was being stolen at the time. If that sounds confusing, bear with us for a few minutes.

TERRY JEAN MOORE: I was just sitting in the car while I was giving directions. I went through this purse that was beyond — below my feet, and just so happened I seen it, and I figured I'd take it.

REASONER: There was just five dollars in it?

MOORE: Yeah, just five dollars.

REASONER: You knew what you were doing?

MOORE: I didn't call it robbery, I wouldn't call it robbery, because I didn't stand there and hold a gun on anybody or nothing, you know.

REASONER: Arrested a few hours later, she ended up pleading guilty to unarmed robbery. Then the wheels of justice seemed to grind her up. Terry, who had never been arrested before, had never even had a traffic ticket, was sentenced to spend twelve and a half years behind fences, where she became pregnant and ended up with a baby girl sharing a cell with her. It doesn't sound like justice, doesn't it? Well, maybe it wasn't. But then again, maybe it was.

By her own admission, Terry was no angel. She had been on her own since she got out of high school in Youngstown, Ohio, in 1974, more or less a drifter. On August 13th, 1977, she was out of work, homeless and broke in Orlando, when her sister's brother-in-law, Ralph Ralston, came to visit her. He suggested they hitchhike to New Orleans. She agreed. But then they made their first mistake — they took a loaded .45-caliber automatic with them.

MOORE: Well, the night before, a friend of ours was showing his — his gun to my friends. And so, he left the next day for about four or five hours, and Ralph suggested to take it . And I says, if we take it, will be for our own protection. And so he took it, and we started off. And so, we started hitchhiking.

REASONER: According to Terry, Ralph then decided to use the gun to steal the car of the first driver who picked them up. That unlucky driver was 19-year-old Randy Cheevers, a hospital worker. He picked them up on a highway just north of Orlando.

RANDY CHEEVERS: I had some stuff up in the front seat, and I asked them if they'd get in the back, and they agreed.

REASONER: Randy got nervous, because they wouldn't tell him where they were going. As a matter of fact, they didn't say anything at all until he signaled for a left-hand turn a few miles down the road and told them to get out of the car.

And then what happened?

CHEEVERS: And he pulled the gun right about here, and he said, "Just keep driving." And I said, "No, I'm going to turn. I stayed in this lane to turn." And . . .

REASONER: Yeah. You saw the gun?

CHEEVER: Right. I turned around, and I looked to make sure it was a real gun, and it was.

REASONER: So Randy drove on, with Ralph pointing the gun at him.

CHEEVER: She was going through my sister's purse along this road, and she found five dollars, and she pulled it out and said, "What do we do with this?" Held it up. "Take it or leave it?" Of course, they were sort of agreement, "Yes, we should take it, because we're going to need gas."

REASONER: When they got within a few blocks of an interstate highway, Randy was told to turn off on a dirt road.

CHEEVER: Okay, he told me to stop the car. So I stopped it. And I already had the door part way open, and had my foot out on the ground. And he said, "Don't make a break for it." And just as he said, "Don't make a break for it," I was gone.

MOORE: And when he ran, we ran, because we were as scared as he was.

REASONER: Terry and Ralph hid in the woods for a while, and Ralph gave Terry the gun. She put it in her purse. When they left the woods, they were caught almost immediately by one policeman. While he arrested Ralph, Terry tried to get away.

MOORE: So I took off running, and I threw the gun in some bushes. And I took off running then, but it just so happened the road I ran down was a dead-end street.

REASONER: The police caught up to her there a few minutes later. She was taken to a jail in Orlando. Being locked in a cell for the first time almost drove her crazy.

Were you kind of a hard case? Did you give the guards and people a bad time?

MOORE: Yes, I did.

REASONER: Why, do you think?

MOORE: Well, at the county jail I feel it was because the slam — the slam of the doors, you know, hearing them doors just shut, and then hearing the matrons walk down the halls with the keys. And I was scared and I was lonely, and there just seemed no hope.

REASONER: It was then that Terry set fire to the mattress in her cell. It wasn't much of a fire, but she was charged with arson. But first she had to face an armed robbery charge.

Her attorney was told that Ralph had agreed to testify against Terry. But Ralph, now living in Superior, Wisconsin, says that's not true.

RALPH RALSTON: I never turned state's evidence. I never even appeared in the courtroom at the same time with Terry.

REASONER: But, convinced that Ralph would testify and that Terry had no chance for acquittal, her lawyer did some plea bargaining. She was allowed to plead guilty to unarmed robbery of the five dollars.

MOORE: And I told him I was going to plead not guilty, and that was to ar— armed robbery. And he said, "No," he says, "you could get life." So I figured — and then he said that most likely the most I would get was three to five years, if not probation, at that, since it was my first offense.

REASONER: But when it came time for sentencing on the reduced charge, Judge Robert McGregor made it clear he still considered Terry guilty of armed robbery. He could not give her the Florida sentence for armed robbery – 20 years to life – but he could and did give her the maximum sentence for unarmed robbery – 15 years, seven and a half to be served in prison, seven and a half on probation.

JUDGE ROBERT McGREGOR: You know, armed robbery is a dirty, nasty crime. You look down the barrel of a gun, or have it to the back of your head, you get a — you know, you just don't know whether you're going to be alive for another minute or another day. I — the young man involved was convinced that when they went from one stopping place to the orange grove, where he finally leapt out of the car and took the keys, that he — he was a marked man, that they — he was convinced in his mind, according to his statement, that they were going to kill him.

REASONER: The judge said that he had the impression from your story and from the investigation that you thought you were a marked man, that you might well be dead before the end of the ride. Did you feel that way?

CHEEVERS: Well, I knew there was the option, but I didn't feel like I was going to be dead, no.

JUDGE McGREGOR: I was mindful that it was a first offense, notwithstanding her hardness at the time of sentencing. And I think if I'm to be criticized, I — I might be criticized for being too light upon her.

REASONER: Would that kind of sentence vary in the State of Florida? I mean, if you were in the – say, in the Miami area, where there's a good deal more crime, would a situation like that with a first offender be apt to get a lighter sentence?

JUDGE McGREGOR: I think that's probably right.

REASONER: A few weeks later, Terry appeared before Judge Cecil Brown on the arson charge, and got another taste of strict central Florida justice – five more years in prison. Did Judge Brown think that was a harsh sentence?

JUDGE CECIL BROWN: No, that wouldn't be unusually stiff; and in my views, it would be quite moderate. The maximum penalty for the offense was fifteen years in the state penitentiary.

REASONER: By now, you must be wondering what happened to Ralph Ralston, Terry's companion in crime. Well, things went much better for him. As a matter of fact, he spent only a couple of weeks in jail. Because he was only 17 at the time and a minor under Florida law, he was sent home to Wisconsin on probation, even though he was the one who had carried the gun. He couldn't believe the sentence Terry received.

RALSTON: I was pretty stunned over it, because I thought she was going to get out before me. But I was already home when she'd gotten sentenced.

REASONER: Terry Jean was first sent here to the Florida Correctional Institution for Women. But she had so many personality and adjustment problems that in a little more than a month she was transferred to the maximum security institution at Broward. While she was at Broward, Terry had an affair with a guard. In July of 1978, she became pregnant.
Would you marry the father?

MOORE: I can't answer that at this time, not until I see him.

REASONER: I gather he — he'd just as soon?

MOORE: Oh, he's asked me to marry him. But it's too soon.

REASONER: You hear from him now?

MOORE: No comment. (Laughs)

REASONER: According to Terry, sexual relations between women prisoners and guards is common in Florida prisons.

MOORE: It happens all the time.

REASONER: Does it? Still going on, so far as you know?

MOORE: Yeah. Oh, yeah. Sure. They won't stop it, because — you know, as long as they got keys to places you can get in. But it — oh, it'll happen, and it'll keep happening. As long as there's men and long as there's women, they'll — it'll happen.

REASONER: A prison official told us that birth control pills are among the best-selling items in prison stores. Nonetheless, Terry became pregnant. She was determined to keep her baby; so determined, she kept her pregnancy a secret for more than five months. Then she called the Legal Aid Service in Fort Lauderdale. Attorney Jackie Steinberg was assigned to the case.

JACKIE STEINBERG: When I met her, all she wanted was to keep the baby she was carrying. That meant everything to her.

REASONER: Using a little known Florida law that said a mother could keep a baby born in prison with her for up to 18 months, Jackie went to court and won. Terry's baby girl, Precious, was born in March. Terry and Precious were given a room in the hospital at the Florida Correctional Institution, and Terry's only work detail was taking care of her baby.
Until Precious was born, Terry's case didn't get much publicity, and there had been little talk of parole. But a baby living in prison tends to attract media interest, and the stiff sentence Terry got for her five dollar crime aroused national indigna-

tion. The Parole Board set November of 1980 for Terry's release. Then the date began to change.

STEINBERG: I think maybe knowing that — that 60 MINUTES was coming might have added a little more pressure. Because when I left the parole hearing, they told me November of 1979. And I got a phone call a week later saying, no, they made a mistake, it was going to be August 21st, 1979. And two weeks before I'd gone to the Parole Board, they had said November 1980.

REASONER: So, a few weeks ago Terry and Precious were released from prison. Waiting to meet her were her mother, her sister, and a horde of reporters.

(Terry being greeted by mother and sister . . . indistinct talk, crying)

Terry's now living and working in the Fort Lauderdale area. Are her troubles over?

STEINBERG: I think that the baby has — has rehabilitated her and helped her to — to find herself.

REASONER: As for Terry, before she left prison, she told us there's one thing she's sure of.

MOORE: I'm going to frame a five dollar bill when I get out, so I'll remember not to do it again.

REASONER: The movement to make jail sentences more uniform is not making much headway. It isn't easy. For one thing, you make all sentences as tough as Terry Jean's or as lenient as those in Phoenix, Arizona, where the average sentence for unarmed robbery, first offense, is one year in jail. What do you do about minors like Ralph Ralston, who wielded the gun during Terry's escapade, but went virtually scot-free?

If there's a moral to Terry Jean's story, it probably is, as a lawyer in Orlando told us: If you're going to steal five dollars in Florida, do it in Miami, not in Seminole County.

A Few Minutes with Andy Rooney

MIKE WALLACE: Someone once said, "Take care of the little things in life, and the big things will take care of themselves." Well, everyone should have an Andy Rooney to take care of the little things.

ANDY ROONEY: Something I've been meaning to talk to you about for a long time now is faucets. Faucets and faucet handles.

The first thing I want to say is there are too many different kinds. All these faucet handles are available at just one plumbing supply place. I like the simple ones, like this old garden-style faucet. You knew what you were doing with that. Here's one with four spokes. You can get a good grip on that, and it's clearly "H" for hot. This one, I don't know what this is. It looks — it could double as a bottle opener. Now you take something like this. Now, the manufacturer must have known whether he thought that was hot or cold, but I can't tell. Not only that, if your hands are slippery with soap, it's hard to turn. But it's a lot different to turn water on and off.

The big companies that make plumbing fixtures are all trying to impress us with how clever they are. Their designers must stay up nights thinking of new ways to turn water on and off. Every time you stand in front of a strange sink, you have to figure out what to do with it. It's like finding the windshield wiper on the dashboard of a new car. All we want is water when we go to a sink. We don't want a lot of clever plumbing. A little inventiveness goes a long way in the bathroom.

I sort of like this one. These stick-shift faucets are smarter than I am. Getting warm water is a learning experience. This part here always ends up leaking. What was wrong with this old model? A handle that says hot, another that says cold. You know where you stand with a faucet like this. A lot of public men's rooms — and I guess ladies' rooms — have these spring faucets. You can never tell with them. Sometimes you don't get enough water, and sometimes you get too much. When the timing mechanism breaks on these spring faucets, washing your hands is like a party trick. I'd like to stow these away with those hot-air hand driers. Every hotel and motel shower faucet works a different way too. Can be halfway to checkout time before you figure out how to get wet.

It seems to me plumbing manufacturers are acting like car makers. They're trying to take our minds off some basic shortcomings of their stuff by catching our eye with flashy gadgets. I suggest they all settle down to a couple of simple models, and spend their free time working on a faucet that doesn't drip, a sink stopper that won't leak when you wash a sock, and a plumber we can afford who comes when we need him.

Letters

MIKE WALLACE: The mail this week was heavier than usual, and a lot of it was about our interview with Fidel Castro.

One viewer said: "Do you think the United States could be in trouble when some of us good old country folk back here in Nebraska would just as soon believe what Castro is saying (as believe) what Carter is saying?"

About our story on Northern Ireland, a viewer wrote: "Why did you fail to mention all the Irish men, women and children — Catholic and Protestant — killed or maimed by the IRA? You implied their only victims were British soldiers."

But there was also this: "Despite the Pope's moving appeal for the end of violence in Northern Ireland, there never will be an end to the tragic strife there until the Queen's Catholic subjects are granted human rights equal to those so recently won by our black brethren in America's Deep South."

And finally, in the mail this week was a letter from a woman who is no stranger to any of us. She wrote: "Regarding teenage drug abuse on your broadcast last Sunday, I was suffering all over again with the Moorestown mother who was frightened that her daughter would hate her if she interfered with her daughter's pot habit . . .

"We wouldn't let our children suffer with appendicitis, would we? And yet we let them suffer with a drug problem because we are scared of our own kids and what they might do if we put our foot down. . . .

"I know. I was one of those mothers. My husband and I thought we could fight it alone. Wrong! There are countless free drug abuse programs available . . . Love your kids enough to let them hate you for a while. . . . "You will be grateful to God you did. We are, and so is our daughter." Carol Burnett.

OCTOBER 14, 1979

The Stolen Cezannes

BARRY LANDO, PRODUCER

MIKE WALLACE: A year ago in December, three paintings by Paul Cezanne, three paintings worth a total of three million dollars, were stolen from the Chicago Art Institute.

The case of the stolen Cezannes is not just the tangled tale of those three purloined paintings; it is also a report about the second most lucrative criminal activity in the world today. First comes drug dealing; second comes art theft.

Well, 60 MINUTES decided to take a look inside the thriving business in art theft to find out why art thieves find it so attractive, indeed so easy. This is not Paul Cezanne at the easel, for that esteemed gentleman died 73 years ago, leaving a legacy of innumerable priceless canvases behind. The man painting this copy of a Cezanne, entitled "Apples on a Tablecloth," is Armand Catanaro, who works for CBS. He's working from a slide of the original. That original is worth about $600,000 and was one of the three Cezannes stolen last December in Chicago. We had this copy made to help us find out more about the mechanics of art theft, and to discover just how easy it can be to traffic in stolen art, both in the United States and abroad.

At the Art Institute in Chicago, it seemed to us that the officials had almost invited the thieves to help themselves. Here those three Cezannes, three million dollars' worth, were kept in this modest closet, secured only by a house lock. The FBI later called this essentially a broom closet. Not just the three Cezannes were inside; 25 paintings, among them Toulouse-Lautrecs and Paul Gauguins. Perhaps the Art Institute of Chicago was lucky that not more millions of dollars' worth of paintings were stolen. Laurence Chalmers directs the Chicago Art Institute. He agreed to talk to us about the theft.

You will agree that security here was lax?

LAURENCE CHALMERS: The fact that this — paintings were stolen is — is moot testimony to that fact.

WALLACE: All right, let's say the thief wanted to spirit them out of the country, and let's say that they would be in Paris at this moment. Could he do it?

CHALMERS: It's hard to conceive how.

WALLACE: Well, we'll show you how. With our copy of that stolen Cezanne in his carrying case, 60 MINUTES Producer Barry Lando flew from New York to Montreal in Canada, shadowed by a cameraman with a hidden camera. Lando wanted to make the Canadian Customs authorities believe the copy he was carrying was the real thing. Its value, he declared, was $200,000.

CUSTOMS OFFICER: Two hundred thousand?

BARRY LANDO: Two hundred thousand dollars, that's correct. It's by Cezanne.

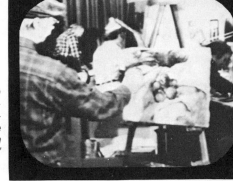

"We had this copy made to help us find out more about the mechanics of art theft, and to discover just how easy it can be to traffic in stolen art, both in the United States and abroad."

WALLACE: In the baggage claim area, Lando was asked to show the painting to another Customs officer.

LANDO: Try to hold it by the edges.

CUSTOMS OFFICER: Do you have any receipt for this —

LANDO: Yes, I do, uh-huh. One from the gallery in Paris.

WALLACE: That receipt was a fake one from a non-existent Paris gallery. The official asked Lando to wait while Customs checked with the international police organization, Interpol, to see if the painting had been reported stolen.

LANDO: I certainly hope it isn't. (Laughter)

WALLACE: Meanwhile, back to Mr. Chalmers in Chicago, who assured us that one reason those stolen Cezannes could not be so easily spirited across the border is that everybody cooperates in the effort to track them down.

CHALMERS: Everyone cooperates in — in an effort of this sort.

WALLACE: Interpol?

CHALMERS: Interpol —

WALLACE: They know about the specific —

CHALMERS: — the Secretary of State, the embassies throughout the world, all of these organizations are informed up front —

WALLACE: Customs officials?

CHALMERS: Customs officials — are informed almost immediately —

WALLACE: Everybody is on the lookout for these things?

CHALMERS: That's right.

WALLACE: But were they? When those Canadian Customs officers queried Interpol's man in Canada, they were told that Interpol had no record of such a picture being stolen. So Lando and that painting, which might very well have been the stolen Cezanne, were permitted to go on through.

LANDO: Okay? Thanks a lot.

WALLACE: That same evening Lando turned around and flew back to the United States with the painting. American Customs officials didn't even bother to look at it. A few days later, Lando flew to Paris. Once again, he had no trouble with Customs. They didn't take a good look at the painting, either.

Now, it was our understanding that Interpol, the international police organization, sends out a constant stream of messages and photographs from its headquarters here in Paris alerting law enforcement agencies around the globe to latest developments in everything from murder to drug smuggling to art theft. On the face of it, an impressive system — except it doesn't always work. Robert Saugier is the Interpol specialist on art theft. He told Lando that U.S. authorities had never even asked Interpol to circulate word of the theft of those three Cezannes.

ROBERT SAUGIER: For this special case, no circulation has been — has been requested by Washington at any time. Unless they ask us either by letter or telegram to make a circulation, we never do it. We could — we can't do it ourselves. It is impossible.

LANDO: Monsieur Saugier, that would seem to mean then that if two weeks from now, three weeks from now, the real thief of those Cezannes, the person who stole them, were to take them again across the border — the real ones now — into Canada, into Italy or into France —

SAUGIER: Umm.

LANDO: — the officers there, the police there, wouldn't even realize what had happened.

SAUGIER: Surely not, if they have not gotten a warning of that.

WALLACE: Back again to Chicago. I showed the Art Institute's Mr. Chalmers the CBS copy of the stolen Cezanne.

Do you recognize this painting, Mr. Chalmers?

CHALMERS: No, I don't.

WALLACE: You don't?

CHALMERS: I should? (Laughs)

WALLACE: Would you like to take a look at it?

CHALMERS: Remember, I'm not an art historian or an artist.

WALLACE: Yes.

CHALMERS: Uh-hmm. That is an interesting water color or oil painting of fruit in a basket.

WALLACE: At that point, I showed him a color photograph of the real Cezanne, the one that had been stolen from his museum.

You know what this is?

CHALMERS: No, I don't.

WALLACE: This is a copy —

CHALMERS: Uh-hmm.

WALLACE: — of the Cezanne that was stolen from that room.

CHALMERS: Really?

WALLACE: Yes.

CHALMERS: That's rather nicely done.

WALLACE: Mr. Chalmers, our producer at 60 MINUTES, Barry Lando, has taken this from La Guardia to Montreal. He has declared it. He has been stopped by Customs —

CHALMERS: Uh-hmm.

WALLACE: — and he has been sent on through.

CHALMERS: It would help if your producer had been stopped somewhere along the line.

WALLACE: You'd think the FBI, you'd think that Interpol, you'd think the Chicago Police Department, you'd think the Chicago Art Institute would have pictures of these three million dollars' worth of paintings circulated to every police agency around the world.

CHALMERS: We thought we did, or they did.

WALLACE: The foul-up on the stolen Cezannes is no exception. Another case in point: that Rembrandt, worth a million dollars, also stolen last December, but from a San Francisco museum. It was a full six weeks before Interpol in Paris got the word to put out an international alert.

SAUGIER: I am not criticizing anybody on — on the case, you know. (Laughs) But of course, you — it is very long. And not only — not only in this country, but in many other ones too, you know.

LANDO: You mean, it's not just the United States that takes months to let you know about paintings having been stolen?

SAUGIER: Not only for the States, but as I tell you, for many other countries.

WALLACE: Why the recent epidemic of art theft? The thieves are simply following the market. This is Sotheby's Gallery in London, where one evening earlier this year ten and half million dollars' worth of paintings were auctioned to buyers from Kyoto to California in less than two hours.

AUCTIONEER: One hundred and thirty thousand pounds then. A hundred and thirty-five thousand . . .

WALLACE: The very rich know that their cash is bound to diminish in value in these inflationary times. So do the thieves. But paintings, they feel, will keep pace with inflation or even outstrip it. This masterpiece by Monet brought $215,000 fifteen years ago. At this auction, the buyer paid $840,000 for that same painting. These huge prices caused a stir not only among the bidders here at Sotheby's, but undoubtedly in other circles, like the people who attended this recent gathering in New York City.

DETECTIVE ROBERT VOLPE: Good evening, ladies, gentlemen, art lovers, active art thieves, and any aspiring art thieves who may be among us tonight looking to pick up some pointers . . .

WALLACE: Detective Robert Volpe heads the art unit of the New York City Police

Department, and he is in ever increasing demand to talk to worried dealers about art theft. The value of art stolen each year in New York City, says Volpe, is ten times greater than the amount of cash stolen in the city each year in armed bank robberies. Volpe told us about the special aura, the special prestige, that distinguishes the art thief from the money thief.

VOLPE: "My son the drug dealer" has a heavy connotation. However, "my son the art thief" becomes poetic; it's creative, it has that movie-like character.

WALLACE: You serious?

VOLPE: Oh, sure.

WALLACE: You mean, you're a more prestigious thief if you're an art thief than a dope dealer?

VOLPE: It has a cultural ring to it.

(On phone): What is the people's name on it?

WALLACE: Despite the growing importance of art theft, not even the FBI has a man assigned full-time to the field. And though New York is now a major clearing house for stolen art from all around the world, Detective Volpe has been given only a tacky corner in Manhattan's run-down First Precinct headquarters for his one-man operation.

VOLPE: This is not only the Art Unit of the New York City Police Department; this is the art unit for the United States.

WALLACE: You mean no other police department has one?

VOLPE: No.

WALLACE: With a budget of how much?

VOLPE: No budget.

WALLACE: But New York City is one of the major art communities in the world. A lot of art theft either takes place here or goes through here.

VOLPE: Correct.

WALLACE: So, the three Cezannes from Chicago, Rembrandt stolen in San Francisco, even a Renaissance painting, let's say, stolen from a villa in Italy within the last few months or so, they could all be right here in New York looking for buyers or waiting for ransom right now?

VOLPE: Absolutely.

WALLACE: Some dealers say, "Oh, you — you're not going to steal a well-known painting, because you can't get rid of it, you can't sell it." You laugh?

VOLPE: Oh, I find that amusing. I've heard that statement made by museum directors and people within the art community, and I'm very surprised at that statement. There's a market there. There are collectors. There are outlets.

WALLACE: Right.

VOLPE: We now have a more sophisticated, organized thing, a theft-to-order kind of situation.

WALLACE: Theft to order?

VOLPE: To order, in which the thief will selectively remove pieces from a collection; leave a total collection behind, but maybe removing four or five pieces.

WALLACE: Why those four or five?

VOLPE: Okay. Again, on a commission basis. Somebody had said, "This is what we want. You go in and get it."

WALLACE: A man who knows at firsthand what Volpe's talking about says that a good deal of art theft today is managed by organized crime, and he should know. For years he was an informer for the FBI, posing as a buyer of stolen works of art.

Let's say that I had my eye on some gorgeous object of art that I really wanted. You could get it for me?

MAN: If the piece was available when you came to me, yes.

WALLACE: Well, let's say it's hanging in a museum.

MAN: Then it would depend on price, depend on how much you want to pay for the object.

WALLACE: Or in a dealer's showroom, or in a church.

MAN: It — it could be had, there's no two ways about it.

WALLACE: It's just a question of how much you're willing to pay?

MAN: Yes. They have the means. They can reach right out and put their hands on any piece of art work they want, if it be in this country or Europe.

VOLPE: We've had cases quite recently. At gunpoint, thieves have entered a gallery here in the Madison Avenue area; at gunpoint, walked to the back of the shop, went to a locked cabinet, cut it open and removed four pieces, selectively removed pieces, and left.

WALLACE: How do you get rid of stolen works of art? How does the thief sell them if he doesn't have a buyer set up ahead of time? Detective Volpe told us it's not difficult. Legitimate galleries, he said, sometimes unwittingly become fences for stolen art.

VOLPE: The bulk of my recoveries are made in the hands of legitimate dealers and legitimate collectors.

WALLACE: To test just how carefully legitimate galleries do check the ownership of paintings brought to them for sale, with the cooperation of a friend we took this Utrillo from her wall and sent 60 MINUTES researcher Allan Maraynes out on Madison Avenue to see if he could unload it, just as if he had stolen it. All he had to prove his ownership was this phony bill of sale from our non-existent Paris gallery. So armed, he paid a call on New York's prestigious Sotheby Parke Bernet auction gallery, which gave him a receipt and told him they'd be pleased to put it up for auction. A few minutes later I showed up, and asked to talk to Shary Grossman, an assistant vice president. She admitted that though the painting might indeed have been stolen, nonetheless it very well could have wound up in their June auction.

SHARY GROSSMAN: It could have. Yes, it could have. And not —

WALLACE: And it could have been —

GROSSMAN: — not through, of course, any kind of dishonesty on our part, you understand.

WALLACE: Why, certainly not.

GROSSMAN: Yeah.

WALLACE: Just — you haven't — you don't check. Everything seems, on the face of it, to be sensible.

GROSSMAN: Someti— yes. I mean, sometimes you unwittingly can be brought into it.

WALLACE: And even somebody like, behind you, Sotheby Parke Bernet, Inc —

GROSSMAN: Uh-hmm. Uh-hmm.

WALLACE: — can occasionally be had.

GROSSMAN: Absolutely.

WALLACE: Let's say that I want a million-dollar painting —

MAN: Uh-hmm.

WALLACE: — but I can't afford a million-dollar painting. How much can I buy that painting for, if it is a stolen painting that I'm buying?

MAN: They'd probably hit you with a figure of a hundred thousand.

WALLACE: About 10 percent.

MAN: Just what an insurance company would pay to buy the painting back.

WALLACE: An insurance company would — would pay —

MAN: Ten percent recovery of that painting, yes.

WALLACE: To organized crime to get it back?

MAN: To anybody that could — that produced the painting.

WALLACE: You are offering a hundred thousand dollar reward for what, Mr. Chalmers?

CHALMERS: For information leading to the safe return of the three paintings.

WALLACE: And you don't really — I'm sure you care, but if you don't get the thief, you'd rather have the paintings?

CHALMERS: It's a good deal like a kidnapping. The first concern is the life of the victim, and then — and only when that's assured, do the police and the FBI focus in on the apprehension and conviction of the thief.

WALLACE: So the art-napper, the art thief, conceivably, can go scot-free?

CHALMERS: Quite possibly.

WALLACE: Well, in the case of the stolen Cezannes, did that thief go scot-free? This what happened. Six months after the robbery, one Nick Pace, a 28-year-old former employee of the Chicago Art Institute, went to museum officials to tell them he had been asked to act as intermediary for the person who had the paintings. The museum could have them back, he was told, for a quarter-million dollars. So the museum president, Laurence Chalmers, arranged to get the quarter-million from his insurance company, and shortly after he handed it over in a Chicago hotel. But when Nick Pace left the hotel, he was arrested. He was not the intermediary, police said. He was the thief. He is currently on trial in Chicago.

Wimpy

HARRY MOSES, PRODUCER

DAN RATHER: With labor support draining away from Carter and toward Kennedy, the candidacy of the senator from Massachusetts looks more and more like a sure thing. The man who started labor's drum beat for Kennedy is William Winpisinger, known as "Wimpy" to the almost one million members of the powerful union he heads, the International Association of Machinists and Aerospace Workers.

It was Wimpy who back in July organized the nationwide "Draft Kennedy" direct mail campaign. Ironically, back when Jimmy Carter was "Jimmy Who," Wimpy's union was the first big one to support him. But Winpisinger now calls Carter the best Republican President since Herbert Hoover, and he's not bashful about saying why.

WILLIAM WINPISINGER: A hypocrite's a hypocrite's a hypocrite, whether it's me, the President of the United States or the Pope. Because I can't call it something different just because his name is Jimmy Carter. If I were the President of the United States, I wouldn't sit in the Oval Office and give the gas producers of this country an annual 10 percent increase in the price of their product up to 1985 and after that the sky's the limit, and then turn around to a worker and say you take seven. We're at least as good as the gas producers.

RATHER: Ted Kennedy's your candidate?

WINPISINGER: Absolutely. I think he has outstanding credentials. He has the — that intangible — charisma, a lot of people call it — to define that in laymen terms that are understandable by the American people, and they rally to him. And as long as that's the case, I feel pretty comfortable that he'll answer the call and run. But if he doesn't, I'm still basically an ABC guy — Anybody But Carter.

RATHER: Wimpy's IAM is the fifth largest union in the country. His fiefdom includes installations like this giant Boeing plant in Everett, Washington. Boeing's business has never been better, and Wimpy's workers share the fruits of that success. The top ones earn close to $11 an hour. Wimpy fights hard for these wages, but he fights even harder for other issues: social issues that he feels are creating a permanent rent in the fabric of American life. He has been so outspoken about this that he is considered the only card-carrying radical among labor union presidents.

WINPISINGER: The labor movement drew its initial strength from underprivileged masses — people that were rebelling against the society because the society wasn't doing anything for them. So the name of the game has to be: be the friend of the guy below you, not the enemy, because those we leave behind suddenly view us no longer as an ally or as a natural vehicle to atta— attach to and bring themselves along, but as an enemy in terms of every nickel we get makes their life more miserable, either through higher prices or whatever. Uniquely, as an American, you save all the contempt in your gut for the poor, miserable guy that's below you on the economic totem pole. You never save a doggone bit for the guy that's causing all of it up at the top that owns it all.

RATHER: Wimpy is headquartered at the IAM Building in Washington. A meeting we filmed had his staff reporting to him on a wide variety of issues: how to stop the proliferation of nuclear power; the machinists' court suit against OPEC nations for price fixing — a suit they eventually lost; the status of the Draft Teddy movement. Hardly your typical nuts and bolts union meeting fare.

Wimpy's favorite subject is what he calls the corporate state, and he reserves his most biting comments for it. He blames corporate power for preventing the labor law reform bill, designed to restore organizing powers originally granted to unions, from getting through Congress. He takes this message to union halls everywhere.

WINPISINGER: The companies own the Senate. It's as simple as that. The companies declared class warfare on the American workers, because they told us by that single action — with that outpouring of venom, the paranoid response they had to modest, legitimate worker demands — that they were going to deny them to us; deny them to all of those who are affected by that law and who work at the very bottom of the economic pyramid in this country. All of the people who don't own anything. That 25 percent of Americans that live from paycheck to paycheck, if they're lucky enough to have a job. All of the Americans that are out pounding the street looking for jobs. All the Americans that are unequipped to hold a job by virtue of a substandard education or no development of their skills, potential skills. And that lies out there, and we've been paying the price ever since. You go ask a guy that doesn't have a job today if it's — if there isn't a class struggle on in this country. Go ask a poor black man that can't make more than the lowest labor-grade wage rate where he works whether or not there's a class struggle in this country. Go ask anybody below the level of 16,000 bucks a year if he thinks there's a class struggle in this country, and I'll bet you you'll get more yeses than noes. And the noes, you give me five minutes to talk to them, they'll be yeses.

RATHER: You say you're not a Marxist, never have been, never will be —

WINPISINGER: No way.

RATHER: — and denounce that, but you don't back away from the word "socialist".

WINPISINGER: People tend to think that anything that's publicly owned or operated in the public interest is a socialistic institution. If that is, I'm a socialist, because I believe we have to do that. I don't see how we solve some of our problems, until we manage to work up the national will to do that.

RATHER: You wouldn't hesitate to nationalize the oil companies?

WINPISINGER: Until they show me a willingness to sit down as one — as one — and operate in the national interest of the United States of America and not the world community, until they show me a willingness to show the same allegiance to the flag as American workers are expected to show, show me the same dedication to our national identity as American workers are — as American citizens are supposed to do, yes, I would maintain that threat to nationalize them. The seven of them go on the world market and they bid against each other, especially in the spot market transactions, to deliberately drive the price up, because every time they drive it up another notch — Standard against Exxon, and Exxon against Gulf, and Gulf against Texaco — it's more bucks of profit in their pocket.

RATHER: It's not only the profit that bothers Wimpy; it's that so few have so much of it.

WINPISINGER: The biggest thing that's wrong in this country today is the lopsided distribution of wealth and income, and everybody forgets to talk about it. On the altar — if you say anything about this class struggle, again, you're the victim of some kind of foreign ideology. Well, I don't hink that's foreign ideology. I can count, and when I see that less than five percent of the adult American people own almost everything there is to be owned in this country, I get concerned. That's a concentration of power that threatens my ability to survive.

RATHER: How much clout does Wimpy have in the American labor movement? How seriously is he taken when it comes to determining policy? We tried to find out at the AFL-CIO Executive Council meeting in Chicago, but the few union leaders who would talk to us about Wimpy did so reluctantly. What turned them off the most was Winpisinger's position on George Meany, the aging head of the AFL-CIO, whose resignation Wimpy has called for publicly. Lloyd McBride, head of the steelworkers, is not a Wimpy fan, period.

LLOYD McBRIDE: Well, I — I don't — I don't think that his pronouncements and — and the style in which they're delivered represent the thinking of the mainstream of the labor movement, no.

RATHER: Fred Kroll, head of the railway clerks, is a true-blue Meany man.

FRED KROLL: I think some of his attacks on George Meany have been unwarranted. And, you know, it's easy for somebody to get their name in the paper by attacking George Meany today.

RATHER: Lane Kirkland, Secretary-Treasurer of the AFL-CIO and George Meany's heir apparent, wouldn't discuss Wimpy at all.

LANE KIRKLAND (laughing):   I pass.

RATHER: Let's talk about George Meany. You've had some harsh things to say about Mr. Meany staying on. I'm going to give you an opportunity to retract those statements.

WINPISINGER: Are you kidding?

RATHER: You think he's stayed too long?

WINPISINGER: Absolutely. The evidence proves it.

RATHER: You think he's been out of touch with the union membership rank and file?

WINPISINGER: I think anybody 85 years of age still trying to conduct a high-powered operation like the leadership of the American labor movement is out of touch, absolutely.

RATHER: You're talking about a living legend. You're talking about a man who's going to be in the pantheon of American labor leadership 200 years from now.

WINPISINGER: I take absolutely nothing away from him. He's had a brilliant career. And what I want him to do is enjoy a retirement that he's earned many times over for what remaining years he has.

RATHER: Wimpy's message seems to have gotten through to George Meany. Shortly after we filmed this interview, Mr. Meany announced that he would not seek re-election. Winpisinger emphasized that he has no interest in succeeding Meany.

As with his calls for Meany's retirement, Wimpy doesn't duck strong positions on controversial issues. For instance, SALT II and the MX missile. Winpisinger represents some quarter of a million aerospace workers at Boeing and elsewhere. It is widely believed by union members that SALT II's passage would hurt workers' paychecks; a ceiling on new hardware means fewer government contracts and fewer jobs. But Wimpy is for SALT and against the MX missile. And in a visit to a nearby tavern Boeing workers frequent, he took them on. Considering that Boeing is a prime candidate to build the MX, it was like walking into a lion's den.

WORKER: If we don't build the MX, our defense, national defense, slowly goes downhill. We build them, it creates jobs, does it not?

WINPISINGER: Is the MX gimmick to make jobs or to protect the country? Because I, for one, am fed up with the notion that we have to be blackmailed day in and day out by spending our tax dollars for defense to prop up the economy on the altar that democracy can't exist or survive on any other basis than building destructive implements.

WORKER: You might as well build more. It creates jobs.

WINPISINGER: I'm telling you, you can get more out of — these missiles, you can't eat them. Highly inflationary.

WORKER: We're not just talking missiles; we're talking aircraft, we're talking submarines, we're talking naval vessels of all types and sizes.

WINPISINGER: Why always hardware? None of them can be eaten. And if you happen to be a starving American, all of that junk on the shelf is worthless. What would you say if I told you I had right on my desk a research study done by this union — your dues dollars paid for it — to establish once and for all the mythology that defense spending is the only way to create jobs; that a billion dollars invested in defense generates forty-odd thousand jobs, and the same billion dollars invested in the private sector almost anywhere will create over 400,000 — ten times as many.

And I'm telling you this union has passed the time where we're going to any longer have class self-interest as our guiding light. We're going to talk about what's in the people's interest, what's in the interest of all our members.

WORKER: And national defense isn't in the people's interest?

WINPISINGER: National defense is primary in our interest, and I'm satisfied we've got plenty enough to defend the country without spending another $70 billion on a worthless piece of junk. The — the part that you guys can't get down your gullet is that there's no such thing as a superior offense. If you can blow up the goddamn world, that's the end of everything. There's no quid pro quo, no moving a checker here or there. It's all over. Curtains. End. Finis.

WORKER: So what you're saying basically is that, hey —

WINPISINGER: Let's build something you can use, I can use —

WORKER: — let's build something we can use.

WINPISINGER: — we can eat it, play with it, drive it, fly it, do anything with it.

RATHER: Critics of Winpisinger tell you that the solutions he proposes are much too simplistic; that the world is more subtle, more complicated by far than he perceives it; that the problems of society cannot be seen through such black-and-white colored glasses. Wimpy will have none of it. What is simplistic to others he sees as simple common sense. By and large, he thinks Americans see things the same way. The people, he says, are smarter than their leaders, and they're crying out for a new kind of leadership.

WINPISINGER: Jimmy Carter has spent the entire time he's been in office — and the trip from the — to the mountain, from the mountain, proves what I'm going to say — trying to find out where in the hell the American people are, in order that he could be there. A real leader would divine where he thinks America ought to be as a nation for the benefit of her people, and lead her there. And that's the difference. And I want a guy who will lead us there, the guy who can envision the American dream and do something meaningful about advancing our progress toward that dream.

The Grapes of Wealth

JOEL BERNSTEIN, PRODUCER

MORLEY SAFER: Back in the 1930's in the novel *The Grapes of Wrath,* John Steinbeck wrote about that awful period of drought and ruin when American farmers lost their land and their lives to the Dust Bowl. "The Grapes of Wealth" is quite another story. It's not about poor farmers going bust, but about rich farmers getting richer; and about the Farmers Home Administration, one of those federal agencies set up back then to help save the family farm; specifically, to come to the rescue of farmers after a natural disaster.

There's no limit on the amount of money that agency, the FmHA, can lend, and always at very low interest rates. Hardly anyone would fault its original purpose: save the family farm. But today, even farmers themselves are shocked at the free and easy way the FmHA lends millions to some people who are already millionaires.

ARNOLD KIRSCHENMAN: If there was a $500,000 limit, there'd be no controversy. Nobody would care. Nobody — nobody's worried, no farmer, no taxpayer, they're not worried about the guy out there in the bib overalls planting his corn and harvesting his corn, he has a windstorm or some disaster, the government helping him. I think people accept that.

SAFER: Uh-hmm.

ARNOLD KIRSCHENMAN: I don't think they accept the fact that a man's got a $18 million loan and he's got a tennis ranch.

SAFER: This is one of those stories that I suspect will not move you to tears. It's about one group of Americans, mostly millionaires, feuding with another group of Americans, mostly millionaires. And what they're feuding about, of course, is money, federal taxpayers' money, a kind of welfare for the rich. And it's happening here in the San Joaquin Valley in one of the richest counties in the country.

If you have an appetite for vegetables, fruit or nuts, you can thank the farmers of Kern County, California, for satisfying a good part of it. Kern County is the third largest agricultural producing county in America. Last year the value of all crops grown here was near a billion dollars. But lately, the farmers of Kern County have had more than produce on their minds, for this is a place passionately and bitterly divided.

COOKIE BIANCO: I don't have any tears for anybody. Nobody should guarantee anybody anything in this country. It's out there to make — make it for you if you can ma— if you're — if you're smart enough and lucky enough.

PHIL JEFFRIES: This program, in my family's case, was a life-saver.

ARNOLD KIRSCHENMAN: Well, Jesus Christ, let's be honest about it. You mean to tell me the federal government — I mean, really, should they finance a horse farm?

SAFER: These are traditionally conservative men arguing over one of the country's most liberal federal programs: a disaster aid program sponsored by the Farmers Home Administration, the FmHA. It's a program that's funneled billions of dollars in taxpayers' money to American farmers like Sig Hoffman, George Nickel and Phil Jeffries — each already had millions in assets — but not a penny to farmers like Arnold Kirschenman and Eugene Nalbandian. They're not exactly poor, either. Kirschenman's worth two million dollars; Nalbandian, 17 million. So, to some extent they both suffer from a slight case of sour grapes. They're among those farmers, the majority, who did not qualify for FmHA loans. Why? Because they're good credit risks and can get bank loans at 12 or 13 percent interest. What set their teeth on edge is that some of their wealthy competitors who were turned down by the banks became eligible for government loans, with interest as low as three percent and rising to only nine percent.

ARNOLD KIRSCHENMAN: A man goes in there, the way I understand it, if he lost, say, 200,000 in a year, if the government gave him 200,000, none of us would be here tonight. We wouldn't care about it. That's fine. But guys are going in there with a $200,000 loss, they're getting six, seven, eight, nine million dollar loans. They're bankrolling the whole deal.

WAYNE KIRSCHENMAN: What you basically have to do in this program is destroy your credit at the bank — by going to Las Vegas and spending your money, or doing something — in order to qualify for all this cheap interest.

SAFER: This would suggest — and certainly farmers aren't stupid — that if you arrange your affairs so that it — it appears that you're in trouble, you're going to get an awful lot of money at very low interest rates.

WAYNE KIRSCHENMAN: This is exactly the case. This is exactly what's going on.

ARNOLD KIRSCHENMAN: Just keep expanding. The government keeps pumping the money in. You don't have to pull in your belt. You got a yacht, you got a — an airplane, you got a fancy homes, you got fancy cars, just keep going. That gets you in a worse cash flow position, which qualifies you for more money.

SAFER: Well, you — you toss off the fancy cars and the airplanes and the yachts very easily. Are there people who have fancy cars and boats and airplanes who borrow money at these cheap rates?

VOICE: Oh, yeah, yeah.

SAFER: Who?

ARNOLD KIRSCHENMAN: We've got a fellow out here named George Nickel. I guess you want a name. He's borrowed somewhere between seventeen and eighteen million dollars.

GEORGE NICKEL (playing tennis):   That's another nice shot.

SAFER: Seventeen and eighteen million?

ARNOLD KIRSCHENMAN: Right. He owns a large tennis ranch. His great grandfather was the largest landowner in California. I mean, that's how far back this money goes, okay? He's what I call a so-called millionaire.

SAFER: George Nickel is more than a "so-called millionaire." He farms 14,000 acres of land worth about $40 million, and he does indeed live in what Arnold Kirschenman calls a "fancy home" tucked safely away along the banks of the Kern River. He's not only a farmer, but a land developer as well: the builder of condominiums, hotel owner, and the owner of the Rio Bravo Tennis Ranch.

Mr. Nickel, just how much FmHA money have you received in loans?

GEORGE NICKEL: Approximately $15 million.

SAFER: The documents we've seen show it's more like 17 million.

NICKEL: .No, that — that's not correct. Nickel Enterprises is the entity that had the $15-million. I was involved in a partnership, Carmel Ranch Partners, that received approximately another million nine hundred thousand dollars.

SAFER: So, it's not completely out of line to say that you, one way or another, are the recipient of $17 million.

NICKEL: Well, I'm a participant. I've got eight children and eleven grandchildren, and they're all in the same partnership with me. So it's — I'm one of them.

SAFER: It's a very attractive interest rate, is it not?

NICKEL: Compared to the bank rates today, that's correct.

SAFER: For how many years is the loan?

NICKEL: It's a 40-year loan.

SAFER: Forty years?

NICKEL: Right.

SAFER: Look, how do you qualify for a loan like that?

NICKEL: Well, you qualify, number one, by the federal government declaring a disaster area. That's what makes the emergency loan available. In Kern County here and other parts of the San Joaquin Valley, we had a number of disasters that occurred one right after the other.

ARNOLD KIRSCHENMAN: In December of '77, we had a windstorm that was tremendous, and it was a disaster, and it blew off half this valley here. You know, it was a 150 mile an hour. Well, since that time — and then we had some floods afterward. But since that time, we've had some rains in the spring, we've had rains in the fall, we've had a frost on our citrus — which is normal, common occurrences of farming. But the government has declared all of these things disasters, to get people in this program.

SPITZER: If — normally, if you'd be farming, within two months you would have a personal disaster of some kind.

SAFER: So — so a disaster is quite normal.

VOICE: A common occurrence.

SPITZER: Thi— this is part of farming. It's like planting and harvesting. Disasters happen from planting till harvesting.

VOICE: That's the chance you take.

ARNOLD KIRSCHENMAN: We believe in free enterprise. We — we fly by the seat of our pants. That's the business we're in. We wait for a guy — some of the guys on the bottom side to go under, and then the guys that can hang on will make money. Way — that's the way of life. That's the way my father brought me up, you know.

SAFER: It's the marketplace.

ARNOLD KIRSCHENMAN: But the government is taking that away now.

NICKEL: This was not my idea, this federal loan program. It was one that was offered to the farmers and — and those were — that were eligible, and — and I certainly needed it and welcomed it. I was appreciative of it, and so were a great many other people in the San Joaquin Valley here.

SAFER: Could you just give me some examples of someone who did not manage his affairs terribly well in the agricultural business?

ARNOLD KIRSCHENMAN: I — the guy's a friend of mine. I don't think Sig Hoffman particularly has managed his affairs well. He's always been in trouble. I don't think he's got a chance. I — personally. He's a good friend of mine. I don't think he's got a chance to make it in agriculture.

SAFER: And how much did he get?

ARNOLD KIRSCHENMAN: Near as I know, a million six, million seven.

SAFER: How much did you put up in collateral?

SIG HOFFMAN: Everything I have.

SAFER: Which was how much?

HOFFMAN: I don't have that figure. I would say it would be around three and a half million dollars.

SAFER: Uh-hmm.

HOFFMAN: I think the ultimate result, that if I had not have got this loan from — loan; it's not a grant, it's not a gift, it's a loan collateralized to be paid back — I — we would have went out of business.

ARNOLD KIRSCHENMAN: If they went under, the land would wind up in a more efficient operation. In other words, I go back to this spectrum, okay? The guys in the middle cannot qualify. These are the guys that are going to feed this country for now and forever.

VOICE: The 95 percent.

ARNOLD KIRSCHENMAN: It's — it's not — the 95 percent right in the mainstream.

HOFFMAN: I don't want to criticize anybody. I came down here 25 years ago. I had absolutely no money. I came down here with 15 cents in my pocket. I didn't inherit any farms from my father. I didn't — nobody made any gifts to me.

SAFER: But what — don't you think some of your neighbors have a case –

HOFFMAN: No.

SAFER: – the ones who haven't gotten – haven't gotten this money?

HOFFMAN: No, they do not. They don't need it. I would love to be in their shoes. I would like to be in their shoes.

EUGENE NALBANDIAN: Let me cite you another company. There is a farmer here named Phil Jeffries —

MRS. JEFFRIES: This one we named Fizz Time?

PHIL JEFFRIES: Fizz Time, yeah.

NALBANDIAN: — has a nice ranch. He's got a nice home on it. Adjoining the house is a million-dollar horse stable. Now, I think that — I think if this person needed any money to farm with, should have got rid of the stable. I don't think the government should come to the rescue of the filthy rich.

SAFER: You borrowed $4.8 million, correct?

JEFFRIES: Correct. Uh-hmm.

SAFER: You have $4.8 million in assets?

JEFFRIES: That's correct. That's correct. I have equivalent — the wife and I together have $7 million in assets.

SAFER: So, you're a rich man.

JEFFRIES: Subtract 4.8 million from it; and then, if we were to liquidate and to pay the capital gains taxes, I don't think that we'd be considered a rich man. I think that I'd have to continue working.

SAFER: And how much did you pay in actual income taxes last year?

JEFFRIES: I didn't pay any income tax. I had over a half-million-dollar loss last year.

SAFER: So you paid no taxes.

JEFFRIES: No.

SAFER: You got near $5 million from the government —

JEFFRIES: Correct.

SAFER: — at — at bargain-basement interest rates.

JEFFRIES: Correct.

SAFER: So you're a lucky man, really.

JEFFRIES: I'm very fortunate that we have the government that we have.

SAFER: The fact is that, directly or indirectly, Phil Jeffries' race horse breeding operation and George Nickel's Rio Bravo Tennis Ranch are also benefiting directly or indirectly from this money, and they're not doing the country a damn bit of good.

JEFFRIES: Well, the similarity I cannot see between a tennis club and — and a breeding farm. I believe that horses were the original power that — mobile —

SAFER: These are race horses, though. Come on!

JEFFRIES: A horse is a — is a horse.

(Whinnying of a horse)

SAFER: A horse is a horse, and a fact is a fact, and Phil Jeffries, Sig Hoffman and George Nickel were able to borrow $23,504,350 at very, very low interest rates. And there's one more that really rankles people in these parts: it's a gentleman farmer who lives out of the county. He got a loan of $650,000. But that part-time farmer is the full-time president of an oil company. In the past year, the FmHA Kern County office has made 206 emergency loans worth $205 million. Throughout the nation, the figure is near three and a half billion.

If you're wondering why you're looking at a custom Cadillac, it's because the farmer who drives this car, Mr. Elmer Rossi, got a loan of $8.3 million from the FmHA. Farmer Rossi also owns a Rolls-Royce.

By now, you've got the idea that farming here in Kern County is no hayseed operation. But just who is it that hands out those millions, or recommends that those millions be handed out to men like George Nickel and Phil Jeffries and Sig Hoffman? Well, as you might expect, there's one over-worked civil servant in a modest office here in the Federal Building in downtown Bakersfield. He's the county FmHA supervisor, and his name is Howard Holden.

Why do we give this favorable — and some might say even pampering — treatment to farmers?

HOWARD HOLDEN: Well, our agency was based on farm problems in the early thirties — started in the old Dust Bowl days — and from disasters. And Congress wrote our rules and regulations to help the farmers, and the idea was supervised credit on longer terms and — and better interest rates. We were to help the farmers. Rather than going down the drain, we were to help them to come on up the ladder.

SAFER: I think most people would understand that. But when they think of it, they think of a — of a farmer and his family surviving. They don't think of millionaires owning tennis ranches and — and horse-breeding operations.

HOLDEN: But he qualified — had a qualified loss, and they're eligible.

SAFER: But do you sense the frustration that a lot of people who don't get those loans might feel when they see, say a man like Phil Jeffries, who paid no income tax last year, zero, got near $5 million at cheap interest rates from the federal government, and is living like a prince.

HOLDEN: Standard of living — that's his standard of living. He had a natural disaster, and we are to keep him in business.

SAFER: Without affecting his standard of living?

HOLDEN: Right, yes.

SAFER: So, as far as you're concerned, if a man had five gold Cadillacs parked in his driveway but he had a crop failure —

HOLDEN: If that's what he's been driving, we don't ask him to get rid of them and drive an old pick-up or something like that. Procedure says you can make the loan. So it comes down to the — the procedure, which was mandated by Congress, and we — we have to go — abide by that.

ARNOLD KIRSCHENMAN: You know, I had an old friend when I was very young — I was in high school — he told me something. He was a very well-read man, and he told me something that stuck with me all my life. Talking about Communism. Maybe not the place to bring it up. He says, "All Communism is, in one sentence: takes away your right to fail." Okay? That's what they've done here. You can't fail any more. Conversely, you can't succeed.

See Letters, October 21, 1979, page 82 .

A Few Minutes
with Andy Rooney

DAN RATHER: Tonight, Andy Rooney takes issue with President Carter not about SALT or inflation or energy, but about — well, let Andy tell you himself.

ANDY ROONEY: A few months ago, President Carter suggested people ought to burn more wood and less oil. I thought that was a terrible idea. People are finding all sorts of reasons now for cutting down trees on their property. Trees that would make great boards two feet wide and 50 feet long are being sawed into fireplace length to be chopped for burning. As an amateur cabinet maker, I could weep when I think of all the potential tables and chests of walnut, maple, cherry that have gone up in smoke.

I bring this up now because our best trees are being used up faster than they're growing. Don't let anyone convince you this isn't true. Trees are under attack from every side. The great fires that sweep the forests of the West are taking too many. Disease we can't control is taking all the elm trees in the East and Midwest. The paper makers grind up millions of trees every year. In some parts of the country, everyone has a wood stove. Sometimes the woodpile by the house is bigger than the house it was cut to heat; has to last the winter. The giant lumber companies are chewing into irreplaceable forests faster than ever. They've promoted the idea that trees are a renewable resource. Renewable resource — this is a promotion man's slogan. So is oil a renewable resource. If we left everything on earth alone for several hundred million years, we'd have more oil. When they speak of trees as being renewable, this is what they mean. They don't mean this. These trees are two years old, being grown under ideal conditions at the New York State Tree Farm. In two years, 10,000 of them might be the equivalent of one redwood.

I'd prefer not to get a lot of angry letters from lumber companies or people with wood-burning stoves. I have one myself. All I'm saying is our great trees are not really very renewable. If we start thinking of a tree as a replacement for a barrel of oil, Vermont's going to look like Iran.

Letters

MIKE WALLACE: In the mail this week were several letters about our story on the man in London who was murdered with a poisoned umbrella, ostensibly by a Russian KGB agent. One viewer wrote: "Surprise! Surprise! I thought only the nasty old CIA assassinated people. Amazing what one can learn from watching CBS."

In that same vein, another viewer wrote: "It is frightening what the KGB can do . . . (but) our own CIA couldn't (even buy the umbrella) without the approval of Congress."

About our interview with Clare Luce, a viewer noted her complaint that she had outlived her enemies. Not so, he said: "Please inform her that I'm alive and kicking and would be honored to be at the top of her list."

Another viewer noted a question in that interview about "bitchy women" and wrote: "Just what do you call that remark? I call it bitchy."

And finally, about our story on the woman who stole five dollars and became pregnant in prison after an affair with a guard, a supervisor for the Maryland Division of Probation wrote: "Please advise how I can get a job (at that prison). The fringe benefits sound great."

OCTOBER 21, 1979

Edward Rubin, M.D.

MARION GOLDIN, PRODUCER

MIKE WALLACE: The MediCal Fraud Unit inside the office of the California attorney general is conducting an intensive criminal investigation into the activities of one Dr. Edward Rubin. Now, the State of California spends more than $4 billion every year on MediCal. That's what they call Medicaid out there. It's medical treatment for folks who couldn't otherwise afford health care. And it's paid for by you and me, the taxpayers. The money goes to doctors and hospitals, clinics and labs. And the Dr. Edward Rubin who is the object of investigation by the MediCal Fraud Unit in California is typical, we are told, of those physicians nationwide who are building empires on these public medical dollars. Rubin has been doing it for almost as long as the programs have been in existence, and his medical and financial practices have been under scrutiny by federal and state authorities for years. Nonetheless, he continues to operate. We wondered why and how.

Our story begins in downtown Los Angeles at the Washington-Main Medical Clinic, across the street. That is the hub of the health empire of Dr. Edward Rubin. That is where his office is. We arrived here about an hour ago to try to see Dr. Rubin, and we went to the front door, the entrance. This is what occurred.

The clinic that advertises it is open 24 hours a day was suddenly shut tight, at least to us.

(Man locks the door on Wallace): What's that?

The clinic that is licensed to serve the public was locked — iron gates drawn across the entrances. It's obvious that they just don't want 60 MINUTES cameras coming into the Washington and Main Clinic. Why? Perhaps because they thought we would find what Dr. Joel Hendler found. He worked for Rubin for eight months, and was an eyewitness to the way that medicine was manipulated to make big money.

DR. JOEL HENDLER: People came in, and they went out in one of two directions — with lots of lab tests or into the hospital. Or lots of medicine, because I believe Ed had a piece of the pharmacy action as well. They also had lots of X-rays, because I believe Ed had a piece of the X-ray action as well.

WALLACE: Rubin also owned the hospitals that most of his clinic patients were sent to.

68

DR. HENDLER: Every morning, one of the technicians would bring around a mimeographed form, and on top of it would say, "A Friendly Reminder." And then would be the — listed the hospital names that Ed was involved in at the time. They changed often enough.

WALLACE: You mean, like —

DR. HENDLER: Imperial Hospital, Beverly Hills Doctors Hospital —

WALLACE: Stanton?

DR. HENDLER: — Stanton Hospital.

WALLACE: Uh-hmm.

DR. HENDLER: And here would be: "Number of beds — 100. Number of Patients — 46. Number of Empty Beds — 54." It didn't say fill those beds up —

WALLACE: But the message was —

DR. HENDLER: — but the implication was clear.

WALLACE: Now, Dr. Rubin knew, and his doctors and nurses quickly learned, that MediCal would pay only if the symptoms of potential hospital patients were described as serious, urgently needing attention.
You go to the clinic. You have a headache.

DR. HENDLER: You go to the hospital, and they write down "suspected meningitis," and they do more tests than anyone would need for that diagnosis. Then the patient gets sent home. Hallelujah, no meningitis! Tension headache. Meningitis suspected; none found.

WALLACE: Hallelujah? A bill for perhaps a thousand dollars, paid by MediCal. And that, says the California attorney general, was typical.
In this room at the California attorney general's office are half a million documents, seized by the MediCal Fraud Unit, involving Dr. Rubin, his patients, his clinics and hospitals. It is reported that Rubin's various medical enterprises have collected as much as $20 million from MediCal, another $12 million from Medicare. And the investigators here believe that as much as 40 percent of all that — 40 percent — may have gone for fraudulent or unnecessary care and services.
For four years this woman was a nurse in one of Dr. Rubin's hospitals. She, as well as Dr. Hendler, was willing to tell us on the record what other Rubin nurses and doctors told us privately.

NURSE: MediCal will only pay for certain illnesses written down in certain ways, so you have to know how to word things correctly. If a mother brought a baby into the emergency room and it had an ear infection —

WALLACE: Yes.

NURSE: — the baby would be admit— admitted to the hospital with a diagnosis of acute otitis media, which is an acute ear infection.

WALLACE: We've heard that the word "acute" was one that was frequently —

DR. HENDLER: Good word. Good word —

WALLACE: Yes.

DR. HENDLER: — used.

WALLACE: Expensive word to the taxpayers.

DR. HENDLER: Probably so.

WALLACE: Did none of the doctors ever object?

NURSE: Oh, yes, there were days when, in a 24-hour period, say, somewhere between 15 and 20 patients were admitted. A responsible physician would come in the next day and discharge all of those patients that had been ad— admitted in the previous 24 hours.

WALLACE: And?

NURSE: And those patients would go home, and all those tests would be cancelled. And the doctor would soon disappear.

WALLACE: What she means is the doctor would soon lose his job.
What percentage of the patients, would you estimate, are admitted to hospitals unnecessarily out of Washington and Main?

DR. HENDLER: Minimum, 80 percent.

WALLACE: It was also common practice, we learned, for Dr. Rubin's mother, who was in charge of the money at Washington-Main, it was also common practice for the woman known as Mama Rubin to ask patients who forgot their MediCal I.D. to give her partial payment in cash up front. Sometimes the money was refunded to them later when they produced their MediCal I.D. But frequently, according to Gail Yockley, who worked under Mrs. Rubin for four years, frequently the clinic kept the cash and still billed MediCal for the full amount.
Miss Yockley, are you absolutely sure about this double billing?

GAIL YOCKLEY: That's right.

WALLACE: Didn't you ever say anything about it to the people, for instance, to Mama Rubin? Say, "Ma— Mrs. Rubin, look, that — that poor person gave you $15 in cash."

YOCKLEY: Oh, are you kidding? You wouldn't do anything like that to Mama Rubin, because it was like you knew what was being done, Mama Rubin knew what was being done; they were doing it, they'd been doing it, and they were going to continue doing it.

WALLACE: Gail Yockley, Dr. Hendler and others had told us that MediCal patients, Medicare patients, indeed patients with any kind of insurance, were given many more expensive tests and procedures than patients who paid cash. We sent two persons to the Washington and Main Clinic to find out about that. Each complained of lower back pain. Each saw the same doctor. There was just one difference: Kathy paid cash, Lionel used his MediCal card.

KATHY: The first question I was asked literally was, "Do you have insurance?" I said no. And by the time that my chart got back to the examining room, it was marked in red "Not Insured."

WALLACE: So the difference, apparently, between you is that you're a cash patient. They didn't run tests on you. They just gave you a reasonable —

KATHY: Right, and I think that was due to the fact that it said "Not Insured" at the top of the chart.

WALLACE: And as far as you're concerned, blood tests, X-rays, urinalysis, two visits — all paid for by MediCal?

LIONEL: All on MediCal.

WALLACE: Kathy's visit cost $23 in cash. Lionel's visits, X-rays and tests cost the taxpayer $240 in MediCal and Medicare money. And remember, they both went in complaining of the identical ailment — lower back pain.

This is Dr. Edward Rubin. He ignored our letters and telephone calls requesting an interview. Nonetheless, we did manage to photograph the silent Dr. Rubin coming to work.

Dr. Rubin, I wonder if I could talk to you just for a moment, sir. Dr. Rubin?

Shortly after Dr. Rubin disappeared inside the clinic, I came out and got back into the van where we had been staking him out for the past few days. Once inside the van, an employee of Dr. Rubin handed me a note inside here that said "Call Mr. Dalton." Mr. Dalton, it turned out, was Dr. Rubin's attorney, and he and I negotiated the terms under which Edward Rubin would come out of his clinic and let himself be photographed.

My understanding is that your attorney says that until these legal matters are over, you don't want to talk, and he's advising you not to talk about it. Is that correct?

DR. EDWARD RUBIN: Yes, he's — yes.

WALLACE: If this is where Dr. Rubin makes his living, this is where he lives, under the palms of Beverly Hills. While we were out here, we learned that he had just put that house on the market for $1,950,000, but was willing to take a million six. We could not find out whether he was planning to move to more lavish or more modest quarters.

The Rubins millions are generated, as we have said, in places like this — Stanton Hospital. Now, according to this memo from the California Department of Health, the percentage of MediCal business at Stanton increased by 331 percent from 1974 to '76, after Dr. Rubin and his partners bought the hospital. The emergency room is the golden door, for most of the MediCal patients here come in that way. But it's not just the money that intrigued us; it was the quality of medical care.

The quality of the doctors?

DR. HENDLER: Awful.

NURSE: There were one or two good ones. The rest of them were all losers.

WALLACE: Roberta Gordon was 30 years old when she was brought to the Stanton Hospital emergency room by Dennis Stillwell, then her boyfriend, now her husband. She was doubled over in pain, and was diagnosed, correctly, as suffering from a tubal pregnancy. Then began the nightmare for Roberta, the wife Dennis calls "Bob" for short.

DENNIS STILLWELL: Bob's breathing stopped, just completely stopped, and so for a while was without oxygen to her system and, you know, especially to the brain. That—that might have not—that might not have happened if I.V.'s had been started or if Bob had received blood. And as you know, what happened is that the laboratory technician, he left. From the time of coming in and seeing the emergency room physician till the time she was operated on, it was four hours.

WALLACE: In pain?

STILLWELL: Right.

WALLACE: With no blood transfusions, no intravenous feeding?

STILLWELL: Right.

WALLACE: The result? Roberta suffered severe brain damage that has left her unable to speak.

The doctor who admitted Roberta Gordon that night is this man, Jerome Rehman. He was head of the emergency room at Stanton for more than a year. The only picture we could get of him is this mug shot taken when he was booked on criminal charges in 1962.

You, Bobby, knew that his — his license had been revoked after he'd been convicted of and served a jail term for conspiracy — quote — "to commit acts injurious to the public health, and for performing unnecessary surgery and tests for profit?" (Roberta shakes her head) You didn't know that.

After that conviction, Dr. Rehman's license to practice medicine was taken away in 1968. That license — he is a Doctor of Osteopathy — was restored in 1974, before he signed on at Stanton. Rehman left there in 1977. Now he's head of the emergency room at this hospital in Cerritos Gardens, California. When we found him there, he didn't want to talk to us.

The only way Roberta Gordon can "talk" is with the help of an electronic communicator, and we asked her to tell us who she holds responsible for what happened to her.

(Roberta punches message into communicator . . . hands tape to her husband . . . who hands it to Wallace)

(Wallace reads tape): "All of the people involved in the hospital."

Roberta Gordon sued Stanton Hospital and Dr. Rehman. Before the case could go to court, they settled. She received a lump sum of $300,000 plus $2,000 a month for life.

As we said earlier, Dr. Rubin has been at this game for a long time. He has owned Washington-Main Clinic since 1961. He was one of the first to see the potential windfall of California's pre-paid health insurance. Tom Moore has known of Ed Rubin since those days. Moore was then an assistant director of health for California, with direct responsibility for those pre-paid plans.

I have here a memorandum from the Department of Health Care Services here in the State of California way back in 1970. Quote: "The most salient aspect of the meeting with Dr. Rubin was his apparent expectation of very significant profits from the project." Why has he survived?

TOM MOORE: Well, physicians don't like to talk about other physicians. They are not likely to — to go to the public or go to a law enforcement agency and ask for action against one of their own members.

WALLACE: It is said that one of the reasons that Dr. Edward Rubin has prospered for so long is that he has friends in high places, friends described in this confidential report prepared by California's Department of Justice; friends that include California State Senator John Briggs, who got a $77,000 insurance contract from Rubin; and former California State Senator and Lieutenant Governor Mervin Dymally, whom he rewarded, according to this report, with campaign contributions amounting to $13,000.

One of the many politicians who became aware of Dr. Rubin's activities as far back as the early seventies is Senator Edward Kennedy.

He sent two of his investigators to California back in 1971 to take a look at Dr. Rubin. And this never-published 157-page report is only part of what they found. "It is quite apparent," said the Kennedy report back in 1973, "it is quite apparent that a substantial portion of the income generated by Dr. Rubin's enterprises can be attributed to improper and excessive utilization policies found in Rubin facilities."

You got to wonder about why Senator Kennedy apparently, or somebody in his office, put the quietus on this report.

MOORE: Well, be a good question to ask him.

WALLACE: We wanted to, but Senator Kennedy refused our repeated requests for an interview; refused to tell us why he never held hearings, and why the report was never made public, though it had cost upwards of $75,000 to produce that report.

We also asked another presidential hopeful, Governor Jerry Brown, to talk to us about his fellow Californian, Dr. Edward Rubin. He declined, and refused to talk to us about why he twice vetoed a $125,000 appropriation for nine more MediCal investigators.

MOORE: He never supported strong surveillance or monitoring efforts by the state. In fact, he said one day, somewhat proudly, to the papers in Sacramento that he doesn't believe in government as a manager. Well, that pretty well says it.

WALLACE: Again, Dr. Joel Hendler.

DR. HENDLER: I said to Ed, "There's a lot of money in medicine, Ed. Can't we make money doing good medicine? Do we have to make money this way?" And he would always say, "Well, let's fix it up." I wish I could tell you, Mike, that he'd say, "Ah, the hell with it. I want to practice bad medicine." He never said that.

WALLACE: We were not surprised that Dr. Edward Rubin didn't want to talk to us, but frankly we did wonder why it was impossible to get any responsible public official, state or federal, executive or legislative, to come forward and explain why Dr. Rubin is still practicing the brand of medicine he practices; why they would not talk to us about what some of them privately describe as the biggest case of MediCal fraud in California, the biggest case of Medicaid fraud in the United States.

Be that as it may, a Los Angeles County grand jury commences an investigation of the Rubin matter beginning November 1st.

*See Senator Kennedy's response, Letters,
December 9, 1979, page 181.*

Deep in the Heart
of Scotland
WILLIAM K. McCLURE, PRODUCER

HARRY REASONER: "Deep In The Heart Of Scotland" is a story about an oil strike and Texans and some of the roughest waters in the world. And because it's oil we're talking about, it's worth the money and effort and the hazard to go anywhere at any price to find it. Even here.

MAN (over BBC shortwave radio):   Attention all shipping. The meteorological office issued the following gale warning . . .

WOMAN (over BBC shortwave radio):   . . . eight. Occasionally severe gale force nine . . .

MAN (over BBC shortwave radio):   . . . during the night. Wave heights on North Sea will reach 50 feet.

REASONER: If you didn't have to have something that was here, you wouldn't come here, would you? This is the North Sea. It is routinely almost unbelievably violent. There's a lot of oil beneath those waters. Already, production is almost as great as Kuwait's — a million seven hundred thousand barrels a day. That's worth about $39 million. That's enough to help a lot of countries in the West, and to set Britain free from bondage to OPEC.

The oil is controlled and divided by Britain, Norway, Denmark and Holland. Sixty American companies are involved in exploration or production or in building the pipelines that take the oil ashore to Scottish terminals. They are headquartered in Aberdeen, which has become as near as the North Sea has to a Houston.

"Already, production is almost as great as Kuwait's—a million seven hundred thousand barrels a day."

It doesn't look much like an oil town. It looks more like one of those travel ads you see that say, "Come to unchanged Scotland sleeping in 2,000 years of history." But the signs are there, if you hunt for them. Those flags are the flags of the new lairds of oil, and the old manor house is now a technical training center. And elsewhere, lying low-profile in city and landscape, are the other evidences of one of the century's great oil booms and all the problems that go with it.

(Scottish bagpipes-and-drums music over montage of faces)

I suppose one of the fairest things in the world to say about Scots is that they are not hysterical. If they were, the centuries of their poverty and oppression would have made those who didn't emigrate hopelessly neurotic. They didn't scream; they went out and helped Britain build its empire. But they have never been invaded before in just this way; and if not in a panic, they are frequently puzzled. They have to keep telling themselves that all the oil and the oil money and the oil people mean things are better. That's the view of an Englishman who was the Labour Party's minister of energy when the North Sea oil mushroomed, Anthony Wedgwood Benn.

ANTHONY WEDGWOOD BENN: Well, we are in a better shape, because of course it has completely lifted from us, or will have done by the end of this year, any burden of buying oil from abroad. Now, if you take the American balance of payments, one of the major problems that President Carter has to face is the need to finance every year, by some means or another, the importation of the oil that the United States economy needs to keep it going. That will have completely gone from us by the end of this year; and throughout the eighties and the nineties, we will be spending not a single pound sterling in buying oil. Indeed, we'll be selling oil. We'll be net exporters of oil. We are the only country in the Western world which is entirely self-sufficient in oil, and will be for some 10, 20 years ahead.

REASONER: If Britain is self-sufficient, it is with the help of a great influx of oil people, the people who make the plans of the great multinational companies work. They always seem to be on the move, so it is at the airport that Aberdeen looks most like the boom town it is.

AIRPORT ANNOUNCER: . . . who have not yet checked in, please do so now at the (Indistinct) check-in desk.

REASONER: People like Jim Tweedy of Occidental come in here and may never see downtown. Their Scottish experience is off the jet from America to what may be the world's busiest heliport, where the hundreds of daily flights keep the oil people moving to and from the platforms out at sea, where the oil is.

This is the most visible sign of the 25 platforms out hidden between the waves, of the 12,500 men who commute to them, of the 20 to 30 years of oil reserves under the water, and of the costs — capital costs up to ten times what they would be on land: little items, like the $2,000 an hour it can cost to run one of these helicopters. Tweedy runs a platform that is code-named "Piper." When he's aboard, he's like a ship's captain.

Whether you were developing an oil field in Nigeria or Texas or Saudi Arabia or hundreds of feet down in the North Sea, chances are you start with Texas technology and Texas technologists. Much of the work force Jim Tweedy supervises is now British, but the basic know-how is still American. They knew how to build this platform on legs that drop 500 feet beneath the surface, build it so it can stand up to the waves and bring oil out at a price now competitive with OPEC, especially since OPEC has raised the price.

It's not exactly a spartan life. While there is no alcohol, there's plenty of food, there are movies, there are cassettes of television shows. They drill 24 hours a day, so far in 25 separate wells. These are roughnecks; gentle men, perhaps, but long ago labeled roughnecks from the nature of the work. As North Sea oil jobs go, they aren't even very well paid. Maybe $250 a week, maximum.

There is an elite among the oil men — an elite of hazard. These are the divers. Quiet men like Jerry Smith, once a Californian, ex-Navy diver, without much idea of the future, except that when his fitness for this work dwindles, he might open a diving school somewhere. In the meantime, he goes down in a bell and out along the underwater apparatus to fix things or build them. These are jobs that would be hard enough on dry land. Jerry also inspects the pipelines that carry the crude over a hundred miles along the sea bed to the main land terminals. A saturation diver can spend as many as 28 days at this kind of thing. When he's not actually wet, he's in a decompression chamber, playing chess or reading; no cigarettes, no alcohol, only the consciousness that he's making, for the moment, a lot of money — and the consciousness that in this kind of work 29 divers have died and dozens more have been injured.

Nobody knows how long you could stand life out in the North Sea, even working on the surface. Nobody wants to find out. So, the choppers bring out new people, and take the old ones in to land for a kind of R & R. It's always a livelier flight on the way to the shore.

(Scottish bagpipes music)

Aberdeen has made some accommodation to the oil men's needs. Some of the bars are open night and day — not the Scottish custom. These are men who think they need a drink after two weeks, and a cigarette. You'd think a diver who hadn't had a cigarette in 28 days might take the occasion to kick the habit, but they don't.

Jerry Smith made $14,000 this trip. But the thing about divers is they would probably do it anyway, even when, as in the case of Jerry and Ev Thompson, it also gives them problems at home.

Does this kind of a job bother your wife?

THOMPSON: Yes.

REASONER: It does?

THOMPSON: Yes.

REASONER: If she were here, what would she say about it? Wha— what would she say was wrong with it?

THOMPSON: Oh, well, what she'd say about it probably isn't repeatable on TV.

REASONER: It's a hard place for families. This is the oil field where a husband is gone not for the day or a couple of days but for weeks. The wives do what they can, sharing their loneliness at the Petroleum Wives Club. The companies do what they can. They even hired Mark Ellington, an American-born Scot whose major achievement in life may have been the restoration of this medieval castle. They hired him as a kind of consultant on how to make on-shore life at least as bearable as off-shore life.

MARK ELLINGTON: There's a cultural similarity between a lot of people in the oil industry and their background and people in this part of the world. So I think, you know, it — it wasn't quite the cultural shock that one had expected. I mean, the first time anybody appeared on Union Street in Aberdeen wearing a kilt and cowboy boots, I think that sort of —

REASONER (laughs):   You've seen that?

ELLINGTON: Oh, I have indeed, yeah. It's — it is a mind-blower. There's nothing like python skin and tartan, you know, to sort of — (Laughter)

REASONER: It isn't only the cowboy boots that the Americans want with them in Aberdeen. The American food store stocks the whole mystique of home — the juices and the cake mixes, the Texan specialties. It has the familiar atmosphere of a small-town general store. It's the feeling of home. So it's not surprising that the Texas flag flies over the stern granite house of Dr. Maitland Mackie and his wife, Pauline. He's Scot and she's Texan, and they know what a Texan wants to do at a party: he wants to burn some choice beef. The Scots in general are not opposed to people cooking beef; they grow the cattle for it. But they have some doubts about this friendly invasion. Dr. Adam Watson is an environmentalist.

DR. ADAM WATSON: There certainly is resentment about the high cost of living. There's resentment about the fact that the best jobs have gone to foreigners. And there's resentment about the fact that — people having to live in these towns without facilities.

REASONER: Is there any specific resentment of Americans? Are we behaving badly?

DR. WATSON: Not badly, I think. But people — many people do feel that the way the Norwegians have done it has been better, because they have said, "We're going to take the oil much more slowly, and we'll get some of the Americans and other foreigners who know about oil to come in and instruct our own people to do the — some of the top jobs as well as the bottom jobs." So there — there has been some resentment about that.

REASONER: The resentment probably would not have been decisive even if it had been greater. Aberdeen still doesn't look much like an oil town as you walk up and down the rainy streets; but the oil is there, and it is so important to all the West that Aberdeen really has no choice but to live with it. And there are benefits. In traditionally poor Scotland, there is work for almost everyone here. The jobs may not pay for the inflated prices of what housing there is, but there is work.

(Scottish bagpipe music)

I guess what you'd say is that the Scots are living with it; they are not necessarily enthusiastic. But when, since Robert the Bruce, were the Scots enthusiastic about anything? They don't rebel and shoot from ambush like the Irish, but they also, I suspect, feel that once again they have been a bit used by the English.

The English conscience is clear. Anthony Wedgwood Benn thinks the whole thing has been well-handled and beneficial.

ANTHONY WEDGWOOD BENN: . . . oil, and we don't want to see the North Sea exploited as ruthlessly as the Middle East was, with all the gas flared off and the oil run out and then the oil companies pull out their stumps, as we say in cricket, and move to another oil field. We want to pace it so that it fits in with the — the — the general pattern of our own economic and industrial policy. And on the whole, the oil companies have understood that.

REASONER: Mark Ellington, the adopted Scot and a ballad writer, has doubts.

(Ellington with guitar singing ballad about the exploitation of North Sea oil over visual montage)

By Design

SUZANNE ST. PIERRE, PRODUCER

MORLEY SAFER: Most of us go through life using all kinds of objects, eating all kinds of food, that comes out of all kinds of packages, without giving them a second thought. Well, the shape and the look of those objects does not just happen, it happens by design. It is the art of industrial design. There have been great successes — say, the Coca-Cola bottle and label — and great disasters — say, the Edsel car. Industrial design truly identifies us. All those familiar objects reflect what and who we are. Well, there's one industrial designer who is truly the father of the art. He's a transplanted Frenchman named Raymond Loewy.

He's been designing for 70 years, and there's not a person in the country who does not recognize his handiwork. We are surrounded by it. He redesigned the Shell sign, and was responsible for turning Esso into Exxon. When Coke wanted a better way of dispensing itself, it went to Loewy to design a machine. Way back when a tractor looked like this, International Harvester got him to redesign it so it looked like this. Then they got him to redesign their logo, which looks like this. And Pennsylvania Railroad once had trains like this, and Raymond Loewy made them look like this. Greyhound buses looked this way, until Loewy made them look this way. When the Post Office got tired of its old symbol, Loewy gave it a new symbol — though some would say the horse moved faster than the eagle.

But wheels have always been his passion. He took the old Studebaker and gave us the 1947 Studebaker. It revolutionized motor car design. His '53 Studebaker took the revolution a step further. Then he took that Studebaker and, in 1961, designed the Avanti. Studebaker folded, they say through bad management, but Avantis are still made for purists. He gave that "up, up and away" look to TWA, he put this package around Lucky Strikes, and made Schick razors go from "push-pull, click-click" to "buzz-buzz." When President Kennedy got Air Force One, he went to Loewy to design the soft, warm interior and the imposing presidential exterior. Everyone making almost everything went to Loewy — from beer containers and vitamin bottles to department stores and ferry boats and sewing machines and popcorn machines and tables and chairs and cups and saucers — all our worldly goods, and even goods for outer space. When NASA wanted Skylab, they went to Loewy to make it an "earthly" place for men to live 300 miles up in space.

Loewy himself lives in great comfort, partly in a chateau outside of Paris and, in the cold months, in a house he designed in Palm Springs, California. He is 85 years old now, but his eye and his mind are as sharp as they ever were.

RAYMOND LOEWY: A good design is a design that does not get obsolete, number one, that stays classic like a Greek statue. That's good design. Secondly, it should be humble; it should not jump at you. It should blend with the surroundings. That's good design. Anything violent, brutal, for me is — is vul— cheap, vulgar. That's junk. A good design is simple. When you look at it, you have the impression of great simplicity, the beauty of simplicity. If it looks gadgety and complicated, it's not good design.

SAFER: Beca— I'll tell you something. I see something here right in your studio. I'd say that's good design —

LOEWY: Yes.

SAFER: — and I would say that's bad design.

LOEWY: This is — this is absolutely awful. It's the only thing I could find in Palm Springs 25 years ago or 30 years ago with three lights on. As soon as I can, I'll discard that. I think it's junky, it's terrible. But that's the art of 25 years ago, and I did not design it, believe me.

SAFER: Loewy started designing in Paris. He got a patent on a model airplane when he was only 15. He arrived in America in 1919, and took a job as a fashion illustrator; then started doodling, improving on the look of things.

His first real assignment was from the Gestetner Company. In the twenties, he took their Rube Goldberg duplicating machine and transformed it. What he has designed could fill a museum, and many things have been placed in the Metropolitan, the Smithsonian and the Museum of Modern Art, including his own office that he designed in the early thirties.

Loewy is one of the founders of streamlining. You can see it in his 1934 Hupmobile. The design was not only for aesthetic but for aerodynamic effect. His point was to make commonplace things easy to look at and easy to use, and that is visible in all of his work. Even things that seem old-fashioned now have a classic look to them.

In Palm Springs, we asked him to cast his eye on some recent designs in one of the biggest shops there, the Alan Ladd Hardware Store.

LOEWY: Now, I'll let you guess, Mr. Safer, how — how — how you can tell time from that clock.

SAFER: Well, there's a square with some fabric, and then inside it another square, and then a black piece of glass. Well, I — I can guess.

LOEWY: Wait, clap your hand in this — (claps hand . . . laughs as time appears in small window) Yes, here is the time. But please — please — Yeah, okay. Now, above it is a much less sophisticated clock, but at least it tells you what time it is.

SAFER: Easy to read.

LOEWY: And it's cheaper. A phony adaptation of technology, because this is high technology, you know. Look at that, this is fantastic. (Laughs)

SAFER: What about the packaging?

LOEWY: This package — well, those three — three roaches seem to look at television. (Safer laughing) I'm sure it's not 60 MINUTES, but they — (laughter) — are looking at television, anyway. I think it's —

SAFER: You don't feel it's threatening enough?

LOEWY: No, I —

SAFER: I mean, as packaging?

LOEWY: — I think it's a dreadful package. But these batteries, for instance, are very well designed —

SAFER: And packaged.

LOEWY: — and packaged. It's plain, it's simple, it's nice.

SAFER: But what would you do? What would you have, a roach being stomped on? Or — or what?

LOEWY: No, I would show them on their back with legs up, killed, which I think — I think is the purpose.

SAFER: Can we find something good?

LOEWY: Oh, here — here's a — well, this is a beautifully designed hook. You don't see the fasteners, you don't see the screws, you see?

SAFER: Is good design more expensive than bad design?

LOEWY: No, it's usually cheaper. That's one of my main — most irritating thing for me, that the added artistic — artistic touch adds cost and makes the thing usually, if not ugly, at least a little bit vulgar. Oh, here's a very interesting little gadget. Oh, this one is very expensive. It's — how much? A hundred —

SAFER: A hundred and thirty-three dollars.

LOEWY: A hundred and thirty dollars, but I've not been able to find out what —

SAFER: What does it do?

LOEWY: I don't know. I don't know. It probably —

SAFER: Ah, hold on.
          (To salesman): What does this do?

SALESMAN: It's a wine opener.

SALESWOMAN: A wine opener.

SAFER: A wine opener.

LOEWY: Oh! oh, oh.

SAFER: It's not a nut cracker.

LOEWY (laughing):   Oh, excuse me.

SAFER: Here's one for $2.50.

LOEWY: These not — these aren't good. Oh, my God! Yeah, look — look at that one.

Can you imagine a poor kid who has been told that he must go to the — to the toilet, and gets there and sees that? Must be frightened stiff. (Laughter)

SAFER: Put a tiger in your tank.

(Laughter . . . indistinct cross-talk . . . garbage truck blows horn)

Is there art in − in something as familiar as a − as a garbage truck?

LOEWY: Yes. Well, I wouldn't say art, but it's designed purely for function, and usually what expresses function correctly, directly, is good, and has permanent value, aesthetically speaking.

SAFER: Among all the things that you've designed, what was the biggest challenge, the most exciting?

LOEWY: NASA, without any doubt. NASA, Skylab. My assignment was to make sure that three men could stay three months in space. And they asked me, "Would you accept the responsibility?" And I accepted it with — with great, great pride. And spent many nights wondering if I'd guessed right, because what we did had to be educated intuition, rather than anything else.

SAFER: No experience.

LOEWY: No experience whatever. We had to establish in space a 1-G atmosphere ambiance, 1-G being, well, gravity one, which is the earth gravity, compared to zero-G, which is no gravity in space. But mostly, and the most important, they all agreed that I wanted a porthole, that is, a window on the world. So, by putting a porthole in, they spent most of their free time looking at the earth. They could see highways, they could see cities. They were not isolated from the world, and that did a — a great deal for the morale.

SAFER: This could be the best representation of Raymond Loewy's work − uncluttered, unself-conscious. The Avanti was designed about 20 years ago; a look and shape that, it would seem, will never be out of date.

In what way did this car revolutionize design? It does not look like a practically 20-year-old car.

LOEWY: First, I eliminated the grill, so the intake (indistinct) is way down there, where it should be. All racing cars, they pick up — the closer you are to the ground, the more air you get in. Secondly, I wanted an off-center treatment. I don't like balanced design. Large window here, good rear vision.

SAFER: Well, this is pretty standard stuff on cars now.

LOEWY: Yes, yes, accepted now or taken for granted, but it was new at the time in '61. To appreciate this job, one has to feel it flowing, you know. By touch, you sense a form. I — at least I do; even better with my eyes closed.

SAFER: Does the look of a thing really make any difference? I mean, does it matter to consumers?

LOEWY: I think the best way to answer that is at a dinner party here in Palm Springs about two years ago, I was sitting next to a charming lady, who said, "Mr. Loewy, you are a designer?" "Yes." "I understand you designed the Exxon sign. But why did you design it that way — with two X's?" I say, "Why — why do you ask me?" "Because I couldn't help notice it." "Well," I said, "that's the answer. When you design a sign, it's to attract attention, and I attracted your attention." I'm not saying that's the difference between success or failure, but it's maybe between success or great success, and that's what it happened to be. And when you are talking about mass selling for companies like that, any — any — any ingredient or any — any accent that might in — attract attention more to that station than to the next one is very important.

SAFER: Have you ever refused commissions? Are there certain things you would not design?

LOEWY: Yes, two. One is a casket, because anything's got to do with — with death — death doesn't scare me, I'm — I'm used to the idea, but it bores me terribly. The other one, I was invited here for lunch by someone, by a friend of mine. Say, "I'd like you to meet a manufacturer, who is a very bright man. He has a new product he'd like to talk to you about." He says, "We've developed a new hand grenade, and we would like to increase the fragmentation to — so we get perhaps smaller fragment but more of them."

SAFER: More killing power.

LOEWY: More killing power or — or wounding power. And I was so — so shocked that I left the table and the lunch and came back here. I think it's the most shocking thing to ask me to design. I'd nev— never touch a thing like that. And both are connected with end of life, as you see.

SAFER: What is the most perfectly designed thing that you've ever seen?

LOEWY: For me it's the egg, because the form of the egg is absolutely streamlined, functional. It goes through the — the chicken with a minimum of — of friction. If it were cubed, for instance, the life of the chicken would be unbearable, I imagine. (Safer laughs) So I think it's a perfect design.

SAFER: The egg may be just about the only thing that Raymond Loewy has not thought of redesigning. At 85, most men have become conservative in their ideas, and prefer the present or the former shape of things to new ideas. Not so with Loewy. He still works day and night at his drawing board, looking for ways of improving the most ordinary objects — a design for living that is as beautiful and practical and painless as the egg.

A Few Minutes
with Andy Rooney

DAN RATHER: Everybody is sore about something or other that costs more than it used to — a gallon of gas, a quart of milk, a phone call. Andy Rooney is no exception.

ANDY ROONEY: The two things I can think of that have gone up most in price in the last 10 years are hotel rooms and candy bars. All these nickel candy bars here are 30 cents now. At least the hotel rooms are still the same size. These are all smaller. Anything that provides continuity to our lives is a good thing, even if it's only a candy bar. All these bars have been around for a long time now. I remember almost all of these from when I was a kid on Partridge Street.

Baby Ruth, Butterfingers, Oh Henry, Bit-O-Honey, Clark Bar. We used to freeze Milky Ways. I wonder if kids still do that. Do you know the best-selling candy bar right now? You'll never guess it. There it is, Snickers. We have these laid out in order of their popularity. Reese's Peanut Butter Cups is next, then M&M's, Hershey with nuts, 3 Musketeers, and so on. Here's one of my favorites, number 14, Mounds. Their listed ingredients look pretty good. I used to like Heath bars. They were small, but pure gold. They used to make them with butter. But look at some of these ingredients now. Milk chocolate, almonds. Fine. But hydrogenated soybean oil? Mono- and diglycerides? Beta-carotene? This is candy?

They keep trying to put things that are good for us in some of these candy bars. Hershey has a nutrition chart on the back. You know, riboflavin, calcium, iron, that sort of thing.

That's not what I care about when I eat candy. It's like putting vitamins in gin. The way I look at it, if I'm going to eat an unhealthy number of calories, I want to eat the best-tasting calories there are: sugar, butter and chocolate. Hold the hydrogenated soybean oil, please!

Letters

DAN RATHER: Most of the viewers who wrote to us after last week's broadcast were incensed that millionaire farmers could get low-interest loans from the government.

One of those viewers said the American system had become a case of: "Capitalism for the poor . . . socialism for the rich."

Another viewer said it was a case of: "Old McDonald had a farm with a Rolls-Royce (here and a tennis court there)."

But we also heard from the Department of Agriculture, from the man who administers those loans. He wrote: "We have taken steps to tighten procedures and ask that Congress change the law so that all emergency loans can be held to a limit."

About our art theft story, several viewers asked virtually the same question about the president of the Chicago Art Institute: "How could a person in his position fail to recognize a valuable Cezanne stolen from his own institution and also be unable to distinguish an oil painting from a water color?"

And another viewer said: "I hope it wasn't he who was sent to make the ransom exchange. If he was, I would advise the Art Institute to take a closer look at their retrieved Cezanne."

And finally, about our story on union leader Bill Winpisinger, a viewer wrote: "If (he) was so wrong about Jimmy Carter in '76, what makes him think he's so right about (Kennedy) in 1980?"

OCTOBER 28, 1979

Holy Smoke

JEANNE SOLOMON, PRODUCER

DAN RATHER: One of the things we Americans have always accepted is that people have a right to practice their religion, no matter how unorthodox, without being molested by the law or by the rest of the community. But there's church in Florida now that lawmen say is stretching that proposition a lot further than most people can accept, at least a lot further than they can accept.

The issue will be decided by a case before the Florida Supreme Court that could eventually wind up before the United States Supreme Court, and that issue is whether or not the state can prosecute members of a church who believe marijuana was given to them by God, and that smoking pot is for them a holy ritual. Our story begins on Star Island in the coastal waterway between Miami and Miami Beach.

Over the years, the people who've lived in this part of Miami Beach often have been famous, sometimes have been notorious, always have been wealthy. The Duke of Windsor, the abdicated King Edward VIII, often stayed with friends in the island neighborhood. Gangster Al Capone once had a not-so-small castle over there. But even Al Capone could not have disturbed his neighbors as much as have the current residents of Number 43, Star Island.

(Coptics chanting)

The call themselves the Ethiopian Zion Coptic Church, a religion these white Americans claim has its roots in black Jamaica. Their outraged neighbors and many law enforcement officials call them a fraud, a group of rich dopeheads who have been allowed to laugh at the law and get away with it. That's because the Coptics insist that marijuana, which they call by its Jamaican name, ganja, is their sacrament; as valid and as necessary to them, they say, as wine is to Catholics during communion.

These services take place three times a day, but the Coptics appear to partake of their sacrament just about all the time. Their leader here on Star Island is a six foot seven inch former Catholic from Boston named Thomas Reilly. He prefers to be known as Brother Louv.

BROTHER LOUV: Well, let's start from the beginning, page one of the Bible, Genesis, book one, verse 29: "Behold, I have given you every green herb bearing seed, which is upon all the face of all the earth . . . " Now, is there any dispute that marijuana is a green herb bearing seed that grows all over the earth?

RATHER: All right, let's — let's address ourselves to the truth. Is the basic message you should smoke ganja?

BROTHER LOUV: The basic message is you should stop your sin. When you and I are neighbors and I have the security that you are a man who keeps the commandments of God, then I know you're not going to rob me, you're not going to murder me, you're not going to covet me. So that's the only security that people can have is to stop their sinful ways, stop becoming homosexuals when they know what the Scripture says about homosexuality; they know what wisdom shows you about destroying your own seed of life. They should stop their abortion. They should stop their birth control. They should stop their oral sex, their hand sex, and any way that they're destroying their own life and their own seed life.

They should stop those things immediately. And they should have known to be smoking ganja from a long time. For how is it that I know too?

RATHER: The Coptic Church bought this house in 1975 for $270,000, paid for in cash. It's a kind of luxury commune with about 40 members, but a commune that adheres to the Bible, Old and New Testament teachings; a kind of combination of Billy Graham fundamentalism and kosher law. Though there is no formal marriage ceremony, the Coptic women must be faithful and subject to their husbands. But the women, and even the Coptic children, are encouraged to smoke marijuana, and that's where the trouble first started.

It was in early 1978 that the local Miami media began focusing in on activities of the Coptic Church. While it was the constant chanting and the smell of marijuana that upset close neighbors on Star Island, it was those scenes of the Coptic children smoking marijuana on local television that brought protests from the city as a whole. Then in November, 1978, news broke of the mass deaths of the People's Temple cult in Jonestown, Guyana, and many Miami residents were shocked into wondering if they might not have a potential Jonestown on their doorstep.

BROTHER LOUV: I have no knowledge of Jim Jones except what I read in the paper. And I read in the Bible that the wages of sin is death, and I understand he ran a homosexual, perverted, wife-swapping, adulterous, lecherous camp somewhere in the jungle, and that many of the people were murdered and some committed suicide, and I'm not the least bit surprised.

RATHER: Nevertheless, the furor caused by the Coptic Church's activities led the state attorney to take action against them. A civil action for public nuisance was brought against the Coptics, rather than a criminal charge for possession of marijuana. The state attorney's office had in fact offered to drop all charges if the Coptics would move out of Star Island to some place where they were less conspicuous. The Coptics flatly refused. Instead, they hired the best and most expensive lawyers in town. Milton Ferrell, Jr. is their chief defense attorney.

MILTON FERRELL, JR: All right, so it was a civil action; went before the judge. The judge decided that, yes, this was a church under the definition of a church for First Amendment purposes, right?

FERRELL: He decided it was a religion. It was a —

RATHER: It was a religion. And now the question before the Supreme Court is whether it is or isn't.

FERRELL: No, the question before the Supreme Court — the Supreme Court's not concerned as to the sincerity of the religious belief, or as to whether or not marijuana's essential to the conduct of the religion, nor whether the religion is a religion under the First Amendment of the United States Constitution. Those findings can't be challenged in the Supreme Court. Those have been found as a fact already. There's no controversy about that at all. The controversy in the supreme court of Florida is this: whether the State has a compelling state interest sufficient to override the fundamental interest of any citizen of the United States to practice their religion without governmental interference in it.

RATHER: The implications of such a confrontation, says Florida Assistant State Attorney Henry Adorno, extend far beyond the Coptic Church.

HENRY ADORNO: If a court were to rule that the Coptics do have a First Amendment right, then I think that would be the opening of the floodgates for possible legalization of marijuana in Florida. I, as a prosecutor, would then have to go around and decide who to arrest for possession of marijuana. They obviously would then come up with the defense, "Well, I'm a Coptic," or "I have, you know, I believe that marijuana is my sacrament," which would then muddle the criminal system to no end in trying to defend or trying to prosecute a case where the defense is First Amendment grounds.

RATHER: Meanwhile, quite aware of all the legal problems they have caused, the Coptics continue their activities at Star Island. While the constitutional issue is debated, a federal civil rights ruling allows them to go on smoking marijuana unmolested. One court battle, the right to be considered a church, has already been won. But just what sort of church is it?

The Coptics claim that their mother church is on the Caribbean island of Jamaica. Brother Louv and his American brethren first came to Jamaica in the early seventies. They were all graduates of Haight-Ashbury and the campuses of the sixties, a remnant of a lost generation. They came looking for marijuana, and they found it and bought it in the slums of Kingston from this Jamaican, Keith Gordon. At the same time, Gordon introduced them to an obscure Christian sect. This was the Ethiopian Zion Coptic Church, which claimed for years that the blacks of Africa were the original Jews of the Bible, and the slaves of the New World were their direct descendants. Marijuana, or ganja, was the "holy herb." Ripe for a new spiritual experience, these Americans could have found nothing better than a religion that extolled the poor, the black man and marijuana all in one tidy package.

Coptic Heights lies 30 miles outside Kingston. The Coptic Church owns as far as the eye can see. They have roads. They have trucks, lots of trucks. They have a dozen corporations trading under different names. To the average Jamaican, these Coptics are efficient, prosperous and highly suspect.

DAWN RITCH: What they're doing is, on an organized basis, exporting marijuana to Miami.

RATHER: Jamaican journalist Dawn Ritch.

RITCH: The group in Miami at Star Island, they are the backers. They're the people with the money. They control this thing that they would like to pretend is a church. It is no church. That is a factory for the export of ganja.

RATHER: Law enforcement agencies say that with his new-found American friends, Keith Gordon's marijuana business took off like a turpentined cat. From being a small-time pusher, he quickly grew to head an organization that controlled cultivation and large-scale distribution right into the United States. Today, the majority of marijuana grown illegally in fields such as this throughout Jamaica has already been pre-sold to Brother Keith and the Coptics. It's prime marijuana that's much in demand.

RITCH: Colombian marijuana, Mexican marijuana, is between two and four percent THC. Our marijuana is between four and eight percent. So we are genuinely the source. Also closest. But Coptic has, I am told 7,000 acres of farm in Colombia, as well. We are now a branch, you see. They claim, in — in Florida, that we are the source, we are the home of this church. We are simply a branch of a multinational corporation operating on the wrong side of the law.

BROTHER LOUV: When — when you talk about smuggling, what do you mean by smuggling?

RATHER: It is not a fact that you are in the business, the business, of smuggling marijuana into the United States?

BROTHER LOUV: I have no knowledge of even what you're thinking about, much less what you're talking about.

RATHER: The United States Coast Guard here in Florida long has been interested in activities of the Zion Coptic Church, as have the FBI, the Federal Drug Enforcement Administration, the Florida Department of Criminal Law Enforcement, and even the Miami Beach police.

One of the Miami Beach police who, as an undercover agent, recently spent a lot of time investigating the Coptic Church is Sergeant Rick Baretto.

Tell me, if you can and if you will, what I am dealing with when I'm dealing with Brother Louv and Star Island. What is this about?

SERGEANT RICK BARETTO: I don't know. I really don't.

RATHER: You looked into it for two years and you don't know what it's about?

SERGEANT BARETTO: That's correct. They obviously have had — been in a financial situation where they can afford a lot of very high-priced attorneys. So they've been able to successfully tie us up time and time again and — through litigation.

RATHER: That's the way the system works, isn't it?

SERGEANT BARETTO: The wheels turn slowly, yes, sir.

FEMALE PATROL BOAT PILOT: This is Coast Guard 459, Coast Guard 459, over.

RATHER: On at least two occasions in this state alone, members of the church have been arrested in very large drug busts. November, 1977, Marion County, Florida: 13 tons of marijuana found hidden in a tunnel on a farm owned by the church. February, 1978, Citrus County, Florida: 20 tons of marijuana taken off the vessel Our Seas, owned by the church; 16 persons arrested, including Brother Louv's fellow church leader, Keith Gordon of Jamaica. However, none of the charges stuck. May 14th, 1979: Marion County charges dropped. May 22nd, 1979: Citrus County charges dropped. Lack of solid evidence cited as the reasons; that the state had found church members around marijuana, but was unable to establish a direct link between the members and the confiscated dope. So, the fact remains – and this is important – that not a single member of the Zion Coptic Church ever has been convicted of possessing so much as a single ounce of marijuana in any court in the State of Florida.

Is this whole church, based so conveniently in Miami and Jamaica, just a cover for large-scale organized crime? Well, no, it's certainly not as simple as that. All the law enforcement agencies who have investigated the Coptics agree: they cannot be faulted on the sincerity of their religious views. Moreover, the Coptics have never, never been linked in any way with the smuggling of hard drugs, cocaine and heroin, that right now is so rampant throughout Florida. Nor with other activities associated with so-called mafioso crime, such as prostitution, gambling and gun-running. None of these would be consistent with the Coptics' professed beliefs. Marijuana, and only marijuana, is what the Coptice are about. To them it is a holy mission.

(Coptics singing in religious ceremony)

RATHER: Back in Miami, the Coptics are pursuing that mission with all the zeal of a political candidate running for office. They recently hired a production company to film their every move, and they study their screen performances with great care. They advertise themselves, together with a biblical plug for marijuana, in the Miami telephone book Yellow Pages. And they publish an expensive newspaper which details with relish their latest costly legal battles. Where does Brother Louv say he gets the money to do all this?

BROTHER LOUV: I want you to consider that you're talking to a spiritual person who has solved the physical problems, and we should be talking about the matters that could uplift everyone who's hearing us right now.

RATHER: Well, where will the money for this thing come from?

BROTHER LOUV: Do you read the Scripture money is the tool of the devil. The love of money is the root of all evil. We love the blessing. Within blessing we've found a higher way of thinking than dollars and cents. Money is a tool. A worldly tool.

RATHER: How do you feel about the Internal Revenue Service case, which is several (indistinct cross-talk) –

BROTHER LOUV: They're a bunch of robbers and thieves and whores!

RATHER: The Internal Revenue Service?

BROTHER LOUV: Robbers, thieves and whores.

RATHER: On what evidence do you (indistinct cross-talk)?

BROTHER LOUV: They have no integrity. They have no foundation. They all have little soft, pink, fleshy little hands. They sit in offices all day long trying to rob the people.

RATHER: Brother Louv's brotherly love clearly wears a little thin when reminded of the Internal Revenue Service. Recently, estimating the value of automobiles, property, boats and the amount of marijuana seized so far, the IRS and the U.S. Customs presented the Coptics with a bill for back taxes and penalties totalling $18 million. Privately, law enforcement officers hope that the tax man may succeed where the police have so far failed, and bring down the Coptic Church. The Coptics have simply refused to pay, and to them it's just one court case among many.

Their minds, and a great deal of their money, are right now tied up in a legal battle of greater significance which they are determined to win, if necessary by going all the way to the United States Supreme Court.

If you were to become Brother Louv's defense attorney, an unlikely prospect, I think you'll agree —

ADORNO: I agree.

RATHER: — and you were advising him, where is the greatest danger to him legally?

ADORNO: Legally it's in the decisions that are — in the mood of the — of the country. I don't think this country is ready for the legalization of marijuana, or at least the state of Florida is not ready for that. And I think that for him to win his battle, he's going to have to fight the greater battle, which is not — not only allowing Coptics to smoke marijuana, but take the one step further and having marijuana legalized. I think that's the only way that he's ultimately going to win his battle.

BROTHER LOUV: Not — from the time you say legalized, that to me sounds like whisky, and whisky's something you can buy from the government but if you make your own they'll put you in jail. So that does not apply to marijuana. Marijuana, ganja, is free. We're not fighting for the freedom or the legalization. We're declaring that it is and always has been free.

See Letters, November 5, 1979, page 113 and Update, November 25, 1979, page 154.

The Pink Panther

JIM JACKSON, PRODUCER

MORLEY SAFER: "The Pink Panther" is not another episode in the adventures of the renowned Inspector Clouseau. No, this "Pink Panther" is a great grandmother in Dallas, Texas, whose instinct for doing business and making money is as finely tuned as a jungle cat going for the kill. Her method, however, is gentleness itself, and quite simple: mobilize the women of America, especially those who would call themselves homemakers; offer up the bait of a dollar or two or a hundred or a thousand, and stand back and see what happens. And one thing more: keep the money green, but color everything else pink.

(Women singing enthusiastically)

While the doomsayers in hundreds of corporate inner sancta warn of the recession to come, this place has a song in its heart.

(Women singing enthusiastically . . . woman singing "I've got that Mary Kay enthusiasm up in my head . . . ")

They may be singing just because they like to sing, and they may be singing because it's the beginning of a new day. And guess who's coming to work.

Every morning around 9:30, a pink Cadillac turns the corner into a parking lot on Corporate Row in Dallas, Texas. It slips into the reserved space along with the other pink Cadillacs. Pink is the color of success at this company, and this is Space Number One, reserved for the chairman of the board.

And out she steps, the chairwoman in this case, herself a symphony in pink. Mary Kay Ash, age unknown and never to be told, the founder and driving force behind:

WOMAN (on telephone):   Good morning. Mary Kay Cosmetics.

SAFER: A direct-sales company begun 16 years ago when this retired grandmother decided to go into business for herself. Today there are 50,000 salespeople, almost all of them women, selling her products. And the company now grosses a hundred million dollars a year.

MARY KAY ASH: My objective was just to help women. It was not to make a tremendous amount of sales. I want women to earn money commensurate with men. I want them to be paid on the basis of what they have between their ears and their brains, and not because they're male or female. But at the same time, I would like women to remain feminine, because I have found that it's an asset to be female in a man's world.

VOICE: I think we're getting a really, really nice look . . .

SAFER: If you haven't heard of Mary Kay, you soon will. The products bearing her name cannot be bought in a store. Like Tupperware, they can only be bought at an event, usually held at a friend's house.

BEAUTY CONSULTANT: We're going to dot here, here . . .

SAFER: The Mary Kay beauty consultant — she is never called a saleswoman — might invite half a dozen people to a beauty demonstration. She is not a Mary Kay employee. She is a free-lance businesswoman who buys the cream or tint or goo wholesale from the Mary Kay plant, and then sells it at a profit over the dining room table.

BEAUTY CONSULTANT: Okay, the basic starter set sells for $37 . . .

MARY KAY: Two of our girls this year — and I think this phenomenal — reached the million-dollar mark in earnings.

SAFER: Earnings?

MARY KAY: And this is less than 15 years. This is not on sales, I'd like to make that clear. This is when you progress up that ladder to the point where you are helping teach other women to go out and do a tremendous job.

SAFER: And what do you think those women would have done otherwise without this, without you?

MARY KAY: They would be home looking at "Days Of Our Lives."

SAFER: The essence of Mary Kay-ism is the cultivation of a spirit that is part religious, part sorority, part military. It's a life, like, say, the Marine Corps or the Carmelite Nuns; but instead of vows of silence, they've taken vows of enthusiasm. An army of loyalists who burst into songs of praise at the least provocation.

(Women singing enthusiastically "I've got that Mary Kay enthusiasm up in my head . . .")

What Mary Kay pours back to her consultants, aside from the profit, is an intense personal relationship between herself and the Mary Kay family. All letters are answered personally; all 50,000 birthdays are remembered.

MARY KAY: If you were to ask me what is it that women need across America, Australia and Canada, I would have to say it's confidence. Here's a woman who's never had any praise at all for anything she's ever done. Maybe the only applause she ever had was when she graduated from high school. She wants recognition, so we praise her for everything good that she does. We praise our people to success.

(At awards meeting): And we thank you so much for what you've done . . .

SAFER: The slightest effort is recognized. Trophies are handed out for anything, for just being wonderful.

WOMAN: Oh, I don't know what to say! (Laughter)

MARY KAY: Well, you don't have to say anything, except that you'll have this every day to remember that we think you're wonderful.

SAFER: The consultants wear their Mary Kay decorations with the pride of veterans of foreign wars.

WOMAN (showing off decoration):   This you see here is the ladder of success, and this goes on a quarterly basis of production; and then you build each quarter on your ladder all the way up to the top.

WOMAN (showing off decoration):   This beautiful add-a-diamond ring can be won for production in Mary Kay.

WOMAN (showing off decoration):   On the pin there are two shovels, one large and one small. The small shovel signifies all the good that we give out to others; and if we do that, that God will give us back a large shovel for it.

(Organ music . . . clapping)

SAFER: In most companies, promotions are given in the boss's office — a handshake and a memo to the staff. At Mary Kay, there's a public investiture into the privileged ranks of the sisterhood. Mary Kay herself administers the sacred oath.

MARY KAY: And believing that our company is built —

WOMAN: And believing that the company is built —

MARY KAY: — on the concept of the Golden Rule —

WOMAN: — on the concept of the Golden Rule —

MARY KAY: I solemnly pledge to uphold and project the Mary Kay image.

WOMAN: I solemnly pledge to uphold and project the Mary Kay image.

MARY KAY: I hereby proclaim that you are now a director!

(Fanfare . . . applause)

(To Safer):   We have as our company adage: God first, family second, job third. And I talk to analysts sometimes, and they say to me, "How in the world do you ever get off the ground with that kind of thing — putting your job in third place?" But you see, I understand women, and I understand that to most of us our families are terribly important, and our religion is important, and that it is important to us to keep our lives in the proper perspective. And somehow — and I really don't know how it works — I only know that in that order everything works and out of that order nothing works.

WOMAN: Mary Kay, welcome to . . .

SAFER: Women and other people tend to reserve their starry-eyed looks and squeals for pop singers and other highly visible celebrities. Rarely do you get this kind of greeting at an airport for a mere corporate executive. But when Mary Kay Ash travels on business, like this tour of her Canadian operation, she and her husband, Mel, are given the full treatment.

WOMAN: Oh, Mary Kay! Thank you. You get to drive in my Cadillac, my pink Canadian Cadillac, the first one up here!

(Organ music . . . clapping in rhythm)

SAFER: Big-shot male executives are said to have a presence. They exude power. And wherever they go, there is the hush of deference from the lesser men whose lives they control. When Mary Kay comes to town, it's exactly the opposite. The air is so thick with upbeatness you can practically cut it.

WOMAN: Ladies and gentlemen, it is with a — a great deal of pleasure that I present to you our leader, our motivator, our inspiration, our first lady, your chairman of the board, Mary Kay.

(Organ music . . . applause)

SAFER: No Mary Kay person, including Mary Kay herself, lets more than a minute go by without invoking God. It's as if the road to heaven is paved with cosmetic sales.

MARY KAY: I sincerely feel that we are not as smart as the balance sheets would show, that God has blessed this company beyond all belief, for the simple reason that we came along at a time when women were coming into their own. And He wants you to become the beautiful person that He knows He created.

SAFER: Do you think that's really fair, in terms of marketing, to inject God into it, as though there was some religious experience involved in either working for, buying, selling?

MARY KAY: Let me say this. I really feel that our company is where it is today and has been blessed beyond all belief by the fact that God is using our company as a vehicle to help women to become the beautiful creatures that He created.

SAFER: But do you think, in a sense, you are using God?

MARY KAY: I hope not. I sincerely hope not. I hope He's using me instead.

WOMAN: Hi, Mary Kay.

MARY KAY: How are you, darling?

SAFER: Mary Kay beauty consultants are only seen carefully coiffed and made up and wearing dresses, never jeans. No liquor is served at Mary Kay functions. Do you tell your people no drinking, no smoking?

MARY KAY: Yes. Well, we suggest that if you smoke, please don't smoke during the beauty show. You can do without a cigarette for two hours. But as far as alcohol is concerned, no alcoholic beverages are served at any Mary Kay functions.

(Organ music . . . clapping in rhythm)

SAFER: Like other chairpersons, Mary Kay has thoughts that touch the very essence of life. The ages of woman, for example.

MARY KAY: To the age of 14, a woman needs good parents and good health. And then from 14 to 40, she needs good looks. From 40 to 60, she needs personality. And after 60, I'm here to tell you what you need is cash! (Laughter . . . applause)

SAFER: However she's done it, it all works. Mary Kay has learned the secret of turning the common clay of American womanhood into an army of true believers.

ALICE FIORE: Hello. My name is Alice Fiore from South Boston, Massachusetts, and Mary Kay has meant a new life for me. It's all my dreams come true. (Organ music . . . applause)

JOAN FINK: My name is Joan Fink. I'm from Edina, Minnesota, and Mary Kay means to me the most beautiful career in the whole wide world. There is no place that I could work as little as I work, have the fun I have and make the money I do! (Laughter . . . applause)

SAFER: But this is merely routine. If you want to get a sense of something special, then you must attend the annual Mary Kay seminar in Dallas. Eight thousand women pay their own way to come to Texas for this crowning event in the life of a Mary Kay person.

WOMAN: Seminar's bigger than life. You can't experience it until you get here.

WOMAN: There's no way you can go back home and tell all your people and all your customers and all your girls the excitement that goes on here, because it's absolutely super. You learn so much.

(Women singing about ". . . m-a-k-i-n-g m-o-n-e-y!")

SAFER: This is a blatant, unapologetic tribute to Mary Kay and capitalism. Other corporate giants walk on stage. Mary Kay levitates.

(Musical number heralding Mary Kay's entrance on stage)

Busby Berkley would not be embarrassed by the show or the budget. A million dollars just to throw this annual three-day bash in Dallas that leads finally to awards night. These are the best for the whole year. There are more queens crowned in one night in Dallas than in 400 years of Westminster Abbey. But finally, the queen of queens, the numera una in the nation, the top sales director at Mary Kay.

(Man announcing top sales director at Mary Kay . . . cheers, applause)

If women, when they are girls, have fantasies of dizzying lives, clinking diamonds, clothed in mink, they quickly lose them to the mortgage and the children and the rest. But Mary Kay Ash, with a touch of marketing genius, proves it can all come true for anyone in middle life. There's a rich pink world out there, and all you got to do is sell.

WOMAN (singing):   "Welcome to my world."

MARY KAY: "Won't you come on in."

WOMAN (singing):   "Won't you come on in."

MARY KAY: "Knock and the door will open."

WOMAN (singing):   "Knock and the door will open. Seek and you will find. Ask, and you will be given the key to this world of mine."

MARY KAY: "I'll be waiting here — "

WOMAN (singing):   "I'll be waiting here — "

MARY KAY: " — with my arms unfurled — "

WOMAN (singing):   " — with my arms unfurled — "

MARY KAY: " — waiting just for you."

WOMAN (singing):   " — waiting just for you."

MARY KAY: "Welcome to our world."

WOMAN (singing):   "Welcome to our world." (Applause)

The Great Depression

LUCY SPIEGEL, PRODUCER

HARRY REASONER: A fairly good estimate of the people watching this broadcast is that six out of ten of you are under 50 years old. If that's so, six out of ten of you really don't have any personal memories of the Great Depression. There's been nothing like it since, and there will probably be nothing quite like it again.

The things that made it happen began early in the 1920's, but for drama and convenience, most people say the Great Depression started 50 years ago this week.

(Swing music: "Sittin' On Top of the World")

Black Tuesday, the biggest day of drama and shock in the history of Wall Street. Within weeks, American Can, which had sold for 181, was down to 86; AT&T, which had hit 304, lost more than a hundred points, and sold for 197; Union Carbide fell from 137 to 59. But Wall Street was only the symbol of the Crash. The whole country crashed. It was, in the slang of a later era, something else. And we thought for the six out of ten who don't remember it, and for the four out of ten who do, we'd put together some thoughts about it. Because however old you are, it changed your life, and it changed this country forever.

(Band music)

You have to understand two things about how it was then. First, the warning signs. The great problems of the 1920's did not seem like warnings to very many people, because economics was an even more uncertain science then than it is now. Farmers were going broke. European governments were collapsing. England was instituting an unheard of thing called the dole. But this did not stir people the way that kind of news would now. And the signs of flamboyant wealth among a minority in the United States did not bother most people. If you objected to that kind of thing, you were a Bolshevik.

(Swing music . . . dancing)

Second, when it all began to happen — when the stock market crashed, when bread lines began to appear in the cities, when banks began to close — the great difference was that at first no one expected the government to do anything about it. It never had before. The idea that the government had an obligation to feed anyone or find a job for anyone or use taxes and incentives to tune the economy — those notions would have seemed to most middle-class Americans immoral, if not vaguely obscene. So the country just sat and took it.

They assumed it would go away, as had previous panics. Calvin Coolidge, who wrote a newspaper column after he quit being President, wrote, "When large numbers of people are out of work, unemployment results." Nobody argued with that. And President Hoover said a lot of things.

PRESIDENT HERBERT HOOVER: To each and every one of us, it is an hour of unusual stress and trial. You have each of you your special cause for anxiety, and so too have I.

REASONER: Hoover and the Congress did take some action, creating the Reconstruction Finance Corporation, for example, to make loans to businesses in trouble, and the Commodity Credit Corporation to help farmers. But things just kept getting worse. In Iowa, which in many ways is the most naturally rich piece of the world, farmers in 1932 burned their corn, kernels and all, in their stoves and furnaces, rather than shelling it and selling it for nine cents a bushel. When the price of milk dropped below the cost of producing it, farmers refused to let it go to market.

AUCTIONEER: . . . ten. Who'll give ten for it?

FARMER: Six cents.

AUCTIONEER: Six cents bid. Who'll give ten . . .

REASONER: Iowa farmers, by nature and tradition conservative and law-abiding, Iowa farmers gathered in groups with pitchforks and sometimes shotguns and went to foreclosure sales. Somehow, looking at those solid citizens ringing the auction block, frequently no one dared to make a bid.

In a way, very few of us, over or under 50, can understand what it was like. President Carter talked recently about a crisis of confidence among Americans. In 1931 and 1932, there was no crisis because there was no confidence. The banks kept closing, and there were no jobs, and there was no money. It was deflation, and deflation so bad the memory of it has helped a lot of older folks live with the idea of inflation. People who'd invested their life savings in stocks and bonds now papered their walls with worthless certificates. The dollar was worth more than what it had been worth in 1928. Do you see how different that was from the kind of statistic we hear now? It was not necessarily better — unless you had a dollar. Nobody did.

And maybe because nobody did, people turned to the movies. People who found a dime for a ticket — a dime which also got them a piece of tableware — wanted fantasy, but they also wanted a kind of Tin Pan Alley gallows humor.

(Girls in musical film singing "We're in the Money")

All right, so what happened? In 1932 and 1933, when solid citizens of humble Iowa stocked their cellars with canned goods because they thought there might be a revolution coming — a revolution in Iowa, for God's sake! — what happened? Well, Franklin Delano Roosevelt happened.

(Dance band music: "Happy Days Are Here Again")

PRESIDENT FRANKLIN D. ROOSEVELT: This great nation will endure, as it has endured; will revive, and will prosper. So, first of all, let me assert my firm belief that the only thing we have to fear is fear itself.

REASONER: Roosevelt happened, but did he solve the Depression? No, he never did. But he did give the country back the feeling that it was not dying. There was a thing called the National Recovery Administration, for instance, a law which encouraged businesses and labor to make agreements on prices, wages and jobs. The Supreme Court quickly declared the NRA unconstitutional, but before it did, there were a lot of parades and a lot of enthusiasm for the Blue Eagle.

MAN: A city afoot, heads erect, hopes high, united in the common bond of a patriotic purpose, they tread the road to recovery. There can be no turning them back now. The greatest peacetime offensive in the history of the world is underway.

(Band music: "The Stars and Stripes Forever")

REASONER: Roosevelt attempted to breathe new life into this nation by creating an alphabet soup of organizations — the WPA, the CCC, the AAA — all to get the unemployed population off the bread lines and into jobs, any kind of jobs. He kept trying, changing direction, buying any kind of pragmatic suggestion. Never an economist, but always a confidence builder.

PRESIDENT ROOSEVELT: To some generations, much is given; of other generations, much is expected. This generation of Americans has a rendezvous with destiny.

(Music)

REASONER: Well, what we had a rendezvous with was Adolf Hitler and Tojo. But we never went back to the old ways. Maybe we should have. A lot of conservatives remember that in the 1932 campaign Hoover said that if Roosevelt were elected grass would grow in the streets of our cities. And they say now that Hoover was wrong only in his estimate of how long it would take. But we never went back. And what you should do now is look around at the things we have that would have been unthinkable in 1930.

The presence of government in every area of our lives: Social Security, and the Securities and Exchange Commission, food stamps, day care centers, federal job training programs, federal money for highways. None of these things would have been around if it weren't for the Great Depression. Federal money for schools, for the arts, for home insulation or land conservation or for growing or not growing wheat or corn. Federal money to discourage smoking, along with federal money to encourage growing tobacco. Federal money for health care, unemployment insurance, and the Federal Deposit Insurance Corporation to protect your bank account.

Now we have inflation: twelve percent interest on your money instead of three and a half percent. But are we any richer in the quality of our lives? From the two out of ten of you watching right now — those of you over 65 — there's no doubt of the answer you would get: Nothing was as bad as that was. Nothing was ever like it. It must never happen again.

(Voice of Bing Crosby singing "Brother, Can You Spare A Dime?" over visual montage of Great Depression scenes)

A Few Minutes With Andy Rooney

MIKE WALLACE: They call it the Sunday paper, but if you're like me you don't get around to some of the sections until Tuesday or Wednesday. Chances are right now there's a section or two still unread over there on your couch or on your coffee table. At any rate, it's one of those familiar, comfortable institutions that have been a part of all our Sundays ever since we can remember. Andy Rooney, who likes to look at American institutions, tonight takes a look at this one.

ANDY ROONEY: Newspapers are always reviewing television shows, but television rarely reviews newspapers. Well, newspapers aren't really all that fault-free, either. I thought I'd review Sunday newspapers in general.

In the first place, I'm very suspicious of a serious newspaper that puts the funny papers on the outside. And who wants eight pounds of type staring him in the face Sunday morning? This is 582 pages. I can hardly lift it, let alone read it in one day.

Here's *The Cincinnati Enquirer,* paper with a great tradition, good town — but is there really that much going on in Cincinnati? I thought I'd go through this and see what I have left that I'd want to read after I throw out what I don't want to read. Here's the news section. I'll read that. Metro, sports, business and financial. Now, here's classified advertising, 58 pages of classified ads. The news section was only 12 pages long. I have a job. Then there are several other miscellaneous sections here. I'll read those. The at home section — you know, nine interesting things to do with a leaky bathtub, or 47 ways to stuff an eggplant. And if they have an at home section, can the housewares section be far behind? This looks like advertising for a department store. Here's another department store section. I don't read sections when all of page one is an ad. Here's a 20-page section on the Bengal Tigers, the football team. Here's section N — ten solid pages of advertising, all ads, ads, ads, ads. And here on page 8, one news story. Rest all advertising.

And here's the stuff that falls out when you pick up the paper on the front porch in the morning. I'll keep the funny papers. Here's a magazine insert advertising *Time* magazine. Something called "Good Ole Times" sale. Here's *The Enquirer* television magazine. I'll keep that in case my name's mentioned. Here's something called "Gold Circle." They seem to be selling socks. Here's an at home — home sale, all advertising. Here's a dollar sale. And look what I found here? "Lookin' Good." A whole section called "Lookin' Good" bought and paid for by — guess who? — CBS. The Nat— *The Enquirer* magazine — that looks good. And here's a nasty-size thing: the Quaker Oats insert here, with all those little things you cut out to save ten cents. I don't know what this is — some wonderful way to save money by spending it, I suppose. And look what I have left. I mean, a paper about the half the size of what it was.

I like newspapers, but I worry about them. If they keep going this way, critics are going to start laughing at newspapers the way they laugh at television now.

Letters

MIKE WALLACE: Most of the mail this week was about our story on the California doctor who's being investigated in connection with medical fraud running into the millions, and about the report on him that has never been made public. More than half the letters were in this vein: "It's quite obvious why Senator Kennedy's investigators buried that report on medical abuses. It gave a crystal clear picture of what we could look forward to if the Senator's National Health Program is enacted."

Another viewer said: "I'm sure the Medi-Caid [sic] ripoff artists can't wait for Teddy's new folly."

Another viewer, noting our story two weeks ago on agricultural loans to farmers with Rolls-Royces and tennis courts, said: "Ye Gods, last week millionaire farmers (feeding at the public trough) . . . this week millionaire doctors. Is it any wonder we have no faith in government?"

Also tonight, an update on a story we reported a year and a half ago — "No Kids Allowed." That's what we called our story about landlords who could legally refuse to rent apartments to folks with children in Santa Monica, California, and in most other parts of the country. Well, in Santa Monica, at least, that's changed. The city council there has voted to ban the practice.

Now back to the mail. About our story on designer Raymond Loewy, a viewer wrote: "For an exceptionally talented and tasteful designer, somebody sure dresses him funny . . . a polka dot ascot under a striped shirt and a plaid sport coat with checked slacks . . . Oh Dear."

And finally, there was this: "Since Mr. Loewy is so successful with logo designs, perhaps you should have him take a look at yours. I'm sure that stopwatch is getting a little wound down by now."

NOVEMBER 4, 1979

Swine Flu
NORMAN GORIN, PRODUCER

MIKE WALLACE: The flu season is upon us. Which type will we worry about this year, and what kind of shots will we be told to take? Remember the swine flu scare of 1976? That was the year the U.S. government told us all that swine flu could turn out to be a killer that could spread across the nation, and Washington decided that every man, woman and child in the nation should get a shot to prevent a nationwide outbreak, a pandemic.

Well, 46 million of us obediently took the shot, and now 4,000 Americans are claiming damages from Uncle Sam amounting to three and a half billion dollars because of what happened when they took that shot. By far the greatest number of the claims — two-thirds of them — are for neurological damage, or even death, allegedly triggered by the flu shot.

We pick up the story back in 1976, when the threat posed by the swine flu virus seemed very real, indeed.

PRESIDENT GERALD FORD: This virus was the cause of a pandemic in 1918 and 1919 that resulted in over half a million deaths in the United States, as well as 20 million deaths around the world.

WALLACE: Thus the U.S. government's publicity machine was cranked into action to urge all America to protect itself against the swine flu menace.

(Excerpt from TV commercial urging everyone to get a swine flu shot)

One of those who did roll up her sleeve was Judy Roberts. She was perfectly healthy, an active woman, when, in November of 1976, she took her shot. Two weeks later, she says, she began to feel a numbness starting up her legs.

JUDY ROBERTS: And I joked about it at that time. I said I'll be numb to the knees by Friday is — if this keeps up. By the following week, I was totally paralyzed.

WALLACE: So completely paralyzed, in fact, that they had to operate on her to enable her to breathe. And for six months, Judy Roberts was a quadriplegic. The diagnosis: a neurological disorder called "Guillain Barre Syndrome" — GBS for short. These neurological diseases are little understood. They affect people in different ways.

As you can see in these home movies taken by a friend, Judy Roberts' paralysis confined her mostly to a wheelchair for over a year. But this disease can even kill.

Indeed, there are 300 claims now pending from the families of GBS victims who died, allegedly as a result of the swine flu shot. In other GBS victims, the crippling effects diminish and all but disappear. But for Judy Roberts, progress back to good health has been painful and partial.

Now, I notice that your smile, Judy, is a little bit constricted.

ROBERTS: Yes, it is.

WALLACE: Is it different from what it used to be?

ROBERTS: Very different. I have a — a greatly decreased mobility in my lips. And I can't drink through a straw on the right-hand side. I can't blow out birthday candles. I don't whistle any more, for which my husband is grateful.

WALLACE: It may be a little difficult for you to answer this question, but have you recovered as much as you are going to recover?

ROBERTS: Yes. This — this is it.

WALLACE: So you will now have a legacy of braces on your legs for the rest of your life?

ROBERTS: Yes. The weakness in my hands will stay and the leg braces will stay.

WALLACE: So Judy Roberts and her husband have filed a claim against the U.S. government. They're asking $12 million, though they don't expect to get nearly that much.

Judy, why did you take the flu shot?

ROBERTS: I'd never taken any other flu shots, but I felt like this was going to be a major epidemic, and the only way to prevent a major epidemic of a — a really deadly variety of flu was for everybody to be immunized.

WALLACE: Where did this so-called "deadly variety of flu," where did it first hit back in 1976? It began right here at Fort Dix in New Jersey, in January of that year, when a number of recruits began to complain of respiratory ailments, something like the common cold. An Army doctor here sent samples of their throat cultures to the New Jersey Public Health Lab to find out just what kind of bug was going around here. One of those samples was from a Private David Lewis, who had left his sick bed to go on a forced march. Private Lewis had collapsed on that march, and his sergeant had revived him by mouth-to-mouth resuscitation. But the sergeant showed no signs of illness. A few days later, Private Lewis died.

ROBERTS: If this disease is so potentially fatal that it's going to kill a young, healthy man, a middle-aged schoolteacher doesn't have a prayer.

WALLACE: The New Jersey lab identified most of those soldiers' throat cultures as the normal kind of flu virus going around that year, but they could not make out what kind of virus was in the culture from the dead soldier, and from four others who were sick.

So they sent those cultures to the Federal Center for Disease Control in Atlanta, Georgia, for further study. A few days later they got the verdict: swine flu. But that much-publicized outbreak of swine flu at Fort Dix involved only Private Lewis, who died, and those four other soldiers, who recovered completely without the swine flu shot.

ROBERTS: If I had known at that time that the boy had been in a sick bed, got up, went out on a forced march and then collapsed and died, I would never have taken the shot.

DR. DAVID SENCER: The rationale for our recommendation was not on the basis of the death of a — a single individual, but it was on the basis that when we do see a change in the characteristics of the influenza virus, it is a massive public-health problem in this country.

WALLACE: Dr. David Sencer,   then head of the CDC — the Center for Disease Control in Atlanta — is now in private industry. He devised the swine flu program and he pushed it.

You began to give flu shots to American people in October of '76?

DR. SENCER: October 1st.

WALLACE: By that time, how many cases of swine flu around the world had been reported?

DR. SENCER: There had been several reported, but none confirmed. There had been cases in Australia that were reported by the press, by the news media. There were cases in —

WALLACE: None confirmed?

Did you ever uncover any other outbreaks of swine flu anywhere in the world?

DR. SENCER: No.

WALLACE: Now, nearly everyone was to receive the shot in a public health facility where a doctor might not be present, therefore it was up to the CDC to come up with some kind of official consent form giving the public all the information it needed about the swine flu shot. This form stated that the swine flu vaccine had been tested. What it didn't say was that after those tests were completed, the scientists developed another vaccine and that was the one given to most of the 46 million who took the shot. That vaccine was called "X-53a."

Was X-53a ever field tested?

DR. SENCER: I — I can't say. I would have to —

WALLACE: It wasn't.

DR. SENCER: I don't know.

WALLACE: Well, I would think that you're in charge of the program.

DR. SENCER: I would have to check the records. I haven't looked at this in some time.

WALLACE: The information form — the consent form — was also supposed to warn people about any risks of serious complications following the shot. But did it?

ROBERTS: No, I had never heard of any reactions other than a sore arm, fever, this sort of thing.

WALLACE: Judy Roberts' husband, Gene, also took the shot.

GENE ROBERTS: Yes, I looked at that document. I signed it. Nothing on there said I was going to have a heart attack, or I can get Guillain Barre, which I'd never heard of.

WALLACE: What if people from the government, from the Center for Disease Control, what if they had, indeed, known about it, what would be your feeling?

JUDY ROBERTS: They should have told us.

WALLACE: Did anyone ever come to you and say, "You know something, fellows, there's the possibility of neurological damage if you get into a mass immunization program?"

DR. SENCER: No.

WALLACE: No one ever did?

DR. SENCER: No.

WALLACE: Do you know Michael Hattwick?

DR. SENCER: Yes, uh-hmm.

WALLACE: Dr. Michael Hattwick directed the surveillance team for the swine flu program at the CDC. His job was to find out what possible complications could arise from taking the shot and to report his findings to those in charge.

Did you know ahead of time, Dr. Hattwick, that there had been case reports of neurological disorders, neurological illness, apparently associated with the injection of influenza vaccine?

DR. MICHAEL HATTWICK: Absolutely.

WALLACE: You did?

DR. HATTWICK: Yes.

WALLACE: How did you know that?

DR. HATTWICK: By review of the literature.

WALLACE: So you told your superiors — the men in charge of the swine flu immunization program — about the possibility of neurological disorders?

DR. HATTWICK: Absolutely.

WALLACE: What would you say if I told you that your superiors say that you never told them about the possibility of neurological complications?

DR. HATTWICK: That's nonsense. I can't believe that they would say that they did not know that there were neurological illnesses associated with influenza vaccination. That simply is not true. We did know that.

DR. SENCER: I have said that Dr. Hattwick had never told me of his feelings on this subject.

WALLACE: Then he's lying?

DR. SENCER: I guess you would have to make that assumption.

WALLACE: Then why does this report from your own agency, dated July, 1976, list neurological complications as a possibility?

DR. SENCER: I think the consensus of the scientific community was that the evidence relating neurologic disorders to influenza immunization was such that they did not feel that this association was a real one.

WALLACE: You didn't feel it was necessary to tell the American people that information?

DR. SENCER: I think that over the — the years we have tried to inform the American people as — as fully as possible.

WALLACE: As part of informing Americans about the swine flu threat, Dr. Sencer's CDC also helped create the advertising to get the public to take the shot.

Let me read to you from one of your own agency's memos planning the campaign to urge Americans to take the shot. "The swine flu vaccine has been taken by many important persons," he wrote. "Example: President Ford, Henry Kissinger, Elton John, Muhammad Ali, Mary Tyler Moore, Rudolf Nureyev, Walter Cronkite, Ralph Nader, Edward Kennedy" — et cetera, et cetera. True?

DR. SENCER: I'm not familiar with that particular piece of paper, but I do know that, at least of that group, President Ford did take the vaccination.

WALLACE: Did you talk to these people beforehand to find out if they planned to take the shot?

DR. SENCER: I did not, no.

WALLACE: Did anybody?

DR. SENCER: I do not know.

WALLACE: Did you get permission to use their names in your campaign?

DR. SENCER: I do not know.

WALLACE: Mary, did you take a swine flu shot?

MARY TYLER MOORE: No, I did not.

WALLACE: Did you give them permission to use your name saying that you had or were going to?

MOORE: Absolutely not. Never did.

WALLACE: Did you ask your own doctor about taking the swine flu shot?

MOORE: Yes, and at the time he thought it might be a good idea. But I resisted it, because I was leery of having the symptoms that sometimes go with that kind of inoculation.

WALLACE: So you didn't?

MOORE: No, I didn't.

WALLACE: Have you spoken to your doctor since?

MOORE: Yes.

WALLACE: And?

MOORE: He's delighted that I didn't take that shot.

WALLACE: You're in charge. Somebody's in charge.

DR. SENCER: There are —

WALLACE: This is your advertising strategy that I have a copy of here.

DR. SENCER: Who's it signed by?

WALLACE: This one is unsigned. But you — you'll acknowledge that it was your baby, so to speak?

DR. SENCER: It could have been from the Department of Health, Education and Welfare. It could be from CDC. I don't know. I'll be happy to take responsibility for it.

WALLACE: It's been three years now since you fell ill by GBS, right?

ROBERTS: Right.

WALLACE: Has the federal government, in your estimation, played fair with you about your claim?

ROBERTS: No, I don't think so. It seems to be dragging on and on and on, and really no end in sight that I can see at this point.

JOSEPH CALIFANO: With respect to the cases of Guillain Barre . . .

WALLACE: Former Secretary of HEW Joseph Califano, too, was disturbed that there was no end in sight. So a year and a half ago, he promised that Uncle Sam would cut the bureaucratic red tape for victims suffering from GBS and would pay up quickly.

CALIFANO: We shouldn't hold them to an impossible or too difficult standard of proving that they were hurt. Even if we pay a few people a few thousand dollars that might not have deserved it, I think justice requires that we promptly pay those people who do deserve it.

WALLACE: Who's making the decision to be so hard-nosed about settling?

CALIFANO: Well, I assume the Justice Department is.

WALLACE: Griffin Bell, before he left?

CALIFANO: Well, the Justice Department agreed to the statement I made. It was cleared word for word with the lawyers in the Justice Department, by my HEW lawyers.

WALLACE: And that statement said, in effect?

CALIFANO: That — that statement said that we should pay Guillain Barre claims without regard to whether the federal government was negligent, if they — if they resulted from the swine flu shot.

GENE ROBERTS: I think the government knows it's wrong.

JUDY ROBERTS: If it drags out long enough, that people will just give up, let it go.

GENE ROBERTS: I — I am a little more adamant in my thoughts than my wife is, because I asked — told Judy to take the shot. She wasn't going to take it, and she never had had shots. And I'm mad with my government because they knew the facts, but they didn't release those facts because they — if they had released them, the people wouldn't have taken it. And they can come out tomorrow and tell me there's going to be an epidemic, and they can drop off like flies to — next to me, I will not take another shot that my government tells me to take.

WALLACE: Meantime, Judy Roberts and some 4,000 others like her are still waiting for their day in court.

Pavarotti

RICHARD MANICHELLO, PRODUCER

MORLEY SAFER: There may be no more dangerous occupation for a performer than being an operatic tenor. He's the tightrope walker of opera. In almost every performance, there are notes that if missed can destroy him professionally. That may be true for any singer, but for a tenor the notes — the high notes — are distributed as in a mine field. That's why the critics of music and opera are so sparing in their praise. It's rare, say every 20 years or so, that a tenor comes along who's considered truly memorable, important or great, someone who can be compared with Caruso.

(Luciano Pavarotti vocalizing)

We're lucky to be living in a time when there is someone to be compared with Caruso: Luciano Pavarotti, a great bear of a man. If you'd asked the boy Pavarotti what he wanted to be, he would have said a soccer star. Some ambitions are just never fulfilled.

(Pavarotti sings "Tu Me Partiere" . . . applause)

Pavarotti, like most opera stars, is loaded with ego. Perhaps the heroic nature of the stories and the roles somehow affects the performers. But Pavarotti has given more thought to this than most, and the man, in fact, is quite modest. The voice is another matter. He thinks of the voice as another person.

LUCIANO PAVAROTTI: Sometime when I speak, I say "we," because I mean me and my voice. We are two — two different things, absolutely.

SAFER: How?

PAVAROTTI: My instrument —

SAFER: How can you be two different things?

PAVAROTTI: It must be two different things in the terms of thinking. I — I — I must think I have here an instrument who is — is mine because God give to me. But I — I have to treat like he's a piano, like he's a violin, like he's another instrument. Then it cannot go to my head, because I know I cannot — I cannot do anything without him, without her, without the voice.

(Pavarotti vocalizing)

SAFER: A voice is not something that can just be turned on. It is like a piano that must be tuned every day. There is as much tedium of warm-up for a singer as there is for a dancer or an athlete.

(Pavarotti sings "Che Fiero Costume")

And there are days when it seems that the whole affair has turned to rust.

PAVAROTTI (coughing):   I need somebody with hot tea.

These — these muscles, then they are sometime tired, sometime sick, sometime — you know, you never know how they are. You never know if they respond to you immediately, and you work until they respond, or until — until when you think they respond.

(In hotel lobby): Che testa grande . . .

SAFER: Pavarotti's base is the Metropolitan Opera, but he spends most of each year on tour.

PAVAROTTI: Chicago. Let's go.

SAFER: A tenor's prime is short and the most must be made of it. He can get more than $20,000 a performance and he's booked up years in advance. Pavarotti, more than anyone lately, is responsible for bringing opera within reach of all America, not in actual opera production, but in concert and recital.

(Pavarotti sings "O Paradiso")

Pavarotti plays to the audience, but he does not pander to it. Much of his repertoire is unfamiliar Baroque music, the less popular music of Beethoven, Liszt and others.

(Pavarotti sings "Recondita Armonia")

Arias that a general audience does not know. All those songs of death and unrequited love. He does not compromise with his instrument or with his selection of pieces. He does not choose the easy ones, and he does not hold back, whether he's playing the Met or Chicago or Erie, Pennsylvania.

(Pavarotti sings "Una Furtiva Lagrima")

But then he'll relent with a nice big plate of musical pasta.

(Pavarotti sings "Torna a Surriento")

What is it about the voice, about the tenor voice, that makes it so appealing, so absolutely universally appealing?

PAVAROTTI: I think the — the reason is because it is the wildest voice, is the most unnatural voice, is the most construct voice.

SAFER: Most unnatural?

PAVAROTTI: I think so. The natural voice of the man is the baritone voice, talking and singing. Tenor is higher and more sparkling. And like — I don't know if you are an expert of soccer, but he's the number nine, the tenor; he's the man who must make goal.

(Pavarotti sings "Recondita Armonia")

He must make the — the public scream. And the audience are always ready to hear the tenor make a mistake, never a baritone. In my country, for example, they say, "Let's go to boo the tenor." They never say, "Let's go to boo the baritone." Because they know then, instinctively, if is somebody who can make a mistake, is the tenor, because he has the most difficult voice.

(Pavarotti sings Liszt's "Sonnetto di Petrarca: 47")

SAFER: You, I think it's fair to say, are fearless in the manner in which you attack something. So you hit those impossible notes or those challenging notes, and the C's and the D's, over C even.

PAVAROTTI: I take the risk.

SAFER: That is a terrible risk —

PAVAROTTI: I am a risky —

SAFER: — to take.

PAVAROTTI: — I am a risky person. I am a person who like take the risk until — until my instrument respond. I want — I want to do the — the thing more difficult than is — than is possible.

SAFER: The biggest risk he ever took was in 1978: a full recital from the stage of the Metropolitan Opera House in New York televised live to a national audience. It had never been done before. And with it, Pavarotti moved from being an important tenor to *the* tenor.

(Pavarotti sings "Mattinata" . . . applause)

PAVAROTTI: I remember my manager when he booked me for — for — for the first recital, Liberty, Missouri. Mr. Breslin went to me and he says, "Go there to see if you like the audience." Not if the audience like me. It was right. He was very right. I went there and I say, "I like — I like the audience. I really — I am born to stay in the middle of the audience."

(Pavarotti on stage . . . applause)

SAFER: The rise to the top took some time. There are no prodigies in opera.
Pavarotti was born 44 years ago in Modena, Italy, a town that produces singers the way other towns produce stone masons. His father, a full-time baker and a part-time singer, spent a lifetime wishing it were the other way around, and part of a lifetime exposing the baby Luciano to the records of the best tenors of the day. The exposure worked, and the then-slim young athlete, with some regret, chose opera over soccer.
(Pavarotti sings "Torna a Surriento"...applause)
A great tenor is an event in itself. There are the entourage, the grand hotels, the private jet planes.

PAVAROTTI (in dressing room):   Whoop! (Whistles) Why you are not using this thing? I cannot believe you are using this . . .

SAFER: There's the enormous set of evening clothes, material enough to suit perhaps a dozen lesser men, the great bearded face, the look of an educated pumpkin, the flowing handkerchief, Satchmo without the trumpet – but the instrument is there.
(Pavarotti sings "A Vuchella")
And wherever he goes, the groupies follow. They are a more sedate set of groupies than most, the hoi polloi of City X, Y and Z.
He takes it all with great fun, great jollity. There may be a darker side to Luciano Pavarotti. There must be. No one whose art, whose life, really, hangs by the fragile tissue of a vocal cord, whose existence can be threatened by a common cold, can be so constantly filled with good fellowship the way he seems to be. Perhaps he takes out whatever meanness is in him on his stomach. If he treated his voice the way he treats his stomach, he wouldn't have made it to the chorus.
Pavarotti's favorite recording artist is Pavarotti. He loves the voice so much he cannot resist singing along with it.

(Pavarotti driving . . . sings along with recording of "Vicino Mare")

Miami may not be the opera capital of the world—

(Pavarotti driving . . . sings along with recording of "O Sole Mio")

—but he prepares for Miami as if it were Milan.

Do you feel that your voice now, at age 43, is at its best, or do you have some — some distance to go yet?

PAVAROTTI: I think now is at its best. Is already two, three years that is at its best. And I am prepared, around 50, to be a little down.

SAFER: The appeal of a Pavarotti is not unlike the appeal of a Tutankhamen. People will go to see and hear him not understanding a word of the lyrics or knowing a single piece of music. They will go because they sense it is a once-in-a-lifetime event; because that night, that performance, might be the most magical in a schedule that demands magic every night.

(Pavarotti performing at the Denver Center)

You said if the audience doesn't stand up and pour their hearts out to you with thanks and pleasure and everything else, then it's your fault?

PAVAROTTI: I think so. I have no doubt about that. No doubt. Faults can be from — a reason can be then the voice don't respond can be that I am not concentrate, can be from for — more than one reason. But certainly, the audience is the best thermometer. I think they are always right, especially the audience who come to see me in concert, because they really come to see me. And if they don't give the applause, this mean I don't deserve.

(Pavarotti sings "Nessun Dorma")

SAFER: It is with grace and absence of fear that Pavarotti says that one day the voice will darken — when the instrument will not be able to challenge the music the way it does now week after grueling week. But that is not really worth thinking about. What is important is to listen to Pavarotti now — the voice at its prime, the man at his best. Combined, they present a force that is almost frightening in its beauty.

(Pavarotti sings "Nessun Dorma" . . . applause)

"Give Me Your Tired . . ."

STEVE GLAUBER, PRODUCER

DAN RATHER: Illegal immigrants are flooding our shores — by land, by air, by sea, from Korea and Vietnam, Mexico and Colombia, Haiti and Honduras. How many aliens are here illegally? Nobody knows. Estimates vary from four to twelve million. Mostly they come here for jobs, and while it is illegal for them to be here, it is not illegal for employers to hire them. What kind of jobs do they get? Mostly jobs that nobody else wants.

(Immigration officers seeking out illegal aliens)

IMMIGRATION OFFICIAL: Definitely somebody in there.

(Illegal alien caught)

IMMIGRATION OFFICIAL: Hey, how are you doing?

RATHER: When they're caught by immigration authorities, as in this raid in Los Angeles, the punishment is deportation back to where they came from.

(Commotion in factory)

RALPH RAIMOND: I'm with the U.S. Immigration. What — what country are you from?

RATHER: Another raid. This time, New York.

RAIMOND: What part of the West Indies are you from?

WOMAN: Jamaica.

RAIMOND: You have residence here?

WOMAN: Uh-huh.

RAIMOND: Do you have your card with you? Huh?

WOMAN: I leave it home.

RATHER: Ralph Raimond of the Immigration and Naturalization Service is in charge of this raid.

RAIMOND: We're only going down to the car.

FACTORY MANAGER: (Indistinct). Don't worry about it. Okay?

RATHER: How much fear do these undocumented employees have that they're going to be turned in?

RAIMOND: I think they live a life of fear around the clock, every one of them. It's indicated to us when we walk into a factory and they run helter-skelter. And naturally they don't want to be caught. They don't want to go back. They've made a — may have given several hundred dollars just to get here, maybe their life savings, and when we catch them, their dreams go down the drain.

RATHER: Down the drain for workers like these, who always fear that one day they'll be caught.
If an employer chose to use that fear to his advantage, he wouldn't have any trouble doing it, would he?

RAIMOND: No, siree.

RATHER: The garment business hires more aliens — legal and illegal — than any other non-agricultural industry in the United States.

JOE RAZO: If all the undocumented workers were deported today, the garment industry would shut down today.

RATHER: Joe Razo recently headed a California State probe into garment business practices in Los Angeles.

RAZO: Workers work for very low wages because they have no choice, and they will take whatever job is offered to them.

RATHER: During the last decade, California's garment industry has grown 98 percent, and it's no coincidence that illegal aliens were pouring into the Los Angeles area during this same time. The California investigation found that 90 percent of the firms do not pay the minimum wage or overtime. Instead, workers are paid by the piece: so much per button or sleeve or whole dress. But no matter how fast they're turned out, the piece rate almost always comes out lower than the federal minimum wage.

How much is the most you've ever made here in a full week?

MAN (interpreting for woman):   Eighty dollars.

RATHER: What's the least you've ever made?

MAN (interpreting for woman):   Forty dollars.

RATHER: And how many hours did you work that week?

MAN (interpreting for woman):   Approximately forty hours per week.

RATHER: Do you know that the federal law in the United States of America is that everybody must make at least two dollars and ninety cents an hour?

MAN (interpreting for woman):   She didn't know.

RATHER: If she didn't know the law, her boss should have. When we went to find him, he wasn't in. This teenager was.

MAN (interpreting for teenager):   She says she doesn't know at this point what she is really going to get paid, but they have pointed out to her that he will be paid seven cents per blouse she irons.

RATHER: How many blouses has she ironed today?

MAN (interpreting for teenager):   She's ironed 11 and then 16, so 27.

RATHER: And she's done 27 —

MAN (interpreting for teenager):   Right.

RATHER: — at seven cents a blouse.

MAN (interpreting for teenager):   Right.

RATHER: Her piecework came out to 47 cents an hour. And in the next room, the now fashionable blouses were ready for delivery.

This clothing bears the label "Georgie Originals." Georgie Originals is one of the biggest, most respected labels in the State of California. Georgie Originals sells clothing to, among other places, Bullocks. Bullocks is one of the biggest and most respected department-store chains in the nation. While in this sweatshop, we also found this contract for work with "Cathy of California." Cathy of California is one of the most prestigious firms in the state, and they sell to Sears Roebuck, among others. Other firms that make clothing under similar conditions sell to J.C. Penney, Korvettes, Macy's, Alexanders — wherever clothing is sold.

INVESTIGATOR: They all just hit 9:01 at the same. Four, 9:01. Five, 9:01. Everybody has 9:01.

RATHER: This violation is taking place in New York's Chinatown, where a Federal Department of Labor investigator suspected that the time clocks were being punched by the employers, not the employees, and that the employees were working a lot longer day than the time clock gave them credit for.

INVESTIGATOR: Who punches these time cards?

EMPLOYER: You know, usually is — is — they punch it.

RATHER: Who?

EMPLOYER: The worker punch it.

RATHER: Who?

EMPLOYER: The worker, they punch it.

INVESTIGATOR: The workers punch it?

EMPLOYER: Yeah.

INVESTIGATOR: Then — then how could the — 16 be at 9:01 and 15 at 9:02?

EMPLOYER: I don't know. You know, they maybe come in the same elevators.

INVESTIGATOR: That's a very small elevator. How could 15 get off the elevator at the same time?

RATHER: Just one week after the inspector had been in that shop, we went back and asked if we could look at the same time clock.

Thank you. Uh-huh, the same thing as last week. You see the problem? Nine o'clock, nine o'clock, nine o'clock, nine o'clock. Every card is nine o'clock. Everybody can't punch in at nine o'clock . . .

So one week after the inspector was there, nothing had changed. Shortening hours is, of course, illegal. Illegal, also, is a prevalent practice called "homework." This woman told us she had worked three straight days at home, nine hours each day. Total pay: $38.70.

You might expect that the garment manufacturers employ the garment workers. Well, most of them do not. They find it cheaper to send their materials to so-called "independent contractors" and have them hire the workers, thus insulating both manufacturers and retailers from any legal responsibility. And who are these contractors? Mostly recent immigrants themselves, often here illegally.

EMPLOYER: Problem is the manufacturer. If they — if — if they pay me more, I can pay more to the operator.

RATHER: But why don't you ask them for more?

EMPLOYER: Well, when I asked for more, they told me, okay, they give me a five- or ten-cent break. You take it. Or sometimes, they don't give me nothing. You take it or you leave it.

JIM QUILLEN: But the problem is you've got a — you've got a structure in this industry that will per— not permit the thousands of contractors to bid on goods and make a profit unless they chisel workers.

RATHER: Jim Quillen is Labor Commissioner of California.

QUILLEN: And so the contractor is faced with that Hobson's choice: Do I chisel the workers, do I pay them less than the minimum wage and make a profit, or do I run a clean operation and go out of business?

RATHER: Bernard Brown, the spokesman for the California clothing industry, acknowledges these practices do go on.

BERNARD BROWN: There are pockets that — that it could be very true, but that does not represent the industry. And we have plenty of laws now that can take care of the violations if the agents get out there, take these people and cite them; and, of course, if they're repeated violations, that the fines are greater, or — or whatever the penalty is, the penalty be greater. But we don't want the law so prohibitive that it's going to drive so many people out of business that we're going to have

120,000 unemployed people in the State of California, for example, because the apparel industry will move elsewhere.

RATHER: That elsewhere could be a place like Korea, where workers are legally paid only pennies per hour. But Bernard Brown says there is a solution: a contract which California manufacturers drew up and have agreed to sign with their contractors requiring the contractors to pay legal wages.

Jody Toteek, which grosses $60 million a year, is one of the dress houses that has signed this contract. Jack Weingarten, the board chairman of Jody Toteek, deals with 60 different contractors.

Now, this is a form in which the contractor says that he will obey the law.

JACK WEINGARTEN: Yes, that's right.

RATHER: Do you require all the contractors to sign that?

WEINGARTEN: Yes.

RATHER: Now, so far as you know, do the contractors obey the law?

WEINGARTEN: I — I really — I really hope so. Let's say it this way, I really hope so, that the contractors who work for us obey it.

RATHER: But the question was, do you know that they do?

WEINGARTEN: I don't.

RATHER: Max Wolf is with the International Ladies Garment Workers Union, and he insists manufacturers do know.

MAX WOLF: They know that it happens on an extremely wide scale. No efficient garment manufacturer, or jobber, does not know what is happening to every single one of his garments and where the seams are sewn and how they're sewn every minute of the day. And when they tell you that they are removed from it, I don't believe it, and don't you believe it.

RATHER: Law-enforcement efforts to curtail exploitation have all been aimed solely against the contractors, and all these efforts have failed. Few shops are caught. Those that are simply change their names and not their practices. Only in California has there been even a legislative proposal to make manufacturers liable as well as contractors, but after vigorous lobbying by the clothing industry, that bill was defeated.

MANUFACTURER: And I'll tell you why, because it's almost an impossibility for a manufacturer to be able to control the actions of a contractor, and I'll tell you the reason for it. First place, as manufacturers we sometimes have as many as 60, 70 different contractors we're using. Number two, some of the contractors are local and some of them are even in other states, let alone in the State of California. Number three, these contractors work for other manufacturers as well as they work for us. And that means that we would have to be in there in each one of these plants continually on a daily basis.

RATHER: And what do the retailers say? Well, to us, they refused to say anything, apparently believing that public recognition of the problem is bad public relations. The refusals came, not only from some of the biggest retailers in the country, but also the the Retail Merchants Association, which is supposed to speak — but in our case, will not speak — for some 35,000 retailers all across the country.

Now, as long as their stores are not identified, retailers admit that their major concerns are quality and price. What garment workers earn or do not earn in Los

Angeles or New York, or for that matter in Korea or Taiwan, is, from the retailers' standpoint, somebody else's problem.

And the garment unions? In California, they have little impact, for there are 3,000 contractors, each of whom can close down when the union shows up, then open for business next door. Instead of gaining members during the industry's treamendous growth, the California union has lost two-thirds of its members.

In New York's Chinatown, where nearly every shop is unionized, workers' wages are just as low as elsewhere. Union leaders say it's because workers are afraid to enforce their rights. But union organizers told us privately it's because labor leadership goes along with the bosses, wants to hold on to what it already has. Caught in the middle, the workers are just plain scared.

I know— it is not a matter of speculation, I know — that employers use this as a kind of hammer over the heads of their employees, do they not?

RAIMOND: In some cases they will, yes, very definitely.

RATHER: And they always have the option to just pick up the telephone and call you anonymously and say, there are — there are eight undocumented workers at this location?

RAIMOND: Unfortunately, that's been done, especially in — they've tried to do when there have been labor disputes, and we don't really want to get in there and bust up any unions or — We're forced at times to get involved.

RATHER: Is there anything you can do about that?

RAIMOND: Well, when a — a call comes to us indicating there are a — a hundred persons that should be checked out, we have to go check them out.

MAN: What do you have back there?

RATHER: No matter how much they are victimized, the illegal aliens cannot raise much public support, nor can they muster much support from immigrants who arrived here legally years ago or just yesterday. They are blamed for throwing citizens out of work, for dragging wages down, for pulling welfare costs up.

(Immigration officials checking illegal aliens' documents . . . speaking in Spanish)

That many economists claim that these aliens contribute more to the economy — by paying taxes and Social Security payments — than they ever cost in taking government benefits cannot change one dominant fact: the aliens are here illegally, and thus can be politically ignored.

A Few Minutes
with Andy Rooney

HARRY REASONER: Andy Rooney likes to browse, and the other day he found a book that — well, let him tell you about it.

ANDY ROONEY: This book contains the 3,000 most common last names of people in the United States. They're listed both alphabetically and in order of how many people have the name.

What would you think the top ten names are? There's only one surprise: number two. Smith is still first. About two and a half million Smiths have Social Security cards. Williams is third, Brown fourth, Jones fifth; Miller, Davis, Martin, Anderson and Wilson. And number two? Johnson.

Rooney is the 1,845th most common name in the country.

I have some statistics on first names, too. Seventy-five years ago, these were the most popular girls' names. Mary led the list. Fifty years later, Mary was still up there, but Linda was number one. By 1978, look what happened. Linda, Mary and Barbara were all gone. More people were naming their girl children Jennifer than anything else: Jennifer, Melissa, Nicole, Christine — an amazing list.

And look at the boys. In 1900, John and William and Joseph were up there. Then, 1950, Robert was on top, John was number two, James was next. But last year, Michael took over the number-one spot: Michael, David, Jason, Christopher. I think Michael and Jennifer will make a nice couple. John is still hanging in there.

Some people just use their initials, of course: J.P. Morgan, T.S. Eliot, J.C. Penney. Others use their middle name and their first initial. It always sounds sort of pretentious to me: J. Paul Getty, F. Lee Bailey, J. Edgar Hoover.

It's sort of funny that we don't get to choose what we're called all our lives. We're born with our last name and our parents give us our first name. We don't even get to pick our own nickname, because our friends usually do that. A nickname comes from the way people feel about you.

That's why I don't even think the President of the United States should insist we call him Jimmy when his name is James. We'll decide what to call him. If we feel friendly towards you, that's what we'll call you anyway, Jimmy.

Letters

HARRY REASONER: Most of last week's mail was about our story on the Ethiopian Zion Coptic Church of Miami, which claims marijuana comes from God and smoking pot is their sacrament. That story, we were sorry to learn, caused embarrassment to parishioners of churches with similar names, and the rector of one of them asked us to please point out: "This group has no relationship to the true Coptic Church of Egypt, nor to the Ethiopian Orthodox Church, nor to any other Coptic organization."

Another viewer said about the claim that there was biblical justification for smoking marijuana: "If Brother Louv could put his joint down long enough, he might be able to finish reading Genesis 1:29, (which) says, 'Seed-Bearing Fruits are to be used for food . . . Food is to be eaten, not smoked.' "

Biblical justification or not, the Florida Supreme Court ruled last week that, although the church is a legitimate one and that smoking marijuana is for them a genuine sacrament, the court ruled the state has a compelling interest in forbidding the church to indulge in that sacrament. The court ruled, further, that the presence of the church on an island off Miami violated zoning laws and that the church would have to move.

Brother Louv says he will take his case to the United States Supreme Court, and we'll keep you posted.

And finally, about our story two weeks ago on Doctor Rubin and medical fraud, we heard from a man who appeared in our report, the former Assistant Director of Health for California. He wrote: "(You) left out the fact that . . . former Governor Ronald Reagan's . . . top health officials protected Rubin and ignored complaints until they heard that Senator Kennedy was conducting an investigation. At one point, officials of the Nixon Administration were also whitewashing the scandal."

NOVEMBER 11, 1979

Looking Back

See Memory of Vietnam, *May 25, 1980, page 560*

Marva

SUZANNE ST. PIERRE, PRODUCER

MORLEY SAFER: Who is Marva Collins and why is everyone saying those wonderful things about her? Well, Marva is a 43-year-old woman who lives on the West Side of Chicago. She's not an elected official. She has nothing to do with government or show business. She's not a social worker. But she's one of those people who is out there quietly, but profoundly, changing the lives of the people she deals with day in and day out. We begin on the street where she lives.

You have it all here on West Adams Street, all the familiar big city blight: the forever-broken windows, the burned-out flats, the disemboweled abandoned cars — all that look and smell that even a crystal afternoon cannot change. And up the street or around the corner, you have a school that, for whatever reason, does not teach, and children who, for whatever reason, do not learn — castaways to that ever-growing legion of unskilled black teenaged unemployed.

And then you have 3819 West Adams, just another tired-looking house with a blank face staring out at a mean street. But come on in 3819, come on in and take a look. And what you find on the inside could not be more different from what you see on the outside.

MARVA COLLINS: Good. Very, very good. Very good, Michael. May I have them. (Indistinct) fairy tales are by whom?

CHILD: Geoffrey Chaucer.

COLLINS: They're about whom? How may pil—

CHILD: The Canterbury Pilgrims.

COLLINS: How — well, how many were there?

CLASS: Twenty-nine. Twenty-nine pilgrims.

COLLINS: There were 29 pilgrims, and they were going to Cant—

CLASS: To Canterbury.

COLLINS: Right. Thomas Becket had —

CHILD: And each one of them had to tell a story.

COLLINS: Each one had to tell a —

CLASS: A tale.

CHILD: And they were going to go to see the shrine.

COLLINS: Right, they were going to see the shrine of Thomas who?

CHILD: Beck.

CLASS: Becket.

CLASS: Of Thomas Becket, okay.

CHILD: He — he got killed.

SAFER: It is the West Side Preparatory School in the West Garfield Park District of Chicago — a one-and-a-half-room schoolhouse that goes against the grain of modern corporate education. In no way is West Side Prep the product of a committee. It is the product of this woman's determination. She is Marva Collins, a veteran public school teacher, who four years ago, utterly disillusioned with the school system, its rules, its unions and its failures, started her own school upstairs in her own house. There are about 30 children in the school, from four to 13 years old, including two of her own. It is a licensed private school, and there is a modest fee. There is very little of what these kids call "baby work."

COLLINS: Okay, Kyle, want to come to the board? Okay: Cleopatra. Cle-o-pa— pa-tra. Very good. Watch, make that "a" a little bit better, okay? Make a round circle back. My goodness, make that an "a!" "Egyptian" — put your ligature on your t-ash. Okay, an Egyptian queen. Very, very good. How — where did you learn to spell "compliment"? We used to just put a "c." Very, very good, Kyle!

SAFER: There are no frills at West Side — no art classes, no music, no gym, not even recess. There are also no discipline problems. The emphasis is on basic education, with an even stronger emphasis on literature and composition. They must read one very tough book every two weeks, and they must write a composition every day. Erica is nine years old.

ERICA (reading): "I hear from the voices of the wind. /They sing within a friend, /A friend who is truthful, honest and brave, /And is there when trouble has already been engraved."

SAFER: School is non-stop. The children arrive each morning just before nine. Children with working mothers get there as early as eight. Except for a 20-minute lunch break, they go right through to three. There are no teacher breaks, no teacher desks. She is on her feet and over their shoulders all day, pushing them, cajoling them and praising them.

COLLINS: Very, very good, Tolisa! Very, very good. Cum laude. And what did I say?

CLASS: With praise.

COLLINS: With praise, in what?

CHILD: Latin.

COLLINS: In Latin. Okay . . .

SAFER: And the results are apparent even to a casual bystander: alert and challenged children being pushed way beyond the boundaries most school systems set.

I was watching you today, and it's a very, very structured classroom, which seems to fly in the face of some current drifts of education, education techniques. For example, a lot of people say it's not — doesn't matter how you speak, as long as you are expressing yourself in the class. But you insist on the King's English.

COLLINS: If children are going to go out into the world and command a job in our society, they have to be able to speak standard English. No one wants to hire a secretary who cannot spell. No one wants to hire a president of a corporation who is not articulate. I think we need to stop saying, "This is all right for this area," and become more universal.

SAFER: Marva unashamedly imbues her class with her own values. Some might call them predictably middle class, but no one can doubt her commitment. She is not a product of the black inner city. She grew up in Alabama in a close, financially secure family; went to college in Atlanta and Chicago; and to the dismay of her own family, she and her husband, Clarence, bought a house on West Adams Street, not in one of the fashionable suburbs.

I notice a very strong moral tone in the class: in the kids' essays, and in your teaching. You are always moralizing.

COLLINS: Even when the four-year-olds begin to read *The Little Red Hen,* I point out the moral that if you don't work you don't eat. I never miss that opportunity. Children want structure. I — I — I think we've given them so much freedom that they really don't know what to do with it. I think they're really destroying themselves.

CHILD (reading):   "This world needs boys who are willing to take on a task that is difficult. Knowing that it is difficult does not mean impossible."

SAFER: What about the recess and the gym and the — the necessary horsing around of kids?

COLLINS: If you watch this area, these children get recess and gym until eleven or twelve o'clock at night. Which would you rather have, a child who reads well, computes well, thinks well, feels good about himself, or a child who runs through art, music, gym and still can't read?

CHRISTOPHER: "Why I like school. In this school, we do not have gym, recess or play all day. We learn to read hard words, hard books, and this school makes our brains big. We like . . ."

SAFER: Chris is seven years old. Very big brains indeed, and a very big voice. And like most of the kids here, very proud of himself.

How is this school different from the other schools you've been to?

CHILD: Well, at first when I came here, I just liked to play. I thought — and when she said, "You're going to do your work," I said, "Wow, this teacher really has herself together!"

CHILD: When I was in my other school, they liked to fight, have fights in the classroom, and we don't fight here.

SAFER: Kyle, what do you do when you get home?

KYLE: I read.

SAFER: Don't you play at all?

KYLE: Uh-uh.

SAFER: Don't you want to?

KYLE: Uh-huh. (Laughter)

CYRUS: Well, sometimes when my mother tells me it's time, she — she takes my books from me and hides them.

SAFER: Why does she hide them?

CYRUS: Re—

SAFER: It's bedtime, right?

CYRUS: And then I like to read in the bed, so I could dream about what I read.

SAFER: I'd like to get some idea of — of who your favorite authors are, what your favorite books are. Look at — who's your favorite author?

CHILD: Geoffrey Chau— Geoffrey Chaucer and Shakespeare.

SAFER: Geoffrey Chaucer! That's very grown-up reading. That's very difficult, isn't it?

CHILD: No, not really, if you know how to learn — if you know how to read.

CYRUS: My favorite author is Booker T. Washington and Hans Christian Andersen, and my favorite book is *The Greek Myths*.

SAFER: *Greek Myths?* Uh-hmm?

CHILD: Emerson, Henry David Thoreau, and William Shakespeare.

SAFER: And Patrick?

PATRICK: I like Fyodor Dostoyevsky and Dante Alighieri and Shakespeare.

SAFER: And your favorite book?

PATRICK: *Divine Comedy.*

SAFER (laughing):   Okay.

CHRIS: I like Ralph Waldo Emerson and Henry David Thoreau, and I like Charlotte Bronte's *Jane Eyre*. That's my favorite book. And I also like Marjorie Kinnan Rawlings, who wrote *The Yearling*. And I like Geoffrey Chaucer also, and Shakespeare.

SAFER: I talked to your — the kids in here today, and if I hadn't seen it with my own eyes, it would have looked as though they'd been conditioned to answer, "My favorite book is . . . by Thoreau or Emerson or Shakespeare or Chaucer." And it is kind of remarkable for eight- and nine-year-olds.

COLLINS: I think it's the kind of standards you set for the children when they first begin. And they meet those goals. I think once they learn how to learn, they kind of live to learn, and that's the attitude in here. They've learned how to learn, and I don't think there's any stopping them now. And they call everything else baby work. "I don't want to go to those schools where they're going to give me that baby work."

SAFER: Even the babies do not get baby work. Mrs. Collins' assistant, Mrs. Vaughn, teaches them in much the same way: always the emphasis on words, their correct spelling, correct meaning and correct pronunciation.

MRS. VAUGHN: Go to the board and write the word "dictation." "Dictation." After the Spanish, we will do dictation. "Dic-ta-tion."

SAFER: How special are these children? A lot of people are going to watch and say these are very special kids in this class. And I would suspect that they come from homes, rich or poor, in which education is a very important thing.

COLLINS: I have not seen a parent yet who wants their children to fail.

SAFER: No matter how indifferent they may be?

COLLINS: No matter how indifferent. Statistically, West Garfield Park is one of the very poorest areas in this city. I — I know how proud these parents are of their children. I think invariably it's just the opposite: the very poor black parent wants their children to excel.

SAFER: What sort of example do the older people set for the kids in a neighborhood like this — men sitting around —

COLLINS: Well — well, when I look at this area, I could really scream at all the monies that are being spent on programs, all the monies that are being thrown away, and not a doggone thing has changed in this area for the last 17 years. And that's how long we've lived here. I haven't seen any change at all. They couldn't read when we moved here; they can't read now. They didn't have jobs then; they don't have jobs now.

SAFER: The statistics bear her out. The two nearby schools show reading scores way below average, and declining the longer the child stays in school.

COLLINS (greeting man on the street):   Hi, sweetheart. Hi, how are you?

MAN: Hello, Morley.

SAFER: Hi, how are you?

MAN: Fine. How are you doing? She used to be my teacher when I was (indistinct) going to school.

COLLINS: Proud of that —

SAFER: Pretty good teacher?

MAN: Right. A real good teacher.

COLLINS: Yeah, and I'll still get you (indistinct).

MAN: She's the best teacher in the City of Chicago.

SAFER: And there are people who would say to you the street language, black colloquial language, is good enough and we should be proud of it, and it's quite all right to use that.

COLLINS: But what happens when they go to apply for a job? That same standard of English is not good enough. So what we are really doing is really playing games. The child comes to me knowing that language. Again, I repeat, "teacher" is a Latin word meaning "to lead or draw." If I teach a child no more than what he comes to me with, then I have not really taught anything.

SAFER: But is every child teachable?

COLLINS: You pick the children, you bring them to me, and you come back one month later, and I'll show you a different child; not through beating, not through screaming, not through yelling.

SAFER: Through what?

COLLINS: Through constant talking, through telling that child every day that his only hope is a good education; that in order to make it in this world, no one is going to give it to you, you have to earn it.

SAFER: Do you carefully select the ones who you know are going to make it, the ones who need —

COLLINS: The children — how do I know —

SAFER: — who need a — a Marva Collins?

COLLINS: I have the very children who came from this school who are sitting there. Why — why don't you talk to the parents tonight?

MRS. RIDLEY: Well, he was in Delano, and I was there two and three times a week.

SAFER: That's the big school right up the block?

MRS. RIDLEY: Yes. Two and three times a week.

SAFER: For what reason?

MRS. RIDLEY: Because I was concerned about him. He was having problems in school. He didn't want to continue to go to school. He made excuses to keep from going to school. He never wanted to study. And now, every night when he goes to bed, I got to take books out of his bed. (Laughter)

WOMAN: Well, you know —

MRS. RIDLEY: He goes to bed with books, paper, pencil. He is always reading.

SAFER: How about his grades?

MRS. RIDLEY: His grades have gone up like three levels.

SAFER: Really?

MRS. McCOY: Before, when Erica was in another school — she was only like five years old; she hadn't made six — and then they told me — she'd only been in that school about three weeks too — and they called me up for a conference, and said that Erica couldn't read, she wouldn't learn to read that year, she might not never learn to read. As a matter of fact, they were even saying that, you know, maybe she was slightly retarded or something was wrong. She might not learn to read —

SAFER: This little girl slightly retarded?

MRS. McCOY: Yes. Before, she would always say, "Well, I can't do that." Today, there is nothing in the world that she thinks that she can't do.

SAFER: Mr. and Mrs. Brunner, is — is this the only school that Craig has been to?

MRS. BRUNNER: No, Craig has been to two other schools.

SAFER: Well, how would you say Craig has changed?

MRS. BRUNNER: Craig has changed quite a bit. He has a lot of confidence in himself.

MR. BRUNNER: He used to do a lot of playing. He — he — he wouldn't get his lessons out. He wouldn't study. But since he's been coming to this school, now he does his homework without any problem, and he loves to come to school every day. I'm just so overwhelmed, you know, I — it makes me feel good.

SAFER: Do you think what happens here in Mrs. Collins' school, could you make that happen on a grand scale in the big public schools?

WOMAN: Only if you had a grand scale of Marva Collins, you know. That's what it's going to take.

COLLINS: I feel that almost anyone who is willing to really work and walk from desk to desk could do very well what I'm doing here. I wouldn't want to have to think that a union would have to protect my job. I have enough pride about — because I reach a high when I'm teaching anyways.

SAFER: Do you think anything can be learned by the educational system from this room?

COLLINS: Well, I think the major thing that could be learned is that it certainly doesn't take monies, because if monies kept a school going, we would have had to close our doors four years ago.

SAFER: The money is the least of West Side Prep. The parents who can afford it pay $80 a month; those who can't pay nothing. Some friends of West Side in a distant suburb raise some money, and Mrs. Collins picks up fees from occasional workshops she gives. She started the school with $5,000 she withdrew from her retirement fund. Education, it seems, can be inexpensive, if the emphasis is simply on teaching.

COLLINS: We keep spending more and more monies. The lower the scores are, the more monies we spend. If I had all kinds of audio-visual equipments here, all kinds of fun and games, all kinds of gimmicks, then I would not only have chaos, but declining scores too. Buildings do not teach. People do.

See Update, December 23, 1979, page 210.

It's a Doozie
AL WASSERMAN, PRODUCER

DAN RATHER: "It's a doozie!" — that's what people used to say about a Duesenberg. In fact, that's where the word "doozie" came from. Well, the Duesenberg has all but disappeared, but people still say "It's a doozie!" And it still means "the cat's pajamas," "nifty," "swell," "wow." Today, hardly anyone can get that worked up about a 1970's car, but let an old car — a Duesenberg or an Auburn boat tail Speedster — come down the street and their eyes light up. Take Harry Reasoner, who thinks any fine old car is a doozie.

HARRY REASONER: If you're like me, you've probably had the fantasy of buying a fine old car for your very own, fixing it up so it's in mint condition, driving it around occasionally so the neighbors can admire it, maybe even winning a prize with it at some fancy car meet. Well, for more Americans than you think, old cars are more than a fantasy. They're an obsession.

Looks like you got some work left to do, even after two years, Mr. Kirby. Did it run when you got it?

CHARLES KIRBY: Oh, no! Oh, it was a basket case. My goodness, those pistons in there were froze up.

REASONER: In Portsmouth, Ohio, we found a gentleman named Charles Kirby. For the last two years, he's been restoring an old car, and he figures he still has about another year to go. This is the car Kirby bought for $2,000 — as he says, a basket case. The Kirbys run a florist shop, but Charlie's real work is his car.

How many hours would you guess he spends a week on the car?

MRS. KIRBY: Oh, it'd be hard to say. He comes down here sometimes at night. Sometimes he'll work till midnight. Sometimes he'll start in the morning, and he'll spend (indistinct).

REASONER: Does he spend as much time on the car as he does on the flower business?

MRS. KIRBY: Oh, yes. He's not even in here. (Laughter) We have a time getting him to deliver a basket. (Laughter)

KIRBY: I'm retired.

REASONER: Kirby's car is a 1919 Scripps-Booth touring car, an undistinguished car made by an almost-forgotten manufacturer. When Kirby is through fixing it up, it may be worth around $10,000 — not much profit for three years' work. But money wasn't the reason Charlie Kirby searched for 40 years to find this particular car. You see, back in 1919, Kirby's father bought a Scripps-Booth tourer. It was the car Kirby grew up with as a boy. You didn't need a license to drive then, so Kirby's father actually let him drive it to school.

KIRBY: And it was around those days, in the horse and buggy days, some of the kids — well, they looked on my brother and I like we were astronauts.

REASONER: Even now his adventures aren't over. He's just learned that there's a fellow in Colorado who also has a 1919 Scripps-Booth tourer. So what's Kirby planning to do on his vacation? Naturally, he's going to drive up to Colorado with the missus and take a look.

(Old recording: song on being wild about automobiles)

The thing is, people who have old cars like to get together with other people who have old cars, particularly if they have old cars just like theirs. Now, if you collected fine art, it probably would not occur to you to start a Matisse club or a Rembrandt club. But for owners of old cars, there are Bugatti clubs, Rolls-Royce clubs, Edsel clubs, what have you. There's even a National Woody Club for owners of cars with wooden bodies. Now, what we have here is the Horseless Carriage Club, Denver chapter. These cars are all different, but they have one thing in common — they were all built no later than 1915.

MAN: I let her cool off a minute, and I gave her a crank, and then . . .

REASONER: Horseless carriage buffs have a thing going of their own. It's not just the cars themselves, with their shiny brass fittings and the tender loving care they demand.

It's a chance to imagine the past, a way of acting out in fantasy a period of history they're all too young to remember — those gentle years before World War I when Americans were still discovering that marvelous new invention, the automobile.

(Music)

It's one of history's larger ironies that the horseless carriage entered the scene as the answer to environmental problems created by an earlier conveyance, the horse. When you consider that the average horse produces 22 pounds of manure a day, the quality of life in big cities at that time isn't hard to imagine. So, as far back as 1899, that august publication, *Scientific American,* hailed the motorcar as the answer to horse pollution, the way to eliminate a greater part of the nervousness, distraction and strain of city life.

Of course, it wasn't a simple matter, taking a ride in one of those early motorcars, and some people wished they had stayed with the horse. But what the car gave in exchange was a kind of personal freedom unlike any that had ever existed before. If you could come up with $500 or so, and if you could afford 15 cents a gallon for gasoline, you could write your own ticket to adventure, take off for parts unknown whenever it pleased you, and go wherever you wanted to go.

(Sound of old car engine straining to start)

Of course, being an old car hobbyist is not entirely a bed of roses. Take Don Schoenfeld of Los Angeles, who's having his problems. (Sound of old car engine straining to start) Schoenfeld is trying to resurrect an old Rolls-Royce Silver Ghost, but the engine seems to be suffering from some strange disease. (Sound of old car engine straining to start)

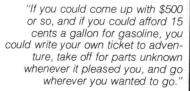

"If you could come up with $500 or so, and if you could afford 15 cents a gallon for gasoline, you could write your own ticket to adventure, take off for parts unknown whenever it pleased you, and go wherever you wanted to go."

DON SCHOENFELD: I assumed that this engine was in perfect condition, and it's not.

REASONER: But the engine is the least of Schoenfeld's problems.

SCHOENFELD: When I purchased the car, I assumed that the chassis was 1914. Now, upon checking it out further, I find that it — that isn't exactly true, although parts of it are of that era.

REASONER: Now, the difference in value between the car Schoenfeld bought and the one he thought he bought is staggering. When this car is fully restored, chances are it'll be worth around $35,000. But an authentic 1914 Silver Ghost in top condition is worth at least triple that amount. So, while you can't exactly call a wreck worth $35,000 a lemon, if you could, that's what Don Schoenfeld got.

AUCTIONEER: Who'll give $100,000 on one of the finest Silver Ghosts in the world?

REASONER: It's hard to talk about old cars these days without talking about money, and for the best of the cars the money is substantial indeed. Here's a 1930 Duesenberg belonging to a wealthy California collector, Riggs Cunningham. If you're interested, it's a dual cowl Phaeton; body by LeBaron. And if it were for sale, the price would probably be well over $200,000. If your taste runs to racing cars, there's this rare 1929 Mercedes SSK, worth maybe $250,000.

Then there's Gary Cooper's old Duesenberg SSJ. Figure around $250,000 for the car, plus an extra $50,000 for the Gary Cooper connection. And if you want the ultimate and have about a million dollars to spare, you might think about buying a Bugatti Royale. There are only six of them, and for size, power, luxury and styling, they stand alone. So, with all those dollar signs floating around, inevitably, when you look into the hobby of old cars, you come to the business of old cars.

A lot of the business is conducted at auctions, hundreds of them each year, like this one in Tulsa, Oklahoma. Old cars are in the same league now with gold, diamonds and Tiffany lamps — as fashionable hedges against inflation. But if you're thinking of buying one as an investment, you'd better know what you're doing; or better yet, bring along your own expert.

BOB GOTTLIEB: Shilling is the practice of bidding a car for the seller. And many, many sellers will have their friends bid a car to, let's say, $25,000. Then the next man who bids $26,000 has bought it, and the car really isn't worth that. It's reached really a point to where you don't know what a car is worth.

REASONER: Bob Gottlieb is an attorney and a collector of old cars. He also writes and teaches about them as investments. We walked around with Gottlieb, getting his opinion of the cars that were going up for auction. They all looked pretty good, but on a lot of them it was clear that the beauty was only skin deep.

GOTTLIEB: Well, many times cars are poorly restored, and plastic or bondo or lead or putty is used in the cars. And there is a way to find that out. First, the best way is by the human eye. If you sight down a car, you can generally pretty well tell. But most people who are collectors or investors carry with them a little magnet like this, and if there's any bondo or putty or anything like that, the magnet isn't going to stick to it. This is a fiberglass fender. The magnet falls right off.

REASONER: The condition a car is in naturally has a lot to do with what it's worth. What's even more important is just how authentic it is.

GOTTLIEB: What you have to be careful of would be those people who might mislead you.

REASONER: There are a few in the business?

GOTTLIEB: There are many in the business, unfortunately. We have a — a tremendously large number of people who would take a — let's say a Packard sedan. Take the sedan body off, because a closed body is not worth as much as an open body. The first buyer may know that he's buying a reproduction car, and so may the second; but pretty soon along the line somebody forgets, and you may be . the —

REASONER: Forgets intentionally, maybe?

GOTTLIEB: Maybe intentionally, maybe unintentionally. I've seen people pay a hundred and fifty thousand dollars for reproduction cars that should have sold for $30,000.

REASONER: If buying a car at an auction is no game for the innocent, neither is selling one. The way things traditionally work at auctions, if you want to sell a car, you pay an entry fee, usually a hundred dollars. Then, if the car is sold, the auction company pays you the money, minus their commission. Sounds simple. But a lot of sellers have learned otherwise.

GOTTLIEB: Many, many times sellers don't get paid for their cars. They — they put a car up for sale and the car is sold, and they lose their car, they don't get paid. There have been a number of auction companies that absolutely went bankrupt, and a couple of them where the money just disappeared.

DEAN KRUSE (auctioneering):   Eight thousand . . .

REASONER: Even the biggest car auction firm in the country has been having its problems. That's the company conducting this auction in Tulsa — Kruse Auctioneers, a family-run operation.

KRUSE (auctioneering):   I got 75. Now, wait! Get ready to roll it out!

REASONER: The Kruses were farmers in Indiana. Their style is down-home and high-voltage.

KRUSE (auctioneering):   Ninety-five. Ninety-five. Are you bidding 95? Help him. Drive it out! Drive it out! Ninety-five . . .

REASONER: The president of the company and the man who does most of the auctioneering is Dean Kruse.

KRUSE (auctioneering):   Forty-one thousand. Forty thousand dollars . . . bidding of forty-one. Anybody else . . .

REASONER: In just a few years, the Kruses built up a $50-million-a-year business. But along the way, they managed to accumulate a couple of million dollars in debts, leaving a lot of car sellers with nothing but promissory notes.

KRUSE: There were a lot of people who were angry, and I don't blame them. I'd be angry too. And the — you know, I — I've been threatened to get beat up and shot and everything else.

REASONER: One of the things that's complicated life for the Kruses and helped give them a reputation for at best poor management was an auction last year in Las Vegas from which the proceeds disappeared.

KRUSE: Our accounting people that handled the money there put the money and the titles in a briefcase, and they took it — they were not suppose to check it, but they did check it on United Airlines.

REASONER: Ordinary baggage?

KRUSE: As ordinary baggage.

REASONER: How much money?

KRUSE: Well, there was $485,000 in checks and money. I believe there was around $80,000 in cash. And of course, there were titles in there for another million dollars' worth of vehicles.

REASONER: The briefcase finally showed up. But as you might expect, it was empty.
   (Old recording: song on being wild about automobiles)
   By now, the moral of our story should be pretty clear. If you get into the old car hobby to make money, watch your step. But if you're in it for love, enjoy.
   (Old recording: song on being wild about automobiles)

A Few Minutes
with Andy Rooney

DAN RATHER: We started this broadcast with a visit to three veterans of the Vietnam War. Andy Rooney, on this Veterans Day, has some thoughts about another war.

ANDY ROONEY: Anyone my age lost a lot of friends in World War II. I was co-captain of my high school football team with Obie Slingerland. Obie was a dear friend, although you don't think of friends that way when you're a boy in high school. He became a Navy pilot, and I bet he was a good one. He flew from the deck of the Saratoga, and he died in the Pacific. I often wake up nights, those nights that are so hard to get through, thinking about Obie and how he would have lived the life he never had. It seems so sad. I'm not easily moved by music, but I often start humming "The Ballad of Rodger Young" when I think of my friends who died.

(Burl Ives singing "The Ballad of Rodger Young" over visual montage)

The war, even heroism, wasn't usually as dramatic as the story of Private Rodger Young. Heroism in war, like in peace, is mostly just doing what you ought to do. Most of us don't make anything of Veterans Day. I'm not much for it myself. We owe Obie Slingerland and Rodger Young waking up in the middle of the night to think of them more often than Veterans Day comes along. We owe the men in Veterans Hospitals anything in the world we can do for them. The rest of us who served but didn't die, weren't wounded — no one owes us anything. We got what we had coming — a free country.

Letters

DAN RATHER: Most of the mail this week was about our story on illegal aliens. Several letters were like this one. "When the welfare system is made so attractive that it is more profitable to collect a public check than hold a job, no wonder illegal aliens are welcomed by employers."

About our story on the swine flu inoculation program and the complications that followed it, a viewer wrote: "Pressure for this monstrosity came . . . from Gerald Ford's White House . . . something dramatic was needed to make Ford look good . . . What better than having him come on during the closing weeks of the campaign as the protector of the nation's health?"

And finally, about operatic tenor Luciano Pavarotti, a viewer said: "The only sour note was the derogatory remark about my home town — Erie, Pennsylvania . . . How would you like to become a soprano, Morley Safer?"

NOVEMBER 18, 1979

The Ayatollah

BARRY LANDO, PRODUCER

DAN RATHER: Iran's Ayatollah Khomeini today was interviewed by Mike Wallace, the first interview by an American reporter since the ordeal of the hostages began. The interview came early during a day in which later three hostages were put on display, pending their promised release, and amid reports that the Ayatollah and others now were mentioning possible trials for remaining hostages if the former Shah of Iran is not handed over by the United States.

During the interview, you sometimes will hear an interpreter translating from our studios in New York. At other times, you will hear the official interpreter present at the interview with written answers to some of the questions, which we had to submit in advance.

MIKE WALLACE: If there is some turmoil in Teheran, there was none apparent this morning in the Holy City of Qum a hundred miles to the south. There, guarded by a lone soldier on a rooftop, is the modest compound of the Ayatollah Khomeini. This morning in his reception room, the ground rules for the interview were carefully spelled out. No question could be asked unless it was approved ahead of time. No questions about Iran's internal politics. No questions about a lack of freedom under the Ayatollah. But there seemed no pattern to those questions that were disallowed; about half of those we proposed were simply forbidden. The interpreter said he would refuse even to ask the Ayatollah any questions that he, the interpreter, deemed inappropriate.

To begin with, of course, we wanted to learn about the hostages held in the American embassy compound.

Do you still say, Imam, that if the Shah, the ex-Shah, is not returned to Iran, that those American hostages in the American embassy compound will not be freed?

AYATOLLAH RUHOLLAH KHOMEINI (through interpreter):   In the name of God, the most merciful and gracious. This issue has to do with the people. The 35 million population of Iran want this, and we must investigate why the population wants the Shah returned. And unless he is returned, the hostages will not be freed.

RATHER: Then, reading from a prepared text, the Ayatollah's official interpreter said, "The Shah has to return and tell us where his money is, and we have to know the extent of his treason against our people."

AYATOLLAH KHOMEINI (through interpreter):   There are two main reasons for the people's insistence for the Shah's return. One, that this is a — a nation with a poor economy; that the wealth of these people have been plundered by the Shah and his relatives, have been taken out of the country, are being deposited in various U.S. and European banks. And these are the monies which, indeed, belong to the people — to these poor people.

WALLACE: Right.

AYATOLLAH KHOMEINI (through interpreter):   And therefore, he has to come. He has to return and tell us where are these monies and why they are there.

The second, which is even more important than the first reason, is that we want him back to show the extent of the crimes committed by this person during 37 years of his rule. We have to know the extent of his treasons in this country. This is why that he has to return and he has to be tried, and then the courts will decide.

WALLACE: But that is not an answer to whether the hostages will be freed.

AYATOLLAH KHOMEINI (through interpreter):   I just gave an answer. The people will it, and we can't go against this will.

WALLACE: Then the — then the hostages will remain there in the American embassy compound, what, for life? Forever?

AYATOLLAH KHOMEINI (through interpreter):   They will remain until the Shah is returned. It is in the hands of Carter. Carter can free them by returning the Shah.

WALLACE: Imam, President Carter accuses your government of practicing terrorism, and says that your regime will be held accountable if those U.S. hostages are harmed.

AYATOLLAH KHOMEINI (through interpreter):   The 35 million people of Iran are terrorists? Ask Carter. You interpret politics like this? You call our people terrorists? I have heard what Carter says of them and it doesn't make sense. He says they are not students. They are bums, mobs; they are terrorists. You know these as terrorists? This is an insult to the students and people across the nation. You consider our people terrorists? Your un— understand them — of politics is that we are a nation of terrorists? We are Moslems. If — this is an insult.

WALLACE: Imam, President Sadat of Egypt, a devoutly religious man, a Moslem, says that what you are doing now is — quote — "a disgrace to Islam." And he calls you, Imam — forgive me, his words, not mine — "a lunatic." I know that you have heard that comment.

IRANIAN INTERPRETER: . . . a lunatic, madman, or — ?

WALLACE: That's — yes, that's — that's what I heard President Sadat say on American television —

IRANIAN INTERPRETER: Yes.

WALLACE: — that the Imam is a disgrace to Islam —

IRANIAN INTERPRETER: Yes.

WALLACE: — and he used the word a "lunatic."

AYATOLLAH KHOMEINI (through interpreter):   Sadat states he is a Moslem and we are not. He is not, for he compromises with the enemies of Islam. Sadat has united with our enemies. Sadat knows well what is occurring south of Lebanon and with the Palestinians. He knows the crimes of Israel, yet he still considers Begin a friend and himself a Moslem. You must try to evaluate what he is doing then through Islam. The Egyptian people do not back Sadat.

RATHER: And once again, the official interpreter reading from his prepared text.

AYATOLLAH KHOMEINI (through interpreter):   I demand that Egyptian people try to overthrow him, just as we did with the Shah.

WALLACE: He calls upon the Egyptian people —

IRANIAN INTERPRETER: He does.

WALLACE: — to overthrow Sadat —

IRANIAN INTERPRETER: He does.

WALLACE: — the way the Iranian people overthrew the Shah?

IRANIAN INTERPRETER: Exactly.

WALLACE: What — we hear, Imam, that today, perhaps today, some black hostages and some female hostages will be released from the American embassy compound. Is that true?

AYATOLLAH KHOMEINI (through interpreter):   The freedom of the women and blacks will be given. Women are given great dignity in Islam, and the blacks have been oppressed in the United States. Great injustice was done unto them. They were under pressure in the United States, thus they came here. We are doing this owing to the tenets of Islam. In return, we ask nothing for their freedom. We want the Shah. Carter must return him. The world's international law agrees with this principle.

WALLACE: I ask you, as an American and a human being talking to an Iranian and another human being, is there no room for compromise? Or is — Or is Iran now, in effect, at war with the United States?

IRANIAN INTERPRETER: I'm sorry, I can't answer — ask that first question —

WALLACE: Will that —

IRANIAN INTERPRETER: — because that one was crossed out.

WALLACE: Imam — Imam, are you, is Iran, in effect at war with the United States now?

AYATOLLAH KHOMEINI (through interpreter):   What do you mean by war? If you mean our armies against the United States' armies, no, there is no such war. If you mean it is a battle of nerves, it is Carter's doing. We are against war. We are Moslems. We desire peace for all. Carter does not allow this. Carter should put aside his so-called humanism and return the criminal Shah, so that we can conclude this matter. The Shah is a criminal, we all know this. This spy nest you call the U.S. embassy then can be returned to a place of humanism and diplomacy. Carter must return the Shah. We have nothing against the people of the United States.

WALLACE: But if the President says he refuses to return the Shah and if the Imam says he will not free the hostages, then what — what can be the answer?

IRANIAN INTERPRETER: I am not sure if I can get the answer, because this was not in the questions —

WALLACE: Please ask him. I'm sure it's a very simple, straightforward question.

(Interpreter telling Khomeini in Farsi that Wallace's question is not in the approved list of questions)

WALLACE: He will not discuss it?

IRANIAN INTERPRETER: He's not even going to listen to it because —

WALLACE: All right.

IRANIAN INTERPRETER: — it's not in here.

WALLACE: All right.

If the Imam was so convinced that the U.S. embassy was a spy center, why did he not close it down and break off relations with the United States? Why did he wait for this group of young Iranians to take it over?

AYATOLLAH KHOMENI (though interpreter):   We didn't think an embassy could be a center of spying. I didn't realize this until our students found the necessary evidence. I didn't realize Carter, going against all international law tenets, would allow this spying and conspiracy at the American embassy. Now that our students have done this, taken the embassy with the backing of all the people of Iran, we have now realized — we have now realized that the American embassy has been a center for spying.

"We didn't think an embassy could be a center of spying. I didn't realize this until our students found the necessary evidence."

WALLACE: Imam, could you, would you, permit me to go to the American embassy compound and talk to the hostages who are there?

AYATOLLAH KHOMEINI (through interpreter):   Okay. Yes, you could.

WALLACE: I can go?

AYATOLLAH KHOMEINI (through interpreter):   It does not matter. Allow him to go and observe. Our young are there, and they will show him the Americans are safe and healthy. There is no problem in going. They are under protection, and nothing will occur to them. Islam protects the prisoner, and Islam is humane. We are Moslems. Our students are Moslem students. They will protect the prisoners. I have asked my son to observe and insure their safety. He reported to me that they are all well. I personally wish and hope for their safety. The prisoners — the prisoners at the United States embassy must ask Carter to allow the Shah to return, so they may again gain their freedom.

RATHER: Well, despite that, Mike Wallace was not allowed into the embassy. But this afternoon, Iranians brought three of the hostages before cameras for what they called a brief news conference. The three were: Katherine Gross of Cambridge Springs, Pennsylvania, a part-time embassy secretary; and two Marine sergeants – Ladell Maples of Earle, Arkansas, and Williams Quarles of Washington, D.C. These three Americans, it was said, would be released later. Whether they are the only three to be released was not made explicitly clear.

The Foreign Legion

See June 15, 1980, page 610

Wellness

LESLIE EDWARDS, PRODUCER

DAN RATHER: Wellness. Now there's a word you don't hear every day. It means exactly what you might think it means – the opposite of illness. It's a movement that is catching on all over the country among doctors, nurses and others concerned with medical care. Wellness is really the ultimate in something called self-care, in which patients are taught to diagnose common illnesses and, where possible, to treat themselves. More than that, it is a positive approach to health, what one doctor calls "recognizing that health is not simply the absence of disease."

NURSE: I'm going to teach you how to take your blood pressure, Russ.

RUSS: Oh, good.

RATHER: The do-it-yourself approach to health care is growing in popularity. Ordinary people are taking more responsibility in meeting their medical needs. They're learning how to handle stethoscopes, how to take blood pressures.

NURSE: Tighten it up.

RATHER: Women have been learning how to administer self breast examinations and Pap smears.

NURSE: Use the whole hand.

RATHER: And in some cases people have been performing their own elementary surgery. It's all part of a movement that's become known as the self-care surge. And one of the leading exponents is Dr. Tom Ferguson.

DR. TOM FERGUSON: People coming into a primary care facility for a first visit, anywhere between — depending on the population — maybe half to seventy percent of those people could probably deal with the problem just as well by home treatments.

RATHER: Wait a minute, Doctor. Are you telling me that somewhere between fifty and seventy percent of the people who go into a doctor's office, and are there for a first visit, shouldn't be there?

DR. FERGUSON: No, I am not saying that. They go in many cases because they don't have the knowledge or the training to — to convince themselves that it's safe for them to stay home and apply home treatments. Most of us have been brought up to think of the doctor as being the person responsible for our health. I think we're now realizing increasingly that we're the people that are responsible for our own health.

RATHER: Dr. Ferguson started his work in self-care several years ago while still a student at Yale Medical School. What caught his attention was that most of the patients he saw as a student had diseases which they themselves could have prevented. Now, you might think that a doctor with Ferguson's training would have a successful practice in some major city. But Dr. Ferguson doesn't practice any more. Instead, he lives and works in Inverness, California, a town just north of San Francisco. There he publishes the quarterly magazine *Medical Self-Care*.
How do doctors who practice traditional medicine feel about patients taking care of themselves? Dr. Michael Halberstam a Washington, D.C. heart surgeon who writes on health, has given that a lot of thought.

DR. MICHAEL HALBERSTAM: We do fail in educating our patients in terms of good health habits, but some of my most brilliant patients are the least educable. I've got very bright patients whom I start to explain something to, and the guy says, "Look, I'm an expert in international finance. You're in inter— you're an expert in — in medicine. I'll take your word for it. I don't — I don't care for your explanations. I've got — I'm — I'm too busy to — to learn about this stuff." I find that a valid point of view.

RATHER: Be that as it may, more and more people are turning to self-care.

DOCTOR: . . . could be a problem. That twist that you see . . .

RATHER: The foundation of the self-care and wellness movements is teaching people to diagnose illnesses and treat themselves whenever possible. Health fairs, such as this one outside San Francisco, are one technique used to do that.

DR. FERGUSON: The purpose of this fair is to provide the community with access to a number of different resources and different kinds of resources having to do with health. Hopefully, they can find something here to educate themselves or to get some — some professional services from people who are experts in the area. What I'm interesting in doing is in supporting and facilitating lay people — individually, in family groups, and in other kinds of groups — to be able to provide health care for themselves, not as a replacement for it, but as a — in addition to the services available from experts.
I think that there are some cases when you should definitely call the doctor. And one of the things that's taught in the self-care classes that we write about and that — the one's that I have taught is what are the real danger signals? When should you definitely and without question call the doctor

RATHER: Give me three fast examples of when you unquestionably should call the doctor.

DR. FERGUSON: Okay. If you cough up blood, if you pass blood in your stool, and if you notice a breast lump.

RATHER: Aside from having a thermometer, a stethoscope, a blood pressure cuff in the home, self-care advocates suggest that people read a number of recently published books geared to the general health consumer. Most of these books tell people how to recognize a symptom, when to call a doctor, how to better report what is troubling you. But if there's one way more than any other that self-care information is spreading rapidly, it's in community clinics such as this one.

DR. TIM RUMSEY: Obviously, you wouldn't be able to diagnose heart disease or anything, but we — trying to relieve a little bit of the mystery that goes on in — in an exam.

(To child):   Can you hear a beat? That's your heart.

RATHER: The Helping Hand Clinic in St. Paul, Minnesota, is one of the few clinics in the country with self-care built right into its services. Although there are no nationwide figures, Dr. Tim Rumsey's clinic had 10,000 patient visits last year.

NURSE: We're checking for infection, and we're checking for low blood.

RATHER: For several years now, patients have been working as partners with doctors in every aspect of treatment.

NURSE: Now, I'm going to put one of the white cells underneath here for you to see.

RATHER: They learn how to examine their own blood and urine samples through microscopes. Parents are taught how to examine ears and other parts of children's bodies. Computers are used to analyze diets for nutritional value. Patients read self-care material on symptoms and illnesses. They're exposed to techniques such as bio-feedback and hypnosis. And the clinical staff here does not wear the traditional white garb.

DR. RUMSEY: We don't talk down to them, use big terminology, and so on. There's a lot to us, a real wonder that we want to share with them. And I think that's really what preventive health care's all about. It starts with a positive attitude, being fired up about just ourselves.

RATHER: Dr. Samuel Bessman is chairman of the Department of Nutrition and Pharmacology at the University of Southern California. Dr. Bessman uses strong language to denounce the self-care and wellness movements.

DR. SAMUEL BESSMAN: Don't forget that every quack has a whole slew of people who'll swear he's very good. They go to court and they swear — it's very hard to prove a quack is a quack. And — because the people who deal with them are mesmerized into thinking they — he done them some good. What's being proposed by the — by the high priests of these cults is that we diminish medical research.

DR. FERGUSON: I think that we've put all our eggs in the basket of academic medicine, too many eggs in for too long, and we need to get some of those eggs out. Not all the eggs. We need — we need to keep what we have. We don't mean to throw out existing academic medicine. But we need to broaden our scope of — of our considerations of health.

RATHER: One of those people who broadened her scope of health is Theresa Rose. She's a former nurse who turned to self-care after suffering for years with painful muscle inflammation. Unable to find a cure with regular doctors and specialists, Theresa gave up traditional medicine — entered a program of self-care known as "wellness." This is a new and developing concept that takes self-care to its farthest point. Noted for his work in this field, Dr. John Travis established a wellness program soon after finishing medical studies at Tufts and Johns Hopkins Universities.

Can you give me a definition of wellness?

DR. JOHN TRAVIS: It's recognizing that there's more to life than the absence of sickness, that health is simply not the absence of disease. It's an on-going dynamic state of growth.

Just because you aren't sick, you don't have any symptoms and you could go get a check-up and get a clean bill of health doesn't mean that you're well. It doesn't mean that you're going to prevent disease further down the line.

THERESA ROSE: I had been in and out of the Cleveland Clinic. I had seen numerous specialists in various area(s). And I just was so tired and so fed up being in so much pain. And I'd spent I would give you a ballpark figure of about thirty-five thousand dollars over the last nine years in medical care.

RATHER: Traditional medical care?

ROSE: Yes. And had achieved nothing.

JULIO ESPOSTI: One-fifty-two, three . . .

RATHER: Julio Esposti joined self-care for the same reasons. He's an executive with a major West Coast firm. For years he suffered from constant headaches and physical pain. Doctors told him it was due to stress in his work. But any test or X-ray doctors administered to Julio proved negative. Like Theresa, Julio says he didn't find relief until he entered a program called wellness.

RATHER: Now, is what you're into a substitute practice of medicine?

DR. TRAVIS: No, absolutely not. It is an adjunct to, and quite different from, the practice of medicine. We don't treat, diagnose or prescribe. Our role is to help the person discover why they're sick.

RATHER: Travis does this by looking at a person's whole life style: their diet, work habits and physical activities. What solved Julio's illness problems was biofeed-back.

DR. TRAVIS: As the tone gets lower, you're warming, and you've just raised your hand temperature one degree . . .

RATHER: Biofeedback basically is an electronic device used to measure the amount of tension or stress in a person's body. After several sessions, Julio learned not only how to relieve his pain, but also how to handle stressful situations at work.

ESPOSTI: I was getting headaches about three times a week.

RATHER: This is before you started going to the wellness center?

ESPOSTI: That's true.

RATHER: And how often do you have headaches now?

ESPOSTI: I guess I get one about once a month now.

RATHER: When you first started going to the wellness center, did you say to yourself, or did someone say to you, "That's a crazy thing to do"?

ROSE: A few people in my — my life said, "What is it? Have you checked out the credentials? And where were they educated?" And, you know, all of those sort of questions.

However, I — at that point I really felt that I had spent all those years going to your credentialed individuals, and so when I found someone who was willing to talk it out with me, that was pretty receptive to me. Not tell me what was wrong with me, but help me to find out myself.

RATHER: Revived interest in self-care is reaching the health profession. Twice a year now, health professionals — surgeons, nurses, therapists and others — meet with Dr. Travis to learn methods of wellness which they can use for themselves as well as for their patients.

Critics of the wellness movement, particularly, they say, well, what would you expect in Marin County, California? It's another one of those kookie — (laughter) Okay, that's what the critics say to me. Yes?

WOMAN: Well, I don't like labels, especially with all the latest publicity on cults in the San Francisco area. And I think that wellness as a concept doesn't need to have a culture or a subculture added to it.

RATHER: A doctor from Southern California — I'm talking now about a physician who's very critical of the wellness movement — said, "Mr. Rather, what you're dealing with is a — a middle-class cult."

WOMAN 1:   That's anti the whole concept of wellness, to — to follow blindly. We are not cheap. And the whole thing we're learning here is to take responsibility for ourselves, to question, and to use what fits for me.

WOMAN 2:   And in wellness, you are the leader. You're your own guru. And you're the perfect person that is trying to make your life better and more full.

MAN (at health professionals' meeting):   If more and more people become involved in wellness and, indeed, do take care of themselves and think more of themselves and are able to function more appropriately without disease, then that's going to cost organized medicine money. And there's an economic incentive then, I think, to — to call the movement a cult and hope it does disappear.

DR. BESSMAN: I always like to ask the question, is the individual who's telling me how good I'm going to be taking care of myself, is he making a lot of money from that? He doesn't even have to take care of me and he makes money.

RATHER: Well, answer your own question. Is he making a lot of money?

DR. BESSMAN: Sure he's making a lot of money. (Laughs) It's a business.

DR. FERGUSON: Well, I think that most of the — that charge can also be leveled at the majority of medical-care institutions in this country. Most private physicians make their living by the fees that they charge for their clinical services. And I can't see much difference between charging someone to diagnose a sore throat or teaching them to diagnose it for themselves.

RATHER: To try and judge what impact the wellness movement may have on hospitals, we visited one in Denver, Colorado. The Swedish Hospital is the first institution in the country of its kind to offer a full wellness center along with regular medical care.
Though the program has been in operation only a year or so, already 50 experts in various areas of health promotion are working to help patients and others to progress from illness, to absence of illness, to wellness. Courses are offered in stress management, diet and nutrition, and there are classes in aerobic dancing to strengthen the heart. (Music)

EXERCISE CLASS LEADER: Now right foot. Jump forward . . .

RATHER: Hospital administrators say the program, besides benefiting the general community, will also lower their patient load. But Dr. Bessman of USC is not impressed.

DR. BESSMAN: I think that any movement which removes the patient from contacting his physician when he thinks he needs help is a bad movement. It's a retrogression.

DR. HALBERSTAM: There's always going to be enough illness, I'm — I'm afraid, for — for physicians, and I —

RATHER: You're not fearful of losing patients to self-care and wellness?

DR. HALBERSTAM: No, and — and I'm — I'm — I'm — and I'm — be glad to lose some patients, some illnesses, to self-care and wellness. I just — I'd be delighted to. It would give me a chance to — and my colleagues a chance to concentrate on the things that we can do best.

RATHER: Now, is it going to take a revolution to accomplish that?

DR. FERGUSON: I think we are in the midst of one.

Letters

HARRY REASONER: Every once in a while we on 60 MINUTES are privileged to introduce you to someone who touches a responsive chord in all of us. Last week's story on Marva Collins and her ghetto school was a case in point, and the mail has been heavy and glowing. For instance: "Although I am a firm opponent of forced busing, I would gladly send my children halfway across the state to attend her school."

And there was this: "(If we made her) Secretary of Education, in a few years we might not need a Department of Welfare."

There was also a letter that said: "If her students perceive public-school education to be baby work, it would seem to confirm the growing public suspicion that a large number of today's teachers are merely expensive baby sitters."

But a public-school teacher wrote: "How can she say she's dealing with the same sort of child the rest of us get . . . her kids come from homes where parents really care. Her kids are well-fed, well-clothed and well-loved. (My kids) have parents who show no interest."

Finally, a viewer wrote: "Could you please clone Marva Collins for every school in the United States . . . and send the first one to Great Falls, Montana."

NOVEMBER 25, 1979

Roy Innis
MARTIN PHILLIPS, PRODUCER

MIKE WALLACE: Many Americans remember CORE, the Congress of Racial Equality, at the forefront of the civil rights movement in the sixties — demonstrating
peacefully against segregation, demonstrating for equality in housing, employment, opportunity, a leader in the fight for civil rights for black Americans. But
what about CORE today? What has become of it? We hear of PUSH and SCLC, of
the NAACP and the Urban League, but little about CORE.

Well, over the last several years it has been wracked by charges that Roy Innis,
national chairman since 1968, has been running CORE as his own private
fiefdom; that he has ordered violence against CORE members, dissident members who get in his way; that he and other CORE officers have squandered money
raised ostensibly for CORE programs. And in recent months, the State of New
York has taken CORE to court, charging that Roy Innis and other officers of CORE
have systematically looted CORE funds, used the money for themselves; that,
allegedly, they are involved in fund-raising fraud.

We sat down at CORE headquarters with Roy Innis and the two other defendants
named in the suit — Mary Dennison, his former wife and deputy, and Wendell
Garnett, CORE treasurer — to review New York State's charges. Looking on was
Innis's attorney, Ray Lefler.

Isn't the State of New York calling you, in effect, a thief?

ROY INNIS: If one could believe these allegations, yes. And if they're calling —

WALLACE: Are you a thief?

INNIS: I'm not a thief. And if they are calling me a thief, they should pull me into
court. I want them to prosecute, not persecute. What they are doing now is a
game, a press game, an assassination, attempt to assassinate one's character,
moral assassination, psychological warfare. It's persecution.

MAN: Mr. Roy Innis. (Applause)

WALLACE: New York State's investigation of Innis began with charges that CORE
fund-raisers harassed and threatened contributors into making donations. State
investigators then subpoenaed all of Innis's books, his bank accounts and
credit-card records. Dan Kurtz, head of New York State's Charity Fraud Bureau,
told us what he found.

DAN KURTZ: There were payments for personal residences of officers and family members, payments of travel expenses for, again, what we re— believe to be personal travel, unrelated to CORE's business; and in addition, travel for family members and children of CORE officers, hotel and restaurant expenses clearly of a personal nature, purchase of furniture, clothing, jewelry, liquor, similar items.

WALLACE: In other words, Roy Innis and his colleagues were using CORE money as their own private bank account, in effect?

KURTZ: To a significant extent, we believe that's what took place.

WALLACE: Marvin Peay was for a long time one of Roy Innis's closest colleagues. Until 1976, he worked for Innis as his so-called "chief of national security" — his enforcer.

MARVIN PEAY: If someone was abusive to the organization, in Innis's words, he — he needs to be dealt with. And my job was to see that he got dealt with.

WALLACE: Dealt with? I'm serious. What do you do? How do you "deal with"?

PEAY: Well, physical abuse.

WALLACE: Serious beating?

PEAY: Yes.

WALLACE: Ever killing?

PEAY: No. Fortunately, no.

WALLACE: When you say "fortunately no," did he never tell you to kill anyone?

PEAY: Yes, but I never killed anyone and I never implement that assignment.

WALLACE: One assignment that Peay insists he did implement was to deal with Ray Cunningham. According to Peay, Cunningham, a former fund-raiser for CORE, had stolen a list of CORE contributors and was using that list to raise funds for another civil rights organization. So one day, as Cunningham was on his way to his car, Peay and three others beat him up.

RAY CUNNINGHAM: They knocked me to the ground, and I got up, and they proceeded to start beating me with mallets, kicking, and I basically tried to defend myself.

WALLACE: What damage did they do to you?

CUNNINGHAM: I had a crushed left sinus cavity. I had severe head injuries all over my head from the mallets. As a metter of fact, I was hit — hit so hard with the mallets that the handle physically broke off. That's a fact.

WALLACE: Peay was later convicted of assaulting Cunningham, but he is appealing that conviction. He insists he was operating on instructions from Innis, who was infuriated that Cunningham had stolen the list of CORE contributors.

PEAY: He said, "Deal with it!"

WALLACE: What did you do?

PEAY: We dealt with it.

WALLACE: Well, apparently you beat him around the head with mallets, rubber mallets. I mean, you smile, but that's — that's the way it happened.

PEAY: That's the way it happened.

INNIS: Marvin Peay is an A-1 certified bandit.

WALLACE: He was your director of national security. Why would Peay go to assault Cunningham unless he was operating under your orders?

INNIS: Let me say, Mike, that if I had a problem with Cunningham, I will deal with that problem myself. Now, I can handle myself pretty good. And you must have seen Cunningham, I can handle Cunningham with one hand tied behind my back. I don't need Marvin Peay and a bunch of goons to go deal with Ray Cunningham.

WALLACE: These men were fund-raisers for CORE in Los Angeles along with Ray Cunningham back in 1976, a year in which CORE raised about four million dollars. Each one of them got 20 percent of what he raised. Some of them made as much as $30,000 that year. But they, too, were skeptical about where all the money they raised was going.

MAN: When I first came to the operation, you know, within a month's time, every weekend there was a — there was a party at the Hyatt House. They'd rent the whole suite, the whole floor. They'd rent the whole floor.

WALLACE: And that money would be money which you fellows had raised on the telephone?

MAN: Sure.

MAN: Right, money that was raised at the Congress of Racial Equality, was indicated that there were — that they were for programs. You know, I physically saw no programs, you know. After not seeing programs and — you know, I have to go along with Virgil, you know, there were certain parties at the Continental Hyatt House; there were certain personal endeavors that Roy Innis and other upper staff within CORE used the money for.

WALLACE: Personal endeavors?

MAN: Right, personal endeavors. This —

WALLACE: What does that mean?

MAN: In other words, good times, dinner engagements, trips; you know, parties; you know, things of that nature.

WALLACE: Today, despite a New York State injunction forbidding CORE from raising money from the public by any means, these telephone fund-raisers are still working in CORE's New York office, still calling business firms around the country.

MAN (on telephone):   (Indistinct) a personal contribution of $50 per year. And we won't get back to you again till 1980, because we know you're in a jam, but we're in a jam, too. We have a school to open up by September 1st. We don't know where to turn to . . .

WALLACE: The donations these firms send are supposed to pay for CORE programs — schools, housing programs, employment and prison programs. But two years ago, former CORE officers and employees told the New York State attorney general that most of the money allocated to such programs never went there, because those programs were simply shells.

The state looked into one vaunted CORE program — its New York day-care operation — and what they found was this: a small storefront that is now the A-OK Hardware Store. But back in 1976, it was the home of a CORE day-care center that the state says took care of just five children, though Innis insists it was a much larger number. But Assistant Attorney General Kurtz says the state's figure is right, and that the annual cost for the five was $58,000.

KURTZ: That means they were spending approximately eleven to twelve thousand dollars per child, which is absolutely implausible sum. In addition, there were substantial charges for areas that seemed completely unrelated to day-care: $10,000 during that period for travel expense; $3,500 for telephone expenses. That led us to believe that the program was in fact a — a nonexistent one, but one which merely had been created to support the fund-raising activities, to give some legitimacy to it.

WALLACE: And the State of New York concluded there was, quote: "A systematic looting of funds solicited for charitable purposes. During the fiscal year ending May 31st, 1976," they said, "a grand total of almost half a million dollars was found to have been drained for the personal living expenses of the corporate officers and directors."
Is it possible that, instead of looting, it's just bad management?

KURTZ: Bad management is certainly, I think, an element of what CORE's problem has been. But I think that it's more than bad management; it's using these funds for personal benefit.

WALLACE: Who's the boss of CORE?

KURTZ: Roy Innis.

WALLACE: Can't he give himself an expense account if he wants to?

KURTZ: Every nickel taken in by a charitable organization is someone else's money. It's not for the personal benefit. Obviously, there are legitimate expenses that an executive of a charitable or business corporation have. But what we are questioning are the — are expenses that appear to have no legitimate basis — money spent on family members of officers and directors, money spent for purely personal travel, money spent for household furnishings, clothes.

INNIS: Where — where is the evidence? Where is the ounce of evidence?

WALLACE: An ounce of evidence?

INNIS: Right. More than allegation.

WALLACE: All right.
At that, we went through documents that had been uncovered last December, when Louis Lefkowitz was the New York State attorney general, documents uncovered by his assistants, William Lee and Herbert Wallenstein.
The state says that hundreds of thousands of dollars were diverted by you for furniture, payments to your African wife.

INNIS: Uh-hmm. And where's the evidence? That's an allegation.

WALLACE: I have in front of me here —

INNIS: Is that evidence?

WALLACE: I — Wait just a second! Checks from CORE dated January of '76 just to March of '76.

INNIS: And what does it show?

WALLACE: Check numbers. Twenty-five hundred dollars for Dor— Roy Innis and Doris Innis's apartment. Two thousand dollars for the same. Two hundred and nineteen dollars more for that. For carpet, eight thirty-five. For DeVern Motors Limited, ninteen hundred. For Royale Draperies, about a thousand dollars more. For Busch Jewelry, five hundred dollars more. For cash, six, thirteen, sixteen, nineteen-fifty, about three thousand dollars cash per, quote, "special R.I. project" – which is special Roy Innis project.

INNIS: You know what's cute, Mike? If you look at the date of those checks —

WALLACE: Yup?

INNIS: — you will find that I was in Angola during most of that period. You will find that I was traveling Africa. So I'm saying that the kind of research, the kind of investigation —

WALLACE: Was somebody doing this behind your back?

INNIS: I am saying it's a figment of the imagination of the corrupt-minded Wallenstein and Lee. That's what I'm saying. I'm saying that none of this can be substantiated in court. I'm saying that this is the most criminal ne— criminally negligent investigation that I have ever seen.

WALLACE: At that, Mary Dennison interrupted to insist that Innis should not be discussing the specifics of the case on television.

MARY DENNISON: One of the agreements we have with Kurtz is that we're going to—

INNIS: Sit down with him.

DENNISON: — is that he was never given a complete set of explanations and answers.

WALLACE: Mary Dennison, all I can tell you is that he, the head of the Charity Frauds Bureau of the Attorney General's Office, State of New York, sat down and made all of these allegations on film with me. What's he trying to do – talk, and keep you quiet?

INNIS: All right. Let me tell you something — Let me tell you something, Mary. We're making a serious mistake. The battlefield is here, right here, not in court. Hold it! Hold, everybody! Everybody, hold it! Damn it, I'm telling you, there's nothing legal in this fight. It's not a court fight; it's a PR fight. That's the only goddamn thing. That's what Lee did to us. That's what Wallenstein did to us. That's what Kurtz is going to do to us now.

And I'm saying that we're going to fight the goddamn war PR, like them, we're going to lose. Let's fight the goddamn war PR, give all the goddamn answers. Let's not get confused. You hold your goddamn ammunition, and Kurtz will kill you on the goddamn tubes. All right? And you'll go —

DENNISON: You know —

INNIS: And you will go into court with a goddamn statement.

WALLACE: One of CORE's severest critics today is James Farmer, the man who started CORE way back in 1941. Today he leads a group of disenchanted CORE members who believe that, unless Innis goes, CORE will die.

JAMES FARMER: Well, if the accusations which have been made by people who were his confidants and who worked closely with him are true, if the accusations of the hit jobs and the contracts out on people are true, if the funds which have been raised for the benefit of black Americans have been used for extraneous purposes, then he should be in jail.

WALLACE: Roy Innis vows that these allegations against him are part of a conspiracy by James Farmer, by the likes of Marvin Peay, by the press, even by the attorney general's office — allegations, he says, stirred up by just a mere handful of dissidents. And to show us how much support CORE still has, he took us into the streets of Harlem, just around the corner, a walk we later found out had been carefully set up.

People on the street, how many work with or have great respect for the Congress of Racial Equality?

(Muffled cheer)

Do you know anything about CORE?

CHILD: Yeah.

WALLACE: What do you know?

CHILD: Well, I know that it's the center of the black world.

WALLACE: Who told you that?

CHILD: My father and my mother.

WALLACE: Is that your dad standing right there?

CHILD: Yes. (Laughter)

WALLACE: Why would Louis Lefkowitz, Nelson Rockefeller's good friend, the attorney general, why would Bob Abrams, the new Democratic attorney general, why would they want to keep on going after Roy Innis and destroy CORE?

INNIS: Well, I certainly don't want to add to the increasing tension between black folks and Jews in America. But let me say that a lot of folks in — in the black community are speculating about an attack that comes against CORE by a Lefkowitz and Wallenstein, and if it is —

WALLACE: And an Abrams?

INNIS: I don't — I do not know if Bob Abrams has inherited, at least in — in spirit, this fight. If he has, then we are going to deal with him exactly the way we dealt with Lefkowitz and Wallenstein. We'll call the shots straight and let the chips fall.

WALLACE: And you've hired a white Jewish lawyer to defend you?

INNIS: Fight fire with fire.

WALLACE: Last April, as we said, a New York State judge ordered CORE to stop raising funds, pending a trial or some settlement in the dispute between the State of New York and Roy Innis. Said the judge in his order: "An injunction is necessary to prevent any further misuse of monies contributed by the public for charitable purposes."

But as we found out during our visit to CORE, its fund-raisers are still working the telephones, still raising money coast to coast. And in developing that information, we learned about more irregularities in the fund-raising practices of other civil rights groups. That follow-up to the report you just saw will be broadcast soon.

See reply from Roy Innis, Letters, December 2, 1979, page 171; and Update, April 6, 1980, page 452.

Justifiable Homicide?

MARTIN PHILLIPS, PRODUCER

MORLEY SAFER: Some months ago, we got a letter from a woman who claimed that a cousin of hers was sentenced to 15 to 25 years in prison unjustifiably. It was a case of murder in which the cousin, a woman, was found guilty of arranging to murder her husband. But if the whole story of this couple were known, she said, it would have been considered a case of justifiable homicide. The whole affair is one of those small, awful little American tragedies, but it raises a fascinating debate, and it raises something fundamental to this society: that everyone has a right to live, even the worst among us.

The man you will not meet in this story is Bernard DeVillez, who was shot down five years ago by a young man he'd never seen before in an alleyway of a suburban motel. Bernard DeVillez was 43 years old when he was buried in St. Joseph's Cemetery in Evansville, Indiana.

When he married in 1951, he was 20 years old. His wife was 15. As she tells it, she was pregnant and had to get married.

Joyce today is 43 years old, serving a sentence of 15 to 25 years at the Indiana State Prison for Women. She pleaded guilty to second-degree murder of her husband after seeing that police had clear evidence of her involvement. So there was virtually no trial. She's a slim, not unattractive woman, a star prisoner who's earned a college degree and is allowed to wear her own clothes and works in a prison library. Authorities say she is an exceptionally intelligent woman.

If you were an artist and you were going to paint a picture of the DeVillez at home, what would you paint?

JOYCE DeVILLEZ: I'd probably try to capture the fear.

SAFER: Fear of your husband?

JOYCE: Yes.

SAFER: Children's fear of your husband?

JOYCE: Yes. He usually threatened to kill us. So we were threatened with death all the time.

SAFER: How close did he come to it during those 23 years of marriage?

JOYCE: My son's skull was fractured by him at one time. I — I always felt that when he would choke us and we would pass out, I always thought that we were very near death, although there's no broken bones or — or — to see.

SAFER: You say that almost casually — that when — when he would choke you, you'd almost pass out. Was this a —

JOYCE: He did.

SAFER: — a regular form of —

JOYCE: Yes, he did that more than — more than, say, beating with his fists.

SAFER: This was the DeVillez home for most of the time they spent in California, a tract house on Monte Vista Street in Alta Loma, just outside of Los Angeles. It is a fairly inoffensive-looking street and inoffensive-looking house. But according to the DeVillez children, who we asked to come back here and talk about their lives and their parents, it was anything but inoffensive.

The oldest is Roxanne, 27 years old and recently separated from her husband. Kevin, 24 years old, recently married Marcella and lives in Houston. Kirk is 21 years old.

I read somewhere in these documents that you were raped by your father.

ROXANNE: Yes.

SAFER: How old were you?

ROXANNE: Eleven or twelve. It wasn't — it wasn't —

SAFER: You were sexually abused?

ROXANNE: Yes.

SAFER: And you never told anyone?

ROXANNE: No.

SAFER: You didn't tell your mother?

ROXANNE: Not — I was under threats of death if I did. I had been close enough to death from him enough times that you don't tell someone.

KEVIN: He'd come in and beat me. He'd get a hold of my arm and twist it, so I'd be on my belly on the bed, whip me on my back with a belt, like a hundred and ten — a hundred and ten whacks.

SAFER: Did you strike back?

KEVIN: I was too young when it first started.

SAFER: Forgive me if I suggest something here, but I do believe that you kids would do anything, say anything, perhaps even exaggerate, to help your mother, to help her get out of jail.

KEVIN: No. See, I loved my father, but I didn't like him. I didn't like him as a person. I loved him — I loved him for being my father, because, you know, he was my father, he gave me birth; but as a person I hated him, because the way he was. And it's not — You know, people after death, usually: "Oh, he wasn't such a bad man!" But he was bad.

SAFER: What would have happened if you'd just taken the kids, moved into a neighbor's house — I don't know — barricaded yourself in, called the cops, called his bluff, in a sense?

JOYCE: For one thing — okay, I — I went to my parents' house when I had just Roxanne, and I said that I didn't ever want to see him, and I — and I was afraid of him. And he came to the door and busted his way in and took me home with him, took me back to our apartment, beating me.

SAFER: The family moved to Evansville, Indiana in 1972. For the first time in her life, Joyce had to go to work. Bernard had been laid off from his job and spent most of his time at home.

JOYCE: He resented anyone even looking at me. He'd walk between — when there was a man, say, in an aisle of a store, he would walk between me and the man, even if there were four feet, five feet there between us.

SAFER: Did he suspect you of playing around?

JOYCE: Always.

SAFER: Did you?

JOYCE: Rarely. (Laughing) Don't put that on! Twice. But he was unaware — he didn't know about that. And I knew that I had my life in my own hands when I was doing it. (Laughing)

SAFER: She says the beatings were random. In a fit of some private anger, he would strike out. One day, just after picking her up from work, he drove into a back alley.

JOYCE: He took me back there and he beat me. I mean, he was just furious when he picked me up from work. He beat me back there. That entailed, say, choking me, knocking my head against the steering wheel, hitting me a few times. We get to the apartment and it continues, and all night, the next night, three nights in a row. And the next time I went to work — I think I missed two days' work after that, because of bruises. But when I got to work the next day, I made the call.

SAFER: That call was to a woman in another city, someone she'd never met, someone who had boasted to a relative of Joyce's that she could arrange just about anything. So Joyce called her.

JOYCE: I had said that I heard that she knew people, and she said she did. And I said that I was looking for an illegal service, and she said, "What?" And I said it wasn't that easy to go into. And she said, "Feel free." And eventually, I said, "A — a contract." And she said, "Fine."

SAFER: Just like that?

At about one o'clock on June 5th, 1974, a young man called at the DeVillez garden apartment, number 3907. At home at the time were Joyce DeVillez, her husband, Bernard, and their son Kevin. The young man, a boy of about 17 named Terry Walker, said he wanted to buy Bernard DeVillez' pick-up truck. He said he'd left his money back at his motel, and if Bernard would accompany him there, he'd pay him.

So they came here to the Jackson House Motor Inn at the corner of First and Walnut Street. And while young Kevin waited in the truck, Walker got Bernard DeVillez to come to the motel with him on the pretext of paying him the money for the truck. The next thing that happened: three shots were heard, and DeVillez' body was found lying behind that chain-link fence.

Terry Walker, the killer, was caught in Detroit. He led the police, not to Joyce, but to this woman, Charlotte Hendrix. Charlotte soon confessed. She said Joyce had contacted her by phone several times. Charlotte told police that Joyce had wanted her husband killed and would pay $1,500 to have the job done. The police got Charlotte to call Joyce. The bereaved widow said she would call back as soon as she could.

This is the phone — the phone outside the Burger Farm Restaurant — that Joyce used to call Charlotte Hendrix. The contract had been kept and now payment had to be arranged. What Joyce didn't know the day she called Charlotte was that Charlotte had already cracked and her conversation was being recorded by the police.

(Tape-recorded conversation)

VOICE OF CHARLOTTE HENDRIX: I hadn't — I hadn't tried to call you.

VOICE OF JOYCE DeVILLEZ: Uh-huh.

CHARLOTTE: You know, because, I — I didn't —

SAFER: That's Charlotte?

POLICEMAN: This is Charlotte Hendrix.

CHARLOTTE: — I didn't know — in the first place, I didn't think you'd go back to work.

JOYCE (laughing):   Oh!

CHARLOTTE: See, and I didn't —

SAFER: And this is Joyce laughing.

CHARLOTTE: You know, I couldn't —

JOYCE: It looked bad, but I couldn't help it.

CHARLOTTE: You know, I figured — (Laughter) I just didn't figure you would.

JOYCE: I tell you, staying at home was a real sad — you know, and everybody coming around, and —

CHARLOTTE: It's hard to be sad when you're glad, huh?

JOYCE: It — Oh, it — it was hard. It was hard. After this great performance, I just, you know — (laughing) — awful!

(Both laughing)

Oh, God! I mean, you know, instead of life, I should have an Academy Award. (Laughter)

SAFER: She clearly suspects when she says instead of life — meaning a life sentence, obviously — she should get an Academy Award for her performance.

POLICEMAN: Right.

SAFER: Her performance in front of you people, among others.

POLICEMAN: Right, right.

POLICEMAN: Yeah.

In front of us, in front of the world, you might say.

SAFER: That's Sergeant Bob Overby, the investigator in the case. Doug Knight was the state's attorney who prosecuted Joyce.

You hear it again and again. People say it, and I suspect that Joyce herself believes it, that had she picked up a gun herself, in the kitchen or whatever, and shot her husband dead, she probably could have claimed self-defense and gotten away with murder. What do you think?

DOUG KNIGHT: Probably so. That's a very difficult type crime to detect and prosecute because, as you say, she and her husband would have been the only witnesses. He'd be dead, couldn't testify, so we'd have to rely only on physical evidence and possibly some confession by Joyce, and it would have been unlikely that she would have confessed to that kind of crime.

SAFER: Uh-hmm.

KNIGHT: So she may have gotten away with it scot-free, as you say.

SAFER: As murder goes, does the judicial system look more harshly on murder by contract than normal — if I can call it that — murder?

KNIGHT: Oh, yes. Certainly, there is a distinction between somebody who kills out of sudden anger and a person who does it coldly and in a calculated manner, which obviously Joyce did. It took a great deal of — you know, calculation, and cold-blooded murder is what it is.

SAFER: Do any of you have any anger at all towards your mother for having done this?

ROXANNE: My only anger is that she did it so foolishly.

KEVIN: No. Don't — your anger is, don't you think, like when you bring up dad and talk about him, you get angry, mad, you want to bust a window or kick the door down or something? When you think of dad and what he did to us, don't you get angry inside?

ROXANNE: No.

KEVIN: I sure do. Times I drink beer or something like that, and I think of my father and what he did to mom and me, I've broken d— doors down in bars and things like that.

SAFER: Joyce, people are going to look at this and say there has to have been another way. We live in a free and mainly compassionate society.

JOYCE: I didn't see any freedom and I didn't see any compassion.

SAFER: No person, no neighbor, no priest, no policeman, nobody to turn to?

JOYCE: Nobody that I knew of.

SAFER: Given the way you kids were raised, particularly the two boys, do you think that there's any possibility that you will become wife-beaters yourself?
(Kevin laughs)

Or have you become one? Kevin?

KEVIN: Oh, I don't know. I'm pretty — I get pretty violent.

SAFER: You do?

KEVIN: Yeah. But it has to be something — she has to do something to make me that way. But otherwise, I'm nice.

SAFER: But you — do you hit her?

KEVIN: If she hits me, I'll hit her back. (Laughs)

SAFER: Does he hit you?

MARCELLA: All the time.

KEVIN: Do you hit me?

MARCELLA: When we're just playing.

SAFER: Kevin, do you think you are normal?

KEVIN: That's a pretty good question. I try to be not —

SAFER: I mean, you admit to hitting your wife, which I — I don't think can be considered —

KEVIN: Well, I don't hit her. I smack her. You know, if — if she gives me what I think is reason to, I've smacked her, yes. But I don't like it. I try not to do it. I think of him and just hope to God I'm not like him.

SAFER: What about children? Do you think you would abuse your children that way?

KEVIN: None of us have kids or want any.

SAFER: You don't?

DeVILLEZ FAMILY (in unison):   No.

SAFER: Why not?

KEVIN: I guess it has something to do with our lives.

SAFER: Roxanne?

ROXANNE: The only time that I felt like I really wanted a child, I would like a daughter to let her know that it can be better than what I had. Mom wrote a story, and in the story I read parts about myself, and as I read it, I remembered things that had happened to me. And I wanted to hold that baby so bad. I wanted to hold her and let her know it's all right. And that was the strongest desire or need that I had for a baby ever in my life. I really wanted one then.

SAFER: Are you sorry now that you did it?

JOYCE: I — I feel that the kids are safe and I feel that I'm safe. And if I had to make a choice — going back to that or staying here in prison — I would have to choose staying here.

SAFER: Dr. Paul Shriver and Ron Branca are psychologists at Indiana State Prison. They've seen Joyce and counseled other women who have killed their husbands, and they feel that in most cases, the women tend to exaggerate their husbands' brutality.

DR. PAUL SHRIVER: When you begin to think of a person as "my problem" or "this monster" or "this abomination in my life" — if that's the perception — you're taking the first step on a line of logic that leads you to see something that needs to be gotten rid of.

SAFER: If this were a movie, I think this is the way it might end. We'd have Barbara Stanwyck or Joan Crawford walking out of the prison gates and the door would clang shut behind her, and there'd be a huge grin on − on − on her face that would say, "I got away with it!"

DR. SHRIVER: In two years, that will happen. Whether she'll be grinning and feeling she got away with it is something we have no way of knowing.

RON BRANCA: But the irony is that the prison is inside her. She's her own jailer.

SAFER: Forever?

BRANCA: Forever.

SAFER: Justifiable homicide or cold-blooded murder? You decide.

Who Pays? . . . You Do!

PAUL LOEWENWARTER PRODUCER

HARRY REASONER: The American nuclear power program is in trouble, and not only because of Three Mile Island and the Presidential Commission's report on hazards. It's in trouble because the cost of building the plants has gone crazy — a China Syndrome of costs.

Take Illinois Power, for example, which wants its customers to help pay for a nuclear power plant whose costs have gone up three times since the original estimates. If the customers don't pony up, the company's financial rating, their ability to sell bonds and meet their customers' energy needs, is in trouble.

We went to Clinton, Illinois, where Illinois Power, a medium-sized utility, is building a nuclear plant. And it wants its customers — its territory covers a third of Illinois — to start paying 14 percent a month more on their electric bills at least three years before they can light a bulb or toast a piece of bread with electricity from Clinton.

This is what a million dollars a day looks like, thirty million dollars a month..Out of all this expensive and complex fun and games will come electricity, to go off there to homes and factories and fast-food restaurants — electricity which, if they figure right, will eventually be cheaper than if they made it out of the coal we've got or the oil we haven't got. The question here: Is this place costing just too darned much in time and money? At a million dollars a day, time is certainly money.

In terms of time, this plant is now two and a half years behind its original schedule. In money, it was supposed to cost $430 million. Now the company says it will be one billion, three hundred million. But you can make book around here that there will be more slips in the schedule; that it will not open, as the company claims, in December of 1982; and that the cost could go up another billion dollars. Critics say part of the blame lies with the cost-plus contracts that govern most nuclear construction, and that, here at Clinton, nobody had any incentive to hold costs down. Ultimately, the consumer would pay.

60 MINUTES producer Paul Loewenwarter talked with David Berg, who was a cost engineer for the contractor in 1977 and 1978.

DAVID BERG: Why did they have two guys on the wall and seven guys standing down below watching them, including two foremen? And why did one shift tear down this — the previous shift's work and rebuild it, and the first shift do the same thing to the second shift? We weren't getting concrete answers to these problems.

FORMER CONSTRUCTION SUPERINTENDENT: I was never approached any time I was out there to work on decreasing my costs or getting some of my costs under control or doing operation more efficiently.

REASONER: This man was a construction superintendent at Clinton, has a crack reputation, works elsewhere now, but fears retribution if his identity becomes known.

FORMER CONSTRUCTION SUPERINTENDENT: Any time I came up with what I thought was a — a — a valid point to reduce costs or do an operation more efficiently, I was usually put down for it, told to forget it; that there was people above me that were paid to do the thinking, I was there to do the — the work.

LOEWENWARTER: Is this something that adds up to thousands of dollars, millions of dollars, conceivably tens of millions of dollars?

BERG: In my areas, I would say that I increased the estimate tens of millions of dollars myself.

REASONER: The company's sharpest critic is Steve Radcliffe, who had been hired by Illinois Power in 1976 as a cost engineer to try to get construction dollars under control.

STEVE RADCLIFFE: It's like Watergate. They've got themselves committed. They went into it and, all of a sudden, they've got a bear by the tail and they don't know how to let go. And they don't have the moxie to say, "We've made a big screw-up here, and we don't know what to do about it."

REASONER: In this complex story, you can imagine that Illinois Power disputes Steve Radciffe and the other ex-employees. And when you talk to the company's executive vice president, Bill Gerstner, it's as though there's no problem at all.

BILL GERSTNER: The job is going very well currently. We're on schedule and on budget.

REASONER: That's not always been the case.

GERSTNER: We've had our ups and downs in the past.

REASONER: We've heard people charge that by the time it's opened, it may be the most expensive nuclear plant for its size ever built.

GERSTNER: That is untrue. Actually, the Clinton plant rise in cost was considerably more — is considerably more than the original estimate, but it is very little different than any other major construction project, utility-wise, going in the United States today, either nuclear or fossil.

REASONER: Gerstner chooses his own favorite nuclear projects for comparison. Our own comparisons showed that, against other plants of similar design, Clinton cost overruns are well ahead of the pack. In any case, Illinois Power now admits that it did not know what it was getting into when it started building this plant. It was their first nuclear project, and the first for their contractor, Baldwin Associates.

The company has an excellent reputation for turning out power cheaply and efficiently at its coal-fired plants, and Baldwin has built some of them. The power company's electric rates are the lowest in Illinois. So it was a shocker for management to see how nuclear construction − the quantities of materials needed, the time necessary for intricate work − how that could suddenly put a successful company into financial trouble.

To an outsider, any construction site looks chaotic and disorganized; this one, with almost every operation hand-tailored and one-of-a-kind, more than most. The company claims that it has it all under control now. But even if that is true, both the company and its customers are cursed with the cost overruns of the past, with the company wanting the customers to share those costs.

Which brings us to this hearing before the Illinois Commerce Commission, with the company pleading for the right to raise its customers' bills by 14 percent to pay for Clinton. The Commerce Commission says it will decide this case on Wednesday. Illinois Power's attorney, William Hart.

WILLIAM HART: What we are concerned about is cash. The company needs cash. It needs it in order to carry out its financing and construction program.

DEBORAH SENN: The project is costing too much, we submit, because it is mismanaged and out of control.

REASONER: Arguing the case for the consumers, attorney Deborah Senn.

SENN: The Clinton project, which the company says will cost $1.286 billion, is going to cost upwards of $2 billion. At that point, we think that this plant — and we have no doubt that it's going to rise to $2 billion — will be one of the most expensive nuclear power plants in the country.

HART: The most expensive thing you can do, in my opinion, is to put the company in a position where it has to halt construction, because we know what happens then. The costs continue. There are certain sum costs. They continue. They mount. And we've seen what has happened with other utilities faced with that problem outside the State of Illinois.

REASONER: Over months of hearings, some of the anti-company forces have been the anti-nuclear groups. Though they carry their usual placards, this time their arguments were about dollars, not safety. All the opponents want to prevent Illinois Power from getting a rate increase, to force it to hold down costs at Clinton. And even the usually neutral staff of the Commerce Commission joined in asking that the rate increase be denied.

The staff members would not talk to us, for fear of prejudicing their case in the public media, but in their testimony they noted that the company now estimates total costs will run three times over original estimates. And they said, with further work slippages, total cost could be six times the original estimate: $2½ billion. They said the estimates are subject to the company's internal politics and lack credibility. And they said there is little evidence that the top management and the board of directors of Illinois Power have been vigilant in dealing with cost overruns and schedule slippages. They simply acquiesced.

GERSTNER: Well, that's certainly a very, very wrong impression, and I would not want to leave that to lie that way. We have regular management meetings to review the budget, for instance. We have regular meetings of management to review the Clinton progress.

RADCLIFFE: Before I came on board, they had never had a written report on schedule status or cost status on any of their projects — coal plants or anything else. And after my four reports, they have not had any written reports to top management since then. They've all been oral reports.

REASONER: What Radcliffe did was to compare Clinton to other nuclear construction projects and to show his management that Clinton's schedule was running slower and its costs running higher.

Okay, so you got this information and you put it together, you give it to management and they say, "Hey, thanks a lot. We'll get right on this." Is that what happened?

RADCLIFFE: No, as a matter of fact, the last week, I think, of July '77 and August 1st, the day before my birthday, I got a termination notice. And —

REASONER: They fired you.

RADCLIFFE: They fired me.

GERSTNER: The job he was hired for was one of implementing and develop—helping develop a scheduling system for the Clinton plant. For whatever reason, it wasn't done. Therfore, we let Mr. Radcliffe go.

REASONER: Your position would be that you already knew what he was reporting to you and that he was not reporting to you on what you had told him to do?

GERSTNER: That's correct.

REASONER: Whatever the facts of the firing, Steve Radcliffe and the other former employees agree on the charges of mismanagement at Clinton.

GERSTNER: Most of them were brought by disgruntled employees, who either left of their own accord because they were dissatisfied with their pay rate or with their position, or perhaps were discharged.

LOEWENWARTER: Why did you leave?

FORMER CONSTRUCTION SUPERINTENDENT: Partially because I was dissatisfied, partially because I was asked to.

LOEWENWARTER: Why were you asked to?

FORMER CONSTRUCTION SUPERINTENDENT: I was told at the time and — that — due to the questions I was asking and getting involved in other things outside of my area that I was making some people nervous.

LOEWENWARTER: What do you mean, outside your area?

FORMER CONSTRUCTION SUPERINTENDENT: Well, they like to have you contain yourself to your portion of the work, do strictly what is assigned to you, what you are told to do. If you run out of something to do, just waste the rest of your day; just don't bring it up to anybody, don't take it to anybody above you that you're not working efficiently or anything.

REASONER: If more time means more money, the question now is whether Illinois Power can hold to its schedule to produce electricity in December of 1982.

GERSTNER: That's our best estimate.

REASONER: Uh-hmm.

RADCLIFFE: And I think they will not make their schedule by at least a year and a half and possibly two years. My feeling is closer to two years.

REASONER: The Nuclear Regulatory Commission also wants to know if a nuclear plant is on schedule. So, when Illinois Power builds a plant like this one, it has to keep the NRC posted each step of the way.

This now is the latest report provided by Illinois Power to the Nuclear Regulatory Commission. But with the help of some experts, we found some questionable claims here – the company claiming, for instance, that it can accomplish some jobs in record time.

For example, there are some critical safety leak-rate tests that will have to be done later on. On the chart, Illinois Power claims that will take only two weeks. No other company has done it in less than a month. Some have taken seven months. Even more, look at the two weeks the company says it will take to complete the full system tests, before the Nuclear Regulatory Commission will permit the loading of nuclear fuel. Again, Illinois Power says it will take just two weeks. But the median time for all nuclear plants for these tests is 14 months. Some have done it in as little as two months; some have taken 26 months. So, in just these several steps, Illinois Power says it will accomplish what no other nuclear builder has ever accomplished that fast before.

RADCLIFFE: I think if they are able to do it that they should be written up in Ripley's Believe It Or Not.

REASONER: Illinois Power was proud that it met one critical milestone in its schedule, albeit a revised, updated, 2½-year-behind-schedule schedule. It installed its nuclear reactor vessel right on the new timetable, and called out the media to witness it one balmy day in October. But the work to come is far more complicated, the kind that has caused mistakes and delays at most other plants, forcing them to fall behind schedule. Illinois Power insists that won't happen here. But if the charts are right, it will happen here, and costs will rise again.

The thing is, someone has to pay for all that. That someone, of course, will be, one way or the other, sooner or later, the customers of Illinois Power. But what Illinois Power and its critics have learned about nuclear power, if they have, is important to us all, because all energy is going to cost a lot more — so much more that anything extra from lessons not learned is simply something we can't afford. From the standpoint of a utility company, or its customers, or a nation, there's no percentage in solving an energy crisis by going broke.

See Letters, January 27, 1980, page 294.

A Few Minutes
with Andy Rooney

DAN RATHER: A few weeks back, Andy Rooney took a look at faucets — how they worked, or maybe more accurately, how they didn't work. Tonight, Andy gives equal time to electrical outlets.

ANDY ROONEY: Be right with you, sports fans. Sorry, they were in here vacuuming last night and somebody unplugged my lamp.

Will someone tell me why it is that every time you want to plug an appliance into an electrical outlet it's like an Easter egg hunt? Why do they hide them? Have electrical outlets got something to be ashamed of?

If there's one obvious place in a room to put a big, heavy couch or a desk, they always put the outlet right in the middle of the wall behind it. You have two choices: you can move the couch or crawl under it.

And why are they so tight with outlets? They put one fixture in the wall, like this, with two outlets in it, and you're supposed to plug in two lamps, the television set, a radio and a record player. What you do, of course, is you get one of these that makes three outlets out of one. The trouble is, if you try to put anything in the side of it here, like this, then you can't use the other outlet behind it here.

The day you have to use the vacuum cleaner is the day you louse up the whole system. First, of course, you crawl under the couch, which should have been vacuumed before you crawled under it. So you find that the vacuum cleaner, or whatever appliance you have, has this thing with three prongs on it. The outlet has two holes. Well, you don't have to be an electronic genius to realize that this isn't going to fit into this, so you have to buy an adapter.

If adapters are such a good idea, why don't they adapt them in the first place? And here's where I give up. This adapter won't fit into this, because this is a special polarized adapter, with these two little nibs on the side. What I should have bought is one of these, a regular adapter, without those on it. And I don't know what this is, but you don't dare ignore it, because you don't want to get electro- cuted.

You just can't be too careful with electricity. Let me show you the arrangement I have under my desk. There it is. I've left this one open for the vacuum cleaner tonight.

Update

DAN RATHER: Tonight, an update. Remember Brother Louv and his Ethiopian Zion Coptic Church, the church that says marijuana comes from God and smoking pot is for them a sacrament? Well, a Florida grand jury this week indicted 19 members of that sect, charging them with operating a nationwide marijuana smuggling operation. The indictment alleges the church used eight ocean-going vessels, operated through at least five corporations, and made themselves a fortune.

DECEMBER 2, 1979

Equal Justice?

LESLIE EDWARDS, PRODUCER

DAN RATHER: Tonight, the strange case of Mims Hackett, a schoolteacher who was sentenced to 30 years in prison for a kidnapping that may never have occurred. Was Hackett afforded the equal justice under law that is guaranteed to him and every American by the Constitution, a guarantee carved in stone above the Supreme Court? Do we always make good on that guarantee? No, not always, especially when a defendant happens to be a black American, and that's what this story is about. It is true that we have made tremendous strides in eliminating race from our judicial system, but the fact is, a residue of racism remains.

Mims Hackett found out the hard way. Hackett is a 38-year-old high-school biology teacher, former football hero, self-educated, father of six, active in the Parent-Teachers Association, youth groups and church. Most who know him describe him as an ideal citizen. He had never been in trouble with the law until he decided to run for the city council in Orange, New Jersey.

Orange is a town of tree-lined avenues, single-family homes and family-owned businesses. It's an old town, and many of the residents have lived here most of their lives. Changed a lot over the years, though. It is now more than 50 percent black, but the political power structure remains white. Bill Cook, long active in local politics, knows well both the Hackett case and the City of Orange.

BILL COOK: This town is a mixture of everything. Sometimes I call it Peyton Place, but it's a different type of Peyton Place. Peyton Place to me was a sex-oriented town. This is a — a political Peyton Place, maybe.

RATHER: What was Mr. Hackett's basic mistake?

COOK: His fatal mistakes probably were being born black, which he couldn't do anything about, and being born black and running for political office in Orange, which he could have done something about. That might have been his fatal mistake. Do you think the public will understand that?

RATHER: In 1975, Mims Hackett decided to try to become the second black on Orange's seven-member city council, promising that he would not be a token. But from his tiny hole-in-the-wall headquarters, he promised to represent both white and black down the street at city hall, because, he said, his major reason for running was to make Orange's schools better for his kids and everybody else's. But prison, not the city council, is where Hackett wound up.

In early 1976, as he was moving into his council campaign against four white candidates, including a policeman, local white authorities tried to get him indicted for kidnapping. A grand jury declined to do it. Later that same year, when it appeared certain that Hackett would win the election, those same authorities took the unusual step of again seeking an indictment. One week before the election, they got it, and the word was quickly leaked to newspapers. Hackett lost by 80 votes the election he had seemed certain of winning. He was tried and convicted to kidnapping Larry Moss and, as a first offender, was sentenced to 30 years.

Did you beat Larry Moss? Did you hit him?

MIMS HACKETT: No. No, I didn't.

RATHER: Did you drive the car in which other people took him away?

HACKETT: No, I didn't.

RATHER: Did you harm Mr. Moss in any way, shape or form?

HACKETT: No, I didn't.

RATHER: Did you have anything to do with his being hurt?

HACKETT: Nothing whatsoever.

RATHER: Police Officer John Farley says the alleged kidnap victim, Larry Moss, came to him the night in question to file charges against Hackett, and that police handled the case routinely and fairly.

JOHN FARLEY: When I reported for duty at 7 PM, I was advised by a desk officer that there was a Mr. Larry Moss at the desk who wished to speak with the detective. I then went and spoke with Mr. Moss. He indicated that, in his words, he's been abducted, beaten, taken to East Orange and was severely beaten by three men, one of the men being Mr. Mims Hackett. Mr. Moss alleged he was the operator of the vehicle which he was taken away in from North Bay and Washington Streets.

RATHER: Excuse me, he alleged Mr. Hackett was the operator of that vehicle?

FARLEY: Yes, sir, he did.

RATHER: Police made a major point of the fact that Hackett's car definitely had been involved. Hackett says what happened was that his home had been burglarized, that he loaned the car to a relative to scout around in the streets to see whether his stereo equipment and other things stolen could be recovered, and that the relative, in turn, loaned the car to somebody named Clarence Williams. Hackett insisted that this Mr. Williams had the car at the time of the alleged kidnapping.

Rocco Zarillo, now the city's director of public complaints, worked inside the

Orange Police Department for 20 years. He is no friend of Mims Hackett. He is an authority on the town's politics.

ROCCO ZARILLO: I would have to say that, at this stage of this matter, I would have to say that there were personal individuals involved in seeing that this thing was pushed to the extreme.

RATHER: The police, no question in your mind, opened the second grand jury investigation of the Hackett case?

ZARILLO: No question in my mind whatsoever.

RATHER: Now, did they do that as a tool to knock him out of the race?

ZARILLO: I would have to say that is a fair assumption.

RATHER: Do you know who went to the prosecutor's office to demand reopening of the Hackett case?

ZARILLO: Yes, sir.

RATHER: Who?

ZARILLO: Captain Frank Possert.

RATHER: Captain, did Mims Hackett get a fair shake from you, from Detective Farley, from the Orange Police Department?

CAPTAIN FRANK POSSERT: Yes, sir, he did.

RATHER: What's at issue here is the claim by Mr. Zarillo that you had a long-standing personal ill-feeling toward Mr. Hackett.

CAPTAIN POSSERT: That's not true, sir. Don't even know the man.

RATHER: Now, Mr. Zarillo says that there is a direct causal relationship between Mr. Hackett announcing for the city council and the decision to go to the prosecutors and seek, for the second time, an indictment. Is that true?

CAPTAIN POSSERT: No, sir. That's not true.

RATHER: Did it have anything to do with your deciding to seek the indictment the second time?

CAPTAIN POSSERT: No, sir, none whatsoever.

RATHER: Why wasn't Hackett's case downgraded? Here you got a case, a guy with no previous record, he's facing a 30-year mandatory sentence if convicted on this charge. It — it strikes me — correct me if — if I'm wrong — that, in looking at that, that a prosecutor would, under normal circumstances, just offhandedly say, "Look, that's too much. Downgrade that."

CAPTAIN POSSERT: No, sir, not in a crime of violence.

ZARILLO: I think they put too much effort behind this Mims Hackett matter. I know cases that are more serious than Mims Hackett case in this town; I never seen the case even go to court in this town, because of political influence. When you know the system the way I know it, when you want an indictment, you get it; when you don't want an indictment, you do not receive it.

RATHER: Well, now, tell me about that. That's not the way the system of justice is supposed to work.

ZARILLO: I'm sorry, that's the way this system works in this county.

RATHER: Hackett was stunned by what happened to him so quickly: indictment, then losing the election. But he still had to face trial. Hackett came to trial in this Newark courtroom, November 1976. In the first court trial of his life, Hackett faced charges of atrocious assault and battery, two counts of threatening to kill, and kidnapping.

The trial lasted a week. For Hackett, the proceedings took several bizarre turns. A few days after the trial began, Hackett's attorney dropped the case and went on vacation, leaving it to an assistant. On the witness stand, the chief witness for the prosecution, the alleged kidnap victim, Larry Moss, his brother Anthony and a friend identified Hackett as the driver of the automobile.

This is Larry Moss, the man Hackett was convicted of kidnapping. He says he was used by the police to frame Hackett. Moss describes himself as a long-time paid informer for the police.

LARRY MOSS: Mr. Hackett wasn't involved in no way. This was all, you know, the detectives' idea, that they had something against him, you know, and they didn't want him around for — for no council. They said only council that he'll run for is a jail cell.

RATHER: The police insist Moss never was a paid informant, that they never had anything against Hackett, and that they never threatened, harassed or even cajoled Moss. After the trial, Moss eventually disappeared and went underground. We found him hiding out in another state. To us, he insisted Hackett had been railroaded.

MOSS: He's innocent, and, like I said, and I'll say it again, if I had to go to jail to go see him get out, I'd rather do it and get it over with, because it'd be on my conscience seeing a man doing big time when I know he didn't do it, and I'm the one got to face reality, you know; you know, thinking about, wow, you know, I've got somebody sent away for something they didn't do on account of me trying to help the police out.

RATHER: But you swore in a court of law that the statement that you gave to Officer Farley was basically correct.

MOSS: The reason I did that, because I was scared of them. I had to see Farley and them every day, not the judge, not — not nobody else. They was harassing me, picking me up on the streets; you know, turning all my friends against me, saying that, if they see th— me in the car with them I get busted, everybody's going to jail.

RATHER: Police point out that before we found Moss an appeals court heard about and did not believe a similar recantation of Moss's trial testimony. And police emphasize Moss flunked at least one lie-detector test. Moss has told a number of conflicting stories.

But two witnesses who would have testified that Hackett was at home during the time of the kidnapping never have changed their stories. Trouble is they didn't testify at the trial. In the case of one of them, the judge refused to allow the testimony, ruling the prosecution had not been notified in time. That was PTA President William Blake, who would have told the jury he was at Hackett's house with Hackett at the time of the alleged crime.

And was Mr. Hackett here the whole time?

WILLIAM BLAKE: Mr. Hackett was here all that same time.

RATHER: I know that you're a friend and admirer of Mr. Hackett. What are the chances that you're wrong in your recollections?

BLAKE: I wouldn't lie for Mr. Hackett, Dan Rather, anybody, because it's not in me. That's all there is to it. But that day is a day I'll remember, because I was here.

RATHER: Another witness who never appeared before the jury, because he was never even subpoenaed, Police Sergeant Chuck Bowles, who told us he also talked to Hackett at Hackett's home about a stolen-car report shortly after 4 o'clock in the afternoon, the time when the kidnapping supposedly was happening.

Now you came to the Hackett home how? In response to a request from headquarters?

SERGEANT CHUCK BOWLES: That's correct. It came over the radio.

RATHER: You went there, and there's no doubt in your mind you saw Mr. Hackett there?

SERGEANT BOWLES: That's correct. I had a conversation with Mr. Hackett.

RATHER: Now you got that call at about what time?

SERGEANT BOWLES: Well, I reported on duty at 3:45. It was shortly after four that we received the call.

RATHER: But *the* most important witness the jury never heard is Clarence Williams. Remember that Hackett has always maintained relatives of his loaned Williams his car the night before the alleged crime. The prosecution questioned at the trial whether Clarence Williams ever actually existed. The police said they certainly couldn't find him. After nine months' investigation and search, we found him. He agreed to talk only if we would not show his face.

As you know, we've been a long time trying to make contact with you.

CLARENCE WILLIAMS: That's what I hear.

RATHER: About nine months. And we find you a long way from Newark. But no matter. The critical things are: Was Larry Moss, the man you describe as the Little Dude, whose name you said you didn't know until recently, was Larry Moss kidnapped?

WILLIAMS: No, he wasn't. There was never no kidnap.

RATHER: He got in the car on his own?

WILLIAMS: Of his own free will, that's right.

RATHER: Was Mims Hackett involved in any way?

WILLIAMS: No.

RATHER: Was he there?

WILLIAMS: No, he wasn't.

RATHER: Was he in the car?

WILLIAMS: No, he wasn't. Wasn't no kidnapping involved.

RATHER: Mims Hackett went to prison November 1978. His wife, Bernice, wrote us asking for help. We told her, frankly, we were reluctant and doubtful, especially since a jury already had spoken in the case. But in January, we began calling local and state officials asking some of the unanswered questions. By February, local and state authorities were calling us, saying it had been decided Hackett should be considered for parole. They clearly were hoping we would drop our story.

We did not. In July, with our story nearing completion, Hackett was paroled.

Governor Brendan Byrne paroled him, but refused a pardon. Hackett had served eight months in that hole of a cell in prison, an eternity for him; but considering his 30-year sentence, parole after such a comparatively short time indicated that state officials, whatever they may have thought of Hackett's actual guilt or innocence, certainly were concerned about publicity raising the equal-justice question.

Hackett now is back teaching science at Union City, New Jersey, High School. He remains, however, a convicted felon, on parole, and, as such, he cannot run for public office. Mims Hackett wants a pardon, full and complete, to clear the record and to restore his good name. If a pardon is not to be, the next best thing for him would be a new trial. A federal judge is considering his request for that.

HACKETT (to high school class):   What's your favorite sport? Football? Basketball? All right. All right.

Safe Haven
JOHN TIFFIN, PRODUCER

MORLEY SAFER: Supposing you had a couple of hundred thousand dollars or a couple of million stashed under the mattress and you needed a safer haven than that for both profit and peace of mind, or supposing you wanted to pay a heavy bribe to a politician somewhere and needed a place that had banks that do not go running to the IRS with information, or supposing you were a nervous potentate with a mob at the palace doors wanting your blood and your wealth — to whom could you turn? You think we're talking about Switzerland, don't you? Uh-uh, there's another place.

(Chimes)

It's the kind of place that, if someone told you there were elves and trolls and gnomes about and things that go bump in the night, you'd have no trouble believing them.

(Chorus singing)

Or if you were told that you'd wandered onto the stage of yet another Rudolf Friml confection, you could not argue.

If all of the above happened to you, then you'd be in one place and one place only. You'd be in Liechtenstein. And this is how you get in the country. (Band music) You just walk in.

(Band music)

You could be excused if you thought Liechtenstein didn't exist at all. It's very easy to miss. A tiny, independent principality between Switzerland and Austria with a native population of 16,000, who, up until a few years ago, mainly occupied themselves making hay, producing nice, fat cows, and taking part in such familiar Alpine diversions as long-distance yodeling — (sound of Alpine horn) — the blowing of very large, very, very large horns, and gazing at some of the most spectacular scenery in Europe; meanwhile, dressing the way people only dress for postcards. They're still in the business of making hay, but we'll get to that a little later.

A country this small (you can drive through it in under 15 minutes, if you make both traffic lights) can be forgiven if it's obsessed with its own importance, its own facts and figures; and the Swiss-German roots of these people demand precision that would drive a Frenchman or Spaniard or American crazy with frustration. For example, we were told that Liechtenstein has 5,897 head of cattle, not 5,898, roughly (a word never used here) 2.643 cows per person. There are exactly 30 policemen and never are they busy: one jail, with no prisoners. Permission to film it was denied on grounds that, if they let us in, everyone would want to see it. There's a military budget of zero and a corresponding army. All that and more, as they say on television, makes Liechtenstein the richest nation in the Western world.

And it is ruled by one of the richest men in the Western world, the Prince of Liechtenstein, who lives high up on the mountain in the family castle. It's a rambling old place that was built in the thirteenth century. It's not one of those open-to-the-public castles. The Liechtenstein family uses the whole thing. The family bought the country, lock, stock and castle, back in 1699, when the previous owners, the Counts of Hohenems, renowned for their brutality and profligacy, went bankrupt. The last count, known as Jakob the Spendthrift, sold it to the first Liechtenstein, known as Johan the Rich. The present prince, who's here some-where, was the first Liechtenstein to actually live in the castle or the country. He moved in in 1938 and declared the country neutral just in time for the Second World War. He moved in with probably the most valuable private art collection in the world.

And at last, here he is: His Serene Highness, Franz Joseph II Maria Aloicious Alfred Karl Heinrich Michael George Johans Ignatius Benedictus Gerhardus Majella, fourteenth Prince, Von and Zu Liechtenstein, Duke of Jagerndorf, Graf von Reitberg, and Knight of the Golden Fleece. And Her Highness the Princess, the Countess von Wilczek of Hungary, can match him name for name, but her friends call her Gina.

Reading the history of this country and — and the — and of your family, it's fascinating, because originally Liechtenstein was purchased by your ancestors. I mean, they —

PRINCE OF LIECHTENSTEIN: Yes.

SAFER: — they bought themselves a country.

PRINCE: Yes.

SAFER: I read somewhere that you've just recently bought a — a — a ranch in Texas that is bigger than the country of Liechtenstein.

PRINCESS OF LIECHTENSTEIN: It's not bigger.

(Laughter)

PRINCE: About, yes, in income. One in Arkansas and one in Texas.

SAFER: One in Arkansas and one in Texas. Together they're bigger than Liechten-stein, surely?

PRINCE: Yes, for — for we had three.

PRINCESS: No, but —

PRINCE: And also another in Texas, and we — (laughter) —

PRINCESS: Well, I don't think they really are bigger. Well, Hans, I don't (indistinct). I don't know how big they are. I forgot, because I never —

PRINCE: The three. The three —

PRINCESS: Well, we don't have the three anymore.

PRINCE: Yes.

PRINCESS: We had them for — for a month, a year.

PRINCE: The third we — we — we — we sold —

PRINCESS: But anyway, they were bigger, I quite agree, but —

PRINCE: — we sold, and now we have two.

PRINCESS: But your — your properties in Czechoslovakia were about 20 times as big as Liechtenstein.

PRINCE: Not — not so.

PRINCESS: Yes, really.

PRINCE: Sometimes bigger.

SAFER: Is the United States a good country to invest in, do you think?

PRINCE: I think yes. Better than in Europe.

SAFER: But Europe is still a mecca for Americans, who make up a large proportion of the 77,455 tourists who stop for a moment on their way from here to there in the capital of Vaduz, population 4,632. All the buses stop at a souvenir shop. All the tourists are greeted by the owner, the Baron Edward von Felz-Vein. (Applause)

BARON EDWARD VON FELZ-VEIN: Here we are . . . Thank you a lot for your nice welcome . . .

SAFER: His barony is not, by the way, in Liechtenstein. It's in the distant Ukraine and was seized by angry peasants 62 years ago. Each busload tries its best to clean him out of his expensive gewgaws, chachkas, anything that ticks, all the fun of the fairground, the best and the worst of nearby Switzerland and far-off Taiwan. And the Baron loves every minute of it.

BARON: Wonderful!

TOURIST: If you'll give me your card, we'll mail you the wine.

BARON: Yes? Yes, yes, yes, I signing this, so you'll remember to who you've been talking.

SAFER: Happily signing anything offered with the signature of an honest-to-God baron.

As we said, the tourists stay barely an hour, then push off for the greater glories of the next frontier. If they stayed a little longer, they'd discover the world's most industrialized state. In the past 10 years or so, all of those yodelers and Heidi's have moved down the mountain to take jobs in factories that mainly make all the things you never think much about: specially treated glass for missions to outer space; sausage skins for Germany; and for the entire civilized world, false teeth by the hundreds of millions. Liechtenstein is, in fact, the world's largest supplier of porcelain molars, cuspids and canines. Tooth heaven in the Alps.

The government of Liechtenstein — and, by the way, the entire government is housed in a couple of offices in that building over there — the government is sensitive to this kind of reporting. The world's press, with nothing better to do, ascends to poor little Liechtenstein full of bad jokes, smart-aleck remarks and easy shots. Well, the fact is they've pulled something off in this country and they have every right to be just a little bit smug about it: no enemies anywhere; a standard of living that's the envy of most of the world, with one-percent inflation, rapid industrialization. And all that without suffering the trauma, the decline in standards, that's been so much a part of so-called progress everywhere else. But they've been very careful not to buy the entire package that modern times had to offer. Their real lives are much the same as their grandparents' — only better. (Band music) All the old virtues have been maintained, and there seems to be no psychological or material loss. (Band music)

So, if you're exhausted by the high drama of life in the United States, you may be attracted to the simpler pleasures of Liechtenstein. If so, we've got even more good news for you, especially if you have a little larceny in your soul.

Liechtenstein has produced a number of lawyers, arrangers and fixers and a number of laws, all designed to make a haven for people in other countries who've managed to evade paying their taxes. For a very small fee, you can start up a company here that will never bear your name; its profits will never be reported. The local word for such a company is "anstalt," and to have one all you have to do is see one of the 65 arrangers of anstalts in Liechtenstein. They are men whose discretion is renowned. Their silence makes Swiss bankers seem gabby.

WALTER KEIKER: No comment. (Laughs)

SAFER: No comment.

WEIDEKER: We can't. We can't. We are not allowed to.

KEIKER: That's one of the questions you shouldn't ask. (Laughter)

SAFER: And there's no way I could get that out of you?

HANS-PETER GASSNER: I'm very sorry, you can't.

SAFER: Apart from ordinary, otherwise law-abiding tax evaders, the anstalts are regularly used by American corporations to pay illegal commissions or bribes and by more organized criminals with more cash flow than they know how to handle.

GASSNER: You see, Liechtenstein today is the ultimate tax haven. It is the one place where a person of substance can feel that his money is safe, politically and economically.

SAFER: Supposing I set up an anstalt with, say, $10 million —

KEIKER: Yes.

SAFER: — that $10 million was earning me in interest here and there —

KEIKER: Yeah.

SAFER: — and everywhere, $2 million a year, say —

KEIKER: Yeah.

SAFER: — how much taxes would I pay on the initial capital of 10 million and on the annual interest of 2 million?

KEIKER: You'll pay on the initial capital one-tenth of a percent per year. That's $10,000. You don't pay on the $2 million earnings if you have an anstalt, not even if you distribute it.

SAFER: One-tenth of one percent in taxes?

KEIKER: Yes.

SAFER: That's marvelous.

KEIKER: Yes. It's, as I say: $10 million, 10,000.

SAFER: If someone confesses to you, as he is about to open an anstalt, that — that this is money, this, say a million dollars, that he's managed to withhold from —

KEIKER: Yeah, that's not declared.

SAFER: Not declared as taxes?

KEIKER: Not declared, yes.

SAFER: You have no problem accepting his business?

KEIKER: No, that's not our business. As long as he is in order and keeps the dollar — pres— legal prescriptions in Liechtenstein, it's not our business to try to keep order in foreign countries. They shall keep to their problem themselves; we keep to ours. You see, it must not always be immoral if you — (laughs) —

SAFER: If you don't pay your taxes.

KEIKER: — if you — if you prefer put money aside.

SAFER: Yes, I'll try to remember that. (Laughter)
And if you can imagine for a moment that I was an agent of the IRS, what would you say to me if I said, "Tell me about Case X"?

GASSNER: He would never get an answer from us. So he would try, and there have been such cases, to collect information in illegal ways.

SAFER: What sort of illegal ways?

GASSNER: By trying to question employees, for instance, by trying to get hold of mail or bug telephones and so on — all illegal ac— activities, of course.

SAFER: Have they tried that? Have they bugged phones here?

GASSNER: Yes, indeed.

SAFER: Sometimes your clients are less discreet than you are?

KEIKER: Very often. You would sometimes be astonished what all is told and — to friends in a bar, or what they tell here and there, they — they themselves, and sometimes there are other people there just listening.

SAFER: Tourists, for example, can be notorious talkers, and the Baron is a patient listener.

TOURIST: And my friend —

BARON: Yes?

TOURIST: — my — my friend, Bill Harbert, Harbert Construction Company, has a lawyer here —

BARON: Yes?

TOURIST: — here in Liechtenstein.

BARON: Yes? And he have a — he have a company, too, I'm sure.

TOURIST: Yes, uh-huh. They — they just — just — just — they have just signed a $500 million contract to build the airport in Is—

BARON: Brrrrrrrrrr. It's not true!

SAFER: Just the kind of thing a man wants to hear spread over national television.

TOURIST: No, no, he is a — he's a friend of mine, my very closest friend.

BARON: Oh, I see.

SAFER: I wonder if Mr. Harbert is still a friend.

Would you take, if I were in the airplane business and I said, listen, I want to set up a — an anstalt to make certain payments that could be called commissions or could be called bribes, say in the Middle East, would you accept that sort of business?

GASSNER: Oh, yes, of course. Paying bribes is something entirely normal, in my opinion, and it has been a standard procedure in the world for the last 2,000 years. I see nothing wrong with that.

SAFER: Nothing wrong?

GASSNER: Absolutely not.

SAFER: And you would be under no obligation to tell anybody, if there was, say a big investigation, a big international investigation of this attempt to bribe officials?

GASSNER: I would not be, and I am not, in fact, under any obligation to divulge any information on the dealings of my clients.

SAFER: What a Liechtenstein lawyer's job is, in essence, is to find secure ways of getting around other countries' tax laws, particularly the IRS. In fact, to keep one step ahead of the law.

GASSNER: That's what we try to do.

SAFER: Or two steps ahead?

GASSNER: That's even better.

The Brethren

MARION GOLDIN, PRODUCER

MIKE WALLACE: Back in 1968, nine months before he was named Chief Justice of the Supreme Court, then-Appeals Court Judge Warren Burger said this in a speech to some fellow judges: "A court which is final and unreviewable needs more careful scrutiny than any other. In a country like ours, no public institution or the people who operate it can be above public debate."

Well, The Brethren, published this week, puts the Burger Court under just such scrutiny. Written by Bob Woodward, who helped uncover Watergate, and his Washington Post colleague, Scott Armstrong, The Brethren is a painstaking, carefully researched and therefore explosive look inside one of this country's most respected institutions. The information cited in the book and in this interview comes from four Supreme Court justices and 175 former law clerks who talked to Woodward and Armstrong about the first seven years of the Burger Court. And what emerges, to begin with, is a shattering view of the Chief Justice.

Case in point: The Brethren tells of Justice Lewis Powell's concern about Burger's intellectual inadequacy, his inability to write coherent decisions. Bob Woodward tells of Justice Powell's reaction to Burger's majority opinion in the Detroit busing case.

BOB WOODWARD: Powell read the Chief's first draft and said to his clerks, "If an associate in a law firm, the law firm I worked in in Richmond, had written this, I would fire him."

WALLACE: Justices Lewis Powell, Potter Stewart, Byron White are said to be the leaders of the Burger Court, and we asked Scott Armstrong what those three men think of Warren Burger.

SCOTT ARMSTRONG: They have a low opinion of his intellect. They have a low opinion of his — his willingness to work toward a consensus in the Court. And they have a low opinion of his level of effort.

WOODWARD: Stewart was reflecting to his — his clerks about the Chief, and he said it's like an ocean liner. You have a show captain and a real captain. You have somebody who runs around, who takes the ladies to dinner, and you have somebody who's up there driving the ship. And he said, "We have a show captain, the Chief. All we need now is somebody to drive the ship."

WALLACE: Potter Stewart on Warren Burger: "He was a product of Richard Nixon's tasteless White House, distinguished in appearance and bearing, but without substance or integrity." You know that he said that?

WOODWARD: Yes.

WALLACE: You're sure he said —

WOODWARD: There's no question about it. Again, it is a — it is a mosaic that is so clear; it is a reflection in true language, but it is also a reflection of a fundamental attitude.

WALLACE: Warren Burger on Watergate, telling his clerks, off the record: "Watergate," he said, "was purely political. The news media were on a witch hunt, character assassins, vindictive." That's you, Bob. "Apart from the morality, I don't see what they" — the Nixon people — "did wrong." You're sure he said that to his clerks?

ARMSTRONG: Many times, sure, he said that. And there were many sources there.

WOODWARD: Again, we — what — what is so fascinating about this, as you immerse yourself in it, as you talk to dozens and — and hundreds of people, the— these justices tell the same stories to so many people and to each other, and a coherent picture emerges.

WALLACE: Woodward and Armstrong uncovered a memo from the Chief Justice on the subject of obscenity in which he writes, "A little chill will do some of the pornos no great harm, and it might be good for the country."

WOODWARD: Burger says we need to restrict obscenity. Does he give a legal reason? Does he even give a moral reason? No. He says a little chill will do some of the pornos no great harm and might be good for the country. In other words, he is — he is acting like a legislator. A — a law professor I talked to about that said, "If you have that memo, if, in fact, Warren Burger wrote that, he is wiped out as a strict constructionist."

WALLACE: We moved on to other justices they write about.
You make Thurgood Marshall sound like the most entertaining, the laziest and the least intellectually fit justice on the Supreme Court.

WOODWARD: Somebody who turns over his work to his clerks, good clerks, the best clerks on the Court. They do what he wants, but he is not intimately involved in it himself.

WALLACE: Lewis Powell, you write, was stunned by Marshall's sloppiness, inattentiveness, laziness.

WOODWARD: And Powell himself asked the question to his clerks, "Who is the justice down there?" Because, in the opinion writing and back and forth, Marshall didn't know what Powell was talking about. But at the same time, in terms of the result — who is going to win, who is going to stand up for — for — for what's important to Thur— Thurgood Marshall? — there's no — he doesn't turn that over to anyone.

WALLACE: And when Lyndon Johnson wanted to appoint Thurgood Marshall Solicitor General before he named him to the Court?

WOODWARD: And the final argument Johnson gave to Marshall was, "Look, I want the tourist people to come to Washington and go down to the Justice Department and see that sign that says 'Mister Solicitor General' and look in there and say, 'My God, it's a nigger!' "

WALLACE: This is Lyndon Johnson to Thurgood Marshall?

WOODWARD: Marshall then says, "I have no choice but to accept."

WALLACE: Yes.

We talked about age, sickness and justices of the Supreme Court.

Hugo Black had a stroke while playing tennis. It was covered up. Public never got a chance to know. Stayed on the Court. Black, the very man who suggested that Cardozo, Brandeis and Holmes had stayed on the Court too long.

ARMSTRONG: Justice Black, we have great reason, that we suggest in the book, to — to believe that there were times when the other justices were very concerned about whether or not he was senile, whether he really was voting the way he would normally vote.

WALLACE: And then, of course, the case of William Douglas, who was incapable of performing his function, hung on.

WOODWARD: When Douglas had his stroke and was in the hospital for so long, they had a problem: a disabled justice. And they sat down and informally decided to literally take away his vote and say, "We are no longer going to count Bill Douglas's vote."

WALLACE: Now, wait. Not counting a vote? There are nine men.

WOODWARD: The decision was 5-4, and Douglas was in the majority, they would not let it be announced.

WALLACE: Those cases were simply held over until Douglas's vote was no longer the decisive vote.

And the public never knew?

WOODWARD: Correct.

ARMSTRONG: Here was a situation in which Douglas desperately wanted to continue in his role. He desperately wanted to be the voice that he felt was lacking from the Court, a voice on behalf of blacks, Chicanos, a voice on behalf of the poor, the disenfranchised; that Douglas considered himself the last civil libertarian on the Court. As he put it, he would just watch to see the — which way the Chief Justice voted and voted the opposite way.

WALLACE: Did not Justice — say that again.

ARMSTRONG: He would wait and see which way the Chief Justice voted and vote the opposite way.

WOODWARD: After Douglas finally resigned, he came back in the status of a retired justice, and he had an office there, and he tried to rejoin the Court as a tenth justice.

WALLACE: You mean after John Paul Stevens had been nominated and he was on the Court, he tried to —

WOODWARD: He — after Stevens was there, he — Douglas literally said, "Put a tenth chair up there." Douglas wrote an opinion and — and had it published and — and wanted to distribute it to the press. He ordered a clerk to do it and the clerk refused, and he — Douglas called him a traitor. Finally, Douglas's colleagues, left, right, center, his best friends, Marshall, Brennan, signed a letter, all of them: Dear Bill. You're off the Court. You can't come to oral argument. You can't write opinions. You can't publish opinion. John Paul Stevens has taken your place. Forget it, effectively. And he finally acquiesced after receiving that letter.

WALLACE: They reveal that former heavyweight champion Muhammad Ali almost went to jail during the Vietnam War.
He almost was not found to be a conscientious objector. Originally, the vote was going to go against him. What happened?

ARMSTRONG: Justice Harlan, who was assigned the opinion by the Chief Justice, was supposed to write an opinion that — that justified se— sending Ali to jail and, in fact, as he examined the record, as his clerks examined the record, then as he examined it himself, he became convinced that he was a legitimate conscientious objector, and one by one he got the other votes to change.

WOODWARD: As the vote shifted, at one point Burger was alone going to be the only one saying, "Let's send Ali to jail." And he would have to write that opinion himself —

WALLACE: And he did— he didn't want to be in that position.

WOODWARD: — and he then joined, and it came out unanimous — I think the — one justice was out of that case — 8-0, freeing Ali, and Ali came out and made a great statement about "I thank the Supreme Court, and I thank Allah," not knowing how close he — he came to going to the slam.

WALLACE: I can't imagine going to a Supreme Court justice to try to influence him. And yet, Tommy "The Cork" Corcoran, who was in, I guess he was in the Roosevelt "Brain Trust" back in the thirties, went to, not one, but two justices and did it?

ARMSTRONG: Mr. Corcoran, we're told, saw fit to talk to Justice Black and then to Justice Brennan —

WALLACE: What'd they do?

ARMSTRONG: — and to su— well, to suggest to them that a case that had been — that had been decided the previous year should be reheard —

WALLACE: The El Paso natural gas case.

ARMSTRONG: and — and, implicitly, to be decided differently.

WALLACE: And I gather that the Ch— Chief Justice was not all that upset about the fact that Corcoran had made the approach to Black and Brennan.

WOODWARD: Well, he just — I think Burger thought it was stupid, and both Justice Brennan and Black threw Corcoran out of their office.

WALLACE: You mention, Bob, something about Justice Brennan's diary? You have a copy of a diary written by Justice William Brennan?

WOODWARD: We have copies of portions of it. What — what Brennan did since joining the Court in 1956 is assign his clerks to do what he calls case histories of the major cases, and each of them goes around and gathers all of the memos, all of the drafts, talks to Brennan, reviews the conference notes, the secret conferences that the justice has, goes to other chambers, talks to other justices, other clerks, and compiles a case history.

WALLACE: Wait, I don't — I'm not sure that I understand. He, Brennan, his clerks, over a period of years, have, in effect, done a running account of everything that goes on in the Supreme Court. It is on paper. Why did he do it?

WOODWARD: Well, the reason he — he gives is that he — he just makes one copy of it and locks it in his safe, and he's going to give it to his grandchildren.

WALLACE: William Brennan will be referred to as the Deep Throat of the Supreme Court. The — the — does he know that you have it?

ARMSTRONG: I think we'd — we'd rather not answer that.

WALLACE: In the Brennan diary, there are 77 pages devoted to a blow-by-blow account of the behind-the-scenes maneuvering to get Warren Burger to agree to accept a majority opinion in the Nixon tapes case written by everybody else on the Court, but, nonetheless, bearing the name of the Chief Justice as its sole author.

WOODWARD: Everyone wrote a part of it.

WALLACE: You —

WOODWARD: Blackmun wrote a part. White wrote a part of it. Stewart wrote some of it. Powell wrote some of it. Brennan wrote some of it. And they literally sat down and said, "You take A; I'll take B; I'll take C." They would send those proposals out, and then the other brethren would send out little notes and (indistinct . . . cross-talk).

WALLACE: And Potter Stewart, Bob, Potter Stewart really told his law clerks that the Chief's initial draft of the tapes decision would have got a gra— a grade of "D" in law school; it had been raised to a "B"? You nod your head yes, Scott.

ARMSTRONG: Yes.

WOODWARD: The justices, one by one, and finally, collectively, have rejected his leadership — just do not let him write opinions, do not — he may assign himself, but they will write the opinions and force-feed and cram it down his throat. And if he wants his name on it, so in the — in — in the public it will appear as if he authored, say, the tapes case, that every crucial part was written by somebody else.

WALLACE: What good does this "Emperor has no clothes" tearing down of the Supreme Court do?

WOODWARD: An example: When Burger first became Chief Justice, he inherited some memos that Earl Warren, the former Chief Justice, had — had left for his clerks that instructed the clerks on how to deal with petitions from prisoners, the tens of thousands of people who are locked up in this country who petition the Court as the last resort, often on hand-scrawled le— yellow legal pads, saying, "I want my constitutional rights reconsidered." And Earl Warren had a policy which he wrote out in a memo, which we have, to his clerks, saying, "You, the clerk, the young, bright lawyer, are to be this poor SOB's lawyer, effectively, and if he has not made all the — all of the legal arguments that he might make, you be his counsel."

WALLACE: Uh-hmm.

WOODWARD: Burger got that and said, "What is this? Absolutely not!" And changed the policy just like that in — in his first months being Chief Justice. Now, I suspect there are lots of justices who don't know that. The poor SOB's who are off in jail sending these petitions in certainly don't know that. And maybe Warren Burger was right, maybe Earl Warren was right, but the point is there's been a significant policy shift that no one is told about.

WALLACE: A postcript. I asked Bob Woodward if he wasn't, in effect, dealing in stolen goods in the case of the memos, the first drafts and the Brennan diary. "I don't regard it as theft," he said. "Everyone who gave us material had authorized access. They were no more stolen (than) the documents that get out of any government institution. And besides," said Woodward, "that whole dilemma was resolved some years ago in the case of the Pentagon papers."

A Few Minutes
with Andy Rooney

HARRY REASONER: Andy Rooney is the type who likes to type other people. You know the type – the type who come to conclusions.

ANDY ROONEY: There are only two types of people in the world, Type A and Type Z. It isn't hard to tell which type you are. How long before the plane leaves do you arrive at the airport?

Early plane catchers, Type A, pack their bags at least a day in advance, and they pack neatly. If they're booked on a flight that leaves at four in the afternoon, they get up at 5:30 that morning. If they haven't left the house by noon, they're worried about missing the plane. Late plane catchers, Type Z, pack hastily at the last minute and arrive at the airport too late to buy a newspaper.

What do you do with a new book? Your Type A reads more carefully and finishes every book, even though it isn't any good. Type Z skims through a lot of books and is more apt to write in the margins with a pencil.

Type A eats a good breakfast; Type Z grabs a cup of coffee. Type A's turn off the lights when leaving a room and lock the doors when leaving a house. They go back to make sure they've locked it, and they worry later about whether they left the iron on or not. They didn't. Type Z's leave the lights burning and, if they lock the door at all when they leave the house, they're apt to have forgotten their keys.

Type A sees the dentist twice a year, has an annual physical checkup and thinks he may have something. Type Z has been meaning to see a doctor.

Type A squeezes a tube of toothpaste from the bottom and rolls it very carefully as he uses it, puts the top back on every time. Type Z squeezes the tube from the middle, and he's lost the cap under the radiator.

Type Z's are more apt to have some Type A characteristics than Type A's are apt to have any Type Z characteristics. Type A's always marry Type Z's. Type Z's always marry Type A's.

Letters

HARRY REASONER: When we get mail, we really get mail, and it flooded in after our story about the woman who had her husband killed because he beat her and their children. Most viewers who wote were incensed that she had been sent to prison. "She did the world a favor by getting rid of such a monster and should be allowed to rejoin that world. I applaud her."

About the two male psychologists in that story, who were not sympathetic and were not ready to applaud her, a viewer wrote: "Starsky, Hutch and Kojak need not take all the blame for TV sexism."

About our story on Roy Innis of CORE, we heard from Roy Innis himself. He wrote: "Et tu, Brute. On the flimsiest of evidence and the allegations of common criminals and malcontents, you have seriously injured the many sincere, dedicated CORE members."

Mr. Innis went on to say that we failed to mention CORE programs that are currently functioning with no burden to the taxpayer. He has a point. One CORE program that didn't exist during the period covered in our story is a CORE school in New York, now serving 116 youngsters. He's right. We didn't mention that.

Finally, from the communications coordinator of CORE, there was a telegram to Martin Phillips, the producer of that story. It said: "My dear and trusted Martin: I have installed you in the Hall of Fame of hatchet swingers, but don't fret. You're in great company with George Washington, who chopped down a helpless cherry tree, Paul Bunyan, who flattened a beautiful forest, and Lizzie Borden, who savagely murdered her parents . . . P.S., our lunch date is off."

DECEMBER 9, 1979

It's No Accident
STEVE GLAUBER, PRODUCER

It's No Accident has been omitted from this book because of pending litigation at the time of publication.

Helping
AL WASSERMAN, PRODUCER

MORLEY SAFER: — when we feel there's nothing we can do. But somehow we feel better making that rather empty offer. But helping can be very positive medicine to both the person giving it and the one receiving it. It has, in fact, become a form of medical treatment. We don't know if the people you'll meet in this story were born special or if their illness has made them special — so articulate and so strong. But we were impressed, and we think you will be too.

TONY BOTTARINI: I'm here because I had bone cancer on my leg and I needed help and I needed some support from . . .

SAFER: Tony Bottarini is 11 years old. Seven days before this meeting, doctors amputated his left leg after bone cancer was diagnosed. He meets perhaps once or twice a week with other children as sick or sicker than he is. The place is the Center for Attitudinal Healing. It is not a hospital that treats the body, it is a place that tends to the spirit — that part of medicine that doctors often ignore. Some of these children will survive their illness. Some of them will die.

The serious illness, the death of a child, would seem to be the most cruel, the most unfair of all the afflictions we suffer. And so, we approach this story with some hesitation. We do not want to be voyeurs at someone's private agony. But it's not that kind of story at all. The setting could not be more perfect: Tiburon, California, overlooking San Francisco Bay. And as you'll see, it's about a way of looking at life and death and pain squarely in the eye, and even overcoming them. In the convenient language of journalism, this is an upbeat story — upbeat in the sense

172

that the people who live with their illness, at least the ones who come here, seem so wise. The members of this rather exclusive club can be as young as six or as old as these young people. Sally is 21; Jim is 18, and so is Debbie.

JIM: Sympathy is the biggest problem — or — no, the biggest mistake that anybody can make. You know, one person treating me natural was one hundred times better than, you know, all — everybody here, you know, saying, "Poor little Jimmy, he's got cancer," you know.

SAFER: The center was started by Jerry Jampolsky, a psychiatrist who feels that there is more to be done for a person, especially a young person, than radiation, chemotherapy, sympathy and empty, lonely death. There's another kind of healing.

SALLY: You have a lot of things built up in you that you hold inside so you don't worry people — your parents, your friends, your brothers, your sisters. You figure they have enough problems of their own. You know, this is your problem. You got to deal with it. And then you come to the Center, and you find out that these problems, whatever, can be shared, worked out among these group of friends.

SAFER: The friends meet perhaps once a week. No one pays anything. The Center is supported by volunteers and by people in Tiburon who believe in what Jampolsky is doing. It is all very low-key, a place where trust and understanding happen, rather than pity or institutional therapy.

BOY: I close my eyes and I think about a land that I'd like to go to, and then I go there. And then . . .

SAFER: Pain, for example, has been the companion of all of these children. They have learned to diminish it, to think it away through imagery, through detaching the healthy, thinking self from the body that hurts.

BOY: What my parents say is, "Think about something good." And I do it. And my Dad came up as getting a warm bath, because I like soaking in my bathtub. And I just — and if you don't think about the needle going inside of you, then maybe you won't — well, you won't feel it, hardly.

TONY: Okay, while everyone is in this room, don't mention needles to me, okay?

(Laughter . . . cross-talk)

BOY: Come on, Tony!

SAFER: The children seem to have some natural gift for coping with life as it is. For parents, it is often more difficult. Jampolsky meets with them too. He says the Center is an exercise in mutual healing: children and doctors and parents.

MR. BOTTARINI: I had gone through this — this stage of crying and — and getting it all out, and I said — I said to you at that time that I was through with that; now is the time for feeling good. And you said, "Well, that's fine, but you should — you should also be honest with your emotions." And I thought that was good. So I — I've come to a happy compromise since that time. I no longer try and pretend about my emotions with Tony.

DR. JERRY JAMPOLSKY: Tony, you got some company here . . .

SAFER: And the brothers and sisters of a sick child have their difficulties.

DR. JAMPOLSKY: . . . that you could share with us?

CHILD: Sometimes I feel like my Mom doesn't love me, and then I just go up to my room and I just — I just lay in bed for, like, a few minutes, and then I come — go back downstairs, and she likes me again.

DR. JAMPOLSKY: I see.

WOMAN: There's a person who wants to talk to you . . .

SAFER: The Center extends way beyond itself through the power of the telephone. The kids have phone pals all over the country. The helping process seems to work at both ends of the phone.

CHILD (on phone):   Hi, Jeff.

CHILD: Hi, Garrett.

SAFER: The shared intimacy of cancer creates a bond as strong as love.

"The center was started by Jerry Jampolsky, a psychiatrist who feels that there is more to be done for a person, especially a young person, than radiation, chemotherapy, sympathy and empty, lonely death."

CHILD (on phone):   I have a brain tumor. You have . . .

SAFER: Jampolsky says the children do not need much encouragement. Helping is almost instinctive.

DR. JAMPOLSKY: What's impressed me so much is that the children wi— that we're working with, it's almost like part of their whole context of their being is that they have looked at their illness in — in a fashion that they are here to help other people. To see what could be a — a tragedy or — or — or something that would be the worst thing possible, to turn that around and say, "Well, all things are lessons God would have me learn. There must be something positive here that I can relate to and to teach." And one of the things that these children seem to relate most in, in terms of — in their enthusiasm, is — is to see that this is an opportunity of helping another person.

SAFER: Tony Bottarini's left leg was amputated the day after his bone cancer was diagnosed. His strength and will are remarkable. Within days he was out skateboarding in front of his home in Marin County. Tony is a novice in cancer, but he is a game fighter full of determination.

A continent away in New Canaan, Connecticut, there is 14-year-old Paul Johanson, a seasoned veteran of the wars. Paul is seriously ill with brain cancer. Doctors say they cannot operate on the tumor. At first glance you might think he has neither the strength nor interest to help anyone. But Paul Johanson is made of very stern stuff indeed, and he's using it to help a boy he's never met over the first painful, frightening, confusing days of his treatment. (Telephone rings)

TONY (on telephone):   Hello?

PAUL JOHANSON (on telephone):   How're you doing, Tony?

TONY: Pretty good.

PAUL: That's good. I got some more jokes for you. Are you ready?

TONY: Yeah.

PAUL: Okay. What do you got when a bird gets caught in your lawn mower?

TONY: Uh — hmm. What do you got when a bird gets caught in your lawn mower? I don't know.

PAUL: Shredded tweet.

SAFER (laughing):   Oh, dear!

PAUL: Pretty good, huh? (Safer laughing)

SAFER: The conversation is mainly nothing special: sports, the awful puns and jokes that two boys inflict on each other. And without batting an eye, with no solemnity whatever, it turns to more substantial matters.

TONY: No, nothing new, but how do you go about chemotherapy? How — were you scared the first time?

PAUL: Well, it just — it depends. Like what kind of chemotherapy are you going to have?

TONY: I stay in for three days, and then after three days if I feel good I could go home. So, you know.

PAUL: Yeah. Well, I'd say there isn't anything to be scared about. You know, just keep your mind off it.

TONY (laughing):   I'm trying.

PAUL: Yeah, I remember when I got chemotherapy, I was really scared. I was scared I was going to turn into some sort of — I don't know, some sort of weirdo or — you know. But, you know, after it, I was glad that I did it, you know . . .

SAFER: The boys now call each other simply as friends, not just as fellow cancer victims. The matchmaker was Dr. Jampolsky, who met Paul on a visit East at a time when Paul was deep in self-pity.

PAUL: And before he came to our house for a visit, I was — I was in a terrible place and I had a big problem and didn't know what it was. And we talked, and we were able to pinpoint the problem, and the problem was I wasn't helping anyone. And so he gave me Tony's phone number, and I called up Tony and said, "Can I help you?" And he said, "Sure."

SAFER: Your problem was, he said, that — that you weren't helping anyone?

PAUL: Right. When you're really sick, and you're sick and tired of being sick, and something's good — you want something good to happen, you can just sit back and take on the pity party.

SAFER: Pity party?

PAUL: And then just fall in depression. And otherwise, you can help other people and you won't fall into that depression.

SAFER: Your conversations with Tony, has he — has he indicated to you that — that he feels better because of them, that it's helped him in any way?

PAUL: I—I hope it's helped him. He—he seems a bit, you know, he—like the first time he didn't talk much, and now he's willing to share anything.

TONY (on phone, while getting chemotherapy):   I don't know, but I can feel it going in right now, and — no, that — that doesn't hurt, but, you know. No, I don't even see it going in. It's just one big tube. I can feel it. It's cold.

SAFER: Back in California, Tony begins the long, painful ordeal of chemotherapy. And the anesthetic, of a kind, is the phone and a friend.

TONY: Yeah. Yeah, do you mind if I scream?

SAFER: The leg was − was one thing, and now you −

TONY: Yeah.

SAFER: − you're beginning this. You got − it's going to be a pretty rough −

TONY: Yeah.

SAFER: − year and a half ahead of you. Can you take it?

TONY: I don't know. (Laughs) I guess so.

SAFER: Can *you* take it?

MR. BOTTARINI: Well, he's the one without the leg and he's the one with all the needles in him. If he can — if he can handle it, I think I can.

MRS. BOTTARINI: Believe it or not, this whole catastrophe there's been a lot of good. I've seen Tony help a little boy that's very ill, iller than Tony is right now, with cancer. And I've seen him help Tony.

SAFER: You're talking about Paul?

MR. BOTTARINI: Uh-hmm.

MRS. BOTTARINI: Yes, uh-huh, Paul. And what those two have done for each other is beautiful.

SAFER: In what way does a boy like Paul, who is now growing very weak, in what way does Paul help you?

TONY: Well, he lets me understand the way — the ways of, you know, growing up and living. And he's did a lot of growing up, because he has to take all this, you know.

PAUL: It really does help to have someone say, "I know how it feels," you know.

SAFER: And really know how it feels.

PAUL: Yeah. Like, if your parents just say, "Oh, sure, I know how that feels," you know, it doesn't really help your inner self. It may help your mask that you're putting on, but it's not really going to help you.

SAFER: So you feel now that − that you're not only being helped, you're kind of giving some help in return?

PAUL: Yeah, by helping whoever needs it. And hopefully some day I won't — well, not hopefully. I shouldn't say that. But maybe some day I won't have to help somebody that's sick. But that — that will be a sad time for me.

SAFER: I find it very difficult to talk to a young man like Paul, or even to a young man like yourself, about death. Yet it is something that you handle awful easily. Has your attitude about living and dying changed a great deal since this?

TONY: Yes. I find, because of I might have died, that life is really nice. And, you know, I haven't thought about it before. What I think — think about is that I'm living. You know, I don't really care. I have a sense of humor that's not really a sense of humor, because I can't really make up jokes, and — but I just laugh at — I'm laughing at myself right now, because I look funny, and I'm laughing at this whole thing. And — and instead of worrying about it, I laugh about it, you know, and it does— and it doesn't make as much fear, and not as much pain also.

SAFER: Do you feel more in touch with life than other children your age at school?

PAUL (sighs):   I feel I am. But, I mean, you're going to die some day, and if no one's there to reach out and touch you, then it's — it's a total waste of living.

SAFER: Not long after we completed this story, Paul Johanson died. His life certainly was not wasted.

Garn Baum vs. the Mormons

RICHARD CLARK, PRODUCER

MIKE WALLACE: Last week in Virginia, a bishop of the Mormon Church excommuni-cated a woman who criticized her church's opposition to the Equal Rights Amendment, and that story has focused attention on the hierarchy, the patriarchy, who run the Mormon Church in Salt Lake City. Nowhere in the country does a church have more influence on the press, politics, business, even on the legal profession of one state, than does the Mormon Church in Utah. Which brings us to another story, another Mormon, a man named Garn Baum, who has been trying for five years to win an antitrust suit against the Mormons — the Church of Jesus Christ of the Latter Day Saints. And as Harry Reasoner found out, that is not easy in Utah.

(Choir singing hymn)

HARRY REASONER: One of our biggest problems doing this story in Mormon country has been getting people to talk to us. Church officials are reluctant to discuss Mormon financial matters, but they don't strongly dispute a recent report that put its income at well over a billion dollars a year – from contributions, of course, but also from a multinational business empire: hospitals, banks, shopping centers, publishing and broadcasting, and tens of thousands of acres of farmland and orchards. For the members of the Church of the Latter Day Saints, it's a dream finally realized.

That's what's left of Garn Baum's dream. This rusting derelict used to be one of the finest fruit processing plants in all of Utah, located next to some of the finest orchards in the state, especially cherries, which have become a lucrative crop. Pie cherries alone have gone from 15¢ a pound six years ago to fifty cents a pound today; hundreds of tons to be stemmed, pitted and packed in 30-pound cans.

GARN BAUM: Each one of these tanks holds approximately six tons of cherries.

REASONER: Garn and Peggy Baum used to process a large share of that fruit. They did it so well, they claim, that some competition, including an employee of the

Mormon Church, conspired to get what they had. What they had was a plant built with Baum's own hands, from plans that are only in his head. He's a mechanical genius, and a man possessed. His high is packing cherries a few seconds faster and a few cents cheaper than anybody else, and without pits. That's important, because pits in cherry pies tend to cause lawsuits for restaurants.

BAUM: So, we invented a machine that would actually pit cherries, and — pitless. We had a sample grading of — it was — I think it was eight thousand and some-odd cans graded, and there was a pit and a half in eight thousand cans.

REASONER: In eight thousand cans.

BAUM: So I call it a pitless pack.

REASONER: Baum's business depended almost totally on big growers in the Salt Lake Valley. He bought their fruit by the ton, processed and resold it to national distributors. But five years ago something happened, and Baum claims it all began here — Alberta Farms, 14,000 acres of prime fields and orchards owned by the Mormon Church.

Baum says that one Clyde Lunsford, who is closely associated with Alberta Farms, was a ringleader among a group of his competitors who started a whispering campaign, saying Baum was in financial trouble that year, would not be able to pay the growers for their cherries. One of the growers has said under oath — quote — "Lunsford told me the growers in Utah County are going to see to it that he don't get any cherries this year, and we'd advise you not to sell to Baum because you'll never get your money." Baum's banker insists Baum was financially sound that year, but the growers apparently listened to the rumors and took their business elsewhere, which prompted Baum's lawsuit against, among others, the Mormon Church.

You're — you're Mormon. Your family are Mormons. Why would the church do this to you?

GARN BAUM: Oh, it's been mind-boggling to me, the same question. And I think it all boiled down to there was a few, a couple or three, just greedy people that wanted what I had, so — and they were Mormons and they were paid employees of the Mormon religion.

REASONER: We asked for interviews with church officials close to the Baum case, but none came forward. Hebrew Wolsey is director of public relations for the church.

Has there been a conspiracy?

HEBREW WOLSEY: I can't talk for all of the ones that he's referring to. But as far as the church is concerned, I can give you an unequivocal answer: that the church is not involved in the conspiracy against Mr. Baum. Everything that we did in this case we feel was — was legal and ethical and appropriate. We have no animosity toward him at all. We have no reason to want him to have difficulties.

REASONER: The name that keeps cropping up when you talk to Mr. Baum is Clyde Lunsford. What's his position with the church?

WOLSEY: He's not an official representative, as far as making a decision. I'd better rephrase that. He's a consultant to the church on our church farm. But in this case, he is a defendant and we are defendants.

REASONER: And the alleged boycott was only part of Baum's problem. The rest, he says, was political. And in the State of Utah, it's hard to separate the body politic from the Mormon Church. Seventy percent of the population is Mormon. The entire congressional delegation and the governor are Mormon, as is ninety percent of the state legislature. It was here, to the state capitol, that Baum had to come for a license to operate his plant.

One of his competitors was also an official of the State Department of Agriculture, which got a law passed permitting it to raise Baum's required performance bond from twenty-five thousand to one hundred thousand dollars, more than ever before required from any processor. The department later investigated itself for possible conflict of interest, and found itself not guilty. That was the last gasp for Garn Baum's processing plant. The property, valued at about two million dollars, was sold at a sheriff's auction for half a million. The buyer: the Mormon Church.

If there is direct evidence linking high leaders of the church with the Baum case, we've not found it; but we did get a taste of what it's like for a Mormon to sue the Mormon Church in the State of Utah.

Start with the fact that no devout Mormon will question church authority. It cannot be wrong, because the leader of the church is the voice of God. To challenge that can be a sort of self-excommunication. None of the people Baum says ruined him would be interviewed. People sympathetic to Baum will tell you privately that they heard the whispering campaign against him, even the Department of Agriculture official warning growers not to sell any cherries to Baum. But when it comes to saying these things publicly, these same friends tend to be "on vacation."

BAUM: They really don't dare raise their hand and say, "I'm for you, Garn." But in the background, it would really please them if we could win our case. But to come marching right out and say, "I'm for Garn Baum," they don't dare, because once — it could affect their business. In Utah, probably two or three steps from wherever their business is, they're going to run into the Mormon influence.

BISHOP RICHARD LOSEE: I've known the Baums for many, many years.

REASONER: One person who did agree to be filmed is Richard Losee, Garn Baum's Mormon parish bishop.

BISHOP RICHARD LOSEE: It's pretty well common knowledge around here what Brother Baum feels took place. And if you're asking me what I think, it wouldn't make any difference, really, because there are stacks of depositions of people who have given testimony in court, and this is pretty well going to have to be resolved in court, evidently.

REASONER: I think it might make a great deal of difference. You know the Baums very well, and you know the hierarchy of the Mormon Church. I think your opinion would be very interesting.

BISHOP LOSEE: Well, it might be interesting, but I'm still going to maintain it myself.

REASONER: Gary Smith is an author, and a free-lance journalist for, among other publications, the *New York Times* and *National Geographic*. He did the only thorough story we could find on the Baum case.

GARY SMITH: I entered a land of "Deep Throats" very quickly. I was entering an area where there exists a climate of fear — fea— a fear — people were afraid of being retaliated against if they spoke on the record. So, a lot of my work had to be done off the record or con— or — or the use of confidential protections for the sources. I don't know if this is a justifiable fear that they had, or if it's just a — a matter of self-imposed fear or self-imposed censorship.

REASONER: And he talked about a different story. Two reporters for the Associated

Press did a three-part series on the financial holdings of the Mormon Church. They won a Sigma Delta Chi award for investigative journalism.

SMITH: The irony was that no Utah paper that subscribes to the Associated Press wire service used the story. So, the story that the — (laughing) — that — that was probably of most interest to Mormons and to Utahans never got ran in Utah.

BAUM: We have really had a hard time getting legal counsel.

REASONER: Why?

BAUM: Because of Mormon influence. We've asked some big firms about taking our case, which they admit it's very meritorious, a good case, but they say, "Well, the bottom line, Baum, is that we'll lea— we'll lose all of our —

MRS. BAUM: Clientele.

BAUM: — clientele."

REASONER: Ask about that in Salt Lake City and some lawyers will say nonsense, others concede maybe, and still others, like Brian Barnard, will say it's true.

BRIAN BARNARD: The church is a major financial institution. The mere fact that your name is tied into a lawsuit against the leadership of the LDS Church or against a corporation of the church would be an influence that would frighten many attorneys. I've talked to several other — other attorneys, out-of-state attorneys, that Garn Baum had requested me to talk to, to explain to them that I would help and — and be involved. I also personally checked around to find the names of antitrust attorneys in Salt Lake, and I gave Garn Baum those names and suggested that he talk to them and pursue the matter. And those attorneys declined to get involved.

REASONER: Would the church, perhaps unwittingly, be a force in being a pressure to keep them from representing Mr. Baum?

WOLSEY: The — the answer is that the church wouldn't try to make any decision on who Mr. Baum should have as legal counsel.

REASONER: I suppose the question comes down to the fact that historically, whenever any church has had extreme wealth and temporal power, it has usually led to abuses. Is there something wrong with the Mormon Church being as big a factor in the State of Utah as it is?

WOLSEY: In Boston, I suppose you'd feel the presence of the Catholics; in Salt Lake City, you'd feel the presence of the Mormons. The important thing is: How do the individual people conduct their businesses? How do they conduct their lives? How do they conduct their relationship with their friends and their neighbors? And from that point of view, we try very hard to see that we are good neighbors.

REASONER: How has this affected your Mormonism? Are you still a good Mormon?

BAUM: The principles that my mother taught me, I mean, I still go by those.

MRS. BAUM: He does.

BAUM: And the principles that I have ran into of the hierarchy of the church, that wasn't what I was taught when I was growing up.

REASONER: For five years now, Garn and Peggy Baum have been in legal limbo. They and their children have taken a lot of their frustrations out on this mountain, where he built a cabin right at the timber line. He's spent a lot of time up here, trying to forget what's happened down below since the church got his property. For instance, the plant has not been maintained. The church is waiting until the court suit is settled before making a move. And there was apparently no attempt to keep up the irrigation on 18 acres of orchard that had been in the Baum family for years.

Are they ever any good again?

BAUM: No. Once you've dried them up like this with water, they're totally — it's gone. You had — the only thing you could do now is bring a caterpillar in and just start all over again.

REASONER: And those special Garn Baum cherry pitters he invented? He's got them hidden.

BAUM: I mean, I would rather take it out in Utah Lake and dump it in the middle of the lake, rather than to turn it over to the industry, because it was meant for me.

REASONER: You are stubborn, you'd admit that?

BAUM: Well, I — I'd like to see — on my case, I think I deserve my day in court, and I — I — and if I can go to court and they whip me in court, then I'll — I'll say, "Yes, you beat me." Shake their hand, and they beat me.

REASONER: It is not completely clear to us whether this is a case of good guys and bad guys, jealousy and greed, or simply people well-intentioned on both sides who got stubborn. But what does seem clear is that for facilities like Garn Baum's processing plant to fall into rust and for these living fruitful trees to die is — in either business or religion — a sin.

WALLACE: Garn Baum has now found a lawyer who will argue his case, but a federal judge in Utah says there isn't enough evidence for a trial. So, Baum and his attorney are appealing to a federal court in Colorado.

See Update, February 24, 1980, page 360.

Letters

MIKE WALLACE: Tonight, a letter from Senator Edward Kennedy — not to us, but about us. This letter refers to a story we did a few weeks back on the questionable practices of a certain Dr. Edward Rubin in California, who was still practicing medicine more or less the way he did eight years ago when Senator Kennedy sent two investigators to look into allegations concerning the doctor and his clinics and hospitals. We said in our report that the senator, for reasons that we couldn't fathom, had never published a 157-page report his investigators had prepared on Dr. Rubin. Well, now the senator is crying "foul" and telling his constituents, in a letter about us and signed by him, that his office had turned over to the Justice Department pertinent materials referring to Dr. Rubin. What the senator failed to tell his constituents is that those materials were turned over long after the statute of limitations had run out.

His letter also says the staff director of his health subcommittee was made available to answer our questions, but that we held out to interview him. Well, he's right. We did. He is the elected representative in whose name the investigation was conducted, and he was the one we wanted to talk to. The senator says in his letter that it would have been "inappropriate" for him to comment on something that had become a legal case. We didn't ask him to comment on the case; only to explain why a probe his investigators began eight years ago was never completed, though it had cost upwards of $75,000. If the senator is worried about what he calls our "incomplete and misleading" picture, why didn't he get in touch with us? The plain fact is he wouldn't talk to us while we were preparing that report, and he doesn't want to talk to us now.

Senator, while you haven't made yourself accessible to us, we are always accessible to you. Call us. Write us. We'd be happy to talk to you.

DECEMBER 16, 1979

The Hooker Memos

HARRY MOSES, PRODUCER

MIKE WALLACE: Tonight, "The Hooker Memos" provide a rare inside look into an American company that some have called a "corporate outlaw." The company is the giant Hooker Chemical. Even before these memos surfaced, Hooker's image was in trouble. Back in 1977, residents of Love Canal in Niagara Falls had to evacuate their homes because soil contaminated by Hooker's hazardous waste had seeped into their basements. Last October, Hooker said it would spend $15 million to clean up damage caused by its chemical pollution of a lake in the State of Michigan. And now the State of California is investigating Hooker on charges that the company's Occidental Chemical plant at Lathrop, California, for years dumped toxic pesticide waste in violation of state law, polluting the ground water nearby. Hooker officials deny the charges, but the Hooker memos seem to say the company knew what it was doing and, nonetheless, just kept on doing it.

The man who wrote these memos, Robert Edson, is Hooker's environmental engineer at their Lathrop plant. He wouldn't speak to us, but his memos speak for themselves.

On April the 29th 1975, Robert Edson wrote: "Our laboratory records indicate that we are slowly contaminating all wells in our area, and two of our own wells are contaminated to the point of being toxic to animals or humans. THIS IS A TIME BOMB THAT WE MUST DE-FUSE."

June 25th, 1976, a year later, there was this: "To date, we have been discharging waste water . . . containing about five tons of pesticide per year to the ground. . . . I believe that we have fooled around long enough and already overpressed our luck."

A year after that, on April 5th, 1977, Edson was still writing memos. "The attached well data," he says, "shows that we have destroyed the usability of several wells in our area. If anyone should complain, we could be the party named in an action by the Water Quality Control Board. . . . Do we correct the situation before we have a problem or do we hold off until action is taken against us?"

And on September 19th, 1978, more than a year later, Edson again pointed out to his management: "We are continuously contaminating the ground water around our plant."

And this is that plant, the huge Occidental Chemical complex where Bob Edson's memos say chemical waste was being dumped and was poisoning the ground water. Back in 1968, the Water Quality Control Board for the region came to an understanding with Oxy Chem about what this plant would be permitted to discharge as waste. Oxy Chem agreed to discharge no substance that would cause harm to human, plant or animal life. But back then, the water board thought that Oxy Chem was dealing only with fertilizers and with nontoxic fertilizer waste. It turned out that was not the case. What the water board did not know, had no idea of, was that another kind of waste was being dumped in here, toxic waste from pesticides, which were also manufactured over at that plant but were nowhere mentioned in Occidental's agreement with the water board. Hooker Chemical, itself a subsidiary of the giant Occidental Petroleum, headquarters in Houston, Texas, and we wondered if Hooker's president, Don Baeder, would talk to us about the Lathrop plant and those Edson memos. He would. But he maintained that the water board in California had known about and had okayed Occidental Chemical's discharge of pesticide wastes. And he told us that Robert Edson simply didn't know that.

DON BAEDER: Mike, it's unfortunate, but Mr. Edson didn't take on the environmental assignment until 1972, so he was unaware of this visit by the state to our facilities. And —

WALLACE: May I see that a second?

BAEDER: Yes, you may. I wish you'd read the last paragraph, too.

WALLACE: "We wish to thank Occidental Chemical for the spirit of concern and cooperation in which this problem was met and to commend you for the thoroughness of your approach." Signed Charles Carnahan, the executive officer of the California Regional Water Quality Control Board, and this is dated 4 September, 1970.

BAEDER: Does this sound like a company that was not concerned with the environmental problems back in 1970, Mike?

WALLACE: I'm at a loss, then, to understand why your own Mr. Edson would say some five years later, "Recently published California State Water Quality Control laws state we cannot percolate chemicals to ground water. The laws are extremely stringent about pesticides. And to date, the Water Quality Control people don't know about our pesticide waste percolation." This is your own man.

BAEDER: Yes, and Mr. Edson —

WALLACE: Chief environmental engineer for Oxy Chem at Lathrop.

BAEDER: Mr. — and Mr. Edson is a good man. And Mr. Edson somehow felt it necessary to — to steel the management to action with these kind of statements. But they didn't need steeling.

WALLACE: June 25th, 1976, a memo from R. Edson to A. Osborne. Who's A. Osborne?

BAEDER: I believe he's another engineer at the plant.

WALLACE: "For years," he says, "we've dumped waste water containing pesticide and other ag-chem products to a pond southwest of our plant. Our closest neighbor's drinking water well is located less than 500 feet from the subject percolation pond and, fortunately for the management, no pesticide has yet been detected in his water. I personally would not drink from his well." This is Edson, this fellow that you respect so.

BAEDER: I do.

WALLACE: This fellow who should have known what — wh— Why didn't you show him this letter that you've shown me?

BAEDER: I don't — I think the important thing, Mike, is —

WALLACE: But —

BAEDER: — what actions that we took to —

WALLACE: No, wait just a second. Why didn't you, someplace along the line, say, "Hey, Bob. Don't you know that the California Water Quality Control Board back in 1970 sent us this letter? They — you're — you're — you're — you're talking through your hat, Bob Edson, because the California people knew all about this all the time."

BAEDER: The fact that certain of our people in our organization didn't know about it isn't — isn't germane. The fact is the Water Quality Control Board did know about it.

WALLACE: But Charles Carnahan, the man who signed that letter Don Baeder had shown us, Charles Carnahan, the executive officer of the water board, told us that when he wrote that letter, he had no idea that Occidental was dumping toxic pesticide waste.

CHARLES CARNAHAN: The waste that they were dumping we figured was the — was the waste from their fertilizer manufacturing.

WALLACE: How do you feel about it now that you've learned differently?

CARNAHAN: Well, I feel kind of stupid. I feel stupid because I think that we took them at — on good faith and we were fooled.

WALLACE: But Don Baeder, who still maintained that the water board did know, also insisted that no harm was done, and that, he said, is what is really important.

BAEDER: No one has been hurt at Lathrop. No one. From our discharges, no one has been hurt and no one will be. No one will be.

DR. ROBERT HARRIS: When you contaminate ground water, you do so, for all practical purposes, irreversibly.

WALLACE: Dr. Robert Harris is an expert on toxic chemicals, recently appointed to the President's Council on Environmental Quality.

DR. HARRIS: The reason is that ground water moves very slowly, and that these contaminants that are now present in the ground water will continue to be there, will continue to migrate towards population centers, towards individual wells, for decades to come. This water will not be cleansed easily.

WALLACE: This past summer, the folks here at Oxy Chem drilled 12 test wells to find out just how contaminated the ground water had become. Five of the wells showed quantities of a pesticide called DBCP, and this well, number seven well, contained it in excessive amounts. Enough, according to Dr. Harris, to increase the risk of dying from cancer by as much as 25 percent if the water from this well were to be consumed over a normal lifetime.

DR. HARRIS: These are not small concentrations of these particular chemicals.

WALLACE: Is it possible they just didn't know, that the state of the art at the time that this kind of thing went on was such that they didn't know what they were doing?

DR. HARRIS: They should have known. They should have known that DBCP had and did cause sterility in laboratory animals more than a decade ago, and they should have known that DBCP was being tested at the National Cancer Institute, and that preliminary results showed that it was a very potent carcinogen as early as 1973. This is information that was available to the general public, and I assume was — was made available to Hooker.

BAEDER: As soon as we found out it caused sterility, as soon as we found out it caused cancer, those operations were shut down.

WALLACE: When was that?

BAEDER: That was in 1977, I believe, the summer of '77.

WALLACE: Shortly after you took over as president?

BAEDER: Yes.

WALLACE: All right. And you don't want to go back into the business of making DBCP?

BAEDER: We are not going back into the business of making DBCP.

WALLACE: You don't want to go back in?

BAEDER: I don't want to.

WALLACE: Well, then, how come I have a memo here, dated December 11th, 1978, to D. A. Guthrie from J. Wilkenfeld, subject: "Re-entry to DBCP Market"? Why would you — why would your company inquire into the possibility of — quote — "re-entry into the DBCP market" if you don't want it? You're the president. This happens in 1978.

BAEDER: Mike —

WALLACE: Why — why would they be exploring it, Mr. Baeder?

BAEDER: Mike, if the government permits it and we develop safe — safe systems for handling it to eliminate any exposure, any potential harm to people, it — it could be and will be produced. It's an important — it's an important chemical to the agriculture of California. Now just because if something is mishandled it is toxic or it causes cancer does not mean that that same material cannot be handled safely. And I can assure you that the State of California would not allow anyone to produce that under risk of these kinds of — of — of problems without markedly changing the procedures under which it was produced.

WALLACE: It is my understanding, according to this memo here, that the State of California has rejected requests for permission to use the material, and the government of Mexico has shut down the two manufacturing plants for DBCP that were operating in that country. And yet, your Acting Vice President for Environmental Health and Safety, Mr. David Guthrie, says, "We've reviewed the proposal for re-entry into the DBCP business and we have no environmental or health objections." Jerry Wilkenfeld has no technical objections. Who's Wilkenfeld?

BAEDER: Mr. Wilkenfeld is a — is responsible for environmental health safety at the Occidental level.

WALLACE: For environmental health and safety?

BAEDER: At the Occidental —

WALLACE: Let me read you what he says.

BAEDER: You did read it.

WALLACE: "Assume" — Oh no, I haven't read the whole thing.

BAEDER: Oh.

WALLACE: "Assume that 50 percent of the normal rate for these people exposed may file claims of effects from the exposure. Determine the number of potential claims for sterility and cancer, based on the insurance department's or legal department's estimate of the probable average judgment or settlement which would result from such a claim. Calculate the potential liability, including 50 percent for legal fees and other consis— contingencies." One gets the impression that profits are more important to the Hooker Chemical Company than care for human health.

BAEDER: We went out of DBCP as soon as we found out it presented any harm or exposures to the people or the workers.

WALLACE: And a year ago you were back in the business of looking at the possibility of going back into the business.

BAEDER: People are looking at it, but we are not into it. And that would have been a very deliberate corporate decision to go back into it. And I — look, Mike, before I'm a president, I'm a human being.

WALLACE: Uh-hmm.

BAEDER: We would not have gone back into it. Again, you're — you're dealing in studies that people make. We make a lot of studies. Why do you hammer us on something that might have happened but hasn't happened?

WALLACE: The only reason I'm hammering it is: Is this the way that America does business?

BAEDER: America looks at many options in doing business. It looks at many options.

WALLACE: And one of the options is, can we afford —

BAEDER: No. No. Mike, there is a risk in making almost an— there's a risk in making drugs. Mike, your drug people look at this same thing in every pharmaceutical drug they put on the market. There is a risk. There —

WALLACE: Do you know how this — this memo e— ends up? It says, "Should this product" — DBCP — "still show an adequate profit, meeting corporate investment criteria, then the product should be considered further." That's the bottom line.

BAEDER: Mike, I tried to tell you that profit is not the primary consideration. Mike —

WALLACE: It's your own memo.

BAEDER: Mike, it's a memo by a — a young man in the corporation. It's not the policy of the corporation. Young people do not set policy. Mike, I tried to tell you that over the last three years in environmental health and safety, we've spent more than a hundred and thirty million dollars. That's more than our profits have been.

WALLACE: I wonder why.

BAEDER: Why? Because —

WALLACE: Yeah. Why have you had to?

BAEDER: — because environment is important. Mike, we're a — you know, we — we have a concern for our people —

WALLACE: Fine —

BAEDER: — we have a concern for our neighbors, and that's why we're spending this money.

REPRESENTATIVE ALBERT GORE (D-Tennessee): Well, I want to believe him, and I hope that what he says is true. I hope that this company and the chemical industry generally will accept the very great public responsibility that it has.

WALLACE: Congressman Albert Gore is a member of the House subcommittee that has been holding hearings on hazardous waste disposal, and he is genuinely alarmed by the extent of the problem.

REPRESENTATIVE GORE: Two or three decades from now, in many parts of the country we'll be facing widespread water shortages. This is a very precious resource which must be conserved and protected, yet we are systematically poisoning it by dumping 80 billion pounds every year into the ground. It was formerly thought that the ground was just like a big sponge that could soak up all of the poison that we could pour into it, but it's not the case.

WALLACE: How bad is Hooker Chemical, Congressman? Is it one of the worst or just in the middle of the catalogue of chemical corporate outlaws?

REPRESENTATIVE GORE: The — the problem is industrywide. They are every day making hard calculations, just like this company did, as to whether or not the risk to other Americans is worth it for them to make a good deal more money.

BAEDER: The State of California, most states, permit certain discharges to the environment, because it's their belief that they can be tolerated. When we learn otherwise, we change. The problem we have is that, with today's knowledge, there's no question we would have done something differently. The real issue is: Should we be judged by today's knowledge on past practices? And I think that's the issue. I think the American people have got to understand that.

GEORGE DEUKMEJIAN: The evidence appears to us to indicate very clearly that they have done this willfully and knowingly.

WALLACE: George Deukmejian, California's attorney general, is currently asking that Hooker Chemical pay millions of dollars in fines. But are fines an effective deterrent? Or, we wondered, would jail terms for corporate officers whose companies break the law be a more effective deterrent?

DEUKMEJIAN: I don't really feel that we need to have additional laws as much as we need to enforce the laws that we do have. And I think that if we do that, I feel that we will be able to control this type of practice. Also, when you get into the criminal law area, you're talking there about the need, I suppose, to prove a criminal intent, and that might be difficult, if not im — impossible, to do in a case of this type.

WALLACE: What do you think about the suggestion of criminal penalties for corporate outlaws?

BAEDER: Mike, I think that criminal penalties for criminal acts are completely justified.

WALLACE: Is it a criminal act to poison, sterilize, whatever, if it can be proved that it was done with knowledge?

BAEDER: Mike, if it can be proved that causing sterilization by violating the law, by — by operating in a way that you know is unsafe —

WALLACE: Hm-mmm?

BAEDER: — I would say that's a criminal act.

WALLACE: And who should serve the time or pay the fine?

BAEDER: I think the people that are involved?

WALLACE: The top man or —

BAEDER: I think the buck always stops at the top, sir.

WALLACE: Since we filmed this report, there has been this late development. California Attorney General George Deukmajian will file a lawsuit this coming week against Hooker Chemical. The suit will ask Hooker to pay fines and clean-up costs in excess of $15 million for the damage caused by their Lathrop plant.

Earn It!

STEVE GLAUBER, PRODUCER

MORLEY SAFER: How would you like it if you came home some night, found someone had broken into your house, that he'd been caught, and that a judge had sentenced him to a job instead of to jail? That's the idea behind a program in Quincy, Massachusetts, called "Earn It," in which convicted offenders are sent not to jail but to work, to earn money to reimburse their victims. It's one of many such programs that are springing up round the country. But as Dan Rather found, some people in Quincy have big doubts about it.

POLICE SERGEANT DON RILEY: In the first instance, let's try and give a kid a break if we can. In the second instance, let's give him five or ten days in the Dedham House of Correction and let him fight off the fairies for five or ten nights, and let him just see how much romance is involved in being a hard guy.

DAN RATHER: But the judge who can sentence men to the Dedham jail doesn't think jails do much good.

JUDGE ALBERT KRAMER: Their failure rate, or recidivism rate, is high. Maybe close to fifty, sixty percent will go back and commit crimes. And they don't pay a penny to their victims or do anything to make up for their offense to the community.

BAILIFF: Hear ye, hear ye . . .

RATHER: Massachusetts District Court Judge Albert Kramer started the Earn It program, and the case before him today is typical. Two teenagers are on trial for vandalizing a municipal ice-skating rink, setting fire to part of the building and causing $25,000 worth of damage.

DEFENSE ATTORNEY: Your Honor, young Mr. Barris is deeply remorseful for what he has done. Some people don't want to admit that they are sorry for some wrongdoing that they have done, but Mr. Barris has done so.

JUDGE KRAMER: May I interrupt by saying that I don't know if all people are sorry, but when they seem to come to court, on this day they tend to express that to the court.

RATHER: The decision? Not jail, but some alternatives.

JUDGE KRAMER: — is if you're willing to go to work, beginning immediately, and to make up for those damages, and that would include from 12 to 14 weeks of five days a week, more than three months of labor, without any fee, so that you can begin to work right at the rink where you caused the damage, would you agree to do that as a condition of this sentence?

BARRIS: I agree, Your Honor.

RATHER: Earn It sentences such as this one are given not only to teenagers and first offenders but to adults with prior records. The usual sentence: turn over two-thirds of what you earn to repay the people you wronged. These men, unable to earn enough to repay the $25,000 in losses they caused, spent the summer working for free at the skating rink they damaged. Jobs are provided by local agencies and businessmen after given a hard sell by Judge Kramer, whose loudest sales pitch is that Earn It helps not only the perpetrators of crime but the victims.

JUDGE KRAMER: The victim has been the forgotten person in this process. The victim is the one that's often left out of the process. The victim is the one who neither often appears in court, and doesn't even know what the sentence is, nor gets compensated. It is no secret that the public has lost confidence in a system that has failed to either rehabilitate the offender or protect the community or compensate a victim in any way. There's a simple reason for that, and that is because traditional sentencing has but a couple of options, both of which are ineffective and unacceptable. One option is to either send somebody to jail. Or the other option, which is used most of the time, which is, if you don't send him to jail, send him back out in the street with just a promise that he won't do it again.

RATHER: Whether crime does or does not pay can be debated. But once a criminal is caught and put in jail, there is no debate about who pays the bill. You do, of course. And the cost is staggering. A day in jail now costs as much as some motel rooms, and a new jail cell costs more than the average whole house in some of the suburbs of this country. Here's why I say that. Last year, the federal prison system spent about $25 per day per prisoner. In Massachusetts, the cost was far greater. And to build a new maximum-security prison now costs $51,000 a bed.

JUDGE KRAMER: There's no way that we can start building jails and trying to put all kinds of people behind bars in which to protect the community. We need alternatives to that.

RATHER: Those who like the alternatives most are crime victims, like Keo Kiriakos. His office was broken into and some of his property destroyed. The offenders were sentenced to repay him.

KEO KIRIAKOS: It's the first time I've ever been reimbursed in the two years I've been here, and there've been a half a dozen breaks I've never even reported. Yes, it does make sense.

RATHER: But lots of people think it does not make sense. Quincy Police Sergeant Don Riley.

SERGEANT RILEY: His programs have become, more or less, the butt of a joke. They refer to a — or allude to the possibility of creating a program for exposers called "Flash It," a program for cooks at the pancake house called "Flip It." I think there's no fear of the law. There's certainly no fear of the police. The only thing that bothers them is the immediate inconvenience of possibly getting a ride in the wagon and spending a couple of hours in the lock-up. They certainly have no fear of being in court.

RATHER: Criticism comes not just from law-and-order police but from liberal academics as well. Harvard law professor Alan Dershowitz.

PROFESSOR ALAN DERSHOWITZ: Restitution programs are very seductive and very alluring. They go back to the primitive instinct to make people whole, but there are lots of practical problems. First of all, restitution programs can be used as a kind of extortion: We will use the criminal law against you really as a collection agency. Second of all, it discriminates against the poor. There are a great many people who simply cannot make restitution. Third of all, it simply applies to a very small number of people. Very few people are caught, and only people who are caught, of course, can make restitution; indeed, only people who are convicted.

JUDGE KRAMER: If the criminal is not caught, I can't deal with the issue. Now let's talk about what I can deal with, what comes into my court. The victims that come to my court, I can deal with all of them. And if I have 1,400 defendants paying victims, that means I'm dealing with 1,400 victims in this court. That's not insignificant, and that's one court. If this was mu— if this were multiplied across the country — and that's just a hundred thousand dollars in this court — think of all the money that would go to victims.

PROFESSOR DERSHOWITZ: I think it presents a false hope to victims of crime that they will actually get money for their suffering. And it won't happen with restitution programs.

RATHER: One objective of Earn It is to humanize the system.

JOYCE HOOLEY: First of all, let me introduce you. This is Mr. Michael Acoin.

VOICE: How do you do.

HOOLEY: That's Christopher McInerney.

RATHER: All victims are invited to meet their offenders. In this case, the offender had stolen a car and then smashed it into three other cars, one of which was owned by Michael Acoin.

HOOLEY: What is the extent of the damages to your car?

MICHAEL ACOIN: Oh, well, it was totaled.

HOLLEY: Was totaled?

ACOIN: Yeah.

HOOLEY: Okay.

ACOIN: Yeah, the — the whole — you know, he hit the rear end of the car and pushed it right back to the windshield. And then the — hitting it in the back, it caused it to hit another car in front, so the front was smashed too.

HOOLEY: Okay.

CHRISTOPHER McINERNEY: Yours was the first car?

ACOIN: Yeah.

McINERNEY: You were in the first car?

ACOIN: Yeah.

HOOLEY: Do you remember that, Christopher?

McINERNEY: No.

HOOLEY: You don't?

McINERNEY: I also — all's I can remember about the whole thing basically is just running.

HOOLEY: Just running?

McINERNEY: Afterwards, yeah. I thought I had passed out, because when I — I opened my eyes and there was blood on the dashboard and everything, I couldn't see out the front or anything. I just opened the door and I started running.

RATHER: The final goal of these conferences is to sign a contract agreeing to an amount the offender will repay the victim. Here, the agreement was quick and cordial. At the next conference, nothing was quick or cordial. This young man also stole a vehicle, a pick-up truck owned by this young man.

LEO: I just went out and my truck wasn't there, and there was all kinds of stuff all around it, where you kind of threw everything about. You remember that?

LEONE: No.

LEO: Oh, I'm sure you do.

LEONE: Kind of threw everything about? What do you mean by that?

LEO: Well, kind of ripped out the inside of my truck where everything was in.

HOOLEY: (Indistinct) did you say something about —

WOMAN: The keys?

HOOLEY: — the keys were in — in the car? Is that —

LEONE: There was one — there was one silver key. It was — it was stuck in the ignition.

LEO: No, it wasn't. There's only one key to that truck. Don't lie.

LEONE: I know —

LEO: And I got it. So, don't lie. This is not the first thing you're lying.

LEONE: All right, so how did I — so how did I get it going?

LEO: I know how you got it going. You want me to go over to my house and show you?

LEONE: Don't tell me I'm lying.

LEO: I know you're lying.

LEONE: Oh, you know I lie.

LEO: Right.

LEONE: That's what that estimate is. That's also a lie.

LEO: You want me to go out to a store and maybe buy some beer or something and me go over to your house and steal your father's car? How'd you feel about that?

RATHER: The final disposition? The offender went to work at McDonald's to repay the victim $875. But before sentencing, this offender, like all others, was scrutinized by probation officers and psychologists, who get together to consider whether or not to recommend Earn It sentences to the judge.

PSYCHIATRIST: This young man has been struggling for some time with . . .

RATHER: All this attention and consideration given to offenders aggravates lots of Quincy residents, but nothing aggravates them more than the court actually finding jobs for offenders who are unemployed. Job seekers complain that jobs should be given to law-abiders instead of lawbreakers.

SERGEANT RILEY: Good kids and bad kids are not treated equally in this town. It seems that there's an incentive for a kid — I have five of my own, and I'd be very inclined to tell my oldest boy that if he wants to get a good education, don't bother to work hard, go and stick up a gas station and Judge Kramer will get him a good job and get him into a good school.

JUDGE KRAMER: I don't think it's fun to go out and work 40 hours a week and make a hundred and twenty dollars and turn over $90 of your money to somebody else and keep thirty for expenses, and do that for a whole summer or maybe a whole year. I don't think that's fun at all. I don't think that's a break. I think that's a real penalty.

RATHER: Judge, that sounds terrific. But you know there are any number of people — and I want to be candid with you now, and I find myself thinking — there is your classic "bleeding heart liberal" point of view; that most of these offenders don't care where that brick lands, they don't care about the victim of the mugging. All they're looking for is to get out of it once they're caught, and then they'll be right back doing the same thing.

JUDGE KRAMER: The point of the court is, if you don't make up, if you don't take advantage of this, we're going to pull you right back and we're going to begin to apply pressure, oftentimes sentencing weekends, until you do conform. If you can't do that, I'll give them a long sentence.

RATHER: Alternative sentencing schemes vary. In some states, both male and female inmates are released daily to work at outside jobs to pay their victims. In some other states, jobs are provided within prison walls. And now the federal government is starting to pour millions of dollars into various experimental programs.
Do you think this is an idea that's going to catch on?

PROFESSOR DERSHOWITZ: I think it is an idea that's going to catch on. There is a lot of popular appeal to a program which is symmetrical, which takes something from the assailant and gives it to the victim, which tries to create a situation of making the whole thing whole. I think it's shortsighted in the sense that it really does cost the government money. The vast majority of people who would be making restitution are people who can't even support their own families, who have obligations which come even prior to the obligation to — to support the victim. And to the extent money is diverted from them to the victim, it's going to have to be made up some other way. It's going to have to be made for — by welfare, by payment to their attorneys. There's no such thing as free lunch, even in restitution schemes.

RATHER: And the victims themselves? Well, even some of them who were repaid, like this woman, remain unsatisfied.

MARTHA CLEMENTS: You know, I believe if I'd have caught the teenagers, if I was just young enough and fast enough to catch that car, I would have — for the first time in my life, I would have killed somebody, I was just so mad.

RATHER: Martha Clements is a hospital secretary and the sole supporter of two teenage sons. She says she worked one and a half years, twelve hours a day, to afford to buy a used car for $600. Soon after she drove it home, it was stolen and wrecked by a young woman and two accomplices. All were apprehended and sentenced to repay Mrs. Clements.

CLEMENTS: She didn't just steal my car. You know, she stole more than that. She stole everything that I believed in, of everything I had to work for to get this. This wasn't handed to me. You know, I worked for that car.

RATHER: They caught the people who did it. Restitution was attempted.

CLEMENTS: Well, the restitution repairs the damage to the car. It didn't repair the damage that it did to me and my family.

RATHER: Honestly now, do you think after going through this program that these same young people would have any hesitancy about doing this again?

CLEMENTS: They will continue doing it as long as they're getting away with it.

RATHER: And you think they did get away with it?

CLEMENTS: Yeah, they did, sure.

RATHER: The final judgment on alternative sentencing is not yet in. But one thing is clear. It is not the cure-all promised by over-zealous advocates. The number of victims helped is small. The amount of money saved is questionable. Jail population is not significantly reduced. And offenders given alternate sentences continue to repeat crimes at the same rate as those sentenced the traditional way.

JUDGE KRAMER (in court):   — to the victims until they are all paid in full. Is that your understanding?

RATHER: But while not a cure-all, alternatives can provide some modest remedies. And given the widespread discontent with the current court system, alternatives like Earn It have increasing political appeal.

JUDGE KRAMER: What is interesting is the tremendous support we get from conservatives and liberals. Conservatives saying it's about time they're made to go to work and not just given a break. And liberals will say that jail is a crazy system; it's good that you give them an opportunity to work back.

Snake Venom

DREW PHILLIPS, PRODUCER

HARRY REASONER: There aren't very many people in this country who don't know someone — family member, friend, themselves maybe — with multiple sclerosis, one of those few maimers and killers left where no one knows what to blame or what to do. In that kind of situation, the patients and the people who love them will stretch for any thread of hope. We heard of one thread and tried to follow it back and test its strength. The idea is not to raise any false hopes; but the idea too, among everyone in medicine and research, is not to miss anything just because it sounds a little bizarre. This one sounds a little bizarre.

Karen Messner is 28 years old and has a four-year-old daughter. She's been in a wheelchair for four years. She'd been told by doctors that her condition will gradually get worse until she loses control of her body completely. She has multiple sclerosis, a disease that hits the central nervous system and messes up the signals the brain sends to the muscles.

KAREN MESSNER: I just want to be able to speak again. Forget the walking. That's not important.

REASONER: MS is one of the remaining medical mysteries. Researchers have no cure for it; they don't even know what causes it. And they don't know why some cases are mild, while others, like Karen's, leave the victims crippled. In this situation, Karen has to believe the doctors are wrong, or the days might be unbearable. She thinks she'll get her voice back, will see clearly again, maybe will even walk again. She believes this, because she's using a controversial new drug called PRO-ven — not really tested, not licensed.

What's in PRO-ven? There are only two active ingredients, two ingredients you would normally avoid like the plague itself: venom from cobras, and venom from a snake without the cobra's reputation that is even deadlier, its little cousin the krait. The thing is Karen is not necessarily living in a dream world. There is just enough of a possibility that the venoms indeed might arrest or repair the damage caused by MS so that some doctors are interested, and there's going to be some testing. We went to see how much is dream and how much is desperation.

To begin, you go to the Miami Serpentarium where the cobras and kraits are; the cobras and the kraits and the owner, a 69-year-old man named Bill Haast. Haast has been fascinating audiences with his handling of the snakes for years.

(Oohs, shrieks and laughter as Haast handles poisonous snake)

But it's more than just a show. The venom Haast milks from the snakes is purified and shipped to hospitals all over the world for use as an antidote to snake bites and in research in many diseases. It's also used to produce Haast's own venom formula, which he calls PRO-ven. Why did Haast develop PRO-ven? That's a story in itself.

Haast immunized himself against cobra bites by injecting small amounts of cobra venom into his body. He's been bitten 140 times by cobras without much ill effect. But when he was bitten by a krait in 1954, he was critically ill for two days, and his nervous system went completely out of control.

BILL HAAST: And I went through such symptoms of nerve stimulation that it just registered on me that if this can do to my nervous systems — I mean, it keyed it up to you can't believe, as if turning up the voltage — that why wouldn't this stimulate then a failing nervous system?

REASONER: He sent some of his purified venom to a doctor in Germany, who tried it on MS patients and reported good results. But it wasn't used on a large scale in America until Haast got together with Dr. Ben Sheppard. Dr. Sheppard, who had treated Haast for snake bites over the years, had arthritis in his hands.

DR. BEN SHEPPARD: Bill Haast really believes that snake venom can cure everything from ingrown toenails to dandruff. He persuaded me to start it on my hands, and it got beautiful results. Now I just have one deformed finger. And then he asked me to try it on some friends of his who had some multiple sclerosis.

REASONER: And so he expanded his clinic into an abandoned schoolhouse. They come here to the clinic of Dr. Ben Sheppard in Miami because he offers them hope, something which is in short supply if you have multiple sclerosis.

And that hope brings people to the clinic by the hundreds on canes, in wheelchairs — hope that injections of Bill Haast's PRO-ven will make them feel stronger, see or hear more clearly, perhaps even walk again.

DR. SHEPPARD: Clinically, I am convinced that we can help 40 to 60 percent of the MS cases. We've had more than several whose eyesight has been restored, because one of the principal signs of MS is the optic neuritis and the double vision and the — and that sort of thing, and we've been able to help them. We've been able to have them walk with the aid of a cane, where formerly they were in a wheelchair. And I'm sold on it.

REASONER: Both Haast and Sheppard insist the clinic was started to help people, and not to make anyone rich; and from what we saw, that's true. Haast provides the PRO-ven free of charge. Patients at the clinic get 20 injections under close medical supervision for $150. That comes to $7.50 a visit. Checked the cost of an office call lately? In addition, the patients are given venom solutions so they can continue their injections when they get home. There's no charge for that. There were more than a hundred MS patients at the clinic when we were there. Almost every one of them insisted PRO-ven works.

WOMAN: My energy level is much better. I'm much more limber than I was. I — at the hotel, I can walk without holding on to anything.

MAN: I know the serum is helping me, because I have movements within my body that I know are moving that did not take place before. I can feel my leg waking up; my fingers were all asleep, and they both work beautifully well. My — I can rotate my shoulders, my hips. I can pick up my legs up to my knee, which wa— I couldn't do before.

WOMAN: I haven't had a headache in three days, and I was taking 12 to 15 aspirins a day.

REASONER: We followed the progress of Karen Messner and two other patients from the first day they went to see Dr. Sheppard. Karen's mother was taught how to continue the treatments after they returned home to Tilton, New Hampshire. We visited them there. After 50 injections, Karen has noticed some improvement.

KAREN: Well, I think I speak better. This is because people tell me that, people that are friends and wouldn't say it unless it were true. Also, just small things. I move my bowels better. My feet, which were cold, are warm now.

REASONER: Bob Wilhelm of Wheat Ridge, Colorado, has had MS for 15 years. He and his wife both felt his condition improved after only 15 shots.

BOB WILHELM: The pain through my shoulders and my back — or hips have all gone away, and my energy has come back in the last week. And what else?

MRS. WILHELM: He's definitely walking better.

REASONER: Walking better?

MRS. WILHELM: Yes. He can walk without the cane now down the hall.

WILHELM: For — not very long, but at least I can start out without it.

REASONER: And a lot less pain?

WILHELM: No pain. That — you see, before, I couldn't sleep.

REASONER: Uh-hmm.

WILHELM: Now I can sleep.

REASONER: Donna Cowart, 39, has had MS for four years. She lives in south Miami with her three children, so she has easy access to the clinic. But after 60 injections at the clinic and at home, she has noticed only minimal results.

DONNA COWART: There's been ups and downs. You know, some — some days I think I feel pretty much stronger. I mean, I can't say that I can get up and walk around again, but I probably will go on with the series.

REASONER: Although we were told a lot of stories about partial or complete recoveries of MS patients at the Sheppard Clinic, we saw no really dramatic changes ourselves. But we did notice that most of the patients were in good spirits, and some were moving better. Was it because of the snake venom, or were other factors involved? Advanced MS patients usually cannot move very well and, perhaps more important, have little or no bladder control; so they tend to be shut-ins, and many become deeply depressed. But in Miami, they usually live in the same hotels near the clinic. Just being with others who share their problems buoys their spirits, and their conversations are filled with hope.

MAN: You know, a lot of people that have, you know, come out okay, you know, that he's talked to, I've talked to, you know. And so, maybe it'll work. I don't think it'll work for everybody, but —

MAN: Oh, no. Everybody will feel something.

MAN: Something.

THERAPIST: The first thing, you go right out . . .

REASONER: The Sheppard Clinic has its own rehabilitation classes, and this therapist is an expert at getting coordinated movement out of muscles that have gone unused for years.

THERAPIST: Now, I want you to take your left and put it back. Good girl. Now bring your right. Now, you did not think you could do that, see?

PATIENT: No.

THERAPIST: See, you've been . . .

REASONER: Neurologists think high morale and physical therapy could lead to improvement in MS patients, but they have serious reservations about the snake venom treatment. Like all new drugs, snake venom must be licensed by the Food and Drug Administration's Bureau of Biologics before it can go into general use, and PRO-ven is not yet licensed. That's why Haast and Dr. Sheppard have used it only in Florida and have not shipped it across state lines.

Dr. Harry Meyer, the director of the Bureau of Biologics, feels the encouraging results reported in Miami could be misleading.

DR. HARRY M. MEYER, JR.:   And that is, anyone who's desperately ill wants to get better, and doctors want to make them better. And so, if a doctor gives somebody something and says, "I really hope this will make you better," many patients will feel that they're better, even though the material, say, has no biologic effect.

REASONER: And Dr. Guy McKhann of the Johns Hopkins Medical Research Center warns against putting too much faith in random cures such as snake venom and clinics like Dr. Sheppard's.

DR. GUY McKHANN: From what I have read and from what I have heard, I think the group in Miami is putting the cart away ahead of the horse. I don't see the data for claims that are being made. I don't see the data for trying to introduce this to the general public. I think that what is needed for this or any other approach to therapy for multiple sclerosis is for a group to do a carefully designed clinical trial that I or anyone else can interpret as to whether or not I think it's either helpful to patients or safe for patients.

WOMAN: Why is orthodox medicine so afraid? Why —

MAN: Politics. Politics.

WOMAN: If it works, it works.

WOMAN: Yes.

WOMAN: And what is happening to all the money which the Multiple Sclerosis Society is supposed to have in its coffers? Why don't they come down here?

REASONER: We took that patient's questions to the National Multiple Sclerosis Society in New York, and the MS Society did exactly what she wanted it to do. Dr. Byron Waksman, the Society's director of research, went to Florida and looked over Bill Haast's venom production facilities.

DR. BYRON WAKSMAN: We have in fact arranged with two of the leading neurology groups in the United States to set up carefully controlled tests of the venom treatment to compare with treatment with placebos, treatment by other means, and to get a clear answer — we would hope within a few months, or a year or two — as to how effective this treatment really is. I would suppose that there are a lot of things in cobra venom that might act on the patient and might act on the patient's nervous system, so that there is a genuine possibility that this treatment might do something.

REASONER: But until tests are completed, MS victims will continue to crowd into the Sheppard Clinic and put their faith in snake venom.

A Few Minutes
with Andy Rooney

MORLEY SAFER: Andy Rooney goes around sizing up things — faucets, electrical outlets, what have you. Tonight, he sizes up sizes.

ANDY ROONEY: It seems to me we're all mixed up the way we designate the size of things. Look at these boxes of stuff. Which size would you think was the bigger: the jumbo, the giant, or the king-size? The king-size looks bigger, but it turns out that this jumbo box weighs nine pounds, and the king-size only weighs five pounds. This giant box here weighs two pounds. Eggs: a jumbo egg is large, extra large is regular, large is small; and medium, you need two.

This all comes to mind now because it's Christmas, and some of us are trying to buy clothes for our friends as presents. Clothes sizes are the worst mess of all. Look at this. I wear a size eight and a half shoe, but I wear a size eleven sock. Does this make any sense? On the same foot? Why does every piece of clothing have a different size scale? Why do I wear a size seven and a half hat but a size sixteen and a half shirt collar? Doesn't that sound as though I could put my shirt on over my hat with my collar buttoned? Why is the average suit size for a man a 40 and the average dress size for a woman a 12? We're not that much bigger.

Every year I go into a store, I want to buy a present for one of my daughters, maybe. I know what she looks like, but I don't see her every day any more. The clerk says, "How big is she?" I say, "Well, you know, about — well, you know, not very big." "Is she my size?" "Yeah, she's about your size, but not quite so — you know." Well, the clerk doesn't know at all, of course, and I have very little chance of getting anything that fits. The average woman might wear a size 12 dress, 34 blouse, size 6 shoe, size 10 stocking and a size 7 glove. If you go to a real fancy store and want to buy something made in France, of course that's different. A size 12 is about a 42, unless she's a junior. Merry Christmas. You can always take it back.

Letters

MORLEY SAFER: Now the mail. About last week's story on the Mormon Church and its influence in Utah, we heard from a Mormon who wrote: "(What does) the church do with its holdings? It builds temples, provides for its members and keeps (them) off government welfare roles . . . we are . . . God-fearing . . . hard-working people . . . truly led by a prophet of God."

Far and away most of the mail was about last week's story on the two boys who were helping each other cope with cancer. One viewer said: "It was truly poignant to see a youngster who should perhaps be tremulously considering his first date coming to grips with his ultimate one in a fashion that would put many of his elders to shame."

And finally, "With all the pain American hearts are going through at this time . . . (those) two young boys showed there is still some real America left. Merry Christmas!"

DECEMBER 23, 1979

"Who Gives a Damn?"

See June 15, 1980, page 615

The Sheik

DON HEWITT, PRODUCER

HARRY REASONER: Last Thursday, the meeting of OPEC — the Organization of Petroleum Exporting Countries — broke up in a kind of chaos in Caracas, Venezuela: no price ceiling, no price floor, arguments over price between Iran and Saudi Arabia and the others. On Friday, Mike Wallace sat down in the very hotel suite where much of the fruitless private negotiations took place, sat down with the Sheik, Ahmed Zaki al-Yamani, Saudi Arabia's oil minister. They talked about OPEC and oil, about Islam, the Ayatollah Khomeini, Yasir Arafat, Russia, and about the United States.

MIKE WALLACE: I read that there are a million more barrels of oil produced every day in the world today than are consumed. A million more. Now, that means that there — the supply is greater, apparently, than the demand.

SHEIK AHMED ZAKI AL-YAMANI (Saudi Arabian oil minister):   Right.

WALLACE: And yet the price keeps going up. Why?

SHEIK YAMANI: Well, why? Because there is a psychological factor involved. They fear that something might happen in Iran which will cause another sharp decrease in the supply of oil. And therefore, the oil companies and certain nations, they buy the oil and they stock it at a very high price. It is the fear more than anything else.

WALLACE: You say there's going to be a glut of oil by the end of the first quarter — by the end of March, the beginning of April? Really?

SHEIK YAMANI: May— maybe even before.

WALLACE: Then you would think that the price would go down.

200

SHEIK YAMANI: Very clear to me.

WALLACE: Well, if that's so clear to you, why in the world would you — and I say you; Saudi Arabia — raise the price of oil not from $18 to $19 or 18 to 20, but by a full thirty-three and a third percent?

SHEIK YAMANI: The difference between the $18, which we had in the past, and the $24, which we now raised, is what the oil companies were making for their own pocket. We didn't want them to make that windfall profit. I think it is fair to take it away from them.

WALLACE: Take it away from them, and what? Keep it for yourself, is that the point?

SHEIK YAMANI: Why not? We are entitled to get it. I don't think that Exxon, Mobil and the others are — are — are more entitled to the benefit of the natural resources produced from Saudi Arabia. I don't think it is fair to see that their profit is doubling and tripling for no reason, except that the Saudi crude is so cheap in the market and they make the benefit out of it.

"I don't think that Exxon, Mobil and the others are . . . more entitled to the benefit of the natural resources produced from Saudi Arabia."

WALLACE: Saudi crude is cheap in the market?

SHEIK YAMANI: Yes, because they take it at $18, they refine it, and they sell it as products in the market. And the price of products, the net back of pri— of the price of products, reflects at $24 per barrel. So the difference is their profit.

WALLACE: That's in the — their foreign market, not in the United States.

SHEIK YAMANI: Well, their foreign market is so great, so big.

WALLACE: But you say "their" foreign market. You own Aramco. You own 60 percent of Aramco. You tell them what to do. You're the boss.

SHEIK YAMANI: I —

WALLACE: You know that the — that the four companies in Aramco, the American companies, they belong to you. If you wanted to cut them off tomorrow, you could.

SHEIK YAMANI: No, it's not true. I don't own Aramco outside Saudi Arabia. I own the oil production facilities. But the Aramco owners, they have an empire of their own in Europe, in the United States, in Japan and elsewhere, and this is where they make the profit from my crude.

WALLACE: You know, Sheik Yamani, I really find it almost amusing. The Saudi Arabians come across, and like to come across, as moderates in the oil market.

And yet, in 1973, only seven years ago, a barrel of Saudi light crude cost in the market $2.10. To produce, it cost you a quarter; maybe a dime, but let's say a quarter. Seven years later, that same barrel of light Saudi crude cost $24, and it perhaps costs — I'm overstating — a half a dollar to produce. Forgive me for using the word greedy, but it sounds to me as though — I mean, you talk about American profits. What about your own?

SHEIK YAMANI: Well, let me tell you something. The price of oil in 1974, in real terms, is still more than the price of oil in 1979. Now, if you take the inflation rate into consideration and the fluctuation in the value of the dollar, we have to have a price of oil of $25 to be exactly at the same price of 1974.

WALLACE: You predict that some OPEC countries are going to slash — that's your word — slash the price of oil fairly early in 1980.

SHEIK YAMANI: It's the law of supply and demand. When there is a surplus in the supply of oil, price will go down. When there is a shortage, the price will go up. It is as simple as this.

WALLACE: Oh, yes, but you've just gotten through saying that the law of supply and demand doesn't work because there — the psychological fear of what might happen to Iran, which will continue to keep the price of oil up as people build their reserves and say, "I've got to get my hands on oil in case Iran goes out of business."

SHEIK YAMANI: But what is demand? Demand is how much oil you buy. This is demand. Part of it you consume, the other part you store.

WALLACE: Right.

SHEIK YAMANI: In the past, you don't store more than what you need. Today, there is a psychological factor — the fear that you might need more — and therefore your demand goes up. So the law of supply and demand is working. But until you reach the maximum physical limit of your ability to store oil; then demand will be exactly your consumption. There is a difference between demand and consumption.

WALLACE: So, the oil glut takes over when you have bought as much oil as you can use and store?

SHEIK YAMANI: Right.

WALLACE: And when you can no longer store oil, then the glut develops and the price comes down?

SHEIK YAMANI: Oh, it's coming. I see it very clearly — unless something happens politically which will interrupt the flow of oil.

WALLACE: What —

SHEIK YAMANI: Then that's another case.

WALLACE: — what could happen?

SHEIK YAMANI: Anything.

WALLACE: Well, you have suggested in the past that perhaps the Palestinians would sink a super tanker or two in the Straits of Hormuz at the mouth of the Persian Gulf, and that would stop the flow of maybe 19- to 20-million barrels of oil a day out of the 31 — million that OPEC produced.

SHEIK YAMANI: It might happen sometime in the future, if we don't solve the Arab-Israeli problem and the Palestinian issue.

WALLACE: Yes —

SHEIK YAMANI: But today, something else might happen.

WALLACE: What?

SHEIK YAMANI: Well, you're talking about a military invasion to Iran, for instance, because of the hostages there.

WALLACE: Uh-hmm.

SHEIK YAMANI: If this happens, I don't expect the flow of oil to continue from Iran at the same level. There might be an interruption, if you do this. That's only one example.

WALLACE: Do you expect a military invasion of Iran by the United States?

SHEIK YAMANI: Well, I hope not, because the price for you is too heavy.

WALLACE: That price would be —

SHEIK YAMANI: Oh, it's not only the flow of oil. I think it's long-term relationship with that nation. It is the door you will widely open to the Russians to get in and have a permanent foothold in Iran.

WALLACE: Would you regard Khomeini as a fanatic?

SHEIK YAMANI: No, not really. I think Khomeini is a different person with different mentality, different values than your own, probably than ours, but he is a man who — who is a leader. You cannot really argue against that. He was able to mobilize the Iranian public opinion against the regime there and to kick out the emperor of Iran, the Shah of Iran. I cannot say that he is lunatic.

WALLACE: You cannot say that he is a lunatic?

SHEIK YAMANI: No. I think it is difficult to say this, if you are objective. You might disagree with him, but you have to be fair to yourself and to him.

WALLACE: And you would say, what, to Jimmy Carter.

SHEIK YAMANI: I will exactly tell him objectively, don't use military forces. Try to talk to the Americans and tell them the reality of the situation. The price is so high.

WALLACE: Just the Russians perhaps com—

SHEIK YAMANI: That's enough.

WALLACE: — coming across the border?

SHEIK YAMANI: Oh, that's quite enough. If the Russians have an access to the Persian Gulf, that is a very difficult thing for you. It will enable them to dictate. The oil is so precious. I don't have to tell you that.

WALLACE: So, we are, in effect, a pitiful, helpless giant.

SHEIK YAMANI: I don't take it that way.

WALLACE: Oh?

SHEIK YAMANI: You are a giant. You are strong. If you are strong and a giant, it doesn't mean that you react like a weak person. Patience is a character of a strong man. It's not a character of a weak man.

WALLACE: Let us posit for a moment that there is a Palestinian state and Yasir Arafat is the head of this state. Here is a man who seems to be the darling of the Russians

— he's constantly making pilgrimages to Moscow — and you don't want the Russians in the Middle East. You said, "Keep Communism out of the Middle East."

SHEIK YAMANI: To start with, I don't know whether he will be the head of the state, or someone else. This depends on the Palestinians. I don't see him really as the head of the state. Number two, I don't think that the Russians love Yasir Arafat. They hate his guts.

WALLACE: Why?

SHEIK YAMANI: But he's the only one with whom they deal.

WALLACE: Why do they hate Yasir Arafat's guts?

SHEIK YAMANI: Because — because he is not their man. But he needs them. You treat him badly, and you really don't help him. Where else he can go? He goes to Russia to — to get some help.

WALLACE: And you don't worry that Russians would infiltrate that Palestinian state that you're talking about, that Russian weapons would be on the borders?

SHEIK YAMANI: I worry about the Russians preventing a real peaceful settlement in the area. I don't worry about them once we have peace in the area.

WALLACE: There is talk about anti-Americanism growing in the Middle East general-ly, and in Saudi Arabia particularly. When I talked with the Shah of Iran some years ago, he expressed a certain sense of wanting to get back at the United States — the "blue eyes," he said — because of the indignities that had been inflicted upon him over the years. And I sense that certain Arabs, even some Saudis, feel, "Well, it's our turn now. We're getting back. Yes, the price is high. Yes, we can make you dance to our tune." None of that?

SHEIK YAMANI: We don't — we don't have these feelings against the Americans. We have so many things in common. I think our friendship is proved beyond any doubt. If you go in the streets of Riyadh or any city in Saudi Arabia, you will know to what extent we have affection to you.

WALLACE: Currently you are producing nine and a half million barrels of oil a day. Can you see — if Iran, let's say, were to go out of action as far as oil is concerned, or if some other countries decided to withhold production; keep the price up, keep their oil in the ground — can you see the circumstance under which you would raise your production to ten and a half or eleven and a half or twelve million barrels a day in order to stabilize the oil market?

SHEIK YAMANI: You don't need that. If something happens in Iran, there will be no glut. The price of oil will stay as high as it is — 24 for the Saudis, 30 and more for the British, the Algerians, the Nigerians and the Iranians. But the absence of two and a half to three million barrels from Iran does not really change the picture, as such. The Saudis are doing so much. You know that we are accumulating a surplus? We are depleting our resources. We are antagonizing our public opinion inside Saudi Arabia. They're still asking what the American did for us. They didn't any— they didn't do anything for the Palestinians, so far. They are waiting for you really to do something for us.

WALLACE: You ask what the Americans did, Sheik Yamani. The Americans discov-ered the oil in your country. The Americans developed the oil in your country. True?

SHEIK YAMANI: Yes, and we are appreciative. We are the only nation who kept your interest in the area. We did not kick you out.

Hypnosis

IGOR OGANESOFF, PRODUCER

DAN RATHER: Over the years Americans have explored various ways to make themselves healthier and and happier. Religious cults, exotic diets, you name it. Well, you might think that hypnosis is just another one of those, but this is different from most fads. For one thing, the medical profession itself more and more is becoming convinced that hypnosis is not just a stage trick, that its use for minimizing human suffering may just be starting. 60 MINUTES went into this fast-growing field to learn what hypnosis can and cannot do.

MAN (from movie excerpt): You shall see nothing, hear nothing, but Svengali!

RATHER: This is what Hollywood thought of hypnosis in the thirties. Svengali — "I have you in my power" sort of thing. Trick eyes and all to do the trick. And all the myths about hypnosis.

MAN (from movie excerpt): Those fellows can make you do anything and say anything you want. Lie, steal — anything!

MAN (from movie excerpt): And then they make you kill yourself when they're done with you.

RATHER: That's make-believe. This is for real.

DR. HERBERT SPIEGEL (to subject under hypnosis): You're three years old, one year old, six months old; today you are one month old. Anything special today?

RATHER: The leading expert in the country, perhaps in the world, is Dr. Herbert Spiegel, clinical professor of psychiatry at Columbia University's College of Physicians and Surgeons. The occasion is a conference of doctors, dentists, psychologists and other professionals. Dr. Spiegel is using a highly hypnotizable subject to demonstrate how she can go back to her earliest years under hypnosis. This technique is said to be useful in psychotherapy to bring out forgotten childhood traumas that might be causing emotional problems later.

DR. SPIEGEL: Hi.

WOMAN (under hypnosis): Hi.

DR. SPIEGEL: What's going on?

WOMAN (under hypnosis): I'm six.

DR. SPIEGEL: You don't seem to be very happy about it.

WOMAN (under hypnosis): I don't like being six.

DR. SPIEGEL: Why?

WOMAN (under hypnosis): I don't like where I live.

DR. SPIEGEL: What's wrong?

WOMAN (under hypnosis): I don't know. There's nothing to do, and everybody's fighting all the time.

RATHER: How does Dr. Spiegel know she's not just acting?

DR. SPIEGEL: It's possible that some of this can be faked, but there are some very subtle tests we can do that, if these can be faked, then the ability to fake so cleverly is in itself more phenomenal than the hypnotic phenomenon itself.

RATHER: Most experts in the field agree that a person cannot be made to do anything under hypnosis that seriously conflicts with their life style or morality. Nothing out of character. No personality changes come out of it. This is also a hypnosis session, this one at New York City police headquarters. The hypnotist is Sergeant Charles Diggett. The young man, Jerry, was witness to a holdup in his uncle's grocery store. The uncle was shot to death before his eyes. But without hypnosis, Jerry was unable to recall details.

SERGEANT CHARLES DIGGETT (to subject under hypnosis):   This is a night that you will never forget. It's about 8:30 PM.

JERRY (under hypnosis):   And these two men took out shotguns out of their belt.

SERGEANT DIGGETT: Can you see the two men clearly now?

JERRY: Yes.

SERGEANT DIGGETT: Uh-hmm. What are they wearing?

JERRY: One of them is wearing a long raincoat, white ski hat . . .

RATHER: For legal reasons, we were not permitted to film Jerry's physical description of the criminals because, although they were caught and convicted, the case is still on appeal. But Jerry's description under hypnosis was so accurate detectives were able to identify one of the men immediately. Police are never allowed to use hypnosis on a suspect or a defendant.

SERGEANT DIGGETT: Well, all of the information that we get from a witness under hypnosis has to be corroborated, just as if he had given us that information in the waking state. As a matter of fact, we tell all of our investigators to try to corroborate the information so much that the hypnosis becomes incidental.

RATHER: Well, if you can use hypnosis to solve a crime, can you use it to induce someone to commit a crime, even an assassination?

DR. SPIEGEL: I suspect that it has been done, except that the people who do it don't go around telling that they've done it. It is quite possible that something is consistent with what they'd like to do, but because of the sanctions of society, the person is afraid to do it. Now, with that extra cover that he has by somebody else telling him what to do, that, reinforcing his own desire anyhow, can make that difference that enables him to do it. The official position of the profession is that you cannot force somebody to do anything they do not want to do. But my unofficial position is that I think it can be done under the proper circumstances.

RATHER: There's a lot of money today in the hypnosis business. The Glover Clinic in Houston, Texas. An average of 500 people go through here every day at $15 per session to lose weight through group hypnosis; others come to stop smoking.

WOMAN: Cal, you have lost some weight!

MAN: Yeah. I need to lost forty more.

WOMAN: Uh-hmm.

DR. SCOTT GLOVER (to large group under hypnosis):   You're not going to eat anything high in carbohydrates . . .

RATHER: This clinic is run by Dr. Scott Glover, a physician who's been practicing hypnosis for 45 years. Dr. Glover estimates that only one out of a hundred or so fail his program, which means perhaps that nearly everybody is hypnotizable to some extent.

DR. GLOVER (to large group under hypnosis):   You are going to feel better physically, and at the same time you're going to be . . .

RATHER: What's going on in this auditorium is a session in mass hypnosis. Dr. Scott Glover has 80 persons in a hypnotic trance. The purpose is to induce patients to eat differently, which means essentially to eat less. In other words, hypnosis is supposed to help patients stick to their diets. In that way, it is not sheer will power.

Doctor, what is hypnosis? You're aware that there are any number of people who think it's nothing but an act.

DR. GLOVER: Well, it's far from that. We do not know actually what hypnosis is or how it works. I regard it as a state of altered consciousness in which the mind becomes increasingly recept— receptive to suggestions which when made, that person then tends to carry out.

RATHER: The pin-ups make the point. Hypnosis requires a suggestion, an incentive.

WOMAN: And I couldn't do it by myself, so I think this is just giving me the extra push. My girlfriend lost 76 pounds here. And I figured if she could lose 76, I could lose 30 or 35.

MAN: I lost 68 pounds. So, it's — it's doing real well.

RATHER: A lot of people think hypnosis is sleep. On the contrary, it's supposed to be a state of relaxed but intense concentration. That's why some athletes all over the world sometimes use hypnosis before a competition to strengthen their drive and concentration.

Is it true that a person, to be an ideal subject, has to be willing to be hypnotized?

DR. GLOVER: No. They do not have to be willing, nor do they have to believe in hypnosis. But if a person, for instance, is in pain — say they've been burned — they — they want to get rid of the pain, so they are extremely well-motivated and they will do anything to get rid of the pain, so they'll go right into a hypnotic state to get rid of their pain.

RATHER: Could anything go wrong under hypnosis?

DR. GLOVER: At parties. Some joker there knows how to use hypnosis. Anybody can learn to use hypnosis. Hypnosis is so simple to learn, it's ridiculous. But I remember I had one call to the hospital one time. This individual had been at a party, and left the party and was brought to the emergency room just scratching their skin, and it was bleeding. Well, obviously, something had happened at the party to give this person such a tremendous itch. And then it comes out that they had been hypnotized, and the suggestion had been made that insects were craws— crawling on their arm, and then the suggestion was not removed.

RATHER: Hypnosis clinics are springing up all over the country like fast-food chains. Some of them will promise you almost anything you want, supposedly curing everything from phobias to sexual impotence. Some employ well-trained hypnotists with solid credentials in psychology or medicine; others are well-meaning amateurs; and some are just out for a fast buck. One California outfit recruits would-be hypnotists in newspaper ads, promising a new, exciting career that pays up to $40,000 a year. We visited a branch of a chain of clinics in Long Island, called the New York Hypnosis Center. This chain deals mainly with weight reduction and smoking. Wade Genthner runs the chain. He's an experienced hypnotist, but that's all.

Do you have a graduate degree?

WADE GENTHNER: No, I do not.

RATHER: Do you have a bachelor's degree?

GENTHNER: No, I do not.

RATHER: Do you treat drug addiction here?

GENTHNER: Very, very rarely. That, in most cases, is much too complicated a problem for us.

RATHER: Yet, it was Wade Genthner, a hypnotist with no other credentials, who personally admitted a heroin addict to his program.

WOMAN: I was desperate. I was just desperate.

RATHER: A young woman, who was taking heroin twice a week, chose to remain anonymous on our program.

WOMAN: . . . help me, and he said that, okay, he would take me on. It would take ten weeks to rid me of this problem.

JOE ALTA: He found that she was appropriate for the clinic, which really startled me, because nobody in the clinic had any experience with drug counseling.

RATHER: Joe Alta, a social worker with a master's degree, freshly trained in hypnosis, was employed at the center at that time and on this case.

ALTA: It was just horrible, I felt.

GENTHNER: She said, "I can stop the heroin at any time. It's how I feel about myself." She had been off heroin for a period of time, and she was simply going back to it on the weekends. It was the only time she was using it.

ALTA: The girl was in very bad shape. It's very possible, obviously, to OD and kill yourself on heroin. It's a life-threatening situation.

RATHER: His claim is the clinic takes in people that have no business here, that there's no way you can help someone who shoots heroin twice a week.

GENTHNER: That's the most foolish thing I've ever heard.

RATHER: You tore up the contract of this heroin addict?

ALTA: That's correct. I referred her on to a — a psychologist which I know at Peninsula Counseling Center.

WOMAN: The best that could have happened is — is I would have been all right for a few months. But I have to do something permanent, you know. I have to go to an analyst, see what the real problem is.

RATHER: Places like the New York Hypnosis Center may not be committing any great wrongs most of the time; they may not be doing anything wrong any of the time; and they probably help some people. But it's worth considering that when it comes to clients with deep emotional problems who might react badly to hypnosis, they could do more harm than good.

DR. SPIEGEL: There is no treatment where hypnosis alone is the — because hypnosis alone is not treatment. By and large, most drug addiction has to be treated with more formidable environmental control, especially during the withdrawal period. And if they're hypnotizable, you can enhance that somewhat.

RATHER: It's estimated that some 11,000 doctors and dentists now routinely use hypnosis for pain relief, as an anesthetic. Dr. Kay Thompson has been pulling teeth for years without chemical anesthesia for the patients who are readily hypnotizable. Incidentally, one of the minor attributes of a good hypnotist is to be able to talk soothingly and monotonously.

DR. KAY THOMPSON (to patient undergoing hypnosis):   All the things that need to happen — start happening. There's that switch for the anesthesia.

RATHER: This patient is having an impacted wisdom tooth pulled while under a trance.

DR. THOMPSON: Okay, fella. You done good.

BROOKE JANIS: Do you feel any sort of pain or discomfort?

MAN: No. I really don't.

DR. HAROLD WAIN: I think we need to be very careful, those of us who are exploring what hypnosis can do; before promising what it does, is to research it more effectively.

RATHER: Dr. Harold Wain is a psychologist at Walter Reed Army Hospital near Washington. He works with physicians and surgeons using hypnosis to control pain.

DR. WAIN: Because hypnosis is not a panacea, it's an outstanding adjunct.

RATHER: About one out of five persons is capable of going deep enough into trance to block off all pain during difficult surgery. The technique is to make the patient imagine he's somewhere else; in this case, on a beach in Puerto Rico.

DR. WAIN: . . . pleasant. You can feel some wind coming in from the sea . . .

RATHER: David Ramirez, a physician himself, underwent this operation at Walter Reed for a deviated septum, which meant that a piece of bone had to be chiseled from his nose so he could breathe normally. No anesthetics were used. Instead, Dr. Wain, on the right, kept a stream of hypnotic suggestions going. The patient's upraised finger was a constant sign that he was continuing in the trance state and was okay. An anesthesiologist was standing by just in case he was needed. He was not.

DR. DAVID RAMIREZ: All I remember is going down there, laying there on the beach, and the lights of — of the operating room being, of course, the sun.

RATHER: Fine. But what about that chisel?

DR. RAMIREZ: That was not painful at all. I was instructed I was only going to hear Dr. Wain, and then the — the chief surgeon, who was Dr. Henderson. And it's kind of funny to be lying there on the beach and have the surgeon saying, "Well, this is the piece of bone that was obstructing his breathing," as he was taking that thing out. And you know, it was not exactly the kind of conversation you hear on a beach. But otherwise, I felt very well. As a matter of fact, I was out of bed that same afternoon.

DR. SPIEGEL: The hypnotist projects nothing at all. What he does is he shows the person how to tap a capacity that either they have or they don't have. If they have this capacity, he shows them how they can use it. Our mind is an incredible instrument.

Letters

MORLEY SAFER: Now, briefly, here's the mail.

About our story on the Hooker Chemical Company memorandums, a viewer said: "If a company dumping toxic wastes is so sure that they're not harming anything, then they should be required to drill water holes around the dump site and the management and the company should be required to drink the water daily without testing it."

On our story "Earn It!" — about a Massachusetts system of having the criminal pay back his victim, a number of viewers were divided; some for it, some against it. This letter bridged the gap: "Make the perpetrator of a criminal act provide restitution to his victim and then serve a jail sentence. Both conservatives and liberals would be pleased (though not concurrently)."

The story on snake venom and the medical doubts about its use on the victims of multiple sclerosis brought this: "If the doctors are skeptical of snakes, how come the American Medical Association uses a serpent in its symbol?"

Update

MORLEY SAFER: And an update on our story on Marva Collins, the Chicago school teacher. That story brought a deluge of mail to both 60 MINUTES and to Marva Collins. A lot of viewers sent her money, money enough for Marva to be able to expand and train other teachers in her no-nonsense method of educating. And two of Marva's students, one boy and one girl, were offered scholarships by two of the most prestigious prep schools in the country — Hotchkiss in Connecticut, and Andover in Massachusetts.

HARRY REASONER: Eleven years ago, in my previous incarnation on this broadcast, I did a little Christmas piece. It seemed like a good idea to repeat it. The basis for this tremendous annual burst of buying things and gift-giving and parties and near hysteria is a quiet event that Christians believe actually happened a long time ago. You can say that in all societies there's always been a mid-winter festival, and that many of the trappings of our Christmas are almost violently pagan; but you come back to the central fact of the day in the quietness of Christmas morning — the birth of God on Earth.

It leaves you with only three ways of accepting Christmas: one is cynically, as a time to make money or endorse the making of it; one is graciously, the appropriate attitude for non-Christians, who wish their Christian fellow citizens all the joys to which their beliefs entitle them; and the third, of course, is reverently. If this is the anniversary of the appearance of the Lord of the universe in the form of a helpless baby, it is a very important day.

It's a startling idea, of course. My guess is that the whole story — that a virgin was selected by God to bear his Son as a way of showing his love and concern for man — it's my guess that in spite of all the lip service they have given it, it is not an idea that has been popular with theologians. It's a somewhat illogical idea, and theologians love logic almost as much as they love God. It's so revolutionary a thought that it probably could only come from a God who is beyond logic and beyond theology. It has a magnificent appeal. Almost nobody has seen God, and almost nobody has any real idea of what He's like; and the truth is that among men the idea of seeing God suddenly and standing in the very bright light is not necessarily a completely comfortable and appealing idea.

But everybody has seen babies, and most people like them. If God wanted to be loved as well as feared, He moved correctly here. If He wanted to know His people, as well as rule them, He moved correctly here, for a baby growing up learns all about people. If God wanted to be intimately a part of man, He moved correctly, for the experience of birth and familyhood is our most intimate and precious experience.

So it comes beyond logic. It is either all falsehood, or it is the truest thing in the world. It is a story of the great innocence of God the baby, God in the power of man; and it is such a dramatic shot toward the heart that it — if it is not true, for Christians nothing is true.

So, if a Christian is touched only once a year, the touching is still worth it. And maybe on some given Christmas, some final quiet morning, the touch will take.

DECEMBER 30, 1979

Big John
PHILIP SCHEFFLER, PRODUCER

MORLEY SAFER: Big John is a survivor. A former Secretary of the Navy, three-term Governor of Texas, Secretary of the Treasury, lawyer, businessman, cattle rancher. John Connally has survived charges of vote fraud when he managed Lyndon Johnson's senatorial campaign. He survived an assassin's bullet in Dallas the day President Kennedy was shot. He survived criminal charges that he was paid off by the milk processors association; a jury found him not guilty.

Tonight, John Connally, the once loyal Democrat who wants to be the Republican candidate for President, talks to Mike Wallace.

MIKE WALLACE: Back in 1962, you called Jack Cox, who was running against you for governor of this sovereign State of Texas and who had changed parties from Democrat to Republican, you called him a "renegade turncoat opportunist." Does that make John Connally a renegade turncoat opportunist?

JOHN B. CONNALLY (laughs):   In the minds of some it sure will, and I've been called that. It's been used against me. It's going to continue to be used, notwithstanding that I changed at a time when no one could successfully accuse me of really being an opportunitist — opportunist. I changed at the depths of the fortunes of the Republican Party in 1973 —

WALLACE: Oh, but wait a second —

CONNALLY: — when it was at the lowest ebb that I guess it's ever been.

WALLACE: Sure, but you were for Democrats for Nixon in 1972. You headed Democrats for Nixon —

CONNALLY: That's correct.

WALLACE: — in 1972 and turned against all your old buddies.

CONNALLY: No, no, I didn't turn against them at all. I simply led Democrats for Nixon because I — I did not subscribe to the philosophy of George McGovern then, nor do I now.

WALLACE: I get the feeling, Governor, that you want to be President so bad that you can taste it, and I'd like to know why

212

CONNALLY: Mike, I want to be President because this country's in trouble. What's happened is that the political leadership of this country, number one, hasn't informed the American people of the problems ahead. We haven't anticipated those problems, and we haven't reacted to solve those problems. And as a consequence now, we're in a — we're in a crisis situation almost every single month. I think I can do something about it. I think I can make this government function better than it does.

WALLACE: John Connally is so much better prepared intellectually, psychologically, by way of experience and so forth, the John Connally — well, you have said, "I can begin to turn this country around in 48 hours."

CONNALLY: Yeah, I think I can.

REP. HENRY B. GONZALEZ (Democrat, Texas):   Connally is an opportunist.

WALLACE: Texas Congressman Henry Gonzalez says John Connally in the White House would be a nightmare. Gonzalez' largely Mexican-American district, he says, simply could not vote for Connally based on his record.

REP. GONZALEZ: When it comes between, say, ambition and honor, it'll be ambition that'll win out. If it comes to between ethics and victory, ethics is going to lose. See, the record shows that.

CONNALLY: Well, he says I'm overly ambitious. In what way? You know, what — you know, people — it's easy to make these statements. In what am I — I just told you I passed up a chance to go to Congress when I was 31 years old. I twice passed up a chance, in my judgment, to go to the Senate. I didn't run for a fourth term. Where is this overly ambitious bit?

WALLACE: Well, you wanted to make money.

CONNALLY: Oh, well, sure, I wanted —

WALLACE: You wanted to make money. There's nothing —

CONNALLY: I wanted to — I wanted to make some money —

WALLACE: As a matter of fact, you say all the time —

CONNALLY: I wanted to make some money, that's correct. I never wanted to be in a position to where I would in the least compromise my own views or my real principles in order to hold a political job. It's the — exactly the opposite of what Henry Gonzalez does — says.

WALLACE: "He ain't no Lyndon Johnson," he says. I asked him why. "Because Lyndon Johnson, regardless of defects and whatever, had a gut feeling for people, and was genuinely feeling for people. John Connally doesn't." (Connally laughs) You hear it over and over again, Governor.

CONNALLY: Yeah, well, that's — there again, I would — I would think that Henry, as a Democrat, would be looking for something to say about me that wasn't too kind.

WALLACE: Former Texas Congresswoman Barbara Jordan, now a political science professor at the University of Texas, feels Connally cannot expect much support from black voters, in part, she says, because of his reaction to the death of Martin Luther King.
Did John Connally say to you, upon hearing of the death of Martin Luther King, "Those who live by the sword die by the sword"?

BARBARA JORDAN (former U.S. Representative from Texas):   Governor Connally made
that statement when Martin Luther King was assassinated. He did not make the
statement directly to me, but I heard him express that, because I recall my
distress at the time.

WALLACE: In those words.

JORDAN: In those words.

WALLACE: He'll deny it.

JORDAN: He very well might.

WALLACE: Governor, whether or not you said what Barbara Jordan remembers you
as saying, there is a tape recording of your saying this about Martin Luther King:
"He contributed much to the chaos and the strife and the confusion and the
uncertainty in this country, but he deserved not the fate of assassination" – which
seems like a mild epitaph for a man of the accomplishment of Martin Luther King.

CONNALLY: Well, I think you have to view that in the light of — of the time in
which it was said, Mike, and the circumstances that existed at that time, and I —
and I don't think it was a — I don't think it was an unfair statement.

WALLACE: It was not a compassionate statement.

CONNALLY: No, it was not a compassionate statement, that's correct. I think that's
right. It was not a compassionate —

WALLACE: If you had the –

CONNALLY: It was not as compassionate a statement as I would — as I would make
today. And if I had to do over, I'd do it differently.

WALLACE: John Connally antagonized yet another group of voters last October with
his speech on the Middle East, in which he talked about the importance of oil and
outlined his plan to bring peace between Israel and her Arab neighbors. The
speech brought headlines and defections from his campaign by prominent
Jewish supporters, among them an old friend, fund-raiser and close political ally,
New York attorney Rita Hauser.

RITA HAUSER: More than anything else, forgetting even the details of his peace
plan, he linked the question of oil in Israel, and implied throughout his whole
speech that if Israel were to give up the various territories it holds, that the Arabs
would then be nice fellows and give us oil at reasonable prices in reasonable
amounts. That's false. There's no single basis of showing that that would ever
happen. It's a pernicious argument and it's a dangerous argument.

CONNALLY: Well, Mike, let me — let me just say that that's the view of some, but it's
an unfair analysis of my speech. Who first linked oil to Israel? I didn't. The Arab
nations. When we supported Israel in the October war, the Yom Kippur war, in
1973, we got embargoed. We were embargoed by the Arab nations. They said
don't — we will not ship the United States oil. They began — they used, for the
first time, oil as a political weapon. Out of that grew OPEC. That's who linked oil
to Israel. I didn't.

WALLACE: You've taken a fair amount of heat on this subject, haven't you?

CONNALLY: Well, I think — I think I have, and I think really unfairly and unjustly.
I —

WALLACE: Unfairly, unjustly. I – across the board. I don't care who – all of your

Republican opponents, some of your Democratic opponents, and most of the press read your speech as saying, in effect: Israel, you be — you give up certain things —

CONNALLY: What I said in the speech —

WALLACE: — and — and — plus a Palestinian state of some kind, and then chances are men like Khomeini and Qaddafi and the Saudi Arabians and so forth are going to be more reasonable about oil pricing and keeping the oil flowing. Now, that's the general perception.

CONNALLY: Well, you know, the general perception doesn't make it right.

WALLACE: And I get the feeling that as President of the United States, John Connally would keep pressure on — honestly now — Israel to be perhaps more forthcoming, more realistic, because of what you perceive —

CONNALLY: No.

WALLACE: — to be the vital interests of the United States.

CONNALLY: No. I would — I would not try to impose any kind of pressure on Israel that would cause her to do anything that would be inimicable to her interests and her security and her preservation.

WALLACE: You've lost support, you will agree —

CONNALLY: Sure, sure.

WALLACE: — in the Jewish community.

CONNALLY: Sure, I have.

WALLACE: And Barbara Jordan says you're not going to get much support in the black community.

CONNALLY: Well.

WALLACE: And Henry Gonzalez says you're not going to get much support in the Mexican-American community.

CONNALLY: Well, I — you know, in the black community, President Ford got eight percent, and I dare say I'll get considerably more than that. I don't think I'm going to carry the majority of blacks nor the majority of Mexican-Americans in this country.

WALLACE: The business community. They've — I don't know, how much you got — seven, eight million dollars in your kitty so far raised?

CONNALLY: No.

WALLACE: Seven.

CONNALLY: Not quite. I wish it was. But almost seven.

WALLACE: Seven. A lot more than anybody else.

CONNALLY: Yeah.

WALLACE: Why is business so devoted to John Connally?

CONNALLY: For the simple reason I've been a part of it, they think I understand it, and they think I know better than any of these other candidates in either party the role that business plays in this country. Because I talk about it and I defend business, and I say business provides five out of six jobs in America, not government. Business is responsible for the standard of living in this country, not government. Business creates jobs in America, not government. Business creates wealth in America, not government. Government's a consumer of wealth. Government is a — a —

WALLACE: So you have respect for the business leadership of this country. And yet, Governor, you are quoted as saying — and I know that you said it — "There's an amazing —

CONNALLY: Well, if I said it, I'm not going to deny it.

WALLACE: "There's an amazing amount of mediocrity, even among the top, top businessmen. I know. I've seen them. Ninety percent of them are mediocre, pompous, narrow, stupid Neanderthals." End quote, John B. Connally. Really?

CONNALLY: I wou — I would — I don't know when I made that statement, but I would say that percentage is a little high. But I would say that a great many of them fit that category.

WALLACE: And these are the people who support you.

CONNALLY: Well, Mike, they are in the sense — you know, again, this is taken out of context. What — what I'm saying is, in that statement — and I am — I'm sure I made that statement. It's — I'm also sure it's an exaggeration. When —

WALLACE: By John Connally.

CONNALLY: Yeah, it's my exaggeration. Ninety percent — who knows? I don't know whether it's 40 percent or 90 percent. But beyond any question, there is a high degree of mediocrity in the highest business councils in this country. Take the oil companies most recently. I don't defend the — I don't defend the — the oil companies, per se. I defend the principles of capitalism. I defend the profit motive in this country. But I think the oil companies have been stupid in the way they've handled their business, very frankly.

WALLACE: Well, wait a minute. You said just the other day that you're not sure whether or not oil company profits are excessive. "I don't know. I haven't analyzed them."

CONNALLY: I haven't.

WALLACE: Do you know who's analyzed them?

CONNALLY: No.

WALLACE: The Saudi Arabians.

CONNALLY: Well, maybe they have.

WALLACE: Know what they said, reported in the *Middle East Economic Survey:* "It's now clear the Saudis feel, particularly in view of the colossal third-quarter profits registered by the ARAMCO parent companies, Exxon, Standard Oil of California and Mobil, that the benefits of the lower Saudi prices have gone to the oil companies rather than the customers."

CONNALLY: All right.

WALLACE: And you say, "I haven't analyzed them. I don't know if their oil company profits are excessive." And —

CONNALLY: Well, what — how do you define excessive? Let me sa — let me say this. I don't think there's an oil company in America whose — whose profits as a result of return on — if analyzed as a return on assets or a return on equity, will equal CBS Network's. There may be a few that you could pick out, but any major oil companies that I know, your profits are higher than the oil companies'. Now, which is excessive, and what is excessive? That's all I'm implying. I'm not trying to criticize CBS. All I'm saying is, when you say — you ask me, "Are their profits excessive?" Compared to what?

CONNALLY (before group of supporters)   We're going to say to America that you — we have to use coal and we have to use oil and gas, we have to use nuclear power. And we're going to say to the world and this country that we've got to quit taking scientific advice from Jane Fonda and Tom Hayden and Ralph Nader — (cheers and applause)

WALLACE: Of course, it was those extreme environmentalists who warned us that something like Three Mile Island could happen. They weren't all wrong.

CONNALLY: What happened at Three Mile Island?

WALLACE: What did happen at Three Mile Island?

CONNALLY: Well, no one was killed. No one was injured. So far as we know, there's no residual damage. The plant performed just as it — as it was supposed to perform.

WALLACE: Governor, did you really say, "More people died at Chappaquiddick —

CONNALLY: No, I did not.

WALLACE: — than at Three Mile Island?"

CONNALLY: No, I did not.

WALLACE: You're sure?

CONNALLY: I'm positive.

WALLACE: If I could show it to you on tape —

CONNALLY: I don't care —

WALLACE: — would you be surprised?

CONNALLY: I — no. If you did, you — you were taping something you shouldn't have been taping.

WALLACE (laughs):   Ho! Then — then —

CONNALLY: If you did, you taped a private conversation. Sure, I've repeated it in our own home, because it was a joke that's going around, and it's been on — it's been on bumper stickers. I have never said it publicly. Never.

WALLACE: Publicly.

CONNALLY: No, sir. And if you've taped it, you shouldn't have.

WALLACE: Well, we didn't tape it —

CONNALLY: Okay.

WALLACE: — but it has been taped. And —

CONNALLY: Well, whoever taped it should not have.

WALLACE: You said it. Why would you say, about Teddy Kennedy, "I never drowned anybody?"

CONNALLY: Mike, I get asked by a newsman, "Do you think that Chappaquiddick and the milk fund are identical?" Or words to that effect. And I said, "No." I — In — in effect, I said, no. In the — in the — in the milk fund matter, I didn't — I didn't do anything. I didn't admit to anything. I denied that I had done anything wrong. And I — I did then, and I do now. There — obviously, whatever he did, Senator Kennedy did it. I said a person was drowned in Chappaqui — is that comparable to what the milk fund was? That's the — that's the context in which I answered that question, and that's the context in which I used it. I'm not going to talk about Chappaquiddick in this campaign. I don't —

WALLACE: You're not?

CONNALLY: No, I'm not, and I don't enjoy bringing up a subject like that, and I didn't bring it up. I —

WALLACE: What do you think — what do you think of —

CONNALLY: I was asked about it, just as you asked me about it.

WALLACE: What do you think of Ted Kennedy?

CONNALLY: I think he's a — I think he's an able senator, and I think he ought to stay there and serve his country.

(To group of supporters) How many of you would like to nominate somebody next summer that could beat Teddy Kennedy? (Cheers and applause) All right. Well, get your — get your jogging clothes on and your running shoes on, because that's what we're going to do. We're going to — by the end of this — let me tell you, by the end of this year, it's going to be clear that we've closed — you know, I don't mind mentioning him. I'm not going to say anything bad about him. Governor Reagan, he's a nice man. He's a great elder statesman of this party. (Laughter) But by the — by the end of this year, it's going to be obvious that he — this race is between the two of us.

WALLACE: With all of this, with everything that you say — and you're a very persuasive stump speaker and a very persuasive fellow on television — why aren't you doing better in the polls, Governor?

CONNALLY: Well — (Laughs)

WALLACE: I mean it.

CONNALLY: Mike, I'm doing well in the polls. The last — the last poll, the — the Lou Harris poll, had me coming — in six months, I've come from six percent to eleven percent in June. The end of September, I was eighteen percent. I was the only one that made any substantial gain.

WALLACE: Well, *Time* magazine took a poll, and it says nearly as many people find him unacceptable as President as find him acceptable, 40 percent to 42 percent; 42 percent say they — quote — "just don't trust him."

CONNALLY: Well, the — you know, polls will tell you anything that you want them to tell you.

SAFER: Well, the polls are not telling John Connally what he wants to hear. He's got the money. He's got the image. But that doesn't worry Ronald Reagan. That two-man race Connally talked about now looks more like a runaway than a race.

Come Fly with Me

IGOR OGANESOFF, PRODUCER

DAN RATHER: Last weekend, 36 people died in 16 separate crashes of private airplanes. For the year 1979, 1,700 people died in private aircraft. That's more than eight times as many as were killed in commercial airline accidents. What's wrong with private planes? Nobody can agree — neither the FAA, the manufacturers, nor the pilots. One thing almost everybody does agree on is that there are good light planes and bad light planes. And while commercial airlines fly less than 3,000 aircraft in the United States, private planes number a quarter of a million, and they've become the ultimate status symbol.

One thing that amazed us was that the FAA, which is supposed to certify all planes for flight worthiness, actually delegates this watchdog function to the manufacturers themselves. The FAA only spot checks. It takes the maker's word that a plane is fit to fly safely.

LANGHORNE BOND: Now, that doesn't mean we take our hand out of it, because in almost every case we do flight tests and check, and we have people in their factories.

RATHER: The head of the Federal Aviation Administration, Langhorne Bond.

RATHER: So it's true that — that you allow them to inspect themselves?

BOND: Oh — yeah, we are not quality control inspectors. They —

RATHER: Nor design inspectors.

BOND: Nor design inspectors, that is correct. We license their program and check their process.

RATHER: The most publicized victim of a recent plane crash, of course, is Thurman Munson, the Yankee baseball catcher. He had only 41 hours of flying time in his new twin-jet Cessna. Munson apparently failed to lower his landing gear in time, and he dropped short of the runway. He died in the flaming wreckage. But there are a lot of small plane crashes that you never hear about, because only two or three people died, not the scores or hundreds when a commercial airliner goes down.

The Big Three makers — Cessna, Beech and Piper — all make good planes, and some not so good. But it's pretty clear that the experience level of the pilot is a definite factor. The average small plane pilot, the average, flies only 50 hours a year. And many, such as the occasional Sunday pilot, as few as 10 hours a year. So many pilots do not really know what they or their planes can do safely.

JACK EGGSPUEHLER: The manufacturer gives us an airplane, and says this airplane will be safe if you operate within this operational framework.

RATHER: Jack Eggspuehler is president of the National Association of Flight Instructors, and a highly experienced pilot himself.

EGGSPUEHLER: Too often the user, the pilot, tries to stretch that; exceeds the limitations of the aircraft or exceeds his own limitations. And that can be very disastrous, as you well know.

RATHER: Spins account for a large percentage of airplane fatalities. A spin comes from stalling, when the plane hasn't enough forward speed to keep flying and skids to one side.

EGGSPUEHLER: Okay, now I've got the yoke — I'm going to pull it all the way back into the stall, and watch it start to rotate. Boy, she's really winding up.

RATHER: Many new planes are virtually spin-proof, but countless older ones are still around and very spinable.

EGGSPUEHLER: We don't have people having problems with spins at five or six thousand feet where we demonstrate these. We have it in a situation where they're turning onto final approach, when their attention is diverted to other matters. And then it is so fast they couldn't begin to recover from that altitude. They're too low.

RATHER: Everybody says that in a great percentage of the cases trouble develops because the pilot pushes the weather. True?

EGGSPUEHLER: Yes. Most common mistake is that you take off on the basis of good information. Weather deteriorates, doesn't go according to forecast. The person says, "gee wiz, what's my home base, where I'm — my destination airport? The weather is good there." They get a case of get-home-itis. It is just so amazingly fast how much trouble he can get into before he really knows what's happening.

RATHER: This is what can happen.

EGGSPUEHLER: Many people have, I'm sure, inadvertently penetrated clouds. And when they do that, here again we start this what we call the "graveyard spiral." They can't handle the aircraft by reference to instruments. And you'll see, Dan, as we enter the clouds — I should have stayed out of these clouds, but now we're in it. Well, I'm not going to turn back. My inner ear tells me that I'm flying straight and level. My body tells me that I'm flying straight and level. But my instruments, if I would just look at them, would tell me — my Lord, I'm in a terrible diving spiral! Notice when we come out of the clouds, speed is increasing. And I say, gee, my nose is down. I'm going to pull my nose up. And look at what happens to it. I don't realize that all I'm doing is banking more and more and more. Gee, that airspeed is picking up even more.

The airplane has every right to have it's tail come off, because that's the design of the aircraft and this is what we understood at the outset. But look at that ground coming up. And then it's too late, and they're going right down to the ground.

RATHER: Boy, that seems remarkably easy to have happen to me.

EGGSPUEHLER: It is remarkably easy, and this is why we continue constantly to urge people not to fly into weather that they're not trained to fly in.

RATHER: Well, is it the pilot's fault if a plane crashes? Michael Antoniou is an engineering test pilot.

When one talks about pilot error, real or imagined, one frequently hears from the manufacturers, from the FAA, and indeed, from pilots themselves: the pilot should have known; it's in the manual.

MICHAEL ANTONIOU: In the typical manual, the level of accuracy is entirely inadequate. There is one airplane in particular, the actual climbing performance of the airplane, as compared to the performance that was shown in the manual, the actual climbing performance was approximately fifteen percent lower. And in fact, the climbing performance was low enough so that the airplane should not have been certificated.

RATHER: What aircraft is that?

ANTONIOU: That's the Cessna Cardinal.

RUSS MEYER: There is no question in my mind that the data with respect to the Cardinal or any other airplane that we manufacture is accurate, it is complete.

RATHER: Russ Meyer is president and board chairman of Cessna Aircraft, the largest small plane manufacturer in the world.

MEYER: The data that's put in our manuals, every one of our manuals, is taken by engineering test pilots, every one of whom has an aeronautical engineering degree.

ANTONIOU: With regard to the take-off performance of this airplane, that distance was given as 4,000-plus feet. And I found that the airplane required something on the order of 6,000-plus feet to clear that 50-foot height. And in order to get that airplane to clear that 50-foot height in that distance required extreme skill on my part, and I am a highly skilled engineering test pilot. If your good old average light plane pilot, with the level of training and the level of expertise that he possesses, would have tried a take-off under those conditions, it is very likely that he would have crashed.

MEYER: Well, I don't know who made that statement or where he was flying, but I would say this: that the comment that we don't put anything in there about what the airplane will not do is not true.

RATHER: What is in the manual and what is not is sometimes the subject of law suits. It depends on which manual and which plane. Test pilot Antoniou flew the original model of the Cardinal, not the later one in which Cessna installed a larger engine. Antoniou is a witness for the plaintiff in a civil suit against Cessna regarding a Cardinal that crashed.

Incidentally, Cessna has been pretty responsive to criticism, and pilots now agree their latest manuals are okay. But then, take the Beech V-tail Bonanza, one of today's most popular single-engine aircraft. A lot of pilots swear by it, but there's one problem. The record shows it falls apart now and then.

DR. BRENT SILVER: Now let's be fair. The scenario is generally a weather-related scenario. Pilot gets into weather; maybe he can't handle the weather. It's hard to tell exactly what happens, because all you're left with afterwards is the smoking rubble, the pieces on the ground, and dead pilots and passengers. They don't live through it.

RATHER: Dr. Brent Silver is an aeronautical engineer and pilot who specializes in aviation safety studies.

DR. SILVER: The pattern shows an accident record there that's very high. And let me make an interesting comparison. Beech makes another airplane, a straight-tail Bonanza. A straight-tail Bonanza has a tail like that — conventional tail. V-tail Bonanza has a tail like that. Nowadays they're almost identical airplanes, except for the tail. This airplane doesn't fall apart. That airplane —

RATHER: The conventional tail.

DR. SILVER: — that airplane does — 24 times more often than the straight-tail version.

RATHER: (Whistles) Why doesn't Beech just go to the straight-tail, and forget about the split-tail?

DR. SILVER: That's a good question. I think it's styling.

RATHER: Is it a question of styling? That's a simple enough question, but Beechcraft executives wouldn't answer that or anything else unless they could control what we put on the air. And you've already heard the head of the FAA say his agency doesn't get involved in design.

It is not our intention to turn what for many thousands of persons is the joy of flying into a fear of flying, but there are some things to be concerned about when it comes to small aircraft. For example, the death rate in small planes is ten times that for automobiles, and a hundred times the rate for commercial airliners. Eight out of ten fatal air crashes occur in single-engine planes.

ANTONIOU: The light airplane manufacturers resorted to the sort of advertising that is commonly used by Detroit — the three-color paint scheme, the new paint scheme for this year's model. They changed the color of the seats; they moved some instruments around. But they didn't do very much to the basic engineering of the airplane.

"Eight out of ten fatal air crashes occur in single-engine planes."

RATHER: But what's wrong with that?

ANTONIOU: There's lots of things wrong with that. There are lots of things wrong with that. Because if you buy an automobile that has a three-color paint scheme and a leaking gas tank, that may be an inconvenience, but it won't kill you. Now, if you buy an airplane that has an improperly designed gas tank, that can kill you. If you have an airplane that won't recover from a spin, that'll kill you.

RATHER: Now, I want to read you a direct quote from someone who is in the field, says that the problem is the marketing and design people have more to say about an airplane than the engineers. Is that true?

MEYER: Well, that is categorically not true, and is certainly not true of Cessna, nor do I think it's true of anyone else in the industry. We work very closely with the FAA, and we certainly follow the regulations just as carefully if it were delegated or if it were not.

RATHER: But some engineers say that the FAA regulations and specifications are too loose and too old. Nevertheless, you can't blame everything on the FAA or the manufacturers. Most accidents officially list the cause of a crash as pilot error. But there's an area in between that causes a lot of crashes. It is called "design-induced pilot error."   ·

GERRY STERNS: For instance, on a twin-engine aircraft, there are six control levers which control the throttle and the pitch and the mixture.

RATHER: Of the fuel.

STERNS: Right. And those are vital to the operation of the airplane. And for years they — it has been urged that those knobs be of different shapes, rather than colors, because often that fellow's flying at night, you see, and he can't see the colors.

RATHER: Gerry Sterns is a lawyer specializing in airplane cases for victims and their relatives.

STERNS: You've got two handles that the pilot has to reach down; they're both the same shape and both the same size, you see. One drops the flaps, one drops the gear. He grabs the wrong one by mistake because they — they don't have different feel. And they are critical to the pilot because of these judgment errors he has made, which would be, you know, something that you'd expect of a Lindbergh or a Neil Armstrong. And I say, "Wait a minute. I mean, who did you have in mind when you designed this airplane?"

RATHER: What he's talking about is this. A fuel gauge might easily be switched to the wrong tank. Cockpits are not standardized, though a lot of pilots think they should be. The fuel pump on one plane may be where the landing lights are on another. The altimeter is in a different place. All this adds to confusion for the inexperienced pilot in an emergency. Cessna is one of the makers that is trying to correct these problems in its new planes.

EGGSPUEHLER: I'm not going to say, because I don't believe it to be the truth, that the people who are in charge of developing light airplanes sit around the table and say, "Well, that's okay. We're going to lose a few of those in spins, and some people are going to get killed, but we don't care about that. It's going to cost too much money to fix it." I don't think that happens. The problem is that the process of developing these airplanes puts them into a position where the pressures that are applied — the economic pressures, coupled with their ability to rationalize as good human beings — allows them to make these decisions and to make them in good conscience.

RATHER: That's where the FAA is supposed to provide a watchdog role.

EGGSPUEHLER: That's correct. Yes, yes. The FAA is supposedly there to say, "Oh, oh. You just rationalized too far, and we're not — we're not going to buy that, because this is going to hurt you, but you're going to have to fix it." The FAA needs to be there early on in the design process.

RATHER: And they're not there?

EGGSPUEHLER: They're not there.

DR. SILVER: The FAA is a schizophrenic monster. It's been charged by Congress with the promotion of general aviation and also its regulation, and it can't do both.

EGGSPUEHLER: The manufacturer has certified his own airplane. All the major light airplane manufacturers — Cessna, Piper, Beechcraft, possibly North American Rockwell — all the large light airplane manufacturers have this authority.

RATHER: To certify their own aircraft.

EGGSPUEHLER: To certify their own aircraft, sure.

RATHER: To give it the FAA seal of approval.

EGGSPUEHLER: Right.

RATHER: Which brings us back to where we began. Incredible as it seems, the FAA mostly takes the maker's word that a plane is fit to fly. It is not unreasonable to think that the agency charged with looking after safety in the air should have more of a role in looking after the quarter of a million private planes and 800,000 pilots flying today in America.

Roy Cohn
JOSEPH WERSHBA, PRODUCER

MORLEY SAFER: Here's how to cause a fuss at a gathering of American judges or lawyers or just thoughtful people. Merely say the name Roy Cohn. People will leap at you with allegations against the man going back to his association with Joe McCarthy — some is sheer invention, some true but unprovable, and a lot that's true and proven. Among the current allegations: that it was Roy Cohn who started the rumor that Hamilton Jordan used cocaine at the Studio 54 disco; he denies he started it; that Cohn is the secret beneficiary of a number of dubious cash-only businesses. Cohn denies it. You will get very few people to praise or even defend Roy Cohn. Many, if not most, regard him as something of a snake. Let's take a look.

SENATOR JOSEPH McCARTHY: The committee will come to order.

SAFER: The Roy Cohn of 1954. The arrogant young man always at Joe McCarthy's ear. McCarthy was impressed by Cohn's work in helping to send the Rosenbergs to the electric chair on the charge of spying for Russia. Roy Cohn, one of the authors of McCarthyism.

ROY COHN: One thing I've always admired Senator McCarthy for was the fact that he was one of the few people I've ever run across in Washington who had guts, and the guts to stand up for what he believed in, and didn't care about the — the "gentlemanly fellow senator" rules and all of that hogwash. He cared about this country. I cared about this country.

SAFER: When McCarthy and McCarthyism died, a lot of people thought it spelled the end of Roy Cohn. The brash New York lawyer, destroyer of reputations, whose venom had no limit, was washed up, finished. Not so. Today, the rich and the powerful and famous seek him out for the biggest of big-money law suits. Benson Ford, for example, who is suing his uncle Henry for scores of millions.

BENSON FORD: I hired Roy Cohn because he is a tough son of a bitch.

SAFER: If I can compare this with a Western, it's — it's like bringing in a hired gun.

FORD: That's right. Because it seems like in Michigan, the — which is — seems to be Henry Ford's town, his word is very strong and his image is very popular back there. And I wanted to get a good street fighter in there to take away that image and break it down and — and clean it up a little bit.

SAFER: It isn't a gentlemen's fight, is it?

COHN: It ain't going to be a gentlemen's fight, Morley, not this one.

SAFER: "Don't Mess With Roy Cohn" has become a motto Roy wears with pride. The man who wrote the *Esquire* cover story, Ken Auletta, is a reporter who regularly measures Roy Cohn's impact on politics, business, and the law.

KEN AULETTA: People come to him because, as I called him in that piece, they think of him as a legal executioner. A husband or a wife goes to Roy because they want to kill, all legal, their mate. Or a business partner or former business partner goes to Roy because they want to get back at a former associate. Or — or Benson Ford goes to Roy because he wants to get back at his uncle. And it's all legal.

COHN: I want to be prepared to the teeth. If I have a witness on the stand for an adversary, I want to know everything about that witness from the year one, every application he filed for a driver's license, to show inconsistencies, to show tendencies which demonstrate lack of credibility. And I want to be armed to the teeth. I don't go for this theory that my magnetic personality or my toughness is going to win over a jury or a judge.

AULETTA: He believes that — that it's war, and that outside of his small circle of friends, he inhabits the jungle. And all of these forces out there, be they the federal government or the U.S. Attorney's office or journalists or others, are out to get him.

SAFER: One man who was out to get him was another young — some might say arrogant — lawyer attracted to Joe McCarthy — Robert Kennedy. Roy and Bobby served the senator loyally, but neither man could bear the presence of the other.

COHN: I don't know why Bobby and I never hit it off together. There could have been — one reason could have been he wanted the job of chief counsel, which I got.

SAFER: But the vendetta continued.

COHN: Well, there's no question about it. I think the — the authority for that, Morley, is one of his assistants, a man named Irving Younger, now a law professor at Cornell, wrote an article for Commentary a couple of years ago —

SAFER: Admitting it.

COHN: Oh, yes. He had been called in by the United States attorney in the presence of Attorney General Kennedy, and said the Justice Department wants to get Roy Cohn. "It's your job to get him and report to us." And —

SAFER: Why?

COHN: He didn't like me.

AULETTA: You cannot hurt Roy Cohn. He's — he's just invulnerable. Because he recognizes that the more publicity he gets, no matter what the publicity is, he benefits.

COHN: I would do anything that is legally permissible to do to get my client to win. Yes, I would. That's my job. There isn't anything I would not do, because I believe there is only one answer in an adversary profession like law, and that is winning.

SAFER: It's that attitude that brings in the clients.

COHN (talking to woman client):   If we make what I feel is a reasonable workout of everything, okay. If we don't make a reasonable workout of everything, I fight all the way?

WOMAN: You fight all the way, but I leave everything in your hands, because you know what the article says: "You never mess with Roy Cohn." (Laughs)

COHN: As long as you — as long as a few people believe it.

SAFER: If you hang out in Cohn's office, you get a taste of the kind of clients he gets and the reason they come to him. A lady who feels she got the wrong end of a business deal. Benson Ford and his millions. And this grandfatherly man.

COHN: Sit down.

CARMINE GALANTE: No, no, I'm going to leave in the morning. I'm going to the country.

COHN: Good. What are you going to do when you get to the country?

GALANTE: I'm — well, I mean, I plant peppers last week. Now I'm going to plant tomatoes.

SAFER: His name is Carmine Galante, the late Carmine Galante, who, the papers said, was the godfather of the Mafia.

COHN: You think that had an influence on the federal judge when he held that you were right and the parole commission was wrong?

GALANTE: I think so. I think so.

COHN: He thinks a farmer ought to be able to seed, right?

GALANTE: I think so. I mean, it's very well known that that's what I do.

SAFER: A few months after this meeting, he was gunned down as he sipped a glass of wine. And to law students who object to Cohn's defense of underworld clients, he offers no apologies.

COHN: I don't have to believe a person is innocent, like — we keep talking Galante or Tony Salerno or someone like that. I don't have to believe in their innocence in a particular case. I have to believe one of two things. Number one, that that person is innocent in the particular case; or that there are some extraordinary circumstances which make the prosecution unfair.

SAFER: Roy Cohn's had his own troubles with the law. He's been tried three times on criminal charges that could have put him away for years, but he was acquitted each time. That's helped his reputation that if you're in trouble, get Roy Cohn. The client is an Italian countess. She gets the royal treatment at a smart New York restaurant, and a ride in Cohn's Rolls-Royce. The lunch is a business deduction, and so is the Rolls.

AULETTA: It's interesting and ironic, because that is the criticism he makes of Henry Ford, that Henry Ford is using corporate funds for his peronsal use. What Roy does, he lives off an expense allowance estimated between three and four hundred thousand dollars a year, all of it charged to the business — on the theory that he is conducting business all the time. I think that's very questionable.

SAFER: Roy Cohn manages to spend, I guess, a half a million dollars a year as expenses without paying a penny of tax on it.

COHN: When we talk expenses, now, that isn't so. First of all, I paid an astronomical amount of taxes. I guarantee you I have paid more taxes than any of the last three Presidents of the United States added up together. I probably hold the world's record of never having a — had a completed audit by Internal Revenue Service for over twenty years. I'm supposed to remember now in 1979 who I had dinner — dinner with February, 1958. I very frankly don't want to earn any more than I have to earn to subsist the way I want to subsist, because I don't like the way this country punishes the workers, the middle class, the blue-collar people, the white-collar people, middle America. I think it's lousy.

SAFER: There are people who think that Roy Cohn's takeovers are lousy. They say there's a pattern in which Cohn takes on a client, and then somehow ends up as the beneficiary of that client's business assets.

COHN: As far as businesses are concerned now, I'll tell you one thing, I have no interest in business of any kind. I don't have an interest in any businesses. I'm interested in practicing law. I don't want assets. I don't have a family. I don't need assets.

SAFER: For a man without assets, Roy lives quite well — in a grand New York townhouse whose ownership is unclear; a house that also houses his law firm, a law firm in which he is not even named as a partner. All of which may be helpful in getting around certain tax obligations. Despite Cohn's reputation as being invincible, he has lost a number of cases. It's just that he always makes them sound like victories.

AULETTA: He recognizes that if you are tenacious, if you are a killer, if you are willing to go to any length to make your point or appeal your case, most people are going to back off.

SAFER: In the musical *Pal Joey,* the song goes: "A canopy bed has lots of class/And so does a ceiling made of glass." Cohn has them both in his ornate bedroom, which is also a kind of recreation room and office and gallery for his collection of frogs — stuffed frogs, china frogs — and toy soldiers. He admits to a certain vanity — religious about doing his 200 sit-ups every day. All this while dictating to his male secretary, Vincent Millard.

COHN: Did you remember I had a lunch date with Barbara Walters?

VINCENT MILLARD: When is that?

COHN: Today.

SAFER: Cohn maintains a permanent expensive tan. In the harsh months, he somehow finds a business reason to head for Acapulco or Hawaii. He's a familiar figure in the best restaurants and tailors and barber shops, and regularly gets the works in places like the Beverly Hills Hotel. He is a sybarite who manages to take his pleasures with at least one ear tuned to business.

COHN: Somebody have a pencil?

SAFER: Cohn has no small talk. He'll tell you unrepeatable gossip about his enemies, and he will praise his friends. The rest is just business. It is always business when he visits Studio 54, that over-publicized disco parlor in New York. Here gather the hip and the old and the odd. Any night, it is the mob scene from a Fellini movie. Cohn may look and feel uncomfortable in this goofy setting, but he goes. Lately, he goes because the owners of the place are his clients, and they've pleaded guilty to income tax evasion. Federal authorities say they've skimmed millions in cash from the place. They'll be sentenced next month. Cohn also goes because he likes to be seen with this week's jet set. Once in a while he'll escort a model, but New York's matchmakers have given up on him. He's just not the marrying kind, though at one time, he says, he and Barbara Walters almost got married. Barbara won't comment, except to praise Roy for his loyalty.

COHN: We're getting married when we're both sixty. Although I must say, in fairness to her, she disagrees with me politically like about a hundred percent, because she's far more liberal than I am in practically every area.

SAFER: Well, why haven't you gotten married?

COHN: I always felt that being a controversial person and being a person that people are always going to be fighting about and over and always destined to be always in some kind of battle or other, that I could go through it better if all I had to worry about was myself, not a wife and kids who are going to have part of the heartache pushed over on them.

SAFER: Roy Cohn came to law with good connections. His father was a gentle-mannered New York state judge, and young Roy met all the right people.

COHN: When I went down as chief council for the McCarthy committee, I totally broke with my own background, with my own past. In other words, here I was, a young Jewish Democrat from New York, supposedly the most liberal — one of the most liberal cities in the United States, going down to become chief counsel for a fellow like Joe McCarthy.

SAFER: To what extent was — was Roy Cohn the — the — the Jewish lawyer from New York going to — out to prove that he was as good an American as any Irish Catholic or WASP lawyer?

COHN: I buy your thought, and I think there is something to it, but the script was a little bit different than that. I did resent very much the idea of associating Jews with a — a sympathy toward Communism. And I — I do admit the fact that this is something that has always bothered me, and I've tried in every way I can to make it clear that the fact my name is Cohn and the fact of my religion has nothing to do except perfect compatibility with my love for America and my dislike for Communism.

SAFER: In the mosaic of New York politics, Roy Cohn is all things to all men. This registered Democrat feels perfectly at home at the East Side Conservative Club. He drifts through a crowd of well-wishers who might fear him, or admire him, or might feel that one day they'll need him. It's hard to say how much political influence he has, but a lot of people believe he has it, and that can be enough. It's all very New York. The Irish bagpipes of the very Irish New York City detective band serenade the Jewish lawyer and his good buddy, the Cardinal's representative.

AULETTA: But how did this man bounce back and become so respectable? Roy, oddly enough, benefitted from a kind of an innocence by association. He — he developed, and throughout his boyhood he had, close friends, and he went to their parties all the time. And people would see Roy, this pariah, in the corner, and others would — Ed Weisl, Cyrus Vance, others — would be talking to him. So they came to feel, well, he can't be that bad.

COHN: I don't think it was a question of pulling anything off. I've tried to give loyalty and I've tried to give friendship. And I find in life when you gi — extend friendship and you extend loyalty, you get it back.

PROFESSOR ROBERT BLECKER (introducing Cohn in a law class): We've seen Roy Cohn twice. What have we seen? A person of great charm, intellect, misstatement, accomplishment and hypocrisy.

SAFER: Do not be deceived. Regard this as a friendly introduction of Cohn at New York Law School. Professor Bob Blecker prepares his students for a series of Roy Cohn lectures.

PROFESSOR BLECKER: Mr. Cohn is a person who thinks very little of truth, but much of genuineness. He's a master of deception, and yet a detester of ceremony. A nice guy who's done and does some lousy things. A protector, a paladin, a friend in court of organized crime.

RATHER: Roy Cohn is not an enigma. He's simply a man who is seen differently by different people. If you engaged in amateur analysis, you might say that Roy Cohn was the kid on the block that all the bullies beat up on. And so, when Roy Marcus Cohn was growing up, he was determined to get rich and get even. And he has.

Letters

DAN RATHER: About last week's story on Micronesia,* we heard from Henry Kissinger, who took exception to our quoting him as saying, "There are only 90,000 people out there. Who gives a damn?" Dr. Kissinger's rejoinder: "I have no recollection of ever having said anything like that. I do not know the context in which it was alleged to have been said. It certainly does not reflect my views about Micronesia."

If Dr. Kissinger is upset, the man he should be upset with is Walter Hickel, who served with him in the Nixon Cabinet. According to the former Secretary of Interior, "who gives a damn" is exactly what he was told by the former Secretary of State.

---

*This segment, *"Who Gives a Damn?"* was originally broadcast on December 23, 1979 and was repeated on June 15, 1980. See page 615.

JANUARY 6, 1980

CCCP-TV in Moscow

WILLIAM K. McCLURE, PRODUCER

HARRY REASONER: People as diverse as E. B. White, Edward R. Murrow, Newton Minow and Captain Kangaroo have worried about what America has done with the great potential of television. But what about television when it's controlled, when it grows in accordance with a philosophy and not a market, when the people in charge are determined to make it a force for good and progress, according to their lights? Is the product much better, or even much different, from the American commercial enterprise that just grew?

There's a great laboratory to study this question. Those aren't the call letters, but they could be. And 60 MINUTES went there and found television as popular as it is here — and sometimes even more tiresome.

In 1970, the Soviets finished Ostankino, a depressingly monolithic building that was designed to have the latest facility for every kind of TV production. Ten thousand people work in this structure, but the parking lots are never full. They come by bus or tram. Security is tight. Even accredited visitors must be checked in and out with escort. But let's be fair. Security is tight at CBS, ABC and NBC, too. Something about television attracts people who require security screening, as Karl Marx might have said, if he had thought of it. And, as in all Soviet enterprises, there is a great emphasis on working hard for the state. If you are a high achiever, you get your picture up on the bulletin board. There are high achievers who are performers, too. A favorite: Alla Pugachova, who could probably make it in any political system.

(Alla Pugachova singing)

From the TV tower in Moscow, the city's tallest structure, with, sure enough, a restaurant two-thirds of the way up, and subsidiary centers dotted in the Soviet Union's 15 federated republics, programming is available to 90 percent of the country's 260 million people across eight time zones. Some programs help to preserve the diversity of a land where 120 languages are spoken, but there's probably more emphasis on TV as a unifying, standardizing message.

I don't know exactly what we expected to see, but it's not all gray and grim. There is a sugar coating of diversity around the service of the state — a spoof on American Westerns, for instance. (Music) In some ways, the Soviets are still in the "Ed Sullivan Show" phase. (Music) They have no fear of classics, like this war film from the early work of Eisenstein. (Film theme) There's nothing against some rather heavy-handed satire, as long as it's satire about Western culture. (Music) Many times the arts are handled straightforwardly and beautifully. If this is propaganda, it's hard to argue against it. (Ballet music) Fred Silverman, properly briefed, might even recognize an elementary form of situation comedy. (Excerpt from television show) Talk shows. You know about talk shows. The difference is in Moscow you are more apt to get cosmonauts being modest and patriotic than double entendre between Johnny Carson and Zsa Zsa Gabor. (Applause . . . music: "Bridge on the River Kwai") Sometimes even a little sex creeps in. (Music)

This is not the sex. This is the message. (Leonid Brezhnev shown) Lenin never saw television, but he knew how to use the media. "The role of the press," he said,

"Some programs help to preserve the diversity of a land where 120 languages are spoken, but there's probably more emphasis on TV as a unifying, standardizing message."

"is not only that of a collective propagandist, but also that of an agitator." From the standpoint of what a Communist government wants to do with its population, television might have been invented for the rulers of today's Soviet Union.

In a way, the specially guarded news area reflects that awareness and, in a way, they treat news in some of the same manner American television does. The news producers have every facility an American network would have: Associated Press, UPI, Tass, Agence-France Presse. But then comes what they do differently with the facilities. You have to remember this about Soviet journalism. They don't feel guilty that they use only news that is helpful to the state. They think, instead, Americans are crazy to let their journalists report discord and diversity, trivialities and, to them, pointless violence.

These people are deciding on the order of items for a news broadcast. The order. The nature of the items has already been decided at a higher level. Henrikus Jushkevitshus, a vice chairman of Soviet television who has wide acquaintance with Western broadcasting styles, explained.

HENRIKUS JUSHKEVITSHUS: We are state organization, and chairman of state television and radio committee is member of government, so it's not our task to criticize government. Our task is to help government, but, of course, on television you can see not only positive stories, you can see also negative stories.

REASONER: Could a journalist in the — the Soviet Union expose a Watergate situation?

JUSHKEVITSHUS: We don't have Watergate. (Laughter)

REASONER: That's — that makes things simpler, if you don't — if you have no problems. But you couldn't do it, even if you did? You could not expose it?

JUSHKEVITSHUS: It's theoretical question. I am practical man. (Laughter)

REASONER: In news broadcasts, the Russians do not use correspondents in the American sense, anchors who are also reporters. Their men and women anchors are presenters, announcers, who essentially read what they are told to read, which doesn't prevent them from becoming popular. They don't get American-style salaries, but they get a lot of mail and a lot of perquisites.

This pair is one of four teams on the daily showcase of Soviet television news. "Vremya," a half-hour summary of what the Russians regard as all the news that's fit to broadcast, on in the primest of time every night. (Music) "Vremya," which means time and is labeled an information program, likes to begin with some upbeat domestic news: no crime or violence, but maybe an interminable paean of delight that the harvest is coming in. Almost every night we watched there was a harvest story. The suspense was bearable. (Voice of newscaster) Then, maybe a story about energy and how important it is. You can watch coal being carried from one place to another for five minutes. This has two effects, one intended: you realize the importance of energy; and you go to sleep. There is an apparently obligatory weekly story on the progress of the new Trans-Siberian Railroad. Each new link is celebrated on the air. The viewers have several years of new links ahead to look forward to. (Voices in Russian) Americans critical of American policy understandably get more time on Soviet television than Russians critical of Russian policy. (Jane Fonda shown) There are other regular news-oriented programs. "Today in the World" is a daily commentary, occasionally using Western sources to make an anti-Western point.

I was introduced a few years ago to a man named Valentin Zorin, and he was described as the Walter Cronkite of Soviet television. Not exactly. What he is is sort of a biased Charles Kuralt, frequently on the road in the United States for the folks back in Moscow, on the bad roads, mostly.

We talked about journalism to Volodya Posner, a commentator whose parents were Soviet officials living in New York when he grew up, accounting for his completely American English.

VOLODYA POSNER: The fact of the matter is that people here are very — very much aware politically. They are interested in what's happening around the world. And traveling, I've — I've come to the conclusion that these people, the Soviets, are probably the most politically oriented; that is, interested in what's happening in other countries, not only in their own.

REASONER: In programming in general, what's the emphasis on? Is it on cultural — drama, music, that kind of thing — or education or propaganda?

POSNER: Well, propaganda's a — is a — is a — ambiguous word. I believe Woody Guthrie, you probably know, used to say that, to the five o — five-year-old little boy that doesn't want to go to sleep, a lullaby is propaganda. Depends how you look at it. Sixty percent of our program is — programming is culture, music, sports, education in the narrower sense of the word — that kind — re — you know, that kind — entertainment. About 12 percent is news, 10 percent is political commentary, and the rest is miscellaneous.

(Music)

REASONER: The rest, the miscellaneous, includes commercials of a sort. They are packaged once or twice a week into separate programs, and they serve the state, urging people to buy products that happen at the moment to be in good supply. (Excerpt from Russian commercial) They are defended as being just as informative as the rest of the programs, and they do mirror the glacial movement of the Soviet Union toward humoring the consumer.

(Music)

These are consumers. Soviet television is broadcast in excellent color, but most ordinary citizens see it in black and white. A worker can buy a black-and-white set for an amount equivalent to one or two months' salary, but he can get convenient time payments. The average family spends 12 hours a week watching one of television's four channels: the national network, local or regional stations, and the educational channel.

(Music)

There are no Nielsen ratings as such in the Soviet Union, but they know which programs are the most popular, and we spent some time at one of the most successful. It's called, roughly, "Let's Go, Girls." It's part game show, part beauty contest, part propaganda. It's 90 minutes long, and they rehearse each show for two weeks. Its production values, as they say in the trade, are fairly rich: a live horse and a carriage to bring the contestants to the studio, a live audience, celebrity judges.

(Voice of master of ceremonies)

There was a master of ceremonies, not much different from masters of ceremonies on "Let's Make a Deal" or "The Dating Game." He cheerfully introduced a visitor in the audience.

MASTER OF CEREMONIES: (Speaking in Russian . . . introduces Harry Reasoner . . . applause).

REASONER: For "Let's Go, Girls," the producers pick a different industry each time. The day we were there, each contestant represented a different job in transportation. There was a streetcar driver, an airline stewardess, a train guard, a stewardess from a passenger ship and a subway attendant. (Excerpt from show) After some intellectual tests, each of the young women danced with a partner. (Music) The rationale for what might be called a sex-exploitation show in the United States is that the wit and wisdom of the young women is the really important thing. That's what they say in the Miss American Pageant, too. (Music . . . applause) The producer of "Let's Go, Girls" explained the prizes don't mean much, but the contestants do become celebrities. They get lots of letters, and a good many of the letters are offers of marriage or acting jobs.

You see a good deal more of this kind of thing on Soviet television now, more than just a few years ago, and it's probably done more smoothly — but the staple for informing and educating the Soviet citizen remains heavier fare. (Singing at Soviet parade) For example, Soviet television covered, live, the whole long Red Square ceremonies for this year's remembrance of the October Revolution — three hours of mass pageantry and military display — and that night a reprise of those ceremonies was not only the leading item on the news, it was the only item on the news, for an hour. (Singing)

And that's the way it is in Moscow. (Singing)

And this is the way it is in Moscow. All of those stirring pictures of Soviet soldiers and tanks in Afghanistan that you've been seeing all week on the news, none of them have been seen in the Soviet Union. And last Wednesday, "Vremya," that major nightly news program, used two domestic stories before getting around to reading the Tass story about Afghanistan, without pictures.

B.M.O.C.

ALLAN MARAYNES, PRODUCER

MIKE WALLACE: It's a new year — every place, that is, except at Boston University. There, it seems, the more things change, the more they are the same, because for years BU's "BMOC" — Bad Man On Campus — has had that place in an uproar. The BMOC is John Silber, president of Boston University. His faculty voted recently by two to one to urge Silber's dismissal. And that followed by only a couple of weeks BU's condemnation by the Massachusetts Civil Liberties Union on charges of violating civil liberty and academic freedom. BU is a university in turmoil, traceable, almost everyone there will be happy to tell you, traceable to the methods and the philosophy of President John Silber.

DR. JOHN SILBER: A university is certainly not a democracy, if it is any good. The more democratic the university becomes, the lousier it becomes.

WALLACE: John Silber, who was born with a withered arm, announced when he came to Boston from the University of Texas eight years ago that BU was a patient near to death and that he, Silber, was the surgeon who had been called in to see if the patient could be saved. Silber has been engaged in surgery ever since and, for his pains, he is known on campus as a dictator. They call him a censor. They regard him as a kind of educational fascist.

STUDENT: There's no freedom of speech at Boston University. There's no freedom of the press at Boston University. And there's not even any freedom to think at Boston University.

STUDENT: The central administration of Boston University has established dictatorial powers over students, faculties and employees, showing contempt for the university community. We declare our lack of confidence in this central administration and call for its replacement. I'd like for all those in favor to stand! (Cheering)

WALLACE: What you're looking at is Harvard University on the banks of Boston's Charles River — a school with an unassailable academic reputation, a huge endowment and, in the late seventies, a placid campus. Further down river is MIT — the Massachusetts Institute of Technology — another giant of higher education, prosperous and quiet. And just across the river, their poor neighbor, BU, Boston University, with an endowment that is minuscule compared to Harvard and MIT. It also has a faculty bitterly vocal about the president of the university.

PROFESSOR ARNOLD OFFNER: John Silber has alienated every single constituent element in this university.

WALLACE: Arnold Offner is a Professor of History and a winner of Boston University's Metcalf Award, given annually for excellence in teaching.
Why should John Silber want to turn the BU college community against him? Why?

PROFESSOR OFFNER: I don't know why he would want to do it. I can only describe what it is he has done. Anyone whose definition of excellence is different from John's, then he assumes that that person is either weak or corrupt or ineffective and the voice has to be stilled or stifled, discouraged in terms of achieving any kind of justice or fair play under the system.

STUDENT: He alienates the students. He alienates the faculty. He alienates the people who work in the administration.

WALLACE: Why would he want to do a thing like that? He's —

STUDENT: Because he runs this place like a corporation, not like a university.

STUDENTS: Yeah!

WALLACE: Silber would undoubtedly plead guilty and promptly point out that it's a successful corporation, its balance sheet showing it in the black, an accomplishment that many private colleges across the country only dream of.

DR. SILBER: I didn't come in with a mandate to maintain the status quo, because the status quo was sto — was so instable that the university would have been destroyed. It would have been bankrupt right now, had not drastic changes been made. It's been necessary to say to some, "You aren't good enough. Your tenure is denied." And to say to others, "You are good enough, but you're not the most outstanding, and we're going to save the highest salary increase for those who are better."

WALLACE: That infuriates the faculty. In 1976, the faculty senate voted three to one that they had no confidence in the administration of John Silber.

When you first came here you said, "Unless I have the confidence of all concerned, of the university community, I don't want to stay around." And yet, in '76, apparently you didn't have the — the confidence of your faculty?

DR. SILBER: Well, you — you have greater confidence in the meaning of that vote than I have.

WALLACE: Why?

DR. SILBER: When the faculty votes that I can't manage the university successfully, they'd better look at a few of the facts. One is that Boston University was in a deficit position when I got here, and it has now had six uninterrupted years of balanced budgets. It has built its reserves. It has built its faculty. Its reputation is much enhanced. Now, after all of those accomplishments, for somebody to conclude that it's been mismanaged by John Silber, it puts the burden on them, in my opinion, and I would just rest on the record instead of resting on a show of hands.

WALLACE: Arthur Metcalf is founder and head of the Electronics Corporation of America and chairman of BU's Board of Trustees. It is after him that the coveted Metcalf Award is named. What does he think about the BU administration of John Silber?

ARTHUR METCALF: Well, the proof of the pudding is in the eating. We have more students, better students, more faculty, better faculty, and more outside fiscal support.

WALLACE: Then what in the world is the reason for all the tension across the river at BU, at least among certain groups?

METCALF: He is driving, he is ambitious, he is brilliant. He doesn't suffer fools gladly. And like some of the rest of us, he perhaps exhibits a little bit of impatience.

PROFESSOR OFFNER: But by and large, he has created far more chaos, far more havoc, and needless — absolutely needless — tension and trauma on this campus than is required.

WALLACE: Do you know a Professor of History by the name of Arnold Offner?

DR. SILBER: Yes.

WALLACE: Good professor?

DR. SILBER: No.

WALLACE: He won the Metcalf Award.

DR. SILBER: Oh, you see, again, what — what — let — shall we start over on that one?

WALLACE: Why?

DR. SILBER: Hmm?

WALLACE: I asked you a question: "You know Offner. A good professor?" "No."

DR. SILBER: Yes, I — I — I would not regard — I would not regard Offner as a man I would recruit.

WALLACE: Professor Offner says, "John Silber has alienated every single constituency in this university."

DR. SILBER: Well, he is — he is just not true. He doesn't claim that I have alienated the trustees. Surely not! He does not claim that I have alienated the alumni. He wouldn't have a chance of making good on that claim. If he claims that I have alienated the students, then he makes up the evidence, because the evidence won't support it.

WALLACE: Well, he has alienated some of them. These students run a newspaper called *BU Exposure,* bitterly critical of Silber and all his works. They claim he is a censor because of Silber's new publication policy that provides no financial assistance to student-run newspapers.

STUDENT: Let me show you four or five of the things of the student publications that have been killed on campus —

WALLACE: Killed?

STUDENT: — that are no longer with us.

WALLACE: Killed by the administration?

STUDENT: Dead, gone. This is *Commonwealth Monthly* magazine. It's award winning. It was award winning. This is the BU *Women's Yellow Pages.* That, along with their newscenter, is dead. This was a 61-year-old weekly.

DR. SILBER: We decided it is a mistake to be publishing a student newspaper, because either you are held responsible for the slip-ups, for the — the infelicities that students get engaged in, that students are responsible for, or you end up having to censor them. And we wanted to do neither. We don't intend to — to censor any student newspaper and, consequently, we don't intend to be in the newspaper business. They can publish whatever they please, because we don't — we don't have any responsibility for them.

WALLACE: The *BU Exposure* was pleased to publish an allegation that Silber had sold admissions to BU's medical and law schools, a charge Silber denies. One second-year law student confronted him with that allegation and came away shaken.

STUDENT: He compared us — our tactics, that is — to the KGB, an inference, I thought, was rather unwarranted. But the man was incredibly abusive. I walked out of that office in a state of shock.

DR. SILBER: He came into my office and read me an anonymous letter which accused me of all kinds of — of activities that were completely false, such as selling admissions to the law school and irregularities with regard to admissions in the law school.

I then picked up an anonymous letter and read it to him, and said, "Here, I have an anonymous letter which reports that your anonymous letter was written by a professor in order to gain sexual favors from a student. Now, which anonymous letter shall we believe?" And I said, "What I do, and what any civilized and decent man does, is to throw anonymous letters in the wastebasket. You, by contrast, behave like the KGB, and on the basis of an — of an unnamed and unknowable informer, you try to go out and get an indictment against somebody." I said, "Save that for a totalitarian regime." You may find that abusive. I don't. I find that just trying to explain to a second-year law student something about due process of law. I think it's pathetic when a law student doesn't know more about it than that young man did. Now the fact is, the student had already been admitted, so we were not using money as a substitute for academic quality, hence we were not selling the indulgence. He was already in school. What we were doing is doing some perfectly straightforward fund-raising after the fact of admission had taken place.

WALLACE: I read back to Silber something he was quoted as having said about the people responsible for *BU Exposure*.

This is what you say about the people who run *BU Exposure:* "I think what you've got are short-pants Communists who want to be real tough revolutionaries to bring about a new world order. They absolutely despise freedom of speech, despise the First Amendment, will hide behind it or any other thing they can find in order to produce their own totalitarian claptrap."

DR. SILBER: Uh-hmm, that's pretty good. That's a pretty fair description of what they're about.

WALLACE: Really?

DR. SILBER: That's right. They really believe that you can engage in a kind of yellow journalism and — and change the institutions of the society around. And what they lack is the class. They lack the class and the knowledge and the ability to — and the respect for truth that is required to really change things.

WALLACE: Understandably, it is candor like that that has alienated much of the student body, and a fair number of faculty members as well.

PROFESSOR HOWARD ZINN: Well, you feel that somehow some group of men has been planted here by a foreign power and is occupying Boston University. (Cheers)

WALLACE: Political Science professor Howard Zinn.

Something special happened when John Silber took over? What?

PROFESSOR ZINN: A change in the atmosphere. A sudden beginning of awareness that from now on we were in the clutches of somebody very tough and very hard who had no particular concern for people as human beings — a man quick to call the police, a man quick to suppress dissent, a man quick to fire people who disagreed with him. And it didn't take long for a certain atmosphere of fear, something close to fear, to develop.

DR. SILBER: He has the right to be that ignorant.

WALLACE: He's an ignorant man?

DR. SILBER: Yes, he's an ignorant man, about me. He doesn't know anything about it. I'm a figment of his imagination.

WALLACE: Why, do you imagine?

DR. SILBER: Because I think Mr. Zinn has a political purpose that doesn't have anything to do with the truth. He's probably read Sol Olinsky's rules for radicals, and he knows if you take rule number thirteen, personalize the issue, that you can arouse quite a few people against that old demon Silber. When he organizes a student rally he leaves before the police come, over and over again. I point that out to the students every time he's engaged in a rally. I say, "Watch Mr. Zinn, and when Mr. Zinn leaves, you leave with him because then you won't get arrested."

WALLACE: And why do you think he leaves before the police come?

DR. SILBER: Because I think he's a Judas goat. He leads his little lambs to whatever slaughter he can arrange in order to create a media event. When you can come on a campus and you hear that every member of that faculty is perfectly prepared to talk to you and tell you how wrong and how bad and how wicked I am, it must be that, at the very least, there is no intimidation on that campus and remarkable freedom of expression.

STUDENT: We cannot quit until Long John Silver is out of our lives and back on a cattle ranch in Texas, where he belongs. (Clapping)

WALLACE: But if the students are free to take their whacks at him, he is no less candid in describing what he perceives to be one of his functions as president of Boston University.

DR. SILBER: I essentially give students the bad news at Boston University. I think if a child walks up and down the piano, the — the greatest favor you can do to the child is to tell him to get off the piano.

When I first came here, I was asked by the students to visit the dormitories, and I was supposed to discover how bad they were architecturally. What I discovered was that most of the rooms were filthy. And I came out with the conclusion that, evidently, the students believed that filth was a cultural achievement, and I was not impressed. Now that, I don't think, won me very many friends among the students at the time, but I think that — that the students who didn't like it when they heard it, many of them went back and cleaned their rooms.

METCALF: There are many great men — and John is a great man — like George Patton, who have a spectrum of personality qualities and some faults.

WALLACE: And you know what people will say? We don't want a general running a university.

METCALF: Well, I hadn't thought of George Patton so much as a general as I thought of him as a great leader.

WALLACE: I know.

METCALF: And you certainly want a great leader in Boston University. Boston University has established a record that is as day is to night since John Silber has first joined the university.

DR. SILBER: I'll be quite satisfied, if when I leave Boston University, Boston University is solvent; it is substantially better than it was when I came, as it clearly is right now; and if everyone who knew me while I was here says, "I — I sure don't like him." I really don't care about that. I can't win all the fights. I will try to win the important ones. And the important ones are making this place academically sound and meaningful, and addressing students as if they were adults.

(Music)

WALLACE: Last May's graduation ceremonies went smoothly enough with no incident to mar the day, though the tension on campus persists. Meantime, donations to the university increase. They have risen four-fold since John Silber arrived. Government and nongovernment grants and contracts have tripled in that time. The caliber of the faculty has improved. The number of applications for admission to BU has risen by half in the last five years. And the SAT scores of entering freshmen are now high above the national average. And still and all, John Silber remains the most hated man at Boston University.

Native Sons

JOHN TIFFIN, PRODUCER

MORLEY SAFER: "Native Sons" is about black Americans who returned to Africa, long before Alex Haley and *Roots,* to found the first republic on that continent; Liberia, a nation on the east coast of Africa whose roots are in the United States.

Most of the news of Africa, independent Africa and southern Africa, has been a catalogue of brutality, tribal war and insane slaughter. Well, Liberia is free of those things, but it suffers from a different, less newsworthy kind of African sickness. The sadness and seediness, petty corruption and grand larceny, black and white mischief – you'll find it all in Liberia.

Liberia calls itself a republic. In fact, it is an oligarchy, ruled by a few, by the few that belong to 300 families descended from the original settlers, families who are at the top and see to it that they stay at the top.

A hundred and fifty years ago, American philanthropists and freed slaves had the idea of a state in Africa. It was in no sense a return to a promised land, but an escape from a land that held no promise.

The Liberian Declaration of Independence is modeled on the American one, except for some key language. It states that Liberians were originally Americans who were forced by conditions to seek asylum abroad from their deep degradation. And so, they landed on this beach as colonists, American colonists, who imposed themselves on what they called the uncivilized natives.

Africa was as alien to them as it was to the first white settlers elsewhere and, just as in the white settlements, everything that was done was done in the name of Christian civilization.

(Church bells tolling)

They brought with them their Western religion and proceeded to convert the natives to it. The result has been a unique Christianity with echoes of an Africa as old as life. (Music) But to those pilgrim fathers, America was the old country. They named places "Maryland" and "New Georgia" and "Virginia," and they built houses that have that same Southern look, a cross between the old slave quarters and the old plantation house.

The absence of a colonial legacy has its disadvantages: no tradition of civil service, terrible communications, primitive education and medical care. In

Liberia, they started from scratch, with little outside help, not even the conscience money its neighbors received from former colonial masters. All it got from America was a memory. The grand old flag with 49 fewer stars. The currency is the U.S. dollar. The mail boxes are American. The cop on the beat wears a New York City Police Department uniform. The capital is Monrovia, named after U.S. President James Monroe. Liberia is stable – stable without the paratroop enforcers you find in so much of black and white Africa.

This is the Liberia most familiar to Americans, the Liberia of President William Tubman. He ran things as an elected dictator for 27 years. It had the look of nineteenth century American in blackface. Tubman insisted on things like silk hats and frock coats. Everyone, diplomats included, sweated it out in the West African heat. But the clothes clearly defined the classes. The only thing the colonialists had in common with the natives was the color of their skin. It was rule by elite, by the top 300 families who could trace their lineage back to the exodus.

Well, Tubman's gone. He died eight years ago, and was replaced by this man, William Tolbert. The president still sets the rules for dress. The leisure suit has replaced the frock coat. There have been other changes, but mainly in look and style.

(Crowd cheers President Tolbert)

It is still rule by elite, by the top people, who regard the nation as a private inheritance. The president disputes this, says Liberia is a democracy. It does have an American-style constitution, a Senate and a House of Representatives, and free elections. But there's only one party, and that's been the case for all of this century.

Liberians resent things like the report that Ambassador Andrew Young described them as a bunch of Uncle Toms. And they're angry with President Carter, who passed through the country on his trip to Africa. No way to be treated by the mother country!

ETHEL DUNBAR: You see, the President passed through here and went to Nigeria and stayed here for days and came here for a few hours. That's your daughter? You pass by your daughter and go somebody else place, and stay two, three days, and you lay — (don't) even lay your head on one pillow in her house? Tell her we don't like it, and she must change her ways. Thank you. (Laughter . . . clapping)

SAFER: The top families, known as Honorables, number about 40,000 out of Liberia's 1.7 million people. They have names like Carter and Phillips and Dennis. This is a wedding party that the Coopers are giving for the Campbells.

There are impossibly complicated cross-connections through intermarriage in these family trees. It insures that power and money remains in the same hands generation after generation. And the American connection is continually being reinforced. Most young Americo-Liberians are educated in the United States, and they often bring back American brides.

That's what one of the Bernard brothers did. They've both just returned from college at North Carolina and western Michigan to take up the family fortune amassed by the their late father, the former director of police.

So, there's the transportation company, the car rental, the bus service, the —

BERNARD BROTHER: Yes.

SAFER: — heavy trucking of gas?

BERNARD BROTHER: Right.

SAFER: There's this extraordinary beach-front property that's going to become a holiday hotel?

BERNARD BROTHER: Exactly. Apartments, farms.

BERNARD BROTHER: Other real estate here and there.

SAFER: This is not, I got to tell you, an image of Africa and Africans that most Americans have.

BERNARD BROTHER: We do have a mixture of the indigenous African and then what some will call the civilized African. We are sort of a blend of, you know, both.

(Chanting, singing crowd)

SAFER: One of the reasons for the blend is that marital fidelity in Liberia is almost unheard of. President Tolbert himself has only one wife, but he has children by many women and is said to be as virile at 65 as he was in his twenties. He's a Baptist minister and former head of the World Baptist Alliance, but he feels no moral or ethical conflict.

You know, one of the fascinating things about life in this country, particularly for an outsider, are these — these — the family relationships. I mean, how it works, so that a man may have a wife and a couple of mistresses, and have children that are born out of wedlock that are, nevertheless, brought into the family. In — in your own youth, I gather, sir, that you fathered children outside your immediate family. How does it work?

PRESIDENT WILLIAM TOLBERT: It worked well. Li — Liberian life, it's peculiar life. In fact, we are a close-knit people. If you touch one, you touch more or less all. Those who are not related by blood, somehow or another, they are close. We have what we call the extended family life.

SAFER: The Bernard boys had the same father but different mothers — one the father's wife, the other their father's friend.

It isn't a question of many wives?

BERNARD BROTHERS: No, no, no.

SAFER: Just one wife.

BERNARD BROTHER: It's the —

BERNARD BROTHER: We don't — it's not a matter of polygamy. It's — it's — there's only one wife. My father's only had one wife, at a time, and it's — it's not a matter of just —

SAFER: He had one wife, but how many children did he have by women other than that one wife?

BERNARD BROTHER: Oh, about 13.

SAFER: Really?

BERNARD BROTHER: Yeah.

SAFER: Liberia has great wealth, and has a reputation for being a easy pickings for the international conglomerates, providing they deal with the right families. Firestone Tire owns most of the rubber, along with eminent Liberians. The field hands earn $7.50 a week. And there's iron. A foreign consortium extracts the ore, and the government extracts half their profits. And for special people, special shares were created. So, a few benefit grandly from this joint venture.

And Liberia has the world's largest shipping fleet registered under its flag, a flag of convenience, the convenience being tax breaks and casual scrutiny of crews and ships. And there's talk of oil, and there's uranium and gold and diamonds, and vast resources of timberlands that are just beginning to be exploited. But the fact is, most of the wealth that all of those natural blessings Liberia has stays up there among the 40,000 people at the top of the heap.

And no one is more top than William Tolbert. This great-great-grandchild of slavery, who can trace his roots back to South Carolina, has farms and rubber plantations and family connections with businesses all over the country.

(Native music and dancing)

He is president of a republic, but he lives like a feudal prince — or, more correctly, an enlightened African chief. (President Tolbert handing out money) All up the west African coast it is called "dash," the small gift to a servant who has performed well — crisp, new U.S. currency to his workers and their families and, while the cameras are there, to just about anyone who asks.

President Tolbert deplores the very idea that anyone might believe that Liberia is controlled by family compacts. Well, take a look at the country's biggest private business. The Mesurado Corporation is involved in many things. Its biggest enterprise is fishing — catching and freezing shrimp and lobster for the export market. It also has a monopoly on commercial fishing for the domestic market. Vice president in charge of Mesurado fishing: Richard Tolbert — Harvard, Columbia Law School, and the president's nephew.

RICHARD TOLBERT (on telephone):   If you need to get any more people on a temporary basis, do.

SAFER: Over at Mesurado's headquarters you'll find more Tolberts: Stephanette, vice president in charge of everything; Cietta Tolbert, working her way up through the finance department; and Laurie Tolbert, in charge of retail sales.

It's rare to find a — a — a firm anywhere that's such a family firm as this one.

STEPHANETTE TOLBERT: If there's any crisis, the family automatically binds together, so that if you're in any kind — if there're any kind of problems, it's just a matter of picking up the phone and saying, "I need you," and everybody comes, and that's the way we've been brought up.

SAFER: Business is business, politics is politics, and family is family. President Tolbert says he'll not run again when his term is up in five years.

PRESIDENT TOLBERT (on telephone):   We don't have $750,000 to give you, either.

SAFER: Among the most likely candidates are Shad Tubman, son of the former president and son-in-law of Mr. Tolbert. But the man most people in Monrovia say is the hottest candidate is this man: A. Benedict Tolbert, trained at Oberlin University, a gentleman farmer, a dynamo of a politician — and the son of the president.

A. BENEDICT TOLBERT: I am the chairman of the Foreign Affairs Committee of the House of Representatives. I am also the co-chairman on the Committee on Education. I'm also a member of the Committee on Information and Cultural Affairs. Out of government, I am the president of the Liberian Federation of Trade Unions. Also, a minister of the Gospel, an Evangelist and spiritualist.

SAFER: That's pretty full — full day you've described.

A. B. TOLBERT: That's right. (Laughs) Personally, I am a child of the universe and I belong to the school of a Senate Master's teaching called the Great White

Brotherhood. There are several hierarchies in the universal cosmological world, and so you have a master in charge of wealth, who's called the Master Fortuna. You have a master in charge of governments and nations of the world called El Moyer. You have a master in charge of freedom of the universe called Saint Germain. You have a master for justice called Porshe. You have a m — master for wisdom called the Goddess of Mercury. But this does not bring about blasphemy, nor does it make them out several gods. It doesn't bring about a pantheon of gods. And if it were not so, I would not have told you.

SAFER: Tell me, in purely practical terms, and one hears this rumored about in political circles here, that you're a pretty good candidate to be the next president of Liberia.

A. B. TOLBERT: I believe I am because of the way I live. You see, God doesn't make many leaders. He makes few leaders. If he made many leaders, then he wouldn't have followers. (Laughs)

SAFER: But in a — in a purely personal way, does this — does this cause some family quarrels or tensions?

A. B. TOLBERT: Not at all. Not at all. I am not ambitious to become president. I only regard myself as a presidential timber because I know I'm capable of governing not only Liberia but the whole of Africa. And if I — if — if the great divine master of human events decides through the minds of the people to use me as a presidential candidate, not only will I rule Liberia, but will I — I shall endeavor to rule the whole of Africa by uniting the continent. (Laughs)

SAFER: Into one?

A. B. TOLBERT: I — this is my goal, my — my — my objective and my aim in my lifetime to see Africa united.

SAFER: With A. B. Tolbert as president?

A. B. TOLBERT: Maybe. (Laughs)

PRESIDENT TOLBERT (laughing):   A chip from the block.

SAFER: And I gather you were a chip off your old man's block?

PRESIDENT TOLBERT (laughing):   Yes.

SAFER: Liberians, at an official level, deny that the country is ruled by nepotism, but at the same time they point to a number of things: that in white America, it is not unknown for certain powerful families to be in politics and business at the same time, or for the same old names to keep getting all the good jobs, or for networks of relatives and friends to look after their own, or for men in public life to be unfaithful to their wives. It's just that in the United States, hypocritically, we try to cover it up. That, rather refreshingly, is not one of the American qualities those African pilgrim fathers brought with them when they came to the dark continent.

See Letters, January 13, 1980, page 261.

Letters

DAN RATHER: Now the mail. About our story on light airplanes a viewer wrote: "If civilians (got) half the training required of military pilots, accidents would be reduced by 90 percent (in the case of many crashes) a mediocre army liaison pilot could have landed the plane and walked away."

About our interview with John Connally, most of the mail was like this: "You should be ashamed of your vicious attack on Governor Connally." And this: "After seeing your program on Governor Connally . . . if he receives only one vote, it will be mine." And finally this: "If John Connally can handle the Presidency as well as he handled (Mike Wallace) he will be a heck of a President."

JANUARY 13, 1980

Deee-fense

DREW PHILLIPS, PRODUCER

HARRY REASONER: The government in recent years has gotten involved in all kinds of occupational hazards, with rules and regulations to protect workers in a great number of dangerous lines of work. But there's one high-risk area it has hardly touched.

This is a man who got hurt on the job. Except for some movement in his head and shoulders and his right arm, he is paralyzed. His name is Darryl Stingley, and he was hurt one Sunday afternoon in Oakland, California. And while his injury many have been unusually severe, everyone in the National Football League gets hurt.

At the end of this season, almost 20 percent of the players in the NFL were on the disabled list, and another 20 percent had missed at least one game because of injuries. But statistics don't tell the story. More important is the fact that many of the league's most talented and exciting players went out. Among them: Dallas running Tony Dorsett with a separated shoulder; Miami running back Norm Bulaich, when his face mask was crushed into his face; the Jets' wide receiver, Wesley Walker, with a dislocated knee; Patriot tight end Russ Francis with broken ribs. And the quarterbacks, 14 of them, including: Baltimore's Bert Jones with a badly re-injured shoulder; Dan Pastorini, who cracked his ribs making a tackle; Pittsburgh's Terry Bradshaw a number ot times, various injuries.

When the cry "Deee-fense!" goes up at the Super Bowl next week in Pasadena, the quarterbacks will start to go down; so will a lot of other players. What we wanted to know was this: Is this the nature of football, a part of its appeal, or could you cut down on the bad knees and the bad backs and the broken fingers and still keep it the same game? To try to answer that, we looked into all of the factors said to be involved in pro football injuries. The first was artificial turf.

Artificial turf is literally a carpet, and like a carpet, it has a certain amount of underpadding. But beneath that is a hard base, usually asphalt. It's a good deal harder and more abrasive than grass. A study done for the NFL in 1974 showed a significantly greater number of major and minor injuries when a game was played on a synthetic surface. Some people would argue with that, but almost all the players we talked to couldn't agree more. Steelers quarterback Terry Bradshaw and running back Rocky Bleir.

TERRY BRADSHAW: Well, I don't like Astroturf. It's extremely hard. The burns that you receive from falling on the turf are very infectious. You get a lot of infection from them, a lot of discomfort; they're very painful.

ROCKY BLEIR: Astroturf, you know, has no cushion. All the stress and strain is within the shoe itself, and within the ankle joints and knee joints. When you practice on it every day, and when you play a majority of your games on it every year, it definitely takes its toll.

REASONER: Fourteen of the twenty-eight teams in the NFL play on artificial turf. Ed Garvey, head of the NFL Players Association, thinks he knows why it became so popular.

ED GARVEY: Well, initially, Monsanto argued in their publicity that it was going to reduce injuries, and I suspect a lot of people bought that line —that it would reduce knee and ankle injuries. The when the — that was proven to be fallacious, they started arguing that it was a lot cheaper to maintain, and I think a lot of the owners and the stadium people felt that they would cut down their costs. If they put in artificial turf, they could eliminate the grounds crew and so on. I think all of those arguments have now proven to be fallacious, but that accounts for the initial installation of artificial turf.

REASONER: NFL Commissioner Pete Rozelle knows how the players feel about artificial turf, and is sympathetic. But he says it's probably here to stay.

PETE ROZELLE: One of the key problems there is that the — the club does not have total say over the turf. A community puts up a stadium, they want maximum utilization; they — they want to be able to have a rock concert on Friday night, a baseball game on Saturday, and a football game on Sunday. And that's why a number of those new stadium turfs are artificial, so that they can maximize their utilization.

REASONER: A few weeks ago, Oilers quarterback Pastorini went back to pass in a playoff game, tripped on a seam in Houston's artificial turf, and ended up with a pulled groin muscle. There's no doubt football is a violent game; that's the reason for its wide appeal. As someone once said, "Football is not a contact sport, it's a head-on-collision sport." But to most players, including the Pittsburgh Steelers all-pro linebacker Jack Lambert, injuries are just part of the game.

JACK LAMBERT: I separated my shoulder the day before the Baltimore game, which was about eleven, twelve weeks ago, I guess.

REASONER: But you went out and played anyhow.

LAMBERT: Right. I've been pretty fortunate. I broke my ankle in the first Super Bowl, and I had a little knee problem — I stretched some ligaments in 1977. Other than that, besides the broken fingers and broken nose and what have you.

REASONER: Just routine stuff.

LAMBERT: Pretty lucky, yeah.

REASONER: Steeler defensive tackle Joe Greene.
What about cases that aren't really within the rules, but where players take action against other players that could cause injuries that don't really help the game. Is there much of that?

JOE GREENE: There is a bit of it, and I've been guilty of that. It's —

REASONER: Are — are you repentant?

GREENE: Oh, no, no! (Reasoner laughs) It's — it's — you have to take care of yourself.

REASONER: Is Joe Green's attitude common in the NFL, and is it a problem? Darryl Stingley thinks it is.

DARRYL STINGLEY: I would say that, you know, some players probably, you know, they definitely do have a problem like that. You know, from being coached from the peewee league to high school on throughout, you know, they've been coached and motivated, you know, in a certain way to get the adrenalin up, to so-called get the best of their ability, perform to the best of their ability. And you know, sometimes while they're being motiva — motivated, the — the aggression and which builds up in them, you know.

And they come out on the field, they're not thinking in — in — in — terms of that they're playing against another human being and how much, you know, pain or whatever that they can inflict on them. And they have that — that killer-type attitude that, really, pro football can do without.

REASONER: The win-at-any-cost, go-out-and-kill attitude is being taught to ten-year-olds in peewee leagues.

COACH (at peewee league game):   You go down after that ball, you come up and hit somebody, you understand? You're out here like this, looking around. What are you looking for? What are you looking for, son? Nothing, right? When you go back in there, you better knock somebody down, young 'un! That's what this game's all about. Now get in there for Bussy. And block!

(Excerpt from movie North Dallas Forty)

REASONER: These scenes are from the movie North Dallas Forty, based on the book by former Dallas receiver Peter Gent.

(Excerpt from North Dallas Forty: trainer injecting Novocain into player)

BRIG OWENS: Many scenes were, you know, very close to what happens in this game today.

REASONER: Former defensive back Brig Owens.

OWENS: As a player, you're almost really playing out of fear. You're afraid to let anyone take your job, feeling that if you are injured and you don't play that Sunday afternoon, there is going to be a guy that's going to come in and — and take your job, and just do such a great job that Sunday afternoon that you're not going to get a chance to come back in and play.

REASONER: Former Denver defenseman Dale Hackbart.

DALE HACKBART: Not being in the locker room for the — you know, for the last four or five years, I — I don't know if players are still taking bennies or pep pills or if they're, you know, taking Novocain to — to deaden an injury pain. I know it happened when I was playing. I have taken Novocain, you know, to — to deaden the pain in my ankle and in my hip to — you know, to get me through a game. And I — you know, I saw other players — players doing it. It was just — it was something that was expected if you wanted to play and — and if you could endure it.

REASONER: What about rules changes? Over the past four years, the NFL has approved twenty new rules designed to prevent injuries. Most, but not all, of the more vicious kinds of blocking and tackling have been banned; and an attempt has been made to protect quarterbacks by blowing the play dead as soon as defensive players get a hold of them. Most defensive players think the rules have been changed too much already. Most offensive players like them the way they are. And Terry Bradshaw, although grateful for the help he's been given, is afraid more changes could ruin the game.

BRADSHAW: I've been a strong advocate of no rule changes. It's very hard game, it's a very physical game, and it's one which the people certainly enjoy watching.

But when you start making rule changes to — to try to make the game safe and everything, protect people, you're going to start taking away from what has made the game so — so exciting.

REASONER: How about rules changes? Any of those that you think ought to come?

LAMBERT: Yeah, I think the quarterback should have to wear dresses — (Reasoner laughs) — so that we can —

REASONER: Terry, I have to report that one unidentified Steeler defenseman said quarterbacks ought to wear dresses.

BRADSHAW: Well, I wonder who said that? (Laughter) Well, that was Jack Lambert, and I think Jack is — is just reiterating what I said earlier about the more you change the rules to protect people, the less exciting are — the more you take away from what the game has been built on.

REASONER: Well then, what about equipment? Back in the good old days, helmets and pads were thin and soft, mostly made of leather; but plastic changed all that. Since hard plastic helmets and pads were devised, head injuries are down, but other kinds of injuries are up. Why?

BRADSHAW: The better the equipment, the harder it's used. And so, therefore — which is good (indistinct) it protects us. But still in all, players — you know, twenty years ago they used to arm tackle. Now they head tackle and they stick their head in the numbers and — and they drive with their legs, and then you land on an artificial surface which is very hard. So, the better the equipment is, the harder the blows.

REASONER: Hard shoulder pads have drawbacks too, according to Joe Greene.

GREENE: There is a — a large space between the hea — the shoulder pad and the neck, which causes the neck — a lot of free room in there. And this is what, in my opinion, causes neck injuries.

REASONER: At Wayne State University in Detroit, the National Operating Committee on Standards for Athletic Equipment has devised sophisticated tests for helmets. The results of these tests have established standards that have virtually eliminated head injuries from football. But Dr. Voigt Hodgson, one of the committee's directors, admits he is finding evidence of what Joe Greene complains of.

DR. VOIGT HODGSON: The helmet is doing the job of protecting the head very well nowadays. What we find about the neck is that it's very difficult with practical equipment to protect it. The only thing that we have found strangely enough so far on the — any kind of a humanoid model that we've had on here is a material called Silly Putty, which helps to strengthen the neck laterally and transfer some of the load from the helmet into the shoulders and shoulder pads.

REASONER: There's a man in Houston, Texas, who may have a better answer than Silly Putty. Byron Donzis is an inventor. He doesn't have a college degree, but he has a great knowledge of space age technology, and a knack for finding practical applications for it. He developed new lightweight pads for the Houston Oilers that kept many of their better players playing after they were injured.

He first became famous in football circles by inventing what has come to be called a "flak jacket" for Oiler quarterback Dan Pastorini — a lightweight, chest-high pad to protect Pastorini's ribs after the quarterback had cracked them this season for the fortieth time in his career.

DAN PASTORINI: This thing is a tremendous — tremendous asset, and hopefully it'll prevent a lot more serious injuries.

REASONER: He found a way to improve defensive end Elvin Bethea's shoulder pads so Bethea could play with a badly injured shoulder. And he devised new pads for running back Earl Campbell so Campbell could keep playing, in spite of a deep thigh injury, well enough to win the NFL rushing title. Campbell wasn't available to show off his pads, but Donzis demonstrated the principle behind it — on me.

This is where you're going to show me how it works? (Laughs)

BYRON DONZIS: This — you're right. I'm going to take your kneecap off and —

REASONER: Have I got it in the right place?

DONZIS: Yeah, we'll put it right up here, okay? And we'll just — I'll start off easy, and then we'll —

(Donzis covers Reasoner's knee with a pad, then hits it with a bar)

REASONER: If that weren't there, I'd have a broken knee.

DONZIS: I would think so.

REASONER: Donzis isn't just interested in keeping injured players on the field; he thinks he can perfect completely new, lightweight protective gear for players that will speed up the game and prevent injuries. Donzis has been given financial support from the NFL, and is using it to try to re-outfit football players from head to toe with pads that he says will give them much more protection but cut the weight of what they wear from an average of 26 pounds to three and a half pounds.

Can you show me on the — on the drawing how the helmet would work.

DONZIS: We'll have an air-inflated, foam-filled helmet, and it will have straps that — like your seat belts in your car, that will come around to a pulley on the shoulder and then to an inertia reel, and will allow you, so that when you're hit from one side or the other or whatever motion that you can make the normal motion; but if you take a fast blow, the inertia belt will take it and disperse the energy into the upper torso.

REASONER: So you won't jerk your neck, damage your back.

DONZIS: All those things, right.

REASONER: Coach "Bum" Phillips of the Oilers thinks Donzis is on the right track.

"BUM" PHILLIPS: I'm familiar with what he's talking about, and if he can come up with it — it will be the answer. They type of — of strap, that he's talking about putting on it, I'm really interested to see, because that is the one area that — that — you know, your ribs will heal up; your head and your neck don't heal up quite as fast.

REASONER: So the answer to our original question is, apparently: some injuries can and probably will be prevented in the future. Better fields, better equipment and better coaching can cut down the number of seriously hurt players. But there are other factors that make it clear there's no way to eliminate injuries completely. One of those factors is player size. The human body is constantly improving; getting bigger and faster. Back in the 1930's, the difference in weight between lineman and running backs averaged fourteen pounds. Today, the difference is forty-eight pounds.

BLEIR: I think that the biggest rule change is that somebody who would tackle you — they'd have a designated tackler — would have to be the same size that you are. (Reasoner laughs) Now, it's very difficult when you're five-nine and 200 pounds and you got a guy that's six-five, 270, he's taking swipes at you. It's just not fair. (Laughter)

REASONER: Another intangible in injuries is the player's concentration, according to Steeler coach Chuck Noll.

CHUCK NOLL: If you're concerned about injuries as a player, you're going to get hurt. It comes down to that. If you're distracted, if you have a family problem at home, your chances of injury go up considerably.

REASONER: And some experts say still another factor in injuries is the owners' attitudes toward players.

GARVEY: There's such a surplus of talent available from the colleges every year that the owners sort of take the position that, look, every player is replaceable. If a player goes down, that's because the — the game is a dangerous game and the — the knee was not made for football and things of that nature. Because there are always these replacements available to come in and take the place of the injured player. So, they have sort of a — a callous view of it, saying that no matter what you do there are going to be injuries, so therefore, let's not worry about it.

REASONER: After mulling over all we'd learned about plastic fields and plastic helmets and cheap shots and Novocain shots, we realized there's another factor involved. Author Bob Yeager, who has just written a book about sports injuries called *Seasons of Shame* , agrees. When you scrape away everything else, he notes, you find an underlying cause of injury – you and me, the fans. When you cheer violent men for their violence, they become more violent.

STINGLEY: I'd hate for anybody to go through what I've been through and what I have yet to go through, and the — the personal grief it's caused not only me, but my family and everyone involved in my life that knows me, you know. It's kind of had an effect on everybody. And I'd just hate to see that happen to anybody else.

REASONER: There have been some developments in the last few days in one of the areas we were concerned about – the idea of senseless violence for the benefit of the kind of people who used to go to the gladiator fights in Rome. Jack Tatum is a defensive player for Oakland. He's the man who, perfectly legally, hit Darryl Stingley and ended Stingley's career. Tatum has written a book called *They Call Me Assassin.* He says he's paid to be a brute. He says, "When you give someone your best shot and he's still able to think, you've failed." He says, directly, "My idea of a good hit is when the victim wakes up on the sidelines with train whistles blowing in his head."

Darryl Stingley's lawyer wants the NFL to kick Jack Tatum out of football. Pete Rozelle, the NFL commissioner, wants to read the book first, but he says he is outraged, and that pro football won't tolerate that kind of philosophy. Somebody, including the fans, has to decide – don't we?

See reply from Monsanto, Letters,
January 20, 1980, page 279.

Off the Books

JIM JACKSON, PRODUCER

MIKE WALLACE: "Off the books," for those of you unfamiliar with the phrase, means cheating on your taxes by working strictly for cash and not declaring that cash to the IRS. More people do it than you would ever imagine. Now, you would think that a person working off the books would be reluctant to admit it. Not so with the people Morley Safer talked to.

MORLEY SAFER: You work in a — in a fancy private club in this unnamed city, correct?

WAITRESS: Yes, sir.

SAFER: How much do they pay you?

WAITRESS: A dollar thirty-three an hour.

SAFER: As what? As a —

WAITRESS: Cocktail waitress.

SAFER: Dollar thirty-three an hour?

WAITRESS: Uh-hmm.

SAFER: How much do you actually earn?

WAITRESS: Probably average $200 a week.

SAFER: Two hundred dollars a week in tips — that's three days a week?

WAITRESS: Yes, sir.

SAFER: What do you declare for your tax purposes?

WAITRESS: Oh, approximately eighty, ninety dollars a week.

SAFER: You declare $90 a week. You earn more than double that. What about all the other people in the place?

WAITRESS: We all do the same thing. It's basically common knowledge that that's what they do in the restaurant business.

SAFER: Most restaurant workers are paid a token salary plus tips. How much? Well the maitre d' of most smart restaurants is the man who knows everything.
If a waiter is making say $600 a week — which is roughly $30,000 a year — in actual income, how much does he tell the IRS he is making?

MAITRE D':   Maybe $10,000 a year.

SAFER: Ten thousand?

MAITRE D':   Ten thousand. He's going to have twenty thousand for himself, definately. That's why there's a lot of change in waiters in every restaurant. They don't stay in the same place.

SAFER: It seems that more people are keeping more money off the books than ever before. Until a few years ago, Americans were the most tax-abiding people on earth. But lately, we are catching up with the Europeans in ways to what the British call fiddle the tax man. It all goes into what the economists call "the subterranean economy," a world of cash without receipts — no checks, no credit cards, no social security, no unemployment insurance and, above all, no income tax.

In the world's oldest profession, for example, it's hard to imagine any of these industrious, self-employed entrepreneurs sitting home filling in their 1040 forms. Dope dealing is another business venture in which balance sheets are scrupulously avoided. Whether it's out on the street or among the rock stars in Beverly Hills, it's just not done to pay by check or ask for a receipt. The IRS tries to keep track of the high rollers in Vegas, but unless it mans every crap table and poker game, it cannot hope to get its share of the winnings.

But then there's this family somewhere in America — mama, papa and all the kids happily working at just about every odd job you can think of. They'll help you move, fix the plumbing, electricity, look after the garden. You name it, they'll do it — for cash. And it's a pretty good living.

How much do you figure you make in a year?

WIFE: In order to — to live — we have five children, so it costs at least a thousand dollars a month to live. So we make at least a thousand dollars a month just to pay a house payment, your utility bills, clothing for school and food.

HUSBAND: If I wanted to, you know — I mean, if we really got out and hustled — there's a lot of people that need help, and if you're an honest man, I can make $50,000 a year. I go and do electrical work or something like that, and they'll — they'll pay you cash. And it's not, you know, it's not hard to do. A lot of time I'll go on a job — what I used to do when I was working a regular job, I'd go on a job and the person would ask me to work on their furnace, okay? And I'd tell them, "I'll come and work on your furnace for $25 an hour if you pay me by check, $15 an hour if you pay cash." Well, they're going to pay in cash, because they don't want to pay that extra ten bucks an hour.

SAFER: His wife has been working off the books for years, demonstrating products at supermarkets, department stores and trade shows.

How much money can you make during these demos?

WIFE: On a weekend, say your work — usually a demonstration's on Thursday, Friday and Saturday — sometimes they don't want them on Sunday — that would be like $90, because you — you would get $30 a demo.

SAFER: Clear?

WIFE: Clear, right. So that's $90 clear. Now, say you get into a show. I do — I do a lot of shows. You have the builders show. The builders show runs ten days. Flower and garden show, the same thing. You can make — if you want to work the full show, you would make $700.

SAFER: You're in fact being employed by very big corporations.

WIFE: Correct.

SAFER: And there's never any question of — of a check with deductions and all of that.

WIFE: No be —

SAFER: It's all in dollar bills.

WIFE: Right. There's never any Social Security even mentioned.

SAFER: Cash.

WIFE: It's not — you Social Security number — you have a number you go by — it's not mentioned. It has nothing to do with anything. They hire you —

SAFER: Do they pay you by check or by cash?

WIFE: Usually cash.

SAFER: With all that, you pay no taxes at all, correct?

WIFE: No, not on what we're doing now, no, uh-uh. Just our house tax. Now for years, he — well, when he worked the printing, he paid tax. I've never paid tax.

HUSBAND: You see, I don't — I don't feel bad about not paying taxes, because I paid a lot of taxes. There's a lot of people around that make a lot of money, and they don't pay taxes. And I don't really think I'm robbing the government, because I'm not blowing it, I'm not investing it. It's just to survive, you know.

WIFE: Just to survive.

SAFER: Are you receiving any government support? Any direct aid in welfare ?

WIFE: No, uh-uh.

SAFER: — food stamps —

WIFE: Never.

SAFER: — aid to dependent children?

HUSBAND: No. We do everything on our own.

WIFE: Everything on our own.

SAFER: Those people, relatively speaking, are the nickel and dime off the books practitioners. The big money is made or skimmed in the retail business — boutiques, restaurants, drug stores, bars; any kind of small — to medium-sized business that deals mainly in cash. Take this man, for instance, who, apart from his determination to not pay taxes, is a legitimate businessman. He wheels and deals in the sunnier parts of America, and is an old hand at keeping everything he earns to himself.
You're in the restaurant business.

RESTAURATEUR: I have been in the restaurant business for some time.

SAFER: How does it work? How do you go off the books in the restaurant business?

RESTAURATEUR: Off the books in the restaurant business is simply a matter of reading out the cash register at — at some point and closing out for the week, and leaving the tapes off the register until you're ready to pick up again. And the money that comes in in the interim period is generally money that goes off the books. I would say that I know probably maybe 400 restaurant operators fairly well. I would say that 300 of them are off the books with part of their income.

SAFER: What — what part of their income, what percentage?

RESTAURATEUR: Twenty-five to thirty percent.

SAFER: Twenty-five, thirty percent?

RESTAURATEUR: Yeah. Some of them more than that. I think that's an average.

SAFER: What sort of restaurants are we talking about now? All kinds, or — or the — the franchise —

RESTAURATEUR: Mostly in — mostly in the franchised and the fast-foods that are operated by individual owners. But you also have to remember that the restaurant operator has to have some cash; in a lot of cases, it's necessary for him to pay some of his employees in cash, because a lot of employees simply will not work if Social Security and income tax is withheld from his pay.

SAFER: There are three ways, pretty much, of paying of restaurant bills: cash, credit card and personal check. What happens at the end of the day when the restaurant closes and they total up the receipts?

MAN (restaurateur):   Okay, you have all your credit cards, your check and your cash. Now, credit cards you have to have a record of. Check, not really; and cash not at all. You can play with those two items, with cash and checks, and that's where the money is, the real money.

SAFER: When you say "play with," you mean —

MAN: Play — declare some, and put some on the side or whatever, you know.

SAFER: Would it be fair to say that all the money that a restaurant takes in cash goes off the books?

MAN: Most likely, yes.

SAFER: Most likely, yes? That can mean an extraordinary amount of money in a — in one of those —

MAN: Why, sure.

SAFER: — fancy restaurants.

MAN: Definitely.

SAFER: In the restaurant business, is it a general understanding that everybody works, one way or another, off the books?

MAN: Uh-hmm. Oui.

SAFER: The IRS acknowledges that this goes on on a large scale, but the IRS refuses to discuss the subject on the record. We did find one tax collector who would — James Zagel, director of the Illinois Department of Revenue.

JAMES ZAGEL: I think when you're dealing with cash businesses, there's a — a good possibility that half the businesses are skimming something.

SAFER: Half?

ZAGEL: Half.

SAFER: That's a huge amount of dollars.

ZAGEL: Well, it is a huge amount of dollars collectively, because there are a lot of cash businesses. But the level of skimming varies substantially. There are people who skim such small amounts that it's difficult ever to catch them; and there are other people who are just outrageous.

SAFER: I get the impression, though, that the number of people who think they can get away with it is increasing substantially.

ZAGEL: Well, it's hard to say. If you want a — a kind of a shirttail estimate, I think it is true. I think that economic squeezes, increasing inflation, a recessionary economy, are the kinds of things that put people in — in financial jeopardy. And when people are in financial jeopardy, the temptation to hedge and take a little off the top before you report your taxes increases.

SAFER: No one knows just how much money is involved in this, in this underground economy, but it is somewhere in the billions. One economist in New York says it might be as high as $250 billion. That's 10 percent of the entire U.S. economy. Well, if it's anything like that, it puts just about every economic statistic that the government issues completely out of whack. There are fewer people unemployed than the government tells us. Our productivity is much higher than the government tells us. Our net income is much higher than the government tells us. And the number of Americans living below the poverty line is much lower than the government tells us. In other words, we're richer than the government tells us, because government statisticians do not take into account the millions of people who keep billions of dollars off the books.

Going off the books, really is a form of theft, isn't it?

RESTAURATEUR: I don't see it that way; because the progressive income tax in itself is — is really a vehicle by which wealth is redistributed. And I feel that if someone is going to redistribute the products of my labor, I should have more of a say-so, so to speak, in how and to whom it's redistributed. Basically, there are two kinds of people in our country, and there are those who produce more than they consume, and then those who consume more than they produce. And I — I feel that it's not theft. I feel that it's — it's more of a — of a statement that I don't really like what's going on in this country and with our government, and I really feel that for — to be forced to support it is a form of slavery.

SAFER: Have you ever had a – a day – a moment when you felt any guilt about this?

WIFE: No. No, no, no. Never, never. We've always worked. He's worked his — his butt off at times when it was really hard to make payments and meet this and meet that. In between, your cars are breaking down. You don't have any money. Who's going to give you another car. You take it back to the company, what are they — you know, they're not going to do anything about it. Nobody — nobody will help you when you really need help, unless you're really destitute, we'll say. And besides, we don't want help. We can do it ourself.

SAFER: But you two are, I – I kno – I suspect, otherwise extremely law-abiding, law-and-order kind of people, correct?

WIFE: Definitely. Yeah, yeah, real honest, of course. You know, with five kids, you're going to want your children to be. And —

SAFER: Correct.

WIFE: Right.

SAFER: But here you are, breaking the law.

HUSBAND: I don't think it's really that illegal. I mean, it's — maybe it's illegal to the — to the tax people —

WIFE: Tax-wise, right.

HUSBAND: — you know, but I'm not wasting the money. We're making a living, and I don't care what anybody says, you know.

WIFE: Just what he said, and not asking for help.

HUSBAND: I don't think I — I'll have to go to jail for it. I mean, it would be kind of ridiculous. But is they ever do catch up, you have to pay your taxes.

WIFE: If he had to go to jail, I'd have to go on ADC with five kids, see. (Laughs)

HUSBAND: Yeah, and that's just what happens. The government would have to pay one way or the other, I guess.

ZAGEL: There are ways, if we wanted to pay the price in the society, for stopping the stuff pretty much dead in its tracks. We could make this a truly cashless society. We could be — put cash-operated businesses more or less out of business. But I don't think you really have much sentiment in the — the American public for a situation in which a government or a computer or somebody with access to a computer can tell you how you've spent every dime. There are people who can cheat on their taxes and will get away with it. And the — the methods by which you can reduce that number to zero are really the kinds of methods which I don't think a free society really wants to adopt.

SAFER: Aren't you concerned that somebody from the IRS is going to be watching this broadcast, and they'll say, "I want to talk to that guy."

RESTAURATEUR: Well, I — you know, I could get on the boat and go out to the Bahamas. I don't think they have too many tax problems out there. (Safer laughs)

George Who?

JOEL BERNSTEIN, PRODUCER

RATHER: Four years ago this month, a Democrat they called "Jimmy Who?" went into his party's precinct caucuses in Iowa and — well, you know the rest of that story. In eight days, a Republican they call "George Who?" will go into his party's Iowa caucuses, hoping to repeat Jimmy Carter's success story. This Republican's biggest problem, besides a lack of recognition, is that some people say he's just "too nice to be President." But although it would take a minor miracle for anyone to take the nomination away from Ronald Reagan at this point, it's been said that if anyone can do it, he can. Who is he? He is George Bush.

Fifty-five years old, Phi Beta Kappa from Yale; Navy combat pilot in World War II; a Connecticut Yankee who moved to Texas and made a fortune in the oil business; former congressman from Houston, former ambassador to the United Nations; chairman of the Republican Party during Watergate; former envoy to China, former director of the Central Intelligence Agency.

Let me read you something that John Connally's been saying about you. In reference to those jobs you held, many of them appointed jobs, he points out —

GEORGE BUSH: Clean it up now when you say anything.

RATHER: Connally's quoted as saying — quote —cleaning it up — "George Bush sat on his butt in those jobs. He had those jobs, but he didn't do very much in those jobs."

BUSH: I will adhere, albeit difficult, to the Eleventh Commandment: "Speak ill of no Republican." I —

RATHER: But one of the major questions on George Bush is: Is he tough enough to be President?

BUSH: But is tough being nasty? Or is tough being a leader that people respect? Is toughness shouting and being ugly and trying to stick a knife in somebody? Or is it principle and leadership, where you look over your shoulder and people are following? Let somebody else go out — it's not toughness. Toughness — go out there and say something ugly aout somebody? I don't think that.

RATHER: Well, the *Christian Science Monitor* — and I know you saw this story — ran a story about George Bush, not an uncomplimentary piece. But the headline on it was "Too Nice To Be President."

BUSH: Niceness, sure. Decency — what's wrong with that? Toughness, fiber, strength, perception of the strengths of this country — I've got it. I understand it. But — but I just am not a person who feels you have to be ugly.

RATHER: A lot of Republicans that I talked to say why not go for John Connally? He has broader experience than George Bush.

BUSH: He doesn't. He never built a business. Never. I mean, I — I'd — let's lay down the — lay down the criteria. Broader in what sense?

RATHER: Well, he was the Governor of the — of the State of Texas. He —

BUSH: Okay, And I was a congressman from the State of Texas.

RATHER: Cabinet member. Makes —

BUSH: So was I. Foreign affairs.

RATHER: Foreign affairs.

BUSH: National security, no.

RATHER: Makes a better speech.

BUSH: Yeah. Are we looking for an orator? William Jennings Bryan didn't make it. I don't think so.

RATHER: Do you fear Connally?

BUSH: Fear him? (Laughs) No.
(Campaigning): Hello, hello.

WOMAN: I feel like writing . . .

BUSH: How are you?

RATHER: Bush started campaigning early. He's been at it almost two years. Yet, he's still the least known of all the leading contenders —

WOMAN: . . . president of the League of Women Voters.

BUSH: What a day!

RATHER: — still struggling to be recognized.

BUSH: Nice to see you. Hi. Hi. Again, again. Again, again. Oh, come on. Let's go in.

RATHER: How can anyone with such impressive credentials, who served his country for so long, have achieved such widespread anonymity?

BUSH: By not playing to the cameras. In the last d ays of the Nixon presidency, by not taking the cheap shot. By saying, look, he should be treated fairly; and then saying the party should not be dragged into the ugliness. By not going, when I was at CIA, and calling you up and telling you of all the fantastic changes I made.

RATHER: Wish you had.

BUSH: By making — I know you did. And I'd been better known. But I made

changes. I did it quietly. I su — reported openly to Congress. And then I elevated
the morale of the CIA by making them understand that I knew that an intelligence service cannot be effective if you're not going to protect sources and
methods of intelligence. So I — you know, I haven't played for the crowd. I
haven't been up against the left field fence jumping up there and catching that,
you know, extravagant one. But I haven't needed that. That's not what I've been
trying to do.

RATHER: But what you do need is —

BUSH: I'm trying to do a job, and do it well. And I've done it.

RATHER: What you do need is a base. Where is your constituency? Who out there is
willing to die for George Bush? To use a Texas phrase, there are people who say
George Bush is a nice fellow but he's all hat and no cattle. Which is to say he has
no base.

*"How can anyone with
such impressive credentials,
who served his country for
so long, have achieved such
widespread anonymity?"*

BUSH: Well, let me tell you this. You ever seen Joe Morgan at his best? He's got
class. And I got plenty of class. And I mean it in the sense of accomplishment.
Doesn't matter whether I'm known now. What matters is, in this constituency,
can I get those people in Iowa excited? Can I get them to feel this man can
represent us? I want a national constituency. This old base theory is baloney,
absolute total baloney.

RATHER: One accusation that has plagued the Bush campaign from the very beginning: that he's merely a stalking horse for Gerald Ford. Bush's own campaign
chairman, Jim Baker, who ran the Ford election campaign four years ago, said if
Bush falters — quote — "we could pull it together for Ford in two weeks."

BUSH: I don't know whether he said it or not. If he did, he made the wrong mistake,
as Yogi Berra would say.But nevertheless, it's irrelevant. It's irrelevant.Yes, they
were asking him in April about having a lot of Ford people, and that probably
was a very factual statement. But that was in April. I was an asterisk on these
polls then. But things have changed. And you think I'd drag my carcass around
this country being a stalking horse for Ford or anybody else, you're crazy.
Absolutely nuts. And anybody that thinks that is nuts. I'm working too hard. I
believe too strongly.

RATHER: Let's be specific, and be candid with me. What's your strategy for winning?

BUSH: My strategy? Keep my head down. Don't have to have the big entourage. Go to those small towns in Iowa. Go to those small towns in — Puerto Rico, actually, and in — and in New Hampshire.

RATHER: New Hampshire. We were there one rainy night when a film crew was setting up inside a hanger at the Lebanon, New Hampshire, airport to film a George Bush commercial. The crew was under the direction of Bob Goodman, a media consultant George Bush calls his Cecil B. DeMille. Bush supporters were bought in to be in the film —

BOB GOODMAN: Watch the wires, and be very careful . . .

RATHER: — their role carefully explained by Goodman.

GOODMAN: But when George gets off the plane, we're going to have a kind of a victory aisle for him to walk through. We're all naturally going to be rather excited about his entrance. And then George will come to the mikes. We'll all gather around him, and we'll let him turn us on.

RATHER: For this night, the airport hanger was transformed into a movie set. But the star's arrival — he was flying in from another campaign stop — was delayed by rain. Finally, here he was. Lights, camera, action.

(Applause . . . chanting "We want Bush!" as Bush exits from plane)

BUSH: Nice to see you. (Chanting "We want Bush!") Thank you, thank you. I bring you word from across America. We're going all the way! (Cheers)

RATHER: Goodman was delighted. The show went well. Everyone was happy.

GOODMAN: Really good.

RATHER: Well, almost everyone.

MAN: Now, look, these — I talked to some of these people —

GOODMAN: Originally, we were supposed to fly here.

MAN: I talked to some of these people, and they knew full well that he wasn't flying in.

GOODMAN: But he was supposed to have flown in.

MAN: Yeah, but they know that he didn't fly in —

GOODMAN: But I didn't know that.

MAN: — and they were — and they were — and they were happily going along with this — with this game of the — of having the — the thing filmed as though he had come in on — on a — on a plane. And they were — they were perfectly well playing along with it.

RATHER: Reporters discovered that Bush had in fact arrived at the airport by car — it was raining too hard to fly — had then climbed into a plane only for the short taxi run to the hanger. After all, the script called for an airport arrival, and that was what Goodman was going to get.

Goodman and Bush are convinced that a strong media blitz can help narrow the gap between dark horse Bush and front-runner Reagan.

BUSH: There's something out there on that Reagan thing. I can't prove it to you. He's strong in the polls. I will say nothing to tear him down. But there's some erosion. It's almost — I think it could be the Teddy Kennedy syndrome. Way out three-to-one before you join battle. And then, whip, down you go. Now, for some events that he has no control over, but also because the myth is gone.

You're in there with your sleeves rolled up. And I think it's going to erode, that Reagan strength.

RATHER: What about that commercial that Bob Goodman filmed up in New Hampshire? Well, it begins with a shot of the plane that George Bush did not fly in. Otherwise, it happened as advertised.

(Excerpt from George Bush political commercial)

RATHER: Your slogan is: "George Bush, a President we won't have to train." But isn't that at least a bit deceptive? You were a congressman for two terms.

BUSH: Right.

RATHER: Envoy to China for a year.

BUSH: Yeah.

RATHER: At the CIA for a year.

BUSH: Yeah.

RATHER: You've never been elected to national office. What you did was win two elections in Houston, Texas.

BUSH: Right.

RATHER: Now you say we won't have to train you?

BUSH: Yeah. Of course I got things to learn. But, you know, lay it down there compared to Jimmy Carter. Jimmy Carter went in there and, let's face it, he captured the imagination of the people. "Trust me. I'm from outside." Almost sanctified this thing.

RATHER: And now, he's the best-trained man to be President because he's had these four years?

BUSH: Yeah, but he's wrong on many of the issues. You got to have training, and you got to have experience, but you got to be coming from someplace.

RATHER: In an effort to dispel the notion that his candidate may be too nice to be President, Bob Goodman now is portraying George Bush as:

GOODMAN: The American Eagle. We call him the American Eagle. And George is starting to feel like the Eagle.

BUSH (to Goodman):   Cecil B. DeMille, I believe. How are you? The Eagle is flying.

RATHER: Mr. Bush, why do you want to be President?

BUSH: I believe an individual can make a difference. I believe we can elevate the standard for people in our country by sensible economics. I know we can — we can continue to project our conviction about freedom for countries around the world. And I — added to these convictions is I've been blessed by a breadth of experience that others haven't had. And it's service, I hope in an honorable sense. Yes, there's some adrenalin flowing in there. Smell of grease paint, roar of the crowd.

(Crowd cheering . . . chanting "We want Bush! We want Bush!" . . . applause)

A Few Minutes
with Andy Rooney

MIKE WALLACE: You've heard it ever since you were a kid: save for a rainy day. But Andy Rooney's problem is that he saves every day — rainy ones, sunny ones, summer and winter.

ANDY ROONEY: This is the time of the year we're all faced with a difficult decision: What do you do with the Christmas cards? Some of these are much too beautiful to throw out. Others have names and addresses on the back that you want to keep. On the other hand, most of us are up to here in junk at this time of the year, and something's got to go.

I'm a saver myself. I save everything. I don't think I've ever thrown away a pair of shoes, for example. I have shoes in my closet that hurt so much or look so terrible I'll never wear them again, but there they are. I'm hooked on old peanut butter jars too. We don't eat much peanut butter in my house any more, but I make up for that by saving old jelly and jam jars too. Coffee cans. How can you throw away such a nice clean can with this tight-fitting plastic top. Who knows when I'll need how many for cleaning paint brushes in turpentine. These are all from coffee we've made here in the office. I save them too, even though I don't have to paint my own office.

There are so many things I can't throw away at this time of year. Sometimes I like the boxes things come in better than anything that comes in them. I keep old wine bottles too. We don't drink much more wine than we eat peanut butter, but I keep the interesting bottles on the shelf out in the garage. Up in the attic, there are about six boxes and two big trunks with the really good stuff I've saved. You know, the kids' old school work papers, programs from school plays with their names buried down near the bottom somewhere with the angels — that kind of stuff.

There are two kinds of savers. First is the practical saver, who thinks he's going to save money by keeping string and old bags and aluminum foil and that sort of thing. Then there's the sentimental saver. The sentimental savers can't stand the idea of throwing out any memory of their lives. Unfortunately, I'm both kinds.

Letters

MORLEY SAFER: The mail this week was heavy and interesting.

About our story on television in the Soviet Union, a viewer wrote: "I hate to tell you this, but you and Soviet TV have more in common than you suspect. (They) cover more news of your dissidents than of your scientific achievements. (You) cover more news of their dissidents than of their cosmonauts . . . As an Arab, I find it all highly amusing."

About our story on Liberia, a Liberian student wrote: "It was no surprise to me that the (ruling) family agreed to be interviewed so they could use 60 MINUTES to promote (themselves)."

Another viewer said: "It was simple proof that as a reporter from an imperialist nation, your first step is to cater to the elite class."

We do acknowledge that we goofed when we said Liberia was on the east coast of Africa. But we did not, as one viewer wrote: "Degrade the entire female gender by using the term *broads* in describing the American women who marry young Liberians." What we said was: Most young Liberians educated in the United States bring back American *brides*.

But most of the mail was about our story on John Silber, the president of Boston University, and most of it went like this: "For my money Silber is worth his weight in gold."

However, there were a few negative letters. This was one of them: "Your segment on Generalissimo Silber and his admiring millionaire Board of Trustees should be required study for all who wonder how a Hitler could capture sophisticated Germany."

But there was also this: "The wrong man from Boston is running for President."

JANUARY 20, 1980

Bette Davis

NANCY LEA, PRODUCER

MIKE WALLACE: Though you wouldn't know it from that old photo, Bette Davis is 71 and still working and still the opinionated lady she was when she was the empress of Hollywood. "I do not regret one professional enemy I have made," says the redoubtable Miss Davis. And: "If you aim high, the pygmies will jump on your back and tug at your skirts." Or from this Yankee puritan: "A good percentage of our lives is spent doing things we loathe. Marvelous! It puts starch in your spine."

Well, Bette Davis recently deserted the East Coast, where she had lived for many years, and moved west again to Hollywood, the scene of her old triumphs and her old battles. Among the triumphs, two Oscars. She had 10 Academy Award nominations. Among her battles, her famous losing fight with Warner Brothers that ended in the courts after she'd gone on strike.

It was in Hollywood that we sat down with her to canvass her current views on politics and passion, men and women, money and work. We begin with a grainy glimpse of one of her first Warner Brothers pictures.

(Excerpt from *The Cabin in the Cotton*)

In 1932, Bette Davis appeared in no less than nine films.

(Excerpt continued)

In this one, over the strong opposition of Director Michael Curtiz, who thought she

263

was "unsexy," she was cast as a conniving vixen, the role that would eventually become her trademark.

(Excerpt continued)

BETTE DAVIS (repeating line from the film):   I'd love to kiss you, but I just washed my hair.

WALLACE (laughing):   That's right.

DAVIS: My favorite line in any movie I ever had. Mr. Curtiz was so against my playing this kind of a part, because he said, "That's the unsexiest looking woman I have ever seen in my life."

WALLACE: Well, Mr. Curtiz —

DAVIS: And Mr. —

WALLACE: — was wrong.

DAVIS: — and Mr. Barthelmess wouldn't even test with me, so I had to end up kissing the lens — (demonstrates) — like this. (Wallace laughs) Boy! Every scene I played in that, he said, "Goddamn lousy actress!" "Goddamn!" behind the camera.

WALLACE: Uh-hmm.

DAVIS: They never really understood that — that there was something very peculiar about me and that they could use it.

WALLACE: It may just have been that you were difficult, Bette.

DAVIS: No, no, no, no.

WALLACE: Not difficult, impossible.

DAVIS: With a stupid director. Then it was self-preservation. It was absolutely self-preservation.

WALLACE: Yeah, but before the director had to be the producer, had to be the choice of script, had to be — had to be — I mean, come on, you had a reputation for being a first-class stubborn mule.

DAVIS: About script and bad directors, those were the two.

WALLACE: And apparently with good reason. This was one of the epics Warner Brothers put her in back in 1936. It was after this abomination that she left Warners and went on strike. She simply refused to do more films like this.

(Excerpt from the film *Satan Met a Lady*)

Bette Davis had trouble not just with on-screen lovers and off-screen executives, she went through a tempest at home, too. Miss Davis has had four husbands. First, bandleader Ham Nelson — five years of marriage, then divorce.

DAVIS: Ham, of course, was just — I outgrew him.

WALLACE: Yes.

DAVIS: I got older.

WALLACE: Then Arthur Farnsworth, businessman — two years, and he died.

DAVIS: Was a lovely, lovely guy. Died, you know, Farnie.

WALLACE: I know.

DAVIS: This would have worked. This would really have worked. He had no jealousy of me. He was — had a damned good job himself at Disney's. He was Yankee.

WALLACE: Third, William Sherry, a painter — six difficult years, and out. Sherry beat you.

DAVIS: Yup. He beat me.

WALLACE: Re — really beat you up?

DAVIS: I have this marvelous doctor in Laguna Beach, and after about — taking care of me for 15 years or so, he said, "I have got to ask you something. How could any bright woman like you marry the men you did?" (Laughs)

WALLACE: And finally, Gary Merrill — 10 years, ending back in 1960 in divorce. That was her last try.

Why in the world did you marry Gary Merrill? Fourth time around, so you're hardly a novice. He's a — he's an actor. You shouldn't have married an actor. He's an actor —

DAVIS: I swore I never would. I think I decided because I love marriage, I believe in marriage. I think a — a woman by herself is a perfectly asinine — a — a — a way to live.

WALLACE: Also, you believed that, in order to go to bed with a fellow, you've got to marry him, or at least you believed that.

DAVIS: Oh, yes, I was — oh, I was — oh, I was brought up absolutely no — no hidden corners.

WALLACE: Were you — were you 26 years old —

DAVIS: When I married Ham.

WALLACE: And you were a virgin?

DAVIS: I was a virgin.

WALLACE: You were chaste at the time?

DAVIS: Uh-hmm, I was chaste.

WALLACE: At the age of 26?

DAVIS: Uh-hmmm. He was the fool. I'd known him since I was 16 years old in prep school.

WALLACE: So, if you love a fellow and you —

DAVIS: But my mother I blame deeply for this. I blame — you see, I am so for the change in the morals today. I really am, because it — that is not a reason to marry.

WALLACE: To go to bed?

DAVIS: No. That is not a reason to marry. That is a ridiculous reason.

WALLACE: And then, in your compulsion to work, in your devotion to your career and your mother's devotion to your career, you aborted your first child?

DAVIS: Two.

WALLACE: Two?

DAVIS: He begged me to. I did what he wanted.

WALLACE: This was with Nelson?

DAVIS: He did, my first husband. He did me a great favor, really. If I had had children that young, it's very possible I would have chosen the children to bring up. And I'm fortunate, because, at this age, had I never tried to do what I wanted to do, I'd be a pretty disappointed woman.

(Excerpt from the film *All About Eve*)

WALLACE: In *All About Eve*, Bette Davis played the role of the actress Margo Channing, and people who knew her thought the character struck close to home.

(Excerpt continued: Margo Channing talking about the conflict between a woman's need for a career and her needs as a woman)

But Bette Davis has more than a book full of clippings, she has three children. One of them, her daughter by William Sherry, Barbara Davis Hyman, known as "Beady," lives on a farm in Pennsylvania with her husband, Jeremy, and their two youngsters, Ashley and Justin. Beady adores her mother, though she is candid about her.

Was she a tough mother?

BARBARA DAVIS HYMAN: In certain ways.

WALLACE: What ways?

HYMAN: Discipline, manners. You — you — it was worth your life to forget a please or a thank you. She was always very, very concerned with Hollywood being a place, not a way of life, and she worked very hard at that. She worked very hard to have a home in Maine, which was way out in the country on the seacoast, and to bring us up in the country.

WALLACE: Was your mother a star at home?

HYMAN: No, never. Never. She was in blue jeans and work shirts, and she was a working mother when she was at home. She was in the kitchen. She was tidying up the house. She was weeding her garden, planting bulbs. She was a mother.

WALLACE: You're making this sound like a storybook —

HYMAN (laughing):   No. No —

WALLACE: Well, come on —

HYMAN: — we had our arguments. We certainly did.

WALLACE: You wrote, "If you've never been hated by your child, you have never been a parent."

DAVIS: You sure haven't. You've got to be hated sometimes. I think that is another thing that is going on today. I think parents are afraid of their children. Yes, they — they — they're so overzealous about being loved every minute.

WALLACE: And by the same token, now you do not use your kids as crutches for yourself.

DAVIS: No.

WALLACE: You got your life, they got theirs.

DAVIS: That's the hardest thing you have to learn to know.

WALLACE: Oh, boy!

DAVIS: Ah, I shouldn't have to tell you. Because you really — when the house is empty of children, takes a few years.

WALLACE: Her adopted son, Michael Merrill, is an enterprising young attorney in Boston.

When you would see, as you were growing up, as you were a youngster and you'd see your mother up there on the screen, what was the reaction?

MICHAEL MERRILL: Well, it's kind of hard to say. It's a — it's a difficult thing to see your mother on the screen; especially in the — in the different roles, I could say that that was difficult, because in the one moment here she is your mother walking around the house cooking your meals and everything and there she is playing some glamorous lady in a movie.

(Excerpt from the film *Mr. Skeffington*)

But as I grew older, you know, there's no problem. I saw it as her job and — and I realized how good she was at it.

WALLACE: And then there is Margo.

Margo, your dear —

DAVIS: My darling Margo is still, you know, about six years old.

WALLACE: Really? And she's 20 —?

DAVIS: Twenty-eight.

WALLACE: Adopted. Tragedy?

DAVIS: Horrible! It was horrible! When a — a brain-injured child gets much, much older, it's — it's different, fortunately. It take — it — it levels off a bit. But it was terrible. My mother said, "Send her back." I said, "Would I have sent Beady back? I made a deal." And actually, Margo's had a great life, due to the fact I could afford to have her in a beautiful school.

WALLACE: Uh-hmm. You see her?

DAVIS: Oh, yes, I've se — I've — for 20-some years she's spent every summer with me and every Christmas.

WALLACE: Really?

DAVIS: Uh-hmm. Yup.

WALLACE: What are your vices?

DAVIS: Always blaming myself, anything that happens. Terrific guilt. Terrific guilt. Terrible!

WALLACE: Puritan New England.

DAVIS: Uh-hmm.

WALLACE: But also, your lack of vanity, your honesty, permits you to play — don't get angry — frumps.

DAVIS: Yeah, I'll play anything. But you see that was my basic theory about acting: that the appearance should not be the reason you choose a part. The only time my daughter ever said to me, "Mother, you have finally gone too far!" was in *Jane*.

WALLACE: *Whatever Happened to Baby Jane?*

(Excerpt from the film *Whatever Happened to Baby Jane?*)

Why? Do you need the money, or do you need the work, or do you need —

DAVIS: I need the work.

WALLACE: You really said, Bette, "It has been my experience that one cannot, in any shape or form, depend on human relations for any lasting reward; it is only work that truly satisfies"?

DAVIS: Yes, that stands by you. It isn't that many people don't add a great deal to your life, but I'm talking about as a permanent thing that's the least disappointing relationship you can have.

WALLACE: Is work?

An old friend of Davis', from New York and Hollywood both, was the late Joan Blondell, who lived in Santa Monica. They used to work together.

She's 71. Why do you think that she came back here, this Maine girl, this New England puritan, to lotus land at the age of 71?

JOAN BLONDELL: I'd think that when you crash into the seventies, boy, you better do something exciting. Whatever's left, you know, and that's — that's left to come here and — well, I think it's a — was a good idea for her to do. Action and work comes from here, and I think it'll open up a whole new career for her now.

WALLACE: Was she always ambitious, driving?

BLONDELL: Nothing stopped her, and yet there was a soft quality about her that I loved. You know, who has meant a great deal to Bette and — was her mother Ruthie.

WALLACE: Oh, yes.

BLONDELL: Yeah. One day we went to the funeral of Orry-Kelly, who designed all the lovely clothes for us.

WALLACE: Uh-hmm.

BLONDELL: And the — the crowds were waiting outside the church, and Bette came over to me and took my hand and led me way aside and she said, "Look up there at that knoll. Do you see that white headstone?" And I said, "Yes." She said, "That's Ruthie. And next to her, the place is all paid for, is where I go — next to Ruthie."

WALLACE: Bette Davis, a practical New Englander, has indeed made all preparations. We visited the cemetery, a part of Forest Lawn that overlooks the Disney Studios and the old Warner Brothers' back lot.

DAVIS: I just am glad that it will be simple. I'll be very near. That's one reason I moved to California. They wouldn't have to take that long trip across the country with me. (Laughing)

(Davis puts flowers on her mother's grave)

Here you are, Ruthie darling. It's Mother's Day.

You know what I'm going to have on my tombstone? "She did it the hard way."

WALLACE: Bette Davis recorded this song in 1976.

(Davis singing song about growing older, feeling younger)

The Thunderbirds

RICHARD CLARK, PRODUCER

HARRY REASONER: America has been a little short of heroes lately and, with the way the world is going in the last few months, we might need some. The seventies were hard on heroism, but maybe in the eighties people will start looking for heroes again. If a hero is a man who exemplifies the best in the national character, who is modest and unassuming, who lives in an atmosphere of great valor and hazard, if he is these things, maybe we've found some heroes. Ladies and gentlemen, meet The Thunderbirds.

(Shouts of The Thunderbirds . . . sounds of planes doing maneuvers)

The Thunderbirds, more formally The United States Air Force Demonstration Team, would, of course, deny that they are heroes. That comes with the suit, doesn't it? The Thunderbirds would say, instead, that they are "careful pilots," selected for two-year stints in an exciting but precise and demanding project — which is, essentially, to show how good the U.S. Air Force is, to help morale within the force, and to attract young men and women to join up.

(Sounds of planes)

Lieutenant Colonel D. L. Smith, commander. He flies lead in the diamond formation. He had 353 missions over Vietnam. Captain Ron Maynis. Ron is left wing in the diamond, more than 2,300 hours in jet fighters. Captain Jim Latham. He's right wing in the diamond. Latham was shot down and taken prisoner in one of 328 missions over Vietnam. Major Jim Koziar. He's the slot man, just behind the leader in the diamond, 2,700 hours in jet fighters. Captain Gale Scarborough. Scar is lead solo, 150 missions in Vietnam. These days he seems to spend half his life upside down. As does Captain R. D. Evans, second solo, more than 1,700 hours in jet fighters.

(Sounds of planes)

Every maneuver in every show or practice flight is rated by a pilot on the ground, and after every flight there is a debriefing, in which, minute by minute of the flight, the pilots criticize each other and themselves.

PILOT: I think I bottomed before you did, which makes it harder for me to come up and pick you up, too.

PILOT: Yeah.

(Sounds of planes)

REASONER: Since their origin, The Thunderbirds 25 years ago, The Thunderbirds and their Navy counterparts The Blue Angels have lost 26 pilots — in training, in transit and in air shows. The last casualty was a Navy flyer in November, 1978. Something went wrong for a second, and a second is all you've got. (Sound of plane exploding) But comparing air time for Thunderbirds and Blue Angels with air time for all fighter pilots — in training, not combat — their casualty rate is low.

People come out to the air shows because it's beautiful and it's precise, but some of them come out also because it looks so darn dangerous.

MAJOR JIM KOZIAR: It's a thing that we say often, but I think we feel safer within that flight with people that we've been working with for a year; feel safer there than we do in a situation like on a freeway, where you don't really know what the fellow next to you is doing, or what his condition is.

REASONER: They are professionals and not daredevils or hotdogs, but they are also quite clearly fighter pilots, members of that breed for which the main qualification is unspoken and vague but completely understood and recognized by everyone who has it. The Thunderbirds have it, as author Tom Wolfe puts it, "the right stuff." These guys, unmistakably, have the right stuff, and they don't want to fly their precision stunts with any guys who don't have the right stuff.

MAN: Thunderbirds, attention! Forward, march!

REASONER: Every step and move on the ground or in the air is precisely choreographed. They leave their home base at Nellis Air Force Base in Las Vegas some 153 days a year, and they put on shows.

What The Thunderbirds are worth to the U.S. Air Force maybe can best be measured at an air show, like this one today at their home base at Nellis Base in Nevada. A quarter of a million people this year at Cleveland, a quarter of a million at Fort Worth. All together during the season, five and a half million people come out to see them.

(Sounds of planes at air show)

No one who has seen them has any question that the three and a half million dollars or so that the team costs the taxpayers every year is worth it.

Are they worth it to the country, do you think?

MAN: You bet!

CROWD: Yeah!

REASONER: All right, now, if you had to pay that 3.7 million out of your — I mean, your share of taxes, you're willing?

CROWD: Yeah.

WOMAN: Well, I pay my share of taxes for everything else.

REASONER: You got the leader, you got wing men, you got the slot men, you got solos, is there any particular position that's a favorite with the crowd?

MAJOR KOZIAR: I found that everyone loves the slot pilot.

REASONER: What's your — what's your position?

MAJOR KOZIAR: I fly the slot.

REASONER: You fly the slots.

CAPTAIN D. L. SMITH: The reason that we put Jim in the slot position is because it's the one position that I can't watch when we're flying. (Laughter)

REASONER: Otherwise you'd get depressed?

CAPTAIN SMITH: That's right. (Laughter)

(To crowd): Hi, Dale Smith.

VOICE: Hi.

REASONER: The Birds like to think of themselves as good-will ambassadors for Air Force and nation, and they are certainly natural-born talents at public relations: modest, witty, patient with people, either on the flight line or in a hospital. They are always, by necessity, on.

PILOT (on inter-plane radio):   Do you feel your regulator pressure . . .?

REASONER: One of the things they do is to be nice to journalists, and when they find one who wants to know how things like this feel inside the plane, they help him out. They send him to Andrews Air Force Base for high-altitude flight qualification.

CAPTAIN R. D. EVANS: The first time you hear the word "bail-out" you'd want to go ahead and initiate the ejection . . .

REASONER: Then they show him how to save himself if he has to.

CAPTAIN EVANS: . . . and the first step of that being: assume the proper body position. It's important that you have your elbows tucked in closely to your body and inside those elbow guards. If they were to be over the side, it would conflict with the canopy as the seat came out of the airplane. So it's proper body position, hand grips raise, trigger squeeze, and the parachute would automatically start to come out at that time.

REASONER: All of this stuff would go away?

CAPTAIN EVANS: Yes, you'd lose — this whole seat would simply fall to — to earth.

REASONER: I'd be there with just the parachute?

CAPTAIN EVANS: Yes, and you'd be left in the parachute.

REASONER: And then they take him flying. I spent, on three occasions, around four hours in the second seat. I'm the man in the strange hat. I loved it. When you do what they call "The Thunderbird pull-out," you live with something like seven times the force of gravity. It makes you look even funnier than usual, but you can handle it. How you handle it and fly an airplane at the same time is fortunately something I didn't have to worry about. The fellow on the front seat did that. There was very little fear — a lot of thrill, very little fear. It is careful and precise — and relaxed, as the calm voices on the inter-plane radio show.

PILOT (on inter-plane radio):   One more time, boys, just cruising right along being cool.

PILOT: We're going to fly through the air with the greatest of ease.

(Singing):   Well, we're all going out to have some fun, doo da, doo da. Up and down, we ain't had none, all ma doo da day.

REASONER: Heroes? Probably. After all, heroes are supposed to make others who share their nationality and culture feel good. These guys make you feel good.

PDAP

PHILIP SCHEFFLER, PRODUCER

DAN RATHER: P-D-A-P, PDAP, stands for the Palmer Drug Abuse Program, born eight years ago in the basement of Houston's Palmer Episcopal Church. Few people outside of Texas had ever heard of PDAP until *People* magazine reported that Carrie Hamilton, the 15-year-old daughter of TV star Carol Burnett and producer Joe Hamilton had become a drug addict, and that her parents had sent Carrie to PDAP, where she kicked her habit. Carol Burnett and her husband Joe Hamilton went on "Dinah" and "Donahue" and other talk shows to extol the drug and alcohol abuse program and to praise it's founder and leader, a former addict and cured alcoholic named Bob Meehan.

Now, some see Mr. Meehan as a miracle worker, bringing God and clean living back into young people's lives. Others say he gets those youngsters dependent on him and PDAP in place of their former dependence on drugs and alcohol. Meehan himself leaves no doubt that he has found the answer. His message is: Do it my way or leave.

BOB MEEHAN: Now, I'm saying this is — this program works for a group of people. If it doesn't work for you, try another one. Don't tell me to change this one, because it's already working for this group of people.

It's my way or it's the highway. Go find another program. There are 22 Mickey Mouse programs running around in our area. Go to one of them. You don't have to stay. We're not keeping you here. You're not in chains. You walk out the doors, you live at home, you go to school. You know, we're not controlling you in any way, shape or form. You don't like it, leave.

RATHER: PDAP operates in meeting rooms donated by more than 30 churches in Houston; has branches in nine other Texas cities, and Denver, Colorado; and starting next month, in Los Angeles. There are no membership fees. The two and a half million dollar budget is raised from the community through an increasingly necessary fund-raising campaign. It is not a residential program. Youngsters live at home or on their own, except for a small number from out of town, like Carrie Hamilton, who stay with volunteer families. A substantial number may spend a month or more in a PDAP-affiliated hospital. PDAP is a drug-oriented, youth-oriented version of Alcoholics Anonymous. The members go to meetings: day meetings, night meetings; even a few times a year, 24-hour meetings. No drugs, no alcohol, as little contact as possible with anyone who uses either. It preaches a way of life, and that outside the chosen path lies disaster. Bob Meehan is convinced it works.

MEEHAN: You people, all of you, saw more sober kids at one time than you have ever seen in your lives at this age group and in any group. I don't care if it's a church group, I don't care where it is, there are people getting loaded there. There's nothing like this or in this size that exists anywhere, and believe me I've looked for it.

GIRL (at PDAP):   This is my twenty-ninth day of sobriety. (Cheers, applause)

RATHER: The program's tools are peer pressure and peer support, laced with a heavy dose of getting yourself right with God, with others and with yourself. All of it encouraged and directed by a staff of PDAP trained and paid counselors who are themselves ex-drug abusers.

COUNSELOR: It's real easy to get into a negative place, you know. So what we do up here is we learn how to be positive. Does anybody want to share?

RATHER: Members are told to steer clear of non-members, and to attend as many meetings as they can, meetings which combine the kind of public confessional popular in certain churches with a dose of amateur group therapy.

GIRL: And yesterday, I was in a car accident. I wrecked the only material thing I had that meant anything to me, my car. And it was the only thing I had that could get me to California. And I just sat in the car, and I wasn't angry, where normally I would be angry for what happened. And I didn't want to go get high. For the first time in my life, I did not want to get high. As far as I'm concerned, this is my first day here, because this is the first day I'm giving a hundred percent. I led a meeting yesterday on risk, and I haven't been willing to take that risk. I haven't been willing. I have thousands of people in PDAP that love me, and they — they don't even know me, some of them. And I'm willing to give it all. I'm finally willing.

(Applause)

RATHER: Some of these PDAP members are well into their twenties. But much younger drug users, some only eleven or twelve, attend other meetings.

BOY: I've been having a lot — a lot of problems, because I — I didn't admit that mind-changing chemicals have messed up at least part of my life. And I know that they have, because I've been stealing from my brother, and doing anything just to get high, you know.

RATHER: At just about every meeting, someone gets a monkey fist — a braided leather ball at the end of a leather necklace.

GIRL: Get a 30-days fist by staying straight 30 days consecutively in a row.

RATHER: Kids who already have their fist bear witness.

GIRL: You just came in my life at a real special time. You know, you kind of replaced a void that I was feeling, and I just watched you grow a whole lot. You're real special to me, and I really like having a little brother. I love you.

(Cheers, applause . . . chanting)

MEEHAN: When one walks in the doors, he must think that anybody that takes a drink, smokes a joint, is a complete loser. Pick winners is the — pick people that — that you respect, that you look up to, that — that offer you a way of life that you think you'd like.

(On phone):   See if you can get me Larry Layden.

RATHER: Bob Meehan is a winner. From the depths of drunkenness and addiction, he has risen to head a multi-million-dollar program with a paid staff of more than 300 ex-addicts. Judges, ministers, company presidents, sit on his boards of directors and contribute to his program.

(Meehan performing with rock group Freeway)

He has formed a rock group from among his members; and while PDAP youngsters are discouraged, even forbidden, to attend other rock concerts, they are encouraged to buy tickets to the occasional appearances of Freeway. The music isn't all that good, but there is something refreshing about a rock concert not overwhelmed by the pungent smell of burning marijuana.

Meehan's income has risen as his program has grown — from nearly nothing to more than $100,000 a year in salary from PDAP and from consultant fees from hospitals and corporations as an advisor on drug abuse and its cure. And he says he's worth it.

MEEHAN: I have a great head. I know more about this problem than anybody I know. I'm the most together person I know. And if anybody wants to know what to do about the problem in a business, they consult with me, they're going to get the right answers. And I am very expensive. If I wasn't making money, you wouldn't be here today, partner.

WOMAN: May we have a few moments of silence.

RATHER: Parents too are part of PDAP. Something less than half the parents whose kids are in the program are active. In PDAP parlance, these are the good parents. They also support the organization financially. Parents give 80 percent of the cost of PDAP. The other 20 percent comes from donations from corporations and foundations.

MAN: God, I love you all.

(Group responds . . . applause)

RATHER: Does the program work? Do the kids get off drugs and stay off? Meehan and his colleagues have repeatedly said that they are 75 to 80 percent successful. But when they are pressed, they say that those figures refer only to the percentage of kids who stay straight for 30 days and get their monkey fist. And when Meehan is pressed further, even that doesn't hold up too well.

MEEHAN: First of all, lets take a criteria for success, which is — which is where the general public gets so confused. To me, somebody — I've been on methadone. I — I tell parents that if you want your child on methadone, great. You always wanted a vegetable garden anyway. Put them in the back yard, a little dirt around their feet, they'll be on hold till they die, see. But everybody sits around, saying, well at least they won't steal my color TV. Wrong. Wrong. They're loaded for that whole year that they keep their stats on them, okay? And they're considered a success. What is success? What are we going to use as a definition for success? To me, it's one who has become a dues-paying member of society, has returned to school, no longer has a chemical problem, okay? Is moving on to enjoy life to its fullest, and being part of what you and I consider society. In that area, we are more successful than anybody I know of. What about the bottom line dry statistics? Fine. Mr. Rather, 60 MINUTES, if you care to give me $75,000 to do that kind of study and hire the statisticians necessary to do it, I will.

RATHER: Are you saying to me that you don't have any data to back up your claim that you're 75 to 80 percent successful?

MEEHAN: We have, the data we have is quite different from data anybody else has. And see, we don't keep records on people. You — if — if your child came to us, they don't have to give us their right name. They want help, they stay. They don't, they leave.

RATHER: Pardon me for interrupting, but that — that's part of the problem.

MEEHAN: No stats, yes. We —

RATHER: Again, you see, I find that an absolutely astonishing thing, that you would say, "Mr. Rather, I don't even know the names of most people who come into our place."

MEEHAN: That's right. We're not here for names. We're here to show people a better way to live.

RATHER: Okay, but —

MEEHAN: If you want it, stay. You don't, leave.

RATHER: You can't give me a figure: these are the numbers of people that we had come through our doors nationwide.

MEEHAN: No, we don't have the time. We get 400 calls a day from all over the world.

RATHER: Okay. You don't know how many are coming through the door.

MEEHAN: No.

RATHER: So, how can you say you're 75 to 80 percent successful.

MEEHAN: Because of the times that I ran groups, I knew, when I knew the kids in the group, when I saw how many came in — when I was running a group myself — I saw how many came in, and I knew what it was.

RATHER: Mr. Meehan, I don't doubt for a moment that you did that. But when you boil it down, what you've got is a guess.

MEEHAN: Oh, definitely. Oh, you're right. Definitely, a guess.

RATHER: Okay. So, when you say you're 75 to 80 percent effective, you're guessing.

MEEHAN: I'd like to say 70.

RATHER: All right, let's say 70. Let's — let's take a conservative figure. Do you consider that to be conservative?

MEEHAN: No. Conservative, 65 to 70.

RATHER: All right, 65 to 70.

MEEHAN: Okay.

RATHER: I note that we're already down from 75 to 80 percent down to 65 to 70.

MEEHAN: I — do — you haven't talked to me.

RATHER: All right, you — you say 65 to 70. But I say, is that your guess as to how effective you are?

MEEHAN: That's my guess.

RATHER: We talked to someone in Dallas who is very complimentary about the program. But they noted that in Dallas that your people had said they had 2,000 PDAP members in the Dallas area. But when they actually got down to counting heads, it turned out to be 500. Is that true?

MEEHAN: Very true.

RATHER: You can understand how someone in my position, trying to be an honest broker of information, would come away with at least the impression, number one, their success figures are inflated; number two, their overall membership figures are inflated.

MEEHAN: Yes, sir.

RATHER: But it's not the truth?

MEEHAN: It's really not. It's really not.

RATHER: Your success figures are 65 to 70 percent?

MEEHAN: At least. At least.

RATHER: If Meehan's figures on how many come in, how many stay, and how many actually kick the habit are wobbly, that makes equally suspect his statement to us that he only spends an average $500 per year per member. And that dollar amount doesn't even include the huge hospital costs of an estimated 550 youngsters referred last year by PDAP to this hospital and other hospitals run by the same management company, a company which pays Bob Meehan $50,000 a year as a consultant. Average length of stay in the hospital: four to six weeks. Average cost: at least $10,000 per youngster. That's not paid by PDAP. It's paid by parents and medical insurance. That alone is twice the entire PDAP budget. In the hospital, the PDAP patients get bio-feedback, psychotherapy and other medical treatment. Few of them need detoxification. But what they also get is a concentrated dose of PDAP. PDAP counselors, whose salary is paid indirectly by the hospital, hold PDAP meetings daily. And they treat and manage patients right along with the more highly trained staff. Are all these youngsters really sick enough or addicted enough to need to be hospitalized? Susie Waters was a PDAP counselor at the hospital for five months last year.

SUSIE WATERS: I think that the reason why most of those people were in there was so we could make a big impression on them right from the beginning. It's a way of isolating them, to only get PDAP from the very front. It was troublemakers that ended up in the hospital. It was the people that wouldn't go by the normal rules, that wouldn't stick with winners, or that wouldn't stop going to concerts. It was the troublemakers that ended up there. And a lot of them were just little kids. You know, they were just out having fun. I remember thinking a lot of time, why is this person here, you know. They weren't — I was just the same as a lot of them.

RATHER: The hospital management flatly denies that the PDAP patients they admitted didn't need the medical treatment they got. And they said the consultant fee they paid Bob Meehan was for his advice on drug abuse, and had nothing to do with the fact that PDAP referred so many patients. Meehan couldn't see the connection, either.

And they pay you $50,000 a year.

MEEHAN: At this time.

RATHER: What do you mean "at this time"?

MEEHAN: Well, I plan to tell them I'm worth a lot more, because they've made an awful lot of money at what they — what — because that they listened to me. And — and I think I'm worth more.

RATHER: Right on the surface of it, there is a conflict of interest. On the one hand, you sit at the top of the PDAP pyramid. On the other hand, you have a personal service contract with the hospital for whom you are directly − not just in effect − directly supplying patients.

MEEHAN: No, sir, I am not. The counselors that work for me are going to put their patients, or are going to refer, to hospitals that they think are doing the best job.

RATHER: You don't see a conflict of interest?

MEEHAN: I really don't.

BOB GAFFNEY: Bob Meehan is just — sits on the right hand of God to most of those people. And to me at one time, that's the way I looked at him.

RATHER: Bob Gaffney was a staff counselor for PDAP. He spent five years in the group. This man, who asked that we not give his name, was in PDAP four years, rising to the high staff post of director of the Dallas branch.

Does the Palmer Drug Abuse Program prepare these young people for reality?

MAN: No. As a matter of fact, we're led to believe that we can't make it without the program, which I think is one of the greatest disservices that's done to anybody that goes through the program. Because I think many people who leave, who naturally leave and who could be considered successes of the program, basically fail because the message is there: I cannot succeed without these people and without this program.

RATHER: Is that what is sold on the inside, from Bob Meehan right on down?

MAN: Yes.

RATHER: That you cannot succeed without the program.

MAN: Yes, yes.

RATHER: Well, that makes it never-ending.

MAN: Yes.

RATHER: They are two of dozens of former PDAP staff members with whom we spoke. They are all sober and straight and feel the program helped them; but equally, they feel, the program has serious flaws.

MAN: Power has become as intoxicating to some people as perhaps drugs were several years ago.

RATHER: By "some people," do you mean Meehan specifically?

MAN: Yes.

MEEHAN: I don't even like power. I am a powerful person. That is to — personal power.

RATHER: Well, among the strongest powers is the power to persuade.

MEEHAN: That's right. I have that power. I certainly do. I've been a con all my life. Just now I'm using it in a good way, see. That's the only difference. People come in to me and want to sober up, I don't say — they say, boy, it hurts when you do that.

I don't say, don't do that, all right? They come in and they try to act cool, I say, hey, don't come in here acting cool. Cool people never get to see me, partner, you know. Cool people out there are making it, so don't come in here telling me you're cool. You know, you got problems or you wouldn't be here. Mamma didn't bring you in by the back of your neck because you're cool. That's a con. It's using words he's going to understand. It's communicating. What is my purpose? To get him to think for himself, to be his own man, and make him see where he really is. In that way, I am powerful.

GAFFNEY: They don't look at it like you're coming into this program to recover and move on. They look at it like you stepped into a better way of life than everybody else in the world has. That's the problem. And if you want to leave, you know, there's something wrong with you. Bob, I think, thought that I was really going to be in the gutter with a needle in my arm or something because I was leaving, you know. And they really think that way, you know. To them, when you get to PDAP, you have arrived.

MAN: It comes down that major decisions in people's lives — you know, continuing an education, getting a job, getting married, going steady — all involve other people and what they think about it. Basically, you can — you can lead your whole life in the program and never have to make a decision, except that you're going to let somebody else make decisions for you.

MEEHAN: That's a lie. It's very upsetting. I don't know if these people are getting high again and have the need to somehow knock us. I don't know what their situation is. I think if you go and talk to some of the people that are making it and doing fine, you would hear another story. But remember, they're out there making it. They're not sitting around chewing on my tail. They're doing their thing. They don't have time to sit around and talk to 60 MINUTES, because they're trying to stay on the dean's list. You're going to have to hunt them down. Well, you don't have time to hunt them down. So who do you pick on? The losers that are lurking around hoping to get on 60 MINUTES.

RATHER: Well, I gather that you're concerned about the line of questioning?

MEEHAN: Oh, yes.

RATHER: Why?

MEEHAN: It's my baby. It's my baby. I know that everything that happens here is the most positive — one of the most positive moving forces in this whole nation today. I know that, without a doubt in my mind. I know that just from the shows we did with Carol Burnett and some people, the calls that we've gotten, that people finally took back control of their homes, told their children love does not mean accepting wrong behavior, threw the dope out, took some hot — positive moves in this country that haven't been done in years. You know, I know what we're doing. My problem is, and my mistake is, I've gotten too successful.

RATHER: The extent of that success will have to await a less self-serving analysis. Unquestionably, there are a number of youngsters who have given up drugs and alcohol with PDAP's help, and we have met some of them. Just as unquestionably, a number have gone back to getting high. And no one really knows what either of those numbers are. As for young Carrie Hamilton, she's still straight and drug free, and last week she went home to her parents in Los Angeles.

A Few Minutes
with Andy Rooney

MORLEY SAFER: In the beginning, there was Super Bowl I – Roman "I." Tonight, there was Super Bowl X-I-V. A year from now, there'll be Super Bowl X-V; and on and on and on. But for the moment, there is nothing.

ANDY ROONEY: Could I ask a little favor of some of you tonight? Please don't sit there saying you hate football and you're glad it's over. Don't say that. Some of us are very sad. There's a hole in our lives you could drive a truck through, as Frank Gifford might say. Be kind to those of us who love football as we go through these agonizing weeks of withdrawal. Don't start out right away with saying cruel things. You know, things like, "You can unfasten your seat belt now, dear. The games are over." Or, "You remember your children, don't you? This is Donald. He turned nine while you were gone." No one who has just lost a close friend wants to hear smart aleck remarks. Just be patient and try to help us. We're going to be okay.

In another month or so, we'll be able to sit up and take food again at the dining room table, instead of in front of the tube in the living room. We have a stack of Sunday papers we never got to read, but we have until next fall now to catch up on them. Next fall starts with the first pre-season game on August 8th. We'll be back in touch with the world again pretty soon, too. Pat Summerall mentioned Jimmy Carter during the half-time show a few weeks ago. He is still President, isn't he? Be patient with us now that football's over.

Letters

MORLEY SAFER: That brings us to the mail, and some more thoughts about football.

About our story last week on football injuries, one viewer said, "People who go to football games and encourage defensive tackles to cream offensive backs remind me of the crazy Romans who . . . enjoyed (seeing) helpless people being torn to death by lions."

During that story, Terry Bradshaw and Rocky Bleier criticized Astroturf by name, which prompted Monsanto, which makes and trademarks Astroturf, to write and say, "Astroturf was improperly used as the generic term for artificial turf when, in fact, there are several manufacturers' products installed in NFL stadiums . . . For instance, the Pittsburgh Steelers play at home on a competitive product."

About Commissioner Pete Rozelle's contention that artificial turf is being used on football fields because it enables stadium owners to use the field for other activities, a viewer wrote, "I suspect the real reason they want artificial turf is (because) the uniforms don't get dirty and (that) presents a much neater image to television."

And what did viewers think about our story on presidential candidate George Bush? You pays your money and you takes your choice. One viewer said, "I don't know what your motive was in attempting to put down George Bush, but you were . . . clumsy and obvious about it."

Another viewer, watching that same story, said, "It was the most inspiring, the most gratifying (story) I have yet seen on television about a Presidential candidate."

And finally, about our story on Americans who avoid paying taxes by keeping their income off the books, there was this, "When taxes are perceived as oppressive, the populace . . . does what the government refuses to do: Lower them (themselves)."

And about the yacht owner who doesn't pay taxes and said he would sail away to the Bahamas if the IRS came after him, a viewer said, "Tell that guy to get on his boat, go out to the Bahamas and take all those other (tax evaders) with him. Then the rest of us won't have to pay (their) tab (along with our own)."

JANUARY 27, 1980

Russian Spies in the U.S.A.

GAIL EISEN, PRODUCER

MIKE WALLACE: Detente is dead. The cold war is back on again. And nonetheless, according to a man who should know, a small army of Russian spies continues to operate with remarkable freedom in the United States. The man who says that is Arkady Shevchenko, who, until his dramatic defection to the United States in 1978, was thought to be a Soviet hardliner, close to Brezhnev and Gromyko. It turned out he was something different.

This man who talked to us about Russian spies in the U.S. told the House Select Committee on Intelligence two days ago in Washington that he had defected because "democracy in the Soviet Union is a mockery," and that "elementary human rights do not exist" there. For five years before his defection, Shevchenko served as undersecretary for political affairs in the United Nations Secretariat. In that post, he was in a position to know what went on in Moscow, at the Russian UN Mission in New York, and in the UN Secretariat itself.

I asked Shevchenko how many spies the Russians have now working under cover of UN headquarters in New York.

ARKADY SHEVCHENKO: Half of the Soviet diplomatic staff would be either KGB officers or the GRU officers.

WALLACE: That means that in the United Nations building on New York's East River, among the clerks and ambassadors, the functionaries and reporters who roam these corridors, the Soviets have succeeded in planting literally hundreds of their spies.

SHEVCHENKO: The professional KGB and the GRU, at least 300 it would be.

WALLACE: We wondered whether Shevchenko's figures, his estimates as to the number of KGB and GRU officers — GRU is Soviet Military Intelligence — working under cover of the UN, we wondered if those figures were accurate. For 12 years, FBI officer Larry McWilliams, now retired, worked in counterintelligence against the Soviets in the city of New York.

You would say then 350 would be in espionage?

LARRY McWILLIAMS: Yes.

WALLACE: That's a lot.

McWILLIAMS: That's an awful lot. It's a horrendous task to try and counter.

SHEVCHENKO: The more personnel they have, the more difficult FBI task to follow them, if you have hundreds of these people wandering around in this country. That's why the UN Secretariat is so important for them, because there they can have such a huge army of the KGB professionals or GRU professionals, that gives them advan — advantages. They don't — they don't care about how much personnel. They — they could — if they would be allowed, they would send thousands here. The UN staff member, they — unlike the Soviet diplomats, they could travel without prior identification in this country.

WALLACE: In other words, you, as a member of the UN Secretariat, can travel any place?

SHEVCHENKO: Yes, any place, except the military bases or restricted area, where even American are not allowed to — to come.

WALLACE: The United Nations then, Mr. McWilliams, is the single most important spy nest, if you want to call it that, in the world today.

McWILLIAMS: Hm-mmm. My view, definitely. No doubt about it, because of their basic freedom of travel. But beyond that, they're in a marvelous position in this city that contains everything. It contains the head corporations of industry. It contains finance. They're interested in economics. My gosh, there's no better place on earth to be. You see, it's got — there's so many of the headquarters of industrial empires that deal with sophisticated weapons, communications, all sorts. It's a marvelous place for a spy to be.

WALLACE: A marvelous place, partly because of the opportunities there are here in New York for electronic eavesdropping. For example, at the Russian UN Mission on the East Side of Manhattan, or at their apartment complex in the suburb of Riverdale, at their estate in Oyster Bay, Long Island, and especially at their retreat in Glen Cove, Long Island. The Soviets have the most sophisticated equipment for listening, for electronic surveillance.

SHEVCHENKO: They have the highly sophisticated electronic equipment for — as interception of the telecommunications, the radio communications in this country, eyedropping and all the thing. So that —

WALLACE: Eavesdropping.

SHEVCHENKO: Yes. (laughs) Not eyedropping. It's eavesdropping. Yes.

WALLACE: You mean that they — they do eavesdrop and intercept telecommunications, telephone calls, cables?

SHEVCHENKO: Yes, that's correct. That is — that is exactly so.

McWILLIAMS: Soviet military attache's office in Washington, the Soviet Embassy, just go past them, and you look up and you'll see nothing but a massive amount of sophisticated antenna. And that's used for monitoring of all types of communications — satellites, telephones, radio. Now, if you get into the scientific field and start talking about computerization, (there) are multiple listening devices. My God, they can sit up there with one of those antenna and just listen to thousands upon thousands of telephone conversations wandering around this area.

WALLACE: Of course the FBI can listen too, as they did during an operation against the Soviets in April of 1977. They chose U.S. Navy Commander Arthur Lindberg to flush out some Russian UN spies. Posing as a tourist, he boarded a Russian cruise ship, and on leaving the vessel, he handed over a note addressed simply: "To the Russian Ambassador."

COMMANDER ARTHUR LINDBERG: The note said, "I am a career American Naval officer stationed in the New York City area, and will retire in six years. I'm interested in making additional money prior to my retirement and can provide you with information which may be of interest to you. If you are interested, telephone me at 201-922-9724 at 11:45 AM, August 30th, 1977."

WALLACE: Lindberg reconstructed for the cameras what happened.

COMMANDER LINDBERG: Precisely 11:45 on August 30th, the phone rang and the whole operation commenced. The notes that I would receive at phone booths were generally put in magnetic key containers and left underneath the ledge of the telephone booth.

WALLACE: First, they sent him this questionaire. "Do you have camera?," it asked. "Do you familiar with photo?" was another question.

COMMANDER LINDBERG: They wanted secrets that were dealing primarily with the anti-submarine warfare, and most sensitive Naval secrets that I could obtain.

WALLACE: The Russians put two KGB officers in touch with Lindberg. And then, unbeknownst to them, the FBI monitored every development. This videotape, secretly shot by FBI agents, was to prove crucial in identifying the UN spies. It shows one of the Russians in snowy weather visiting one of the phone booths in the New Jersey area where the operation took place. The technique of the Russians was to move Lindberg from booth to booth, leaving messages, changing routes, making it almost impossible for anyone else to interfere. Unknown to the Russian, his phone call is being tape-recorded at Commander Lindberg's end.

RUSSIAN: You have the stuff?

COMMANDER LINDBERG: Yes, I do.

RUSSIAN: You do. Proceed now to the stop. And just after the Essex Toll Plaza —

COMMANDER LINDBERG: Yeah?

RUSSIAN;   You'll see the phone booth, public phone booth.

COMMANDER LINDBERG: Uh-huh.

RUSSIAN: Now the second phone booth from the right, if you look at, in front of you. You know, right after the booth. The number is seven-four-eight.

COMMANDER LINDBERG: Seven-four-eight.

RUSSIAN: Nine-six.

COMMANDER LINDBERG: Nine-six.

RUSSIAN: Eleven.

COMMANDER LINDBERG: Eleven.

RUSSIAN: Yes. And follow the instructions completely. And you'll find everything there, all right?

COMMANDER LINDBERG: Right. I'll talk to you later.

RUSSIAN: Hm-mmm. Okay, bye-bye. (He hangs up phone)

WALLACE: At the end of the call, the Russian carefully places the magnetic key case, together with the next message for Lindberg, underneath the phone shelf, and he leaves and returns to the car. Incredibly, he was using his own vehicle registered in his own name. Commander Lindberg arrives to enter the phone booth and collect the message in the magnetic box that's been left for him by the Russians. Once the spies had been identified on the tape, Commander Lindberg had to pass real secrets over, so they could be charged with a real offense. The man in the phone booth was Vladik Enger, a Russian UN civil servant.

SHEVCHENKO: I knew that the both of them KGB.

WALLACE: You did know?

SHEVCHENKO: Yeah, I did, because Enger had been working in my department. I was officially told by the Soviet KGB resident that he is a KGB professional officer.

WALLACE: Rudolf Chernyayev was the other spy. He too was a Russian UN civil servant. No real defense was offered at their trial and they were sentenced to 50 years in prison. Eventually, they were exchanged for five leading Russian dissidents.

I asked Mr. Shevchenko about the cost of the KGB operation at the UN.

The United States pays about 30 percent —

SHEVCHENKO: Yes.

WALLACE: — of the cost to the United Nations Secretariat, right?

SHEVCHENKO: Correct. Correct.

WALLACE: And half of the people at the UN Secretariat who are Russians are KGB, you say?

SHEVCHENKO: Yes. Yes.

WALLACE: So —

SHEVCHENKO: Or — or GRU.

WALLACE: Intelligence.   So, in effect, the U.S. taxpayer —

SHEVCHENKO: Yes, certainly.

WALLACE: — is paying Russian spies at the UN in New York.

SHEVCHENKO: Exactly. That — that is — it's — it's exactly so.

WALLACE: Now, in New York, there is a gentleman by the name of Victor Lessiovsky. He's a personal assistant to Secretary General Kurt Waldheim. And the story goes that he is simply well-known as a KGB agent. True?

SHEVCHENKO: I think he well-known as a KGB officer, and — but people sometimes, even knowing that, don't hesi — not only don't hesitate to talk to him and to meet with him, but even interested sometimes to — to — meet and to discuss some of the things with a high-level KGB officer. He's intelligent man, very sociable, and very knowledgeable.

WALLACE: Of what use is he if everybody knows that he's KGB?

McWILLIAMS: He's of great value to them, Mike. They have — he has access to so many Americans that disregard the fact that he's an intelligence officer.

WALLACE: I know of — of reporters, I know businessmen, I know attorneys here in New York who spend a good deal of time socially with Lessiovsky.

McWILLIAMS: If I was in business, let's say, and knew Lessiovsky, and he was exposed as a KGB officer, I'd say, "I'm sorry. I'll talk to a businessman or I'll talk to a legitimate diplomat, but I won't talk to you."

WALLACE: And Victor Lessiovsky declined to talk to us. Neither would Waldheim discuss Lessiovsky or espionage at the UN.

The UN oath, which is taken by everybody who works for the Secretariat, says that they're going to exercise the functions entrusted to me as an international civil servant of the UN and not to seek or accept instructions illegal to the performance of my duties from any government or other authority external to the organization. Now obviously you had to sign that oath. Lessiovsky, everybody signs that oath.

SHEVCHENKO: Well, certainly. Everybody sign that. And a good many — a good deal of people pay no attention of that, but especially the Soviets pay no attention to that at all.

WALLACE: In other words, you are working — you are working for the UN ostensibly, but — but in fact, you are working for the Soviet Union?

SHEVCHENKO: That is correct.

WALLACE: Recently, Shevchenko has been living quietly near Washington with his new American wife, Elaine, and writing a book about his life in the Soviet foreign service. I asked him about the circumstances of his break with the Soviets.

Mr. Shevchenko, shortly after your defection in 1978, there were two private meetings with you held at the request of the Russians. Present at those meetings were the the Russian ambassador here in Washington, Dobrynin, the UN Ambassador, Troyanovsky, your lawyers, and some State Department people. The Russians knew that they had lost you, and they wanted you back. They said that you had been — quote — "reading top secret documents in the Soviet mission up to the last day and sending reports back to Moscow."

SHEVCHENKO: That is so. It's correct.

WALLACE: They must have been stunned.

SHEVCHENKO: I would say so. (laughs)

WALLACE: And — and wanted you back desperately.

SHEVCHENKO: That, they — they tried to do that, but they failed.

WALLACE: Some of what you have seen here appeared first on the BBC in London. We are grateful for their cooperation in this report.

All About Oral
JOSEPH WERSHBA, PRODUCER

MORLEY SAFER: Oral Roberts at 62 is the granddaddy of the electronic preachers. He declares with absolute certainty that God cures the sick by the laying on of his — Oral Roberts' — hands. He claims further that he talks to God, and God orders him to do God's work: build a university, build a medical center in Tulsa, Oklahoma that combines medicine with faith. He calls it the City of Faith. It began with great assurance, but today there's big trouble in the City of Faith, and the Reverend Roberts says if he doesn't finish the quarter-billion-dollar project, he'll lose his soul. Beyond the financial troubles in the City of Faith, there's a movement afoot in Tulsa to stop it on purely secular grounds. We wanted to talk to Oral Roberts about it all, about the City of Faith and his faith healing. First he said yes, then he said no, but his organization generously did let us use a lot of its film.

ORAL ROBERTS: It's time we believed in the King of Kings and Lord of Lords who reached in the burning fire furnace and snatched out the three Hebrew children.

SAFER: When Oral gets the spirit up, stand back. He is not Mister Cool. He is on a warm, first-name relationship with God and in a hot fight-to-the-finish with Satan.

ORAL ROBERTS: What God wants is obedience. What God wants is people with faith. What God wants is people who are willing to suffer and to stand up and look the devil in the eye and say, "I don't belong to you, devil! I'm God's property. Take your hands off God's property. That means me. I belong to God."

(Richard Roberts singing hymn)

SAFER: The organization seems to be pitching Oral's son, Richard, as his eventual successor, and Richard, narrating this film, has no doubt his daddy talks to God.

RICHARD ROBERTS: He is a man who hears the voice of God deep in his heart and obeys it, who sees visions from God and follows them, who feels the healing love of God and shares it, no matter what the cost.

SAFER: He claims to talk to God.

VADEN ROBERTS: Yes, and I don't know about that. I don't know.

SAFER: Vaden Roberts, Oral's older brother, was Oral's right-hand man in the days of his tent crusade. Vaden is loyal to his brother, but on the matter of Oral talking to God, he has reservations.

VADEN ROBERTS: That's the wonderment. I don't know. I'm a — I'm a — I don't want to say anything that would, shall we say, offend God and doubt God's word and doubt God's presence and doubt God's power. For me to say that I don't believe in God, or God talks to anybody, I'm afraid to say that. He don't to me. He has never to me, to — to my knowledge.

ORAL ROBERTS: And I want to tell you what I believe from the bottom of my heart, something about you, and it's this: Something good is going to happen to you!

(Music: "Something Good Is Going To Happen To You")

SAFER: "Something good is going to happen to you" — that has been Oral Roberts' message and ministry for more than 30 years, first by tent, then by television. God is the great healer, and Oral Roberts' hands are His servants.
Do you believe that Oral Roberts' hands can heal?

VADEN ROBERTS: No, sir. Hands can heal? No, sir.

SAFER: Some of those cures that we used to see in the old tent show on television, people getting our of wheelchairs and stuff, were those people really cured?

VADEN ROBERTS: I've seen people that I thought wanted a little attention. You see what I mean?

SAFER: I see what you mean.

VADEN ROBERTS: I've seen people that I thought needed a little attention and seized upon that moment to get a little attention. Now, I — this is a private thought of mine.

SAFER: But one of the prickliest thorns in Oral Roberts' bosom this past year is this book, *Give Me That Prime Time Religion,* an insider's report written by Jerry Sholes, who worked as a writer on Oral's TV shows and also on Oral's fund-raising seminars.

JERRY SHOLES: After these people have given their money, then the next day, after the money is in, he lays hand on them. He prays for the sick. And I've seen people in wheelchairs come in. I've never seen anybody healed.

ORAL ROBERTS: Lord Jesus, loose her!

SAFER: Is it rigged?

SHOLES: I — I'm not — I'm not going to say it's rigged, because I — I — I don't think that's what it is. There are people who, maybe because of the type of illness they have, they use a wheelchair from comfort. They're not totally ambulatory. It hurts their hip sockets to walk. But if they have to get up to go to the bathroom or get into a car, they can do it. These are the people in Oral Roberts' seminars who will get up out of their wheelchair and they may be healed for as long as it takes them to get backstage and behind that back curtain and get back into the wheelchair.

Can you imagine the power that you would really have as an individual if you could indeed heal somebody, whether you did it or God did it through you? That's not Oral Roberts. That's not any faith healer. It's — it's hucksterism at its worst because you're exploiting people who are at the lowest point in their life. And when you're dying, you're going to turn to anything.

SAFER: What's this?

SHOLES: It's a piece of cloth with Oral's handprint on it.

SAFER: How do you get one of these?

SHOLES: You write Oral Roberts and ask for one. You put it anywhere on your body that you feel bad, it'll make you feel better. You believe that?

SAFER: That's the imprint?

SHOLES: That's Oral's imprint.

SAFER: Of his hand?

SHOLES: Yes.

SAFER: "As you place your hand on the imprint of mine, immediately look to the healing and restoring hand of the living Christ." Does this cost something?

SHOLES: The letter that went with this encouraged you to send Oral Roberts $38 for the City of Faith.

SAFER: Dr. C. T. Thompson, a Tulsa surgeon, is not neutral on the subject of Oral Roberts. He's a committed opponent of the Oral Roberts brand of medicine.

DR. C.T. THOMPSON: You know, every time a new project comes up out there, God sort of puts it on him. It used to be that was one of the prima facie evidences that would get you sent to the funny farm, was hearing God talk to you.

SAFER: Dr. Thompson, do you dismiss the healing power of prayer?

THOMPSON: No, sir. No, sir. I've been — I've been a doctor for over 30 years and I think that faith is of a central core of almost all patients' ability to do well and their own sense of well-being. But I don't think that there's a specific faith that will make a cancer go away or that will make a heart attack disappear or that will make a diabetic need less insulin.

ORAL ROBERTS: And then God told me to raise Him up a university, "Raise up your students to hear My voice."

SAFER: And Oral did raise up a university in Tulsa, Oklahoma, and gave it his own name. Everything about it is space-age and computer clean. It is fully accredited academically and attracts students from all over the country, but only those who want a religious atmosphere: tight discipline on alcohol, drugs, haircuts and clothes, and even on fitness.

INSTRUCTOR: On your marks, go. (Students dive into swimming pool)

SAFER: At ORU, fatties need not apply. If they get that way, they are put through the aerobic center. If they don't shape up, they ship out. A religious soul in a healthy body could be the university's motto. ORU's student body is almost all white and its varsity basketball team almost all black. The school recruits as fervently as any school in an attempt to keep its name as up-front as possible. It offered one prominent coach a 10-year, two-and-a-half million dollar contract. The medical and dental schools have not yet graduated doctors or dentists, but the equipment is as good as any school's anywhere. The television facilities are better than some network production centers. From here, Oral Roberts broadcasts his weekly programs — explicit faith, implicit fund-raisings. Big stars help bring in the faithful with four, one-hour variety shows each year. Oral claims 60 million people watch each show. They get his healing message, and they respond with millions of dollars.

Oral Roberts has come a long way from the Bible-thumping, sawdust trail of tank towns and circus tents. Here in Tulsa, Oklahoma, he's built his own New Jerusalem. Over here, University Village, a retirement community that older partners in the faith can buy into. And over there, that exotic looking space needle is the Prayer Tower, a place that they tell us receives something like 2,000 phone calls a day from partners seeking spiritual help. And all around it, Oral Roberts University. And behind me, Oral's pride and conceivably his undoing: The City of Faith — hospital, research center, clinic — a grand design that he says will combine the best of medical science with the best of faith healing.

ORAL ROBERTS: You know, a lot of people don't stop to realize the Almighty God is able to heal cancer.

SAFER: The City of Faith will consist of a 60-story clinic, a 30-story hospital, eventually with 777 beds — Oral believes in lucky seven — and a 20-story research center for cancer, heart and aging. In the front, two bronze hands, supposedly modeled on Oral's raised in prayer, and rising 60 feet over a "river of life." The original estimated cost: $100 million. Oral's people now concede it will run closer to 200 million. Oral's critics think it will cost 400 million. A rough guess might be 250 million. It's scheduled to open in 1981, but Oral's critics are trying to stop that. They argue the City of Faith will destroy the good hospital system already operating in Tulsa.

DR. THOMPSON: I can think of no place in this country that has an actual need for that many hospital beds, any place. The very size and complexity of sort of imposing a giant, almost egomaniacal structure on a medical care system in which there's not been the slightest bit of evidence of need can only attest to me that this is the fulfillment of a giant ego.

SAFER: The medical establishment has gone to court to stop the City of Faith. But

Oral Roberts is a man of some clout in Tulsa. The money and property he controls has put him on the board of the Bank of Oklahoma, the state's biggest bank; Oklahoma Natural Gas, the big utility; the Tulsa Chamber of Commerce. Politicians like to bask in his glory, but his huge undertaking is causing some doubts. and Oral, for the first time, admitted in a letter to his partners, his contributors, that he is strapped for funds, and if they don't cough up, the City of Faith will crumble.

ORAL ROBERTS: If I don't build the City of Faith, without a doubt, the university — the Oral Roberts University, will go under. Everything we have will go. You'll see nothing out here but — but buildings, maybe somebody else in them. If I don't obey God and do what He told me to do, my soul's at stake. I may lose my soul. I know I will if I disobey God.

SAFER: Does anybody have any idea just how much money Oral Roberts raises each year?

SHOLES: I do.

SAFER: How much?

SHOLES: All right, the seminars, as an average, we'll say two million to two-and-a-half million dollars a seminar. If he held ten of them, that's 25 million a year. Through the mail, another 22 to 30 million. That's 50 million a year, 50 to 55 million a year. That's a lot of money.

SAFER: How much of that $50 million a year goes to the benefit of Oral Roberts?

SHOLES: The best way maybe to answer that question is to, first, let's take a look at Oral's reported salary. It's reported as 29,500 per year. Now last year, I — my income tax statement, I paid taxes on twenty-nine eight. I don't wear Gucci loafers. I can't afford them. I don't buy five hundred to one thousand dollar Brioni suits. I don't have a $2 million Fanjet Falcon airplane at my disposal. I don't drive a $30,000 Mercedes or Cadillac Seville. I don't have a million-dollar home in Palm Springs. But my salary was $300 higher than Oral's. Now, I'm doing something wrong. See, it doesn't matter what your salary is once you get to a certain point because of the control you have over this corporate conglomerate known as the Oral Roberts Ministries.

SAFER: You say he takes a salary of around 29-and-a-half thousand dollars a year. But what about his royalties as an author? He publishes hundreds of books and million of copies.

SHOLES: Hm-mmm.

SAFER: Is that a source of income for him?

SHOLES: Well, as far back as 1955, his reported royalties were about $80,000 a year, royalties from books, as (indistinct).

SAFER: Those books are given away. How do you get royalties from books that you give away?

SHOLES: (laughs) All right. (Clears throat) There's a thing called Pinoak Publications. Pinoak Publications was set up to avoid the problem that Oral Roberts was having with a direct conversion of non-profit monies into his own pocket. The IRS frowned on an evangelist using a religious non-profit organization to market giveaways, records or books. Oral Roberts Association gives the book away to the person who writes in for it. And Oral Ro— and the Oral Roberts Association pays Pinoak for the book. Now when you — you look down through the books that Pinoak has a credit on, press runs from a hundred to four hundred thousand copies at a time. It doesn't cost you two dollars a book to turn out a 250 page book. It's less than fifty cents. So that leaves somebody, Pinoak, with a dollar-and-a-half left to play with. And Pinoak is a private family trust.

In one year, 1975, just two books, Oral Roberts gave away two million of them. And when you multiply two million times a dollar-and-a-half, in just one year, there's $3 million there to play with.

SAFER: Just after Jerry Sholes' book was published, he was brutally beaten by an unknown attacker. Sholes does not blame Oral, but thinks it could have come from a follower of his.

SHOLES: One of the people I called was Richard. He didn't offer to have his father come over and lay hands on me and heal my broken cheekbone and take care of my orbital forefracture and my double vision and my concussion. I had to go see a doctor to do that. (laughs)

ORAL ROBERTS: I'd rather go in that furnace and be standing up than to bow down and have him say, "Oh, what a great guy he is."

SAFER: Like Shadrach, Meshach and Abednego, Oral Roberts says he does not fear to enter the fiery furnace and that he would rather burn than bow his head to the critics of his grand design. Well, we asked him, not to enter the furnace, but to answer a few questions on this broadcast. He declined. What we would have liked to have asked him is: How much money does this organization bring in every year? And how much money goes to the benefit of Oral Roberts and his family? And how does a man earning $29,500 a year in salary manage to live like a millionaire? A few questions about his talks with God, and how the hands, and even the imprint of the hands, heal. And a whole raft of questions about building a hospital for a quarter-of-a-billion dollars, a hospital that experts in Tulsa say the city does not want and does not need. Oral does not answer. He hunkers down in his office and speaks only to God and to his flock.

ORAL ROBERTS: And now, take these words of God with you. They're in the Bible. And here are His words to you: "Greater is He who is in you, than He who is in the world!"

The Frontrunner?

JOEL BERNSTEIN, PRODUCER

DAN RATHER: Before last week's Iowa caucuses, we could have put that "frontrunner" label on Ronald Reagan without the question mark. Now, the early frontrunner is running into trouble. One poll has him tied with George Bush for the Republican presidential nomination. We sat down with Ronald Reagan yesterday in California and talked about his campaign.

You took that long lead and basically ran it right straight into the ground. What went wrong?

RONALD REAGAN: Well, for one thing, because of our strategy, possibly didn't put in the time that, as it turned out, we could have put in there. But I have been trying — I haven't been, as some people have been trying to say, some journalists and some pundits, that I've been sitting above the fray and not actually campaigning. I've been beating my brains out.

RATHER: What about the allegation that you delegated too much authority to John Sears, your campaign manager?

REAGAN: Well, no. It's my campaign. I made the decision about the debate in Iowa. My decision about the need to run in 35 primaries, not just pick a few out.

RATHER: You made the decision not to debate in Iowa?

REAGAN: That's right.

RATHER: That was a mistake, wasn't it?

REAGAN: I don't know. I don't know whether that had very much of an effect or not. But my reason for it was not anything to do with thinking I didn't need to go to Iowa. My reason was — and I felt this very deeply, was, one, that I have been against anything that makes it appear that Republicans are running against each other. And I was just fearful that anything that smacked of a debate could lend itself to the kind of devisiveness where we polarized our people, and then part of your people, when the nomination is finally given to someone, go home, instead of joining the campaign. Now, it could be that I'm wrong. Maybe the party is so unified now they can survive those things, and I'm going to take a look at each opportunity in the future and format of each, make a decision on each one. But I have to say that it did not prove divisive in Iowa, and — but that was my position. I knew I'd take some raps for not doing it, but I just felt that strongly.

RATHER: Are you willing to debate now?

REAGAN: I'm going to look at each one and make my decision depending on the format.

RATHER: Now correct me if I'm wrong. I think the translation of that is yes, you'll debate.

REAGAN: Yes. I — I think that's inherent in what I just said. Yes.

RATHER: These are among the things I've heard, that Ronald Reagan has campaigned so sparingly because his aides were frankly afraid he'd put his foot in his mouth.

REAGAN: (Laughs) No. I've read those things too. It isn't true. No one's trying to moderate me. No one's wrapping me in cellophane. I am out there and on my own, as I am right here with you. The campaign is mine. I'm in charge.

RATHER: Reagan was eager to talk about foreign policy. He said President Carter has been creating dangers by being weak and indecisive, waffling first one way then another. Halting grain sales and talk of boycotting the Olympics, Reagan said, are too little, too late, not nearly strong enough signals to the Soviet Union.

REAGAN: We're running the risk of actually being — of — of probably nuclear — possibly nuclear war, simply because of the Soviet Union reading these signals that they're getting, getting the feeling that there is no place at which we would risk war to stop them. And it is time that the United States send them the proper signals that indicate.

The President said, when they crossed the border, or before they crossed the border, when they were massed on the border, he sent a warning. In diplomatic language, it was a very firm warning. The President said to them that if they moved across that border, that would be taken by us as a most serious matter. Now, in diplomatic talk, that really means like two kids in a schoolground, you've knocked the chip off my shoulder. And they crossed the border, and nothing happened. We didn't evidently, take it as a serious matter. Then he said to the American people all these things about how seriously we take this and how we feel, and yet no signals.

Now, I believe, and I have talked for some time now, that some of those signals could be the presence of American forces in the Middle East, be our fleet, which is out there circling around in the Indian Ocean, bases established at Oman and Somalia, Pakistan.

RATHER: But the President is doing that.

REAGAN: No, his words were rather ambiguous. His words separated the Persian Gulf and Pakistan, which is not part of the Perisan Gulf. Pakistan is next in line on the border of Afghanistan.

RATHER: You favor putting troops in Pakistan?

REAGAN: I think that we should pro — be providing arms. The nature of the presence there, that would be followed, of course, I'm sure, by technicians. But whether it requires force there or not. But at least, to indicate — I don't think that the Soviet Union is ready yet. I don't think they have an edge — enough of an edge that they want a confrontation with the United States. And, therefore, I think that if we show a presence, that they're going to have to seriously consider whether they want to move further. But there's more to it than that. There is: How do we move them out of Pakistan? And I think that the United States should have a policy of — what can we do that would be a move comparable to their own move, and a move that would indicate to them that there is some reason why they should withdraw their troops.

RATHER: Pardon me, Governor. When you say move them out of Pakistan, do you mean move them out of Afghanistan?

REAGAN: Afghanistan. I'm sorry. Yes, Afghanistan. For example, why don't we take a closer look at Cuba? Here is their surrogate state over here in the Western Hemisphere, with Soviet military. And again, let me call to your attention that the President, when he discovered that combat brigade was there of Soviet troops, said to the American people, "I will not hold still for the status quo," meaning the presence of that brigade. But the brigade is still there and no action of any kind has been taken. Evidently, he's decided he can live with the status quo. But suppose we look at the options that we might have with regard to Cuba —

RATHER: Governor, you're —

REAGAN: — that would show the Soviet Union how seriously we take this aggression of theirs.

RATHER: I want to make sure I understand this. You're not suggesting that we consider putting — putting the heat on Cuba in retaliation for Afghanistan?

REAGAN: I'm suggesting that we might — we might blockade Cuba and stop the transportation back and forth of Russian arms, of Soviet military that are — submarines are based there. They have airplanes and pilots there. They have troops there on that island. A blockade of Cuba could be an option.

Now, I'm not prepared to name all of the options that we could possibly take, because no one, unless he's actually Pres — President, has the information as to what the options might be. But I'm talking of a process in which you select something that is of interest to the Soviet Union and say to the Soviet Union, "This is how seriously we take what you've done over here in this independent nation, and we're going to do this until you withdraw those troops."

RATHER: You think we're capable of blockading Cuba?

REAGAN: Yes.

RATHER: What would that do to our relations in Latin America?

REAGAN: I don't think it would bother them at all. As a matter of fact, I think a lot of Latin American countries right today are more concerned with our apparent weakness in the face of the Soviet Union than they are about us once again being big old Uncle Sam.

RATHER: If you were President today, Ronald Reagan —

REAGAN: Yeah?

RATHER: — would you actively consider the possibility of blockading Cuba?

REAGAN: Yes. But if I were President today, I would have access to the same information the President has and there might even be better options than that. I am not talking war and I'm not being a warmonger. I am talking of my fear that unless the United States sends the proper signals to the Soviet Union, that they are going to make the wrong choice. They are going to guess wrong and finally are going to make moves that will leave us no choice.

"I am not talking war and I'm not being a warmonger. I am talking of my fear that unless the United States sends the proper signals to the Soviet Union, that they are going to make the wrong choice."

RATHER: Well, you do have experience, two terms —

REAGAN: Yeah.

RATHER: — as governor of a very large state, California. But your foreign policy experience is slim to none, is it not?

REAGAN: Not exactly. I've heard some reference to that on the part of some of our other candidates. And it just so happens that during my terms as governor, a President of the United States asked me to represent him on several occasions abroad. I was meeting with Chiang Kai-shek at the t— time that Henry Kissinger was in Peking making the final details, the arrangements, for President Nixon's visit to China. And I was there to convince Taiwan that this was not a betrayal of them or throwing them overboard. I not only met with him extensively, and enjoyed the visit very much, but I met his son, who then was an official of the government, who is now the president of Taiwan. I was in Japan at the time of the devaluation of the dollar and the whole tension that grew out of the textile business and the — the problems with our textile trade.

RATHER: So, you would argue that you do have foreign policy experience?

REAGAN: I know — I know the present premier of Japan. I have been told that I am the only non-head of state who was granted an audience by the emperor of Japan. I know Margaret Thatcher and have met with her several times. I have met with Helmut Schmidt. I knew General Park, when he was President Park, of Korea, before his assassination.

RATHER: So, you think this is a bum rap?

REAGAN: Yes. As a matter of fact, I've met Brezhnev, and I've met others of the Politburo in their visits to the United States.

RATHER: Governor, I want to ask this question respectfully. But you mentioning Brezhnev, head of the Soviet Union, brings to mind that scene, and I know you saw it, of Brezhnev tottering, teetering at a very important meeting in East Germany fairly recently. And even though he heads the Soviet Union, one found oneself saying, you know, I really feel sorry for the Soviet Union to have a leader that not's quite in control of himself.

REAGAN: Hm-mmm.

RATHER: You know the picture I'm talking about?

REAGAN: Hm-mmm.

RATHER: I wonder if you know how many people who might otherwise be inclined to vote for you fear that that's what we'll wind up with if they vote for Ronald Reagan?

REAGAN: Well, in the first place, he's considerably older than I am. Second place, he's ill. Third place, I have authorized my physician — I have an annual check-up every year — to make public to anyone my condition. And I didn't even ask him what he was going to say. I have been told several times that I am physiologically younger than my years. And I would have to tell you this. If that were ever a possibility, I'd be the first to recognize it and the first to step down. I don't — I don't think there's any danger of that. And I have seen even younger heads of state who also have succumbed to illness. And I've often wondered this. They talk about my age in comparison to other Presidents of the past.

RATHER: You'd be the oldest American President ever at age 70, would you not?

REAGAN: Hm-mmm. But would I actually be, if my number of years — in comparison to the longevity today and the longevity then? How many Presidents were many years past the level of longevity when they became President back in years — not too many years ago, when the average lifespan was in its 40's and we had 50- and 55-year-old Presidents? Well, they were 15 years past the lifespan of the time. I haven't gotten to the average lifespan yet.

A Few Minutes
with Andy Rooney

MORLEY SAFER: Time now for a few minutes with Andy Rooney.

ANDY ROONEY: Do you find it hard to follow directions? I was thinking of installing one of those automatic garage door openers over the weekend. The directions say, "Make certain the garage door is square and straight and that the garage floor is level." Directions always read like that. Is everything in your house straight, square and level? If my house was straight, square and level, I would never have to fix anything. What we all need are directions that tell us what to do when everything is crooked, off-center and all screwed up. You buy a can of paint. You get ready to go to work. The paint seems a little thick, so you read the directions between the drips running down the side of the can. It says, "Make certain the surface is absolutely free of dirt, dust, grease or rust." If the surface was perfect, would I be painting it? The recipe in the newspaper gives you directions. They say, "Have your butcher prepare three six-ounce pheasants." What butcher? All I ever see is a lot of packaged meat in the refrigerator counter, with the fat and the bones hidden on the downside. I don't have a butcher anymore than I have a straight, square and level house. You call the airlines. Ticket-seller takes the information and then give you directions. Says, "Be at the airport to pick up your ticket at least an hour before flight time." Well, if I have to be out at the airport an hour in advance, I might as well take the bus to where I'm going from downtown.

Then I like the directions we get from those consumer affairs people about how to handle these problems. "If you want to get your car repaired," they tell you, "get at least three estimates in writing." Have you ever taken your car to a garage without knowing what's wrong with it and demanded a written estimate from the mechanic on how much he'll charge to fix it? If the pain persists, see your doctor.

Letters

MIKE WALLACE: Several weeks ago, we reported that the Illinois Power Company had requested a 14 percent rate increase from the Illinois Commerce Commission to pay for the escalating costs of constructing its first nuclear power plant at Clinton, Illinois. Well, that was an error. Although part of the rate hike was requested to cover those construction costs, most of it was to cover general inflationary increases. We also reported that the staff of the Commerce Commission had recommended against the increase. Not true. What the staff opposed was including the Clinton construction costs as the basis for part of the increase. They did not oppose the rest of the rate hike. Sorry about the errors.

And now to the mail. About our story on the Houston drug program called PDAP and the man who runs it, Bob Meehan, a viewer said, "Drug pushers are making billions (and) you dare to knock Bob Meehan for making a hundred thousand dollars a year for saving our children from the pushers?"

Another letter writer was incensed that we questioned Meehan's statistics on the number of people he's cured. The letter said, "Are you so ignorant that you can't see that if PDAP helped one person it is entirely a success? Who cares about statistics?"

Well, apparently somebody did. Not about those statistics, but about statistics involving Bob Meehan's apparent conflict of interest. So much so that the Board of Directors announced Friday, following our report and a similar report on ABC's "20/20," that Bob Meehan had resigned as head of PDAP but will stay on as consultant.

About our story on the Air Force demonstration team, The Thunderbirds, a viewer called it, "Pure P.R. pap from the network that gave us 'The Selling of the Pentagon' . . . How quickly you forget."

There was also a letter that said, "In Harry Reasoner's introduction to the Thunderbirds he (defined) a hero as 'a man who . . . ' What would Amelia Earhart have said?"

About our story on Bette Davis, there was this, "Her two abortions, four husbands and her vote for the new morality symbolize the demoralization of the U.S.A."

But there was also this, "What other biggie has passed so unflattened through the Hollywood wringer?"

And finally, "I fell in love with Bette Davis when I was 15 . . . 40 years later nothing has changed. The lady's a dreamboat."

FEBRUARY 3, 1980

Losers

SUZANNE ST. PIERRE, PRODUCER

MORLEY SAFER: Most of the people you'll meet in this next story are losers, but they
started out as winners, all of them superb athletes whose bodies were fed into the
billion-dollar industry that is amateur intercollegiate athletics. For weeks now, a
scandal's been breaking on university campuses from one end of the country to
the other — allegations of fraud, grade manipulation, game fixing. Even Oral
Roberts University, with its superb basketball team and deeply religious administration, was accused of paying athletes. But the victims of the anything-goes
attitude of intercollegiate sports are the players — not the few who will become
professionals, but the thousands who will neither make a career of sports or be
educated. They are the losers.

It is an article of faith in the poor and black parts of America's cities that the fast
way upward is through education, and a faster way is through excellence in
sports. And it is an article of faith for most good black high school athletes that
he'll be another O. J. — (Excerpt from O. J. Simpson commercial) — or Reggie J.
or Dr. J. or Magic J.

What does being a pro mean to you?

BLACK STUDENT: Hey, easy street, you know, good times. You know, because
you're making money —

BLACK STUDENT: You know, a big cars. You know, a car — you know, the kind of
car I want. You know, not settle for no little Datsun, you know.

BLACK STUDENT: Yeah.

BLACK STUDENT: Where I drive a — yeah, you know —

BLACK STUDENT: Be cruising around with your personalized license plate. Everybody pointing at you. All the little kids coming up getting your autograph. Hey,
that's good times. That's life.

BLACK STUDENT: You got you a Benz over here, a Benz station wagon, you know —

SAFER: A Mercedes, you mean?

BLACK STUDENTS: Yeah. Mercedes, you know.

SAFER: The odds against any of these boys realizing that dream are thousands to one. Still, the dream will be nourished. Most of them will receive offers of athletic scholarships, the chance to be noticed by the pros and, at the very least, the chance at a university degree and a decent job. But chances are they will end up like this young man, or this one, or this one: an academic life filled with meaningless classes until their eligibility is used up, then abandoned. No pro contract, no degree. Twenty-one-year-old washouts with broken dreams.

According to Harry Edwards, professor of sociology at Berkeley, collegiate sports play on the myth in the black community that the quick way to success is through sports. Edwards, a former basketball player himself, has for years been trying to mobilize black athletes.

DR. HARRY EDWARDS: The reality is that 75 to 80 percent of the black athletes who go to school on scholarships in this country never graduate. That's — it's Horatio Algerism at its worst: the home run, the knockout punch, rags to riches, the grand slam, the hundred-yard kickoff return. It's the worst kind of — of mythical, purely illusionary, chase that — that one could imagine.

SAFER: But what you say so far, for the most part, could apply to any kid, not just the black kid.

DR. EDWARDS: Yes.

SAFER: The — the hero in America tends to be the sports hero.

DR. EDWARDS: But the difference is that there are so many alternatives for whites who fail. When the dream collapses, the black athlete falls much further.

SAFER: Many college athletes should never have graduated high school. Their grades were too poor. But if a college wants them badly enough, as the University of New Mexico wanted these three players, it can fix that, make them eligible; then keep fixing.

This year alone, at least six big universities have committed serious violations. The most blatant was the University of New Mexico. In the New Mexico case, the FBI wiretapped a conversation between the coach and the assistant coach and found their leading player's degree had been purchased from the dean of admissions of Oxnard Junior College in California. It was ultimately revealed that most of the basketball team was not eligible to play, and the football team too was riddled with irregularities. Everything was expected from the student on the playing field, and very little in the classroom. William Davis is president of the University of New Mexico.

Who — who dis — deals with an athlete's academic progress?

WILLIAM DAVIS: This is —

SAFER: Who's the advisor?

DAVIS: — this is monitored within the athletic department itself, and usually by the assistant director of athletics; and also, it — in — in basketball and football, there — one of the assistant coaches is usually designated to be advisor and to advise the athletes and monitor the — the progress. And obviously, someplace in — in that link the — the system failed.

SAFER: Never mind the coach or the athletic department. It's a shocking indictment of the university to allow this to go on.

DR. EDWARDS: But you have to understand the power of the athletic department. If it — if the department of sociology here at the University of California at

Berkeley had had, over the last 10 years, the kind of graduation rates among its scholarship students that the department of intercollegiate athletics here at the University of California has had over the last 10 years, it — the department of sociology would have been shut down years ago. That's the kind of power that intercollegiate athletics has.

SAFER: But if only 20 percent of your basketball pa – players ever graduate, doesn't that tell you something about your program?

DAVIS: Sure — certainly it does.

SAFER: That it's very successful in terms of basketball, and it's a disaster in terms of academics.

DAVIS: Well, it cer — it certainly is — is disappointing in terms of — of academics.

SAFER: Only disappointing?

DAVIS: Well, it's disappointing, and — and — you know, and we are determined to change that around.

SAFER: But the way athletic scholarships work here and other places, you bring a kid in on an athletic scholarship and what does he study? Theory of basketball or baseball; essentials of football. Why do you have Mickey Mouse courses?

DAVIS: You're talking about marginal students. We also —

SAFER: I'm talking about Mickey Mouse courses.

DAVIS: Right.

SAFER: Why do you allow Mickey Mouse courses in this institution?

DAVIS: Well, what's a Mickey Mouse course to you? Now, the theory of basketball is a Mickey Mouse course?

SAFER: Wouldn't you agree, for a – for a – a – a scholarship basketball player?

DAVIS: No, I wouldn't — I wouldn't think so. I think that the techniques of — of coaching and the — and the theory of basketball can be an ex — excellent course for a — for a student. And certainly, if he was ever to go into the coaching profession, either men or women, that — that it might be a very valuable course, not only for a basketball player, but —

SAFER: But what if he can't speak the English language properly, or read it or write it?

DAVIS: Well, I think he also has courses in English which he — which are — are required and which he has to take in terms of communication and in terms of writing skills, and that these are — are part of his curriculum, too.

SAFER: Even a distinguished institution like Berkeley has its share of Mickey Mouse courses. The transcript of one former football player, Stan Glenn, reveals that while he played he took classes in forest conservation, world of cinema; and then phys ed, phys ed, and more phys ed.

Then you get to the end of his last football season, suddenly he's been asked to take serious university courses in the last two quarters, and he flunks miserably: F's, F's, F's, F's, F's.

DR. EDWARDS: Yes, right here at the University of California at Berkeley. This is typical. This is a classic case. As long as the athlete has eligibility left, then there's always some way of keeping this athlete in school; but as soon as the eligibility is over, he has to sink or swim according to the rules that apply to matriculation for students throughout all other departments. And the results are — are predictable.

SAFER: At some point along the — along the way, did you think you were being educated?

STAN GLENN: Along the way, yes, I thought I was being educated. I thought I had the right counseling and academic department. I thought the courses I was taking was preparing me for my degree.

SAFER: But did your counselor know you were taking this light a load, and did she ever say, "Listen, Stan, you'd better — you'd better take some more serious courses in there"?

GLENN: No, she never instructed me about that, never — never questioned me about that, about me taking too many phys ed courses, physical education courses.

SAFER: Stan Glenn didn't make it to the pros. He works as a courtesy clerk at a supermarket. Through Dr. Edwards' intervention, though, Berkeley is going to give him another chance, this time for an education. But some former athletes at Cal State, Los Angeles, want more than a second chance. They want millions. They're suing the university for failing to educate them. They allege fraud and forgery as well. Neither the university nor the basketball coach, Bob Miller, will talk. The athletes will. Randy Echols, a former basketball player.

RANDY ECHOLS: The purpose of this lawsuit is really to shake up the system, to say, hey, college administrators, be more responsible to those people who are generating all this money: Rose Bowl, $4.2 million; Orange Bowl, two, three million dollars; NCAA finals, million-dollar television rights contract. Those people running around on the field or the track or on the court should at least realize more than some tragedy.

SAFER: What did Coach Miller tell you to do?

INGRAM: Well, basically, he says we didn't have to go to school, just enroll in these classes, these dummy classes or whatever, and not attend. You know, the teachers will take care of it for us. Just stay — just stay healthy enough to play basketball.

MOORE: When I was in school, I was seven different people. (Laughter) You know, I played ba — I — yeah, really, I didn't know — I didn't know if I was in the school or not, you know, that — because I played under seven different names.

SAFER: Hold on. What do you mean you played under seven different names?

MOORE: I played under Andy Potter, Nathan Tyler, and then I — a few more other people.

SAFER: He claims that he was not properly enrolled, so the coach put him in as a ringer, gave him the name of someone with good grades. And then, to make him official with a good SAT test score, he says the coach came up with another idea.

MOORE: And one Saturday after practice, he said, "Let me have your Social Security card." And I said, "For what?" He said, "Don't worry about it. Just give it up." (Laughter) I brought it to him, and then maybe four —

SAFER: This is the coach?

MOORE: Yeah, this is coach. Maybe four weeks later, he said, "You did very well on your SAT test." And I said, "What?"

SAFER: You – a ringer wrote the exams for you? Do you know who took the test?

MOORE: Yes, I know. And the same person took quite a few other people's test.

SLAUGHTER: Yeah, mine got taken also.

SAFER: You didn't take your test?

SLAUGHTER: No, I didn't take mine either.

SAFER: Who took it?

SLAUGHTER: Same guy. If — if I'm not mistaken, I think he took about eight tests.

SAFER: You – for eight different people?

SLAUGHTER: Eight different people.

ECHOLS: You — you have some people who are, sadly to say, functionally illiterate, but will wind up on the dean's list at — at a university that operates like this.

FRED BUTLER (watching football on television):   Get him! Get him!

SAFER: One former Cal State student who is not part of the suit is Fred Butler, age 25, former cornerback; 12 years of public school, four years of college. Fred Butler cannot read and cannot write.

BUTLER (commenting on football):   There, he's got him.

SAFER: Why do you think you never learned to read?

BUTLER: Maybe because — one of the reasons, I was really into sports a lot more than I was going to class and stuff like that. I mean, I was brought like — raised like — sort of was brought up like that. They was always putting me through and sliding me through the classes. But I think it would have been better if they'd just told me I couldn't play football if I didn't go to class. I think I'd came out a little bit better, because then I'd know how to read now.

SAFER: What happened in high school? Did the teachers just push you through year after year?

BUTLER: When I was in the seventh grade, I — I — I got skipped from the seventh all the way up to the ninth grade. I didn't go through the eighth grade.

SAFER: You were skipped?

BUTLER: Yeah, I was skipped, because at the time I was in the seventh grade, most of the kids that were in the eighth grade they were the same size as me or I was bigger than them.

SAFER: What sort of marks did you get in college?

BUTLER: A's, B's and C's. Because, you see, when you play football, you're not allowed to have any F's. I started getting F's after my — all my eligibility was used up.

SAFER: How do you get by? How do you read a menu in a restaurant?

BUTLER: I don't. (Laughs) I don't. I just have to look, just use the pictures of the food. Most places out here, I have one of my friends. Usually people that are close to me know I can't read —

SAFER: Uh-hmm.

BUTLER: — and stuff. Like my girlfriend, she knows I can't read, so she read — reads it and tells me.

SAFER: Don't you fellas feel that you bear some responsibility for this, in that — that you thought — for whatever reasons, you thought that that — bouncing that ball was going to be the passport?

MEN: Yeah, uh-hmm. Yeah.

INGRAM: At that particular time, yes.

SAFER: And so, you were prepared to buy the whole thing?

ECHOLS: Right.

SLAUGHTER: You couldn't tell me that I cou—I wouldn't be playing pro ball today.

INGRAM: You couldn't tell me that I —

SLAUGHTER: In 1972, coming out of high school, you know, I was one of the top players picked in the country coming out of high school, and you couldn't tell me that I wouldn't be playing pro ball. I'd look at you and say, "You must be kidding!"

MOORE: And coming out of high school, that's probably — every young guy that's playing basketball, that's his dream —

INGRAM: That's his dream, yeah.

MAN: — to be a star, a professional basketball player in the NBA.

SAFER: What's the difference between what your lives are like now and what you thought they might be when you left high school?

INGRAM: About $500,000 away from what I expected. (Laughter) That's right, about $500,000 away.

SLAUGHTER: If you — to be frank about it, you know, I'm a bonafide pro ballplayer. Even though I'm not playing, I can go in the pros right now and do my thing. My life — now my life is at a standstill. No education, nowhere to go but to work. And I feel like I've been cheated.

ECHOLS: Most people think that you go from high school to college to pro one, two, three, bam; big contract, long car, big house. It just does not work like that. And ghetto ballplayers are particularly vulnerable to that: gimme, gimme something for nothing. This is not what college is supposed to be about.

SAFER: Maybe a lot of us are naive and really do believe that a game should be played for the sake of playing it, and that a university is a sanctuary of learning, a place that could be looked to by all Americans as a passage to a better life, whatever way they want to define that. But we really are fools to believe it, you know. The games have become phony, and so has much of the scholarship. It's all just so much commerce. So next time you watch an NCAA game on television and hear some announcer pretentiously describing the spiritual and the athletic virtues of this U. or that U., remember that kid who can't read and can't write. All he remembers is how badly he was used.

See Update, February 17, 1980, page 344.

Ezer

BARRY LANDO, PRODUCER

DAN RATHER: "Ezer" is Ezer Weizman, the outspoken, gregarious, ambitious defense minister of Israel, the most popular politician in that country, according to the political polls; a man with his heart set on becoming prime minister. In an Israel beset today by a welter of problems — rocketing inflation, a huge trade deficit, a PLO that is gaining acceptance in the world community — Ezer Weizman seems to be about the only optimist among Israel's leaders. Even the specter of Yasir Arafat, as raised by Mike Wallace, doesn't trouble Ezer Weizman.

MIKE WALLACE: Yasir Arafat —

EZER WEIZMAN: Yes?

WALLACE: — does that name send shivers down your spine?

WEIZMAN: Shivers?

WALLACE: Does it — I say Yasir Arafat. (Snaps fingers) Quickly, is this a horror to you? Is this something that you deplore, abhor?

"In an Israel beset today by a welter of problems—rocketing inflation, a huge trade deficit, a PLO that is gaining acceptance in the world community—Ezer Weizman seems to be about the only optimist among Israel's leaders."

WEIZMAN: Now, what is it that General Patton said? "Don't be a fool and die for your country. Let the other son of a bitch die for his." This is what Yasir Arafat brings up.

WALLACE: You once offered to meet with him.

WEIZMAN: Five or six years ago I said in one of my speeches, and I — I said that I'm — I was willing to meet him, and someone asked me, "What are you going to talk to him about?" And I said I'm going to tell him why we're staying on the Western Bank.

WALLACE: Would it be a disaster, seriously, if you were to meet with a Yasir Arafat or a major PLO leader?

WEIZMAN: Well, first of all, I think that all the talks now about meeting Yasir Arafat or meeting this or meeting that are contrary to the good spirit of Camp David.

WALLACE: But you're an innovator, General Weizman. You're an original. You're — you take chances.

WEIZMAN: I've taken a great chance with the Egyptians. How many chances can you take in one year?

(Sounds of honor guard in Egyptian . . . Israeli national anthem)

WALLACE: A full-dress ceremony of welcome at Egypt's Ministry of Defense for Israel's defense minister, who used to be the quintessential Israel hawk. But after Anwar Sadat's journey to Jerusalem, Ezer Weizman changed radically. He has made more of these visits to Cairo than any other Israeli cabinet minister, and he is persuaded of Sadat's sincerity.

PRESIDENT ANWAR SADAT: Welcome, Ezer.

WEIZMAN: Mister President.

I think he's one of the most out — if not the most outstanding leader in the world today.

WALLACE: Anwar Sadat?

WEIZMAN: Yes. Yes, he is wise and courageous, which doesn't always go together. I'll drive 10,000 miles to see an — an interesting personality. I don't think I'll drive more than a hundred miles to see a sight —

WALLACE: Uh-hmm.

WEIZMAN: — a waterfall or a nice tree. Oh, it's very nice if you bump into it, but I won't go — I've never been to the fjords of — of Norway. You say, you haven't seen the fjords of Norway? No, but I saw Sadat.

WALLACE: But Weizman does like to see the sights of Cairo on his trips there. He got a police escort on this foray downtown. First stop, a Syrian bakery.

(Weizman talking, shaking hands with people)

Weizman likes to press the flesh, to banter with anyone who'll listen to his ragged but serviceable Arabic.

(Weizman talking in Arabic)

And he also knows that such outings make for good press and political mileage back home in Israel. From the bakery to Groppy's, a favorite Cairo coffee house. Weizman spent many off-duty hours here during World War II when he was stationed in Egypt as a – quote – "Palestinian" serving with the British RAF.

Ever here with an Egyptian girl, General Weizman?

WEIZMAN: With a girl, this, that.

WALLACE: Just a few hours earlier, Weizman had learned that Foreign Minister Moshe Dayan had resigned from the Begin cabinet because of sharp policy disputes. That left Weizman as one of the lonely moderates in the cabinet.

Be a prophet. What's going to happen?

WEIZMAN: You saw today how we were received, the delegation and me —

WALLACE: Warmly. Warmly.

WEIZMAN: — in the Ministry of Defense of the Egyptian armed forces, General Ali. You saw the warmth in the streets of Cairo now, in the shops — people that I know and people that I don't know. You see the atmosphere here in Cairo. On the other hand, Moshe resigns.

WALLACE: Dayan resigns.

WEIZMAN: What will be stronger, the peace, the will of the people and the great change that has taken place, or the problems of individual?

WALLACE: Back in Israel, Weizman took us to a military training camp in the Negev. And in his conversations with the officers and men here, it became quickly clear how disillusioned, how bewildered, are these Israelis at their country's assorted problems, mostly its galloping inflation, now running above a hundred percent a year, and its bickering politicians. Some of these soldiers are regulars; some of them students, businessmen or kibbutzniks – reservists on temporary duty.

WEIZMAN: Now wait a minute, I — immediately you see that he is a regular, not a reserve, by at least a better haircut than this one. (Laughter)

WALLACE: Why is the mood of the country bewildered?

WEIZMAN: Because of the peace, that nobody — some of them don't realize where we're — it's heading to. Some — some of it — some of it is not bewildered.

WALLACE: Because of the economy?

WEIZMAN: Be — primarily because of the economy. Primarily because —

WALLACE: Because of the fights in the cabinet?

WEIZMAN: Well, this — this does not add. You see, this does not add. This is why I come here. I come here and I get my morale higher when I talk to him and I talk to him and I talk to the three kibbutzniks.

WALLACE: Yeah.

WEIZMAN: And — and — and leaders also need a booster of morale. I can't sit cooped up in my office all — all week long. And so I go out here, guns are popping, helicopters are flying, architects are smiling.

WALLACE: And the cabinet is meeting at this moment in Jerusalem, yes?

WEIZMAN: Yeah, but I — I got permission to — to be out. (Laughter)

WALLACE: Weizman was born 55 years ago in Israel to a prominent Zionist family. His uncle, Chaim Weizman, became Israel's first president. Young Ezer enlisted in the RAF during World War II. And then in 1948, as the State of Israel was about to be created, he became one of the first pilots in the tiny – and at that time illegal – Jewish air force. He flew this flimsy British Austin.

WEIZMAN: Well, this was the only thing we had, and we used for supplies. We used to drop grenades from time to time. We actually hooked a machine gun on it.

WALLACE: What, you took the door off?

WEIZMAN: We took the door off. We tied it up here with a — with a rope, and a gunner used to sit in the back and boof boof boof boof boof.

WALLACE: Boof boof who?

WEIZMAN: Boof boof Arab terrorists in those days. We were attacked then by all the Arabs around us.

WALLACE: Eventually Weizman went on to run Israel's air force. Then came a few years in private business; and in 1977, he returned to public life, to politics. Though he doesn't much like Menachem Begin, he was, like Begin, a hawk at heart; and he masterminded the political campaign that finally brought Begin to power. Weizman became his minister of defense, and then came Sadat's visit to Jerusalem.

When you first met Anwar Sadat, apparently you talked about your own and his own personal tragedies of the wars between your two countries. Your son, Shaul, and his —

WEIZMAN: His brother, yes. His brother was killed on the very first day of the Yom Kippur War as a pilot on the Sinai, yes. And my son was very badly wounded, and is still — still handicapped from this — from the injuries.
Hello, son. How are you?

WALLACE: From the day his son was born, Weizman doted on Shaul. And then in 1969, while serving in the army near the Suez Canal, Shaul was shot in the head by an Egyptian sniper. At times, Shaul still suffers from neurological disorders. We talked to him in Cairo while he was visiting Egypt with his father.

WEIZMAN: I was asking him how he feels about having been in the wars and — I think — ask him that.

WALLACE: Any bitterness that these are the people who did that to you?

SHAUL WEIZMAN: No, not at all.

WALLACE: Really?

SHAUL WEIZMAN: Not at all.

WALLACE: Because?

SHAUL WEIZMAN: A war, it's a fair fight. A canal, two, three hundred meters between us, a guy that never saw me, I never saw him. He don't know me, I don't know him. I can hate you, you can hate me, because we know each other.

WALLACE: Yeah.

SHAUL WEIZMAN: Yeah. We met already.

WALLACE: Right.

SHAUL WEIZMAN: But people that's never — never got met together, how they can hate each other or love each other or like each other?

WEIZMAN: It's two scarred nations that are healing each other.

WALLACE: King Hussein, you write of him as though he is a jackal, a hyena. "Hussein hates us no less than other Arab rulers, although he covers it up with crafty phrasing to please the Americans." That's pretty tough stuff.

WEIZMAN: Yeah, not bad. Okay —

WALLACE: You believe it?

WEIZMAN: I believed it when I wrote it, definitely. I hope that he's mellowed in time. Right now he hasn't changed, so why should I change my opinion of him?

WALLACE: What's holding him up, do you think? He would seem to have a good deal to gain.

WEIZMAN: Well, I think that he's — he's probably — probably worried about whether he can get what the Egyptians got, and the Egyptians got the whole Sinai. And we've said it time and time again, and we'll say it again —

WALLACE: You're not going to give him back the West Bank.

WEIZMAN: Exactly. But exactly.

WALLACE: The only way really to understand such things as the West Bank and Israel's security, says Weizman, is to let him take you in his helicopter on a tour, Weizman at the controls.

WEIZMAN: Okay, off we go. We're airborne!

WALLACE: We headed north from Tel Aviv.

WEIZMAN: (Indistinct) three very nice hotels ...

WALLACE: Then we turned inland. Within five minutes we were crossing the old pre-1967 borders, the borders to which the Arabs want to return. The distance between that point and the sea, across the entire width of Israel — only eight miles. And that's the width of Israel —

WEIZMAN: That's right.

WALLACE: — at its narrowest point?

WEIZMAN: From a security point of view, this part is miles more important than the Sinai. Imagine here unfriendly troops. Imagine here, for instance, at this valley a tank regiment. One thing the world, unfortunately, must remember: if we lose the war, we lose everything.

WALLACE: You're willing to bet, I understand, that Jimmy Carter will be renominated and re-elected?

WEIZMAN: I've already laid a bet.

WALLACE: And you've put your money where your mouth is.

WEIZMAN: Well, usually a bottle of whiskey.

WALLACE: You like him. A lot of American Jews are skeptical.

WEIZMAN: I suppose skepticism is because America is going through a difficult period generally, and therefore —

WALLACE: Sounds like Israel.

WEIZMAN: Well, you know, I wish we had the problems of the United States.

WALLACE: Like?

WEIZMAN: Inflation, 14 percent.

WALLACE: Yes, you have a hundred, a hundred percent.

WEIZMAN: A hundred percent, yes. Therefore, 14 is nice, 15 is nice, 16 —

WALLACE: Yes.

WEIZMAN: — I'll buy 20. I couldn't really tell you why skepticism among my brethren in the United States, but —

WALLACE: You would advise them to vote for Jimmy Carter?

WEIZMAN: I don't — I don't advise — I don't advise anybody anything what to do in the United States. I just about manage to advise Israelis to do what they should do.

WALLACE: You want to be prime minister?

WEIZMAN: I never said so.

WALLACE: No. You believe, yourself, that you are finally ready for the job?

WEIZMAN: I've never said no to anything in life.

WALLACE: A highly placed friend of yours said:

WEIZMAN: A he or a she?

WALLACE: He.

WEIZMAN: Yeah.

WALLACE: "Ezer Weizman is the Teddy Kennedy of Israel. Great family name, great charisma; shallow and unstable."

WEIZMAN: Was this Ted Kennedy? Is this — is Ted Kennedy like this?

WALLACE: I — I am not suggesting that —

WEIZMAN: Well, first of all, anyone who — who says this is not a friend of mi — a real friend of mine. But —

WALLACE: Probably.

WEIZMAN: — probably. Therefore, your — your first statement is rather incorrect, and you mix with the wrong people. I — I — I can't analyze myself. I can only put my credentials of 37 years of — of adult life, what I've done, what I haven't done, what I did good and what I did bad, and I suppose the next elections or the next period will judge.

WALLACE: You thin-skinned? I think it's very difficult to get that kind of a — a comment —

WEIZMAN: Am I sensitive about criticism?

WALLACE: Yeah.

WEIZMAN: Of course I am. Of course I am. Who the hell likes it if someone says that I'm — that you are shallow? Nobody likes that.

WALLACE: Your real friends say your biggest enemy is your mouth.

WEIZMAN: Yes, I — I — I will not disagree with that. But again —

WALLACE: You told Harold Saunders, who is one of our top officials —

WEIZMAN: Beautiful things I've told him, yeah?

WALLACE: Yes. You said to him, "Don't teach us what to do. You lost everywhere." That's the United States. "You lost Angola, Iran, Ethiopia."

WEIZMAN: Cuba. (Laughter) I don't — I don't go back on a word I said to Hal Saunders.

WALLACE: Your quick tongue, your quick temper, your numerous threats to resign.

WEIZMAN: No, not so many, Not so many. No, no, no.

WALLACE: Five.

WEIZMAN: Did you count them?

WALLACE: Yes.

WEIZMAN: I didn't. Well —

WALLACE: Does that sound like the kind of stable leadership one — a country like this needs?

WEIZMAN: You know, in my career as a commander, I always preferred officers, especially commanders, who I had to rein, to control, rather than push.

WALLACE: Weizman feels he is ready to command the country as prime minister. He feels he understands and knows how to deal with the malaise that grips Israel today.

WEIZMAN: We're going through a crisis now. Suddenly peace is being imposed on us. Nobody knows what it is. Though I think we have far more energy in us, and I think we have far more wisdom in us, we have far more will in us, we have far more gumption, energy, tenacity than we show now in this changing period of a new era. I think it's a passing episode. And if you would have asked yourself two, three years ago whether Sharon, Dayan, Yadin, Begin, Tamir, Weizman will sign a peace treaty that means taking off settlements, you would have said, "You're crazy!"

WALLACE: Taking off settlements in the Sinai?

WEIZMAN: In the — in the Sinai. In the Sinai.

WALLACE: Yes. Uh-hmm.

WEIZMAN: And therefore, let — let — let us rest now a little bit, and see what happens with the mighty process between Egypt and us.

RATHER: Well, that mighty peace process was bogged down, at least on the Palestinian issue. Now it's showing signs of getting back on the track. Two days ago, Egypt and Israel took their first step toward breaking the deadlock on the question of self-rule for Palestinians living on the West Bank and in the Gaza Strip. President Carter's special Mideast envoy, Sol Linowitz, said – and I quote – "I have no question in my mind that very significant progress has been reached in these negotiations. We are much closer to an understanding." U.S. officials are hoping that the agreement will be the first step toward resolving major differences that divide Israel and Egypt on the question of Palestinian self-rule.

Wild to Regulate
AL WASSERMAN, PRODUCER

HARRY REASONER: A few years ago, if you asked an American businessman who was public enemy number one, chances are he would have said Ralph Nader. Today, it's this man. His name is Mike Pertschuk, and he's the head of the FTC, the Federal Trade Commission, a government regulatory agency that watches out for the interests of consumers. As far as businessmen are concerned, and a lot of congressmen, Pertschuk runs a bureaucracy that's out of control, that's just wild to regulate.

MIKE PERTSCHUK: One cong— one senator, who's a friend, said to me, "Let me tell you what my impression of the FTC is. You've got, I don't know, one thousand, five thousand, lawyers down there, and they sit around and if there's a quiet moment in the day, they say, "Who can we regulate next?" And that's just not the truth, but it's hard to catch up with it.

REASONER: Orrin Hatch of Utah is a senator who is not a friend of the FTC.

SENATOR ORRIN HATCH (R-Utah):   I like Mike, personally. He's a — he's a typical bureaucrat, however, and he is one of those people who has come out of the blue and for the last 50 years have controlled this country, who believe in the enhancement of the public sector and the enhancement of the federal government to the detriment of every state and every little person and every small businessman in this country.

PERTSCHUK: Nobody who's the subject of an FTC investigation or rule-making is going to like it, because essentially our job is to go after areas in which businesses, for whatever reasons, enjoy an advantage over the — over the consumer because the marketplace hasn't been working very well. And we want to take that advantage away and give it to the consumer, where it belongs. And — and nobody likes that.

REASONER: The Federal Trade Commission was created by Congress 65 years ago to protect the public from business practices that are unfair, deceptive or that stifle competition — a broad mandate. When Pertschuk and his staff get together, the agenda can range from the sales practices of used-car dealers to the cost of the eyeglasses you wear to the question of a corporate merger.

FTC STAFF MEMBER (at meeting):   . . . now, the retail food merger in California that was . . .

REASONER: Pertschuk has been chairman of the FTC for a little less than three years, but he's an old hand on the Washington scene, having worked for 15 years as a staff member of the Senate. And he remembers the FTC during the days when it was so unobtrusive it was called the "little old lady on Pennsylvania Avenue."

PERTSCUK: You know, this agency was criticized for many years for basically taking on trivial targets, and nobody in Congress was mad at us then. And the answer, I think, is fairly simple: we didn't affect very much.

REASONER: A supporter of yours in Congress is reported to have said to you, "Mike, you've just done a wonderful thing. You've alienated my entire constituency." Is support for the FTC a political hot potato for congressmen?

PERTSCHUK: Yes. Yes, it is. I — I do have friends — as you know, I worked on the Hill — who say — who say, "Well, we think you're doing just about what Congress — Congress wanted you to do in the original act, but it's very tough for us to get out in front. These interests are — are angry, they're well-organized, and we'll try and help you, but I don't think I can really get out in front." I've had that conversation.

REASONER: Pertschuk finds he has to be his own salesman, trying to win friends and soothe enemies.

PERTSCHUK: Much of the reaction by business to overregulation is — is not only understandable but — but needs to be paid attention to.

REASONER: He tries to disarm business audiences by assuring them that the FTC is in favor of free enterprise, that when the agency intervenes in situations of price fixing or monopoly, what they're doing is really the opposite of regulating; they're encouraging open competition in the good old American spirit. This audience of corporate executives restrained their enthusiasm.

PERTSCHUK (to business audience):   . . . years indicate a shift consumer issues have at particular . . .

REASONER: Consumer groups are his natural allies, like this gathering of representatives of senior citizen organizations. He tries to make the agency more understandable by stressing its bread-and-butter concerns.

PERTSCHUK (to senior citizens audience):   Probably the most dramatic and — and effective action we've taken — but it's typical of what we're trying to do — is our eyeglass rule. I think you should know that — that since the commission has moved to free up competition, to allow op— optometrists and opticians to advertise prices, eyeglass dispensing has been one of the areas of health care which has not been caught up in the inflationary spiral.

REASONER: But Pertschuk knows he's fighting an uphill battle. Right or wrong, there's a general feeling in Congress that the agency has gotten too big for its britches, that it has been pushing its powers to the very limits and even beyond. One thing that helped create this kind of image for the FTC was an inquiry by the commission into television advertising directed at children. Some sweeping regulations were proposed that earned the agency a reputation for wanting to become a kind of national nanny.

PERTSCHUK: And — and in fact, what the commission did — but very few people remember this — the staff proposed a series of stringent regulations on advertising directed to children. The staff proposed that all advertising directed to very young children be banned. And the staff also proposed some restrictions on the advertising of highly sugared products. The commission didn't adopt, even on a tentative basis, those proposals. What the commission did was to say: There is a serious problem here. We've heard from — from parents' groups and dentists and pediatricians.

REASONER: Another of those concerned about the problem is Pertschuk himself. He wrote an article criticizing the effect of TV commercials on children, and has since disqualified himself from participating in any rulings on the matter. But he feels the commission's approach is reasonable.

PERTSCHUK: We feel that we have a responsibility to open up a broad inquiry and — and ask these hard questions: What is the impact of television on children? What is the impact of the advertising of these products on children's diets and their attitude toward foods high in sugar and salt? The commission hasn't done anything more than that: just open an inquiry. But now Congress proposes to stop that inquiry in its tracks.

SENATOR ERNEST HOLLINGS (D-South Carolina):   But if we're going to have an entity in government that's going to decide what's fair, then we really got something going, I'm telling you.

REASONER: Senator Ernest Hollings is a member of the Commerce Committee, the Senate committee that oversees the Federal Trade Commission. The senators want the FTC to stop trying to decide what's fair or unfair in commercial advertising, and that's not all they want the FTC to stop.

SENATOR JOHN DANFORTH (R-Missouri):   We do not want you to initiate investigations into the insurance business.

REASONER: What Senator John Danforth is discussing is a ban on allowing the FTC to study the insurance industry. The reason? Well, last summer the agency released one such study. It said that Americans have over $140 billion invested in life insurance as savings, and the average return on these savings is very poor.

SENATOR DANFORTH: And one of the things that has alarmed the insurance industry throughout the country is some kind of staff study to the effect that ordinary life insurance is a fraud. So they have to go running around to everybody because the staff came out and said ordinary life is a fraud. So everybody's been running to the insurance agents all over the country and saying, "Have you defrauded me?" And then you got to explain, "No, I haven't defrauded you."

PERTSCHUK: We didn't say it, and we were very careful not to say it. What we did say is that the — we said two basic things: that the — the rate of return that you get as a purchaser of whole life insurance, part of which is an investment, is — is much lower than other forms of investment, although there are good reasons for purchasing whole life. We also said that the way in which life insurance is sold makes it very difficult for consumers to pick, among competing life insurance policies, the best value. And what we proposed was that the — the states adopt a disclosure — a disclosure system, a uniform disclosure system, so that the consumer could tell how good a deal a particular policy was and compare them with others. That's all we did. Nobody has suggested that that study was a sloppy or ignorant study. They don't like the answers.

REASONER: What upset the committee was not only the substance of the FTC insurance study, but the basic fact that it was done.

SENATOR DANFORTH: We have told them once before that we don't want them to get into the business of investigating insurance. They have done it, despite the mandate of Congress. Now you're . . .

PERTSCHUK: Well, that puzzles me. We reported to Congress each year, in our budget and otherwise, what we were doing. It's right there.

REASONER: What puzzles Pertschuk is that as far as he knows the Senate never complained about the report before it was released, and the House of Representatives actually encouraged the FTC to study the insurance business.

PERTSCHUK: Now, the report made a lot of life insurance people very, very mad, and — and I think they were mad because they didn't like the substance of what we said, not the fact that we were doing it.

REASONER: The Commerce Committee voted unanimously to keep the Federal Trade Commission out of the insurance business, and also approved a number of other restrictive measures for the full Senate to vote on later.

Last November, the House of Representatives had its turn to draw blood. The first casualty was a rule proposed by the FTC aimed at correcting abuses in the funeral industry. Congressman Marty Russo of Illinois led the House fight against the funeral rule.

REPRESENTATIVE MARTY RUSSO (D-Illinois):   Sure, there are abuses. There are abuses in every field. But is the answer to abuses federal regulation? Our free market system lends itself to abuses in the marketplace, and a lot of times the people themselves and consumers of this country can better handle the marketplace than Big Daddy telling them that you don't know enough about it, you're too stupid, so we're going to tell you, we're going to protect you from your stupidity.

REASONER: But Russo's main objection is the FTC's procedures.

REPRESENTATIVE RUSSO: The question is were they fair in — in gathering the information to justify the rule? And my answer is they weren't fair, they were biased, they were inaccurate and they did things to add to their case they shouldn't have done.

REASONER: Pertschuk feels the funeral rule should be judged not by the FTC's procedures but by the end result.

PERTSCHUK: And essentially what we propose to do is very simple: require the funeral director give the — the bereaved family, or whoever is arranging the funeral, a price list — what it's going to cost, and what the different parts of the funeral are — are going to cost. And also on that sheet to tell the truth. Some states don't require embalming, but — but a lot of funeral directors represent to the family that they must embalm the body. It's very expensive. We don't want to stop people from doing it. We just want them to know what they ha— what — what the choices are.

REASONER: However modest the FTC's final proposal, the House of Representatives voted to overturn it.

PERTSCHUK: The fact is that Congress, or the House, moved to kill that funeral rule based upon 40 minutes of debate in the House, without hearings; a rule that had taken us four or five years and thousands of pages of testimony from victims as well as funeral directors to develop — to develop — to develop a— an under- standing of what was going on and to — to move to remedy it. So, they obviously heard from their funeral directors about what their funeral directors had been told by their trade associations the commission was doing, and there wasn't a very good match between that and the truth.

REASONER: Will that have a bandwagon effect, and would that scare you – that every industry that is touched by your regulation will come to Congress?

PERTSCHUK: It does scare me, and in — in fact I think it ought to scare anybody who believes that government intervention in the marketplace can be justified. There is a bandwagon effect, and — and I'm concerned and I think every citizen ought to be concerned.

WOMAN: We go in talking about the merits of the case, and are not able to go in and say, "We will see you at your next $500-a-plate fund-raiser."

REASONER: According to consumer advocates, the problem is that it's not the merits of the issues but re-election that concerns most congressmen.

WOMAN: They know that they can pick up the votes and the contributions of all the funeral directors on that one vote, and they can keep this industry and this profession happy — and hope that the consumers aren't watching.

MAN: But the — the so-called, you know, self-appointed consumer advocates in this country do not represent what the consumers want in this country. I think they're out of step with what they want. Maybe in the sixties and the early seventies the answer was throw more federal dollars and more federal regula- tion at the problem. The mood in the country today is away from that. It's less federal spending, less federal involvement, less federal regulation. And I think that's the reason why they're losing. They're not losing for any other reason. They're not losing because Congress is being bought off.

PERTSCHUK: It's much too crude to talk about this as if the lobbyists were up there buying votes. It's just that, as somebody said, widows, orphans, kids, consum- ers, just don't have access to the same talent that — that — that business groups do. I think that — that those who would like to get out from under government scrutiny have used general public feeling about regulation very skillfully. And they really have the resources to get access to Congress and to — to take the general mood or the general feeling and — and translate it into — into tales of outrage. You know, our most serious problem is that — that most of the congressmen and senators, first of all, they're very busy; and essentially, they — they hear snatches of pleading by the different interests who are affected by the commission, and — and they get a ha— half the story; and gradually there builds up in their mind a— an impression of an agency crazy, wild to regulate.

REASONER: With all of the — that goes on — the confrontations and the trouble and all the problems — do you have any fun in this job?

PERTSCHUK: Oh, it's a great job. It's probably the greatest job going. I mean, we deal with people's real problems. You know, everybody who's pot a — bought a pair of Levi jeans in this country in the last couple of years has had the benefit of some aggressive price competition. You've seen it. There are sales, there are discounts, on Levis. There weren't any sales on Levis until we moved against Levi Strauss, who were fixing the price at — at retail. So that my family and your family can benefit tangibly from the kinds of things we do. And besides that, I don't mind a fight. (Laughs)

REASONER: And a fight is just what he's got on his hands. Before Congress right now are proposals to limit the FTC's powers, exempt certain industries from its jurisdiction, and give either house the right to veto rulings by the FTC when they affect an entire industry. If the legislature goes too far, President Carter is threatening his own veto.

Letters

DAN RATHER: In the mail this week, there were several letters referring to that part of our interview with Ronald Reagan that dealt with his age. One viewer noted the age of two of our former Presidents, and said: "If this country did well under a President in a wheel chair (63 when he left office) and a Missouri haberdasher (68 at the end of his term), I'll put my money on young Reagan."

Reagon will be 69 next Wednesday. If elected, he would be 77 at the end of a second term. That might be what prompted another viewer to say: "Couldn't resist capping the Reagan interview with a Geritol commercial, could you?"

About our story on Russian spies at the UN, a viewer said: "I have an idea . . . take the Olympics out of Moscow, but give them the U.N. . . . . Think they'll go for it?"

About our story on Oral Roberts, we heard from a viewer who described herself as "fat but faithful" and who said Oral Roberts told her that he doesn't like fat people at his college. She wrote: "Does Oral Roberts ever ask (overweight people) to refrain from sending in money? Fat chance!"

Another viewer wrote: "It is no wonder our country is falling apart with people like you attacking Oral Roberts."

But there were a lot of letters like this one: "If Oral Roberts can heal people by placing his hands on them, why does he need to build a hospital?"

Followed by this: "Oral Roberts doesn't have to answer to you. He answers to God."

FEBRUARY 10, 1980

Mr. "X"

DAN RATHER: During the 1940's, the fifties and early sixties, when Washington wanted to know what Moscow was up to, it turned to George Kennan. In 1947, it was revealed that George Kennan was the mysterious Mr. "X," the principal architect of this country's post-war policy of containing the Soviets behind what was then known as the Iron Curtain. This former ambassador to the Soviet Union, now at age 75 a writer and historian, is still considered our most experienced analyst of what Moscow is up to, and he doesn't see what Moscow is up to in Afghanistan as being as aggressive as Washington would now have us believe. What he believes is that the Russians took over Afghanistan only to make their own border more secure.

You think we've overreacted to the Soviet invasion of Afghanistan?

GEORGE KENNAN: I do. I think we have somewhat overreacted to it.

RATHER: Now, how much does that have to do with the fact that we're in the midst of a presidential election campaign?

KENNAN: I would hope that it didn't have much to do with it, but I am afraid that it has, if not in the case of the President himself, in the case of a great many other people. I — I do feel that the atmosphere in Washington these days is a rather dangerous one. You know this atmosphere and probably could describe it much better than I can, but it's one in which there is not only a high degree of militarization of thinking about our problems with the Soviet Union, but it's one in which a great many people seem to have felt that we had to do something to show our muscle, our force, almost regardless of what it is that we do for that purpose. I think this is a highly dangerous frame of mind to get into.

I would not like to be misunderstood here, Mr. Rather. I — I favor the building up, the — the — the improvement of our military capabilities relevant to that part of the world. I think that's all right, but it has to be balanced with efforts in the other line — along the other line: efforts to restore some sort of political communication with the Soviet government; efforts to reassure them that if they want to liquidate their unhappy situation in Afghanistan, we are not going to stand in their way and we're not going to take advantage of it, we're not going to try to make it an opportunity for humiliating them or for winning a prestige victory over them.

314

RATHER: Why did the Soviets invade Afghanistan?

KENNAN: It seems to me that the weight of the evidence would indicate that they invaded it for defensive, rather than offensive, reasons. I have seen no reason to suppose or to believe that they invaded it with a view to going farther and attacking Pakistan and Iran.

RATHER: You don't buy the idea that they're looking for that historical warm-water port?

KENNAN: No, I don't. I think if they had wanted a port of — on the opening out here, it would have been much easier for them simply to go down through Iran, which couldn't have op— posed any resistance to them in the last year or two.

RATHER: Do you expect them to go into Iran?

KENNAN: It would depend, I would think, somewhat on the development of the situation. But I don't think that this has been part of their plans, and I don't think they will do it unless they are in some way or other provoked into it by events in Iran. You see, they could have done it at any time. There would have been no resistance. The— you know — you know as well as I do what's happened to the Iranian armed forces in the past year, and I'm sure it would have been no military problem whatsoever for the Soviet Union. They didn't need even to go into Afghanistan for that. They've got just as easy an access from their own territory right down through here as they would going all the way around through Afghanistan coming across.

Not only that, but I do attach some importance to the fact that they have denied any intention of going from Afghanistan into either of those neighboring countries, and they've denied it in the most authoritative way that they know how now to deny it, and that is by a statement signed by Brezhnev, published on the first page of the *Pravda*. Now I know many of our people in Washington are cynical, and perhaps with some justification, about statements of this nature. But I think that they forget that these are commitments not just vis-a-vis ourselves, but also vis-a-vis the Soviet public and the Soviet Communist Party. When Brezhnev comes out on the front page of the *Pravda* with a statement like this that says we have no intention of going into either of these places, he commits himself before 16 million members of his own party, plus the entire Soviet population, plus, indeed, the satellite countries of Eastern Europe. And this is not to be taken too lightly. Do you see what I mean?

RATHER: You believe him?

KENNAN: I think it's likely that this is a — this is stated in good faith.

RATHER: You know, Professor, that there will be many people, and many of them your friends, who will say George Kennan's a brilliant man, may know more about the Soviet Union than any other man in America, but he's not cynical enough and once again he's being had.

KENNAN: I think I know — I hope I know, as well as anyone in this country, what are the negative aspects of the Soviet political personality. I've been in this, I believe, longer than anyone on either side of the line, over 50 years of involvement with Soviet-American relations. And I've lived through — through the whole Stalin time, and you couldn't live there through that time without being aware of those features of the Soviets' personality which don't appeal to us and which sometimes seem — seem to us to be dangerous. I don't mean to make light out of them. On the other hand, I must, and have tried, to protest bitterly against a frame of mind which yielded to the idea of the inevitability of war. I

don't think that our differences with the Soviet Union have to be resolved by war. I don't think they could be resolved by war. I think the Soviet leaders understand that, if anything, better than we do.

RATHER: Will threatening to boycott the Olympics help in any way?

KENNAN: I don't think that it will. I don't want to speak against the President's decision. He's taken his decision, and I don't think it would do any good to argue about the right and wrongs of it now. But I don't think that is going to do a great deal of good.

I don't think, in fact, that we can do much good there by putting public pressure on the Rusians and giving them ultimata and saying that you must do this and that by a given date or else, because this isn't the way that you induce great governments to do the sensible things.

RATHER: Professor Kennan has no criticism of the way President Carter has handled the hostage situation in Iran. However, he fears the deep psychological effect of prolonged captivity on the hostages and feels that yet stronger international pressure has to be put on Iran to release them. But he's not happy with the way U.S. policy towards the Russians is managed.

Cyrus Vance. Should he stay as Secretary of State?

KENNAN: I would hope he would.

RATHER: Zbigniew Brzezinski. Should he stay as the Security Advisor to the President?

KENNAN: In my opinion, no. I think the whole system of having two secre— two Departments of State, one in the White House and one half a mile away, and having policies in matters of enormous importance handled partly in one place, partly in the other place, I think this whole system is misconceived and, in some respects, dangerous and unproductive.

It seems to me that it's questionable whether it was a good thing to send the President's Security Advisor to Pakistan to spend many hours discussing military matters with the head of state in that country, which I believe he did, going out to the Afghan border and giving the impression that we regard this again as solely a military problem. I'm a little afraid that the wrong signals may be given to the Russians by things of this sort. I would think that they — what you wanted to do there was precisely not to frighten the Russians with the specter of a Chinese-Pakistani-American alliance along their southern border.

RATHER: What about the trip of Defense Secretary Brown to China? Was that a plus or a minus for us in our efforts to deter the Soviets?

KENNAN: Again, I looked at it with certain misgivings. I do not think that the Chinese-Soviet quarrel is our quarrel, and I don't think any good is going to come of our appearing to get into it and favoring one or the other. I have never agreed with what I — I have felt were the ad — the rather exaggerated images of the Soviet — new Soviet colonialism which have been bandied about during these last two or three years. I don't really see that they have accomplished so much. This is the first time in — now in Afghanistan that they have sent their own forces abroad beyond the high-water mark to which they advanced in Europe in 19 — in the last war, in 1945. And this is indeed an innovation. It is indeed a worrisome one, an important one, and I don't mean to make — make light of it. It is something they have not done before.

RATHER: Are the Soviet hardliners, the hawks, taking over in the Kremlin? Is there evidence of that?

KENNAN: There's no hard evidence, because these people keep things so secret, but it seems to me that all the indications suggest that there has been certainly a switch of influential opinion in that direction in recent months. On the other hand, it hasn't gone all the — all the way.

You see, what bothers me is the belief here that only weapons are going to solve this. Obviously, the — the series of warnings we have given to the Soviet government — warnings not to attack this place, not to attack that place, not to attack the Persian Gulf, not to attack Pakistan — these warnings have implied that, in the absence of our warnings, this is precisely what they wanted to do. I cannot accept that, and I think that in — if they didn't want to do these things, then these warnings can be very mischievous. They look to me as though we were pursuing a policy which simply was demanding of the Soviet government that they admit that they were wrong, they accept a great international reverse, they leave again, and leave us and our diplomacy triumphant. That might be all very nice, but it's not the way that problems are solved.

I think that the Russians are aware that they made a great mistake in going into Afghanistan the way that they did. I think they would like to get out. I think this is probable. And I think that if they're permitted to do it in their own way, and without raising too much the questions of prestige, they will do it.

RATHER: How do you reconcile what you've said with the fact that sometimes using surrogates — the North Vietnamese and the Cubans — that the Soviets have enormously increased their influence?

KENNAN: I can't quite accept that. They've had a series of spectacular failures in the last 10 or 20 years in Africa. There are a number of places that were once viewed as dangerous puppets of the Soviet Union which today are anything else but. Look only at Egypt. Look only at China. It's not so long ago we all viewed China as an extension of Stalinist power. But it's not only these — those places. There were a number of other countries in Africa — Guinea and Ghana and others — which at one time or another were supposed to have been under Soviet control. They no longer are today.

RATHER: On this broadcast recently, the leading Republican presidential candidate, Ronald Reagan, rather forcefully called for a blockade of Cuba as a way of making it clear to the Soviets that they will get tit for tat when they do something such as Afghanistan. What's your reaction to that?

KENNAN: Well, you know, it's not on every question of foreign affairs that I would agree with Governor Reagan, but I — in this case, I rather would. I do think that if we can — if the Soviet — if the Soviets are going to remain in Afghanistan and if they attempt to make any use of that for strategic purposes further afield, then it's time that we thought very seriously about whether we can stand a neighbor, which is only a hundred miles or so off Florida, being a — an ally of the Soviet Union —

RATHER: What do you think —

KENNAN: — a military ally. As a matter of fact, this might have been a more logical reaction to what they did in Afghanistan than what we have actually done.

RATHER: Do you think it's too strong to say that we're on the brink of World War III?

KENNAN: Yes, I think it's too strong to say that. I don't think we are. But we are much closer to it than I like to — to feel, and I really do think that this is a — a time where we have to pause and think very, very carefully about what we are doing and where we are going.

"Lenny"

MARION GOLDIN, PRODUCER

MIKE WALLACE: For longer than he cares to remember, Lenny has been the boy wonder of American music, ever since that famous Sunday afternoon back in 1943 when 25-year-old Leonard Bernstein walked onto the stage of Carnegie Hall in New York and, over the radio, into the homes of millions of Americans to conduct the New York Philharmonic in place of the ailing Bruno Walter. Since then, of course, his face, his persona and the music he has written have become familiar to millions all around the world. Next Thursday night, his memorable *West Side Story* opens in revival here in New York City, and he'll be in the audience. But it is Lenny on the podium who has variously dazzled and/or annoyed audiences and critics with his acrobatic brilliance.

(Music)

We have all seen Bernstein's athletic performances on the podium, but during rehearsals we were struck by something else: his obsession with precision. He acknowledges that, at heart, he is a perfectionist.

LEONARD BERNSTEIN: The day that that stops, I'm going to stop. I mean, if I ever become satisfied with myself, that means it's all over. Toscanini said something like that once. He agonized over every performance, and he would come off and he would say, "Stupido! (Italian word) Toscanini!" after a performance. And I heard somebody say to him, a very close friend, "But that was a magnificent performance. It was flawless. It was perfect. The audience was enchanted. They were weeping," And he said, "No, they don't know. Stupid. They don't know. And when it is perfect, I will die."

WALLACE: You kiss the cuff links that Koussevitzky gave you before every performance.

BERNSTEIN: That's my only superstition. It's not a superstition; it's just a way of saying hello to Koussevitzky. It's a terribly close relationship that still goes on. After all, he died in my arms.

WALLACE: Serge Koussevitzky, the man who led the Boston Symphony years ago, a world figure in music, was Bernstein's idol, and Kousse adored the young Lenny, nurtured him, saw his infinite possibilities.But Koussevitzky worried that one thing would stand in Bernstein's way.

BERNSTEIN: It is the name, the nom. He said, "It will be open for you all the gates

from the world, but it will nothing happen then you will not change it the nom."
And then he proposed to me the nom that I should change it to, which was
Leonard S. Berns. I lost a night's sleep over it and came back and told him I had
decided to make it as Leonard Bernstein or not at all.

WALLACE: Koussevitzky was not the only one to worry about the name Bernstein.
(Jamie Bernstein singing)
Lenny's daughter Jamie, herself a budding musician, has felt the pressure of
bearing that now-famous name.
(Jamie Bernstein singing)
Is it a little formidable?

JAMIE BERNSTEIN: Being around Daddy my whole life, I became sort of shy about
being overtly ambitious. It's very important for me to — to have a sense that
whatever I accomplish, I accomplish because of who I am and not because of
what my last name is.

WALLACE: Jamie is Bernstein's oldest child. Alexander, his only son, graduated
from Harvard, Lenny's alma mater, last June. He's beginning now to work in
television news. And the youngest of the brood, Nina, is still in high school. Their
mother, actress Felicia Monteleagre, died a year and a half ago. A month after his
Harvard graduation, Alex turned 25, and his birthday celebration was held at
Tanglewood, where Lenny's two great passions, music and his family, frequently
come together.
In a sense, Tanglewood in western Massachusetts is Bernstein's musical home.
He was nurtured here, and each summer he comes back here to the Berkshires, to
the green lawns and the massive old trees and the music here in the Tanglewood
Shed, to find something of himself again.
(Bernstein playing piano, singing melody)
For two weeks each summer, Bernstein happily repays the debt he feels he owes
Koussevitzky and Tanglewood. He spends hours with aspiring conductors who
yearn to follow in his path, and he spends longer with the student orchestra, until
their sound is virtually indistinguishable from a professional sound.
(Bernstein singing along with orchestra)
Tangelwood was only one stop for Bernstein during the time we followed him. In
just the last six months, he's conducted concerts in Vienna, in London, in Tokyo
and Tel Aviv, in San Francisco and Seoul, in Washington and New York.
Are you in any sense the captive of the necessity of making not just a living but a
huge living to live in the way that you want to?

BERNSTEIN: No.

WALLACE: I mean, there's the house in Connecticut, there's the place in New York,
there is your life style, there is the support of your children, in a certain sense. You
live extraordinarily well.

BERNSTEIN: Money means absolutely nothing to me. I mean, as long as I have
enough to take care of this house and my children and so on, it never occurs to
me to want any more. I sign contracts without reading them. I have no interest in
that —

WALLACE: Really?

BERNSTEIN: — aspect of life.

WALLACE: Bernstein wants — indeed, he seems to need — human contact with his audience. And after each performance, worldwide, they flock backstage to see him.

WOMAN: Thank you so much. Thanks for *The Mass,* too. That's my absolute, all-time favorite.

BERNSTEIN: That's my all-time favorite.

WOMAN: Good! (Laughs)

WALLACE: Celebrity has been a — a fact, a state of being, thus a state of mind, with you ever since you were 25 years old.

BERNSTEIN: Not a state of mind, a state of fact.

WALLACE: A state of fact.

BERNSTEIN: It's very strange, I — I did enjoy it, those first years, in my twenties. I thought it was wonderful. You know what I enjoyed most about being a celebrity? That people asked for me to give my name to causes. And I thought, "God, isn't it wonderful? You mean, all I have to do is say, 'Yes, you may use my name,' and it will help get wheat to the starving South Africans and it will be serviceable in anti-Fascist causes and labor causes and civil rights causes?"

WALLACE: It also got goggles for the Black Panthers.

BERNSTEIN: Oh, please! The theory is that I gave a party for the Black Panthers in my Park Avenue apartment.

WALLACE: Right.

BERNSTEIN: Right?

WALLACE: Right.

BERNSTEIN: That was then called slumming and then radical chic. It was not slumming. It had nothing to do with chic and it had nothing to do with radical. This was picked up by everybody all around the world and turned into a major event, all based, as I say, on lies, which has still not ceased to follow me everywhere I go.

WALLACE: Opening day of the Leonard Bernstein Festival in Kansas City. In just a little over two hours, this hall will be jammed with Bernstein fans who've been anticipating this night for months. It's been an exhausting and an exhilarating day for Leonard Bernstein. He is supposed to be here merely as a spectator. No chance. He has been working all day long.

BERNSTEIN (interrupting musician):   I know what's wrong. I know what's wrong. (Bernstein singing as he plays piano)

WALLACE: Remember, everything you're hearing is a Bernstein composition.

BERNSTEIN: That's when Sono Osato's body was raised.

WOMAN: Ah!

BERNSTEIN: And everybody said, "What a body!" And . . . (begins playing piano). And boy, did she have a body then. Whew! Now, what happens at the end. (indistinct cross-talk between Bernstein and musician).

WALLACE: Like the name, Lenny, people who hardly know him can call him Lenny, but not, he says, not the critics who review his work.

BERNSTEIN: There's even certain press that can call me Lenny, when it's affectionate, but not when they review a concert.

WALLACE: Do they?

BERNSTEIN: Oh, sure. "Lenny's at it again. Lenny's jumping up and down." (Laughter)

WALLACE: Lenny doesn't seem to be jumping up and down as much as he used to, or am I wrong?

BERNSTEIN: I have no idea what I do on the podium. I don't prepare a gesture.

WALLACE: But he is incapable of looking, acting, somehow less than theatrical.
And I am fascinated as I sit here, the way you smoke, the way that your hair is combed, the open —

BERNSTEIN: Is it combed?

WALLACE: — the open — or uncombed. The open throat, the plaid. There is a certain theatricality —

BERNSTEIN: Theatricality? Where?

WALLACE: You hate that word, don't you?

BERNSTEIN: This — no, because —

WALLACE: What in the world is wrong with theatricality? That's what we pay to — to go to see.

BERNSTEIN: But why is this theatrical? (Points to open-neck shirt). Which means this wouldn't be? (Zips up his shirt) Is that your idea?

WALLACE: You know something?

BERNSTEIN: This wouldn't be? (Brushes back his hair . . . laughter)

WALLACE: Right.

BERNSTEIN: What do you want me to do to be untheatrical?

WALLACE: As we said, he is incapable of being untheatrical, on the podium or off. Last May, Kansas City held that four-day festival in his honor. This is vintage Bernstein, capes and kisses, the flamboyance for which he is so famous, which he says that he despises but somehow cannot seem to shed. Those four days in Kansas City were filled with Bernstein's compositions. The Saturday night performance, a melange of Bernstein show tunes: *On the Town, West Side Story, Wonderful Town, West Side Story* again.
(Musical selections from *On the Town, West Side Story, Wonderful Town*)
A San Francisco critic wrote, "He needs, clearly wants, acceptance as a major composer. This has not happened. His concert music is frankly theatrical. Thus far, his serious concert music has been the external music of a performer." Now, you may — you may or may not utterly disagree.

BERNSTEIN: Are you grilling?

WALLACE: I'm asking.

BERNSTEIN: Well, I don't agree with that at all. It is true that my music is theater oriented. All of it is, that's absolutely true. But I don't see anything particularly demeaning about that, because the theater is a great place.

WALLACE: But because Bernstein himself feels he's failed to fulfill his promise as a composer, he's vowed to take the next year off to do nothing else.
You know that there are friends of yours, admirers of yours, who will say that

Leonard Bernstein simply doesn't have the temperament for long-term compos-
ing, that you really can't abide the loneliness, the solitariness.

BERNSTEIN: I love it, actually.

WALLACE: Month after month?

BERNSTEIN: Uh-hmm. Right.

WALLACE: That you return to conducting because it, in effect — that you need it, that it
feeds you.

BERNSTEIN: I return to it because that's part of my nature. Part of me is a performer,
there's no doubt of that. As I've gotten older, some of the things that I always
wanted to do, like perform music beautifully, either at the piano or conducting,
have offered less deep inner rewards than they used to.

WALLACE: The rewards he seeks now are less fleeting, the rewards only his peers
and history can give him as a composer. And he seems almost to deprecate what
has gone before, to focus not on his formidable accomplishments but on all the
things he believes he has failed to do.

BERNSTEIN: Actually, I have written a very small body of music. And since writing
music is — this may sound strange to you — the most important thing I can do,
the main dissatisfaction is therefore that I have written so little music. I mean,
when you add it up, it's not a very long list.

WALLACE: We caught Bernstein last summer at a time when he was a trifle down,
introspective, and very much missing his late wife.
Felicia would probably be very happy that you're about to take this year off.

BERNSTEIN: Oh, yes, she would love it. As a matter of fact, it — the decision was
partly taken through, so to speak, consulting her voice. She's with me a lot. I — I
miss her terribly. Whenever I detect a kind of whine in my voice, I hear her voice
saying, "Are you whining?" And then I stop.

(Music)

WALLACE: Bernstein's last completed work was *Songfest*, which premiered two
years ago in Washington. In it, he sets American poems to music, including one of
his favorites.
Edna St. Vincent Millay.

BERNSTEIN: Right.

WALLACE: Has to do with age.

BERNSTEIN: And lost love.

WALLACE: And lost love. And you are — by the time this broadcast goes on the air,
you will be 61. In *Songfest*, you write —

BERNSTEIN: Sixty-one? Yeah.

WALLACE: Edna St. Vincent Millay's poem —

BERNSTEIN: Means nothing. I'm not counting any more, in the way I don't count
the number of cigarettes I smoke.

WALLACE: — which ends, "I only know that summer sang in me a little while that in
me sings no more."

BERNSTEIN: That's not quite true of my life, though. It does still sing in me. Not as
often as it used to and maybe not as strongly as it used to, but, boy, it sure does.

89```````````````

Otherwise I would have jumped in the lake long ago. If summer doesn't sing in you, nothing sings in you, and if you don't — if nothing sings in you, you can't make music.

(Music ends with a flourish)

(To orchestra): Okay, let's have a break.

The Marketplace

DREW PHILLIPS, PRODUCER

HARRY REASONER: Last spring, we reported that the drug business in and around Miami probably now tops the tourist business, that less than 10 percent of the marijuana and cocaine coming into Florida from the Caribbean gets stopped. What happens when all that marijuana and cocaine reaches the street, the marketplace? If less than 10 percent is stopped coming into Florida, out on the street it seems they stop almost none of it.

IRV SIMMONS: What you got, mama? How much you want for them?

WOMAN: They — fifty cents apiece.

SIMMONS: How much you got there?

WOMAN: Wait a minute.

SIMMONS: Don't take all day to counting out, lady. Goddamn, we ain't got no license to do this, you know.
How — how much is that — those up?

MAN: Three dollars each, two for five.

SIMMONS: Give me ten dollars.
Hey, s—! How much is a quarter ounce?

MAN: Forty dollars.

SIMMONS: Hey, baby, what's happening? Smoke? Got nickel bags?

MAN: Yeah, I got nickel bags.

SIMMONS: Give me — give me two nickel bags. Anybody got any — any blow? Cool . . .

REASONER: The man you've been watching buying drugs all over New York City is Irv Simmons of the Drug Rehabilitation Center, Phoenix House. He agreed to wear a wireless mike while we filmed him with a hidden camera. It surprised us, but it didn't surprise him or the cops that patrol midtown Manhattan that the park behind the New York City Public Library is a veritable marketplace.

SIMMONS: Anybody got any blow?

MAN: Yeah, my man got some.

MAN: Quaalude.

MAN: You got that opium on you.

SIMMONS: Who got opium?

MAN: My man.

REASONER: Technically, our drug buying was illegal, but we had informed New York City Police Commissioner Robert McGuire of what we wanted to do and he told us to go ahead. He had no doubt we'd be successful.

COMMISSIONER ROBERT McGUIRE: We have tried to respond to the complaints of communities, citizens, that we want to move the drug pushers off the street. But you have an enormous market. You have enormous access to contraband. People want to buy it, and law enforcement serves a very limited deterrent purpose, quite frankly. Once it's on your streets, you'd need a massive army of hundreds of thousands of law-enforcement people to truly stop it.

REASONER: We had given Irv Simmons a thousand dollars, put the hidden microphone on him and sent him out to spend the money. He got rid of it in four days at 11 locations in the heart of Manhattan.

SIMMONS: If I were a user, the only thing I would have felt safe with, reasonably safe with, during the entire tour would have been the pills and the — the joints. The Quaaludes could very well be a synthetic Quaalude or, according to the size and the shape of this, maybe a Rolaid. (Laughter)

REASONER: And this is all cocaine?

SIMMONS: This is all —

REASONER: Well —

SIMMONS: — cocaine. I'm — suspect — I — I would think after we have this analyzed we would find a variety of substances, such as mannitol, which is used to cut cocaine, procaine, which gives a similar numb to cocaine, some other local anesthetics, or any other type of white powder that the dealer believes he can get away with.

REASONER: You and I could walk out the door now and, within a few blocks, buy almost anything we wanted?

SIMMONS: Most certainly. If you'd like to do it, I can get — take you where you can buy any of this yourself, and I have no doubt that they would sell to you. I don't think these are people who would recognize you. They don't seem to be the type that you would find in your audience.

REASONER: They're not 60 MINUTES fans?

SIMMONS: They're not 6 — 60 MINUTE — the — 60 MINUTES happens to come on at a prime time, and prime time for drugs is about that time of the evening. (Laughter)

REASONER: We decided to test Irv's opinion, and what better place than Battery Park on a bright, windy, fall afternoon, with the Statue of Liberty in the background? Somewhat nervously, I took two strolls through the park. On my first trip, I had no trouble making my first illegal drug buy — $65 worth of cocaine and heroin.

SIMMONS: You got some coke? Let's get — let's get — let's get coke.

REASONER: That'd be good. I got fifty.

SIMMONS: Okay, give me two tens.

REASONER: Well, that was easy. I think they did recognize us and didn't care. The second time around I was quickly spotted, and suddenly no one in that park was selling anything.

SIMMONS: Got any stuff?

MAN: What, smoke?

SIMMONS: No, a little heroin.

MAN: No, not in this park.

MAN: Down the street, but not in here.

SIMMONS: Got coke? Any coke?

MAN: Got no coke, either.

REASONER: What have you got?

MAN: I don't have nothing.

REASONER: But the fact that I could buy heroin so easily the first time, in broad daylight, convinced me that the drug problem has spread from the ghetto and has become a white, middle-class problem. Our hidden camera confirmed this. Almost all of the dealers are black, but most of their customers are white. For a lot of New Yorkers, the three-martini lunch has become the two-joint lunch. These people are sharing a joint they just bought on Park Avenue. The two women on the left are rolling their own joint at the foot of Wall Street. For harder stuff – cocaine, pills, even heroin – all you have to do is go into almost any of Manhattan's parks. And not all of the dealers are black, either. At Phoenix House, we met a new patient who only a week before had been selling Angel Dust and pills himself.

Any trouble from the police?

BILLY: Not really. More — more trouble with getting ripped off, you know.

REASONER: By other dealers, or other –

BILLY: Right.

REASONER: Yeah.

BILLY: By other dealers or people that were strung out. There was police there, but the — they never really raided the place or anything like that.

REASONER: Why did you quit?

BILLY: I'm fed up with it, you know. I'm — I was using it, a lot of the stuff that I was selling I was using, and I just wanted to make — to straighten out my life, because I'm — young and everything.

REASONER: Billy told us most of his customers were white, well-dressed students and businessmen. Of course, the more affluent drug users don't do their buying on the street. There has been a lot of publicity lately about how easy it is to get cocaine in nightclubs, and the stories make it seem like the fashionable thing to do. (Newspaper headlines about Studio 54) Sterling Johnson, New York City's special narcotics prosecutor, deplores this.

STERLING JOHNSON: Cocaine used to be what they called the champagne of drugs. It is no longer the champagne of drugs. Any and everybody can get cocaine. People who don't regard themselves as drug abusers, who would never think of touching heroin, feel it's the chic thing to do to dabble or snort a — a — a little cocaine to get high. So, it is the "in" thing to do nowadays.

REASONER: Johnson put us onto a man we knew as "Warren Smith," once operations manager for one of the country's top narcotics dealers. Smith is now working with authorities to keep from going to prison and his identity must be protected.

WARREN SMITH: The state, the city police and the federal police consider cocaine a low-priority item.

REASONER: Why?

SMITH: Because it's used by the upper-class people.

REASONER: If it's used by upper-class people, that in — that makes it better?

SMITH: Well, it doesn't make it any better, but police are not going to raid a Sutton Place apartment.

REASONER: Uh-hmm.

SMITH: If they know it was going — it was being sold there, they wouldn't go into Sutton Place, but they'd break a door down in Harlem.

REASONER: But if you're going to buy in the street, you've got a problem. If you look like a transient the dealer is never going to see again, or if you look like an undercover cop, he's apt to go to the pocket with the bad merchandise. We took all our purchases to the Industrial Testing Laboratory. Owner Ken Kohlhof told us that, as Irv Simmons had suspected, we didn't get all we paid for.

KEN KOHLHOF: Cocaine, you were ripped off. Half the samples contained procaine, which is Novocaine. The other half ne — didn't even contain procaine. No cocaine, no procaine.

REASONER: What about the heroin?

KOHLHOF: The heroin samples we did find positive as heroin.

REASONER: Now, in the stuff that I bought, specifically in Battery Park, that was not cocaine, but it was heroin?

KOHLHOF: Yes, you got heroin, but you did not get cocaine.

REASONER: That's an old story to Dr. Mitchell Rosenthal, who runs New York's Phoenix House, and it's part of the reason he says the middle-class users who think they have everything under control are playing a dangerous game.

DR. MITCHELL ROSENTHAL: People who go out and think that they're buying cocaine are often buying other local anesthetics or Angel Dust, which is dangerous. They think they're buying a good grade of marijuana. They may be buying marijuana that's sprayed with anything from Angel Dust to underarm deodorant. The pills that they're getting are of unknown quality and quantity. They're really playing a kind of pharmacologic roulette, where many of them don't know what's happened to them until they wake up in a hospital emergency room.

REASONER: Okay, but we're talking about New York. It couldn't happen in your town, could it?

SMITH: Any stranger can walk into Anytown, U.S.A. and buy whatever drug is being sold.

REASONER: Not just New York City?

SMITH: Not just New York City. I've been all over the United States and I've never found any difficulty in obtaining either cocaine or marijuana in any place I've ever been.

REASONER: So the stuff's out there, just about everywhere. What can we do about it? Commissioner McGuire thinks it will take a total commitment by the public, the police and the entire judicial system to stop open-street sales.

COMMISSIONER McGUIRE: Well, I think the law has to be enforced, and I think that when we make an arrest, given our resources, I think that the criminal-justice system has to treat that arrest seriously. And I think that some of these cases have to serve as examples, because you must — it must have a ripple effect. And I think if the end result of a lot of our time, manpower, resources is that the person does not receive any serious sanction for openly, as you say, and flagrantly violating the law, then I think other people will act with impunity. And I think that we got to turn that around and get the entire system to recognize this is serious.

Our young people are being impacted dramatically. I'm less concerned about a 45-year-old lawyer or doctor who wants to use cocaine. I don't like it, but I — he's at least making a judgment based upon a life's experience. That's not true of young people. So I think there has to be a — a much more aggressive educational effort with young — young men and women that this is not the way to live your life.

DR. ROSENTHAL: The level of drug use has gotten so frightening to parents that we have a new wave of parental concern. That's very significant, because when that voice is heard across this land, I think that our government is going to begin to re-evaluate and restrengthen its efforts in this fight.

REASONER: But in New York anyway, the strengthening of the fight against street sales will have to wait at least another year, because the anti-narcotics budget has been cut. That probably means there will be more street sales, instead of less, in New York in the coming year. And since all governments — federal, state and local — are facing the same financial crisis, the street-sale problem, at least in the short term, will probably get worse everywhere before it gets better.

A Few Minutes
with Andy Rooney

HARRY REASONER: There used to be a popular song that went, "Johnny get your gun." Another one went, "I didn't raise my boy to be a soldier." Does it now follow that someone will write, "Janie get your gun" or "I didn't raise my girl to be drafted?" Probably not. But if we're not singing about the draft, a lot of people are bellyaching about it.

ANDY ROONEY: This argument about the draft is pretty dull, really, because there are only two issues involved. One, should we have a draft at all? And two, if we have one, should we draft women? President Carter could have considered a lot of other alternatives that would have made the argument more interesting, it seems to me. For instance, a 16-year-old boy wrote a letter to my hometown newspaper suggesting drafting only women. Well, now there's an idea for you. Men have been discriminated against in the draft for more than 200 years. Maybe we ought to start an affirmative-action program, draft nothing but women until the total number of women drafted equal the total number of men who have ever been drafted. Even West Point would be all women, you know, with maybe eight or ten token men, just enough for an occasional newspaper feature story about how they're doing there.

Keep in mind, no one is saying men shouldn't serve in the Army at all. Far from it. There are certain non-combat jobs men are especially well-qualified to do. Men make good medics, for example, because they're kinder, gentler, more sympathetic to someone in trouble. I think it would be safe to say that basically they're nicer people.

Wouldn't a proposition like that make the draft argument more interesting? How about using our free-enterprise system to attract people to the service? Offer to pay privates $50,000 a year, but only take the best applicants. There'd be plenty of applicants. This way we'd get good people and the Army and Navy wouldn't have to be so big. Everyone wants to be an officer, no one wants to be a private, so privates would be paid the highest salary. As soon as a private was made a corporal, he'd only make $40,000 a year. Sergeant would make $35,000, and so on. By the time anyone in the Army got to be a general, he'd only be making $7,500 a year, something like that. There are always plenty of people who want to be the general.

Here's another idea. What about limiting the draft to people between the ages of 50 and 60? A lot of us are in better shape than we were when we were 20, and we're a lot smarter, too. Now, some 50-year-olds might protest against registering for the draft, but wouldn't it be a relief to see someone other than students protesting for a change?

Well, there are so many possibilities. What would you think about just drafting cigarette smokers? The ones who smoke more than a pack a day would serve in combat at the front lines, because, well, you know. Well, something to argue about, isn't it?

Letters

DAN RATHER: In the mail this week was a letter from a viewer who said of our story on Mike Pertschuk, the man who runs the Federal Trade Commission: "If you do not get a flood of mail condemning Mr. Pertschuk . . . then perhaps we consumers are indeed as stupid as he believes us to be."

Well, we did get a flood of mail, but not much of it condemned Mr. Pertschuk. Most of it was like this: "Will miracles never cease? How relieved I was to learn that there is still a federal agency that is . . . deserving of our tax dollars . . . Hats off to the Federal Trade Commission.",

Another viewer said: "It's about time some government agency did what it was set up to do . . . Look out for the little guy."

About our story on black athletes who spend most of their college time on the basketball court or the gridiron and very little in the classroom, we heard from the director of sports information at the State University of Buffalo, New York. He called our story: "An unfair indictment of administrators, faculty and athletic staff at . . . institutions of higher learning."

But an associate professor at the University of New Mexico, one of the institutions of higher learning we focused on in that story, said: "College administrators . . . forget their moral and intellectual duties in this area . . . You were too gentle with them."

There was also a letter that said: "Surprising that 60 MINUTES does not recognize that (athletes) aren't held at gunpoint to let others take their tests for them or to sign up for Mickey Mouse courses." That same viewer thought we should have given some time to schools and coaches with higher standards, schools like Joe Paterno's Penn State and Bobby Knight's Indiana. Well, we did. Last season, we devoted an entire story to Joe Paterno, and right now we're preparing one on Bobby Knight.

Finally, a viewer wrote: "If (those athletes) don't have the drive to get that education they missed, that's tuff! (You could say) that's the way the ball bounces."

FEBRUARY 17, 1980

The Death of Edward Nevin

HARRY MOSES, PRODUCER

DAN RATHER: Occasionally we run across a story that is so unusual it seems it should be fiction. The death of Edward Nevin is such a tale. He was an immigrant whose life could be the story of every Irishman who came to these shores. Edward Nevin was a patriot, a man who worshipped freedom, and yet a man whose death, so his family says, came at the hands of the country he loved. Until recently, the death of Edward Nevin was a mystery. It involved a secret government experiment so closely guarded it would be a quarter of a century before it could be told. The year was 1950. The Cold War was at its height.

That same autumn, a man named Edward Nevin, a 75-year-old Irish immigrant who had come to San Francisco in 1905 and fathered seven children, died. Mr. Nevin had just been through successful surgery and had been released from the hospital. Then, suddenly and without explanation, he became ill and was forced to return.

DR. RICHARD WHEAT: I became acquainted with Mr. Nevin when his illness was obviously severe and he came to the medical service where I was a resident and we cared for him until his death.

RATHER: In 1950, Dr. Richard Wheat was a 28-year-old resident at Stanford University Hospital in San Francisco when he noticed that certain patients in his care were coming down with a mysterious illness. By the time the infection had run its course, 11 men had been stricken by a strange bacteria called Serratia marcescens. What puzzled Dr. Wheat was that this particular bacteria had never before been seen in his hospital or anywhere else in the San Francisco area.

DR. WHEAT: Well, at first it was a curiosity, and then it became a concern that perhaps we had something going that we didn't understand or didn't know about. So, with that in mind, we tried to find out where it was coming from and what had caused it, with absolutely no luck at all.

RATHER: So puzzled was Dr. Wheat by the appearance of Serratia marcescens and the illness of the 11 patients that he published an account of the experience in a medical journal. Ten of the men eventually recovered from the infection, but one man did not, a man whose initials were E. N. In November of 1950, Edward Nevin died. It would be 26 years before all the circumstances surrounding his death would be known.

These old home movies of Edward Nevin, taken a few years before his death, are the only remaining record of him. They reveal a vigorous, vital individual who looked and acted far younger than his age, a man who, by all rights, should have been able to resist the bacteria that appeared from nowhere to kill him. And where it came from was a mystery.

We pick up the story some 3,000 miles across the country, at Harvard University, where this man, Dr. Matthew Messelson, is Professor of Biochemistry. In 1965, Dr. Messelson's assistant had told him a story she had heard and kept secret since 1950. It concerned a U.S. Army biological-warfare experiment in San Francisco which, according to the woman's informant, had resulted in the death of a man. The experiment involved the use of live bacteria called Serratia marcescens. The woman was very nervous about telling this to Dr. Messelson.

DR. MATTHEW MESSELSON: She was frightened. She was frightened. She knew that I was then, as I ha— have been for many years, very interested in chemical and biological defense and chemical and biological arms control, chemical and biological weapons. That's why she told me, and also because we were good friends. But she was afraid and asked me not to tell anybody. I then made a search of the medical literature to see if I could find any articles about this, because that would be rather unusual. I knew that it — deaths from Serratia marcescens would be considered unusual. And I found an article, and I called one of the authors, Dr. Wheat.

RATHER: And what did he tell you about the death? Did he tell you that he was pretty sure that it was caused by this? Or caused —

DR. MESSELSON: The death itself was certainly caused by bacterial endocarditis and — due to Serratia marcescens.

But as to the puzzle of where the bacteria came from in that and the other cases, which all occurred within a short interval of time, he was still as mystified as before, though he still, as I recall, believed, as he had written in his paper, that there had been a common source. But what that common source might be, he had no guess at that time.

RATHER: But you had a guess?

DR. MESSELSON: If he did, he didn't tell me. I had a guess.

RATHER: You knew about the test?

DR. MESSELSON: I knew about the test. And I told people in the government that this sort of thing was foolish and that it ought to be stopped. But I didn't know who the right people were to talk to, I don't think.

RATHER: What Dr. Messelson also didn't know was that millions of Americans had already been used by the government as unwitting guinea pigs in more than 200 biological-warfare experiments that took place between 1949 and 1968, when they were finally stopped.

What was the Army trying to learn from exposing millions of Americans to what they thought was completely harmless bacteria? They say it was the only way they could find out how to cope with a real germ-warfare attack should the Russians ever launch one. So, 19 civilian targets were chosen to practice on. One of them was the New York City subway system.

As 60 MINUTES Producer Harry Moses did the other day, the Army's man in New York entered the subway carrying a light bulb; only his light bulb contained live bacteria to be used in the experiment. As the train sped through the tunnel, the man opened the door separating two of the cars, stepped into the opening, and dropped the light bulb on the tracks, releasing the bacteria. Monitoring stations set up by the Army showed that the experiment was a success. The bacteria had traveled from 14th Street all the way up to 59th Street, a distance of more than two miles. Similar tests were conducted at Washington's National Airport, at Greyhound bus terminals in Alaska and Hawaii, and in two tunnels on the Pennsylvania Turnpike. But the biggest and the most bizarre biological-warfare test of all took place in September of 1950 in San Francisco, California.

The object of the test, according to recently declassified Army documents, was — quote — "to study the offensive possibilities of attacking a seaport city with a biological-warfare aerosol generated from a ship located some distance offshore." And so, on a Navy ship, about the size and length of this one, the U.S. Army's secret testing team steamed out into the middle of San Francisco Bay. Attached to the railing on the fantail of the ship were three huge metal canisters containing the biological agent to be used in the experiment, a bacteria named Serratia marcescens, selected because of its supposedly benign characteristics and the bright red color it produces under laboratory analysis. At precisely 1700 hours, the testing team pointed the hoses attached to the canisters skyward, opened the valves of the nozzles and set forth an aerosol cloud of bacteria toward its intended destination, the City of San Francisco.

As the cloud made its way across the bay, three aircraft hovered overhead collecting meteorological data, and 20 ground stations were obtaining figures on wind direction and velocity. While all this was happening, the Army had established 43 sampling stations at various locations throughout the Bay Area to determine how great the bacteria's penetration had been. Volunteers stood by the windows of their homes, of government office buildings, even on their rooftops. All were holding sievelike collectors, similar to this one, which would trap airborne bacteria released from the ship. After these collectors had been analyzed by the lab, the Army learned that 30 square miles, or nearly all of San Francisco, had been exposed to the bacteria. Almost 800,000 persons had breathed particles of Serratia marcescens that September day in 1950.

Why, then, did only 11 people, one of whom died, feel the effects of the Serratia marcescens? The winds that day blew it directly over the hospital where those 11 patients were undergoing treatment that made them particularly susceptible to the infection. A common source for that infection was always suspected by Dr. Wheat, but as Dr. Messelson told us, there was no way of knowing what it was at the time.

The spraying of San Francisco would remain a closely guarded secret until 1976, when an enterprising reporter found out about it, linked it to Dr. Wheat's article, and filed his story. On December 22nd, 1976, the story hit page one of the *San Francisco Chronicle*. No one would feel its impact more greatly than a young trial attorney who had been specializing in medical malpractice cases. He remembers it this way.

EDWARD J. NEVIN III: I take BART from my home in Berkeley to work, and I was waiting for the BART train and I was reading the paper and I came upon a front-page article which was — headline read "Bacteriological Warfare Experiments in 1950, San Francisco." As a trial lawyer, as someone who deals with these kinds of cases, I — I looked at it without surprise, but with a detached sort of objective view, a professional looking at something within his field. I then discovered that the one person who died as a result of these experiments was Edward J. Nevin, a retired San Francisco pipe fitter who died in Stanford Hospital on November 1st 1950. That was my grandfather.

I was stunned. I was angry. I was hurt. The government made a decision with extremely limited thought and preparation and investigation, made a decision to expose 800,000 San Francisco citizens to bacterium, live bacterium, did not investigate the potentials for that bacterium causing disease to an adequate degree, and proceeded, nevertheless, to, in effect, reverse the whole process of the purpose of our military and our defense system — that is, to protect the people of the United States of America. And instead, that very branch of our government attacked the people of the United States of America.

RATHER: What does the Pentagon say about that? It refused our request for an interview, but maintains that any association between the bacteria that was sprayed on San Francisco with the bacteria that killed Edward Nevin is a coincidence.

DR. WHEAT: Of course, it was a fascinating coincidence, if that, since the time of their experiments was on the 26th and 27th of September, and our first case came in on the 29th of September. And Mr. Nevin, our gentleman who died of the disease, first became ill with this organism on the 2nd of October. The timing of those things is awfully interesting.

RATHER: "Awfully interesting" is not how the Nevin family would describe the relationship between the Army experiment and the death of Edward Nevin. His son is far more vehement.

NEVIN, JR.:   Well, I can't help remembering that the enemy did not do this to those 11 people in Stanford Hospital; that it was this government that did it, and it resulted in my father's death.

MRS. BRAY (Edward Nevin's daughter):   It's — it's — it just happened to the wrong person.

RATHER: Mr. Nevin's daughter.

MRS. BRAY: You know, if it was somebody that wasn't a likeable person or didn't do good in the world. I feel that he did good in the world. He was real proud of being an American. And, you know, my mother was, too. They never had any desire to go back. They wouldn't leave America. They loved it. He left a wonderful heritage to all of us. I think we're a remarkable family.

(Sounds of Nevin family celebration)

MAN: Timmy! Open it up, Tim!

(Christmas music)

RATHER: Each Christmas is a time of reunion for the Nevin clan, and each Christmas all four generations of the family gather to celebrate the season. The Nevins are there, of course, and the Careys, too, the Brays and the Gallaghers, the Donohoes and the McFaddens. And from the oldest to the youngest, there is a bond and a resolve and a purpose that joins everyone. For all of these people – all 65 living descendants of Edward J. Nevin – have united to file suit against the Army, the Navy, the Department of Defense and the United States of America for the wrongful death of the founder of this extended Irish-American family. And who will be arguing the case?

EDWARD J. NEVIN III: I'm Edward J. Nevin III. And 30 years later, I have an opportunity to present to the American people my grandfather's story for a very,very important purpose. You do not test people without them knowing it. You do not test in secrecy. You do not risk, no matter what limited risk you think you have you're — that you're taking, without having people knowingly submit to that risk. This is a question for all of us in a democratic society. We have to know.

Anderson of Illinois

NORMAN GORIN, PRODUCER

MORLEY SAFER: In every election, there is one candidate who everyone admires but no one takes seriously, a maverick, an outsider. This year that candidate is John Anderson. No one outside of Anderson's immediate political family gives him much of a chance. He ran sixth in the Iowa caucus. Yet many people say he is among the most capable of candidates. John Anderson has been a congressman from Illinois for 20 years, the first 10 fairly conservative, the second 10 fairly liberal — born again, some would say.

It's almost a maxim of recent political history that Americans do not vote for the people they claim to admire most, which is not to say that John Anderson is the most admired. Millions of voters have probably never even heard of him. But John Anderson is, to John Anderson, a very serious candidate indeed.

REPRESENTATIVE JOHN ANDERSON (R-Illinois):   I don't care whether you call me a liberal. I don't care whether you call me a Democrat or a conservative. All I want you to not say about me is that John Anderson is not a man who is without ideas, ideas to deal with the future. And to that . . .

SAFER: John Anderson is 57, Phi Beta Kappa, University of Illinois, Harvard, State Department, then the Congress for 20 years. While most of the candidates' stance an aggressive, almost warlike America, John Anderson asks for second thoughts.

REPRESENTATIVE ANDERSON: I believe that even now the American people are beginning perhaps to reassess this whole hawkish mood. They're beginning to wonder, do we really want to fight World War III for oil?

SAFER: Do you not think that there is a threat, a serious threat, to the security of this country right now?

REPRESENTATIVE ANDERSON: Well, we have — I think we have to put the problem of Afghanistan in perspective. I do believe that it's one thing to have the Soviets move into Afghanistan and it's another thing to suggest, as some people are wildly proclaiming, that this is just one more step to plant the red flag around the globe. I believe that that kind of — that kind of position represents a convulsive overreaction to what hap— happened in Afghanistan.

(Speaking to audience):   I would say to those who want to be tough abroad, hasn't it come the time when we ought to be tough on ourselves here at home? Let's rid ourselves of some of the self-indulgence and some of the self-complacency and substitute for it some of the self-discipline that has been lacking in our society in recent years.

SAFER: You are said to be the — the hair-shirt candidate, the — the man who's asking America to make great sacrifices.

REPRESENTATIVE ANDERSON: Yes.

SAFER: Isn't that almost a guarantee of defeat?

REPRESENTATIVE ANDERSON: Well, that's what I've been told by my political experts. I've had some extended arguments with them over the last few months. It does supposedly violate the canons of the profession to talk in those terms.

SAFER: And do you think Americans are going to respond to a man who says you're — we want this and that and the other sacrifice, conservation, gas taxes, all kinds of jeremiads?

REPRESENTATIVE ANDERSON: Yes.

SAFER: From John Anderson?

REPRESENTATIVE ANDERSON: Well, of course, even as I deliver that kind of a message, I also try to assure the American people, or those who are listening, that this would lay the predicate for a brighter and a better future. The reason this has become a vital interest — Iran, the Persian Gulf — is because we are importing that one-point-sev— seven million barrels of oil a day from the Persian Gulf. So let's cut back on our consumption. Let's be willing to tax ourselves at the gasoline pump to drive down consumption, use the proceeds to lower Social Security taxes. But let's not go on with business as usual, which I think has been the attitude of — of the Carter Administration.

SAFER: What makes you really different from, say, a Teddy Kennedy or a — or a Jimmy Carter?

REPRESENTATIVE ANDERSON: Well, I believe that Teddy Kennedy is espousing pretty much the old liberal Democratic politics that says that if you throw enough money at a problem, it's — it's bound to be solved. I think that Mr. Carter is very difficult to define what his political ideology is anymore. He's swung so wildly from — from left to right and back to center again, he reminds me a little bit of that fellow who says that if I — that — that politics is like paddling a canoe. If I paddle first a little bit to the left, I paddle then a little bit to the right, somehow I'll end up staying in the center. And that seems to be pretty well what the President has been doing.

SAFER: But John Anderson paddled a lot to the right and now he's paddling a lot to the left. You were — you supported a lot of conservative causes, or — or to put it the other way around, you were against a lot of liberal causes —

REPRESENTATIVE ANDERSON: Yes.

SAFER: — in 20 years in the Congress.

REPRESENTATIVE ANDERSON: Yes.

SAFER: And now you seem to have deserted your old political ideology.

REPRESENTATIVE ANDERSON: No, I don't think —

SAFER: What — what happened?

REPRESENTATIVE ANDERSON: — I don't think that's true at all, really, I saw the civil rights movement develop in this country in the early sixties. I saw the tensions that were produced. I saw the dangers that were inherent in the idea that, unless we solved our racial problem, that we were literally going to become two separate and distinct societies. And so my views changed, and — and I did become an ardent supporter of civil rights causes, and I still am.

SAFER: You're an evangelical Christian. You say the most important influence on your life was the Bible; yet you support freedom of choice in abortion. What about the Biblical admonition against abortion?

REPRESENTATIVE ANDERSON: Well, of course, I don't interpret that Biblical admonition of which you speak to deprive a woman of what I think is the most intimate, personal decision that she has to make, and that is whether or not to carry a pregnancy to term. It seems to me that's a decis— decision that she ought to be able to make with her God, with her physician, and that the state should not, with its coercive power, intrusive force, come in and, in effect, make that decision for her by saying "Thou shalt not." I don't think that's in conflict with my own personal interpretation of — of Scripture.

SAFER: Are you born again?

REPRESENTATIVE ANDERSON: I had a religious — religious experience as a child when I was nine years of age. And, yes, I acknowledge — I acknowledge that fact.

SAFER: Is there a pra— parallel secular experience in politics? Are you a — a born-again liberal?

REPRESENTATIVE ANDERSON: No, no.

SAFER: But Anderson has, at least, seen the light on such issues as Vietnam.

REPRESENTATIVE ANDERSON (during Iowa debate):   But I suppose, as I look back over a career in the Congress and the thousands of votes that have been cast during that time, if I had one that I could change, it would have been the vote that I cast in favor of the Gulf of Tonkin Resolution.
(Speaking to audience):   1980 ought to be the year when we finally get around to ratifying the Equal Rights Amendment. (Applause)

SAFER: Is this — it's a maturation of John Anderson?

REPRESENTATIVE ANDERSON: Yes, I've described it as such. I think it — it is a — it is a process of growth. But basically, I still feel very comfortable with a lot of the orthodox fiscal views of my party. I don't like 18 deficits in 18 years. I do think that when I talk about sacrifice, I'm not just pointing a finger at the American people. I'm looking at a fat, complacent federal bureaucracy. I'm telling mayors, I'm telling governors, at least when I can get them to listen: "You can't continue to expect the federal government to supply one dollar out of every four that you are spending. We're going to have to defer, at least defer for the next couple of years, some of the aid and programs that you've been counting on, because we've got to get inflation under control."

SAFER: Well, so what are you saying? Abandon the cities?

REPRESENTATIVE ANDERSON: No, far from that. Far from that. I just think that we have been very, very sloppy in the way we have designed federal programs, and we've done it on a political basis instead of the kind of rational basis of putting the aid where the aid is needed the most.
(Speaking to audience):   Without exception, every one of the other six candidates who are running, they want every super-sophisticated weapons system, including the biggest boondoggle of them all, in my judgment, the MX mobile

missile. They want all of those things as the price for defending the security of this country.

SAFER: Are you saying that these — these new weapons systems should be scrapped?

REPRESENTATIVE ANDERSON: We need to do something about our naval strength. We need to do something about perhaps improving our conventional weaponry. But to invest billions and billions and billions in a new round of the intercontinental ballistics arms race, I don't think is going to add to the security of this country. For heaven's sake, let's get our priorities straight. Let's begin to reorder those priorities and think about building the strength of the American economy here at home. And that can't be done by promising people bigger military budgets, more spending for — for all these projects, from the MX on down, and at the same time cutting taxes and balancing the budget. That's — that's the old charade that has been played out many, many times before.

SAFER: There are certain aspects of this Republican that are reminiscent of Gene McCarthy and George McGovern and their campus constituencies. Anderson in some way is a voice of the sixties.

REPRESENTATIVE ANDERSON: Jerry Wiesner told me the other night, last week down there at MIT, when 2,000 students crowded into the student union building on that campus, he said, "I haven't seen that many students in one place since they took it over back in 1969." (Audience laughs) And it's not just the draft, it's not just registration, even though I oppose registration and the draft. (Applause)

SAFER: But students are notorious nonvoters. So, do you really expect to get much support from the campuses?

REPRESENTATIVE ANDERSON (to student audience):   To disprove the fallacious notion, and it was stated to me by a rather cynical member of the press corps as recently as today: "Well, so what? You've talked to 5,000 students in the last week. They don't vote. They don't really get out and make that much difference in an election." You can show that, in 1980, history will record that it was the young people of America that made the difference.

SAFER: John Anderson's campaign does not stop traffic. In fact, the candidate has to stop his own taxis. No limousines, no Secret Service, and very little money. And he does admit that the process of getting nominated is not the most uplifting of experiences.

You've said that the process of becoming President, the process of being nominated, is a demeaning and debilitating thing.

REPRESENTATIVE ANDERSON: Yes. Well, I've said that because I really think that what I would like to contribute to this campaign is the creation of a new kind of politics where you didn't select a candidate simply on the basis of the — the fact that he had been able to shake more hands than everybody else.

MAN: How do you do, sir?

REPRESENTATIVE ANDERSON: Well, yes, of course. Nice to see you. Nice to see you.

MAN: A pleasure.

REPRESENTATIVE ANDERSON: Well, thank you for coming.

MAN: My colleagues in Illinois tell me that you're a good man, and I'm proud to be here.

REPRESENTATIVE ANDERSON: Oh, well.

MAN: Shall we move through here?

REPRESENTATIVE ANDERSON: You have political consultants that are supposed to tell you how you avoid any possible misstep as you make your way along this path to the Presidency. Candidates are actually being selected on the basis of whether or not they have the vim, vigor and vitality of maintaining a schedule from 6 o'clock in the morning until 11 o'clock at night, cheerfully accepting some anonymous person's directions as to where they go and what they do, to the point where they become totally programmed.

SAFER: It's hard to believe that this fund-raising party in New York is for a Republican candidate. It's held at the Fifth Avenue apartment of the radical millionaire Stewart Mott. It is a little bit limousine liberal, a little bit literary, and it is largely a traditionally Democratic crowd. The novelist Kurt Vonnegut, for example, is switching from Carter to Anderson.

KURT VONNEGUT: Every Democrat's dream, I think, is a liberal Republican. And —

REPRESENTATIVE ANDERSON: I'm — I'm listening very carefully now, Kurt.

SAFER: I'm thinking of last night. You went to a little fund-raising affair —

REPRESENTATIVE ANDERSON: Yes.

SAFER: — in Stewart Mott's apartment here in New York. And there you were being embraced by the radical chic, I guess you'd call them out in the Midwest, where you come from, that this is kind of a kiss of death to a — to a — particularly a Republican candidate, being embraced by all those people who were last seen embracing Eugene McCarthy and Mo Udall and George McGovern.

REPRESENTATIVE ANDERSON: Well, you know, I'm not concerned about whether or not financial support comes to my campaign from the people that you describe, and I don't know whether they all fit that description of being radical chic. And if they want to help me finance this campaign, give me some of the chance that other candidates have to bring a message to the nation on television or through the print media, I don't think that I am dishonoring my candidacy by accepting their help.

SAFER: For an underdog, Anderson is a gentle soul who does not speak harshly of his rivals, even when you play the candidate game with him.
I'll give you a name, you give me an answer. Ronald Reagan?

REPRESENTATIVE ANDERSON: I'm not concerned about his chronological age. I am concerned about his ideas. They are very aged, indeed.

SAFER: George Bush?

REPRESENTATIVE ANDERSON: I don't believe he's electable. I think he's too conservative.

SAFER: Howard Baker?

REPRESENTATIVE ANDERSON: I'm disturbed about his unwillingness to support SALT II. It's that frame of reference, I think, that bothers me more than anything else about his views.

SAFER: John Connally?

REPRESENTATIVE ANDERSON: Oh, I think that Mr. Connally represents too much the stereotype that people already have of the Republican Party as being in league with big business.

SAFER: It's kind of interesting the —

REPRESENTATIVE ANDERSON: Yes.

SAFER: — the perception of John Anderson. For example, this *Washington Post* headline is: "Dream Candidate Going Nowhere." Tom Wicker, a liberal columnist in the *New York Times,* says the man running on either side can't win. Conventional wisdom. Leo Durocher says nice guys finish last. What do you say to all that?

REPRESENTATIVE ANDERSON: I've heard those things over and over again, and I am sustained in my quest for the nomination because I believe that this time it's different.

SAFER: If you were laying money on John Anderson, what sort of odds would you be getting?

REPRESENTATIVE ANDERSON: Well, I haven't talked to Jimmy the Greek lately, so I don't know what the betting odds are. I continue to be serene in my own mind that I've got something to say, something to offer to my party and to the country, and I'm going to win.

Yugoslavia

WILLIAM K. McCLURE, PRODUCER

DAN RATHER: He is the last survivor of the big names of World War II — Roosevelt, Churchill, Stalin, Hitler, Mussolini, De Gaulle, Chiang Kai-shek — and now he is hovering between life and death. Marshall Josip Broz Tito of Yugoslavia battled Hitler to a standstill in World War II, and then this most fiercely independent of Communist leaders took on Stalin in the post-war period.

In the light of what is happening in Afghanistan, what happens now in Yugoslavia after Tito is a question that concerns the United States more than ever. We visited there in 1978 to report on Tito's Yugoslavia.

Tito was in his 86th year. He was, and looked the part, a kind of Yugoslavian "Big Daddy." He had villas all over Yugoslavia and his own mud baths and wine cellars. His expensive tastes had not diminished his popularity. There are no free elections in Yugoslavia, but even if there were, he would have won them with ease. His image had suffered a bit at home and abroad because of the unexplained disappearance of Mrs. Tito. Since these pictures were taken, they no longer live together. Some said she was being investigated for plotting to arrange Tito's successor. Still others said it was just a case of Tito finding a new woman. He had become interested in a 24-year-old masseuse. All of the villas and the rumors underscored Tito's craving for creature comforts. But he loved being photographed in ways that tended to make him appear, not as a potentate, but rather as a person whose tastes remained those of the common, ordinary workingman.

Tito had always traveled extensively, constantly conferring with leaders of aligned and nonaligned nations. He met all post-war Presidents of the United States. His Washington visits touched off protests from Yugoslav dissidents, especially those demanding an independent state of Croatia.

In the summer of '78, he began his most ambitious travel schedule ever, beginning in Moscow. Brezhnev greeted him warmly, at least before the cameras. In private, Brezhnev reportedly gave blunt warnings against any closer relations with the West or with China. (Marching music in the background) Next for Tito that year was a rapturous welcome in North Korea. This was a stopover on his way to an ironic triumph, his reception in Peking, Mao's successor, Chairman Hua, toasted Tito in the Great Hall, the first direct meeting ever between leaders of the two major countries that succeeded in splitting away from the Soviets. Mao considered Tito's brand of Communism too soft and dangerous. Not so with China's new leadership.

Mrs. Tito, of course, was nowhere to be seen on these trips, nor had she been around even for routine public functions at home, such as this reception where schoolchildren lined up to be kissed by the "Old Man," as he was affectionately called. He loved this sort of performance.

When Tito is in Belgrade, he often comes here to the White Palace, but he doesn't come here as often as he did in the past. Partly because of his health, he prefers warmer places.

The reality of Yugoslavia today, economically, is a contradiction in terms: free-market Communism. What that means is that, instead of the highly centralized economy practiced by the Soviet Union, China and other Communist states, Tito has tried to decentralize. And in so doing, in Yugoslavia he has created, like in no other Communist state, a consumer society.

(Excerpts from commercials on Yugoslav television)

Commercials on Yugoslav television. Just as in the capitalist world, the hard sells generate high demand for consumer goods. This, in turn, has driven Yugoslav industry to improve the quality and quantity of its goods.

(Excerpts from commercials on Yugoslav television)

Lubica Ivancevic, schoolteacher, mother of two, typical of the new middle-class consumer created by Tito's free-market Communism. Her husband, Nick Ivancevic, Communist Party member, the only architect in their village of Korcula, an average Yugoslav island town off the Dalmatian coast. Population: 2,000, mostly literate. Principal industries: tourism and shipbuilding. We singled out the Ivancevics because they speak English and because they seemed so typical of the middle-income family that represents Yugoslavia's new affluence. As long as they toe the line politically, they are well off materially.

Do you have a family goal now? Is there something that you want to buy for your house or your family?

NICK IVANCEVIC: Yes.

LUBICA IVANCEVIC: Yes.

NICK: Hi-fi.

LUBICA: Ne — yes, hi-fi.

RATHER: A stereo?

LUBICA: Yes.

NICK: I have a complete system, you know, with loudspeakers, with turntable, with all these things. But very good one.

LUBICA: And the machine for washing up the dishes, that's what I would like to have.

RATHER: Oh, a dishwasher.

LUBICA: Dishwasher. That's it. Thank you.

RATHER: You have a washing machine for clothes?

LUBICA: Oh, yes, of course.

RATHER: And a refrigerator?

LUBICA: Yes.

NICK: Two of them.

LUBICA: Two of them. (Laughs)

NICK: Not two cars, but two refrigerators. (Laughter)

LUBICA: We need them during the summer. I think that we in Yugoslavia eat very much. I think we are spoiled.

RATHER: So, you have a — a number of aspirations. You want to buy a — a stereo.

LUBICA: Yes. Color television, dishwasher. Yes.

RATHER: Is all of that reasonable to expect that you'll be able to buy that?

NICK: Yes, of course. Why not?

LUBICA: Yes, yes, of course. Many of our friends have got color television and a dishwasher already, so I think we — we wouldn't be any — anything special to have all these things.

RATHER: It strikes me, as you talk, that your life here is very much like middle-class life in the United States or England.

LUBICA: Yes, maybe. Yes. Yes, it is. There is not a great difference.

(Music: "When the Saints Go Marching In")

RATHER: The "scene" in Korcula. It could be Saturday night in Kalamazoo. Dancing to American jazz mixed with Yugoslav rock. In many other important ways, this is happening today in Yugoslav society. Nick and Lubica's combined yearly income of $12,000 does not cover the good life they covet. They are in debt for their house, their car, their appliances. Even these evenings out must be paid for on credit cards.

Another unique feature of Communism Tito-style was freedom to travel. He was the only Communist dictator who allowed comrades to take jobs abroad, particularly in Germany and Italy. Example: the old Iron Curtain line between Trieste and Slovenia, once studded with tank traps and mines; now, hardly a Yugoslav has to do anything more than slow down for passport inspection. Communist leadership everywhere else fears this kind of worker mobility. Tito encouraged it.

Consumer products — everything from telephones and pocket calculators to hand tools and TV sets — are rolling off Yugoslavia's own assembly lines. This plant is operated by Iskra, a kind of Yugoslavian General Electric, with 30,000 employees spread over 47 plants throughout the country. Headquarters: a prestige tower in the center of Ljublijana. I went to see its managing director in his executive suite, and I asked Jose Hujs if his enterprise makes a profit.

JOSE HUJS: Sure we do. I hope every year. (Laughs)

RATHER: That's your job — to make a profit?

HUJS: Yeah. (Laughs)

RATHER: How does this system differ from capitalism?

HUJS: I know the — both systems, let's say, fairly well, and I would say the differences is — differences are quite substantial; substantial in the sense that — that the workers have a completely different attitude to the company and to the — its er— earnings as well.

RATHER: How does it differ from the Soviet system?

HUJS: I would say as much as from the capitalistic one, in certain way. If you put them — each one to side of the table, we are right in the middle somewhere, you know.

RATHER: So, a major difference is that you do not have central planning?

HUJS: No, not at all.

RATHER: It is that decentralized economic self-determination that keeps business energy jumping here. Jose Hujs is allowed to operate on the law of supply and demand and is forced to compete with other Yugoslav industry for operating funds and raw materials. He entertains top executives and foreign buyers at the poshest restaurant in Ljublijana. It's a Yugoslav version of the three-martini lunch.

(Music . . . followed by factory whistle)

Belinka — a chemical factory specializing in detergents. Compared with Iskra, this is no big deal; annual gross income only about $30 million. Its young manager is Marjan Cerrar. He's a good example of the new Yugoslav technocrat: not a party member, but a dedicated believer in self-management.

MARJAN CERRAR: I think the main things of our self-management system is that the alienation of the workers isn't so big, that workers really feel that they — they are responsible for the company, that they must be efficient, so that they must create profit, they must save cost, they must reduce the cost, and so on.

RATHER: How does this system work?

CERRAR: Yeah, it works in such a way that the main government in company is the workers' council, which meets from time to time; it depends on the problems, about — it depends on how the problems heavy are, and so on. It means if workers' council says something or orders something, this must be done.

RATHER: And who owns this company?

CERRAR: This company is owned, by our constitution and legal position, by the whole Yugoslav society. That means all 22 millions of Yugoslavs are owners of this company.

RATHER: The society is?

CERRAR: The society, the Yugoslavs, 22 million of Yugoslavs. We are not centrally planned economy.

RATHER: You are not a centrally planned —

CERRAR: We are a self-management economy. That means everybody has a small proportion in this plant.

RATHER: The theory is that employees must be directly represented on workers' councils, where the rank-and-file argue with and question management decisions and have a vote in all major policy matters. Workers' councils decide on such things as distribution of profits, their own salaries and salaries of the managers. But self-management often creates a cumbersome, slow bureaucracy of its own, and that is the system's chief weakness.

How much bureaucracy do you have to answer to?

CERRAR (laughs): I think there's — bureaucracy's the problem of the modern world; you know, is the bureaucracy in the States, is bureaucracy in Yugoslavia, Soviet bureaucracy, as well as bureaucracy in the federal administration. The more socialism, or the more social a system is, the more bureaucracy you have to introduce, you know.

RATHER: Belgrade, center of the bureaucracy for the decentralized economy, one of the ugliest capital cities in Europe. Inside the old Parliament building, the Central Committee meets, preparing for more discussion on who and what may follow Tito. But the announced plan is to have a rotating group of presidents rule, one from each republic. Yugoslavia is made up of Slovenia, Croatia, Serbia, Bosnia, Montenegro, Macedonia, plus two autonomous provinces. Tito has kept them together, when necessary with ruthless force, repressing ancient differences, especially the hostility between Croats and Serbs.

If, after Tito, there is civil war, Moscow-dominated Warsaw Pact forces might be used to intervene to regain Yugoslavia for the Soviet empire. Many Western experts believe a massive invasion could succeed in six weeks. The Yugoslavs don't think so. They have one of the largest standing armies in Europe and they believe it could withstand any assault from the East.

Tito's "fight them every inch of the way" creed includes his People's Territorial Army, a guerrilla-force throwback to the old partisan days. This propaganda film, shown repeatedly all over the country, illustrates the training given the entire population. As in Israel and Switzerland, everyone is required to serve. It is organized down to the village level, and there are units within factories and schools. (Sounds of soldiers marching) But it is Yugoslavia's full-time professional army that is the key to what happens after Tito. Among the most important questions: Is this army capable of putting down any outbreak of traditional hostility between Serbs and Croats? (Sounds of soldiers training) And is it strong enough to discourage any Soviet strike? In this training exercise, these soldiers were using outmoded Soviet-style weapons. What Tito desperately wanted was modern arms and, in '78, he came to Washington to ask for them.

Tito might not have gotten all he wanted, but last week President Carter told his news conference, "If we are called upon to give any kind of aid to the Yugoslavian people, we would seriously consider it, to protect them as a nonaligned country without being dominated or threatened by the Soviet Union."

A Few Minutes with Andy Rooney

DAN RATHER: You never know what's in Andy Rooney's head, but this week Andy's more concerned with what's on it than what's in it.

ANDY ROONEY: Next to death, commercial bread and the price of gas, I hate the idea of getting bald the most. I'm not really getting very bald yet and I'm pleased about that, but when I do, I'm not going to try and hide it. All anyone who's getting bald looks like when they try to hide it is like someone getting bald trying to hide it.

Some men let what little they have grow long and then spread it around. Someone wears a toupee — it looks like either a good toupee or a bad toupee, but it usually looks like a toupee. This is one of the best toupee shops in the country. A good hairpiece here costs about $800. Of course, over the long run, you make it up in haircuts.

I don't know why we're so sensitive about getting bald. A lot of men look good bald. They often look distinguished and important. Some men are even bald on purpose. It can even be a trademark. Often the amount of hair on a man's head is sort of a political statement. You can tell a Reagan supporter from a Kennedy man.

One of the great mysteries of life is why some men have an easy time growing hair on their face and a hard time growing it on their head. You can't talk to a man about how he likes his hair. On the tennis court, Jimmy Connors looks terrible with long, stringy, wet hair. I suppose he likes the way it looks when he isn't playing tennis, although it doesn't look all that good then, either.

I'm very suspicious of a man who fusses much with his hair. It can be there or not be there, but he ought not to spend half his life arranging it. He ought to comb it once in the morning and maybe once in the middle of the day if he gets caught in the wind. Otherwise, a man ought to leave his hair alone.

Okay, cut. How was that? All right? How did — did I look all right on that? Let's — let's take it again.

Update

HARRY REASONER: During the story we did on college athletes whose grades are doctored to keep them eligible to play football or basketball, we looked at the University of New Mexico. Last week, a federal grand jury looking at that college indicted two of the college's former basketball coaches on just such charges. The indictment said that Norm Ellenberger and John Whisenant had, among other things, prepared a counterfeit transcript to make it appear that one of their players had higher grades and more credits than was actually the case.

Letters

HARRY REASONER: Now the mail, and we got a lot of it last week about our story on Leonard Bernstein. Some of it was like this: "Until your (story) I never fully appreciated the immense wisdom and sensitivity this great man possesses . . ."

But most of it was like this: "Cheap, cheap, cheap . . . How dare you stoop so low as to attack Leonard Bernstein?"

Followed by this: "Mike Wallace should stick to interviewing Arabs and Iranians, not beloved public figures."

Another viewer wrote: "The story warmly depicted a man who for decades has represented the embodiment of all the higher qualities of life . . . But I have one complaint (his cigarette smoking) . . . The talents of Lenny should not be clouded by the exhaust of his only character flaw."

About our story on street drugs, we got several letters like this one: "If the courts weren't so soft on drug cases, things might be different . . . People would then think twice about (using drugs)."

But there was also a fair sprinkling of letters like this: "The only way to stop (it) is to take the profit out of it by making it legal."

And there was also a viewer who wrote: "(You said) drugs spread from the ghetto to the white middle class. Correction: Drugs spread from rich whites to the ghetto . . . Everyone knows the rich can get more and better everything than the poor."

About our interview with George Kennan, who takes issue with the way President Carter is dealing with Russia, a viewer said: "Thank God you are perceptive enough to see that the Carter Administration is running foreign policy like it was Georgia politics. The George Kennan interview was superb."

But that was followed by this: "As I watched (Kennan), one thought came to mind. Give him an umbrella and we have another Neville Chamberlain. Remember him?"

FEBRUARY 24, 1980

Uncle Sam Wants Your Money
LESLIE EDWARDS, PRODUCER

DAN RATHER: It's getting to be that time again, income-tax time, and no doubt in the preparation of your returns you're gathering those little pieces of paper that document how and what you spent and earned. Heaven forbid that we get caught not being able to back up each and every expenditure. Relax, it doesn't have to be all that worrisome. Paul Strassels is a man who should know. Not long ago he was on the other side, a tax specialist for the IRS. Now he's written a book called *All You Need To Know About The IRS*. And he's eager to share on the outside what he learned from his years on the inside.

PAUL STRASSELS: I want you to know that IRS has a plan, a conscious, sophisticated, expensive plan. The plan is to keep you so scared that you won't cheat on your income tax.

RATHER: And it works. When it comes to income taxes, most people are honest.

WOMAN: Down here, you put the balance of the check . . .

RATHER: In fact, statistics show that the United States has one of the highest rates of tax compliance of any nation in the world. Americans pay more than 92 percent of their taxes voluntarily. Strassels says that one reason for the high compliance by Americans is the effectiveness of the IRS plan. That plan sees the taxpayer as the enemy.

STRASSELS: The taxpayer is the enemy. IRS has only 85,000 full-time employees now. They take care of 137 million tax returns, and it's growing by ten percent every year. They only have two billion dollars, and they feel they are terribly outmanned. So what they do is they turn it around. They tru—they take that and put it to their advantage. The taxpayer is dumb, because he's uneducated in the field. People are afraid of the IRS, and as long as they can keep it that way fine. You don't — you don't give the enemy a break. You try and collect as much revenue as you possibly can.

RATHER: If taxpayers are seen as the enemy, Strassels says they'd better know what they're up against. Here's what he tells forums such as this one at a community center in Springfield, Virginia.

STRASSELS: One of their attitudes is, you're guilty. You're guilty unless you can prove yourself innocent. Now I know that goes against every bit of jurisprudence in this country: you know, innocent till proven guilty. But it doesn't really work that way with taxes. With taxes, you have to prove to an IRS auditor that you can back up what you're claiming on your return. You can't prove it, sorry, Charlie, out of luck.

RATHER: The principal weapon the IRS uses to bring taxpayers into line is the audit. Strassels says the audit is used not so much to actually collect revenue as for visibility.

STRASSELS: If you have an individual that's making a hundred, a hundred and fifty thousand dollars a year — a high incomer, in tax language — chances are his financial life is going to be much more complex, and if he's audited, they're going to find many more tax dollars than if they audit somebody who's making $25,000 a year, owns a small home in the Midwest. Just his life isn't as financially complex; doesn't have as many deductions. Well, why in the world would they even bother to audit the person making $25,000 a year? They're not going to find the income. But yet they audit him.

RATHER: Why?

STRASSELS: If they can get you audited, and you tell your neighbors, and your neighbors tell their neighbors that you were audited, and it just spreads. So one audit will touch many lives, not just yours.

RATHER: Theoretically, every tax return goes through a basic audit process. Once your return reaches one of the several regional centers in the country, tax examiners check each one for the most common errors: Simple addition and subtraction. Signatures. Were the proper wage statements included? And so on. If anything vital is missing, a letter is sent to the taxpayer. If all the information is correct, it is entered into a computer and sent to the national service center in Martinsburg, West Virginia. It is in Martinsburg where all the nation's tax records are kept.

This is the electronic nerve center of the Internal Revenue Service. In this highly guarded complex, tax returns from all across the country are rated, graded and evaluated according to secret formulas. Sophisticatedly programmed computers kick out those returns with high audit potential. How does the agency know what's normal? Strassels says there's a special audit program for that.

STRASSELS: It's called a TCMP audit. It stands for Taxpayer Compliance Measurement Program. It's a monster. That's worth being scared about, right there. The most honest person, the most knowledgeable person, about taxes in this entire country can be selected for a TCMP audit. Statistical sampling done through the magic of computers, they select a certain number of returns. Fifty thousand returns are going to be subjected to a line-by-line, item-by-item audit. Fifty thousand of them. And if you're selected for it, there's nothing you can do about it.

RATHER: Returns for the TCMP are randomly selected at every income level. This is how the IRS learns in which areas people may be cheating, and then uses the research to evaluate all other returns. Strassels told us that a TCMP audit can take a taxpayer as long as three weeks to complete, all at his own expense. Which items does the IRS especially frown upon? Well, Strassels says, the areas to be most careful about include tax shelter, family trusts, offices in the home, family businesses, entertainment expenses. In what areas are you less likely to draw attention?

STRASSELS: Energy tax credits. Why? Small amounts. IRS has found people don't cheat there. Charitable contributions. People are basically honest for the small amounts. Professional journals, sales taxes, mortgage interest, moving expenses, political contributions, union dues; capital gains and losses, that's questionable. Small amounts, clean amounts, yeah, people are honest. And these are items you can take on your return, can record on your return, and it's not going to trigger an audit.

RATHER: In addition to the audit program, Strassels says the agency uses informants: people telling on an ex-spouse; a dissatified partner in a business relationship reporting an associate; even bank tellers sometimes come forward with information. He says it's rare that the agency acts on tips, but when it does, it's successful. In one year, the agency prosecuted 500 cases this way. Money paid to informers amounted to less than $400,000. How much did the agency collect? Fifteen million dollars. And when it comes to bank accounts and safe-deposit boxes, Strassels says take special note. Your bank records legally do not belong to you. In many states, with a flash of a badge to a bank manager an IRS agent can look into your records without your knowledge or consent. He also says people should know that banks must report any deposit of $10,000 or more. Amounts for less than that are okay. Strassels adds taxpayers should be extra careful in selecting the person who prepares their returns.

STRASSELS: Ever since Congress and the IRS decided to crack down a bit on less than competent — that's their term — tax-return preparers, IRS has developed a list of those preparers, paid preparers, who don't do the job according to their satisfaction.

RATHER: They keep a list of good boys and bad boys.

STRASSELS: Uh-hmm. Exactly. Exactly.

RATHER: And if — if I happened to have had my return filled out by one who's on this list of preparers —

STRASSELS: Uh-hmm.

RATHER: — am I more likely to be audited?

STRASSELS: Oh, absolutely. Absolutely. Anybody that sits down for an audit, the first two or three questions relate to the preparer.

RATHER: How could I know who's a problem preparer, because I certainly don't want to have my taxes made out by one of these people?

STRASSELS: That's a good question, and I wish I could answer it. But I've asked how you find out who's on the problem preparers list, and I'm told I can't get the answer.

RATHER: He also told us people shouldn't worry too much about the better known commercial tax-assistance centers.

WOMAN: Okay, now, you have some interest income . . . ?

RATHER: With a simple, uncomplicated return, he says, these establishments generally do a good job. With more complex returns, Strassels suggests people should seek more sophisticated help. He warns all: Be wary of tax advisors who say, number one, that they can guarantee you a refund and, number two, that they've never been audited. Strassels says people would be less afraid of taxes and the IRS if they simply developed a personal plan.

STRASSELS: Once they do, and once they start taking care of their taxes personally, thinking about taxes, then they can develop a plan and kind of fight back.

RATHER: And your recommendation is be aggressive?

STRASSELS: Reasonably aggressive. What I'm required to report as income, I will report every dime of it. What the law absolutely specifies I'm entitled to deduct, I will deduct. But there's a gray area in between. There's many items that are — you're not quite sure. And I feel you should be reasonably aggressive. If they don't accept it, you go down, you sit down with them, you talk to them: "You won't allow that? Okay, you won't allow it. Well, let's talk about it. You — That's okay? Fine." View it that way and you can sleep a whole lot eaiser at night. Remember, the law only requires you to pay what it extracts, not a dime more.

RATHER: What's the best time of year to file your return, if you want to avoid audit?

STRASSELS: As close to April 15th as you can get it.

RATHER: Why? Strassels says close to deadline time IRS computers are processing hundreds of thousands of returns weekly, and your return, when it arrives in a flood of mail, stands a better chance of escaping an audit. But no matter when you file, if your personal income is $50,000 or more, Strassels says your chances of being audited are only one in ten. If you make between fifteen and fifty thousand, it's only one in 40. And if you earn less than 15,000, chances are you have nothing to worry about.

Where There's a Will . . .

PAUL LOEWENWARTER, PRODUCER

HARRY REASONER: Ten days ago, a grand jury in Illinois handed down an indictment against a wealthy lawyer suspected of shady dealings in the handling of wills and estates. It happened in Monticello, Illinois, but it could have happened in your town, in any town. We don't know how often it happens. Not even the bar association has been able to come up with figures on that. What we do know is that the bar association tries to crack down on it whenever they can. We decided to look into this story because, if we're lucky, all of us, we'll leave something of value when we're gone. And it may be worth examining what can happen when we do.

There is a vault like this in almost every American community, a place where, in a way, the dead are kept as surely as in a cemetery: in books like this, and records of probate, and reports of executors. This is Piatt County, Illinois. And the story of the lawyer begins with the story of Cordelia Davis and her will.

It's supposed to be that a person's will is a free expression of his or her clear intent, the lawyer acting only in the purest interest of his client. But ever since Cordelia Davis died, folks here in Monticello, the county seat, have been wondering whether Mrs. Davis really intended to leave her estate, mostly farmland, worth millions, to just one man, her lawyer.

Cordelia Davis was 92 when she died in the summer of 1978. She is said to have been warm, gentle, devoted to remaining distant relatives and to friends. Chief among her friends was Carl Canull, almost a son to Cordelia. Carl was her tenant farmer, virtually her partner. He raised his family on her land. And the Davis land, 1,000 acres of some of the richest farmland in the country, worth four to five thousand dollars an acre, four to five million dollars.

And then there's the lawyer, whom you will not meet in this report; he refused to be interviewed. His name is Dwight Doss and he lives in this expensive home in Monticello. He's now 65 years old, but photographs of him are rare. This one dates back to 1949, when he posed with the rest of the Piatt County Bar Association.

The unanswered question is why a 92-year-old lady left almost all her wealth to a man who had been her lawyer for only the last four years of her life? Carl Canull and his daughters mince no words about how they think that happened.

CARL CANULL: The man was a con man from the word go. And I think just think he conned her into it — if she did do it.

JACKIE MORRIS (Canull's daughter):   I feel that if she signed any papers she had no idea what she was signing.

JAN JONES (Canull's daughter):   I don't feel the will that he has in his hand is the one she left. And the only reason I say that is that in December, before she was sick in April, she and I were sitting in the car one day talking, and she explained to me that Dad had been having chest pains and she was terribly concerned. She wanted him to quit farming. And she asked me to take him to a doctor, and she said that if Dad would quit farming, she had left him — which I — apparently I was the only one she had told — she left him two farms and they'd be taken very good care of. And that's the reason I was shocked when I heard who had inherited it. However, everyone kept saying Dwight will come up with all of it.

REASONER: Dwight Doss has his law offices up there, across the street from the courthouse here in Monticello.He's a man in his sixties, said to be charming and affable. We don't know. He won't talk to us. Producer Paul Loewenwarter asked repeatedly for an interview, and after several weeks, Mr. Doss's receptionist told us the answer was no.

RECEPTIONIST: Doesn't desire to be on camera.

PAUL LOEWENWARTER: I see.

REASONER: So this report relies upon publicly available documents and individuals who have deep doubts about Dwight Doss.

The Davis fortune started on this side street in the little town of Beaumont. It came from this building, where the Davis drug store was. People who remember him say that Ward Davis — his friends called him W.W. — would work here every day from 7:30 in the morning until 10:30 at night. With the money he made he bought some stocks, but mostly he bought land, beginning before World War I. W.W. died in 1946, but Cordelia Davis kept the land. Its value kept going up, and that's how, by the time she died, it was worth four or five million dollars.

To give you some idea of what happened to the estate of Cordelia Davis, here is the paper trail. First, this will of March, 1973. It gave her estate to relatives and to the closest of friends, her tenant farmer and his wife. Then there was another will, apparently lost. It presumably said much the same thing as the first. And finally, this will, of November, 1974, revoking the other bequests and giving almost all her estate to Dwight Doss.

Well, you obviously think that Mr. Doss milked this estate.

CANULL: Yes, I most certainly do, because he came here one time and he said, "Who made out the will, the first will?" And he said, "I don't like the will at all. I'm going to tear it all to hell and make out another one." So, I drank coffee with him a few days after that and he said, "I changed the will. I got you half of the land and the house you live in." And I said, "Well, don't you think you ought to ask Mrs. Davis about that first?" And he said, "Oh, you let me take care of her." He said, "I can handle her."

REASONER: There's also a provision in the will in which Mrs. Davis forgives all debts to her.

And it turned out that Dwight Doss owed her $326,000, which he will never have to pay. There was a mention in the will that all debts be forgiven.

CANULL: Yeah.

REASONER: That included, apparently, a debt of $326,000 to Mr. Doss?

CANULL: Uh-hmm.

REASONER: Did you know about that at the time?

CANULL: No, I didn't.

JONES: She just didn't loan money. That was a policy of hers, I'm sure.

REASONER: One interesting note: The First State Bank of Monticello had never been Cordelia Davis's bank, but it suddenly turned up in her last will as executor. Biggest single stockholder in the bank? Dwight Doss.

We may never learn whether there was improper influence or deception, or whether it was all honestly done. Mrs. Davis is dead, the lawyers won't talk to us, and nobody can investigate the handling of the will in court. Why? This agreement. The heirs mentioned in the previous wills challenged Doss, and he backed down. Instead of taking it all, he settled for 40 percent out of court. After taxes, that left him with about three-quarters of a million dollars.

The other heirs split the remaining 60 percent. After all, that was better than nothing. But because of this agreement, signed by all the parties, no court, no prosecutor, can question whether attorney Dwight Doss was Cordelia Davis's choice to inherit the largest part of her estate. The estate is closed.

In spite of that, the attorney for Carl Canull and one of his daughters, Kenneth Baughman, has a lot of questions about the case.

KENNETH BAUGHMAN: The examination of the records in this case, the will itself, raises some questions of ethics, of propriety, of legality and of undue influence with respect to the execution of the will. And that's why the courtroom was full of attorneys on the day that the will was set for hearing for probate. This question was raised immediately and it was apparent to anyone who was present.

REASONER: Was Mr. Doss present?

BAUGHMAN: Mr. Doss did not appear at the hearing for the probate of the will.

REASONER: It may strike you as a conflict of interest for an attorney to be named as almost the sole beneficiary in his client's will. Well, Mr. Doss didn't write this will. Listen to the unusual wording that Mrs. Davis signed: "By way of explanation, the said Dwight H. Doss has for some time been and is my friend, confidant and legal advisor. And I have on numerous occasions requested him to prepare my last will and testament with the provisions as here and above set forth. But he has at all times refused to prepare the same because of his professional association with me." This will was put together by an attorney named Kenneth Kinser of Decatur. Like Mr. Doss, he refused to be interviewed by us. But in a later proceeding, he did admit that he may have discussed the will with Doss before Mrs. Davis's death. And the will names him as attorney for the estate, a $100,000 job.

Over coffee, some farmers who knew both Carl Canull and Mrs. Davis told us how they felt when they learned Canull had been written out of the will.

RALPH MOERY: Well, we were shocked that a large percentage didn't go to Mr. Canull and his family.

ROBERT MORGAN: Well, I thought Mrs. Davis thought enough of him that he would get the biggest part of it, or biggest share of it.

SHELBY CLARK: I know that everybody was sort of shocked and surprised the way it turned out.

REASONER: Shirley Durbin was a close friend of Mrs. Davis, and she and her husband used to do chores for her.

And when you found out about the new will you were surprised?

SHIRLEY DURBIN: Yes.

REASONER: In all the time that you saw her, working for her, eating with her, you saw nothing that would lead you to believe that a change in her will was going to come about?

DURBIN: No. No.

REASONER: How did it happen?

DURBIN: I don't know. I just wouldn't have any idea.

REASONER: Isn't there a suspicion, almost a presumption there, that this attorney either ingratiated himself with her in an improper way or deceived her?

BAUGHMAN: Yes, it's a — it's a permissible presumption.

REASONER: Do you draw any conclusions from this, any advice that you would give to people as they get older, particularly if they've got any money?

CANULL: Well, there's a lot of little old ladies that got out their wills and read them over and took a long look at them. And I hope that they — that they learned something from it.

REASONER: There's concern that there have been abuses of wills and estates, mostly unnoticed, all across the country. But the Illinois legislature is about to investigate the Davis estate, and Representative Tim Johnson is trying to write laws to prevent this kind of result.

STATE REPRESENTATIVE TIM JOHNSON: The relationship that apparently existed between the client and attorney produced a — an outrageous result, and it seems to me that that sort of activity, if it isn't in — unethical, ought to be, and if it's not illegal, ought to be. So I would think either creating a presumption of ind — undue influence or actually prohibiting a lawyer from being a beneficiary under a will when he'd represented the person for three to five years prior to the execution of the will would be a reasonable solution.

REASONER: We said earlier there's another case involving Dwight Doss, fewer dollars involved, but potentially much more serious for Doss. Eugene Bloomingdale is a 53-year-old man who gets a disability check, not enough to live on, even in a modest house like this one. Six years ago, his multiple problems seemed solved. An aunt died and left him 80 acres of prime farming land near Decatur. Even then, a conservative appraisal put the value at $88,000.

And now an interstate highway runs through part of the property and there's commercial development next door, but Gene Bloomingdale and his wife are baffled, as much as anything, by what's happened since. They deal frequently, but unsatisfactorily, with their attorney. Their attorney: Dwight Doss. The Bloomingdales say they go to Doss's office and get handouts of only twenty-five or fifty dollars at a time, plus money for their mortgage, but never a full accounting of the estate.

You have never seen a piece of paper saying the estate of your aunt was worth so much money? You have gotten so much already, there's so much left? You've never seen anything like that?

EUGENE BLOOMINGDALE: No.

MRS. BLOOMINGDALE: No.

BLOOMINGDALE: Never seen any of that. No.

REASONER: Have you asked for it?

BLOOMINGDALE: Yeah. I ask him how much one day there last summer, how much that I had left, and he said he hadn't had it figured up. He wouldn't go into that right now.

REASONER: Have you asked him?

MRS. BLOOMINGDALE: I went in there to ask him before and we never get anything settled. I mean, I — I don't know of — the subject gets changed or something, because I never do find out anything.

REASONER: It's important to note that a legal guardian recently was appointed for Eugene Bloomingdale after his doctor testified he suffers from severe high blood pressure impairing his vision and his mental processes.

Have you ever seen any papers describing how much you inherited or what the land was worth?

BLOOMINGDALE: No, uh-uh, never seen any. He's got it all up there.

MRS. BLOOMINGDALE: For all we know the farm's not sold.

REASONER: You don't even know if it's been sold or not?

BLOOMINGDALE: No.

MRS. BLOOMINGDALE: No. We don't know if it's sold or if it — who bought it, or how much was paid for it, or what's been done to the farm since his aunt died.

REASONER: Th — this has been six years?

BLOOMINGDALE: Yeah.

MRS. BLOOMINGDALE: Hm-hmm.

REASONER: We found out some things from these papers in the Macon County Courthouse in Decatur that Gene Bloomingdale says he didn't know. On the basis of this information, there's some questions we'd like to ask Mr. Doss, if he'd talk to us:

These records seem to show you bought the land from Bloomingdale for the low appraised value of $88,000, yet he says he doesn't know if the land was ever sold, and certainly never heard that you bought it. Why doesn't he know? These records seem to indicate that a few months after you bought the 80 acres for $88,000, you sold off 13 acres for $100,000. Did you consider sharing that stroke of luck with your client, or even telling him? Just consider the $88,000. Is there any record of where it went, apart from the small house payments and the doled-out pocket money? And was it really 88,000? Another document is said to show that you agreed to pay him $188,000 for the land. In either case, did you pay it to Bloomingdale's account, or set up a trust, or what? In summary, why don't the Bloomingdales know what they're entitled to know about the Bloomingdale inheritance?

Those same questions were put to a grand jury in Decatur, and ten days ago, Doss was indicted on three counts: forgery, in regard to the records of the property sale; perjury, in his preparation of the Bloomingdales' state tax returns and failing to file those returns properly. The grand jury found no grounds for an indictment of theft against Doss, but the Bloomingdales are contemplating a civil suit against him to account for their funds.

In the Cordelia Davis matter, an agency of the Illinois Supreme Court is investigating whether Doss violated the code of legal ethics. If he did, he could lose his license to practice law.

Citizen Loeb

JOSEPH WERSHBA, PRODUCER

MORLEY SAFER: In just two days, the New Hampshire primary happens. It should be remembered that in the past 30 years no candidate for President has been elected without first winning his party's New Hampshire primary. There's a whole menu of candidates for voters to choose from, some new some old. But there's one voice that is heard in New Hampshire every four years, and American and foreign reporters drop in on him as if he were the Oracle of Delphi. His name is Bill Loeb, publisher of the *Manchester Union Leader*.

Citizen Loeb is a man with barely a kind word to say about anyone. He's called Ike, "A stinking hyprocrite." JFK: "Number-one liar." Nelson Rockefeller: "Wife-swapper." Gene McCarthy: "A skunk." And four years ago, on the eve of the last New Hampshire primary, of President Ford he said, "Jerry is a jerk." Well, what does Bill Loeb think about this year's crop?

President Carter?

WILLIAM LOEB: Most incompetent — and — President we've ever had in the United States. Way over his head.

SAFER: Ted Kennedy?

LOEB: A coward.

SAFER: Jerry Brown?

LOEB: My favorite California flake. (Laughter)

SAFER: A flake?

LOEB: Yeah. Very witty, very lively and very amusing to talk to.

SAFER: Okay, Republicans. George Bush?

LOEB: David Rockefeller's candidate for the Presidency.

SAFER: Ronald Reagan?

LOEB: Make a good President.

SAFER: Senator Baker?

LOEB: Weakest lady in the United States Senate.

SAFER (laughing):   Oh, dear!
John Connally?

LOEB: Born-again wheeler-dealer.

SAFER: Anderson?

LOEB: The liberals' candidate.

SAFER: Bob Dole?

LOEB: A very nice fellow who'll never get over being tarred by — by his campaign running with — with Je— with Jerry Ford.

SAFER: Now, there are a couple of outside, I suppose, possibilities who are Republicans. There's Jerry Ford.

LOEB: Right. Well, I— I— I— I— I don't think that his sabbatical has improved his intelligence, so I'd hate to see that happen. (Laughter)

SAFER: Oh, dear! And then —

LOEB: It could very well, It could very well.

SAFER: Bill Loeb has never supported a Democrat, and for Republicans, he may be just as much a spoiler as he is kingmaker. In the last 30 years of New Hampshire primaries, Loeb has backed four winners and four losers.

As a spoiler, his paper is credited — if that's the word — with destroying Senator Edmund Muskie's chance for the Democratic nomination eight years ago, not by attacking the senator, but by reprinting from *Newsweek* gossipy, back-of-the-bus conversations about Muskie's wife, Jane, reprinting it three times. Muskie responded on a snowy Saturday, a day just like today. He pulled a flatbed truck up in front of the *Manchester Union Leader* and he began his counterattack. He meant to pillory Citizen Loeb, but instead his emotions got the better of him and he may have ruined forever his chances as a presidential candidate.

SENATOR EDMUND MUSKIE: By attacking me, by attacking my wife, he's proved himself to be a gutless coward. It's fortunate for him he's not on this platform beside me. A good woman — (breaks down).

SAFER: Eight years ago, you ran an editorial that said, "Hold your nose and vote for Nixon." Is there anybody we should hold our nose and vote for, in your view?

LOEB: And a very clever one of my readers said, "You should have said" — cleverer than I was — "You should have said, 'Hold your breath and vote for Nixon.'" (Laughter) No, I— I don't — I don't think so this time.

SAFER: Your newspaper supports Ronald Reagan.

LOEB: Hm-hmm.

SAFER: And staunchly.

LOEB: Hm-mmm.

SAFER: But do you really think he's got what it takes? Honestly, do you ever —

LOEB: Well, I think he's got more— more of what it takes than anybody else in the picture.

SAFER: Well, a couple of the criticisms of Reagan from within the Republican Party, never mind outside.

LOEB: What?

SAFER: His age.

LOEB: Hm-mmm. Well, of course, since I'm approaching my 75th birthday myself, I can't be very sympathetic on— on that one. That's entirely a matter of the arteries and what shape you're in.

SAFER: Won't he divide the Republican Party?

LOEB: I don't think so, because the only people really against Ron in any strong fashion are the — a small group of Eastern elitists, self-appointed elitists, who want to keep control of the party. And, of course, so far, they've managed to reduce the party to a 20 percent— percentage point strength, which I would not say is successful.

SAFER: When you say that George Bush is — is David Rockefeller's candidate —

LOEB: Hm-mmm.

SAFER: — what do you mean by that?

LOEB: Well, he — he is part of the old school tie, a — Eastern Republican type, what I call the self-appointed elitists. And they really have no real relation with the average Joe in the — in the — in the street, what — what his problems are, what he needs or what he wants or what the country needs. And, in that sense, I call him David Rockefeller's boy. I think the media, by and large, are building up Bush today. Most of the Eastern media are on Bush's side, and — and — and I think they're building — I think the media can influence in that fashion; more by the news, I think, than — than by editorials.

SAFER: John Connally, you — you said, born-again wheeler-dealer. But my gosh, a lot of Republicans would say here's a fellow who really looks the way a President should look.

LOEB: No question about it. No question about it. But his negative rating, you know, in the polls is almost as high as his positive rating. The — the man in the street instinctively doesn't — doesn't trust him.
Now, my corporate friends think he's wonderful. He's their candidate, because he looks like them, dresses like them, and he's a very charming individual. She is, too. But he just doesn't go over. He's not going to get anywhere in New Hampshire, in my opinion, at all. And if he loses in South Carolina against Reagan, I would say he's pretty well out of the picture.

SAFER: Do you think John Connally has the brains for the job?

LOEB: John Connally has the brains. But the character, that's another question.

SAFER: Do you trust him?

LOEB: No. I like him, but I don't trust him.

SAFER: Now, Howard Baker, you were very rough on Howard Baker. You said he was the —

LOEB: Weakest lady in the United States Senate.

SAFER: Weakest lady in the United States Senate. That — that challenges a lot of things about him.

LOEB: That — that's the characterization from one of his fellow senators, incidentally. Well, let's put it this way. As you know, most — most Americans, overwhelmingly, we were against giving away the Panama Canal. It was a popular cause. When the leader of the opposition not only gives away a popular cause to — to his — his opponent, in this case, President Carter, and — and at the same time something which really isn't good for the country, I — I don't think much of the brains behind that.

SAFER: John Anderson does have an awful lot of appeal, I think.

LOEB: I did — I did admire him for coming out in favor of the — the grain embargo when all the other candidates fudged, including — including Reagan. And it turned out in the end the farmers in Iowa didn't care much about the grain embargo, so it was selling your soul for nothing. He — he is forthright on all of the issues that he believes in . I think he's wrong on many of those issues, but at least he's forthright on them. And I think that every liberal Republican should be voting for John Anderson.

SAFER: Jerry Ford, some people think, is waiting in the wings.

LOEB: I'm sure of it.

SAFER: You're sure of it?

LOEB: Hm-mmm.

SAFER: Waiting in the wings for what?

LOEB: For the — for the convention to be all tangled up and — and then say, "Well, now, I'll bring peace to the party and unify everybody." And I think he's sorely lacking. I think he's obviously better than Carter, and I would have to — you know, remember my last time. I — New Hampshire did go for Ford. I advocated voting for Ford, because better the fool you know than a knave you don't.

And I still think that would be my judgment this time. I think Ford is more sensible than — than Mr. Carter and — and a little bit more equipped to handle the situation.

Why, I — Mr. Carter frightens me to death. For instance, you know, I'm a hawk, but you've got to be a hawk only when you've got something to back it up with. We — we're not in any position to fight a war with the Russians right now.

SAFER: But, indeed, you are a hawk, and you — you say that you're frightened of Carter. But surely Carter should be your man. He's now —

LOEB: No.

SAFER: It's some of the toughest talk we've had from — from an American President, I guess, since the early days of Lyndon Johnson.

LOEB: But you shouldn't talk tough unless you've got something to back it up, Morley. And he — we haven't got it. I — I can assure you, from the inside, we have not got it to back it up right now.

SAFER: The paper's been pretty rough, pretty vicious on Teddy Kennedy.

LOEB: I could take exception to one adjective, but go ahead.

SAFER: The paper's been extremely tough on Teddy Kennedy.

LOEB: That's all right.

SAFER: Why? It's almost a vendetta.

LOEB: No, I — I — I don't think so. I think it's terribly important to realize — to get the moral aspects of any of these things. And whenever there was a crisis, Teddy ran; whether it was about the — the car ac— incident in Virginia or the — or the matter of — at Harvard. You know, cheating for a — exam in calculus might be immoral, but it might be reasonable, but — but Spanish? And then, of course, we come to Chappaquiddick and —and, again, he flunked out. He ran. I think it's terribly important not to have somebody like that to — in a situation like that.

SAFER: You say that Jerry Brown is a flake. (Laughs) What does that mean exactly? It's not —

LOEB: Well, it's — it's — it's —

SAFER: That's kind of a modern word for a fellow like Bob Loeb to be using.

LOEB (laughing):   Yeah, well, I have to keep up with the parade once in a while. But Jerry is — is — is a charming individual. Anoth— another expression was ding-a-ling. You know, he got a wonderful mind and it's very fast. He was trained by the Jesuits. He's a delight to talk to, you know. I mean, the phone rings from California and the — the secretary says, "Governor Brown's calling." When he gets on, I say "Gee, this is my favorite flake calling." He says, "Yeah, Bill, it's me." (Laughter) Nothing bothers him. But, you know, it all — it's all so light and breezy and — and — and really so — none of it comes out logically in the end.

SAFER: But as a group of— this is, I guess, the best the country can offer a— to choose from.

LOEB: Well, Morley, I— I have wasted a lot of breath— and I'm sure not made many converts— but I keep talking before professional and business groups, constantly saying, you cannot turn over the— the business of government of the biggest organization in the world— the United States of America— to the lightweights that you've been turning it over to. But I said, all you people insist on being so much interested in making money that you insist on going into professions or in business and leaving government to the type of people we've had. And— and you really— there's no mystery to the problem in the United States today. We're suffering from a— a crisis in— in political management, period.

SAFER: Who's your favorite President, not— not of all time, let's say in my time? Your favorite President in the last 50 years?

LOEB: A pretty poor collection all the way around. I suppose I— I liked Harry Truman, except for the MacArthur incident, as much as anything.

SAFER: Truman, you— you— you figure?

LOEB: Yeah, hm-mmm.

SAFER: What— what was the— the quality that made the difference?

LOEB: Well, he was a down-to-earth, honest little fellow, with a lot of— lot of unfortunate friends sometimes, and a few other things. But— and drank a lot of bourbon. But, by and large, you know, you sort of knew where— where Harry was about things. As I said, I think he was very wrong on MacArthur, but he thought he— he thought he was doing the right thing at the time.

SAFER: Bill Loeb is 74, and his office walls are filled with decades of memories, all good and great friends: Mayor Rizzo of Philadelphia, Senator Goldwater of Arizona, the late Jimmy Hoffa, Admiral Rickover of the nuclear Navy; and his godfather, really his godfather, his favorite, all-time President, Theodore Roosevelt. Loeb's father was secretary to Teddy Roosevelt.

LOEB: The— the intellect. You know, he wrote those speeches, he wrote those books himself, without any ghost writers. (Indistinct) he was a great— a great, accomplished naturalist, a recognized naturalist, but he understood foreign affairs. He understood the people he was dealing with. And his tremendous enthusiasm for the future of America were all things. I think the Panama Canal was a great— was a great move. I think his making the peace at Portsmouth between the Japanese and the Russians was a— was a magnificent piece of diplomacy. And I must say his trust-busting, his— his leading. The first conservationist President we had. He touched so many aspects of American life, and did it so beneficially to the nation.

SAFER: Are you worried about the country, Mr. Loeb?

LOEB: Very worried.

SAFER: Do you think we are going down the drain?

LOEB: I—I—I can see tremendous dangers ahead of us, from a military standpoint, from an economic standpoint, and from a general morale standpoint, and largely because there is no knowledgeable, firm hand on the— on the tiller of the ship of state.

Look at the brilliant architects we have, the brilliant engineers, the brilliant scientists, the brilliant medical people. We have some tremendous brains in the United States, but you never see them in politics, do you? And that's the reason why the country is in the bloody mess it's in.

A Few Minutes with Andy Rooney

MIKE WALLACE: You've heard it a thousand times, you've probably even said it yourself: "I like it, but is it art?" Or, "Excuse me, but is that picture upside down?" Chances are the person who says it's upside down doesn't know any more about it than you do. Andy Rooney doesn't know any more about it than you do, either. It's just that he's got the floor and you haven't.

ANDY ROONEY: If you're putting up pictures in your own house, you can decide for yourself what looks good and how much you want to pay to have it look that way. Decorating a city with works of art is a lot harder. Nothing in this country has changed more than our public art, and a lot of people don't like it. For a long while, the statues in little parks everywhere were in the image of traditional old American heroes, or perhaps some local hero known only to the people of the town where it stood. There were tens of thousands of Civil War statues put up, and tens of thousands more memorializing the doughboys of World War I. Statues erected in honor of people who were heroic after 1930 are rare. Maybe heroes are rarer. Sculptors have always liked to make horses. Anyone looks heroic on a horse.

There was never much complaining about the money spent on statuary of this kind. I suppose people aren't so apt to complain about art in honor of the dead. That's not true about the new, modern sculptures being put up everywhere with both public and private money. It seems to a lot of people that artists are trying too hard to be artistic. Most people like art to look like things as they know them to be. That's hard for an artist, and skeptics think that's why artists have changed what they do. If it doesn't look like anything we know, we can't complain that it doesn't look like what it's supposed to. It isn't supposed to look like anything.

A lot of the most modern work has been commissioned by the federal government. Most of us don't have very good taste in art, but government's taste is usually worse. People who like the modern public art refer to it as a museum without walls. Critics who don't like it call it nonsense and a waste of money. A good artist tries to satisfy himself. That's a noble artistic idea, but when the artist is satisfying himself with public money, he has to satisfy some other people, too. Many modern artists work in geometric shapes. They like angles, circles, cylinders. They mix them, balance them, stand them on end. Most of us aren't ready for it. We know the artist is trying to tell us something, but it's a foreign language and we don't understand what he's trying to say. We'd like to see the artist's idea written out on paper in English just once. A lot of us suspect the artist of not having any idea at all, beyond getting a government grant. We aren't sure enough, though, of our own artistic judgment to say so. We know from experience that the artist may just be an artistic Einstein whose work is important and great and just beyond our comprehension.

So the real question is this: Is America ready for art that's smarter than it is?

Update

HARRY REASONER: Several weeks ago, we broadcast a report on Garn Baum, a Utah fruit processor who is suing the Mormon Church claiming a conspiracy to put him out of business. We made two statements in that broadcast that might have misled our viewers. The story dealt with the difficulty Baum said he found in getting a lawyer to represent him against the church, and we concluded the story by saying he now has a lawyer who will press his case. The fact is that Baum has had several lawyers representing him, of which the lawyer we referred to was the latest.

We also said he is appealing the case to a court in Colorado. This may have left the implication that he was doing so because he felt he could not get justice in Utah. The fact is that his case was dismissed for lack of evidence by the Federal District Court in Utah, and any appeal of the District Court of Utah would have to go to Colorado, to Denver, where the Federal Circuit Court of Appeals is located.

We regret any misunderstandings our story may have created.

Letters

MIKE WALLACE: About another Army experiment, in the mail this week were several letters about our story on Edward Nevin, the man who died in San Francisco allegedly as a result of a germ-warfare test conducted by the Army. One of our viewers noted that while only one person died in the tests, millions might have been saved. And she wrote: "I wonder if Mr. Nevin, a patriot, in the words of his family, would really want his lawyer-grandson to (sue the government)."

Another viewer was skeptical about that multimillion-dollar lawsuit: "I am hard pressed to believe that the 65 relatives of Mr. Nevin are suing the government to protect the future safety of other Americans."

About our interview with presidential candidate John Anderson, a viewer wrote: "Out here in Utah where the deer and the buffalo and the giant missiles roam, John Anderson sounds like a Republican/Democrat fantasy come true."

Another viewer wrote: "What impressed me most about Anderson was his remarks about the youth vote. Anyone who is willing to take us seriously has my vote."

That, however, was followed by this: "John Anderson and 60 MINUTES would have been as easy to keep apart as fish and chips. Both (of you) are dedicated to a weak, dead America and another generation of sick, sick, sick."

And finally, about our story on Tito's Yugoslavia, a viewer wrote: "(By) presenting a typical middle-class Yugoslav family . . . over-extending themselves on credit . . . (You also presented) a biased promotion for American-style consumerism as the only alternative to the Soviets."

MARCH 2, 1980

The Iran File

BARRY LANDO, PRODUCER

MIKE WALLACE: Today is the 120th day the American hostages have been held captive in Teheran, and today marks the end of the first week of the UN tribunal's investigation into the alleged crimes of the deposed Shah. They have been asked also to investigate Iranian charges of U.S. complicity in those acts.

Why do so many Iranians believe in U.S. complicity, guilt? Why do they so fervently endorse the anti-American Khomeini and the holding of the hostages? Of course, we know the embassy takeover was triggered by the Shah's entry into the U.S. last October for medical treatment. More about that later. But beyond that, the fury in Iran focuses on the undenied fact that the CIA restored the exiled Shah to the Peacock Throne back in 1953, and after that, the Iranians have been told, the CIA helped the Shah set up Savak, the secret police force that has tortured so many thousands of them. A classified Senate Foreign Relations Committee report confirms the CIA's role in forming Savak. It says the CIA provided the Shah money, as well as training, for that purpose. Of course, the brutality came later.

In 1976, in Niavaran Palace in Teheran, I asked the Shah about the continuing reports of torture inflicted by his Savak upon so many of his citizens.

Now, when an outfit like the International Commission of Jurists comes here and then comes out with a report saying that, in spite of what you say, Your Majesty, torture continues —

SHAH MOHAMMED RIZA PAHLEVI: How do they know? Well, they can't continue saying this.

WALLACE: Well, they talk about psychological and physical torture.

SHAH OF IRAN: Physical, I don't believe.

WALLACE: I talked —

SHAH OF IRAN: Not any more. Maybe in the old days. Maybe.

WALLACE: I talked just today to a man, whom I believe, who told about torture.

SHAH OF IRAN: How many years ago?

WALLACE: Within — I want to be very careful. Not yesterday.

SHAH OF IRAN: Ah, well, maybe. I don't know.

WALLACE: The word has gone out to stop it?

SHAH OF IRAN: To stop what?

WALLACE: Torture.

SHAH OF IRAN: But a long time ago, yes.

WALLACE: How long ago?

SHAH OF IRAN: Well, I won't tell you, as you don't tell me.

WALLACE: This was the man who had told me just hours before my interview with the Shah in the fall of 1976, who told me about torture still going on, Raji Samghabadi, then a highly respected Iranian journalist who now reports for *Time* magazine. I spoke to him in New York a few days ago.
When you told me back in 1976, October —

RAJI SAMGHABDI: Yes.

WALLACE: — that torture, physical torture, was still going on, how did you know it?

SAMGHABADI: My brother was released from jail perhaps a week after — before I saw you. There were torture marks all over his body. The physical torture went on, and the psychological torture was worse than physical torture.
My own brother, a political prisoner, was taken once to this dark room and shown the mangled bodies of a few persons, and he was told that relatives of his, including his brother, including his mother and his father, were among the corpses. And he was instructed to identify them. So, he spent hours and hours and hours trying to decide whether this stump of a head, this mashed pulp of a face, belonged to his brother, to his mother.

WALLACE: You mean you?

SAMGHABADI: Yes. And this was a deliberate lie, but he didn't know. So, through a series of psychological tortures, as His Majesty said, they drove him crazy, insane. And he came out, thousands and thousands of dollars went into his treatment, and even now I can't say that he is a complete human being.

WALLACE: Raji Samghabadi spoke then of an episode that took place on the occasion of President Carter's visit to Teheran on New Year's Eve, December, 1977.

SAMGHABADI: We were celebrating New Year's Eve with the American press in the Hilton Hotel, and Mr. Carter was giving a speech that night, saying — I don't — I don't remember the words exactly, but he was saying that America has never had such a good friend, America has never been so close with another nation, with another leader, and it profoundly touches us that the Shah takes care of his people so well and his people love him so well.

WALLACE: On that very night, New Year's Eve, said Samghabadi, his brother was seized with another fit, and he brought him to a mental hospital close to the Shah's palace.

SAMGHABADI: And a doctor there told me that 70 percent of our cases are Savak-tortured people. It is 1978, about two years, perhaps 15 months, after your talk with the Shah and after his claim that torture is not going on.

WALLACE: Max McCarthy, three-term Democratic congressman, now Washington bureau chief for the *Buffalo News,* was press officer at the American Embassy in Teheran in '76. He had put me in touch with Samghabadi.
Raji Samghabadi told us about his brother.

MAX McCARTHY: Uh-hmm.

WALLACE: Did you know the brother?

McCARTHY: I did.

WALLACE: And?

McCARTHY: He was imprisoned, tortured, and I saw him afterward and the poor guy was just a walking dead man. I mean, he — he was a zombie.

WALLACE: As a result of torture at the hands of Savak?

McCARTHY: Right.

(Crowd noise at trial)

WALLACE: A trial of two Savak torturers held in Iran after the fall of the Shah, one of a score of such trials during which these men and others confessed of heinous crimes: sticking hot iron bars in noses and eyes; hanging prisoners upside down to beat them; using everything from thick whips to electric shock; raping both male and female prisoners; torturing one member of a family in front of the other; often victims were then forced to swallow cyanide tablets or taken out and shot. Some other victims, like this young Iranian we filmed a few weeks ago in a London hospital, were permanently crippled. Over three years in an Iranian prison, he was apparently subjected to repeated spinal injections, another form of torture. He is paralyzed, unable to talk. Doctors say he soon will die.
Is it your understanding that we – you in the embassy – knew what was going on with Savak?

McCARTHY: Well, I did.

WALLACE: In fact, it was such acts by Savak and the indifference of the American diplomatic establishment in Iran to such savagery that caused Max McCarthy to resign as press officer there in late 1976. And he wrote a report following his resignation.
In your report you say: "U.S. Mission personnel are regularly warned not to divulge to any American correspondent information that Iranian government does not want disclosed or which tells too much about the U.S. role in Iran." You serious?

McCARTHY: That's right.

WALLACE: In other words, Dick Helms, as ambassador, would say, "Look, the U.S.

role in Iran, we don't want too much news of that in the American press?"

McCARTHY: Co— correct.

WALLACE: Ambassador Helms was pro-Shah.

McCARTHY: Right. Well, he used to say there's no alternative to the Shah.

WALLACE: Which, I suppose at that time, Americans generally believed. And so, in — in being pro-Shah, you — you did what the Shah wanted you to do, in effect?

McCARTHY: Right. There was a — that — that was a very prevalent idea, giving the Shah what he wants. Remember, there were articles to that effect and —

WALLACE: And why was it so important to give the Shah what he wants?

McCARTHY: Well, because he was our pillar in the Persian Gulf, and we built our whole security on this one man.

WALLACE: All right. Therefore, if the Shah committed excesses?

McCARTHY: We had to forgive that.

WALLACE: If we knew about corruption that went on?

McCARTHY: Right. There were more transcendently important considerations than corruption and repression.

WALLACE: So the United States knew, really, what was going on, but was willing to say, "Well, wait a minute. For the greater good of the greater number of people, let's turn our back on these brutalities, excesses, corruptions?"

McCARTHY: I believe that's a fair statement.

WALLACE: It was not just in Iran in the late seventies that Americans knew what was going on. Jesse Leaf was Iran analyst for the CIA in Langley, Virginia, in the early seventies. He had heard reports of Savak brutalities and he wanted to do something about it.

JESSE LEAF: And, in fact, at one point I was going to write a report on torture in Iran and was told not to.

WALLACE: By?

LEAF: By — on division level.

WALLACE: This was in what year?

LEAF: I — it was in — I can't give you an exact year. I believe it was '70, '71, something like that.

WALLACE: Well, who was the head of the CIA at the time?

LEAF: Well, the head of the CIA at the time was — was Richard Helms, but —

WALLACE: He would have known about it?

LEAF: Well, you'd either have to be blind, deaf and dumb and a presidential candidate not to know there was torture going on in Iran. I mean, it was all over the place. Amnesty International has a huge file on — on — on what happened. I — I have seen from various — I saw from various sources descriptions of torture rooms in Savak headquarters in Teheran.

We knew what was happening and we did nothing about it, and I was told not to do anything about it. It — this was an internal Iranian affair. Iran — Savak's job was to keep the lid on dis — dissident elements within the population. Originally it was Communist, then it meant anybody who said — who looked crosswise at the Shah.

WALLACE: Hm-mmm.

LEAF: By definition, Mike, an enemy of the Shah was an enemy of the CIA. They were — we were very close. We were friends. This was a very close relationship between the United States and Iran.

WALLACE: What do you know, Mr. Leaf, about the CIA, Savak, and torture?

LEAF: When the agency set up Savak, they had regular instructional classes. Part of the instructional classes we— were in interrogation techniques. As part of intensive interrogation techniques, torture is covered.

WALLACE: That, Leaf says, was a classroom lecture, although one former Savak agent still in Iran claims the CIA actually showed Savak agents how to physically torture prisoners.

LEAF: I think it's baloney, especially coming from the source. I mean, he's working for — he working for the other side now.

WALLACE: You mean he's testifying in order to save his own life?

LEAF: Oh, I think — I think so. We didn't have to — we didn't have to teach the Iranians torture. I mean — or to torture people. They have a long, long, glowing history in that part of the world of torture. It's — it's an everyday thing.

WALLACE: So far, we've been talking about Savak in Iran. But what about Savak outside Iran? Like our own CIA, Savak also conducted operations abroad. Here is a vivid example. We first told this tale three years ago on 60 MINUTES. It centered on this man, then living in Paris, Jules Khan Pira, an adventurer, a soldier of fortune. Born in the Soviet Union, he lived clandestinely in Western Europe, a stateless man, in and out of prison several times, until finally he was granted an Iranian passport and went to work as a journalist in Teheran. Then, he says, he was contacted by Savak and sent back to France on a mission of political assassination. His first target was to be Sadegh Ghotbzadeh, the man who is now Iran's foreign minister, but who, when we first met him three years ago in Paris, was a little-known supporter of an Iranian religious leader then in exile in Iraq, the Ayatollah Khomeini. Khan Pira, instead of killing Ghotbzadeh, told him the whole story, and told him also that he had been commissioned by Savak to kill another man, an American, Nasser Afshar, a wealthy businessman, formerly an Iranian, now an American citizen, whose home was in Alexandria, Virginia, where he published the *Iran Free Press,* a newspaper filled with attacks against the Shah, his regime and his family.
Why would the Savak want to kill you, Nasser Afshar?

NASSER AFSHAR: Because I'm the publisher of *Iran Free Press.*

WALLACE: Simple as that?

AFSHAR: Simple as that.

ARDESHIR ZAHEDI: My dear friend, Mike, I think this is very ridiculous.

WALLACE: Ardeshir Zahedi today lives in exile in Switzerland. At the time of our report on Savak three years ago, he was Iran's ambassador to the United States.

ZAHEDI: We are not the people who want to kill anyone. We had traitors in the past. Many of them has come back, even the Communists.

WALLACE: But when we checked out Khan Pira's story three years ago, it stood up.

We were satisfied he was telling the truth, though every government agency we talked to at the time denied it. The State Department, the CIA – no one knew anything about it, or so they said.

And there the matter stood, until the Senate Foreign Relations Committee investigated the activities of foreign intelligence organizations in the United States, including Savak. We have secured a portion of that classified report from Dale Vanatta of Jack Anderson's staff, and it confirms Khan Pira's story in every detail. It says the CIA had known of the Afshar assassination plot for more than a year prior to our broadcast; that the Bureau of Intelligence and Research of the State Department had been told about it by the CIA; and that the U.S. Embassy in Iran had also indicated that one Jules Khan Pira had been trained in assassination techniques.

Though Khan Pira never operated in the United States, a network of Savak agents did. How did we learn that? From the Shah of Iran himself, when I spoke to him in 1976.

And they are there for the purpose of checking up on Iranian students?

SHAH OF IRAN: Checking up on anybody who becomes affiliated with circles, organizations, hostile to my country, which is the role of any intelligence organization.

WALLACE: And they are there with the knowledge and consent of the United States government?

SHAH OF IRAN: I think it is.

WALLACE: That statement caused a flap. Henry Kissinger categorically denied U.S. knowledge of Savak activity here, but he promised to make inquiries. Two weeks later, his aide Robert Funseth announced that after an investigation the State Department had – quote – "found no evidence of any illegal or improper activity." Well, that was totally misleading, as the Senate report makes clear. The report confirms that Savak's primary function in the United States was to spy on Iranian dissidents like these students, who could be targets for Savak upon their return to Iran. And the report says also that the CIA itself furnished Savak with information gathered by the FBI. Training of Savak personnel continued in the U.S. And the CIA did not ask that Savak refrain from using in the United States the surveillance techniques it learned here.

And during the Carter years, Savak activity continued here. In July of '78, according to the *Washington Post*, then-Deputy Attorney General Civiletti warned Zbigniew Brzezinski that Savak was involved in significant police, security and non-diplomatic activity in the U.S. But there is no indication, the *Post* said, that Brzezinski made any move to tighten control over Savak's actions.

Why the reluctance of the United States to crack down on Savak, or even to send its agents home? Three years ago, Ambassador Zahedi answered my question about that quite candidly.

And if the U.S. government tells Iran to pull its Savak agents out of this country?

ZAHEDI: If United States government does not want it, we are not going to insist and we shall ask them to leave. At the same time, we shall ask your people to leave my country.

WALLACE: That threat, coming from the Shah himself, was repeated many times to U.S. officials in documents we have seen. The United States was not willing to pay that price. Iran was a vital listening post for the CIA, with a thousand miles and more of border with the Soviet Union.

Former CIA officer, now a political science professor, Richard Cottam, explains.

RICHARD COTTAM: The fact that the Shah allowed our watching operations from Iran, monitoring operations was terribly important to us. But I'd say, more generally, that wherever you have this kind of liaison relationship with another service like Savak that the hold they have over you is very substantial.

WALLACE: Our support for Iran meant turning a blind eye to the excesses of the Shah. And, according to Cottam, it meant failing to recognize the mounting opposition to the Shah inside Iran, and he holds Henry Kissinger responsible.

COTTAM: He coined the phrase "total commitment." Why look at a minor group of opposition people and gratuitously annoy the Shah when the operations that we do jointly are so important to both countries?

WALLACE: What you seem to be saying, Professor Cottam, is that when the question "Who lost Iran?" is finally asked, Henry Kissinger is — is at the top of your culprits list?

COTTAM: I think Henry Kissinger's idea of diplomacy in this sense is — is intolerable. I believe that you should never be in a position of not reading the full breadth of — of public opinion in any country. And Kissinger, to cut us off entirely from — from a major popular force, I think, is — is, to a very extensive extent, responsible for a lot of what's happened, yes.

WALLACE: Two events in 1978 infuriated and unified the legions who oppose the Shah: the January massacre in the Holy City of Qum by Savak and the Iranian police; and then, as the opposition to the Shah solidified, the tragic fire in the Rex Theater in Abadan in August. Hundreds died in that fire, allegedly set by Savak either to capture or kill several key agents of the Khomeini revolution known to be inside. A man charged with some responsibility for those two episodes was Reza Razmi, said by the present Iranian Embassy in Washington to be a Savak agent. He was police chief in Qum in January and in Abadan in August.

Reza Razmi. Do you know the name?

SAMGHABADI: Yes.

WALLACE: Who?

SAMGHABADI: Used to be the police chief of the city of Qum. He committed great atrocities there, had people shot on the streets. And was taken to Abadan and promoted to a general's rank, because he had performed gallant duty.

And in Abadan, during his tenure there as the police chief of the city, the Rex Cinema fire, a very controversial fire, broke out, in which about 600 people, 500 people — I don't exactly remember — a huge number died.

WALLACE: Were incinerated.

SAMGHABADI: Incinerated. Policemen actually prevented the people from breaking a hole into the wall or somehow breaking the walls down or the doors down and getting the people out.

WALLACE: Today, that former chief of police, Reza Razmi, lives under an alias in Fresno, California. We found him there and tried to talk to him, but he refused. We learned he had entered the United States in January of '79. The Iranians have protested to the State Department what they call Razmi's asylum here. They say they want him back in Teheran for trial. And the State Department acknowledges that an informal protest was lodged with Secretary Vance last October by Iran's then-Foreign Minister Ibrahim Yazdi, and that Vance promised to look into the matter, but said he would need evidence on which to proceed. Both sides agree the Iranians have yet to produce that evidence.

The CIA refused us any comment whatsoever on Razmi, but the FBI told us they had learned the date of his entry into the Port of New York, and after he settled in California, they said, Razmi called the CIA for protection. The FBI said the CIA had referred him to them, and the FBI office in San Francisco referred him to the local police. So, the Razmi mystery remains, and remains in Fresno.

We should make it clear that no one we have spoken to, Iranian or American, has suggested there was any collusion between American authorities and the Shah's officials to arrange for Razmi's entry into the United States in January of '79.

Joseph Sisco is today chancellor of American University in Washington, but for 25 years he was in the State Department, his last chore as Undersecretary to Henry Kissinger. And though he acknowledges the excesses that took place in Iran, he says there is another side to the story, the accomplishments of the Shah that too many people are right now unwilling to credit.

JOSEPH SISCO: What I'm trying to suggest to you is, in the present emotional environment, take in Iran, do you think that they're — either the commission or the people in Iran, the leadership in Iran, are able today to look at this in the context of 25 years of Iranian-American relationships? The very fact that the Iranian-U.S. relationship provided a certain umbrella for Iran to permit the country to develop economically, to permit education to be broadened, to permit land reform, to permit a new industrial class. In other words, for there to be 20 or 25 years of progress towards bringing Iran to a modern state.

WALLACE: If that is true, I asked Sisco, why did the Iranians overthrow the Shah? Why do they apparently hate him so?

SISCO: A number of reasons. One, no real opportunity for political expression. Secondly, a certain amount of repression. Third, there's no question, Mike, that in and around the throne, corruption had developed. I don't say there weren't grievances. I think it's important, however, as we look at this, to look at both the positive and the negative elements.

WALLACE: Understood.

SISCO: And we share a measure of responsibility. I don't — I don't either condone —

WALLACE: How much of a measure of responsibility do you think that we bear?

SISCO: Very difficult, because what has developed is the myth of American control in relationship to Iran or, for that matter, to Third World countries.

WALLACE: Let me read to you from a Senate Foreign Relations Committee report, with — with which I'm sure you're familiar. In the 1970's, three or four CIA officials met weekly with their Savak counterparts to discuss common interests. This was at a time when it was well known that Savak agents in the United States, according to this same once-secret Senate report, said significant police security and non-diplomatic political activity is carried out by Savak in the United States, including — quote — "the planned assassination of a U.S. citizen by a man who told the CIA he had been asked by Savak to kill a U.S. citizen." Just one example.

SISCO: Well, you can't possibly condone anything like that, and I don't think — I don't know of anyone who does.

WALLACE: Just today — we're doing this interview on Monday, February 25th, right? Just today, Mr. Sisco, Iran's president, Bani-Sadr, said that he is amazed at the naivete of the United States, of U.S. officials, and said that America still fails to understand the revolution that overthrew the Shah. To break Teheran's American hostage stalemate, says President Bani-Sadr, the United States could clear the unfavorable climate in relations between the two nations by conceding to Iran three demands, this according to President Bani-Sadr. They are: admission of U.S. past wrongs; a pledge not to interfere in our internal affairs in the future; and agreeing not to block our efforts to get back the Shah and the wealth of Iran he embezzled. Are those demands, in your — I mean, you're a trained diplomat. Are those so unacceptable?

SISCO: Mike, in this situation, there can only be one negotiator, and that is the President of the United States —

WALLACE: And he's vowed never to —

SISCO: — who has all of the information at his disposal. Grievances? Yes, they can be aired and they can be discussed, but not in circumstances why — while 50 Americans are paying the price.

SAMGHABADI: They did not have the right to take the hostages, because hostage taking, in my book and in my value system, is thoroughly condemned. The American people do not owe it to the Iranians — okay? — to come out and confess guilt, as you say. They owe it to themselves. They owe it to their Constitution. They owe it to the concept of America as a citadel of democracy and freedom.

WALLACE: Do you think that we are wrong to bring out this material for the American public at this time?

SISCO: No, I don't think that you're wrong in bringing out this material at this time. The reason why I was anxious to talk to you, in response to your query, is that I felt that this material is quite relevant, but it's important that this material be evaluated by the American public, by the world, within the broad context of Iranian-American relationships, without condoning it. I don't — I'm not condoning these actions, as you well know. Within the broad context of Iranian-U.S. relations, as well as the positive benefits to the West and to the Iranian people over a period of a quarter of a century.

WALLACE: Have —

SISCO: Mike, six Presidents and six Secretary of States just can't be totally wrong.

WALLACE: Nevertheless, it was the decision of this President and this Secretary of State, their decision to permit the Shah to enter the United States last October, that triggered the capture of the embassy and the taking of the hostages, a decision about which they'll have some tough questions to answer once the hostages are free.

For example, was the admission of the Shah to the United States an instant response to the plea of a desperately sick man? Not according to a State Department contingency document classified "secret, sensitive" and entitled "Planning for the Shah to Come to the United States" — written three months before the Shah's arrival. It says that once the Khomeini regime is firmly established – quote – "it seems appropriate to admit the Shah to the United States." Three months later, he arrived, presumably for emergency medical treatment. But Washington had been warned by the embassy in Teheran. A cable from the chargé there said, "I doubt that the Shah being ill would have much ameliorating effect on the degree of reaction here." About that reaction, the State Department reported had spelled out the "danger of hostages being taken"; and went on, "When the decision is made to admit the Shah, we should quietly assign additional American security guards to the embassy to provide protection for key personnel until the danger period is considered over." According to Henry Precht, head of the Iranian desk in the State Department, those guards were never provided.

And finally, on the issue of whether the Iranians had assured the Americans that they would protect the embassy if the Shah were to come to the United States, the Americans say the Iranians pledged they would. But yesterday, Iran's former foreign minister, Ibrahim Yazdi, told me that when informed officially just 24 hours before the arrival of the Shah in New York, Yazdi says he warned the State Department, "You are playing with fire. There will be a very drastic reaction." And on that subject, when President Carter asked Secretary Vance if the embassy could be protected, the Secretary told me Friday, "We said we could, but we didn't."

Handcuffing the Cops?

See June 22, 1980, page 624

Letters

HARRY REASONER: The mail this week brought a raft of letters about our interview with a former IRS man who says the Internal Revenue Service operates in large measure by scaring people. One viewer wrote: "What's wrong with the IRS scaring (people)? Do you know a better way to collect (what we need) to run the country?"

Noting our report about the odds of being audited, a viewer wrote: "(You said) if you earn $15,000 or less you have nothing to worry about . . . nothing to worry about except making ends meet."

And there was also this: "Thought you might be interested to know that the IRS' National Computer Center in Martinsburg, West Virginia, is located on Needmore Road . . . Does this tell you something?"

But far and away the most mail was about our interview with New Hampshire publisher William Loeb. Loeb, who had called Jerry Ford a jerk and Eisenhower a stinking hypocrite, and now calls Carter the most incompetent President we ever had, got a dose of his own medicine. One viewer said of Loeb: "Why waste your time interviewing . . . a senile old coot?" Another said: "William Loeb would be better left under his rock." Another pointed to Loeb's calling Jerry Brown a flake and said: "It takes one to know one." Which was followed by: "Who cares what some pompous, arrogant codger thinks about the candidates?"

However, there were a few letters like this one: "It was refreshing to hear from a fine American . . . A relief from the standard . . . media drivel."

But finally, there was this: "At last Morley Safer found someone to interview who was as much fun as Miss Piggy."

MARCH 9, 1980

Oman

MIKE WALLACE: Oman. Though you may have barely heard its name before, though you may have only the vaguest idea of where it is, Oman, a country the size of Kansas, with a population of perhaps three-quarters of a million, Oman at this moment is one of the United States' most valuable allies. Pentagon and State Department stategists have made several pilgrimages there in recent weeks because the U.S. needs help from Oman. Before we tell you more, we'll tell you where it is and why it is so important.

Here is Oman, just south of oil-rich Saudi Arabia, its southern shores washed by the Arabian Sea, in which the carrier battle groups of the U.S. Navy now patrol. To the north, Iran, and Afghanistan, where perhaps a hundred thousand Russian troops are now deployed. And to the west, South Yemen, the People's Democratic Republic of Yemen, where Russian, Cuban and East German troops and advisors are now deployed. And finally, Oman sits at the choke point of the Persian Gulf, the Straits of Hormuz, through which flows almost two thirds of the oil which fuels Japan, Western Europe and the United States.

(Sounds of marching band)

Oman's ruler is the 39-year-old Sultan Qaboos bin Said, America's friend, Russia's enemy, who fears the Soviets intend to move against not just Oman but every oil-rich country that rims the gulf, despite Soviet protestations to the contrary.

The Russians say they had no intention. They've said it again, they have no intention of moving toward the gulf.

SULTAN QABOOS BIN SAID: Well, do we believe them?

WALLACE: Appa— Apparently you do not.

SULTAN: No, we do not.

WALLACE: You believe that they continue to have a plan to do what?

SULTAN: To expand. They want to get their hands on the wealth of the Arabian peninsula.

WALLACE: That wealth, of course, is oil. And though Oman's oil production is minuscule compared to the giants, nonetheless it is lucrative enough to have transformed Oman, along with the rest of the nations that rim the gulf, from a backward kingdom to a modern Mideast state.

372

Schools and hospitals, highways and factories, Oman has all the requisite symbols of an oil-rich nation, especially in its capital city of Muscat. Muscat is, without doubt, the most picturesque capital city in the Arab world and one of the proudest. They expelled the Portuguese, who built that fort, in 1650, and they, along with their Arab brothers who rim the gulf, have remained wary of colonialists, imperialists, ever since.

(Music)

Which is a problem for the Sultan because, though he is undeniably the boss, he's had to rely on British officers, like these in khaki dress at one of his garden parties, and British civilians to help him make Oman's quick journey out of the Middle Ages. He pays them under contract, or they're assigned to him by the British military. And part of the price he pays for these "Brits," one hears around the gulf, is to be regularly attacked by his Arab brothers as a puppet of the imperialists. Indeed, the PLO points to the Sultan's devotion to Anwar Sadat and his forthright support of the Camp David agreements as further proof of his perfidy. As a result, the Sultan will not permit most Palestinians to enter his country. They worry him.

"Here is Oman, just south of oil-rich Saudi Arabia, its southern shores washed by the Arabian Sea, in which the carrier battle groups of the U.S. Navy now patrol."

And that worry keeps Oman's glorious beaches and tourist hotels mostly empty, for the Sultan doesn't want too many strangers floating about. Even Americans are not especially welcome as tourists.

SULTAN: I don't like people just to come and wander about and maybe sometimes bring trouble.

WALLACE: The trouble he and his British advisors fear most was expressed to us at the Omani Air Force Base on the desert island of Masirah by Wing Commander Gordon Brown.
How important do you think Oman is in the whole configuration out here?

GORDON BROWN: Well, sir, we— we can both read a map, and I like to think of it as the— the nut in the cracker.

WALLACE: The nut in the cracker?

BROWN: To the north, Afghanistan, the Iranian problem. To the south, the Yemeni problem. And here are we, a vulnerable piece of countryside.

WALLACE: So, if you're a Russian military strategist looking at this bottom end of the Arabian peninsula?

BROWN: I would be very interested, sir.

WALLACE: In fact, you don't have to travel to Afghanistan these days to view the Soviet military. A helicopter of the Royal Omani Air Force heading north up the rugged Musandam peninsula of Oman and out across the Straits of Hormuz. We are on our way out into the Straits of Hormuz to take a look at a Russian light cruiser and a Russian frigate said to be here on station.

The ships were there, anchored at the entrance to the Straits, just two miles outside Oman's territorial waters. The largest, number 555, a Kresta-class guided missile cruiser, bristling with sophisticated electronic gear. So was the smaller Petya-class frigate nearby. Their mission, among other things, to eavesdrop electronically on the U.S. carrier task forces just over the horizon. Nothing better symbolizes the importance of this part of the world to both the U.S. and the Soviets than these Straits of Hormuz. On the average, an oil tanker passes through them every 21 minutes.

With their foray into Afghanistan, the Soviet troops are now just 300 miles from the Straits. But more important, they are within easy striking distance of the oil fields of the gulf.

If the Omanis feel they are being squeezed, and they do, with the Russians moving closer from the east and Afghanistan, the western arm of the nutcracker comes from over there, the PDRY, the People's Democratic Republic of Yemen, with Cuban, Russian and East German troops and advisors mixed in with the South Yemen forces. That border there is quiet now. It's now under 24-hour observation from over here. But the Sultan feels that the integrity of his country is most threatened from over there.

That's the threat that is the most serious threat to Oman?

SULTAN: To Oman and to the rest of the Arabian peninsula.

WALLACE: The Sultan's troops on patrol near the border with South Yemen. What he wants to meet the Communist threat, says the Sultan, is discreet help from the United States, not so much money as arms to protect these frontiers.

SULTAN: Well, the first thing I would like the Americans to do, and I hope they will do, that to give us all the means so we will be able to stand on our own feet, to protect our own ground, to protect our own interests and the interests of the United States and the rest of the free world.

WALLACE: Give us the tools, you're saying, and we will do the job?

SULTAN: And we will do the job.

WALLACE: You don't want Americans on the ground here?

SULTAN: Americans or other people.

WALLACE: When Henry Kissinger says that in order to make plausible — to make plausible — the threat of the use of force here, perhaps one division or two divisions of American troops should be here, and then he mentioned your country by name. That's unacceptable to you?

SULTAN: No, that's unacceptable. Unless, as I say, there is a massive attack on us or on the area, then, of course, we will welcome our friends to come and help us.

WALLACE: But in order to come and help, the U.S. needs access to Omani air bases, ports, facilities where they can pre-position fuel, supplies, ammunition, facilities to be used as staging areas for U.S. troops that would be flown in in an emergency. U.S. Ambassador Marshall Wiley explains what has come to be known as the Carter Doctrine.

AMBASSADOR MARSHALL WILEY: I think that we can best deal with this security situation not by attempting to acquire bases with large numbers of American troops present on the ground, but rather by developing our rapid-deployment forces, which can be based outside of the area and which with modern technology and transportation can be moved into the area quickly, if we have to, in times of crisis.

WALLACE: Which brings us to the air base at Thumrait on Oman's western border — one of the spots Americans could move to in time of the crisis the ambassador talks about. This is the most modern base the Pentagon planners have looked at — a first-class working base, five years old, with a runway long enough to take any plane the Americans might want to put in here.

But the prime piece of real estate under consideration by the Americans is this desert island of Masirah, 10 miles off the south coast of Oman, 45 miles long, seven miles wide, and reasonably close to the U.S. carrier battle groups steaming off there in the Arabian Sea. Long enough, big enough, they tell us, to house a division of American troops should they be needed here in the future, and doubly attractive because it's away from the prying eyes of the people on the mainland.

Were you here when the American teams came through to take a look?

BROWN: Yes, I gave both the teams their full briefings on Masirah.

WALLACE: And you are serious that there is room up there for as many as a division of American troops, the water, the— the land, the—?

BROWN: Certainly it was suggested to me that the Americans might be interested in a camp site for up to a division of troops, and were certainly, in the countryside—

WALLACE: Suggested to you by?

BROWN: By the Americans.

WALLACE: Dr. Kissinger talked about the necessity, if we are going to have a credible deterrent here, to have as many as a division of troops on the ground and he suggested Oman. The Americans have talked about the possibility of—?

BROWN: Sufficient camp space for a large number of men is the way that it was put.

WALLACE: And that's not just to service airplanes?

BROWN: Oh, no.

WALLACE: If it becomes necessary to improve the facilities on Masirah, to make them available, to make them more accessible, to make them more up-to-date for American planes, American men?

SULTAN: Well, America should give us the funds to do so.

WALLACE: And America plans to do just that. Negotiations are virtually complete. In fact, we've learned that there has already been more military cooperation between Oman and the U.S. than either side cares to admit. Already last year, Omani pilots, most of them British mercenaries in these Omani jets, were flying joint training exercises with American pilots from the U.S. carrier battle groups in the Arabian Sea.

Who is Sultan Qaboos, our new ally on the gulf? He looks like the model of a modern major general.

(Military music)

But he was, in fact, until 10 years ago, under the thumb of one of the most autocratic rulers on the gulf, his father, Sultan Said bin Taimur. He ruled an Oman that had once been a great seagoing nation, with colonies on the east coast of Africa and the south coast of Asia, with ships trading, centuries ago, as far abroad as China. But that was in the past.

To the old Sultan, progress meant trouble to be avoided at all costs. He stood foursquare against everything from Western dress to sunglasses to education beyond the sixth grade. Nonetheless, he permitted his son, the current Sultan, to study at the British military academy at Sandhurst. And when he returned and announced he had a few ideas for change, the old man had him placed under virtual house arrest.

Work or starve, did he say?

SULTAN: Yes, he did. He always told me that.

WALLACE: Work or starve?

SULTAN: Yes. One has to work or starve, yes.

WALLACE: Finally, in 1970, the British officers who ran the old Sultan's army conspired with young Qaboos to throw his father out.

Is it difficult to overthrow a father?

SULTAN: I think the most difficult thing in the world, yes, to think of you have to tell your father to — to remove himself, really.

WALLACE: But he survived and went to London and lived in the Dorchester Hotel until his death two years later?

SULTAN: Yes.

WALLACE: Did you ever speak again?

SULTAN: We wrote to each other.

WALLACE: Did he approve of what you were doing in Oman?

SULTAN: He did, and he wished me very well.

WALLACE: But under Qaboos, Omanis continue to live under a dictatorship, though more benign. There are no elections, rigid censorship. And to help him keep tabs on things, watching over all, a secret police organization, the Oman Research Department, headed by the Sultan's British advisors.

Some compare the Sultan to the Shah of Iran and predict he'll suffer the same fate. But unlike the Shah, he has not alienated the religious leaders, he still respects tradition, and what corruption there is does not exceed the common standards of the gulf.

Ten years ago, only 800 children in the entire country went to school. Today, there are 80,000 of them, with many more studying abroad, all expenses paid by the Sultan's government. And some observers think that's not a very good idea.

That's what happened to the Shah. The students went abroad, they became educated, they began to understand that they were le— living in a dictatorship, that there were certain excesses taking place in that dictatorship. You are educating your young.

SULTAN: Yes. When they come back they take part in running their country. At the moment, of course, not politically, but they run the administration of the country. They have work to do, because their country needs them.

WALLACE: Some of your brothers here on the gulf seem to worry almost as much about the Americans as they do about the Russians. The foreign minister of Kuwait, for instance, says the gulf must remain aloof from conflicts between the superpowers. The impression that one gets from some of the people up and down the gulf is that the Americans are more interested in that oil and, conceivably, in taking over that oil.

SULTAN: No, I believe the Americans are interested in seeing the countries which have the oil are secure.

WALLACE: Secure?

SULTAN: Secure.

WALLACE: But there is skepticism about American motives here in the gulf.

SULTAN: Is not here in Oman.

WALLACE: When some gentlemen from the White House, from the National Security Council of the President, came here recently, you are reported to have asked them three questions: What took you so long? Are you serious? And what are you prepared to do for me? Is my information accurate?

SULTAN: Almost. We in Oman have a practice to speak out our minds and to say in public what we say in private. And we — if we believe something is going to lead to a good thing, we support it.

Bobby Knight
STEVE GLAUBER, PRODUCER

DAN RATHER: Even if you don't follow college basketball, you've probably heard of Bobby Knight. He's the coach who touched off an international incident at the Pan American Games last summer when he was charged with socking a cop. That came as no surprise to sports fans because Bobby Knight is just that kind of fellow. If he weren't the best basketball coach in the country, and a lot of people say he is, or if his Indiana University team were not a national contender, which it is, we would probably still be doing a story about him. Love him or hate him, and there are plenty of people on both sides of that issue, he is bigger than life and meaner than a rattlesnake.

BOBBY KNIGHT (on basketball court):   You're crazy! The goddamn ball was that far off the bucket! Christ, you can't even see that where you are! The ball is on this side!

RATHER: At Indiana, this scene is as common as a ball going through the hoop.

KNIGHT (in locker room):   We're getting beat because we're just not tough enough in the way we're playing. That's the whole thing. We're not tough enough on the boards, we're not tough enough handling the ball, we're not tough enough moving the ball. Now, let's don't have anything left after 10 minutes. And then we'll just play on guts from that point on. But let's throw everything we've got into the first 10 minutes of this half.

RATHER: At the age of 24 he began coaching at West Point and led the Army teams to the few winning seasons they ever had. In 1972, he came to Indiana and quickly turned them from also-rans into NCAA national champions four years later. But no matter where he is, he always acts the same. He yells at his players.

KNIGHT: Who in the hell is guarding Hanson?

PLAYER: I got Hanson.

KNIGHT: Well, then, goddamnit, get him!

RATHER: He puts down reporters.

KNIGHT: That's just how good I feel tonight, Russ. I'll even say hello to you.

RUSS: You must feel damn good.

KNIGHT (on basketball court):   No, no!

RATHER: He screams at referees.

KNIGHT: Oh, no! He just went down!

RATHER: He even berates home crowds for not yelling loudly enough. But most importantly, he wins. And winning basketball games here in Indiana is as important as a good corn crop is to Iowa or a hit season is to Broadway.
(Band music)
Indiana is basketball crazy. A ball and a net would make a perfect state flag. And as long as Knight is holding the flag, his players march, run and jump to his tune.

KNIGHT (on basketball court):   Let's go. We'll go out this way. Let's go. Let's go!
(To Rather): I say, "Boys, we're going to play basketball my way. This isn't going to be very democratic. We're not going to vote on what offense or what defense or who the hell's going to play or anything, because I've forgotten more about this game than you're going to know, and we're going to play it my way."
(On basketball court): You took a jump shot off the dribble, no passes. Your next shot is a jump shot with one pass. Now, are we running your offense or mine?

RATHER: Both his offense and defense seem more suited to a battleground than playground. He permits little individual freedom, few flashy moves, no one-on-one play. Knight stresses the fundamentals. He considers himself not so much a coach as a teacher. Indeed, one history professor calls Knight the best teacher at the university, period. Other professors say his winning-at-all-costs attitude and intimidating ways make him the worst influence in the state.

KNIGHT (on basketball court):   Tell Bushie one pass and a shot again. We just — damn it, well, tell him!

RATHER: Knight's philosophy is the same off the court and seems wildly out of bounds to many of today's Indiana students.

KNIGHT: It's important that people know what the hell you think when you're the man in charge, and I try to leave little doubt as to exactly what I think about most issues. (Laughter) Somebody says to me, "How do you get your teams to play as hard as they do? Your teams play harder than almost any other basketball team I watch. What's your secret?" Well, there's absolutely no secret. You're either going to play hard or you're not going to play. That's a great motivational device. (Laughter)

CURRY KIRKPATRICK: His method of motivating is— is maybe one of the things that people object to. I think he motivates by fear a lot of times.

RATHER: Curry Kirkpatrick, college basketball writer for Sports Illustrated.

KIRKPATRICK: It's scary sometimes, some of the things he does with young, impressionable college players. Now, I think if he went to the NBA, did the same thing he does in college, he would either have the best team in pros or he would be dead within a week, because some of the pros would— would, you know, beat the hell out of him.

RATHER: Ten of Knight's players have made it to the pros. One of them, Quinn Buckner of the Milwaukee Bucks.

QUINN BUCKNER: When you get out on the court he asks you to do one thing and that's just give you— give him a hundred percent every second that you're out on the court. And I — I personally don't think that's asking a lot. Sometimes he's — he's so intense that — he gets so involved in the game, and I— and— and yelling at some players really destroys them. And I don't mean permanently, just for a— a certain period in their life it was like this was the toughest thing they've ever been through. And my whole goal, as far as being on the basketball court, was winning the NCAA championship. And he motivated me to get out there every day to do that, and he motivated the other guys on the team to do it, and it's hard to argue with that.

RATHER: Enough players have quit to form a team of their own. Some are quoted as saying they were "intimidated," "humiliated," "scared," "frightened." One said basketball wasn't fun any more and called Knight an SOB.

KNIGHT (on basketball court):   Well, hell, don't nod about it, do it! Let's go!

(To Rather): I honestly believe that people respond — who are competitive — best to criticism. I sometimes think that praise makes us a little lazy.

(On basketball court): Come on, be ready! Ready! Be ready!

(To Rather):   Well, see, I'm a great believer that— that none of us works to potential. I believe the most detrimental, singular thing in society is human nature. I think human nature dictates that, instead of working on my jab-step-one-dribble-and-jump shot for an hour, I work on it for 15 minutes and then I go watch what's going on around the swimming pool. You know, I— I think human nature — to you, to me, to players — is the toughest opponent that we have to fight.

RATHER: A former coach who never beat Indiana is Al McGuire, now basketball commentator for NBC Sports.

AL McGUIRE: He expects when you play for him if there's a ball on the floor, you dive for it. You don't have to come up with it, but you must come up with Spalding on your forehead, and you must leave some of your blood on the court. It's a constant maximum effort; that there is no softening, there is no marshmallow type of thing out there. It's almost blood and guts.

(Knight hunting . . .sound of shot)

KNIGHT: I really think that there's a great similarity between hunting and working with hunting dogs and coaching and working with basketball players, because you get a dog that has native talent — it can run, it has some strength, it has a nose that can — that can smell — and then you've got to really develop and perfect that. That's like getting a basketball player that can run, can jump, can do some things that — that embody physical skills, and then you've got to kind of be the mastermind behind the operation as the hunter, just like the coach has to be with the team.

RATHER: During the six-month basketball season, Knight's wife and two sons rarely see him, except as spectators.

MRS. KNIGHT: I haven't watched half the games. My head's been in my lap this year. (Laughing) That's how nervous I've been this year.

KNIGHT: If we can be a very difficult team to score against, then we're going to be a difficult team to beat.

RATHER: As a player, he wasn't even a starter. Then again, he wasn't bad. Number-six man on an Ohio State championship team starring Jerry Lucas, Larry Siegfried and John Havlichek. Knight says he learned from them why some teams win and some teams lose.

KNIGHT: We read reams of copy about the will to win. We hear countless broadcasters talk about the will to win. I want to tell you something about the will to win. The will to win is the most overly exaggerated phenomena that we have in society today. You have to have a will to prepare to win, not a will to win, because everybody's got that. It's the will to prepare to win.

RATHER: Knight demands total commitment to team play. It is the team, not the individual, that counts.

KNIGHT: If we can get the— the kind of boy that I think is willing to say, "All right, I'm going to be a part of a really good team and from that I'm going to get a lot of recognition," which has happened with out players, instead of the boy that says, "Well, how many shots per game will I get in your offense?" Or, "How many minutes will I play?" Or, How will you use me offensively?" If we can determine that the kid will — will think that — that all the recognition that he wants is going to come out of team accomplishment, then this is what we're after, and that's not an easy thing to determine.

RATHER: At high-school games he scouts for future players – players willing to take orders, who after arriving on campus will be molded and formed into Knight's image.

KNIGHT: I think I have to take away individuality, to some degree, to accomplish what I want to accomplish in athletics. They're required to get haircuts; they're required to be clean-shaven. That takes something away from those kids that is a little bit of a sacrifice on their part.

RATHER: Recruiting for college teams is, of course, fiercely competitive. Some high-school superstars not only are wined and dined, petted and pampered, but also offered big money, often in the form of hugh fees for summer jobs not performed. Forty thousand dollars a year is a figure often bounced around in locker-room huddles. Knight refuses to play that bidding game and demands that his players work hard academically. At many other colleges, a lot of players don't graduate. At Indiana, they do.

McGUIRE: He goes after maybe four blue-chip thoroughbreds, blue-plate specials, these Einsteins that every coach in the country wants, and he gets them. So, there has to be a section of this country that believes exactly in what Bobby Knight does. They believe in discipline, they believe in crew haircuts, bow ties, the 40's and the 50's, General Patton, charge into the machine-gun nest, that type of thing, and— which isn't bad. It's — it's more of a conservative type of America.

RATHER: If much of Middle America admires him, many sports reporters do not. For the two seasons before this one, Knight held virtually no post-game press conferences. Instead, one of his assistants handed out mimeographed quotes. Begrudgingly, he changed that policy this year, but at the same time he often closed the locker room to reporters after games.

KIRKPATRICK: I don't think Bobby Knight really understands the rule of the press. If you're not — if you're not a hundred percent for Knight and the Indiana program, you're an enemy. This is a kind of a paranoia.

RATHER: It is also a kind of perverse independence, a belligerent way of letting everyone know that he can win his own way. In a sport cheered for flashy offense, Knight insists on aggressive defense. In an era of permissiveness, he insists on discipline. When competitors insist they simply cannot win without buying recruits, Knight proves that he can. And when other coaches would leap at national publicity, Knight will turn his back if he thinks a publisher ever wrote a bad word about him.

RATHER: What was your reaction to *Sports Illustrated* last fall when they asked you to pose on the cover?

KNIGHT: And I told them that I thought, being what our relationship had been over the past four or five years, that — that what I felt they should do is step out on Sixth Avenue and take the Time-Life Building and stick it . . .

KIRKPATRICK: He's threatened me physically. He's threatened other people on our magazine physically. He threatened to throw another one of our writers out of a second-story window. I mean, I ca— you know, we could go on here. But these are just personal things. And you know, they're — they're laughable.

RATHER: But he says them in jest, doesn't he?

KIRKPATRICK: I hope so.

KNIGHT (on basketball court):   Now we've got three minutes to take this thing into the halftime. You've worked 17 minutes. You've played good basketball for 17 minutes to get it into this position. Let's take it in with three really strong minutes at both ends of the court. Let's help each other out, let's block out, and let's be sure of what we're doing with the ball on offense. Let's go!

RATHER: When it goes good for the team, it goes good for the university. Direct basketball income for this season is projected just short of one million dollars. Add another quarter-million for a successful post-season tournament. And alumni contribute more when the team wins than when it loses — a healthy two million dollars more last year and probably more this year.
Can you lose and survive here?

KNIGHT: I don't think so. I don't think that the university or the — the people in Indiana, the — the atmosphere of basketball in Indiana, would permit you to lose here and survive. I — I don't think there's any way that could be done.

RATHER: Last weekend Indiana again won the Big Ten championship. This weekend they began their quest for a second NCAA crown.

KIRKPATRICK: When Bobby Knight is involved, you lose sight of the players, you lose track of his players. And, after all, the games are for the players, not for the coaches. And I think Knight, subconsciously or not, takes the spotlight to the detriment of the players, all in the cause of winning. All in the cause of winning.

KNIGHT: Maybe I do have tunnel vision in that regard, but damn it, I want those kids to — to be able to get out of here, and I want them to look back and say — now they may not understand why I've said what I did, or what I've said, but I want them to get out of here and — and at some time — it may not be this year or next year, maybe five years — I want them to be able to sit down and analyze education at Indiana University, and say that playing basketball was the greatest form of education I received while being there.

Barry Goldwater

HARRY REASONER: An elder statesman, by one definition, is a leader in whom the fires of personal ambition have been banked. From the coals, the nation then gets wisdom and candor. Well, Barry Goldwater is sort of our elder statesman. He always gave candor, and now a good deal of what he says sounds like wisdom, even to some of the Americans who voted against him in 1964.

He's always been full of paradoxes. The last senator, except for those from Alaska and Hawaii, born in a territory, three years before Arizona became a state. An instinctive conservative who desegregated the Arizona National Guard years before President Truman desegregated the Army. An Episcopalian of part-Jewish heritage who once said he didn't care what color a man his daughter married if the fellow was a hard worker. A senator in whom 30 years in Washington has developed a certain cynicism, but whose patriotism and sense of honor and belief in the nation's future have never wavered.

A few days ago, we sat down and talked to Barry Goldwater — about Afghanistan and Iran, about Richard Nixon and, naturally, about politics.

I remember listening to you in Chicago in 1960, when you said, "Wake up, conservatives, you can take this party over." Well, they did, didn't they? I mean, the Republican Party belongs to the conservatives now?

SENATOR BARRY GOLDWATER: Oh, it always has. About 85 percent of the Republicans who will attend the convention in Detroit will be conservative. Fifteen percent will be what you call moderate to liberal. And that's about the balance, and I don't think it's going to change.

REASONER: So that if — if all the polls showed that John Anderson would win by a landslide, the convention probably still wouldn't nominate him, would it?

SENATOR GOLDWATER: No. Anderson, I don't think, can get the nomination, because I think Reagan has it all put in the bag.

REASONER: Would you be comfortable with Ronald Reagan as nominee?

SENATOR GOLDWATER: Yes, I could — I'll — I'll work my head off for him.

REASONER: As for George Bush, Senator Goldwater thinks his presence might just open the door for former President Gerald Ford.

SENATOR GOLDWATER: If George can keep picking up delegates until he and Reagan go into the convention, say with two to three hundred pledged delegates apiece, and it develops into a hassle where we go through one or two or even three ballots and no choice, then I think you could expect Jerry Ford to pop in.

REASONER: 1976, you supported Mr. Ford.

SENATOR GOLDWATER: That's right. I did that because it's rather customary to support the President if he's a member of your party and you were in the Congress. I wasn't too happy with endorsing him because he didn't run a good campaign. And we wound up with, I won't use the word, a bad President.

REASONER (laughing):   What word wouldn't you use?

SENATOR GOLDWATER (laughing):   Huh?

REASONER: What word wouldn't you use?

SENATOR GOLDWATER: Lousy. (Laughter)

REASONER: You – you don't think that much of Mr. Carter?

SENATOR GOLDWATER: No. I know some other lousy people and I wouldn't want to compare them.

REASONER: Do you see anybody beating him in New York in the – at the convention?

SENATOR GOLDWATER: No. I think Carter has the Democratic nomination sewed up. I think Kennedy had a chance at one time, but old Teddy just couldn't keep his mouth shut and it got him in trouble. I don't think he can make a comeback now.

REASONER: Is there any Democrat who's been mentioned that you'd rather see run than Jimmy Carter?

SENATOR GOLDWATER: No. But there are a lot of very, very good Democrats in this country that would make, in my opinion, a good President. I'm thinking of men like Ed Muskie, who's a very solid, level-headed fellow; Senator Boren of Oklahoma. There are many, many Democrats that can do a splendid job in the White House. We just don't happen to have one right now.

REASONER: Another question: Are Watergate and Richard Nixon still factors? Did he hurt conservatism and the Republicans?

SENATOR GOLDWATER: Mr. Nixon hurt the Republican Party and he hurt America, and frankly, I don't think he should ever be forgiven. He came as close to destroying this country as any one man in that office ever has come. Now, I was very close to that. I worked those last two weeks with General Haig and the other members of the White House and we were teetering on the brink of disaster. And had Nixon decided to stand impeachment, I don't think this country could have survived it. And it was his fault. So, he— he did damage to all of us, Republican, Democrat alike. But as a— of the two parties, he did damage more to the Republican Party.

REASONER: It seemed to me, talking to people who knew Nixon, that the resentment against him is strongest in people like you who were his friends?

SENATOR GOLDWATER: I think that's right. I know he and I worked together 25 years in politics. I campaigned for him he campaigned for me. And one morning on a television show — the day that he went to China for the second time was the same day that Gerald Ford started his campaign in New Hampshire — and I just — something came through my mind, just like in a millisecond, "This guy's dishonest." And I said so. I got home and Peggy gave me hell. "What are you saying that about the President for?" I said, "Sit down and I'll tell you." (Laughs) And I've never gotten over it.

REASONER: I remember a few days later saying to you, "Did you hear from Mr. Nixon?"

SENATOR GOLDWATER (laughing):   Yeah.

REASONER: And you said, "I didn't hear from the 'blank.' " (Goldwater laughs) I don't want to hear from the 'blank.' "

SENATOR GOLDWATER: That's right, and I haven't. (Laughter)

REASONER: Was it a fatal flaw in his character that was there all along that you didn't spot and the rest of the people didn't spot?

SENATOR GOLDWATER: I'm convinced that he — he had it all his life: a — a basic —
I don't like to use the word "dishonesty" — but a basic tendency to think first of
Richard Milhous Nixon and then think of anybody else and the country. As I
look back on many things that he did, he was doing them only for himself and to
get himself in that top slot as President. I can think back, and many people can
think back, of promises that he broke to us. I doubt that he even remembered
them after we left the Oval Office. So, he — he is basically, in my opinion, a di—
a dishonest person.

REASONER: We wondered about Abscam, the FBI's trapping of some politicians
using bribes as bait.
What did you think of that tactic of the Abscam? Is — is that fair?

SENATOR GOLDWATER: Yes, I think it's fair. I don't care how dishonesty is turned
up, I think it should be turned up.

REASONER: Senator, I see, this morning's paper, that Washington's biggest lending
operation, mortgage-lending operation, has gone to 17 percent. You've got a
prime rate of 17¼ percent. We talk about reducing not only government expendi-
tures but use of credit cards by people and everything else. What about wage and
price controls?

SENATOR GOLDWATER: Well, they're not going to work. They sound real good, but
we've tried them before. You tell an American he can't do something and, by
God, he'll find out a way to do it, even if it means cheating. And that's exactly
what's happened when we've tried wage and price controls before. We get the
black market. We find there's ways to buy this, ways to pay you for doing this
without it showing. So, it — that's not the answer. We're not going to get a
handle on inflation until we've chopped federal spending down. But I don't
think we're making the right steps, and I don't know if we have the guts to take
the right steps.

If we could have every member of Congress say, "To hell with getting re-elected,
I'm down here to do a job for the people," then we might get that job done. But
with elections coming every two years, and a third of the Senate running every
two years, the President running every four years, my own feeling is we're not
going to see the end of depre— of inflation in this country.

REASONER: Foreign affairs. The senator, like others, is afraid Russia's presence in
Afghanistan could be just the first move toward the control of crucial Indian Ocean
ports.

SENATOR GOLDWATER: If we don't have control of that Indian Ocean, we don't
have much control over our world commerce, and Russia will have. So that's
why I look on it — and I've told the President — that I think it's probably the
most dangerous thing that's happened to our country in the history of this
country.

REASONER: That's a very strong statement.

SENATOR GOLDWATER: It is, but it's true. I don't think that Russia ever wants to go
to war with us. I think she wants to gain control over us, as she has repeatedly
said, by destroying or controlling our economy. And she's made some pretty
strong steps in that direction.

REASONER: It sounds as if, to some extent, at least, you approve of what Mr. Carter
did about Afghanistan?

SENATOR GOLDWATER: Yes, because the only other alternative would have been to use force. Now, I've been in Afghanistan. Don't ask me why, but during the war, somebody said, "Go there." "Yes, sir." Also I flew over the whole length of the Himalaya Mountains quite a few times, and that's got to be the worst country in the world. Even a right-minded goat wouldn't live in those mountains. And that's what makes it tough. And it would make it a tough military venture for us to dislodge the Soviets, just as the Soviets are finding it very tough to get these mountain people out behind the rocks. The Afghan doesn't look on a flag as any symbol at all that he's respectful of. He— he does what we in the West would call — he protects the back-forty, and he'll fight to the death for his land and his family. And they're pretty tough cookies in very tough terrain. And the Russians have got their hands — they have their hands full.

REASONER: Well, we reacted by some minor trade embargoes, at least not major, and by boycotting the Olympics. Could we have done something else?

SENATOR GOLDWATER: No. I frankly think that boycotting the Olympics is going to hurt Russia more than boycotting grain. Russia had looked on this as an opportunity to show the world what a nice place Moscow is. They were prettying it up, they were getting rid of all the bad element, so that people would come home and say, "Gee, those are nice people, nice city. What's wrong with it?" And now they're not going to have those hundreds of thousands of Americans parading around Moscow to eat up the nice food they've brought in and sleep in the nice clean hotel rooms they've just swept out. So, Russia's not coming out well on it. And frankly, if Russia pulls her troops out of Afghanistan, I think it will be because of the Olympic boycott more than not giving her grain.

REASONER: So, if we made approximately the right response in Afghanistan, what about Iran, what about the hostages?

SENATOR GOLDWATER: I don't know what the President could have done other than what he did do. I can't see the advantage, never have seen the advantage, of going into Iran and just bombing, shooting up people. We need Iran and Iran needs us. So, I would say let's get the hostages home and then do everything we can to get along with Iran.

REASONER: Now, this is a — isn't this a new, moderated Barry Goldwater? Are you mellowing after—

SENATOR GOLDWATER: No, I'm not mellowing. I just — I've been to war and I don't want to see people go to war unless we can accomplish something. Now, I have suggested that we might destroy the refinery at Abadan, where I used to refuel during the war. That wouldn't kill anybody. It would just deprive Iran of kerosene, which she has to have, and some JP for jet fuel and gasoline. But that's as far as I've gone. I have said that if we ever have to use force, I would volunteer to fly the lead ship in to bomb — bomb Kharg Island, because you could see that fire from here. (Laughter) But I don't want to do it.

A Few Minutes
with Andy Rooney

MORLEY SAFER: We all grew up with it: "A penny saved is a penny earned." Well, Andy Rooney isn't so sure.

ANDY ROONEY: It's a wonder we all aren't millionaires, isn't it, with the opportunities we have every day to save money? Just look at some of these. Save $3.44. Save 60¢ on the Flex Fighters — in case you want to fight your flex! Look at all the money you could save on paint here. They mailed this to me. It says "To Box holder." Sort of a little personal touch there. Save $5.50 on every gallon. I don't know what she's doing here. Save $17.50 on an electric pencil sharpener. I wish they had something that would sharpen my typewriter. Save $1,253 on a Saab. I mean, if you bought eight or ten Saabs a year, you can save enough to buy a Mercedes.

Here's a whole page of savings. Save $9 on an adjustable bar stool. Save $15 on crystal-glass chandeliers. Five dollars on a garbage pail. I added it up. It comes to $108. I mean, if I bought two of everything on this page, I could save $216.

Here's one. You can save 10¢ buying soup with this coupon. It's good soup. I don't know about the coupon. You have to read the small print. It says, "Cash value, 1/100th of a cent." It sounds to me as though if you spent a couple of years collecting 10,000 of these coupons, their cash value would be exactly one dollar — except in states where money is illegal, of course.

Here's free Tylenol. Getting something free isn't as good a deal as saving $1.98, is it? I mean, if all you do is get something free, you don't really save a nickel.

There are a couple of ads I've never understood. You hear announcers on radio or television say, "Savings as much as a hundred dollars or more!" What do they mean "and more"? If they mean savings as much as $200, why don't they say so? As a matter of fact, I'm always suspicious of that "and more" stuff.

RATHER: Those stories and more.

WALLACE: Those stories and more.

REASONER: Those stories and more.

SAFER: Those stories and more tonight on 60 MINUTES.

ROONEY: What's that "and more" stuff? Me?

Letters

MORLEY SAFER: And now letters. Our story last week looking into why the people of Iran are so angry at the United States brought an unusually large outpouring of mail. A sampling of that mail indicates that it was about evenly divided between those who applauded us for doing the story and those who were critical of us. If anything, the pro-mail outweighted the anti-mail, but not by much.

We also heard from the families of some of the hostages. The daughter of one hostage said: "My grateful appreciation and respect for having initiated the

American media's first acknowledgement of U.S. indifference towards atrocities committed under the Shah's regime."

The daughter of another hostage: "The broadcast was blunt, marvelous. It showed the American people something they've never seen — the tortures the Persian people went through under the Shah. It was important to bring it out to the American people."

But not all the hostage families felt that way. From the wife of a hostage, there was this: "Your timing on the Iranian program was just great — playing right into the hands of the terrorists. At this sensitive time in the negotiations you probably have set the release of the hostages back many weeks."

Also in the mail were letters like this: "Your report was 120 days overdue."

And this: "Your program bordered on treason."

And this: "I cannot condone the taking of . . . hostages, but at least now I understand the Iranians' fervent desire to gain the attention of a government that virtually ignored the atrocities committed by a regime that it supported."

And finally, there was this: "You made Judas look like a piker."

MARCH 16, 1980

Remember Enewetak!

JOHN TIFFIN, PRODUCER

MORLEY SAFER: There's probably more nuclear know-how in this country than anywhere. We know how to blow up the world, we know how to heat and light it, we can cure disease. But how much do we really know, and will we really ever know enough? This month is the first anniversary of the Three Mile Island accident. Washington and a couple of state governments are struggling with the dilemma of what to do with nuclear waste.

All of this makes us remember just how painfully ignorant even the experts can be in nuclear matters. And we remember something else. Remember Enewetak, once ground zero, the island, the chain of islands, in the Pacific we so casually blasted away at a generation ago. With great assurance, we exploded our bombs and, with equal assurance, we said we could clean up the mess they left behind. It's all worth remembering in this moment of political, military and scientific uncertainty. We begin at the beginning — or almost at the beginning.

(Bomb explosion)

Those acts of creation back in the 1950's: 43 separate nuclear events, as they are bureaucratically called, mainly on the Pacific atoll of Enewetak. What we proved with this hellish technology was that we could destroy the planet if we chose to. What we chose to ignore was that we were destroying one small part of it in the process. I mean really destroying it, like the island that once rested here and was vaporized into a bottomless hole in the Pacific — the earth made a penny's worth smaller. This perfectly balanced little paradise was a perfect place for nuclear events, or so it seemed back in the lusciously simple year of 1947. The only problem was people lived on the islands. The U.S. had been granted them in trust by the UN, and so one day the Navy arrived at Enewetak and ordered everyone off the islands. A hundred and forty-two people who'd lived on 40 islands were all placed on this single island hundreds of miles away. The people cried when they left. The U.S. Navy was more cheerful. The press release said — quote — "The natives are delighted about the atomic bomb which has already brought them prosperity and a new, promising future." But for 30 years they've been demanding their islands back. The original 142 islanders have now grown to 500, and they've got an American lawyer, Ted Mitchell, to help them.

TED MITCHELL: Hello, chief!

SAFER: The old chief, the ivoj, in his crisp U.S. Army uniform, is confused by America. On the one hand, they take his land away, on the other, they send him a lawyer to help get it back.

MITCHELL: I remember the first time that we took the — the ivoj, Johannes, to the United States. For him, it was absolutely inconceivable that there could be so much land available to a single society and that, having so much land, they could go so far away to his island and destroy part of it with nuclear testing.

SAFER: Three years ago, Ted Mitchell finally got the U.S. government to agree to let them return, and the Army was sent in to clean up the radioactive mess.

MAN (at Army briefing):   Good afternoon. What I'd like to do this afternoon is give you an update briefing on the Enewetak cleanup project. Enewetak atoll consists of 41 named islands and is the homeland for two peoples: the Dri-Enjebi in the north and the Dri-Enewetak in the south.

SAFER: Which was precisely the problem the Army faced. Each people, each clan, had almost a supernatural attachment to its own islands, and so:

MAN (at briefing):   The joint task group has the mission of preparing the atoll for habitation by both the Dri-Enjebi and the Dri-Enewetak.

SAFER: On the southern islands, no problem, no nuclear waste. They'd been used to house American personnel during the tests. But the northern islands, where the bombs were exploded, were seriously contaminated with plutonium, strontium, cesium and other dangerous substances. Still, the Congress had granted $20 million to the Army to try to clean up all the islands to a degree that would be acceptable in the United States. That grew to 40 million, and that has now grown to $105 million, about a quarter of a million dollars per islander. (Sounds of planes landing) There's been nothing quite like it in history, one of those massive efforts that Americans take on with such ardor. Everything was heaved into it: machinery invented especially for the job, to scour the islands foot by foot, to sniff out plutonium by detecting gamma radiation. There are certain ironies: one bit of our genius being used to clean up the mess left by another bit.

Contaminated soil from the northern islands was removed bargeload by bargeload. Tons of radioactive metal from test towers was gathered together. One island was needed to store the waste, and this one, Runit, was chosen. Runit had a built-in waste disposal — an old atom bomb crater code-named "Cactus." All this so-called "hot" material was shoved down the crater and it was finally sealed — an eerie-looking, inverted saucer of a tomb. It's supposed to remain leak proof for 200 or maybe 2,000 years. Nobody knows. We do know that Runit will remain hot and off limits for the next 24,000 years. But the Army says even Runit is reasonably safe for a short visit now that most of the radioactive material's been sealed behind those 18 inches of concrete.

Can you understand my concern or, say someone watching this right now, their concern, when they see a whole truckload of people, big-shot colonels among them, all wearing surgical masks, yellow boots, but at the same time we're saying, look, this place is perfectly safe?

COLONEL HALLORAN: We're also saying that it is quarantined.

SAFER: But there is a — there is a — something that doesn't balance, correct? It's clean, but we must do this?

COLONEL HALLORAN: I think I can probably best answer that by, when we get back to Enewetak, getting the expert out that can talk about it.

SAFER: Okay.

The expert is Roger Ray of the Defense Nuclear Agency. He's assistant manager of the cleanup.

ROGER RAY: There's a lot of material that was not cleaned up on the island of Runit. There is a lot of plutonium still in the near surface and surface soils of Runit. There's a lot of other material that — that is hazardous to man on that island. Why wasn't it cleaned up? Well, because to restore the island of Runit would have required as much soil removal on that one island as was done in the en— entire rest of the project. In order to have cleaned up Runit, the island would have had to have been cut in half. It — it simply would have been too great a task to leave any usable island at the end.

"Contaminated soil from the northern islands was removed bargeload
by bargeload. Tons of radioactive
metal from test towers was gathered
together. One island was needed
to store the waste, and
this one, Runit, was chosen."

SAFER: With all the effort, only three of the southern islands are now free of contami-
nation, and those three never received any radiation in the first place.

Runit, of course, is not one of them, and the loss of one island in an atoll of 40 islands may be no great loss. But what about an island like this one, Enjebi, in the northern half of the atoll? A good number of the Enewetakians regard this island as their homeland. Enjebi, in theory, is absolutely free of plutonium. All radioac-
tive junk plus 6-inches of topsoil have been scraped up and shoved down the crater at Runit. The people of Enjebi want to return to their island and they've been assured that there's nothing they can breathe or touch that will harm them. But in order to have people, you have to have palm trees. Coconuts are both a staple and cash crop here. And they're planting palm trees and, in a couple of years' time, they'll mature. But there is a catch, for beneath me, in this plutonium-free soil, there is still cesium and strontium and one or two other elements that are hazardous to your health. And those new coconuts will be just chock-full of them.

For anyone concerned with what the future of the Enewetakians might be, it's worth diverting for a moment to a similar island people who've gone through a similar experience, the Bikinians, who were moved from their atoll to another refugee island, then, after a cleanup, were allowed in 1968 to return to Bikini. But by 1975, it was clear that their coconuts were high in cesium and strontium and there were traces of plutonium in their bodies, and they were running a high risk of getting cancer. So, for the second time, they were banished from their island and have now become refugees, forever to be wards of the United States.

RAY: Considering the — the knowledge that we had at the time, the — the Bikini cleanup was quite a thorough job. We subsequently learned, as we expected to learn, as the crops matured and became available as part of the diet, we learned that Bikini Island was not suitable for human habitation at this time.

SAFER: And — and you say you knew that was going to happen?

RAY: We knew that we didn't have those answers in the 1969-1970 time frame and —

SAFER: But aren't you going to have the same situation as you had in Bikini when they planted crops and when the fruit appeared it was contaminated?

RAY: Well, I suppose that — that you could construct a scenario that would make that similar, but I think we must recognize that Enewetak is — is different in having clean islands in the south. The people of Enewetak are smart people. I think that if they're told, if they understand, that coconuts grown in the north are — should not become a major part of their diet, they'll have an alternative and they'll use that alternative.

SAFER: But — I agree they're smart people, but are we very smart by encouraging the planting of coconuts there?

RAY: I believe we are, because the people have asked us to do so. And the people have asked us to do so with full knowledge that those coconuts may, at some later time, turn out to be not suitable for human consumption.

SAFER: In effect, the government would be saying to the northern islanders, "Grow coconuts, but don't eat them. Travel 20 miles over open water for uncontaminated fruit." The experience in these islands is that people will eat what grows in their own backyard. You can't help but wonder, if this is the best we can do for only 500 people, what would we do if this was a midwestern city of a million people surrounded, not by a forgiving and cleansing ocean, but by millions of acres of delicately balanced farmland?

Enewetak is part of the soon-to-be independent Marshall Islands. Tony de Brum, the Secretary of State, thinks the cleanup has been a mistake.

TONY DE BRUM: I think that there has been such an investment on the part of the U.S. Congress and everyone that got involved in bringing Enewetak back to life that to admit defeat at this point would be too embarrassing for everyone. The United States' scientists want to make a — a point that they can, indeed, render something safe that was radiologically contaminated.

SAFER: So, the suggestion is the Enewetak cleanup is a kind of public relations program?

DE BRUM: Yes. From the beginning it's — it's been a dog and pony show. Next week they'll be meeting there for a dose-assessment meeting, where people who have had barely more than a third- or fourth-grade education will be presented a set of figures on how much radiation is left on what particular land and what particular community section of Enewetak and they're supposed to make a decision as to whether to proceed with the return in April.

SAFER: Public relations, dog and pony act, sincere belief in helping these people — whatever the purpose, the effort is real. A boatload of scientists, lawyers, people from the Defense Nuclear Agency, the Department of Energy, the Interior Department, translators, land on the island of Ujilang, the temporary home of the Enewetakians. The Americans are all members of something called the Dose Assessment Team. They've come to explain the risks of living on the northern islands. It's only a bit ludicrous. The giant brains of our nuclear establishment handing out statistical results of years of research to people who've never seen an electric light bulb, then telling them it's up to them whether they want to return to land unfit for habitation under American federal standards.

ISLANDER (through translator):   Now the question is: Here it states that the U.S. government has established that a person should not receive more than 500 millirem in one year. Five hundred millirem of what?

WACHOLTZ: Radiation.

ISLANDER (through translator):   Of what kind of radiation?

WACHOLTZ: All types.

ISLANDER (through translator):   All types. These figures tend to be misleading to us, because 500 does not seem like a small amount. If we're counting anything, 500 rocks, gee, you can't even pick them up. And so, these, you say, are small amounts, but to us, to listen and see a figure like that on the board, 500, that throws us.

SAFER: There is an element of research of this. It's useful for us to have these Enewetak people go back. We learn more that way.

RAY: Well, certainly we're interested in pursuing environmental research with this setting, because this is a unique setting. But we are not — I am absolutely confident that we are not introducing man into that setting in order to study man's response to it, or with any recognition that — that — that this is harmful to the men who are — to the people who are being re-introduced. The decisions are decisions for the people, and I believe that — that we have an obligation to help them to become informed so they're the right decisions.

(Sound of a pan being struck)

SAFER: The islanders go off for a private palaver and return with a decision. They want to go home — 500 millirems or no 500 millirems.
(Islanders singing)
Why go through this massive, costly effort in the first place? Why not just do eminent domain, or however big, powerful governments do it, and say, "No. No go. No Bikini, no Enewetak, none of these places. Here's a pocketful of money and we'll settle you wherever else you want to settle"? Why this tortuous business?

RAY: I think that would have been unconscionable to — to say we're not going to try. Remember that we spent billions of dollars making this mess and to now say that we can't spend millions to clean it up would be unpalatable to me.

(Islanders singing)

SAFER: There's something more here than a simple "made to order for television" conflict between the friendly but determined natives and the friendly but devious big power and the random unknowns of science and nature. You get a definite sense of epic forces as you look across the breathtaking expanse of the Pacific Ocean and sky. You understand, perhaps for the first time, our limited vision and the infinite nature of time and distance and the terrible act of creation that took place here.
(Bomb explosion)
It's easy now to say we shouldn't have done it or we shouldn't have done so much of it or should have done it more carefully. But it's been done and there's been nothing in history like the effort that's been made to put things right. That, too, may be wrong, but at least we tried. So, the dome at Runit stands, perhaps as a symbol

and a warning to future tinkerers with nature. And a thousand years from now, when some archeologist stands here and gazes at these works, he may well wonder at this odd structure, if it is, as everyone hopes, still standing. He still, by the way, should carry a surgical mask and rubber boots and should definitely not hang around too long.

Blood Money

MARTIN PHILLIPS, PRODUCER

MIKE WALLACE: "Blood Money" is a look inside the business of raising funds, raising money for certain American civil rights groups, especially the SCLC, the Southern Christian Leadership Conference. Ever since the death of its founder, Dr. Martin Luther King, SCLC has been having a hard time of it financially. Donations have dropped off drastically, and so they get their money where they can. And one source they and other civil rights groups in the past have turned to is a white businessman, a professional fund-raiser by the name of Steven Blood, who headquarters in Los Angeles, California. He is resourceful, energetic; some have called him unprincipled. And be that as it may, he can deliver the goods.

These are the headquarters of Steven Blood and his promotion development associates. Inside his offices and a telephone boiler room, which he would not permit us to photograph, were upwards of 20 telephone salespersons, who raise money on behalf of the Southern Christian Leadership Conference and Steven W. Blood. Ray Cunningham used to work in Blood's boiler room.

How much money is raised out of here?

RAY CUNNINGHAM: My estimation is, from what I have physically seen, about two and a half million dollars.

WALLACE: A year?

CUNNINGHAM: That's correct.

WALLACE: And how much of that goes to SCLC?

CUNNINGHAM: A hundred and fifty thousand dollars.

WALLACE: Two and a half million is raised ostensibly on behalf of SCLC and a hundred and fifty thousand goes to SCLC?

CUNNINGHAM: That's correct.

WALLACE: Well, do the people at SCLC, up top, do they know?

CUNNINGHAM: Yes, they do.

WALLACE: Blood raises this money by selling ads in the SCLC magazine, which he publishes. The salesmen in his telephone boiler room, posing as workers for the Southern Christian Leadership Conference, peddle ads which cost from $295 for this simple listing to $1,500 for this full page. The circulation of the magazine is negligible, perhaps 10,000 coast to coast, but though the advertiser knows his ad will reach virtually nobody, he feels it will get the civil rights group off his back. What he doesn't know is that less than 10 percent of the money that he spends will go to the SCLC.

Well, that piqued our interest and we wanted to talk to Steven Blood about it. At first he confirmed over the telephone what we had learned, but then he refused to take our calls. And when we went to his office to try to talk to him, we were turned away by his burly sales manager, John Jackson.

WALLACE: How are you sir? My name is Wallace. What's yours?

JOHN JACKSON: The camera —

WALLACE: The camera and what?

JACKSON: We talked to you guys about this before, okay? No cameras, please.

WALLACE: All right, we'll go. Can I — we've — we've been trying to get in touch with Mr. Blood.

JACKSON: I gave him the message.

WALLACE: And?

WALLACE: Some weeks later, we were finally able to film the elusive Steven Blood. He is a young man for one so resourceful, so successful, but he has been in trouble for his fund-raising techniques. Back in the late sixties, the State of California succeeded in enjoining him for making false statements to contributors and, indeed, secured an injunction putting him out of business all together — though that injunction was later overturned because it was deemed too broad.

Roy Innis, the head of CORE, the Congress of Racial Equality, on whose activities we reported last fall, Roy Innis used to employ Blood as a fund-raiser for CORE. Here's what he has to say about Steven Blood.

ROY INNIS: Early in the seventies, when we had recently just taken over the administration of CORE and we had failed in our attempts to raise funds, since all the old angels of CORE had left, we were contacted by Steven Blood, who offered to raise funds for us.

WALLACE: How much did he charge you to raise money for you?

INNIS: He first started with the Los Angeles chapter and he charged — charged 90 percent of whatever he raised.

WALLACE: You got a dime, he got 90 cents?

INNIS: No, the Los Angeles chapter. We got wind of it, took the Los Angeles chapter out of the — the contract, signed a new contract with Blood, wherein we took, I think, somewhere around twenty, twenty-five percent. Now, we were very calculating in this case because we did not know the business. We put a man into the business with Blood, we caught him in shenanigans, we bounced Blood, we took over the office and we started fund raising ourselves.

WALLACE: Which you're doing now?

INNIS: Which we're doing now. We then proceeded to inform other civil rights organizations.

WALLACE: Did you inform the SCLC?

INNIS: We informed PUSH and SCLC that Steven Blood is a fund-raising shark, that he is a bandit, and that he is a — a leech on the black community.

WALLACE: Well, wait just a second. One man's leech is another man's shrewd businessman.

INNIS: Steven Blood is a leech. I'm saying we have warned our brothers. There's no reason why Jesse Jackson, Abernathy or Lowery must repeat our mistakes.

WALLACE: Nonetheless, Jesse Jackson, the head man of Operation PUSH, signed a contract with Blood, but cancelled it in embarrassment after just one year because of complaints that Blood's fund-raisers were harassing, strong-arming, double-billing advertising contributors.

THE REVEREND JESSE JACKSON: And since fund raising is such a delicate area and since our credibility is the most important thing to us, we just simply had to re-assess that method and try to expand in other areas.

WALLACE: Now he was getting 90 cents and you were getting 10 cents out of every dollar contributed to PUSH?

REVEREND JACKSON: It — it really came down to that, except that was the cost of operations. And I think it can't be measured just in monetary terms because we also had a communications organ that we had not had before.

WALLACE: Of course, not all the money Blood raises from these communications organs, these magazines, is pure profit. This man, a former associate of Blood who did not want to be identified by name, filled us in on the details. Blood's salesmen get a 30 percent commission on everything they raise. All other overhead − offices, telephone bills, the cost of printing the magazines − comes to another 30 percent, and 30 percent goes to Blood. What's left, less than 10 percent, goes to the civil rights group to which the businessman thinks he is giving the money. Incidentally, Blood's former associate estimates Blood's personal income at over half a million dollars a year.

Joseph Lowery is the head of the Southern Christian Leadership Conference in Atlanta. Most of the SCLC budget is covered by the money that comes in from Steven Blood. We reminded Lowery that that's only a hundred and fifty thousand a year out of the millions donated for ads.

You've had this information for a long time, Dr. Lowery.

DR. JOSEPH LOWERY: Some of it I've had, some of it I've not.

WALLACE: Ray Cunningham has written to you about it.

DR. LOWERY: And his suggestions to me, as I recall (I sent the letter to our attorney to deal with), was that he felt we were not getting a fair shake from Mr. Blood, and that's what we'll look at this year when the co— the contract expires.

WALLACE: If I give a hundred dollars to SCLC through Steven Blood, who represents himself as representing SCLC, have I not reason to believe that a good share of that hundred is going to you, to SCLC?

DR. LOWERY: Mr. Blood has no business soliciting money from you or anybody else, or donations to SCLC. Mr. Blood is authorized to sell advertising for a magazine.

WALLACE: A good many people we've talked to, Dr. Lowery, say, "I'm not advertising in any magazine. I know that it's going into a magazine, but that magazine has no circulation. I'm supporting the Southern Christian Leadership Conference. That's what I'm doing when I give that money, solicited over the telephone by Steven Blood's people." And that makes sense to you, doesn't it?

DR. LOWERY: No, it doesn't make sense to me. I would think that any business that wanted to give money directly to SCLC would know how to do that.

WALLACE: Yeah, but if they're contacted on the phone?

DR. LOWERY: All they have to do is say "No, thanks" —

WALLACE: Oh, but —

DR. LOWERY: — and send the money to SCLC.

WALLACE: And so you would think that they really believe that they're getting proper advertising in a proper magazine?

DR. LOWERY: I don't know what they believe. I'm simply saying that —

WALLACE: Well, there are only 10,000 issues, according to your understanding, circulated in all of the United States.

DR. LOWERY: I'm aware of that, Mr. Wallace. I was trying to respond to your question. I don't know what the businesses believe. But I believe that people who have sense enough to run a business would know whether they want to take out an ad or whether they want to make a donation. We'd be happy to receive their donations.

WALLACE: Dr. Lowery makes it sound too simple, for we learned that Blood fund-raisers many times, in order to sell ads in the *SCLC* magazine, permit an advertiser to believe his ad money actually goes as a donation to the SCLC. That practice is described in an affidavit filed by U.S. Postal authorities in federal court in Los Angeles — an affidavit that charges Blood with "a scheme and artifice to defraud." The charge is currently under investigation. But Blood's lawyers assert that if such tactics are employed by his salesmen, it is without Blood's knowledge and consent. And they point to an agreement his salesmen, as independent contractors, sign as a condition of their employment with Blood, which advises that they must be "forthright and honest in all particulars."

Well, having said that, we wondered why, in view of his history of run-ins with the law, why civil rights groups continue to do business with Steven Blood. To get an answer, we questioned the former head of the Los Angeles chapter of SCLC, Bishop H. Hartford Brookins. Until recently, he was also chairman of Operation PUSH. I asked the Bishop, first of all, why SCLC would settle for a hundred and fifty thousand dollars annually from Blood out of the millions that he raised.

BISHOP H. HARTFORD BROOKINS: Because a hundred and fifty thousand dollars, or 10 percent of something, is better than a hundred fifty percent of nothing. And the fact is, Mike, you must understand the whole civil rights movement.

It — there are no government grants that — that support civil rights groups. A group of volunteers come together with an idea and they try to operate. They must raise bucks wherever they can get them, and when you can pick up ten to fifteen to twenty or thirty thousand dollars to keep an office going and a secretary and a telephone, et cetera, you have struck it rich.

WALLACE: So, if even a Steven Blood comes along and guarantees you $150,000 a year, chances are you'll turn a blind eye to perhaps the tactics that he uses?

BISHOP BROOKINS: Particularly if those — those tactics are not infringing on somebody else's person or property. Corporations have a budget which they give out ads for and they do not always discriminate what they give them to.

WALLACE: It's, in effect, conscience money or protection money or —?

BISHOP BROOKINS: Well, if they're giving out conscience money, then that can be no worse off than Steven Blood getting the conscience money. That's nothing but the story of Robin Hood. (Laughs)

WALLACE: And if it's — and if it's protection money or if it's stay-off-my-back money?

BISHOP BROOKINS: Then I think they're serving a good cause — the funds.

WALLACE: The funds are serving a good cause?

BISHOP BROOKINS: That's right.

WALLACE: And Steven Blood is simply operating in the old American tradition?

BISHOP BROOKINS: On the guilt of the corporation, and that's the American way.

WALLACE: And what about Ray Cunningham, the man who first brought Steven Blood to our attention? Soon after he left the Blood operation he went into business for himself under the name of the NBCF, the National Black Community Fund. He said he wanted to see to it that donations went to the black community, and not into the pockets of white profiteers. But he, too, quickly came under a cloud. Four civil rights leaders on the West Coast sent a letter to Los Angeles D.A. John Van der Kamp asking him to investigate Ray Cunningham. The representatives of SCLC, NAACP and Operation PUSH charged that Cunningham was misleading contributors to believe that he was authorized to accept donations on their behalf, but that he had received permission to do so and that he had never turned over a dime to them. A few weeks later, we sat down with Ray Cunningham and went over those charges.
You sent out letters using their names and you didn't —

CUNNINGHAM: No. We sent out letters of announcement to each one of those agencies prior to making a single contact. We sent a letter to headquarters of NAACP in New York, Benjamin Hooks. We sent a letter to Dr. Lowery. We sent a letter to Reverend Jesse Jackson and all of his people. And the letter followed this up with a phone call, was in the process of —

WALLACE: And did you get any answers back?

CUNNINGHAM: No response.

WALLACE: And yet you went ahead and used their names in your fund-raising letters.

CUNNINGHAM: That's correct.

WALLACE: At that, we introduced a Los Angeles computer businessman who had called us after he had been contacted by one of Ray Cunningham's salesmen. That Cunningham fund-raiser, he told us, had called him for a donation, and when he'd refused, the fund-raiser came up with a brand new tactic.

BUSINESSMAN: He said, "Well, let me explain." He says, "Let me ask you this. Have you ever heard of CBS and 60 MINUTES?" So I said, "Sure." "And Mike Wallace, have you ever heard of that name?" I said, "Of course, he's on 60 MINUTES. I watch it all the time." He said, "Well, they thought enough of us, of the NBCF, to come out. Mike Wallace himself came out from New York, brought a film crew out, and is doing a segment on us which will be shown in October. And that's kind of who we are."

CUNNINGHAM: Let me say this —

WALLACE: Why would you use that?

CUNNINGHAM: I heard this being stated and I called a meeting. I said, "At no time can you call CBS and ask them to verify or endorse what we're trying to do as an organization, because they have no idea what we're doing." We did, in fact, ask you to come write a story, to film a story, about improprieties that we wanted to prove that were occurring in the community.

WALLACE: As far as we can make out, you're doing exactly the same thing that you're accusing Steven Blood of doing.

CUNNINGHAM: Not at all.

WALLACE: You're raising money. You're using pressure tactics. You're using us, ostensibly, Mr. Cunningham, as your seal of approval. You have no programs. You haven't given any money to PUSH, SCLC, NAACP or any of the others. You've acknowledged every bit of this. Again I say it's a case of the pot calling the kettle black.

CUNNINGHAM: No, it's not. We do have programs.

WALLACE: In fact, Cunningham couldn't tell us of any programs that had benefited from his efforts. Nor would he tell us how much money he had raised in the year he'd been in business. He said he didn't have up-to-date records. I asked Ray Cunningham why, if he could give us a reason, why the whole business of raising money for certain civil rights groups seems so tainted.

I get a picture of — forgive me — fraud, misappropriation, misperception of where this money is going.

CUNNINGHAM: That's exactly what's been allowed to occur and it's very unfortunate.

WALLACE: Am I misapprehending when I say that?

CUNNINGHAM: This is what — this is what the general conditions of — of things are presently. It has been for many years.

WALLACE: It's hard to raise a dollar for —

CUNNINGHAM: Right, right. Absolutely.

WALLACE: — for civil rights groups.

CUNNINGHAM: Right. You know why? Because civil rights groups never handled their fund-raising activities themselves. They were always handled on a contractual basis by people outside of the black community who had no interest in the black community whatsoever and could give less than a damn about where the money went.

WALLACE: Ray Cunningham is way off base. The NAACP raises funds without scandal, raises its own money in individual communities, from private donations and from top business corporations. The National Urban League does much the same, raises its own funds from the white business establishment, from foundations and from the federal government.

But as we said, since the death of Martin Luther King, the SCLC has come on hard times and so has made the best bargain it could. And for the moment, that bargain continues to operate. Blood continues to sell ads and raise money for SCLC. He gets 90 cents, they get 10. And a new contract between them has been drawn awaiting only the approval of the SCLC board at its April meeting.

See reply of the National Urban League,
Letters, March 23, 1980, page 419.

Cat Burglars

BROOKE JANIS, PRODUCER

DAN RATHER: The next time you go to the grocery store and find the prices out of sight, or try to rent office space and find it will cost you an arm and a leg, or you find your car-insurance bill keeps going up year after year, it may be that it's not just inflation that is putting a crimp in your pocketbook — because there is a new style of burglar operating all over the country who may also be adding to your cost of living. These burglars are stealing farm and construction equipment and the billions they are getting away with are being passed on to consumers in higher food bills, higher insurance fees and higher rents and construction costs. As we said, it's a nationwide problem, but one of the places where it is most acute is Houston, Texas, where cat burglars — robbers who steal heavy equipment such as Caterpillar bulldozers and tractors and backhoe/loaders — are in the machine-rustling business. Like unbranded cattle, machines are an easy mark.

This is a Case 580C backhoe/loader. One way to start it is simply take something like a knife, or any piece of metal, put it across two posts on the solenoid above the starting engine. (Sound of engine starting up) Presto! It's that easy to start it. But if you don't know that, all you have to know is how easy it is to get keys to these things. Now, one key is said to fit any Ford tractor manufactured over the last 20 years. Two keys — either one of these two — will start just about any piece of Case heavy equipment. But even if you don't have the keys, you could just crawl in and take a penknife. This shows you how easy it is to start one of these things and get away with it; you wouldn't believe it unless you did it yourself. You just take a penknife, put it in the ignition and, presto, you can start it right up — (sound of engine starting up) — and within a matter of just minutes, seconds really, can pull it away and load it up on a truck, be all ready to go.

This back/loader is the most stolen piece of construction equipment in the country. It's worth about $30,000. Also on the most stolen list, wheel loaders, worth about $60,000, or track loaders, $100,000, or this bulldozer, $200,000. And where does a piece of stolen heavy equipment go? Often that depends on whose order is being filled, since this is so much a steal-to-order business. You might be surprised who's giving the orders to thieves like Royce Featherston, who has stolen over a million dollars' worth of heavy equipment.

ROYCE FEATHERSTON: I won't give his name, but he was a professor at one of the universities, had a farm and he wanted a farm tractor. So, he paid such a good price for it, I thought, why go out and go to all the trouble of passing checks when I can steal one piece of equipment and do it all in one week?

RATHER: What was the tractor worth?

FEATHERSTON: Apro—approximately, oh, 12,000 then, tractor and trailer. I turned around and sold it for 4,000 then.

RATHER: Featherston, caught for the second time after stealing five big tractors, is now serving a five-year sentence at Darrington Prison Farm outside Houston. You see, what I find difficult to believe, let me be candid with you —

FEATHERSTON: Surely.

RATHER: — is that a college professor would have anything to do with that kind of operation.

FEATHERSTON: You'd find it harder to believe some of the people that are buying the stuff nowadays besides college professors.

RATHER: Buying stolen goods?

FEATHERSTON: Oh, sure.

RATHER: Well, give me an example.

FEATHERSTON: Chairman of the Board of one of the biggest savings and loans.

RATHER: As in most well-organized rackets of this type, you need a middleman, a fence, literally to move this heavy equipment to its final destination. The middleman buys it from the thief and then resells it at a fraction of its real worth. This man, a veteran fence of 30 years who asked not to be identified, has been dealing almost exclusively in stolen heavy equipment for well over a year now, and is out on bond awaiting trial. He has moved 50 pieces of equipment in one year.

But in round figures, how much would that equipment have been worth, one year's worth, 50 pieces?

FENCE: I'll say $350,000 to me.

RATHER: That, of course, is tax free.

FENCE: I should hope so.

RATHER: The equipment frequently is stolen as part of insurance fraud schemes. An equipment owner might move his bulldozer from one site, deliver it elsewhere or even hide it, then report it stolen, all to collect the insurance. Insurance companies pay claims so quickly in many cases that owners and thieves know it's a quick way to make a buck.

Out of every 50 pieces of equipment stolen, based on your experience, how many would you say were stolen for insurance fraud purposes?

FENCE: I would say probably 50 percent of them. In other words, 25 of the units.

RATHER: That high?

FENCE: Yes.

RATHER: With so much equipment being moved, we asked Royce Featherston how he entered the various sites to do the stealing.

FEATHERSTON: Well, that's no problem. Most places aren't even fenced. If they're fenced, I just cut the fence.

RATHER: But most places have a guard, do they not?

FEATHERSTON: Yes, but you can find out what their op — what their schedule is. They'll come back on their scheduled time, but by then you're — we're gone.

RATHER: Well, you make it sound very easy.

FEATHERSTON: Well, I tell you what, I'd rather be out stealing a piece of equipment than doing this right now.

RATHER: It's easier?

FEATHERSTON: It's easier.

RATHER: Ray Higgins, a construction superintendent in Houston, had a tractor stolen from his job site.

RAY HIGGHINS: We never have recovered it. It's worth about $18,000. We lost another tractor off of the other job one night, trawling machines and everything. The whole complete job was taken, and it was worth 30-some thousand dollars on the whole deal. And we have one more job that we lost a tractor off of. They cut the fence, drove it through the back of the property, and we never have recovered any of this stuff.

RATHER: Since large tractors and bulldozers are so expensive to buy, many users rent them from contractors like Varreece Berry, who told us he has had 10 tractors stolen from him; only two were insured. We asked him how much that loss was worth.

VARREECE BERRY: Probably in the neighborhood of six or seven hundred thousand dollars over a period of time.

RATHER: Six or seven hundred thousand dollars.

BERRY: Total also of machine and down time and production cost. Our cost over the period of time has been raised on rentals probably 10 percent overall in — in our cost of our customers. The customers have to pay that and pass it on. It's just the way the economy is.

RATHER: If your backhoe/loader is stolen here in Houston, there is only one detective in the Houston police department available to track it down for you.

DETECTIVE BOB OLSON: Oh, okay, now that's on the tractor that he recovered out of a Kosse?

RATHER: He is Detective Bob Olson, who has been covering this beat for four years. We went with Olson to a freight depot which was thought to handle stolen equipment. We looked at a tractor awaiting shipment out of the country and asked him if there were a reason to believe it had been stolen.

OLSON: Yes, sir. Myself and some other officers have looked it over and — and all the numbers have been removed.

RATHER: Now, straight talk, do you think this piece of equipment is hot?

OLSON: I would suspicion it to be so.

RATHER: Is there anything else you can do about it?

OLSON: No, sir.

RATHER: Detective Olson can't do anything about his suspicions because, first off, there are no proper serial numbers on this equipment to help him trace the rightful owner. Unlike cars or trucks, serial numbers are not stamped into the metal on all machines. That's why thieves find it so easy to change or remove them. But Olson also can't do anything because there is no paperwork trail, no titling or registration.

OLSON: If you bought a — old '50 — '50-model Chevrolet for, say, fifty to a hundred dollars, you wouldn't consider buying that vehicle if you weren't given a title to it. If that particular vehicle is stolen from you, it's got plates on it, it's rolling down the road, an officer can pick up a microphone in his police car, check the license plates on that vehicle. If a piece of heavy equipment's rolling down the road, the officer has nothing that he can check on.

RATHER: There's no license plate required for it?

OLSON: No license plate, no registration.

RATHER: And that makes recoveries of stolen pieces virtually impossible – only one out of ten, compared with seven out of ten for stolen automobiles and trucks. Sometimes the stolen equipment crosses state lines, but the FBI places little priority on trying to stop it. And sometimes it moves through the port of Houston, bound for countries around the world where it brings a far higher price. A lot of it goes overland from Houston to Mexico.

OLSON: Probably 30 or 40 percent, at least.

RATHER: Do you think it's that high a percentage?

OLSON: I believe it's — that's probably conservative.

RATHER: In a matter of only a few moments, a truck can be loaded and driving out of Houston headed south for the 375 mile ride to the Mexican border near McAllen, Texas. Few police patrol here and there are no truck weigh-in scales to delay the hauler.

So, if this were a stolen backhoe/loader — this particular one isn't — it could move practically unnoticed right down to the border. The Mexican border checkpoint at McAllen, Texas is typical. Keep in mind that it is conservatively estimated that $250 million worth of heavy farm and construction equipment pass into Mexico each year. How much of that is stolen equipment, nobody knows. We do know that a lot of it is and the concern of officials is rising, because it's just so easy to move the big stuff into Mexico. All a trucker need do is fill out an SED — that's a Shipper's Export Declaration. The primary purpose of this is to compile statistics for the Commerce Department. So, a trucker can tell the truth about what he is hauling or he can lie. It is not within the jurisdiction of the U.S. Customs to check it out. So, for the trucker hauling stolen equipment, he can just keep on trucking right on to foreign soil. Now, on the other side is where he could have a problem. The Mexican *Federales* are supposed to check out the equipment. So, how do the thieves deal with the *Federales*?

FENCE: Well, you go through your connections at the border and you make your deals ahead of time. You either pay for it or you trade them merchandise for the favors of moving it in. We carried in four vehicles — three new Broncos and one new four-wheel-drive pickup — and they were already ordered to let the machinery come across.

RATHER: To whom did those vehicles go?

FENCE: Straight to the *Federales*.

RATHER: Now there are some small steps being taken to counter this kind of theft. Lightweight equipment, for example, is sometimes suspended at the end of each day from giant cranes. Security fences, although they don't always work, are being erected. Special locks, so you can't steal that equipment quite so easily, are being tried. And some owners are marking their equipment in more identifiable ways — with decals or individual numbers, or with a special paint job. But so far, nothing seems to work.

In your best year, how many cases have you made?

OLSON: Against the people that have bought it?

RATHER: Yes.

OLSON: Two.

RATHER: Twenty-one million dollars' worth of equipment stolen in one year and you made two cases on the buyers?

OLSON: That's correct.

RATHER: How many cases, in your best year, have you made against the actual thief?

OLSON: About 12.

RATHER: So, what to do about all this theft? Well, it appears that the key to the problem so far is very much like that key used to start up all the same tractors and backhoe/loaders. It is for the convenience of the people doing business, and no one seems to be able to agree on the ideal solution.

One possible remedy, law officers say, is registration. But some manufacturers and contractors resist registration, contending that registration would mean more government control, more bureaucracy and more paperwork. Manufacturers also resist it, lawmen tell us, because registration could mean stricter enforcement of environmental standards as well as letting competitors know just how much equipment they produced and sold every year. Registration would mean, also, that manufacturers could no longer sell, say, a 1980 machine in 1985 as a new model — and at much higher prices — with no one the wiser. As for some of the contractors, under registration they would have to admit to the tax man how much equipment they actually own. All of that would add up to more money out of pocket for the people who make, sell and use this equipment.

So, what is the answer? Well, what one pending congressional bill would do — and all that it would do — is begin a study of ways to combat heavy equipment theft nationwide. But many equipment manufacturers and dealers and users are lobbying hard against that bill and appear to be beating it. Apparently, they fear government and taxes more than they fear the thieves.

Letters

MIKE WALLACE: And now here is the mail. About our story on Oman, several viewers reacted this way: "I see a perfect relationship between Oman and the United States. *Oman* has oil and *we* have arms. So Oman *sells* us oil and we *give* them arms. Did I miss something?"

The mail on our story about Bobby Knight, Indiana's basketball coach and teacher, was huge and showed that most of you either loved him or hated him: "Bobby Knight as a teacher! A teacher of what? Profanity? Uncontrolled temper? Conceit? . . . He was both repulsive and insulting."

And this: "Isn't it awful that a grown man has to stand up . . . (and) curse and blame God for everything. Someone needs to stick a sock in his mouth!"

And this: "To me, he's the Woody Hayes of college basketball coaches."

But Bobby Knight has his equally vocal fans. One woman wrote: . . . "He is a vanishing breed. The day America stops asking her youth to commit themselves and give their all, we are in deep trouble."

Another said this: "If we had some Bobby Knights in Washington, this country might not be in the mess it is in today."

And from Washington, from an Indiana politician: "I . . . happen to agree with his philosophy of hard competition in a fair way. I admire the fact that he's a stickler about not engaging in illegal recruiting and that he insists that all of his athletes acquire an education."

And finally, about our talk with another member of the Congress, Senator Barry Goldwater, a viewer asked: "Why *is* it that politicians make the most sense when they're not *running* for anything?"

MARCH 23, 1980

The Riddle of DMSO

MARION GOLDIN, PRODUCER

MIKE WALLACE: DMSO — 15 years ago news of this potential miracle drug flashed across the medical horizon: dimethyl sulfoxide. It was touted as a pain reliever which would also work miracles on burns, on acne, even on spinal cord injuries; a kind of jack-of-all-trades among drugs. The medical literature was full of stories about it, some of it pro-DMSO, but much of it con, skeptical, even derisive. The *Journal of the American Medical Association* editorialized against it. And the FDA, the Food and Drug Administration, refused to okay it for general use; said it has never been proved effective. Nonetheless, two states, Oregon and Florida, have legalized it for prescription. And the black market in DMSO has become nationwide. That's how many Americans get it. Meantime, the puzzling story of DMSO continues.

It is largely fueled by the efforts of one man, Dr. Stanley Jacob, an associate professor of surgery at the University of Oregon. For 15 years, this man — some would say this zealot — has been pushing DMSO because he believes so deeply, despite the doubters, in what DMSO can do.

Dr. Jacob, isn't a drug that has so many alleged uses from arthritis to tennis elbow, from burns to spinal cord injuries, from mental retardation to baldness. Isn't a drug like that automatically suspect?

DR. STANLEY JACOB: No question. And I think that that's one of the reasons it's having problems. And if I had it to do all over again, maybe the major mistake that I made, Mike, in the beginning was to tell it the way it was. I think if I would have said it was good for a sprained ankle, but only if the ankle sprain were on the left side, DMSO maybe might be approved today.

WALLACE: Because its use is legal in Oregon, patients make the journey to Dr. Jacob's office there almost as if it were a domestic Lourdes. As we've seen, Dr. Jacob treats some of his patients topically for their bruises, their aches and pains; but some others of his patients, some of the most desperate, are young people left paralyzed from auto and motorcycle accidents. These he gives DMSO intravenously to relieve the pressure on their damaged brains, to reduce the swelling in the brain or spinal cord. And sometimes, apparently, he gets dramatic results.

MRS. WEBER: It took the swelling out of the spine, and they told my husband on the

405

phone that I would — I'd probably be in a chair, paralyzed, for the rest of my life. And so, we're really excited with the results.

WALLACE: Another Oregonian, transplanted to Georgia, swears by DMSO. June Jones is second-string quarterback for the Atlanta Falcons. Time was, he says, he could hardly raise his arm to throw a football. He said he'd be out of the game without DMSO.

JUNE JONES: My problem is in my shoulder, so the simple thing for me to do is I just put this on like this.

WALLACE: Just that much, about an inch worth?

JONES: I put about an inch worth, and I'll rub it — rub it all around the area. And I'll just leave it sit — sometimes I put on a little bit more than that —

WALLACE: Uh-hmm.

JONES: —and I'll just let it sit like that for, oh, anywhere from twenty minutes to thirty minutes, fifteen to thirty minutes. And—

WALLACE: Boy, it smells, already!

JONES: Yeah, it — in fact, in about, well, maybe in about five minutes, I'll be able to taste it.

WALLACE: That's one small special characteristic of DMSO — it smells like garlic and tastes like oysters.
But if you took a big whack during a game, let's say, and it was black and blue, you'd rub it on?

JONES: Oh, yeah. I do this more when I — when I play basketball in the off-season. Sometimes you get kneed in a — in a charley horse.

WALLACE: Yeah.

JONES: Boy, I tell you, those things are painful for days.

WALLACE: Right.

JONES: I put it on right after, and I may not have any pain the next day at all.

WALLACE: Jones says several of his teammates use it too, but they wouldn't talk about it in public, because talk of any drug, especially an illegal drug, is verboten in the NFL.

JONES: In our business, availability is the most important thing. In other words, if a guy gets hurt, he's— he could lose his job. So, when someone comes to me and asks for — me for it, I give it to them. And — whether I'm legally okay to do that or not, I really don't care, the repercussions, because I know I'm going to help somebody.

WALLACE: Perhaps more typical of the legions who depend on DMSO are those who suffer chronic pain. Emily Rudich suffered searing, unrelenting pain from arthritis for years, and she could find no relief, she says, until DMSO. She'd no longer be playing the piano without it, she told us.

EMILY RUDICH: I have some very badly gnarled fingers from arthritis, and the DMSO eases the arthritis right away. It's not a miracle drug, doesn't really cure it, but it eases it.

WALLACE: And it does other things for her too.

RUDICH: I had a fever blister on my lip. I used DMSO three times, and the fever blister went away immediately. I've cut myself in the kitchen, and sometimes quite badly, and have used DMSO on it and the cuts begin to heal right away.

WALLACE: How does DMSO work? What does it do inside your body that kills pain and helps healing? Dr. Jacob gave us a capsule understanding.

DR. JACOB: One is that it blocks certain types of nerve conduction. These are the fibers which produce pain. Second, it reduces inflammation or swelling. Third, it actually improves blood supply to an area of injury. Fourth — and this could be the key — in the test tube in certain types of injury, it literally stimulates healing.

WALLACE: But is it safe to use? We put that question to Dr. Richard Crout, head of the Bureau of Drugs of the Food and Drug Administration.

How many people have died from using DMSO? How many that you know have gotten ill from using it?

DR. RICHARD CROUT: Nobody's died from using DMSO. It— it's— it's a relatively safe drug, as— as drugs go.

WALLACE: Uh-hmm.

DR. CROUT: It— it causes skin rash where it's put on, or at least redness of the skin. It's caused hives in a few people. May cause headache, nausea, in some people who use it. And it rather routinely imparts a garlic odor to the breath. So it's got side effects that are not entirely pleasant, but it's not been a toxic drug.

WALLACE: It's a safe drug, comparatively safe drug, you would say?

DR. CROUT: Com— comparatively, yes.

WALLACE: So, we come back to the controversy that began fifteen years ago. Dr. Crout insists that, despite these anecdotes, neither Dr. Jacob nor any other scientist has ever really proved that DMSO is effective. They've never proved scientifically that it works for anything other than a rare bladder disease called interstitial cystitis.

DR. CROUT: I think people are— are rooting for the drug, in a sense, rooting for the investigators to come through, give us some — give us the right kind of evidence that stands up under scientific scrutiny.

WALLACE: Well—

DR. CROUT: And that's — that's how simple it is with DMSO.

WALLACE: So, I put a sampling of apparently credible scientific evidence before Dr. Crout.

Are you familiar with "Dimethyl Sulfoxide in Muscular Skeletal Disorders" — *Journal of American Medical Association?*

DR. CROUT: Yes.

WALLACE: "Topical Pharmacology and Toxicology of DMSO" – *Journal of American Medical Association.*

DR. CROUT: Correct. Right. Uh-hmm.

WALLACE: "A Double-Blind Clinical Study" – "for Acute Injuries and Inflammations" – *Current Therapeutic Research.*

DR. CROUT: Yes.

WALLACE: "Treatment of Aerotitis and Aerosinusitis with Topical DMSO." An entire book on the subject of dimethyl sulfoxide by D. Martin and H.G. Hauthal. So it's not as though this is some quack remedy that a few people have used and swear by. There is a considerable body of scientific investigation undertaken –

DR. CROUT: That's right, with some very key holes in that body of evidence.

WALLACE: And that – and those key holes are?

DR. CROUT: Controlled trials demonstrating that it really works for some of the claims that it's — that it's touted for.

WALLACE: But controlled trials with DMSO are difficult, because that would involve something called "double-blind" tests, where neither patient nor investigator knows who is getting a drug, who is getting a placebo. And that can't be done with DMSO, because the smell of the drug gives it away. What the FDA says is needed is proper testing, and that, for instance, is to treat comparable groups of patients with and without the drug over a long enough time to evaluate its consequences, good or bad. And this, say the doubters in the medical establishment, has just not been done with DMSO.
The National Academy of Sciences, you know, looked over a lot of the work that has been published about DMSO, right?

DR. JACOB: Yes, they did.

WALLACE: And the National Academy of Science's committee said, in effect, that only a few were scientifically sound, that most of the DMSO studies had been inadequately set up and carried out.

DR. JACOB: I don't agree with that conclusion, because I personally have published several dozen articles on DMSO, and I've been associated with two New York Academy of Sciences symposia. There was no one on that committee, Mike, who had actually ever treated a patient with DMSO, to my knowledge—

WALLACE: Uh-hmm.

DR. JACOB: —and I think that that makes a difference.

WALLACE: This young mother, Sandy Sherrick of Riverside, California, suffered severe whiplash and nerve damage in an automobile accident two years ago. When we first met her last November, she was in agony. No pain-killer, no therapy, no doctor, it seemed, could help.

SANDY SHERRICK: Oh, the pain was extremely bad. I was to the point where I cried continuously. I did not cook meals. I did not clean. I barely got myself dressed.

WALLACE: And this went on for how long?

SHERRICK: Months. They finally got to the point where they just told me, "You're going to have to live with it. The weather's going to affect you, and you're just simply going to have to live with it."

WALLACE: Then she heard about DMSO. And as a last resort, Sandy Sherrick – as you can see, still very much in pain – flew to Portland, Oregon, to be treated by Dr. Jacob. We went with her. She received her first dosages intravenously.

DR. JACOB: This will run in about an hour, an hour and a half . . .

SHERRICK: I can taste it.

DR. JACOB: You can taste it?

SHERRICK: Yes.

DR. JACOB: Ready? Don't be too disappointed if, after the first intravenous, you're not significantly improved.

SHERRICK: Okay.

DR. JACOB: Okay? Let's just see what happens.

WALLACE: Twenty-four hours later, there was no real improvement. Besides, she had become nauseous from the treatment.

DR. JACOB: Bend it to one side, and bend it to the other. Now, do you have any more mobility, or about the same mobility?

SHERRICK: I think about the same.

WALLACE: By the third day, she was feeling a little better. You began to see it in her face.

SHERRICK: Well, I didn't have to take any more medicine.

DR. JACOB: How long has it been since you haven't had to take medicine?

SHERRICK: Over two years.

WALLACE: Before she left for home, Dr. Jacob showed her where and how to apply DMSO topically to her neck and back.

DR. JACOB: Now, when you put it on, don't rub it too hard. You just have to apply it to the skin and it goes in. Let it dry over twenty minutes to a half an hour. It won't be totally dry, but anything left you can just wipe off.

WALLACE: That was last November. This is Sandy Sherrick two months later back at her Riverside, California, home.

SHERRICK: Oh, the pain's gone. The pain is totally, completely gone from my neck.

WALLACE: You — you're serious?

SHERRICK: I'm telling the truth, the honest to God truth.

WALLACE: You can do anything? Can you do housework?

SHERRICK: Yes, I can.

WALLACE: Drive a car?

SHERRICK: Yes.

WALLACE: Lift stuff?

SHERRICK: I have not found anything I can't do.

WALLACE: We asked Dr. Jacob to come on down and take another look at you and to talk to you and us together. Okay?

SHERRICK: Okay.

DR. JACOB: Now, could you bend your head to the left side? Any discomfort?

SHERRICK: None.

DR. JACOB: Okay, now how about to the right side? Any discomfort?

SHERRICK: No.

WALLACE: Sandy, if you had done this three months ago, four months ago, what would have happened?

SHERRICK: I would have been in pain. He wouldn't have been able to touch me.

WALLACE: When a woman has been in pain for two years, and has an injection of, or topical application of, DMSO and suddenly a miracle happens; when a quarterback for the Atlanta Falcons has been using it off and on for years, and says, "I swear by— I'm telling you my arm is better— I throw faster, straighter, better"; when you get testimonial after testimonial, I ask you, what's wrong with those testimonials?

DR. CROUT: Nothing's wrong with them. They may be right. But they don't get the— the— they don't provide the scientific evidence that's necessary for acceptance by scientists.

WALLACE: It's not just the FDA that's skeptical, not just the medical establishment; the drug companies don't have much enthusiasm for DMSO, either. Why? Jacob and others say it's because DMSO is a common chemical solvent that can be manufactured for four dollars a quart, on which no drug company can get an exclusive patent; therefore, there is not big financial return available.

Did an executive of a major drug company really tell you, Dr. Jacob, "I don't care if it" – DMSO – "is the major drug of our century, and we all know it is, it isn't worth it to us?"

"It's not just the FDA that's skeptical, not just the medical establishment; the drug companies don't have much enthusiasm for DMSO, either."

DR. JACOB: I was told that if DMSO were approved, it would be competitive, and — and they didn't hold the patents. Yes, I was told that.

WALLACE: And you will not tell us—

DR. JACOB: I — I would not tell you the — the name of the drug company or the individual.

WALLACE: Why?

DR. JACOB: That's the only question I will not — I will not answer. I'll answer any other question.

DR. CROUT: I think it's a fact of life that drug companies are not going to invest in something unless they think there is some financial return.

WALLACE: But we come back to the main reason for the FDA's objection to DMSO – that a story like Sandy Sherrick's doesn't take the place of a scientific test.

SHERRICK: Well, that's fine. I can understand their feeling. But they've got to be able to look at the test results and take me as an individual. I have no reason to say it does work or it doesn't. All I can say is what it's done for me personally. It worked for me.

WALLACE: Two footnotes. DMSO is now available for treatment of assorted ailments in Western Europe, the Soviet Union, Japan and Latin America. And tomorrow morning in Washington, the House Committee on Aging begins an inquiry into why DMSO is not available to all Americans for any appropriate ailment, including plain and simple pain.

See Update, April 6, 1980, page 452.

Jarrett vs. Jarrett

JIM JACKSON, PRODUCER

MORLEY SAFER: *Kramer vs. Kramer* is one of the most talked about movies around. The film deals with perhaps the most painful problem any family can go through — divorce and child custody. *Kramer vs. Kramer* has been nominated for nine Academy Awards. But in life, they do not hand out awards. Take the case of Jarrett versus Jarrett. It is about a couple who came apart, settled the question of child custody; and then something happened, something that brought the courts in, might bring the Supreme Court in. At the heart of this story is American morality, but really at the heart of it, of course, are the children.

Jacqueline Jarrett is a 36-year-old divorced woman who lives in a suburb of Chicago. She's the mother of three, has a full-time job, and keeps house with Wayne Hammond, who is 29, a quality controller. They are not married. Except for that missing marriage certificate, they appear to be another suburban couple.

JACQUELINE JARRETT: We are no different than most people that are married, except that we don't have that piece of paper. We have a very good, close, intimate relationship with my children. We are open and honest with them, and we communicate with them. And we listen to what they have to say, because we care about what they have to say, what they think, and what they feel.

SAFER: Three key people you will not meet in this story are the three Jarrett children, the girls, aged ten, thirteen and fifteen. Their father requested that they not appear. Their father, Walter Jarrett, has custody of them. Father and daughters live just eight blocks away from Wayne and Jacqueline. He's a 43-year-old chemist, and he is a devout Roman Catholic. Four years ago, when he and Jacqueline were divorced, he agreed to let her have the children. But when Wayne Hammond moved in with her, Walter Jarrett sued for custody on grounds of her alleged immorality, and he won.

Mr. Jarrett, why did you sue to gain custody of your children?

WALTER JARRETT: I did it because I felt that when their mother had Mr. Hammond move into the house to live with her, that it created an improper moral environment for my daughters to be raised in. That is really the— the whole basis for it.

SAFER: It was as simple as that?

WALTER JARRETT: Yes.

JACQUELINE JARRETT: For myself, I don't feel that what Wayne and I are doing is harmful. I don't feel it's wrong. And if I did feel that way, I certainly wouldn't do it.

WAYNE HAMMOND: Over marriage, we choose to live together. And we feel that we're free to make that choice as adults, as long as we're not harming anyone. And what we're saying is we are not causing any harm. And the courts have never looked at our total environment to see is it a fit environment for those children to be raised in.

SAFER: Now, Mount Prospect, Illinois, is no Malibu Beach, and Jarrett versus Jarrett is not Marvin versus Marvin, but the Jarretts are the center of a legal battle that could have national implications. For the Illinois Supreme Court ruled that, while Mrs. Jarrett is a perfectly fit mother, she lives in an immoral manner that might corrupt the lives of her three daughters. The case of Jarrett versus Jarrett could affect the lives of millions of Americans who regard a living arrangment as none of the court's business, and lives of millions more who think there is only one moral code, a code that can be reduced to the simple phrase, "Not in front of the children."

The court ruled that this was not a fit house in which to raise your children.

JACQUELINE JARRETT: They didn't use the word "wasn't fit." I've never been found to be unfit.

SAFER: That's not what I said. A fit household, not an unfit mother.

HAMMOND: There was no evidence introduced whatsoever to show that our environment had any type of adverse affect on the children. None whatsoever.

JACQUELINE JARRETT: See, when we went into court, we were told by two attorneys that the burden of proof was on my ex-husband. That's the law. He has to show detrimental harm to the children. We went into court believing that there was no harm. He had no evidence, no proof, of any harm to the children. Therefore, the worst that could possibly happen would be that the judge would give us an option, give me an option: "Mrs. Jarrett, I don't like the way you're living. The court does not condone your actions. You either get married or you have the man move out." Two attorneys told me that, that the worst that would happen would be that we would be given an option. I never ever went into court believing they would take my children, because I feel that what we are doing is not wrong and it in no way harms my children. I had talked to my children, and I — I've even said to may children, I said, "Do — do you feel that, by my living with Wayne, not being married, that I'm telling you to do the same thing?" No, they don't, because they know that I want them to grow up and have a mind of their own, to grow up and make their own decisions based on what is right for them.

SAFER: Do you regard the manner in which Jacqueline lives, your ex-wife lives, as living in sin?

WALTER JARRETT: I would consider that to be so, for me, yes.

SAFER: What about that relationship? What was going on there that bothered you — and I know it really did — about the girls living there?

WALTER JARRETT: Uh-hmm. All right, I — I think that that's — their mother is their — is their model, all right? She's their role model. You can tell a child most anything, give them any kind of verbal instructions. What they see you do is what makes the most lasting and the deepest impression on them. So, even though she may like to take another approach to it or deny that she's training them, I think just the very fact that she lives in this particular manner is — is training them by her example.

SAFER: Do you question her commitment, her love, her fitness to be a mother?

WALTER JARRETT: No, I don't have any reason to do that, no. I think she— she cares for the children, certainly. She loves the children. I— I think that perhaps, for whatever reason, she has come to think more in terms of what is best for herself first, and then what is best for others secondly.

SAFER: No case like this one is without its hired guns, the lawyers. One, for the purposes of this case, takes on the mantle of great moral outrage. The other, for the purposes of this case, takes on the mantle of the new morality. And you can't help but feel that both could switch mantles with equal ease. Anyway, in Mr. Jarrett's corner, Arthur Solomon.

ARTHUR SOLOMON: I suggest that the conventional morality of most of the people in this country is still against the way of life Mrs. Jarrett has chosen for herself and her children.

SAFER: In Mrs. Jarrett's corner, Michael Minton.

MICHAEL MINTON: Jacqueline Jarrett wants her children back. She and I feel that she's going to get them back, but she's not going to be required to marry Wayne Hammond in order to continue being a custodial mother.

SOLOMON: The court decides disputes brought to it, brought to it in this case by a sincere father who's troubled about the well-being of his children. They have to decide that dispute. We can't shoot it out on the village green. And they have to decide it according to some standards, and the standards they selected are objective statutory and community standards. They're not the subjective bias of this court. They're standards that most people agree on in this country.

SAFER: "Not in front of the children."

SOLOMON: "Not in front of the children." I'm not sure I want my children to watch me prepare my income tax return and see what compromises I might make, because I teach them to be honest and upright. Not that there's anything wrong with my income tax return—

SAFER: I'm sure.

SOLOMON: —but we all have things — we speak differently in front of our children. We might watch our language, we might behave in many ways differently. And it's not unusual for the court then to demand that a custodial parent act in the way we all believe we have to act in front of our children. You don't have your boyfriend living in the house with three girls. And that is all the court announced in agreeing with Mr. Jarrett.

SAFER: But what the court has done here has— it has stepped in and made a moral judgment. It did not make a legal judgment, did it? It made a moral judgment.

SOLOMON: No, it made— it made a legal judgment, which included within it a moral judgment, because it enforced a statute in this state that says that the court may change custody if it finds that the physical, moral, emotional, psychological well-being of the children is endangered. And the legislature used the word "moral." In a dispute between the father and mother, the state had to resolve that dispute, the court had to resolve it. The statute said that morality was one of the factors it should take into account.

MINTON: The Jarrett case stands for the proposition that if you're one of 20-million single parents in this country, or you happen to be one of the 11 million children of these single parents, and you choose to live with a person of the opposite sex for any reason whatsoever, be it social, economic, physical, psychological, you're going to lose custody of those children unless you marry that person. Now, this is marriage by edict. It has no place in the annals of legal history. It never has, and it never should be.

SAFER: But does she want to make a civil rights case out of this, or does she simply want her children?

MINTON: Jacqueline wants to keep her children, but she does not feel that a court should order her to get married as a qualification for keeping her children. She and Wayne have talked about marriage, but marriage is a very fundamental right; and on the other side of that coin, there's a fundamental right not to marry. Why the court is focusing on this type of conduct is questionable. In this state, if Jacqueline Jarrett were a bank robber, a drug addict, an alcoholic, a tax evader, that conduct in and of itself, without proof of harm to the children, would not be enough to take custody away from her. It would only be one factor among many for the court to look at. But if she lives with someone, that and that alone is used as a basis for not calling her unfit but at the same time saying that you cannot continue to be a mother to your children.

SAFER: If your children were so important to you, if you were putting them first and not yourself first—

JACQUELINE JARRETT: Uh-hmm.

SAFER: —if you weren't being selfish, you could have gotten married.

JACQUELINE JARRETT: At that time, I was— I couldn't have gotten married. Emotionally and mentally, I could not have gotten married. I— especially under force.

SAFER: And today?

JACQUELINE JARRETT: Under— it would be very difficult to get married under force.

SAFER: Even for the sake of your children?

JACQUELINE JARRETT: It's not that cut-and-dry. Where is my guarantee that if I go back into court as a married woman, that they will— that a judge will give me back my children?

SOLOMON: Mr. Hammond and Mrs. Jarrett came into court saying we live together, we're unmarried, we have no intention of being married, and they threw it in the face of the community to approve this. They said we do not believe your standards have any validity, and we are challenging them. And it was that frontal attack on what is still the majority view about the way children should live that brought this court down on Mrs. Jarrett in such an apparently absolute manner. They— they gave the court no out. They would make no concession to what most of the people in this country — not just in Mount Prospect, Illinois, but in the United States — believe about how you raise children. Many people live together in this country; very few of them live together with children.

MINTON: Why have they started legislating morality? Why don't they stick to questions of law and fact, and leave questions of morality to the theologians?

JACQUELINE JARRETT: Wayne and I would not continue fighting this if my children did not want to come back. I could not force my children to live here if they didn't want to.

SAFER: You want to take this case to the Supreme Court of the United States?

JACQUELINE JARRETT: Yes.

SAFER: If you had those justices of the Supreme Court behind that camera right now —

JACQUELINE JARRETT: Uh-hmm.

SAFER: —what do you say to them?

JACQUELINE JARRETT: Give me my children back.

Libya's Qaddafi

WILLIAM K. McCLURE, PRODUCER

HARRY REASONER: Of all the Arab nations, Libya uses its oil as a political weapon more than any other, and on April first that nation will cut its production by almost twenty percent. In this case the cut, ordered by Libya's dictator, Muammar el-Qaddafi, may be more economic than political. Libyan oil, high-priced and high-quality, is for the moment in oversupply. That could change quickly. What won't change quickly is the fact that Qaddafi's Libyan oil fields are the world's ninth largest producer, and account for about eight percent of America's imported oil. So, Libya's Qaddafi is a man to be reckoned with.

(Cheering at meeting of Libya's Revolutionary Congress)

If you had to describe the public perception of Qaddafi by his people, you might think "guru." He has the right combination in his face: a strong and asymmetric handsomeness, like the anti-hero movie stars of the sixties and seventies, along with a persistent withdrawal or contemplation in the eyes, an implied asceticism. He usually gives the impression of being quieter than those around him, especially when the people around him are revolutionary committees, an elite, almost a group of commissars, who keep track of the purity of the revolution, his revolution. He holds no public office; gurus don't have to. Perhaps he sees himself as a combination of Gandhi and Mao Tse-tung.

The Gandhi part is his contention that government and political parties are just ways to cheat people. Government, he says, will wither away, and committees of the people will decide on what is best for them. His role? He is a teacher. Like Mao Tse-tung, he has compiled his thinking into a *Green Book* — actually, a *Green Book* parts one, two and three. It is the "Third Universal Theory" — a blending of the Koran and Qaddafi's own brooding thoughts. The result is something the Libyans call the Jamahirya — the state of the masses. So far, the Jamahirya is mostly an extension of Qaddafi's will, an attempt to reshape the Libyan consciousness in the form of his vision.

His vision is one thing; this is the reality — 2,500 tanks, Russian-built and accompanied by five to six thousand Russian advisors. Qaddafi has spread arms and training money to rebel groups in many African countries. To this parade on the tenth anniversary of his bloodless coup d'etat, September 1st, 1969, Qaddafi invited Syria's Assad, Jordan's Hussein, and Yasir Arafat, even though soon after he withdrew Libya's large subsidy to Arafat's Al Fatah, the most moderate element of the PLO. The most prominent American guest was Billy Carter, who worked briefly for Libya as a consultant. His military equipment, billions of dollars' worth, was there, more than Libya has trained people to operate. Even some of their jet fighters, which we could not photograph, are flown by North Koreans.

Libya is Mediterranean, rather than African. It is surrounded by poorer, more conventional Arab neighbors: Algeria, Tunisia, Sadat's Egypt, which Qaddafi considers an enemy. It is ninety-nine percent sand, not arable in its natural state, except the strip along the sea. For its two and one-half million people, it is huge. You could fit three states of Texas inside its borders.

To find Qaddafi, if you have been invited to see him, you may have to go out into the fields beyond Benghazi to where he prays outside a tent, a tent sort of like those of his Bedouin ancestors, where, you are told, he likes to go to keep away from the corruption of cities and to be in touch with his spiritual roots.

(Qaddafi praying)

In the tent, you hear in his gentle voice the most vicious position on Israel, for instance, of any Arab leader. Any Jew who came to Palestine since 1948, he says, must go away.

MUAMMAR EL-QADDAFI: This is only the way for peace. And without peace, the war is compulsory solution in this area.

REASONER: There's no compromise on this?

QADDAFI: I don't think so.

REASONER: I believe that Libya issued a statement disapproving in general of the taking of hostages in an embassy, but you support the Iranians otherwise. If you were President Carter, what would you do about the hostage situation?

QADDAFI: I consider the behavior of President Carter is good, because he controlled himself. But I am against the concentrating the American fleets and arms around Iran. We consider it as if America declared the war against Iran silently. And from the side, I see the situation is serious. But you must be sure if any aggression takes place in future against Iran, we will be a part of this war.

REASONER: Qaddafi's fierceness has been so far mostly verbal, but the equipment to fight such a war is still arriving at the docks of Benghazi. We were not invited to photograph this ominous cargo, but we established they were Russian-built ground-to-ground missiles. To us, the Libyans preferred to emphasize other aspects of their prosperity.

Libya, say the pamphlets of the Department of Information, is booming, and it is. The oil money is fueling heavy activity in commerce, in housing, in industrialization — a better life for people who just 25 years ago were listed as the poorest in the world. A disproportionate share may be going for arms, but the ordinary citizen is seeing a lot of it too. There is practically no unemployment in Libya, and while imported goods are expensive, Libyan wages are five to ten times as high for similar jobs as in Malta or Egypt, which explains why Libya has no difficulty in importing one million foreign workers — Maltese, Egyptian, Palestinian. This is a new idea of Qaddafi's — modern supermarkets. He hopes they will replace the ancient tangled bazaars. To help, these government-owned and subsidized stores are, on an average, forty percent cheaper than the bazaar shops in old Tripoli.

(Music)

The most omnipresent feature of Libyan urban geography is Qaddafi. His portraits are everywhere, another layer in the long and complex culture of Libya that begins with statues the Romans left behind.

This kind of thing never moves evenly. Qaddafi says every Libyan is entitled to a car, and all day long you get the feeling they already all have one. And they are ordering more, in spite of the fact that cars in Libya cost about twice what they do most places. These cars are a symbol of progress, maybe. In any event, no one rides a camel any more.

Another radical plank in Qaddafi's philosophy is that every Libyan is entitled to a house, but no Libyan is entitled to more than one. The government will help you to buy your home if you have been a renter, or will build you one if you never had one. It's great for the construction industry. This apartment project was designed and built by Italians. When Qaddafi took power, he threw out 60,000 Italians who had stayed on after the former colony became independent. Some of them have since been hired back as contract workers.

The money flows like a light, all-weather oil. This hospital, for instance, more modern than many in Western Europe or America. There's free medical service for all.

And a quarter of a billion dollars for Tripoli's international airport, also designed and built by Italians. No stinting anywhere. Qaddafi provides practically unlimited money for education. This university, built by the British, is in the second city, Benghazi. The country's street signs and all advertisements are in Arabic, but a large part of the university curriculum is taught in English. Arabic texts are not yet available.

Have all these social reforms and development programs made Qaddafi loved by all Libyans? No, there are many anti-Qaddafi Libyans, but most are outside Libya in a resistance movement against him. They told us Qaddafi was a military dictator who takes away the people's freedom and confiscates private property; that while he shows off his humble life in a desert tent, he does not show us his four villas and his multimillion-dollar yacht. The dissidents say he does not live a true Islamic life. He violates the Koran by killing his opponents. They also say when the oil runs out, Libya will return to the poverty of the early fifties, without even any significant upgrading of its agriculture. We found evidence the dissidents are wrong in the case of agriculture.

We went to the Province of Fezzan in the heart of the Sahara a thousand miles south of Tripoli. Here, while attending high school, Qaddafi began to dream and plan his revolution. We found a farmer who may not be typical but is certainly happy. His local people's committee helped him get twelve and a half acres and water. His obligation — to do a good job of farming. On that condition, he can keep his profits. With the farm as a grant goes a house, a car, camels for milk and meat. He also gets a tractor, and for a while a yearly salary. Understandably, he supports the Qaddafi revolution.

The American presence used to be big jets at Wheelus Air Force Base. In 1970, Qaddafi threw them out. But now there is a kind of truce, a marriage of convenience. These are American pilots hired on contract to fly crop dusters. Like many other Americans, they aren't very happy in Libya, with restrictions on their movements and the absence of alcohol, but they are there, not flying military missions but buzzing the oat and barley fields.

And the oil business, the source of Qaddafi's wealth and his arms and his influence, has still a definite American complexion at management levels, and foreign workers at all levels. Libya was the first to increase oil prices, the first to get American companies to give the host nation a larger share of profits. Qaddafi was the first to use oil as a weapon and a threat. In spite of all that, the Americans who helped Libya find and develop its oil are still there. The boss of this concession is Charles Douglas of Occidental Petroleum, who is very candid about why the two nationalities need each other.

CHARLES DOUGLAS: It's — the money is good, and that's the name of the game, whether we like it or not, is — is money.

REASONER: But the game has turned ugly. This is the American Embassy in Tripoli, burned out in the wave of violence that hit the Moslem world after the Iranians seized the embassy and hostages in Teheran. Qaddafi did little to prevent the troubles in Tripoli. This symbolizes his ambivalence toward the United States. He resents the embargo that keeps him from getting American military-related equipment. Qaddafi says we have put Libya on a blacklist, and he constantly threatens to turn off the oil.

QADDAFI: This good policy towards America will not be permanent and will not go longer if America still acts against us as enemy and put us in the blacklist.

REASONER: It might affect Libya's willingness to sell oil to the United States?

QADDAFI: Yes, of course.

REASONER: Like a prince out of the *Arabian Nights,* Qaddafi rides off, leaving behind the question: At what point can the United States afford to antagonize any man who sits on top of that much oil?

A Few Minutes
with Andy Rooney

HARRY REASONER: Tonight, Andy Rooney, looks at some of the signs of the times, and doesn't much like what he sees.

ANDY ROONEY: Someone's always trying to push us around with the signs they put up, aren't they? I mean, what's your reaction when you come up against this sign? (KEEP OUT) Even if I don't want to go in, my reaction is always: The hell with you, fella, I'm comin' in! I think most of us have some kind of reaction to every sign we see that isn't what the people who put up the sign intended us to have. For instance, when I see this one (NO PARKING AT ANY TIME. VIOLATORS WILL BE TOWED AWAY AT OWNER'S EXPENSE) I figure they're bluffing. They've had the sign up for nine years and haven't towed away anyone yet. A lot of signs try to scare you into not doing something. (NO TRESPASSING. WARNING: TRESPAS-SERS WILL BE PUNISHED . . .) Or maybe they'll suggest you're going to get bit. (BEWARE OF DOG) Some signs are very polite. For instance, they'll try to sweet-talk you into not smoking. (THANK YOU FOR NOT SMOKING) Some are more direct. (SMOKING NOT PERMITTED) Some get tougher. (POSITIVELY NO SMOKING) But has any kid ever not done anything by order of the Board of Education? (NO SMOKING – BY ORDER OF THE BOARD OF EDUCATION . . .) Schools have a special, irritating way with signs. This one pretends to be friendly (WELCOME TO OUR SCHOOLS . . . NO . . .) but look at all the stuff you can't do. Any kid reading this never would have thought of playing lacrosse on Sunday until he saw the sign. I don't care much for signs with pictures of things on them. "Deer Crossing," "Cattle Crossing." By the time I've figured out what it is a picture of, I'm past it. I like signs there's no doubt about. I mean, this could only have one meaning. (IN) This is a big new seller for people who make signs. (NO RIGHT TURN ON RED) We passed a law saying you could turn right on red, now we're putting signs up everywhere saying "Except here." I always figure this one means, "It's a shortcut, but they don't want you to go that way." (NO THRU TRAFFIC) And this is an exit, but they don't want you to go out this way. (NO EXIT) There are a few signs you don't fool around with. (RADIATION) I mean, if you really didn't want anybody walking on your grass, this might be the one to put up. A lot of signs are put up too late, of course. Usually by the time anyone puts this one up, people have been dumping there for ten years. (NO DUMPING ALLOWED) You know some signs don't really mean it. (SPEED LIMIT 5) I mean, there is no five miles an hour. The fact of the matter is, most of us don't like to be told anything by a sign.

Letters

MIKE WALLACE: And now, the mail. About our story on the West Coast fund-raiser who solicits advertising on behalf of the Southern Christian Leadership Conference and keeps up to 90 percent of what he raises for expenses and profit, we heard from the head of the National Urban League, who acknowledged that we had reported that his civil rights organization raises its own funds, but didn't think we had said it strongly enough. He wrote: "(You) failed to correct the very strong impression that all civil rights organizations are involved with such fund-raisers . . . The National Urban League raises its own funds (and) expenses for these fund-raising activities amount to only six percent of total income."

We would also like to re-emphasize that the NAACP is not in any way involved with a fund-raiser like the one we reported on. They raise their own funds.

We also heard from the SCLC. One of their regional vice presidents said that after our story he hoped there would be righteous indignation in the black community, and he went on: "Perhaps black America will put its money where its mouth is and support those civil rights organizations which have a history of helping people."

Finally, about our story on the people of Enewetak in the Pacific who voted to return to their island despite the danger of lingering radiation from nuclear testing some 30 years ago, the President has now signed into law a bill to provide health checkups and continuing inspection of food grown on those islands. One of the attorneys representing the islanders wrote: "In arriving at the unanimous decision to resettle Enjebi, the people of Enewetak obtained independent advice from three of the world's leading scientists . . . You left . . . the impression that the people of Enewetak (were) ill-advised."

MARCH 30, 1980

Looking Out
for Mrs. Berwid

NORMAN GORIN, PRODUCER

MORLEY SAFER: This is about murder — murder that could have easily been prevented. While the appropriate institutions were looking to help the potential murderer, Adam Berwid, who was looking out for Mrs. Berwid, the potential victim?

Eleven years ago, Adam and Ewa Berwid emigrated to the suburbs of New York from Poland. Both were engineers and both found good jobs. Adam Berwid found the adjustment to America difficult. His wife did not. She soon was earning more money than he was. He became resentful, abusive. She sued for divorce. A family court ordered him to stay away from her. He didn't. But it was all much more than domestic squabbling. Adam Berwid was insane, committable. But because there was so much pressure to return Mr. Berwid to society, looking out for Mrs. Berwid seemed to be the last consideration.

This was not a happy home. Relations between Adam and Ewa Berwid had deteriorated from coldness to bickering to bitterness. Separation and divorce did put distance between this couple, but it also fed the hatred in Adam Berwid. He regularly threatened and attacked his wife. He was arrested eight times for it, and he was committed to mental institutions — but in the end, Ewa was stabbed to death. Adam Berwid's anger and insanity had beat the system — the system that was designed to protect Ewa Berwid and the rest of society from him. What's so scary about this story is that the system not only was warned it was going to happen, it made it easy for it to happen.

The first strong warning it received was at the Nassau County jail. Berwid had been taken there after repeated attempts to harass his wife. It was here that Adam Berwid first expressed, in writing, the hatred for Ewa Berwid that by now was almost totally consuming him. He sent her this letter, telling her he was going to kill her and how he might kill her. He is clearly a troubled man. "I have a sentence for you. Count the hours of your life. If you get choked, it will be by my hands. The bullet from a shotgun will whistle in your temple, and that will be me. By the time I put you to death, I'm going to push your ribs through your body." And on, in greater, gorier detail. In all, he sent four letters like this, and Ewa Berwid had no doubt he meant what he said, so she called the police. Sending threats through

420

the mail is, at the very least, a misdemeanor. So police took him from here to appear before County Judge Joseph De Maro, who also had no doubt that Adam Berwid meant what he said.

JUDGE JOSEPH DE MARO: After hearing all of the psychiatrists and seeing him on a number of occasions, I was convinced that he was going to kill his wife if he was ever free to do that. There was no doubt in my mind.

SAFER: So Judge De Maro not only asked the State Department of Mental Health to commit Berwid to a secure institution, but he went further. He wrote a personal letter — a warning — to the institution, in fact, red-flagging the Berwid case.

How common is it for you to write a letter like this one?

JUDGE DE MARO: I've never found the need to write such a letter before.

SAFER: The reason I ask is that this letter is not the usual cold-blooded, judicial letter. It's written with some passion. You say, "Adam Berwid is a *very dangerous, insane person* and, if left free, will, in fact, take the life of his ex-wife and probably the lives of his children."

JUDGE DE MARO: The intensity of the man himself led me to fear, actually fear, that this would take place if he were released.

SAFER: Judge, what happened in the courtroom that day? What did Adam Berwid do?

JUDGE DE MARO: Mrs. Berwid had entered the courtroom, and he had screamed at her and moved towards her and was restrained by marshals in the courtroom. If he was released, he would kill her, and I was sure he would.

SAFER: There was a room full of witnesses to those threats here at the Nassau County Courthouse that day. Among the witnesses, an assistant district attorney named Robert Aliano. He was so convinced that Adam Berwid was homicidal, he wrote a letter to the State Mental Health Department urging them to keep Berwid under the closest possible confinement, and, if his status was ever changed, to give plenty of notice to the police and to Ewa Berwid.

ROBERT ALIANO: In open court he stated, in my presence, in the judge's presence, that he intended to kill his wife, Mrs. Berwid. He attempted to assault her in open court, so that's what prompted me to write this letter, because I had no doubt in my mind that there was a real problem.

SAFER: You're not an expert in these affairs, are you?

ALIANO: It's true I'm not an expert, but it's just a determination that I made, one, as a — a human being and, secondly, as an attorney who observed this man's behavior.

SAFER: The last line of the Aliano letter tells us just how convinced he was. It reads: "If Berwid is released, we have no doubt we will be reading about the murder of Ewa Berwid in *Newsday*" — that's the big Long Island newspaper — "at some time in the future." Well, the future appeared exactly 18 months later, on the front page of *Newsday*. (Headline: "Psychiatric Inmate Held in Slaying of Wife")

Sitting alongside Ewa Berwid the day Adam Berwid tried to assault her in open court was her attorney, Charles Macevily.

Why were you convinced he would kill her?

CHARLES MACEVILY: His letters made it very clear that this was not a — a passing emotional frenzy.

SAFER: Was not the system impressed with the bizarre nature of this stuff, that they had a very dangerous man on their hands?

MACEVILY: It wouldn't shock me to discover that this system never read the letters.

SAFER: Berwid was sent to Mid-Hudson Psychiatric Hospital – a forbidding-looking place that houses 350 of the most difficult and dangerous patients in New York State. The director of Mid-Hudson is Dr. Erdogan Tekben.

Did you consider Adam Berwid a – a homicidal man, a dangerous man, a man who might kill his wife?

DR. ERDOGAN TEKBEN: Yes, we did.

SAFER: You took heed of the letters that the judge sent you, that the assistant district attorney of Nassau County sent you?

DR. TEKBEN: We did take into account any information, positive or negative.

SAFER: Given the secure nature of Mid-Hudson, Mrs. Berwid felt secure that she was beyond the reach of her husband. But after nine months at Mid-Hudson, Dr. Tekben's staff reached the clinical opinion Adam Berwid could be transferred to a less secure institution.

When you say you reached a clinical opinion, in laymen's terms that means he'd improved?

DR. TEKBEN: In that specific case, yes, it was the staff's clinical opinion that he did show a marked improvement.

SAFER: So, taking into account the – the – the – the warnings by society – by society, I mean the judge and the district attorney – you still, you and your staff, still felt that he was – had improved enough to be –

DR. TEKBEN: To be cared and treated at the psychiatric center which is in his community.

SAFER: In his community?

DR. TEKBEN: Yes.

SAFER: But another lawyer looking out for Mrs. Berwid's safety, Marjorie Mintzer, wanted Berwid kept under maximum security.

In other words, you were trying to –

MARJORIE MINTZER: We —

SAFER: – do your best to keep him there?

MINTZER: That's right. We wanted to be able to say, "Hey, wait a minute. Have you questioned him about his wife? Is he still delusional about his wife? Do you know that he's okay around his wife and kids?" That — we would — wanted that kind of input. We were not permitted to do that. In any event, Mid-Hudson did transfer him to Pilgrim State.

SAFER: Pilgrim State is enormous, the world's biggest psychiatric hospital. It is, by design, a very open place, easy to get in and out of. When Adam Berwid was transferred here, he found himself back in his old neighborhood, near his wife and children, just where he wanted to be.

Two Pilgrim State psychiatrists were suspended after Mrs. Berwid was murdered, and Dr. Peter Luke was placed in charge of the acute admissions unit.

DR. PETER LUKE: If a patient comes here on a civil status, it's — means that the person is on no different a status than you or I, if we were unfortunate enough to be admitted here; that we have legal rights. We have rights to, for example, get treatment in the least restrictive environment. Apparently some very good psychiatrists saw this patient prior to his coming to Pilgrim and okayed that. And yet the alternative would seem to be we ought to lock him up forever, and then the question is, should that be in a psychiatric setting? My belief would be, no, that is inappropriate.

SAFER: About a month after coming to Pilgrim State, Adam Berwid walked off the grounds. He was picked up at the home of Ewa Berwid, where he had tried to kill her. Police returned him to Pilgrim State. A few days later he escaped again. He was caught again. This time hospital authorities had him shipped back to Mid-Hudson because of his — quote — "unmanageability and threatening behavior." Back here, doctors who only two months earlier had thought Berwid well enough to be transferred out of here were once again treating him for homicidal behavior.

So you begin all over again with him?

DR. TEKBEN: Well, all over, or from the point we found him, yes. As a matter of fact, that it was, clinically speaking, in a much better shape — our record clearly indicates that — during the second transfer.

SAFER: But Mrs. Berwid's lawyers were convinced, regardless of psychiatric opinion, that their client's life would be in jeopardy if Adam Berwid was moved out of maximum security.

MACEVILY: Mrs. Berwid and I went up to Mid-Hudson and asked for Mr. Berwid to have an interview — with this — the treating psychiatrists present — with Mrs. Berwid, since she was the focus of his insanity.

SAFER: This was a demonstration on your part —

MACEVILY: Exactly.

SAFER: — that he would go around the bend when he saw her?

MACEVILY: Exactly. It was denied, because they were more interested in Adam Berwid than the potential victim of Adam Berwid.

DR. TEKBEN: I don't have any record of it and I don't recall it. That's all I could say on that point.

SAFER: Did you meet with them at all?

DR. TEKBEN: No, I did not. My staff did meet with Mrs. Berwid.

SAFER: With — with Berwid present?

DR. TEKBEN: No.

SAFER: But what about this — the lawyer's idea of setting up a — a confrontation with Mrs. Berwid — let him meet her and see what happens?

DR. TEKBEN: As long as the — the patient did not refuse, we would have no objection.

SAFER: But it seems to — to — from what you say that the patient has all the rights and the potential victim has very few.

DR. TEKBEN: Patients do have a — rights, as you and I do have a — rights. As — the law is clear. That's the law.

SAFER: Seven months later, by mid-November, 1979, the doctors declared, once again, that he was well enough to be transferred, once again, back to Pilgrim State.

You, the psychiatric establishment, created the opportunity for Adam Berwid to kill his wife.

DR. TEKBEN: It was not a question of giving opportunity or not; it was a question of the clinical judgment. Again, I'm saying that he was not sent to hotel, he was not sent to a park, he was not sent to home. Again, he was sent to the psychiatric center for further care and treatment because that was a clinical opinion. His condition permits such a transfer.

SAFER: It is November 20th, 1979, and Adam Berwid is back in the same ward at Pilgrim State. On December 6th, Berwid applies for a pass to leave the hospital grounds. He says he wants to buy himself an overcoat. The doctors feel that he's improved enough to be granted a pass until 4:00 PM. But there are some precautions. On Berwid's medical record is this notice to everyone: that if Berwid is missing, the following people are to be notified — the Nassau County Police, Mrs. Berwid, Mrs. Berwid's lawyer.

Ewa Berwid now has only hours to live. Shortly after breakfast, pass in hand, Adam Berwid walks off the hospital grounds. He boards a train and, within the hour, he is only blocks away from Ewa Berwid's home. Instead of buying that overcoat, he goes to a sporting goods store and buys a hunting knife. It's now 4:00 o'clock — the time Adam Berwid's due back at the hospital. He calls the hospital, tells them he's missed his train, he'll be back soon. What actually happened was he came to the house. He came around the back and looked in the window and saw his wife and children. At the same moment, she saw him. As she dashed for the phone, he broke in. She did manage to dial 9-1-1, the police emergency number.

At exactly 5:07, the Nassau County Police received a 9-1-1 call. It was from a woman — frightened, hysterical, screaming. Here's a tape of that call.

EWA BERWID (on tape):   Olga! Call the police! Olga!

SAFER: She says, "Olga!" Olga's the name of the oldest child. "Olga! Call the police!" And then the 9-1-1 operator.

OPERATOR (on tape):   Stop screaming and tell me where you are. Where are you?

SAFER: The woman is shouting, "He's killing me!"

EWA BERWID (on tape):   (Indistinct . . . screaming).

OPERATOR (on tape):   Ma'am?

EWA BERWID (on tape):   He's killing me!

OPERATOR (on tape):   Ma'am? (Ewa screaming) Lieutenant — Lieutenant, I have this woman on this line. She's hysterical. Something's wrong there, but I don't know what. She's calling some guy's name. He don't answer.
Ma'am?

EWA BERWID (on tape):   Oh! Oh, God!

OPERATOR (on tape):   Ma'am?

SAFER: The police could not get a name or address out of her. If they'd been able to, they say, they would have been there in three minutes. And then the line went dead. It was about ten or eleven minutes past five, the approximate time of death of Ewa Berwid.

Later that night, police received a phone call from Pilgrim State asking them to come 'round and warn Mrs. Berwid that her husband was on the loose. What happened?

POLICE OFFICER: At that time, three police officers were sent down, and they came to this house. They knocked at the door five or six times. They checked the perimeter of the house — it was completely secured. And they even remarked that maybe Mrs. Berwid found out about it and she left for the night with the children.

SAFER: Well, the hospital did try to warn her — six hours after she'd been killed, seven hours after Adam Berwid should have been back in the mental hospital. It sent her a mailgram, and it reads: "Adam Berwid left hospital without permission. Contact hospital with any information you may receive." It was delivered two days later, long after Adam Berwid had confessed to murder.

Adam Berwid was a brilliant, masterful liar, or actor.

DR. TEKBEN: That — I entertained that, after the events, that's possible to — does exist. And lying is not a mental illness.

DR. LUKE: A psychiatrist, I think, is no better than anyone else in terms of reading people's minds. We don't. We don't do any better than the general public, you know, and their advice or their suggestions.

SAFER: In the case of Adam Berwid, you did worse than the general public.

DR. LUKE: Apparently. Apparently.

SAFER: The fact is he fooled you.

DR. TEKBEN: If you are talking on the clinical basis, I do not know. If you are talking about on the basis of the event — events took place, yes.

SAFER: Adam Berwid may never stand trial. Two weeks ago, a judge ruled that he was mentally incompetent, and he was sent back, once again, to the Mid-Hudson Psychiatric Hospital. And New York State has just tightened the laws on furloughs for mental patients. Now three psychiatrists must agree before a furlough is granted.

Strike Two!

DREW PHILLIPS, PRODUCER

HARRY REASONER: There's a tough labor dispute coming to a head this spring, and there may very well be a strike. If there is, it will be big news in places as far away as Japan, even though it will involve only around 700 American workers, quite a few of whom are richer than some of their bosses. It happened once before, in 1972. Now they're talking strike two. The issue is whether the owners of 26 baseball clubs can reclaim some control over their ballplayers − and their ballplayers' salaries − that they've lost in the last five years. They say the issue isn't money, but it really is.

Along about this time of year, mornings brighten up for some millions of Americans. There is once again baseball news in the papers, and the man who has been listlessly noting the hockey and basketball and indoor-soccer scores all winter has again something to read with his coffee. Those who cannot be in the training camps in person are there in spirit − on the green outfield in the sun, listening to the crack of bat and sock of ball that says, "Yes, there will be another summer and another season, in spite of ayatollahs and primaries and 17-percent mortgages." Can even this be threatened? It is.

How can this be when players' salaries have risen from an average of $22,000 a year in 1970 to a hundred thirty-three thousand in 1980, an impressive 600 percent? Remember, that's an average. Not by any means are all ballplayers doing that well, but the free agents are cleaning up.

Mets pitcher Craig Swan just signed a contract calling for $600,000 a year for five years. Cardinal shortstop Gary Templeton is now making more than $650,000 a year. Cardinal first baseman Keith Hernandez is up to $800,000. Pitcher Nolan Ryan is making a cool million a year with the Houston Astros. And Dave Parker makes one million, one hundred thousand dollars playing the outfield for the Pirates. He thinks he earns it.

DAVE PARKER: But baseball is — is a very demanding game. It — it exceeds just a two-and-a-half-hour game. A lot of the times we're at the ballpark eight, nine hours a day. The time it takes away from a — a family man and his family is just — it's phenomenal. So, you know, it's — it's — it's really a — a game, like I say, supply and demand, and I think it accounts for what — what's taking place in the game today.

REASONER: All of those players are proven stars who are probably worth that kind of money to teams trying to win championships and attract fans. But some free agents are getting salaries that have some fans scratching their heads.

For instance, Rennie Stennett hit .238 last year, but San Francisco is paying him $600,000 a year. So, it's no wonder that everyone wants to be a free agent. There were none until 1975. For its first hundred years, baseball operated under what was called "the reserve clause." It's now a pale shadow of its former self, which was a kind of legalized slavery. What it meant was that once a player signed with a club he was theirs — to keep, to underpay, to sell. His only option? To quit playing. But the players got a strong union going in 1966, and in 1972 the union and the owners agreed to appoint an impartial arbitrator to rule on salary disputes. That agreement was the beginning of the end for the reserve clause.

It's doubtful that even the most faithful baseball fans remember the name Peter Seitz, yet he may have had more impact on the game than any other single man. Seitz was the arbitrator who, in 1975, declared Andy Messersmith baseball's first free agent, gutting the reserve clause and blowing the lid off players' salaries. Incidentally, the owners immediately fired him.

They took Seitz's decision to court and lost. And in 1976, the owners gave in and allowed any player with six years' experience to become a free agent if he played a full season without a contract. Salaries began to escalate as the owners bid against each other for the best players. The owners say that the bidding war is jeopardizing baseball, that at least 14 teams are losing money. They are insisting on a new contract provision that would sort of protect them from themselves. It would force a team buying a top free agent to give up an established player in return. The players know the free-agent system got the salaries they have today, and before letting it get watered down, they say, they'll strike.

Marvin Miller, head of their union, speaks for the players.

MARVIN MILLER: The average player goes through three or four years in the minors, and then, if he has talent, he gets to the major leagues, and has the further talent to last as long as six years, he's the exception already. And then, for the first time, under our last agreement, that player can have an initiative as to where he's going to work. And that's the first time in his career that he can have that. The owners are saying they now want to put further restrictions on that man. He can become a free agent, all right, but before another club can sign him, that club must give up a regular player to the team that he used to work for. Well, at that point, that player is not a free agent any more; he is the instrument of a trade. He can't go to another club unless that club will give up a regular player. And they are saying that that will not cut into the bargaining power of the free agent, when it obviously would.

REASONER: The owners are just as determined as the players. Clark Griffith of the Minnesota Twins —

CLARK GRIFFITH: We need a program that allows us to more or less program and plan what the future will demand of us. It wouldn't take us backwards. It wouldn't — it wouldn't level off anything. But it would give us an element of control, where we could hopefully keep — keep our costs in line so that the costs that are passed on to the consumer are reasonable.

REASONER: Cincinnati pitcher Tom Seaver — who's in a pretty high salary bracket himself — says the owners are just trying to penalize the players for their own mistakes.

TOM SEAVER: One of the things that owners do, which is — which is — is kind of a contradiction, in the sense they'll sign a free agent for a — for a very big contract and say, "This is great for our franchise and great for a — for a — for our town, et cetera, and it'll bring us a — it'll bring us a pennant." And then out of the other side of the mouth, out of the other hand, is this — they cry that the players are too — making too much money. It's a — it's a — it's a distinct contradiction.

GRIFFITH: It's easy to say that — looking from the outside — that owners aren't sticking together, that owners are — are trying to beat each other so badly that they lose sight of — of reality. But I think you also have to look at what the owner's problems are in his market. He has a star player. He foresees a situation in which he's — he's damned if he loses the player and is also damned if he keeps him. He'd — he'd rather pick his players and have the best possible club, so he gets caught in a situation in which he actually signs a player for what is not a — a justifiable figure.

REASONER: Since ticket prices have almost doubled, from an average of two dollars and twenty cents for a general-admission seat in 1970 to four dollars and twenty cents this year, the fans have a stake in the players' salary spiral. How do they feel about it?

MAN: I say that if the salaries keep going the way they are, eventually they will have some effect on the attendance, because they will be pricing — pricing themselves right out of the business.

MAN: After — after I finished in e— in electrical engineering and went through General Electric Company and was on — and was on the road, I never made over $1,500 a month. Now, what — what do these athletes make? A million dollars in — in two and three years. And they have a good time doing it.

REASONER: While we were in Florida, we ran into Peewee Reese, who played shortstop for the Brooklyn and Los Angeles Dodgers for 16 years and seven World Series in the forties and fifties. Salaries were kept secret then, but it's doubtful Reese ever topped $50,000 a year.

PEEWEE REESE: I tell you the truth, I can't even comprehend the salaries they make now, and I just hope that it stops someplace. I don't know where it's going to stop, and — but I guess if I were playing today I'd be trying to do the same thing they're doing.

REASONER: Even the great Babe Ruth only got a top salary of a hundred thousand dollars a year, but that was in the twenties and thirties, when the dollar was worth six times what it is today. And remember, the Babe paid less than $5,000 in income tax. One of today's great players is Willie Stargell of the Pittsburgh Pirates, who is beginning to fear the free-agent system will get out of hand.

WILLIE STARGELL: I know that the salaries are becoming a problem. I think we all realize that there should be a leveling point. But like everything else, where do you — what — well, what does it take in order to get a leveling point? And I think this is where we're at now in — in our negotiations.

REASONER: Marvin Miller says salaries are not too high, but in some ways they're unfair.

MILLER: Sure, there are inequities. You could probably, without much trouble, pick out two players of relatively equal talent and length of service and find one being paid several times the other.

REASONER: One example Miller points to is pitcher Ron Guidry of the Yankees. Over the last three years, Guidry won 59 games and lost only 18. He was the most valuable pitcher in the American League in 1978. Yet, because he is not a free agent in his fifth year, he is making only about a hundred and twenty-five thousand dollars a year, less than all but three or four of his teammates.

MILLER: It takes six years of major-league service to become a free agent. We'd like to cut the eligibility requirement. We'd like to bring that down to about four years, so that a Ron Guidry, who might still be underpaid for a couple of years, at least would have an earlier opportunity to correct that inequity as a free agent. That doesn't mean he would change clubs. It would simply mean that when he sat down with Mr. Steinbrenner, he would sit down as an equal, rather than as a prisoner.

REASONER: Miller points out that baseball attendance hits a new high every year and television revenues have doubled. He thinks only a few teams are losing money, but he can't find out for sure.

MILLER: In every negotiation that I've been in in 14 years, at the opening session the owners' chief spokesman makes a speech, in which he says, "We have not, we do not, and we will not claim any financial hardship" — thereby removing the issue from the table, prevents us from asking for any data, and — takes it out of the negotiations. That doesn't stop the owners' committee right after that meeting from walking out in the hall, cornering the first newspaperman and saying, "It's terrible. We are all losing money." The newspaperman has no statutory authority to ask for the data and simply prints what they say.

REASONER: Ed Fitzgerald, board chairman of the Milwaukee Brewers, admits there's still a profit in baseball, but it's getting harder and harder to make.

ED FITZGERALD: Where, at one time, if you could get a million fans in your ballpark and make money, that day has long gone. I guess most franchises today, if they draw less than a million and a half or even more, they're going to have trouble making b— making money. Now we drew something — about a hundred thousand less than two million last year, but if we would fall significantly below that, we would not make money.

REASONER: The owners insist they need the changes they're asking for. American League President Lee MacPhail thinks there could be compromise. But the owners are a united front.

LEE MacPHAIL: Some of these are emotional issues. I'm not really sure how much basic effect this is going to have on the structure of the game, but I think it's very important to the clubs that they get some of the things that they're asking for.

REASONER: How about the players? They've voted almost unanimously to authorize a strike. But will the highly paid stars stay on strike long, watching those ten- and twenty-thousand-dollar-a-week paychecks go down the drain? They say they will.

DAVE PARKER: I'm for the players, you know. I'm in there with the Players Association, and the only way that we can fight this misjustice that's trying to take place towards us now is to stay together as a unit. And I'm definitely for whatever the — the Players Association choose to do.

REGGIE JACKSON: We have a very nice benefit plan and — and pension plan, and Reggie Jackson makes a very nice salary because of Marvin Miller and his Players Association. And I will stick with them 100 percent.

MIKE SCHMIDT: I'm willing to sacrifice whatever it takes in order to make it so that the younger ballplayers coming into the game now have the same opportunity that I have.

REASONER: Since Marvin Miller became head of the union in 1966, both sides have been playing hardball. The players boycotted spring training in the 1969 negotiations. They struck for 13 days in 1972. And in 1976, the owners locked the players out of spring training. So, tough talk by both sides has to be taken seriously.

The union meets Tuesday to set a strike date. Will there be a strike? We don't know. But we think you fans better enjoy these scenes. They might be the only baseball you see this season.

With negotiations going nowhere, last Thursday the owners asked federal mediators to step in. Meanwhile, the owners have put together a $7 million strike fund and have taken out strike insurance. A strike could start opening day, April 9th, but there's talk the players would rather wait until Memorial Day weekend — when attendance is at its highest, the TV revenue begins to come in, and they have collected enough paychecks to make it through the summer.

One of Hitler's Favorites

JEANNE SOLOMON, PRODUCER

DAN RATHER: She was one of Hitler's favorites, although she hardly fit the part. The kind of woman Hitler admired was one whose life centered around her children, her kitchen and her church. This woman's life centered around her camera. She doesn't like to be reminded of it, but she will be remembered as the filmmaker who glorified the early Hitler years. And one of the films she made for Hitler was about a sports event many people thought the United States and the rest of the civilized world should have boycotted.

(Marching music)

If ever there was an Olympic Games where sport became consumed by politics, it was here: Berlin, 1936. The German team marched round the Olympic stadium in uniform and jackboots, and the whole spectacular organization was presented to a gullible world as a great Nazi achievement. The games were officially opened by Adolf Hitler in the name of peaceful competition between all nations.

ADOLF HITLER: (Speaking in German).

RATHER: Three years later, Hitler was at war, leading an attack for world conquest.

The Berlin Games were brilliantly documented in this film, *Olympia,* generally considered then and now to be a cinematic masterpiece. Film for the Nazis was as important a weapon of propaganda as sport. But *Olympia* was not the product of the party propaganda machinery. It was the work of the beautiful German movie actress Leni Riefenstahl, who later would not be forgiven for this and other films she made in Germany during the thirties.

Leni Riefenstahl recently spent her 77th birthday in the Bahamas. To some, she remains one of the greatest filmmakers the cinema has ever seen. To others, she was an evil genius who helped celebrate a brutal regime. It was said she recruited gypsies from concentration camps as extras for her movies; that she informed on her Jewish colleagues, and even filmed inside the concentration camps herself — accusations she has always vehemently denied. But because she was attractive and that rare phenomenon in Nazi Germany, a professionally successful woman, the most persistent rumor has centered around her personal relationship with Hitler. "The First Woman of the German Reich" is what the French called her, and in the States she made the cover of *Time* magazine as "Hitler's Leni Riefenstahl."

LENI RIEFENSTAHL: It is written so many things. Look here what is written, a book about Eva Braun, a diary. In this book is written unbelievable things — that I have danced naked for Hitler and this. And the whole book is — not true.

RATHER: It's a lie?

RIEFENSTAHL: No, it's a lie.

RATHER: You were not a friend of Hitler's?

RIEFENSTAHL: No, never. Hitler have — had Eva Braun. She was a friend of him, and he had no other friends.

RATHER: You were not Hitler's pinup?

RIEFENSTAHL: No, not a little bit.

RATHER: Or his mistress?

RIEFENSTAHL: Not a bit. Not one day, not one minute.

RATHER: If she was not Hitler's pinup, she had certainly caught his eye. Back in 1932, Hitler told this former dancer, now an actress and movie director, "When we come to power, you must make our films for us."
In 1934, and now Chancellor of the German Reich, Hitler asked Riefenstahl to film the Nazi Party rally. The rally was to take place at the newly constructed stadium at Nuremburg. And this is what it looks like today — just another crumbling stadium, with grass growing between the stone cracks. But there's an eerie feeling being here, because who can forget Nuremburg? For anyone old enough to have experienced World War II, it burns forever in our memories. This was the spiritual center of Hitler's Nazism; its symbol and its soul.
(Excerpt from *Triumph of the Will*)
This was the film that Riefenstahl was persuaded to make, *Triumph of the Will*, and Hitler could not have been better served. The only person unhappy about the arrangement was the Nazi minister of propaganda, Joseph Goebbels.

RIEFENSTAHL: Hitler wants that I make the film, because he has said, "It's not important that we get a film rally what is interesting for the party. It must be the idea, and Leni Riefenstahl is an artist. And the party people are not artists." And that was the beginning of big enemy between Goebbels and my person. And I have difficulties from the party. And then I told Hitler, "I'm a girl, I can't do this." "You give me only six days of your life," he told me this, Hitler. "The rally are six days. Give me six days. That is not so much." I told, "It is not six days. It means six months to cut." And he said, "Oh, Leni, you are very gifted, and I think you are one of the very few people who are able to make this a good film. Give me —" He — he — he has not said, "You must." He — he begged me. And then I seen it is hopeless. Hopeless? This is right?

RATHER: Yes.

RIEFENSTAHL: Then I have ask for my conditions. I told him, "Good. If I think I must do it, that I never must make the film in — in order from the government, from Hitler or any other; that I am free and that I can make my film what I want to make; and my own company, not under the order of Dr. Goebbels." That was that. Hitler agreed.

RATHER: He agreed?

RIEFENSTAHL: He agreed.

RATHER: Though *Triumph of the Will* has come to be regarded as the definitive work of propaganda in the cinema, it is still considered to be a technical and artistic masterpiece, a truly great film. The city of Nuremburg was turned into one giant film set for Riefenstahl's benefit on a scale that would have dwarfed a Hollywood epic. She even dressed her cameramen in storm trooper uniforms so they would not mar the pageantry. Riefenstahl now claims it was not propaganda. But in a book published under her name in 1935, she said, "Could mere reporting do justice to an experience such as Nuremburg? It would never reveal the meaning of those days."

(Excerpt from *Triumph of the Will*)

RIEFENSTAHL: I have had six months to finish the film, and in this six months I was day and night working to cut the film. And Hitler and Goebbels, nobody, has seen.

And as the film was ready maybe the same day, I have not even shown the film to the censorship. I don't know if it is a good film or not. I've had not a little bit idea. And then the film was shown in the Berlin, and it was a very big success.

RATHER: Was Leni Riefenstahl a Nazi, or was she an ambitious opportunist? Certainly she was never a member of the Nazi Party. Her absorption in her art was such, one of her cameramen told us, that if it had been necessary she would have quite happily worked for Stalin. But with the success of *Triumph of the Will,* which won top awards in Paris and Venice, Riefenstahl joined that closed social circle of Nazis around Hitler and enjoyed a reputation as the only person he would see without delay.

Riefenstahl's next film was the Olympic Games of 1936. Alone, she spent 18 months editing over a million feet of film shot by cameramen using the most sophisticated lenses and equipment available at the time. Riefenstahl claims she received the commission directly from the International Olympic Committee, and financed the project privately. Records in the German archives indicate the money came in fact from the German government, and that her company was only a front.

The Nazis brushed up their image for the Olympics. Signs saying "Jews Not Welcome" were temporarily dismantled so as not to offend foreign sensibilities. "They all came," Hitler exulted afterwards, and Germany did win most of the gold medals — but not all of them. The winner of the 100 meters and a fistful of other medals, much to the annoyance of Hitler and Goebbels, was not the hoped-for blond, blue-eyed Aryan, but a black American by the name of Jesse Owens. Goebbels warned Riefenstahl not to make, as he put it, "heroes of the black race," but she refused to edit Owens out of her film.

(Excerpt from *Olympia* featuring Jesse Owens setting a world record)

So, you were still having trouble with Mr. Goebbels?

RIEFENSTAHL: Very much. A lot — lot of trouble.

RATHER: Why did — did Dr. Goebbels not like you? You — you mentioned — first of all, you were not a member of the party.

RIEFENSTAHL: Yes, it was not the reason. It was not so important that I was not a member of the party. But the normal reason was very easy to understand. He was the propaganda minister and film was under him, and I was a filmmaker. And normally the most film companies are under his hands, and I have refused.

RATHER: So, he didn't like that.

RIEFENSTAHL: Oh, he hates this, naturally.

RATHER: "I admire Hitler," Riefenstahl said in 1940, "but he is surrounded by a bunch of criminals and we are going to lose the war." Arrested by the Allies in 1945, she spent three years in jail. Her property was confiscated, and her recent marriage to a German army officer broke up. Released by the Allies, she then faced years of investigation by the new German courts. At every stage, Riefenstahl was cleared of — quote — "political activity in support of the Nazi regime which would warrant punishment."

Three decades later, Leni Riefenstahl still lives in Germany in a house just outside Munich, and she continues to work. Though there's been no place for her in the post-war cinema, she has in the last ten years carved out a new career for herself as a first-rate still photographer. In two impressive books, she has documented the dying culture of an African tribe known as the Nuba. The years she spent with the Nuba, Riefenstahl says, were the happiest of her life.

Last summer, we went to the Bahamas to watch Leni Riefenstahl at work on her latest assignment. Five years ago, at the age of 72, she discovered scuba diving, and now specializes in deep underwater photography. The fact that only three months before this trip she broke her hip skiing in St. Moritz was not going to put her off. In the face of that, how could we refuse to join her? Leni Riefenstahl's greatest bitterness is that for 30 years she has been unable to make movies. Several times after the war, she set up film deals, but at the last minute the funds always mysteriously fell through. These days this is as close as she can get.

Leni Riefenstahl now is going on down to about 70 feet to feed her favorite grouper. I think I'll leave her with it. "Nothing can touch you from the outside down here," she says. It's as if she now deliberately finds locations that are as far removed from her early career and her memories as possible.

If someone a hundred years from now —

RIEFENSTAHL: Uh-hmm.

RATHER: — or two hundred years from now —

RIEFENSTAHL: Yes?

RATHER: — takes a look at your work, what would you like for them to know about you? What is the most important thing you would like someone a hundred years or 200 years from now to know about you?

RIEFENSTAHL: I think The Blue Light, because it is a key for my life.

RATHER: The Blue Light was Riefenstahl's early film success which first brought her to Hitler's attention. She was the writer, director and star.
(Excerpt from The Blue Light)
Riefenstahl believes that the role she created for herself then in 1931 was to foretell what would later happen to her. She played the part of a young girl whose ideals are misunderstood. An innocent victim, she is persecuted and stoned as a witch.
(Excerpt from The Blue Light)
Others have seen her life differently. A report of the interrogation of Leni Riefenstahl by the American Seventh Army in 1945 concluded with these words: "She has never grasped, and still does not grasp, the fact that she, by dedicating her life to art, has given expression to a gruesome regime and contributed to its glorification."

A Few Minutes
with Andy Rooney

MIKE WALLACE: Tonight, Andy Rooney is in the doghouse.

ANDY ROONEY: The relationship between dogs and people is not only interesting, it's a little strange too when you think about it. Dogs give us a kind of companionship we ought to get from each other, except that a lot of us find that dogs are more satisfactory companions than people are. It isn't hard to understand why. The average dog is a nicer person than the average person.

These aren't average dogs, of course. We took these pictures at the Westminster Dog Show. Dogs are nice. There's just no doubt about it. They like us, no matter what. They forgive us for making them look ridiculous. This dog obviously knows that running back and forth across a floor is a silly thing to do, but he's willing to go along with it if that's what his friend wants him to do. It's presumptuous of people to decide which dogs look best. The dogs ought to decide that among themselves.

We all get our impressions of breeds from specific dogs we've known. The bulldog is my favorite, because I've known two wonderful ones. I understand why people like other dogs too, though. Oh, I don't always understand. The faces of some dogs are so kind and joyous that they make you smile with pleasure at the thought of any living thing being so guileless. And there are dogs so superficially homely but so deep-down friendly and honest that you have to revise your opinion about what homely is. Some dogs remind you of people you've known, or some types of people anyway. Wasn't there a girl in your class in high school who looked like this? And haven't you known an older woman who looked like this? This is what Bo Derek would look like if she was a dog — which she isn't, of course.

Some dogs look as though, if they could speak, they'd speak a foreign language. There are some dogs you only see at dog shows. And of course, a lot of dogs you'd never see at dog shows. Dogs have such a wonderful, friendly way about them. We like that. Even what dogs do with their tails is so much more natural and attractive than what people do with theirs. Dogs are patient, loyal, understanding, and always anxious to please. Dogs have qualities we all look for in our friends, but you can't teach an old friend new tricks.

Letters

MIKE WALLACE: This week's heavier-than-usual load of mail came principally from viewers asking for more information about DMSO, that pain-killing and healing drug the FDA has refused to license but whose use is advocated by Dr. Stanley Jacob of the University of Oregon Health Sciences Center at Portland, Oregon. And we're endeavoring to answer those letters.

One of those who wrote us was Congressman Claude Pepper, chairman of the House Select Committee on Aging. He said: "(My) committee heard testimony this past week . . . that (DMSO) relieves pain, reduces swelling and promotes healing, all without serious side effects."

About our story on Libya's strongman, Muammar Qaddafi, a viewer wrote: "(You attempted) to complete what Billy Carter tried and failed to do — legitimize a Marxist dictator and supporter of terrorists. (It was) indicative of the 60 MINUTES . . . desire to sell out to the oil moguls."

About our story on the child custody battle between Mr. and Mrs. Jarrett of Mount Prospect, Illinois, the mail was more in his favor than in hers. This letter was typical: "Hooray for Mr. Jarrett. If his ex-wife thinks that she is . . . together enough to raise her three daughters, then let her grow up enough to get married and do it right."

But there were also some letters like this one: "Mrs. Jarrett and her co-renter were open and honest about their living arrangement. Apparently her children were taken away because she did not give proper lip service to community taboos. Just what did the judge think they were doing in front of the children?"

APRIL 6, 1980

Inside Afghanistan

ANDREW LACK, PRODUCER

DAN RATHER: Little or nothing in the way of news comes out of Afghanistan. So, the only way to find out what goes on there is to go in and see for yourself. That is easier said than done.

You start by making contact with one of the resistance groups who move back and forth across the Pakistan-Afghanistan border. If they trust you, you sit down and talk. The group we made contact with seemed eventually to trust us — producer Andy Lack, cameraman Mike Edwards, and soundman Peter O'Connor — and they agreed to take us back with them across the border to the war they are fighting against Soviet troops and Afghan army regulars led by Soviet advisors. If the Soviets are winning the war in the cities, and they appear to be, along the southern border in the mountains, where a good half of Afghanistan's 17 million people live, the resistance fighters have the upper hand. Because the American would stand out like a beacon in those mountains, the resistance fighters disguised us as one of them.

I'm standing on the border between Pakistan and Afghanistan, a border that is now closed to most everyone except refugees fleeing the Soviet invasion. These Afghan clothes I'm wearing were part of an operation to sneak me and a CBS News film crew into Afghanistan. The operation succeeded. So far as we can tell, we are the only full television crew to get inside Afghanistan in recent months. The Pakistani government refuses to let journalists cross the border, officially saying they cannot be responsible for our safety.

We were smuggled into Afghanistan by a young Mujahadeen — Mujahadeen, the Moslem word for freedom fighter or fighter in a holy war. In this case, as the Mujahadeen see it, a holy war against Soviets. A war, they say, that if they get weapons from us or anyone else in the free world, they will win.

You have to walk to this war, and what you see first is a stream of refugees walking away from it, and then you see why. An armed Soviet helicopter from the Russian military base in Jalalabad, Afghanistan's second largest city and a Soviet stronghold 50 miles from the border. Our first day in, we reached the mountains that surround Jalalabad and put us just three miles from where the Afghan resistance forces have been launching attacks on the Soviets. There we hooked up with a small band of guerrillas, led by this white-bearded man. His name is Yassini, and he lives on the run, moving from mountain hideouts through tiny villages of straw and mud huts to the opium fields that often provide him and his men cover from the Russian aircraft that circle continuously.

Yassini took us first to a garrison on the outskirts of Jalalabad that he had recaptured from the Soviet-led Afghan army. The Afghan army has dwindled now to about 35,000 men. Defections are high, and in the battle over this fort, the Soviets were unable to keep their Afghan troops in line. We got this story through our interpreter, Eden Naby, a leading American scholar on Afghanistan who came with us from the States.

"So far as we can tell, we are the only full television crew to get inside Afghanistan in recent months. The Pakistani government refuses to let journalists cross the border, officially saying they cannot be responsible for our safety."

EDEN NABY (interpreter for Yassini):   We used to come here and fight, yes. We used to come at night. For — eleven times at night we came and we fought, and there were Mausers over there that were firing at us. And they had other kinds of heavy weapons, also.

RATHER: Russian-made?

NABY (interpreter for Yassini):   Yes.

RATHER: 1976.

NABY (interpreter for Yassini):   It's made in Russia, but we got it — we captured it from Afghan — the Afghan army.

RATHER: Does he have ammunition for this? He has three, but does he have ammunition, a lot of ammunition?

NABY (interpreter for Yassini):   No, we don't — we didn't capture any. We make them ourselves, though, from powder.

RATHER: What kind of weapons does he need?

NABY (interpreter of Yassini):   Anti-tank— r— rocket launcher, anti-tank.

RATHER: There were Afghan soldiers in here?

NABY (interpreter for Yassini):   Yes. Yes, there we — there was all Afghan soldiers with a Soviet advisor.

RATHER: Oh, with a Soviet advisor. Was he killed?

NABY (interpreter for Yassini):   No, he fled.

RATHER: He fled. How many of your people were killed here?

NABY (interpreter for Yassini):   One of us was wounded and another killed.

RATHER: And how many of the Afghan army soldiers were killed here?

NABY (interpreter for Yassini):   About 35 people.

RATHER: Has he seen any napalm?

NABY (interpreter for Yassini):   Yes. You mean the one that throws down fire on us?

RATHER: Yes.

NABY (interpreter for Yassini):   Yes. They also use gas, yes.

RATHER: Does he know that they use gas?

(One of Yassini's men, a doctor, had been directly affected.)

NABY (interpreter for doctor):   Yes, he's a medical man, and now he's a mujahad.

RATHER: Can he describe to me exactly what the gas felt like?

NABY (interpreter for doctor):   He himself was in the trenches when a bomb was dropped, which he says produced an effect. There was a — there were — there was a black smoke, and when that black smoke came, there was also a — a — a smell.

RATHER: He's absolutely sure it was some sort of gas?

NABY (interpreter for doctor):   He says what I can be sure of is that there was a smell, and then when — when that happened, we were all unconscious for about half an hour.

RATHER: Throughout the day, we spotted several types of Soviet aircraft flying in and out of their main supply depot in Jalalabad. Afraid of being spotted ourselves, we began a long march under cover into the nearby mountains with a 14-man patrol. Our goal: a ridge looking down on a Soviet emplacement. The climb was straight up — 10,000 feet.

The unit arrived at the top just as the sun set behind the far mountain. Objective: to scout a possible location of tanks on the perimeter of Jalalabad. The sound of nearby helicopters has stopped the patrol. Yes, there are two tanks. A flare. They just started firing. The resistance fighters have opened up with automatic weapons from the top of the ridge toward the tanks below. (Sound of explosion) Anti-tank gun goes off. Now, again, silence. (Sound of explosion) Artillery shell. (Sound of explosion) Anti-tank round. Impossible to know where it hit or if it struck home. (Sound of explosion) Artillery round struck very close. That's automatic weapons fire from the resistance fighters trying to rake the base of the ridge to keep any patrol from making their way up. It would figure that they're beginning to get our range. We're going to move off the ridge and scramble down below. (Sound of explosion) That round hit the ridge just below us. (Sound of explosion) The mortar hit very close. The last light goes. And I don't know when anybody's been so glad to see stars.

In the morning, we sighted more Soviet helicopters. There were reports that the fighting would soon intensify. Yassini wanted to keep us moving. He took us up to his command post in the mountains.

Excuse me, is he worried about these helicopters back here? I hear that bombing sound in the background.

NABY (interpreter for Yassini):   He says, no, no. It's not going to bother us, don't worry.

RATHER: But it seems to me the airplanes and the helicopters just across that hill could attack him easily.

NABY: I think he's trying to assure us.

RATHER: Do the Russians ever come up here? Do they come out of Jalalabad to try to catch him up here?

The trek took three hours, a walk Yassini often takes two or three times a day. For an eighteenth-century man fighting a twentieth-century war, these mountains are his only safe haven. Once we were there, he wanted to show us the few heavy weapons he had gotten recently in Pakistan. We wanted to see if any American arms had reached him through various rumored CIA operations.

NABY (interpreter for Yassini):   It's about one month that they have resettled in this area since they took the other area from them —

RATHER: Uh-hmm.

NABY (interpreter for Yassini):   — the Soviets.

RATHER: Now, is this his main headquarters?

(His command post, a cave, carved out of the side of a mountain.)

NABY (interpreter for Yassini):   Yes, they — they are — they hide the — the place where this is because they're afraid that it might get bombed.

RATHER: It started by a handful of men on the lookout for Soviet reconnaissance planes. After some tea, some bread and rice, the commander put his arsenal on display.

Now, commander, whe– where did you get this? Where did you get this? This is a real antique here. Could we sit it down and take a look? Sit it down and take a look. How long has he had this weapon?

NABY (interpreter for Yassini):   It's about two months.

RATHER: Uh-huh. Does he know it's World War I?

NABY (interpreter for Yassini):   Their forefathers used to fight with — with swords, and this is all they have to fight with also, because Afghanistan doesn't have technical progress.

RATHER: Is this the only heavy automatic weapon that he has?

NABY (interpreter for Yassini):   No, they only have the Kaleshnikovs.

RATHER: Yeah, that's a hand weapon. This is really heavy. Now, what is this over here?

NABY (interpreter for Yassini):   This is new. They have— they have— they have just gotten it.

RATHER: Is this the only mortar that he has?

NABY (interpreter for Yassini):   No, that's all we have.

RATHER: This is a – says it's a 72-millimeter, Pakistani-made. And those are the best weapons you have, huh? They only have about 20 rounds for this?

NABY (interpreter for Yassini):   That's all. They have 20 rounds, yes. And they know that these are all old weapons, and they really aren't up to doing anything to the Russian weaponry that's around. But that's all they have and this is why they want help. And he was — he is saying that the — America seems to be asleep. It doesn't seem to realize that if Afghanistan goes and the Russians go over to the Gulf, that in a very short time it's going to be the turn of the United States as well.

RATHER: But I'm sure he knows that in Vietnam we got our fingers burned – indeed, we got our whole hands burned – when we tried to help in this kind of situation.

NABY (interpreter for Yassini):   Your hands were burned in Vietnam, but if you don't agree to help us, if you don't ally yourself with us, then all of you, your whole body, will be burned eventually. Because there is no one in the world who can really fight and resist as well as the — as much and as well as the Afghans are.

RATHER: But no American mother wants to send her son to Afghanistan.

NABY (interpreter for Yassini):   We don't need anybody's soldiers here to help us, but we are being constantly accused that the Americans are helping us with weapons. What we need, actually, are the American weapons. We don't need or want American soldiers. We can do the fighting ourselves.

RATHER: Do any of his units have any American weaponry in any of these various odd lots that he's in connection with?

NABY (interpreter for Yassini):   Not one of them, they don't have any American weaponry.

If you — if we don't survive, you won't either. If — if you allow this situation to continue, if you allow the Russians to — to hammer us down, then there is no place in the world that the Russians will not have the courage to go.

RATHER: Ah, but one last question here. The Russians have already hammered them down, have they not?

YASSINI: Nah. Nah.

RATHER: It's a holy war they're fighting, a Jihad they call it, a war they will have to win on faith. Islam is their strongest weapon now, even stronger, they will tell you, than the anti-tank weapons they so desperately need.

(Sound of tractor)

This is not a tank, it's a tractor. But it carries a message in this war all its own: refugees. They pour across the border at night, mostly, safer for the women and children. Estimates run to 10,000 a day. There are, in fact, half a million Afghan refugees registered already with the Pakistani government, and no one doubts that another half a million are on their way. At the current rate of arrival, one out of ten Afghans will become refugees by summer — a staggering figure in so short a time. We followed this long road out with them. It led through a no-man's land of ancient tribal territories to the northwest frontier province of Bajaur in Pakistan, a two-day walk.

Six miles inside the Pakistani border, we found two refugee camps adjacent to one another. The first was filled with widows and orphans whose husbands and fathers had been killed in the village of Kerala. Kerala is a name that one day may be as familiar as My Lai. Eleven hundred men reportedly were massacred in Kerala a year ago for not complying with Russian reforms. A government information officer confirmed the story.

GOVERNMENT INFORMATION OFFICER: The village people said that we believe in our Islamic society and we are not going to accept your communistic and socialistic regime. When they didn't accept, the soldiers opened fires on them and they killed all the people on the spot, at least one thousand and something.

RATHER: Over a thousand?

INFORMATION OFFICER: Yes.

RATHER: We moved on to the next camp where some three thousand refugees had just been settled. New camps are established somewhere in the border area almost daily.

Now, what — what's the outlook? Will there be more refugees coming in?

INFORMATION OFFICER: Yes, surely. The refugees are even on the way — thousands. In battalions they are coming.

RATHER: Perhaps I could talk with some of them here.

INFORMATION OFFICER: Yes.

RATHER: Maybe we can move in here. If you'd be kind enough to interpret where necessary.

INFORMATION OFFICER: Yes.

RATHER: Hello. Hello, my name is Rather. Can he — can he tell me why did he come here?

INFORMATION OFFICER (interpreter for refugee):   Due to the Russians' atrocities.

RATHER: Tell me about those atrocities.

INFORMATION OFFICER (interpreter for refugee):   There was arson and destroyed our villages. They used bombs on our villages and the tanks on the land.

RATHER: Did he actually see this?

INFORMATION OFFICER (interpreter for refugee):   Oh, yes.

RATHER: What — what did you see? Airplanes or helicopters or tanks or what?

REFUGEE: All of them. All of them.

INFORMATION OFFICER (interpreter for refugee):   All of them.
I think he can speak —

RATHER: Can you speak English?

REFUGEE: A little. A little.

INFORMATION OFFICER: A little. A little.
RATHER: You see helicopters?

REFUGEE: Yes.

RATHER: Airplanes?

REFUGEE: Yes.

RATHER: Tanks?

REFUGEE: Yes.

RATHER: Paratroopers?

REFUGEE: I — I not understand. (Information officer explains) Oh, yes. Oh, yes.

RATHER: You did see paratroopers?

REFUGEE: Yes.

RATHER: Russians or Afghan?

REFUGEE: Russian.

RATHER: My friend, let me ask you a direct question. Is Afghanistan lost?

INFORMATION OFFICER (interpreter for refugee):   He's just asking for arms and ammunition, including tanks, planes and helicopters.

RATHER: But he knows that's not realistic.

INFORMATION OFFICER (interpreter for refugee):   Then we are at the mercy of God. What we can do if it's not possible?

RATHER: But he's obviously an intelligent and wise man. He knows that it's over in Afghanistan.

INFORMATION OFFICER (interpreter for refugee):   They have taken shelter here, but they think that they are going again for the holy war.

RATHER: Do you expect to go back?

INFORMATION OFFICER (interpreter for refugee):   They are expecting to go back because their leader is there and he's fighting there.

RATHER: These people tell me it isn't over?

INFORMATION OFFICER: They don't know.

RATHER: So you think Afghanistan is gone?

INFORMATION OFFICER: I think so. I might be wrong, but I think so.

RATHER: How about the chance of their becoming guerrilla fighters in their country, effective guerrilla fighters?

INFORMATION OFFICER: It's impossible, because without arms and ammunitions you cannot fight, and no country is providing arms and ammunitions to Mujahadeen, freedom fighters.

RATHER: So, what happens to these people?

INFORMATION OFFICER: I think they will be permanently — a chronic problem for Pakistan and they will be a burden — an addition to the — Pakistan's population. This will be an addition.

RATHER: This is a training session for new recruits — Afghans who have settled their families in Pakistan and are now ready to go back home and fight. The spirit was there, but the organization and discipline to fight seriously was missing.

Afghan resistance fighters, many believe, have been overromanticized. They have fought among themselves as much as they have fought outside interference. They lack real leadership in the face of overwhelming Soviet might. But the leader of this group, a man named Mujahadee, a prominent Afghan who fled his country several years ago, saw it differently.

MUJAHADEE: I think no power can stop the general rise-up of the public. Now, when the — Afghanistan's 17 million or 19 million people — children, women and old people, young and all people — they have decided that they will fight until the last moment of life. They will contribute to the struggle. And no power, I think, that will be able to stop it. Either the Russian power will destroy all the public of Afghanistan — nobody will be left here — or, by the — by help of God, we shall kick them out.

RATHER: A protracted guerrilla war, if that's what the Afghan insurgency becomes, will almost certainly bring most of the resistance fighters here, to Darra, a town as old and as famous in this part of Pakistan as Dodge City was in the American West. Darra is where you buy guns, any guns.

(In gun shop): How much?

They make copies of them all here, especially the Russian Kaleshnikov.

MAN: Six hundred dollars.

RATHER: A favorite among Afghans, who sell their home-grown opium for the best available weapons.

Now, when the Afghan man buys a — a — a weapon here, when he buys a rifle, does he go back into Afghanistan?

MEN (in unison):   Yes, yes, yes, back into Afghanistan.

RATHER: Back into Afghanistan?

MAN: Yes, yes. Every day is back.

RATHER: Every day is back?

MAN: Yes. Every day is — (indistinct) and back into Afghanistan.

RATHER: So they don't stay here in Darra?

MAN: No, no, no. Only two days here, three days.

RATHER: In truth, there are many who don't go back to Afghanistan, at least not right away. They drift down here to Peshawar, Pakistan's largest city near the Afghan border. In Peshawar, there are now half a dozen rival political factions trying to organize some kind of respectable movement to free Afghanistan.

(Chanting)

The movement has produced more talk than action — but the talk does draw some attention. And one man in particular appears to have a reasonably strong following. His name is Gulbadin Hikmatyar, a 33-year-old former engineering student from Kabul University. He has been compared in some ways to a young Khomeini; a deeply religious man who, unlike other Afghan leaders, wants no American help.

From the United States, you and your party, do you want weapons?

GULBADIN HIKMATYAR: No.

RATHER: Do you want money?

HIKMATYAR: No.

RATHER: Do you want anything?

HIKMATYAR: We don't want anything. So, I — I will explain this one.

RATHER: Please.

HIKMATYAR: The case of Afghanistan is a fight between a superpower who has captured our country and our own nation. And we don't want this fight to be between two superpowers. We don't want Afghanistan to be Vietnam for Russia. These last 20 months, 100,000 of our people were killed, assassinated, and mass killing. I'm asking why America was silent in these 20 months.

RATHER: Hikmatyar doesn't explain why other Moslem countries have been so slow to offer their support. It may be they simply think it's a lost cause. Meanwhile, the reports keep coming in from the battlefields, and the families of the Mujahadeen gather around makeshift bulletin boards for news from home.

Freedom fighters and foreign invasions are almost tradition in this part of the world. You think about that while walking here among the graves in the old British cemetery, just north of where the British invaded Afghanistan a century ago. It makes you wonder now where the Soviets are burying their dead, and how many Afghans will die fighting the Soviets before the Soviets decide whether they need Afghanistan.

The doctors at Lady Reeding Government Hospital in Peshawar are asking the same questions. If you want to see the war in Afghanistan, this is as good a place as any. Eighty war-related cases a day come into the emergency ward here. Ten may be admitted for major surgery.

Doctor, what is the — what's this patient's — obviously she's lost her arm.

DOCTOR 1:   She has — she has come to us as a case of blast injury. She was in the home and she got this by shelling. There was shelling outside and she got that injury on the right upper limb and on the buttock, right buttock.

RATHER: This shelling, was it by artillery or from helicopter, airplane?

DOCTOR 1 (interpreting):   This was not by the plane. This was by the artillery.

RATHER: By artillery.

DOCTOR 1:   Artillery.

RATHER: Okay. What happens to her now, Doctor?

DOCTOR 1:   She has lost her right limb and now she is with us for the infected wound on the right buttock. It is quite deep and we are dressing it daily.

RATHER: Does she have children?

DOCTOR 1 (interpreting):   I think that she has got one daughter, and she is alive. So, she has lost five of her family members in the war.

RATHER: She's lost five —

DOCTOR 1:   Yeah, she has lost five members of the family.

RATHER: Is her husband still living?

DOCTOR 1 (interpreting):   Yeah. Her husband is alive.

RATHER: How old is this woman, Doctor?

DOCTOR 1:   Probably she is thirty years.

RATHER: This is the father?

DOCTOR 1:   He is the father.

RATHER: How do you do?

Did he see fighting as well?

DOCTOR 1 (interpreting):   He says that I (he) was outside in the hills fighting with the opposition.

RATHER: Tell us what happened?

DOCTOR 1 (interpreting):   He says that they were in the hills and they get shelling by the planes. But they used to hide there and then they used to fire on the planes from below.

RATHER: Does he plan to go back?

DOCTOR 1 (interpreting):   He says that two of my brothers, they're still busy there in the war. And the moment he gets — she is better, he'll go back.

(Rather moves on to the bedside of a sick child)

RATHER: Doctor, what is her injury?

DOCTOR 2:   I think she has broken her leg. It's the femur. He said that she is so much frightened, you know, from the bombardment and everything that she can't talk now.

DOCTOR 1:   She's lost her father and some of other relatives as well.

RATHER: Do we know how old she is?

DOCTOR 2:   Seven years.

RATHER: Doctor, you see most of these cases or a — a good many of them.

DOCTOR 2:   Yes, we do.

RATHER: What do these people tell you as a general rule? Tell me some of the stories they tell you.

DOCTOR 2:   Generally, majo— majority of them they go to the war and they get wounded there. But some of them, and especially women and children, old people too, they are — either they're shot in the houses or when they are on their way to Pakistan they're shot.

RATHER: They're shot on their way here?

DOCTOR 2:   Yeah, on their way here.

RATHER: Doctor, have you heard these kinds of stories? Tell me what you've heard from the patients.

DOCTOR 1:   Well — well it's true. Usually the male people. I mean — I mean, the male member of the family, they go to the war, but the female, usually they get wounded because of shelling or because of the bomb blast and all these things.

RATHER: Doctor, do you hear this every day from all of these patients, that they will go back?

DOCTOR 2:   Yes, most of them, they say this is true.

DOCTOR 1:   He says that my country is dear to me and I have to go back.

DOCTOR 2:   He said that he'll go back today, even today. If he's out of here, he'll go.

RATHER: Do you believe they'll go back?

DOCTOR 1:   Well, definitely. If this is the spirit that he has, he will go, definitely.

DOCTOR 2:   He said doesn't matter all these bombs and planes and tanks, you know, he'll try his best what he can.

High-Low Silver

RICHARD CLARK, PRODUCER

HARRY REASONER: A funny thing happened to this story on the way from research to studio. In January, we decided we ought to do a story about silver, which in a few months had exploded from six dollars an ounce to the $50 range. The theory was that there was plenty of silver, but that speculators buying heavily had driven up the price. Chief speculator: Nelson Bunker Hunt of Texas.

Then the price began to drift down and, on March 26th, it plummeted. Hunt, and a lot of people who were riding with him, suddenly had to come up with money, hundreds of millions of dollars' worth, to buy silver that they had contracted for at high prices months before. There was a near panic. A lot of people, including

Hunt, got hurt. He can probably stand it. One acquaintance said, "Bunky Hunt couldn't go broke if he tried."

Anyway, we found ourselves on a yo-yo of a story that wouldn't stand still. But it makes an evenbetter story, and explains why you'll see people smiling with silver at $40 an ounce, a little worried with silver at $16, and concerned with silver at around $10.

The thing about silver is that, unlike gold, it has more than monetary worth. It's a metal indispensable to a lot of American industry.

At the end of last week, with silver trading at around $14, things seemed to have stabilized. But let's look at silver before someone spins the yo-yo again.

This is what it looks like — some 20 million ounces in this room, worth about a billion dollars when silver hit $50 an ounce. This is the stuff that has always been the common man's metal in America, with echoes of free silver politicians demanding a two-metal standard, and silver coined at a ratio of 16-to-1 for gold. And William Jennings Bryan campaigning for silver and shouting, "You shall not crucify America upon a cross of gold!"

Well, now, the common men who own much of it are people like Bunker Hunt of Texas, maybe a hundred and eighty ounces. Bunky Hunt may have overreached himself. The history of great attempts to corner markets in this country shows more people burned than successful. And Hunt has been burned in the collapse of silver prices that began March 26th. We haven't been able to reach Bunky — that's his nickname, which few say to his face — but last January, when silver prices were peaking, Ray Brady of CBS News did talk to him. He is an heir, of course, to H.L. Hunt's billions of oil dollars. He began converting oil dollars to silver, he says, when the value of our paper money began dropping. His critics say he merely wanted to control the silver market. But even beyond financial considerations, Bunky Hunt seems driven to prove that, even in an era of huge multinational conglomerates and computerized technology, that a man alone on a horse can ride out of Texas and hold the world at bay.

RAY BRADY: Estimate says you've got $6.7 billion in silver contracts. How much have you got?

NELSON BUNKER HUNT: Well, I never — I never comment or — I never took the — I never really think about it, to tell you the truth. I think it's bad luck to talk about your money or how well you're doing or to count your money. And so, I'll just keep that — I don't know offhand, but I — if I did, I wo— I don't believe I'd want to say.

REASONER: That's Bunker Hunt. Now let's see the results of what some claim was his lust for silver.

This is silver country. A great geological fault runs the length of this picturesque valley in the north of Idaho, and from it comes almost half the silver mined in the United States. It hadn't gotten much attention until recently, but when the price of silver went from six to fifty dollars an ounce in less than a year, places like Wallace, Idaho, population about 2,000, went on the map.

(Sounds of machinery)

Vertical shafts more than a mile deep had been in production here since the late 1800's, bringing up lead, zinc, and silver.

MAN: This is what pays everything.

REASONER: Pay dirt here used to mean the lead and zinc. This pile of ore he's sitting on would have been worth a few thousand dollars, but when silver hit $50, that same pile was worth a hundred thousand dollars.

Bill Griffith is the president of Hecla Mining Company. He showed us around Hecla's Lucky Friday Mine.

BILL GRIFFITH: Well, we had a good year last year. It's public knowledge. We made $35 million on sales of 67 million. But the year before, we lost 96 million on sales of 30 million, because we had to write off a big venture in another metal, copper, where the market killed us.

REASONER: And what about the Hecla Mining stock?

GRIFFITH: A year ago it sold as low as four and a half, and I think it closed last Friday at about 48.

REASONER: It might have been kind to let us know that that was going to happen! (Laughter)

GRIFFITH: I wish I had known myself.

REASONER: But something seemed wrong. Griffith was happy, all right, but somewhat reserved; cautious is the word. The same with the miners. Most of them owned silver stocks, which were booming. We'd read that Wallace was a boom town. It isn't. In fact, the most Saturday night fever we found was in a local school gymnasium, where a lot of miners and their wives and children went for the weekly dance.

"We've been down too often," we were told. When things are good, as now, they pay off the mortgage and the car loan, because who knows what's around the corner.

(Song)

MAN (at silver exchange):   Offer 500 at two-twenty.

MAN (at silver exchange):   Bid two-ten for a thousand.

MAN (at silver exchange):   Offer 5,000 (indistinct) at 14.

MAN (at silver exchange):   Callahan was $16 a year ago and today it's fif— $51.

REASONER: Ben Harrison runs the Spokane Silver Exchange. He's been at it for 51 years.

Is this whole room a lot busier than it was two years ago today?

BEN HARRISON: It's considerably so. Volume was 16 million in January alone, and that's more than we had in the first six months of last year.

REASONER: I read that gold might go to $10,000 an ounce and silver then to 650. Do you see that?

HARRISON: I don't know about that, but the — the price is plenty good right now. (Laughter)

REASONER: We were told that in the back of the room were several millionaires — but again, something didn't make sense. Silver was close to $40 an ounce that day; some were saying it would hit a hundred dollars down the road. But Ben Harrison told us this —

HARRISON: The Spokane people appear to be selling and the outside people are buying.

REASONER: Funny they should be selling, we thought, because back East, where the experts are, the Silver Commodities Exchange had become an international crap table. Silver hit $50 an ounce and you didn't have to read the financial pages to find that out. A stop at Tiffany's on Fifth Avenue would tell you.

Tiffany Chairman Walter Hoving —

What did it do to your prices? Do you think of an example or two?

WALTER HOVING: Oh, it went— went way up, way up. We had, for example, a tray downstairs that last year sold for $600 and now it's $1590. I mean, it's a ridiculous price, really.

REASONER: Hardest hit by the high prices are industries that depend on silver for their product. For instance, the Gorum Company has, for decades, manufactured fine silver tableware, along with vases, bowls and candelabra. They've had to change prices eight times in recent months. Last year Gorum used two and a half million ounces of silver; this year they guess it will be about a million ounces. Gorum's president, Frank Grezlecki, says people who used to buy sterling have turned to silver plate and stainless steel.

Would you have a rough idea of what sterling percentage used to be and is now?

FRANK GREZLECKI: Well, I would say last year it was probably 80 percent of our pieces and this year it'll probably be somewhere in the neighborhood of 20 or 25 percent of the total pieces.

REASONER: What would have been the price of a— a place setting of your silver say, just a year ago compared to now?

GREZLECKI: Well, in January and February of 1979, a place setting of our most popular pattern sold at retail for roughly a hundred and twenty dollars a place setting. This year, to buy that same place setting, you'd probably pay around four hundred and thirty-five or four hundred and fifty dollars.

REASONER: People are not only not purchasing new silver, they are mining their attics for old.

MAN: These would come out to two dollars and seventy-five cents.

WOMAN: Oh, great!

REASONER: There are companies traveling the country buying everything from eyeglass frames to silver trays to be melted down.

WOMAN: And they bring junk that's been lying around the house, silver that they don't want to polish any more.

REASONER: Stolen merchandise? These buyers check people's identifications and keep careful records. But law-enforcement people say their full-page ads are an open invitation to second-story men.

DETECTIVE RICHARD ROWSELL: We began to see an increase in thefts of silver.

REASONER: Detective Richard Rowsell of the Beverly Hills Crime Prevention Unit.

ROWSELL: The burglar knew, or the thief knew, that he no longer had to rely on the fence. He no longer had to cut the fence into his profit margins. And so, when he stole silver now, he could take it over directly and get full market value for it.

REASONER: And if you've been wondering why photography is suddenly an expensive hobby, Eastman Kodak's Vice president, Kay Whitmore, will tell you what happens to his company when the price of silver goes up more than $40 an ounce.

KAY WHITMORE: Well, we buy about 50 million ounces, troy ounces, of silver a year. So, a dollar increase in the price of silver is $50 million increase in our costs. Well, that's been a dramatic increase in our costs of manufacture of sensitized goods.

REASONER: Medical X-rays are the biggest headline here. Silver is extremely light sensitive; it holds the image you see on the plate. Last September, a package of 500 X-ray films cost $667, up to $1443 when silver peaked in January.

The same is true, to a lesser extent, with ordinary film used by both amateurs and professionals. Silver is essential for an image, and we wondered if there might be some substitute in sight.

WHITMORE: Well, if you used your camera to take a picture with, say, Kodacolor or Kodachrome film, your normal exposure would be, say, one-sixtieth of a second — a fairly short time. But if you used another material, for example, diazo, which is a commonly used material, that's — its sensitivity is nowhere near silver and, as a result, your exposures, if you tried to use that, would be very, very long; in the matter of days or weeks to get the same result.

REASONER: To get this — somebody is sitting there with their beard growing while you took the picture?

WHITMORE: That's correct. That's correct.

REASONER: Kodak has been recovering silver from scrap film for decades, but there's a new intensity about it these days. For instance, you're looking at 825 million sprocket hole punch-outs from six million feet of movie film, which will yield about 465 ounces of silver. That happens here, in a one-of-a-kind smelter built by Kodak to squeeze every drop of silver they can from their refuse. They can get back about 20 million ounces a year.

There are smaller units, like this one, that will wash silver from photographic prints and negatives; some cost under a hundred dollars.

You might think that these painstaking recovery procedures and the January explosion of silver prices mean the metal is in short supply. It isn't. There's plenty. But again, the bulk of it is owned by a handful of hoarders who plunged into the exchanges and almost cornered the market. Their silver sits in vaults, used not for teaspoons and jewelry and appliances and X-ray plates, but for speculation.

Over the weeks we were doing this story, silver users, manufacturers, seemed hesitant to point accusing fingers at the people they believe sent the market into turmoil. Then a couple of weeks ago came a cry from what seemed an unlikely place: Tiffany's. Walter Hoving bought an ad in the *New York Times*.

    We think it is unconscionable for anyone to hoard several billion — yes, billion — dollars' worth of silver and thus drive the price up so high that others must pay artificially high prices for articles made of silver, from baby spoons to tea sets, as well as photographic film and other products.

Why did you put that in?

HOVING: Well, I think that the general public was, more or less, being ripped off there. They were paying very high prices. And we certainly heard from them. They — they told us that they were very high and they were correct. And we knew that Mr. Bunker Hunt was involved in the thing, so we thought that we ought to try to goose this thing so — to get it out in public.

REASONER: And how does Bunky Hunt react when people like Walter Hoving accuse him of making us pay more for silverware, photographic film and X-ray plates?

HUNT: Well, I — I certainly don't think I have that kind of power or that kind of influence. Actually, I bought large amounts of silver, fairly large amounts, some six or seven years ago, and it didn't really affect the price very much for a period of five or six years.

BRADY: You are in a commanding position. You are in a position to squeeze the short and —

HUNT: Well, no, I — I don't really think so. I — I — I don't — I don't really feel that I am, and I certainly never tried to deliberately cause any problem at all.

REASONER: Since that interview, of course, the bottom fell out. Silver, which was at $50 in January, went to about $10 in March. If Bunker Hunt does have a hundred and eighty million ounces, that means its worth dropped about seven billion dollars in two months, and a lot of people got hurt. Lowell Mintz is the chairman of the New York Commodities Exchange.

LOWELL MINTZ: A lot of the people who were not greedy and who played the markets correctly probably did make a lot of money. There have been a lot of people, also, who bought all the way on a scale-up, on a pyramid-type operation, who have gotten wiped out in this downward move. The volatility has been tremendous.

REASONER: Enough to worry you as a long-time silver trader?

MINTZ: Enough to be concerned for the market and wondering, you know, if the market is being used for the wrong thing.

REASONER: As for Hunt, he and some Arab oil people who are associated with him have announced they'll sell bonds backed by silver.

BRADY: How about one last try. How much silver do you own?

HUNT: That's — that's known only to God and to me. And I — the — the Lord isn't talking, and so I won't, either.

REASONER: The Good Lord and Hunt may not be talking, but chances are Hunt has less silver than he did a couple of weeks ago. He had to use a chunk of it, as well as some of his oil wealth, to settle his problems.

And the prices we all pay for products using silver are down, not as low as they were, but down. And a number of investigations by government and the commodity markets are underway to see if rules should be changed to prevent this kind of thing from happening again.

It may turn out that Bunker Hunt has changed the silver market permanently — but not in the way he intended.

A Few Minutes with Andy Rooney

MORLEY SAFER: Bunky Hunt isn't the only one who sits up nights trying to figure out where his money went. Even a little fella like "Bunky" Rooney does that.

ANDY ROONEY: Every once in a while I wonder what in the world I've done with all the money I've made. Do you ever wonder that?

I began buying things with my own money in 1945, just after I was discharged from the Army. The other day I started making a list. This is very rough, but here it is.

Food for a family of six for 20 years, at two dollars a day per person, comes to $87,600. The kids have left home now, but my mother lives with us, so that's three people, for 15 years, at three dollars a day per person — food costs more now — comes to $49,275. That's a total for food of $136,875.

It's hard to remember how many cars you've bought. I think I've bought 18 cars in 35 years for an average of maybe $3,500 a car. That's a total of $63,000 I've spent on cars. We drive a total of about 50,000 miles a year. We have two cars. Gas costs a dollar thirty a gallon now, but it used to only cost 28 cents, say, so an average of 35 cents a gallon. We get maybe 18 miles on a gallon of gas. So, that's 97,000 gallons of gas, at 35 cents a gallon, that's a total of $34,000 we've spent on gas.

We bought the house in 1951 for twenty-nine-five and, with a 20-year mortgage, the bank collected about $50,000 from me.

We put four kids through college, four years each at $6,000 a year apiece. That comes to a total of $96,000 for college. Sometimes I think we should have sent them to cheaper colleges and bought more expensive cars.

Heat, light, telephone, real estate taxes, utilities in general, must have averaged $2,500 for 35 years. That's a total of $87,500.

Then there was miscellaneous: clothes, haircuts, crab-grass killer, sunglasses (I lose a lot of sunglasses), bourbon, beer, shoelaces, appliances, television sets. say, $200,000 for miscellaneous.

Now I'm going to level with you, I've made a lot of money. You know, not a fortune, but more than most people. In 35 years, I suppose I made $1,250,000. In addition to all these items, I guess I've paid about $400,000 in taxes. So, that's a grand total that I've spent of $1,067,375. Now, tell me this. If I've made a million and a quarter and I've spent $1,067,000. what the heck did I do with that other $183,000?

Letters

MIKE WALLACE: Most of the mail we got after last week's broadcast was about our story called "Looking Out For Mrs. Berwid." Mrs. Berwid was the woman who was murdered by her husband, a mental patient who had left no doubt that he would do just that if he ever got the chance.

In our mail was a letter from a doctor who wrote: "It is inconceivable how a man who so cleverly planned his wife's death . . . could be found incompetent to stand trial for his crime . . . (No doubt) he will again outsmart the system . . . When will we ever learn?"

But another viewer said: "(You did) a terrible injustice to the thousands who suffer a mental illness and recover to return to productive lives."

Another viewer noted that the mental hospital warned Mrs. Berwid that her husband was on the loose not by phone, but by a mailgram that arrived after she was dead. And he wrote: "The hospital sent Mrs. Berwid a mailgram? There is more than one insane person in your story."

A lot of the letters about that story were like this one: "My heart is aching. Can you please tell me what happened to the poor Berwid children?"

Adam Berwid did not physically harm his children. They were asleep in their beds when the police came and thought that no one was home. The next day, after Berwid called the police to report the murder, the children were taken away. Where are they? They are safe and sound and, for obvious reasons, authorities are not saying where.

About our story on the cinematographer who made films glorifying the Hitler years, a viewer wrote: "I'm glad you put things in proper perspective. Leni Reifenstahl, for all her talent, was a moral nitwit."

Update

MIKE WALLACE: Now two updates. On DMSO, the prescription drug about which we've received thousands of letters, the Arthritis Foundation, which had heretofore expressed some skepticism as to its value, has announced it is now endorsing limited use of the drug as a painkiller. Says the Arthritis Foundation: "DMSO appears to work as a local analgesic and therefore might be useful in a host of conditions causing pain."

One warning, though. Various doctors have written us that care should be exercised in its use; that it is a prescription drug, not a patent remedy, and should be used only under the supervision of a doctor.

About our report on CORE last November, the Congress of Racial Equality, we reported then that CORE had been temporarily forbidden by a New York State court to raise funds on its own behalf because it allegedly had no programs and its officers allegedly used some of the money for their private purposes. Well, this past week that injunction was lifted. The judge said he was permitting CORE to resume fund-raising because New York State attorneys had not yet brought their case against CORE to trial. But those New York State attorneys tell us they still intend to proceed with their action against CORE, and that they intend to ask that the fund-raising injunction be reinstated.

Now, getting back to the mail, there was quite a bit about our story on the baseball strike. One viewer said: "The fans are the ones who should go on strike and force those overpaid gluttons to go out and earn an honest living."

About a statement in our story by Marvin Miller of the Players Association, a viewer wrote: "After carefully considering the statement by Marvin Miller that Ron Guidry is a prisoner at a hundred and twenty-five thousand dollars per year, I've decided to sacrifice myself for a hundred thousand dollars per year. How do I reach Miller?"

And finally, there was this: "The prospect of not having the airwaves cluttered with baseball . . . is almost too good to be true. Hang in there, baseball owners. It could be the best summer in memory."

APRIL 13, 1980

Scientology: The
Clearwater Conspiracy

ALLAN MARAYNES, PRODUCER

MIKE WALLACE: A couple of months ago, a federal judge in Washington, D.C. sentenced nine persons to prison terms of up to ten years for a variety of crimes to which they had pleaded guilty. Which may not sound unusual on the face of it, except that these nine were among the top leaders of a religion — the Church of Scientology, with a worldwide membership of five million, three million of them in the United States. Scientology has been in the headlines off and on for 25 years now, almost since the time it was founded as a religion by science fiction writer L. Ron Hubbard back in 1952.

Scientology's story is one of a church embittered by what it perceives as harassment by government agencies and by other individuals. Those nine Scientologists convicted in Washington say their crimes were directed only at those they saw as threats to their religion, including the Internal Revenue Service, which had questioned whether Scientology was in fact a religion and therefore tax exempt, and the U.S. Department of Justice, which investigated various illegal activities of church officials.

Raymond Banoun, an Assistant U.S. Attorney for the District of Columbia, details the crimes committed by one or another of those nine top Scientologists who were convicted.

RAYMOND BANOUN: Burglaries, conspiracy to steal documents, conspiracy to forge government credentials, conspiracy to bug and wiretap government meetings, conspiracy to obstruct justice by lying to a grand jury, destroying evidence, submitting false evidence to the grand jury, harboring a fugitive, and kidnapping a witness when he decided to surrender.

WALLACE: Those crimes were committed in Washington, but some of Banoun's attention was focused on Clearwater, Florida.

BANOUN: They had, in fact, engaged in a widespread conspiracy against private organizations, against private citizens, public officials and Clearwater was a prime example of what they had done.

WALLACE: "The Clearwater Conspiracy" is the story of a typical campaign launched by the Scientologists back in the middle seventies. Much of what you will hear is under further investigation by a federal grand jury in Florida. It demonstrates graphically the tactics used by church officials in furthering their religion, and in persecuting anyone they felt was trying to get in their way.

So Clearwater, in effect, was a microcosm of the kind of operations undertaken by the Church of Scientology?

BANOUN: Precisely.

WALLACE: Clearwater used to be a quiet, even placid, town on Florida's west coast, next door to St. Petersburg and Tampa — a popular retirement community, conservative politically, mostly Baptist. But a few years back, Clearwater's economy was beginning to feel some pain. Tourism was off.

The city's downtown area was beginning to dry up some when, in 1975, along came an unknown group calling itself United Churches of Florida looking for a place to settle. And they put up almost three million dollars in cash for two big downtown buildings — the old Bank of Clearwater, and that imposing structure, the Fort Harrison Hotel. Much of the business community was happy, but some city officials and the local press were curious about the identity of United Churches of Florida. Who were they, this church that had that kind of cash?

Well, it turned out that United Churches was, in fact, the Church of Scientology. And that initial deception infuriated these citizens of Clearwater, shown rallying a couple of months ago against the Scientologists. Their former mayor, Gabe Cazares, was bitterly skeptical of the church. He is a key figure in Clearwater's continuing rebellion against the Scientologists.

GABE CAZARES: L. Ron Hubbard has stated that Scientology is extremely wealthy; that it has the money to buy cities and even countries. That destructive cult has to know — let us make it perfectly clear for once and for all — that sparkling Clearwater is not for sale. (Cheers)

WALLACE: Now, spokesmen for the church insist they came in under the cover name of United Churches of Florida only after they had been repeatedly harassed when they tried to set up shop in the open in other cities. But that explanation did little to calm the people of Clearwater, who saw Scientology as a cult and were furious that a good chunk of Clearwater real estate had been taken off the tax rolls. The mayor continued his attacks and, for his pains, he was placed on the church enemies list. They set out to smear him with sexual innuendo, to ruin him politically.

I read to him from a church memo, culled from documents we acquired in our investigation, just what they planned for Cazares: "The purpose of this operation is to actually get real documentation into the files of Mexican license bureau or bureaus stating that the mayor got married in Mexico to some Mexican gal 25 years ago, who is not his wife, so it puts the mayor in a position of bigamy. This can be accomplished either by a bribe or a covert action."

So what you're saying was that they were trying to destroy your chara— assassinate your character?

CAZARES: Without — without — without question. They — they did many things to try to — try to destroy me.

WALLACE: Mrs. Cazares told us what the church did to her.

MRS. CAZARES: Things like this never happened to Gabe and I before. We'd been married 29 years, suddenly I was getting all kinds of mysterious phone calls.

WALLACE: Saying?

MRS. CAZARES: Girls calling, "Is Gabe there?" Tell — telling me there's something personal between "he and me." Asking me if I knew where — "Do you know where Gabe is now?" Things like that, you know.

WALLACE: It was difficult for us to imagine how the tale the Cazares told meshed with the religion that calls itself Scientology. We wondered just who are these Scientologists and what they're doing inside Clearwater's historic Fort Harrison Hotel.

This library is on the tenth floor of the Fort Harrison, which is, in effect, the Clearwater seminary of the Scientologists. Men and women from around the country, indeed around the world, come here to study the gospel according to L. Ron Hubbard.

Scientology, which calls itself "a religious philosophy that can be applied to Christians and non-Christians alike," aims at helping an individual to find himself, herself, through spiritual fulfillment. Its primary religious artifact is something called an E-Meter, used by church ministers, or "auditors" as they are called, to indentify past painful experiences and eventually to blanch them out, to reach a state of peace, or "clear" in church jargon.

CHURCH AUDITOR: Very good. Recall a time in life that's cheerful.

MAN: Yeah, early in the week here I got up and . . .

WALLACE: Church members swear by this E-Meter auditing process. They swear by Ron Hubbard and Scientology to such a degree that they will pay, for instance, $2,255.45 for a Ron Hubbard Personal Ethics and Integrity Course — without the man in person there; he is now a recluse — or a public relations course for $10,525.41. Room and board are extra.

The Church of Scientology will not open its account books, but its assets are reported to run into the tens of millions. They've already spent over ten million in cash for properties they have bought in Clearwater alone.

It was partly the church's real estate acquisitions in Clearwater that attracted the nearby *St. Petersburg Times* to the Scientology controversy. But the Scientologists didn't like the stories the newspaper published about them, so the *St. Petersburg Times* wound up on their enemies list.

Reporter Betty Orsini was doggedly pursuing the story of the church's undercover campaign in Clearwater, and so the *Times* became the object of an all-out attack. Scientologists stole files from the paper's legal offices, its reporters and editors were harassed — only, says editor Eugene Patterson, only because the *St. Peterburg Times* was covering a news story.

EUGENE PATTERSON: That's all we were trying to do — find out who they were, what they were up to, so that we could inform the community.

WALLACE: And what did they do to you?

PATTERSON: They put the heat on. The — the pressure gets pretty — pretty heavy from them.

WALLACE: What about the reporter who was involved in the investigation?

PATTERSON: First they slandered her to me in an effort to compromise her job.

WALLACE: Slandered her?

PATTERSON: Saying she was printing lies, that she was not giving their side, that she was being unprofessional. After that, they went after Mrs. Orsini's husband.

He heads up a small charity here in St. Petersburg, Easter Seals. He's the executive director.

WALLACE: Uh-hmm.

PATTERSON: And once they found they could not get Betty Orsini off the story, or get the *St. Petersburg Times* off it, the next thing we know, an anonymous letter, a poison-pen letter charging criminality to Mrs. Orsini's husband, landed on our city desk and that of two or three other newspapers in Florida. The man was innocent. And I think they thought that we were some bush-league newspaper that they could scare out of the box.

WALLACE: But the most persecuted victim of the Scientologists, speaking here at an anti-Scientology rally in Clearwater, was Paulette Cooper.

PAULETTE COOPER: In 1971, I wrote a book . . .

WALLACE: Paulette Cooper wrote a book back in 1971 called *The Scandal of Scientology*.

COOPER: Now the Scientologists did not want you to read this book.

WALLACE: To try to silence her, the so-called "Guardians Office" of the church cooked up a scheme to steal some of her stationery and make it appear that she had sent the church office two bomb threats. I read from one of the forgeries —

"James, this is the last time I'm warning you. I don't know why I'm doing this, but you're all out to get me and I'll give you one week before Scientology is an exploding volcano. I'll knock you out if my friends won't."

COOPER: Right. And as a result, I was arrested, I was indicted on three counts, I faced up to fifteen years in jail if I was convicted. The whole ordeal fighting these charges took eight months. It cost me $19,000 in legal fees. I went into such a depression. I couldn't eat, I couldn't sleep, I couldn't write. I went down to 83 pounds. Finally, I took and passed a sodium pentothal — or a truth serum — test, and the government dropped the charges against me in 1975.

WALLACE: Another church plot against Cooper was named "Operation Freakout," intended to get her placed in a mental institution until she stopped writing about Scientology. Church officials even launched a graffiti campaign against Cooper.

COOPER: They put my name up on walls in New York City, where I live, with my phone number, so people would call me. They put my name on pornographic mailing lists, so that I would get all kinds of disgusting mail. You see, for years I was saying that these types of things were going on, and people thought, well, what is she talking about? This is a church. And finally, after 11 years, I see that everything I said was true and that Scientology turned out to be worse than anything I ever said or even imagined.

WALLACE: We were frankly surprised that two high church officials agreed to answer the various charges against the Scientologists. The Reverend Kenneth Whitman is the 32-year-old president of the Church of Scientology in the United States. David Gaiman is worldwide head of public relations for the church. I asked him about the church's campaign to discredit Cazares and Patterson and Paulette Cooper.

DAVID GAIMAN: Yes, it sounds dreadful.

WALLACE: And, as a matter of fact, it turned out to be rather dreadful.

GAIMAN: If you judge by the net result, absolutely true.

WALLACE: You set out to smear Gabe Cazares, the then-mayor of Clearwater, sexually — that is, smear him with sexual innuendo — harassed his wife on the telephone. The Church of Scientology?

GAIMAN: Bizarre. I'm — I'm not — I cannot defend the intention and the statements within this documentation, within — within this particular document.

WALLACE: The two church leaders went on to explain that those attacks were made only in response to perceived threats to the existence of the church; that some overzealous members were merely protecting their religion. Still, we found those actions difficult to understand.

You must admit, if I lived in Clearwater, if you lived in Clearwater and weren't a member of the Church of Scientology, you'd say, "What in the world has this got to do with religion?"

GAIMAN: I think that we, that — that part of us, part of we, the Guardians Office —

WALLACE: Uh-hmm.

GAIMAN: — fell into the arrogance of the end justifies the means, which is — which is — which is wrong and alien to Scientology, just as it is wrong and alien to other groups who have gone down the same stony road. It is a crisis point for us.

WALLACE: After confessing wrongdoing by church officials, the two, nonetheless, insisted that the church's founder, L. Ron Hubbard, had nothing to do with such methods. So, I read from a Hubbard policy letter.

"If there will be a long-term threat, you are to immediately evaluate and originate a PR campaign to destroy the person's repute and to discredit them so thoroughly that they will be ostracized."

GAIMAN: That— I have never, ever seen an issue, and I'm familiar with this documentation. I have never seen such an issue.

WALLACE: Well —

GAIMAN: I have —

WALLACE: — have you seen that?

GAIMAN (examines document):   Yes, yes. Then this — and this in this form is —

WALLACE: May I see it just a second?

GAIMAN: Yes.

WALLACE: It says here, "Don't ever tamely submit to an investigation of us. Make it rough — rough on attackers all the way. You can get reasonable abo— reasonable about it and lose. Sure, we break no laws. Sure, we have nothing to hide." Although, you will agree that you did break laws?"

GAIMAN: And the time that that was written?

WALLACE: 1966.

GAIMAN: Right.

WALLACE: "Banish all ideas that any fair hearing is intended, and start our attack" — the Scientology attack — " with their first breath. Never wait. Never talk about us, only them. Use their blood, sex, crime, to get headlines. Don't use us."

GAIMAN: Yes, that's true. Yeah.

WALLACE: That's — that's your man.

GAIMAN: That's right.

WALLACE: Gaiman still insisted we were taking Ron Hubbard's words out of context. He said that Hubbard was against the breaking of any laws, and the Reverend Whitman elaborated.

THE REVEREND KENNETH WHITMAN: And our position is this: that if any Scientologist has broken the law, then he's going to be dealt with per the law.

WALLACE: What you seem to be saying, in effect, is to Clearwater, "Mea culpa, we were wrong, our shame. Now, let's move ahead"?

REVEREND WHITMAN: Exactly, exactly.

WALLACE: And you want us to believe you?

REVEREND WHITMAN: No. Not — not even so. That's why we want you to look. That's all. Look, observe for yourself. Judge us by our deeds and by who we are and what we are and — and what effects we produce in society.

WALLACE: What the Reverend Whitman is saying is that, in future, the church will undertake to atone for past sins by positive contributions to Clearwater.

REVEREND WHITMAN: The people involved in Scientology speak for themselves, which is — which is our best representation.

WALLACE: That sounded fair enough to us, so we sat down with three church members suggested to us by Whitman and Gaiman: Nancy Cass, a former U.S. State Department Foreign Service Officer; Mario Feninger, a concert pianist; and Diana Alfano, a long-time resident of Clearwater. And from the start, it was apparent that, although the two church leaders seemed eager to plead guilty to church wrongdoing, they apparently had not communicated any comparable sense of guilt to these church members.
You say that ethics are very important to a Scientologist?

NANCY CASS: Very. Very, to me.

MARIO FENINGER: Right.

WALLACE: Well, then, please try to help me understand the ethics involved in trying to smear the mayor of Clearwater, in trying to get the job of the fellow who runs the *St. Petersburg Times* — all true and all acknowledged — in the name of religion. Doesn't that make you say, "Hey, my religion would do a thing like that?"

CASS: In the name of survival of a religion? If these people are trying to knock the religion down, what do you do? Sit back? I mean, look, you know, this is not the first persecution of a religion.

WALLACE: And you really believe that Gabe Cazares and the *St. Petersburg Times* and Paulette Cooper were trying to destroy Scientology?

CASS: You (indistinct) I do.

WALLACE: Therefore, you commit crimes going after Paulette Cooper. You forge letters that bring her up on federal charges that she's going to be a bomb thrower. You — you —

CASS: No, no.

WALLACE: — you — you destroy her name. You — you indulge in sexual in — innuendos. A church does does that, Mr. Feninger?

FENINGER: Well, I was not informed about all this, really.

WALLACE: You read?

FENINGER: No, I don't.

CASS: You know what I do when I read that kind of stuff about Scientology? I don't even read it.

WALLACE: Why?

CASS: Because it doesn't interest me. Let the people who have to handle that handle it. Because I have too much to do, and I can't be bothered with that kind of stuff. Let them handle it.

WALLACE: But these are people —

CASS: Because we will survive.

WALLACE: Diana Alfano has a shop across the street from the Fort Harrison. You — you were aware of the — you were aware of all those facts?

DIANA ALFANO: No, I was not aware of all the facts. I'm still not aware of all the facts.

CASS: See, as I said earlier, an attack on the church is not important to us, because Scientology has to survive. It has to.

WALLACE: And Scientology is surviving, not just in Clearwater, but worldwide. The Scientologists have paid $125,000 in back taxes in Clearwater, and they continue to try to persuade the skeptics there that they intend to mend their ways.

But the hostility against them lingers, but the Scientologists insist they are in Clearwater to stay.

Gimme Shelter

SUZANNE ST. PIERRE, PRODUCER

MORLEY SAFER: "Gimme Shelter" is not a bit of rock nostalgia about the Rolling Stones. "Gimme Shelter" is the common plea of a good number of people in high tax brackets, and the shelters they're looking for are tax shelters — perfectly legal ways of reducing the amount of tax you have to pay. We learned about one that could be a honey of a shelter if you're lucky enough to be in the 50-percent tax bracket. You not only save money, you get that nice glow of being a philanthropist. Just buy some things, some pictures or other art objects or some precious stones at a wholesale price. Get an expert or two to appraise them, wait a year, because that's what the law says you must do, then give them to a museum and take a fat tax deduction. Precious stones and minerals are the easiest to understand, so that's the shelter we take a look at tonight.

PAUL DESAUTELS: Tax shelter and tax avoidance are perfectly legitimate, allowable, legal, moral, upright, trustworthy, helpful, loyal, friendly, courteous, kind, reverent, obedient, and a-few-other-thing words. They are used in Internal Revenue literature.

SAFER: Paul Desautels, curator of gems and minerals at the Smithsonian Museum, is speaking to a group of dealers and collectors about a subject as dear to them as diamonds and rubies. Without tax shelters, Desautels says the nation's museums and we, the people, would be a whole lot poorer. Whether it's gems for the Smithsonian or Picassos for the Museum of Modern Art or old masters for the Metropolitan, American museums do not have much cash with which to buy things, so they depend on people's generosity, and American philanthropists would not be so generous in giving away these treasures if they were not rewarded themselves with a juicy tax shelter. So, when Paul Desautels stalks the corridors of the annual Tucson Gem and Mineral Show, looking for unusual stones like peridots —

MAN: Oh, my God, look at the size of them!

SAFER: — or topaz —

MAN: Oh, boy! (Laughter)

SAFER: — or garnets, or exotic rocks to add to his museum's collection, he has that benign look of a man who only does good in life.

You get an interesting bit of Americana at a show like this one. Ordinary rock hounds. People who operate those ma and pa corner gift shops, shops with names like Nature's Bounty and the Good Earth. You get the pack rats, the collectors who just love all things bright and beautiful. And you get the museum curators who come here to see what's missing from their collections and maybe find someone who will fill in the gaps.

MAN: I'd die for that one, yeah.

SAFER: And then you have that other breed of America — the man looking for an honest tax advantage, the man who can confirm that it is, indeed, greater to give than to receive (it can be much, much greater), who practices that fiscal magic that can turn a $20,000 purchase into a $100,000 gift in just a year.

Many of the people at this show are true collectors, who collect for the passion of it as well as the financial reward. In the past couple of years, gems and minerals have risen in value. But beyond that, and very important on the tax side of things, a gem can have a couple of different values: a wholesale price for which it can be purchased; and a retail price, the figure a jewelry store might sell it for, or the figure you might claim as a deduction when you give it away. That's exactly what Willard Dover, a Florida lawyer, did — bought gems wholesale, gave them to the Smithsonian, and took the retail price as a tax deduction.

WILLARD DOVER: My investment is worth five times what I paid for it. It happens that I got a bargain — a bargain buy or a bargain sale.

SAFER: How much did you pay for it? .

DOVER: Twenty thousand dollars.

SAFER: You paid $20,000 and they were valued at?

DOVER: Approximately a hundred and eleven.

SAFER: A hundred and eleven thousand dollars when you gave them away?

DOVER: When I purchased them. The comparable value would probably have been a hundred thousand.

SAFER: You mean you got a hundred-thousand-dollar buy for only $20,000?

DOVER: Sure.

SAFER: What was your tax benefit that year?

DOVER: Well, I don't remember my personal tax benefit, but you can anticipate that people would not be making charitable contributions if they were in, say, less than the 50-percent tax bracket; so just for a gross computation, you'd say, $111,000 minus 50 percent. So your tax benefits conceivably could be $55,000.

Of course, you've got to take into consideration that that $55,000 cost me $20,000.

WAYNE LEICHT: It sometimes happens that there are people who are looking for tax shelters. It sometimes happens there are dealers who are — are looking who have materials which will lend themselves, for various reasons, to tax shelter. And, yes, I frequently will direct a — a dealer to a potential buyer, or a potential biler — buyer to a dealer.

SAFER: Wayne Leicht is a dealer who has worked with the Smithsonian.

I want to buy it at the wholesale price, obviously.

LEICHT: Yes. Oh, yes.

SAFER: You would sell it to me? Would you assist me in finding the museum? I mean, you know what museums want.

LEICHT: Oh, yeah. No, we know what the museums want. Certainly, we'll find things that the museums want. Yes. Uh-huh. No problem there.

SAFER: And within that year, or over a year, I presumably can get an evaluation for it that would be the retail evaluation, the retail market value?

LEICHT: Yes.

SAFER: Another dealer, James Fullwood, says he does big business in the tax-shelter business.

If I give you a — $10,000 and say, "Look, I'm pay — I'm in the 50-percent bracket and I want to reduce my tax obligation" —

JAMES FULLWOOD: I'd take —

SAFER: — what could you do for me?

FULLWOOD: I'll give you an appraisal for a hundred thousand on the material.

SAFER: A hundred thousand?

FULLWOOD: Yeah. As long as it's not cut stones, it's all right. Carvings, some rare — rare pieces. In other words, something that a museum would like to have. We've done a lot of tax shelters. We have a couple of attorneys buy from us all the time, and they — what they do, they make two and a half percent on it to their clients. The stones you're buying from me are going to be bottom-line house sale. And when you go to retail — if I've imported something in the country, sometimes it's gone through ten hands —

SAFER: Yeah.

FULLWOOD: — with everybody doubling it before it got out to the public.

SAFER: If you have big money to spend, there's no problem buying gems at the wholesale price. The dealers, for the most part, do not care whether they sell them to a retailer or an individual, so long as the turnover is quick.

MAN: Look at it this way. I mean, in a way, it's — to a certain extent, the — the government is supplementing the museums, in a — in a — in a way. And that's probably easier than us paying tax dollars, sending it to the top and having it filter down, because every dollar comes down like a nickel. (Laughter) You know how — you know how with the bureaucratic. So, in effect, it's sort of a low level —

SAFER: Subsidy.

MAN: — sub— subsidy of — of museums.

SAFER: That's —

MAN: And God knows they need it, right?

SAFER: Betty Llewellyn likes to think of herself as an angel. She buys and collects but rarely sells. She gives and gives and gives. To who?

BETTY LLEWELLYN: Smithsonian, Carnegie, Pittsburgh, the University in Denver — the museum in Denver. I've given to the University of Utah, Southern Methodist University, Parish Junior College.

SAFER: Have you ever totalled it, toted it all up, how much it was worth?

LLEWELLYN: No, I never have. I never even thought about that until this minute. It might be interesting.

SAFER: Thousands and thousands of dollars' worth, Betty?

LLEWELLYN: Thousands, yes. Usually I find something that I like very much. I enjoy it, and I keep it for a while. And then I think, you know, it's just wrong for one individual to have this piece.

SAFER: Two pieces that Mrs. Llewellyn thought should be shared with the nation were these: a necklace called "The Garden" that she gave to the Carnegie Museum; and this, "The Pomegranate," clusters of diamonds that she gave to the Smithsonian.

How long did you own them?

LLEWELLYN: Over a year, maybe. I'd have to really look that up. Maybe a couple of years.

SAFER: Now, do you recall the tax — what the — what you paid for it and what the deduction was?

LLEWELLYN: No. No, I'm not good at numbers.

SAFER: Come on!

LLEWELLYN: No, I really don't. I really don't know the numbers. If you're asking me, I'm sure that it was — that it went up triple. I'm sure that it was three times.

SAFER: At le— at least three times.

LLEWELLYN: Exa— three times is about what the — what I donate. That usually goes up about three times. The Pomegranate, I was able to get at a very, very good price.

SAFER: Mrs. Llewellyn would not say what she paid for it, but we know she took a tax deduction of around $50,000. The Smithsonian awarded her a bronze medal for her generosity and invited her to dinner.

LLEWELLYN: And I wore The Pomegranate that night —

SAFER: And so that —

LLEWELLYN: — with my chin held high. (Laughs)

SAFER: If there wasn't a tax advantage, would you be giving away quite so much?

LLEWELLYN: If you're asking me, do I realize when I give something that it is a tax advantage, yes, I realize it.

JEROME KURTZ: Taxpayers are entitled, as you know, to the fair market value, and that sometimes is a seriously debatable issue.

SAFER: Jerome Kurtz, the commissioner of the IRS, is the man who ultimately decides on tax shelters. And despite Mr. Dover's and Mrs. Llewellyn's deductions, Mr. Kurtz claims that what you pay for a gem is, in most cases, what it's worth.

KURTZ: We would take the position, in almost all cases, that cost is the best indication of value. After all, value is defined in the law as what a willing buyer would pay a willing seller. If the — there is an actual transaction at a thousand dollars, and then, very shortly thereafter, a gift, a thousand dollars is the best evidence. Now it may be that something unique happened within the year to change it, but the taxpayer would have to show that.

SAFER: From what I've discussed with the IRS on this, the fair market value is what the goods can be purchased for, and if Willard Dover can purchase the goods for $20,000, and Joe Doaks, presumably, can purchase them for $20,000, then the fair market value is?

DOVER: That's not what the regulations say. I don't know what Internal Revenue is telling you, but in — fair market value is determined at retail. I'm not disputing Mr. Kurtz. He's the commissioner. But you have to compare apples with apples, and we're talking about a retail fair market value. You know, a car, for example, can be purchased wholesale or retail, and yet the value of an automobile when it's donated to a charity is the fair market retail value of that car. The fact that somebody is a wholesaler and can buy at wholesale shouldn't say that I, who am holding at retail, have to be constrained by his price limitations.

SAFER: So, you're saying that if the IRS does try to make — make it stick according to the — the gospel according Mr. Kurtz, that they're going to lose in court on this one?

DOVER: I — I would hesitate to say what will happen to the Internal Revenue Service.

SAFER: Betty, has the IRS ever looked at some of these gifts of yours and said, "Uh-uh, you can't do that?"

LLEWELLYN: The IRS has examined my income tax for the year I gave The Pomegranate to the Smithsonian. They examined it and they came out with no change.

SAFER: Do you think it's fair to all those people out there who can't afford to give things away, who can't afford to get this tax advantage?

LLEWELLYN: Well, they should thank me, don't you think, for increasing the wealth of the museums and the schools so that their children and their grandchildren can enjoy it? I don't have to do it, you know.

SAFER: Nowhere in the Bible does it say "Thou shall buy at wholesale and thou shall give at retail." But the Bible has nothing to do with tax shelters. Or does it? A few months ago, this ad appeared in major newspapers all over the country: "Buy Bibles by the thousand at wholesale, wait a year, then give them away at their retail value to your favorite church and take a deduction." This little holier-than-any-of-us shelter was the brainchild of Parker Dale, a California investment broker.

PARKER DALE: We couldn't think of anything more charitable as a concept than the giving of the — of the Holy Bible, assuming that — that you understand I'm a Christian, and so to me that's a very charitable con— aspect. So, we felt that if we could be in a position to distribute a half a million or a million Bibles, we couldn't be doing anything more charitable than that.

SAFER: Exactly how does it work?

DALE: Let's assume that you've got a — and let's just take a Bible. And let's assume that that Bible retails at $30, and so what you're doing is that you're buying that from us at $10. All right? So, by waiting the 12 months, the tax laws indicate that you can make that donation and deduct retail price.

SAFER: How do you find a charitable organization — a church or a missionary, whatever — who want the Bibles?

DALE: Well, we have right here in front of — you know, I would say, I don't know, a hundred letters from all kinds of groups that —

SAFER: U.S. Catholic Conference, Seventh Day Adventists, Assemblies of God, World Witness. You sure do. On and on. And all of these people are interested in gifts —

DALE: Right.

SAFER: — of Bibles?

DALE: Right.

SAFER: One cannot resist the ironies of a situation like this, of giving the Bible and getting a very good —

DALE: Economic return, also.

SAFER: — economic return, including the — the sheer irony of quoting the Bible back at you — that it's more enriching to give than to receive.

DALE: You know, we can always approach everything from a cynical point of view or we can try to look for the best in people's purposes and desires to do things.

SAFER: In a certain way, you're using the IRS to spread the word of God.

DALE: I would like to believe so.

SAFER: You —

KURTZ: We've already ruled on that one.

SAFER: You have ruled on it?

KURTZ: Yes.

SAFER: And?

KURTZ: Cost. Cost. If — if —

SAFER: You mean anyone responding to that ad —

KURTZ: Well, they — they — they can go to court and litigate with us, but they're buying litigation, because our view is, again, it's the same thing. The value is what one can buy it for, and if one can buy it for five dollars, it cannot be worth more than five dollars.

SAFER: What Mr. Kurtz is saying is that the IRS is changing rules in midstream, because up to now they have allowed the retail price as a deduction. It could be a bit of that renowned IRS intimidation, too. We checked with a former commissioner, Mortimer Caplin, and in his judgement, if a case went to court involving precious stones, the IRS would probably lose. In other words, the deduction would stand.

Israeli Arms For Sale
BARRY LANDO, PRODUCER

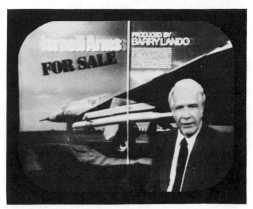

HARRY REASONER: This week, Egypt's President Sadat was in Washington. Next week, it's the turn of Israel's Prime Minister Begin. But while the diplomatic haggling goes on, the countries of the Middle East continue to pour billions of dollars into new weapons. And for Israel, much of that money is spent at home. Defense is not only a major preoccupation in Israel, it is also one of the major industries in Israel, producing not just for domestic needs but for export as well. Of course, Israel's arms sales are dwarfed by the exports of such giants as the U.S., the Soviet Union and France, but still tiny Israel has become one of the world's biggest exporters of arms. Sales of defense and aerospace products bring in a vital $600 million a year in foreign exchange. Recently, the Israelis let Mike Wallace take a look at some of their arms for sale.

MIKE WALLACE: The latest weapon the Israelis let us film is their new Merkova battle tank. Dollar for dollar it's considered to be one of the best battle tanks in the world.

Is it that good?

GENERAL YOSEF MAAYAN: It is the cheapest in its category.

WALLACE: Yes.

GENERAL MAAYAN: And it's leading in its own category.

WALLACE: General Yosef Maayan supervises Israel's arms production.

GENERAL MAAYAN: We found that it's also economically less expensive to produce here in Israel than to buy elsewhere.

WALLACE: Why? One reason is because the 40,000 men and women who work in Israel's defense industries, right to the top engineers, earn about one-third of what they would make in the United States. And so, Israel now produces, at a profit, the whole gamut of modern weapons — from sophisticated radar and electronic gear, to miniaturized guidance systems, to shells of all shapes and calibers. Of course, the most famous Israeli product worldwide is undoubtedly the Uzi submachine gun, still standard gear for the U.S. Secret Sevice. But the current best seller for the Israelis is their Galil — an automatic rifle, dependable even after the most punishing treatment.

(Gunfire)

Israel also produces big guns, which they've sold to about 20 countries. One of their newest, this 155-millimeter cannon, they claim to be one of the best in the world.

EZER WEIZMAN (Israeli Defense Minister):   This is a very good gun. It's usually rather expensive — $300,000 apiece. But we design it and manufacture it ourselves.

WALLACE: For export as well?

WEIZMAN: If a — a proper country with a proper check comes along, we do that.

WALLACE: What's a proper country? The proper check I understand.

WEIZMAN: Oh, no, we don't sell it to anyone. If it was Saudi Arabia, for instance, we wouldn't sell it.

WALLACE: But you might sell it to — seriously — South American countries?

WEIZMAN: Also, again, selective.

MAN: Not to Cuba. (Laughter)

WALLACE: Israeli Defense Minister Ezer Weizman.

Some people would say that the people of the Bible have become the people of the sword.

WEIZMAN: Well, first of all, the people of the Bible weren't so meekish. If you read your Bible, you'll see that our ancestors didn't keep the swords at home. And the — the great thing is to be the — if you want to really be the people of the Bible and be safe, also keep the sword.

WALLACE: One of Israel's most lethal "swords" is this one, the Gabriel, a ship-to-ship missile developed and built in Israel. It delivers a warhead over a distance of 30 miles with devastating accuracy. This Gabriel missile is a mainstay, a big money-maker in Israel's arms-for-export industry. More than a third of a billion dollars' worth have been sold abroad over the past few years. Marvin Klemow is the respresentative in Washington for Israel Aircraft Industries, independently managed but owned by the Israeli government. IAI builds the Gabriel missile.

MARVIN KLEMOW: One of the main marketing features, Mike, of Israel Aircraft Industries products is that — and I say this somewhat facetiously — unfortunately, they are combat-proven. And military people around the world respect the capability of the Israeli military. The Gabriel is the greatest example of that.

WALLACE: To carry those missiles, Israel also produces and exports swift patrol boats. Another big seller, the Shafrir air-to-air missile, one of the most effective low-cost missiles in the world.

But there are some Israelis who are not at all happy with Israel's position as one of the top ten arms exporters in the world today. Uri Avnari is a journalist and a member of the Israeli Parliament.

URI AVNARI: If you have to — to fight to defend yourselves, okay, but selling arms to people who don't really concern you and think — think of arms for money, it's a bad business.

GENERAL MAAYAN: One has to remember that Israel has invested tremendous resources into defense industry.

WALLACE: So, it's pure — I say expediency. It's pure necessity?

GENERAL MAAYAN: It's pure necessity on our part.

WALLACE: There are some deals Israeli officials don't mind talking about — the fact, for instance, that the U.S. buys sophisticated Israeli electronics gear. But when it comes to talking about many other sales, the Israelis are uniformly tight-lipped.

KLEMOW: I cannot answer you any questions on who our customers are. I told you, Mike, our policy is we don't confirm or deny. I read *Aviation Week* to see who it's going to.

WALLACE: The fact is that some countries, many countries, are ashamed to say that they deal with Israel.

KLEMOW: No, I don't think that's the correct word. I don't think "ashamed" is the pros— proper adjective. I think they understand the political realities of announcing that they deal with Israel.

WALLACE: And those political realities are?

KLEMOW: Arab pressure and oil.

WALLACE: In other words, they just don't want it known. Simple as that?

KLEMOW: I don't want to speak for those countries, but it — I think it seems obvious.

WALLACE: That combination — oil and politics — obviously cuts Israel off from the biggest arms market in the world today: The Arab states. But it also blocks its sales to most other Third World nations. However, the Israelis manage to make sales, nonetheless. Some of its best customers are the so-called "pariah" states. Shafrir air-to-air missiles, for example, go to the military regime in Chile. Many young members of Khomeini's Revolutionary Guard in Iran, who daily denounce Israel along with the United States, they also pack Israeli Uzi's, which in years past Israel had supplied to the regime of the Shah. And we have also learned of a multimillion-dollar weapons order placed by the Shah with Israel just before he was overthrown. Gabriel missiles go to the dictatorship in Argentina. Gabriel missiles went to the racist regime in South Africa; also Reshev patrol boats and assorted other weapons. A big favorite with military regimes in Central America, the Israeli-made Arava, a short takeoff and landing plane, promoted in sales films like this for everything from disaster relief to rugged military duty.

(Excerpt from sales film)

Almost to the bloody end, Israel supplied Galil rifles to the Nicaraguan National Guard of Anastasio Somoza, one of the most notorious of Latin America's dictators.

WEIZMAN: We sold arms to Nicaragua. Nicaragua was lost to Castro. Is this good or is this bad? I think it's bad. Therefore, I don't regret having sold arms to Nicaragua.

WALLACE: Look — look, the fact — the fact is —

WEIZMAN: You know— you know what? I think that there's a lot of hypocrisy about this thing, because why is the rea— why was the reason that the United States didn't like aid to Nicaragua? Because of human rights, isn't it?

WALLACE: Yes.

WEIZMAN: Now, if this was a reason not to sell to Nicaragua, why sell it to Saudi Arabia? Human rights in Saudi Arabia? I think that the Saudi Arabia thief still has his arm chopped. And look how much arms you sold to Iran. What is happening in Iran? So, let's not be hypocritical about the thing. And usually when we go selling arms, we usually find big— bigger countries there — France and Italy and Great Britain, and quite often the United States, too.

WALLACE: And the Stockholm International Peace Research Institute says, "Financial payoffs seem to be the main motivation behind Israel's expensive arms-sales campaign. Jerusalem has shown little political restraint in the choice of their arms customers."

WEIZMAN: Yeah, I think — I won— I wonder what the stock— the stockholders of Grumman or Boeing think? What does Boeing sell — or why does Grumman sell F-14's? For the love of it or to make money? People are up in arms when we sell arms to someone else.

WALLACE: Yes.

WEIZMAN: Nobody was up in arms when France sold — sold aircraft to Libya or to Iraq. Why? I think you do find a few French aircraft in South Africa, too. Did anyone ever complain to France?

WALLACE: Morality is only part of the issue. Israeli leaders point out that, on purely pragmatic grounds, attempts by governments like the United States to prevent other countries from getting arms are hopelessly naive. Case in point: the Kfir C-2, a single-engine, supersonic fighter, now standard equipment in the Israeli Air Force. It exists just because back in the late 1960's other countries would not sell the Israelis the weapons they wanted. This Kfir was developed in Israel after the French imposed an arms embargo on Israel following the Six-Day War. Israeli agents secured the blueprints for the French Mirage. Israeli engineers improved on the Mirage concept and installed an American engine. The result, this Kfir, which in Hebrew means "young lion."

GENERAL MAAYAN: I don't think you'll find a finer single-engine aircraft around the world today.

WALLACE: Many other experts agreed, and the Israelis had high hopes that the Kfir, at about $7 million a plane, would be a big sales success — but so far they have yet to export a single plane. The reason? Mainly the U.S. government. Israel was all set to sell $175 million worth of Kfirs to Ecuador, but because those Kfirs contained American-made GE engines, the Israelis had to get the U.S. okay before they could sell abroad. The American government wanted to keep such advanced weapons out of South America, so it blocked the sale.

KLEMOW: I might add that 40 percent of this airplane is American-made, so therefore if that sale would have been made, 40 percent of the revenue would have come to American companies.

WALLACE: So?

KLEMOW: The French moved in and made the sale to Ecuador, and the Mirage that they sold has not had one screw of an American product.

WALLACE: The French picked it all up?

KLEMOW: Totally.

WALLACE: So the lesson of that is, if you don't sell, somebody else will?

GENERAL MAAYAN: There is no doubt that if we don't sell, somebody else will sell.

WALLACE: The case of South Africa, says Maayan, also demonstrates the futility of trying to control the international arms trade.

GENERAL MAAYAN: I can only talk for myself. I didn't feel any embarrassment dealing with South Africa until the United Nations decided on an arms embargo to South Africa.

WALLACE: And now you observe the letter of the law of that embargo?

GENERAL MAAYAN: That's exactly what we do.

WALLACE: No spare parts, no nothing?

GENERAL MAAYAN: For an excellent reason, and that is because the South Africans were doing then, I believe in anticipating such an embargo, to — what we did, the Israelis, in 1968. That is, they have been building an industry that will be able to supply their own spare parts and eventually develop their own arms. It's about time that the fallacy of the so-called embargoes is — is known to the world.

WALLACE: The fallacy of the so-called embargoes?

GENERAL MAAYAN: They — they really don't work. You either find somebody to go around the embargo, or you force the embargoed country to develop its own arms industry.

WALLACE: What would happen if peace were to break out?

WEIZMAN: Where? It's broken, with Egypt.

WALLACE: No, I'm serious. Peace. What would happen to your arms industry?

WEIZMAN: Oh, it'll go flourishing along, because we'll have to guard the peace. Like yours. Are you at war with anyone?

WALLACE: Momentarily, no.

WEIZMAN: So, why do you — why do you produce F-15's and F-16's?

REASONER: War or peace, Israel has plans to produce a new sophisticated jet fighter of its own, called the Lavi, or the lion. And just last week, the United States agreed to permit General Electric to provide the engine for that plane. This time around the Israelis have high hopes the U.S. will not block its exports.

Letters

DAN RATHER: In the mail this week were several letters about our coverage of the war being waged in Afghanistan against the Soviet invaders, the war being waged by Moslem groups known as the Mujahadeen. One viewer wrote: "Why are the Mujahadeen of Afghanistan when they fight against the Soviet invaders called freedom fighters . . . And when the Mujahadeen of Iran fought against the American-imposed Shah, they were called terrorists?"

Another viewer said: "(If) we can't get 17,000 Soviet troops out of Cuba, (how are we going to get) eighty to a hundred thousand of them out of Afghanistan?"

There was another letter that said: "Would you consider taking our Olympic athletes on that same tour of Afghanistan?"

And there was also this: "(Now that you've sneaked into Afghanistan), do you think you could sneak into the White House and let us know what's going on there?"

Finally, about Bunky Hunt, the Texas billionaire who tried to corner the market in silver, a viewer noted that Mr. Hunt said about the amount of silver he owns, "That's known only to God and me, and neither of us is talking." That prompted a viewer to write: "The good Lord is probably not talking to Bunky Hunt either, because the Lord only talks to persons who listen . . . Bunky listens to nothing but the clink of silver."

APRIL 20, 1980

Omega 7
MARTIN PHILLIPS, PRODUCER

MIKE WALLACE: The United States has offered asylum to 3,500 of those 10,800 Cubans jammed into the grounds of the Peruvian Embassy in Havana, refugees from their own government. Eight hundred thousand Cubans have already sought refuge here, most of them now integrated into our society, though they remain passionately anti-Castro. But a small group — no one knows just how many — have banded together into something called Omega 7, and they have gone a considerable step further than mere peaceful protest. Within the past 12 months, Omega 7 has taken credit for bombing the Cuban Mission to the UN, the Soviet Mission to the UN, the New York offices of Aeroflot, the Soviet airline. It is also thought to be involved in the cold-blooded killing of at least two Cuban Americans, including a New Jersey man last November, Eulalio Negrin.

Just what is Omega 7? No one knows for sure, though the FBI says they are a group of Cuban American fanatics masquerading behind the cover of an organization called the Cuban Nationalist Movement.

This man says the FBI is the brains behind the secret organization Omega 7, though he swears he has nothing to do with it. He is Armando Santana, 30 years old, a bill collector by profession. But the FBI calls him a gangster and a terrorist. We talked to Armando Santana and his younger brother, Eduardo, at the headquarters of what the FBI calls their "front organization," the CNM, the Cuban Nationalist Movement, in Union City, New Jersey.

Over and over again, Mr. Santana, we hear that the CNM, your movement, the Cuban Nationalist Movement, is, in fact, Omega 7.

ARMANDO SANTANA: Those are accusations made by the authorities. Who else are saying it except the authorities, right?

WALLACE: The authorities say?

EDUARDO SANTANA: Local branches of the FBI. As far as we know, the FBI in Washington hasn't made such an accusation.

WALLACE: The FBI in Washington believes the same thing. The FBI in New York believes that CNM, the Cuban Nationalist Movement, is, in fact Omega 7 and is, in fact, responsible for the bombings and the killings that have taken place in recent years.

ARMANDO SANTANA: So, all you're doing is just restating exactly what the authorities are repeating constantly.

WALLACE: And you will restate the fact that what?

ARMANDO SANTANA: That this is contrary (indistinct). Nobody in our movement has been indicted or convicted as a member of Om— Omega 7.

DEMONSTRATORS (chanting): Guerra! Guerra!

WALLACE: Guerra, Guerra! — War, War! — has been the cry of assorted anti-Castro Cuban groups like this one for two decades. This is not a meeting of Omega 7, nor of the CNM, though Armando Santana is here. And while it is true, as he says, that no one has been indicted or convicted as a member of the secret Omega 7, nonetheless, Armando Santana himself served a two-year term after being caught in an attempt to bomb New York's Academy of Music in 1976.

BOB SCHERER: They are dedicated. They are fanatical. They are very articulate. They dress well. They present a very good front appearance.

WALLACE: FBI agents Bob Scherer and Carter Cornick have worked on an investigation of Omega 7 and the Cuban Nationalist Movement for the last four years.

CARTER CORNICK: What, in fact, these people do is they intimidate, they extort from, and they actually murder people for political reasons. They murder, however, defenseless, unsuspecting individuals in the same country which has granted them asylum — asylum from the — from the country in which they escaped dictatorship.

WALLACE: On the main street in Union City, New Jersey, I asked passersby how they feel about Omega 7.
Omega 7.

MAN: Yeah.

WALLACE: What about it?

MAN: Is okay.

WALLACE: It is okay?

MAN: Is okay. Everything against Castro is okay.

WALLACE: Perhaps a hundred thousand Cuban Americans live in this area, dedicated to the belief that Omega 7 is the best way — indeed, the only way — to keep alive the anti-Castro movement in the United States.
Is there anybody in this crowd who is against Omega 7?

MAN: Nobody.

CROWD: No, nobody.

MAN: Shouldn't be nobody.

WALLACE: And — and there's nobody who is against the tactics, the bombing, the killing that goes on?

CROWD: No, no, no, no.

MAN: Shouldn't be nobody.

WALLACE: You, young man, you are?

MAN: We may not sympathize with all their tactics, but we are for it, against Communist. We— we're all the way against Communism.

WALLACE: When you say —

MAN: We might not agree with such tactics as bombings and terrorist acts, but we do agree with the Omega 7.

WALLACE: I asked about two Cuban Americans whose names are well known to the Cubans of Union City: Eulalio Negrin and Father Andres Reyes.
You ever heard of Lu— Eulalio Negrin?

MAN: He's a goddamn Communist. He's a traitor.

WALLACE: So, as far as you're concerned, the fact that they killed him?

MAN: That's right.

WALLACE: It was okay?

MAN: That's right.

WALLACE: And Father Reyes?

MAN: That's right.

WALLACE: What?

MAN: He must be killed, too.

WALLACE: Father Reyes must be killed, too?

MAN: Yeah, he's a goddamn Communist.

WALLACE: Father Andres Reyes used to preach in Union City, but he was transferred by his diocese after his life was threatened for advocating a dialogue between Castro's Cuba and the Cuban community in the U.S.

FATHER ANDRES REYES: The only thing I can tell you, that what I did, I did it because I want to be a good Christian. I did it because I'm a Christian. And because of that, I won't hesitate to do it again if I have to — to do it. So, I'm — I'm not pro-Castro, pro-anybody, just pro-Christ.

WALLACE: Eulalio Negrin was shot to death in the street in Union City last November by two masked gunmen. He had acted as an intermediary between Cubans here and the government in Havana. Omega 7 took responsibility for his murder, saying that he was legitimizing Fidel Castro.
Well, you said that he was a traitor and you'd like to give his killer a medal. Your — quoting you.

ARMANDO SANTANA: That's correct. I said that, I don't deny it.

WALLACE: Were you in any way involved in the murder of Eulalio Negrin?

ARMANDO SANTANA: No, I was not involved in the murder of Eulalio Negrin.

WALLACE: A couple of months before you tried to beat him up.

ARMANDO SANTANA: Well, that's because the gentleman provoked me.

WALLACE: And conceivably —

ARMANDO SANTANA: Conceivably what?

WALLACE: You — you know that you are generally regarded by law-enforcement officials as being an accessory to the murder of Eulalio Negrin. You know that.

ARMANDO SANTANA: Yes, I know that.

WALLACE: Yeah.

EDUARDO SANTANA: Well, that's their problem. Since they've had a persistent inability to gather accurate information within the exiled community as a whole, they — they base all their intelligence on supposition. And that's another supposition.

WALLACE: You don't believe in hurting innocent people with your bombs, is that correct?

ARMANDO SANTANA: With — not with my bombs, with the bombs.

WALLACE: With the bombs.

ARMANDO SANTANA: Right.

WALLACE: Look, it was going to be your bombs at the Academy of Music. You served two years. Your bombs.

ARMANDO SANTANA: That — that — that I'll take care of.

WALLACE: You don't believe in hurting innocent people, you say?

ARMANDO SANTANA: I don't believe in hurting innocent bystanders.

WALLACE: Do you know something? The FBI said to me yesterday, "They're just blind lucky that not one or two but a dozen or two dozen people have not been killed so far, and the time is going to come when their plans, their bombs are going to go awry."

ARMANDO SANTANA: Mr. Wallace, I hate to use these figures. I don't want to get into a — a conflict thing, but innocent people sometimes get hurt in wars. The example is in — in Nagasaki and Hiroshima. But I think every effort has been made on the part of the anti-Castro movement to try only to concentrate on the people directly responsible for the Communist existence in our nation.

WALLACE: On a side street in Union City, a storefront advertises that, for a fee, they can send medical supplies to families in Cuba and arrange for visits to that island nation. Inside, we met a woman who'd come to make such travel arrangements, but when we began to speak to her of Omega 7, which threatens those who do business with Fidel, her companion warned her not to answer.
(Companion speaking in Spanish)
What — what does he say?

MAN: I tell her take care when she open the mouth, because, you know, you ask a lot of things, maybe you know —

WALLACE: It's — it's a free country.

MAN: I know.

WALLACE: She — she has the right to answer a question.

MAN: I know.

WALLACE: But you just don't want her answering questions about Omega 7, because —

MAN: No.

WALLACE: Not a question of being afraid. You know what they can do, right?
There is something called the Committee of 75 — its members listed here — that is despised by Omega 7 and by the leaders of the Cuban Nationalist Movement. The committee is sneered at as appeasers of Fidel. Their names are paraded in this publication of the CNM. In fact, the Committee of 75 is comprised of priests,

academicians, professional and business persons — among them, Father Reyes and the late Eulalio Negrin — who say simply that Castro and his Cuba are a fact of life that must be dealt with. They preach, in effect, peaceful coexistence.

These two individuals are members of the Committee of 75, afraid to show their faces here for fear of retaliation. What is it that they do that puts them in jeopardy?

WOMAN: I have been involved in — in — in some activity that — that I believe is fair and just and legitimate.

WALLACE: What's that?

WOMAN: To be involved with a group of people of the Cuban community, to try to bring some political prisoners out of Cuba, and to try to make some kind of arrangement so that Cubans, Cuban Americans, can travel to Cuba and visit their relatives.

WALLACE: In other words, you are — your group, your Committee of 75 — are, in effect, saying, "Look, Castro's here, he's going to stay here, it's a legitimate government and let's coexist"?

MAN: That's right. Just like the Hungarians and the Poles and the East Germans can do with their countries of origin: in a realistic way, to let people visit their families and do things like that.

WALLACE: They regard you as traitors?

MAN: Sure.

WOMAN: Enemies.

MAN: They regard George McGovern and Ted Kennedy as traitors, too. They probably regard you and the press as traitors and enemies and all kinds of ludicrous things.

WALLACE: And I suppose a sensible question: Are you Communist? Are you Fidelistas? Are you dedicated to Fidel Castro?

MAN: Of course not. Of course not. And they have no right to define us in the way they wish. That's outrageous. They run around, they define who in their eyes is a Communist or whatever, and they turn around and say they will execute us.

WALLACE: How se— Execute you?

MAN: That's exactly what they say.

WALLACE: How — how serious, do you believe, are the threats which they level about execution?

MAN: Very serious.

WOMAN: Very serious.

MAN: They have killed two people already. They have carried out numerous bombings in the New York, Miami and Puerto Rico areas, and they're tied to international ter— international terrorist organizations. The — the same group claimed the attempted bombing of a TWA plane going to Los Angeles a year or so ago.

WALLACE: It is that same group that the FBI says conspired to carry out this car bombing in Washington, D.C. that caused the death of a Chilean diplomat and triggered headlines around the world four years ago.

The Chateau Renaissance Motel just outside Union City, New Jersey. It was here, back in 1976, that members of the Cuban Nationalist Movement met with a

Chilean secret agent, Michael Townley. The purpose of their meeting? To tell Townley they would help him with the assassination of a former Chilean foreign minister, then living in exile in Washington, Orlando Letelier.

Former U.S. Attorney Eugene Propper prosecuted the Cubans for their involvement in the Letelier murder. He told us why it was the Cubans had agreed to help carry out that murder.

EUGENE PROPPER: The Cubans had asked the government of Chile, through Townley, to be allowed to use Chile as a government exile, to be recognized as the legitimate Cuban government in exile, to be allowed to send their fugitives there if and when the FBI or local police were after them. They were looking for a safe haven. They were looking for a source of explosives or weapons if they needed it. Effectively, they were looking for legitimacy. And the government of Chile, which is very anti-Castro, was their legitimacy.

WALLACE: So, in order to get the Chilean government to cooperate with them, they cooperated in the killing of Orlando Letelier, is that what you're saying?

SCHERER: Exactly.

CORNICK: Exactly, sir.

SCHERER: Exactly.

WALLACE: Tit for tat?

SCHERER: Tit for tat, exactly.

WALLACE: September 21st, 1976, Sheraton Circle, Washington, D.C. It was past here that Orlando Letelier drove to work each morning. On the day in question, his assistant, Ronni Moffitt, was sitting in the front seat next to him; in the back seat, her husband, Michael Moffitt. As his car reached this spot, it suddenly exploded. Letelier died instantly. Ronni Moffitt made it out of the car; she died 45 minutes later. Her husband, Michael Moffitt, survived the accident with almost no injuries.

Five Cubans from the Cuban Nationalist Movement were indicted as part of the conspiracy to assassinate Letelier. Among them, this man, Guillermo Novo, who used to head the CNM. Back in 1964, he and his brother, as a protest against Castro, fired a bazooka at the UN building in New York. It fell short.

Today, he sits in Leavenworth Prison serving a life term for his role in the Letelier murder.

What is Omega 7?

GUILLERMO NOVO: I don't know. I — Omega is the 24th letter of the Greek alphabet. I've been playing with this to see what — what it means, really. Twenty-four, twenty-four sevens, seven twenty-four; the last of the seventh, I don't know.

I know it was an organization that is doing attacks on Soviet and Cuban property, that's about it.

WALLACE: You know nothing whatsoever about it and its activities?

NOVO: I know about its activities what I have read in the papers.

WALLACE: No, I mean of your own certain knowledge.

NOVO: No, I do not.

WALLACE: You're not a member of it, have never been a member of it, know nobody who is a member of it, don't know anything about the inner workings of Omega 7?

NOVO: No, I don't.

WALLACE: And its relationship to Cuban Nationalist Movement?

NOVO: There's no relationship between Omega 7 and the Cuban Nationalist Movement. I'm not a terrorist. We're not terrorists.

WALLACE: You're not a terrorist?

NOVO: Of course not.

WALLACE: Well, you're serving time —

NOVO: Yes.

WALLACE: — as a murderer —

NOVO: Yes.

WALLACE: — Orlando Letelier.

NOVO: Yes.

WALLACE: You're a mild man, an intelligent man.

NOVO: And I did not have anything to do with the killing of Letelier.

WALLACE: Well, you did not persuade a jury of that.

NOVO: Unfortunately not. The government was very efficient in presenting the lies and the falsifications of evidence that they did present.

WALLACE: Why would the United States government, why would the FBI, be so certain that Guillermo Novo was one of those responsible?

NOVO: I don't think they're certain that I — I — I am convinced that they know that I had nothing to do with the killing of Letelier.

WALLACE: Well, then, why would they finger you and put you here in Leavenworth Prison?

NOVO: Well, I suppose — I don't know. I suppose maybe they needed a scapegoat. Someone had to be chosen, so it was I. It could have been anybody from any other organization — with the proper record, naturally, with a record of anti-Castro activist, with a belligerent record.

WALLACE: Though Novo swears he is innocent, he refuses to back away from his pledge to bring down Fidel Castro.
You're 40 years old and conceivably could spend the rest of your life in this prison. Is it worth it?

NOVO: Yes.

WALLACE: While Guillermo Novo sits in prison for complicity in murder, the man who replaced him as head of the CNM, Armando Santana, with his brother, Eduardo, leads the charge from headquarters in Union City, impatient with the Cuban Americans who have so far failed to free Cuba from Castro.

ARMANDO SANTANA: I'm not criticizing the old generation, but everything in history evolves and new generations take over. Okay? That — that's common history.

WALLACE: Yeah.

ARMANDO SANTANA: But the tactics of the old generation, concentrating on waiting for the green light from Washington, and waiting for the Marines to solve their problem and the CIA to solve their problem for them.

WALLACE: Uh-hmm.

ARMANDO SANTANA: And we don't believe the American government it's — and its interest are ever going to concord with our interest.

WALLACE: You don't —

ARMANDO SANTANA: And if we're going to wait for the Marines to liberate our nation, I'm going to be buried here in the United States.

Anne Lindbergh

JOSEPH WERSHBA, PRODUCER

MORLEY SAFER: There's never been a hero like him, and Anne Lindbergh knew that hero better than anyone: "Lucky Lindy," the first man to fly alone across the Atlantic. That was in 1927. Now he's been brought back to center stage by his wife, the writer, Anne Morrow Lindbergh, who has just published the latest volume of her diaries — diaries that deal with some of the most painful moments of her life with Lindbergh, the years 1939 to '41, when he was a leader in the movement to keep America out of World War II. To many that was his fall from grace. President Roosevelt publicly reviled him, and privately said, "I am absolutely convinced that Lindbergh is a Nazi." After Pearl Harbor, Lindbergh withdrew as a public person till his death six years ago. His wife's diaries will rekindle the old Lindbergh controversy.

Do you think that — that we made too much of Charles Lindbergh?

ANNE MORROW LINDBERGH: Yes. (Laughs) Yes. He was not a demigod. I think the best answer is in an article that said Lindbergh came along at this moment, and he satisfied two ideals of the Americans, two dreams, two self-images: He was the young Lochinvar from the West, all by himself, depending on no one else; and he was also the glory of the machine, the success of the machine age. So, the American people could worship two conflicting ideals at exactly the same time.

SAFER: Anne Morrow Lindbergh is 73 now and has lived a life — many lives. Part of the year she spends here on the island of Maui in Hawaii. She's been the wife of a legend, the mother of five, grandmother to 13. In 1927 she was 21, a beauty, educated, shy, daughter of a banker who was Ambassador to Mexico. He was 25 and the man of the moment. But Lindbergh was the sort of man who never understood what the fuss was about. She was the sort of woman who'd never heard of Charles Lindbergh.

MRS. LINDBERGH: I didn't even know that he'd crossed the Atlantic, because I was in college and I was working in the depths of the library on a paper on Erasmus. And when I came up, I — I say, "Who is this Lindbergh everybody's talking about?" And then he planned to go to my father's in Mexico City for Christmas with his mother, and we were all going down, too. We were in college, the family. I — I was terribly impressed when I saw him. I thought he was an incredible man. And it was this purity of vision, and it is what I have always called the "burning glass" quality. When he looked at you, he looked right through you. I mean, he had this quality of focus, which was extraordinary. And he put this into everything he did, and sometimes he burned.

SAFER: They were married in 1929 — the perfect American couple. The Eagle, the man of action, and the shy, literary violet. They were a team. He taught her to fly and she became his co-pilot and radio operator, and they flew the world. She wrote of the utter peace of it. "We were like birds," she said. "We were of the air." That peace was shattered in 1932, when their 20-month-old first child was kidnapped, then found dead.

MRS. LINDBERGH: Almost everyone has had a tragedy. Almost everyone. And you — you — you die, and then you are born again. I think that's what happens. Many people go through it. Not quite that, but many people go through it.

SAFER: Did that make you a stronger person, that experience? A tougher person?

MRS. LINDBERGH: Well, I don't believe that suffering teaches, although that is a very puritan axiom. I think you need both suffering and — and love, or — and beauty to get through things like that. And I had a great deal of support and sympathy and understanding. But I don't think suffering teaches, not alone. Suffering often embitters people.

SAFER: What about the effect on your husband at the time you lost the child?

MRS. LINDBERGH: He didn't express himself very much about it, and I think — I think that is a Swedish tradition. And I think he held it all in, wheras I wrote reams in my diary. I could get above it by writing about it. He really couldn't bear invasions on his privacy.

"I didn't even know that he'd crossed the Atlantic, because I was in college and I was working in the depths of the library on a paper on Erasmus."

Now there, I think, there was something irrational. He had an irrational feeling about the news, about new— news— newsmen. He felt they intruded on him. I don't think he was quite rational. He had reasons not to be, and we were terribly pursued and — at the time of the baby's kidnapping. The newsmen, some of them, behaved absolutely terribly — broke into the morgue and took pictures of the baby — and he never forgave them.

SAFER: In 1935, to get away from it all, they moved to Europe. The U.S. military asked him to go to Germany to report on the strength of Hitler's air force. He was acclaimed by the Nazis. He met with people like Goering, was awarded a medal. He reported back that the Luftwaffe could beat anything in Europe. He returned home in 1939. There was war in Europe, and he suddenly became a figure of controversy. He stumped the country urging America to stay out of the war. The polls showed most Americans agreed with him. He said President Roosevelt was violating the Constitution by taking the country into undeclared war.

CHARLES LINDBERGH: President Roosevelt and his Administration have never taken the American people into their confidence. (Applause) They preach about preserving democracy and freedom abroad while they practice dictatorship and subterfuge at home. (Applause)

SAFER: In September of '41, just three months before Pearl Harbor, Lindbergh told a Des Moines audience that the three groups that wanted to get an unwilling America into war were the British, the Roosevelt Administration and the Jews. To many Americans who had once idolized him, this was blatant Nazi propaganda — the end of Lindbergh as a hero. And for Anne, it was, next to the death of her child, the most painful time of her life.

MRS. LINDBERGH: I said, "If you give this speech" — I was very upset — "if you give this speech, you will be called the standard-bearer for anti-Semitism in this country." And he said, "But — but I'm not, and I don't want to be, and fix the speech up so it doesn't say that." And I said, "There's nothing I can do. If you isolate the Jews as a group, you may not be meaning to be anti-Semitic, but you're laying the ground for anti-Semitism. It's like lighting a match next to a pile of excelsior and saying you're just doing it in order to show your path."

SAFER: And, in fact?

MRS. LINDBERGH: In fact, he did light the pile of excelsior. It was terribly stupid. Oh, I was horrified. Horrified. I accused him of using this as a threat. He said, "No, I'm — I'm not doing that. I'm just saying the facts."

SAFER: Did you — did you row over it? Did you have a fight over it?

MRS. LINDBERGH: Oh, we — we did. I felt terribly about it, terribly. And he — he just didn't believe me, of course. He didn't believe me. I said, "I think it's worse. I think to rouse anti-Semitism in the country, it's much worse than war. I'd rather have war." But he said, "That's not what I'm doing." He simply couldn't see it.

One — one thing — one thing, I think, you have to realize is that he was not really a great reader. Had he read Goebbels and Hitler and so forth, all of them, he would have known that people who really are anti-Semitic start with these statements.

SAFER: He did have some ideas of racial superiority, though, in terms of warning against the brown or the yellow peril?

MRS. LINDBERGH: Well, I think that was — was a terrible thing. I think that's a much worse thing to say. I think that's a much worse thing to say. You know, when someone that you've lived with for years and that you love and who is — who you know does something that seems to you a total aberration, you don't walk out the door. You say, "Why did he do it?" And I think he did it because of a kind of blindness.

SAFER: Did you — It's a difficult question. Did you love him less for that?

MRS. LINDBERGH: No, I can't say I did. But I pitied him. I — I pitied him. I mean, it was so awful to see this happen to him.

I had a great belief in him, great belief, and I — that was some of the pain. I couldn't bear it that people saw someone that I didn't see, that I didn't think was there.

SAFER: The stubborn Swede that you often describe?

MRS. LINDBERGH: He was a stubborn Swede. He was. And his father was like that.

SAFER: In the privacy of his own home, was he a demonstrative, affectionate man?

MRS. LINDBERGH: Yes. Yes, he was. But only — only in his own family. Nobody else could be there; didn't want to show it off to anybody else. It was the way he was brought up. I was quite shocked when I met him in Mexico City that — for the first time. His mother was there and they shook hands to — good night. To say good night, they shook hands.

SAFER: I can't imagine shaking hands with my mother.

MRS. LINDBERGH: Shaking hands with your mother to say good night! So that, evidently, was something in his background.

SAFER: Your life with Lindbergh, what does — did that tell you about American hero worshiping and hero destroying?

MRS. LINDBERGH: Well, I think it's a very interesting phenomena in American history that we seem to build up our heroes overnight and then destroy them almost immediately. They're tumbled down. I just think — I think we worship success, but we really don't like the successful. (Laughs) We — we feel, perhaps, envious of them.

SAFER: Lindbergh did serve in the war, but it was not easy. A lot of people continued to feel that he was soft on Fascism. Anne Lindbergh lived with the pain of a stubborn man who did not understand the subtleties of the world and with a world that did not understand the man. But she had her writing. It was at once a way to relieve that pain and private demon.

MRS. LINDBERGH: I think if you are a writer you become another person when you're writing, if you're very steamed up about it, and — and you forget everything else. You forget your children, you forget your husband. And it — it — it's a terrible conflict, really. You're possessed of a demon. Yes, I think one is possessed of a demon. And then if — if the — if you've struck a vein of gold, you just have to go on.

SAFER: Has it troubled you or concerned you that you might have been more important or more renowned in a certain way had you not been encumbered by your husband's heroism?

MRS. LINDBERGH: I don't think I was inhibited in the sense that I minded the renowned, but I did want people to like me for myself and not because I was Mrs. Lindbergh. That is something that dogs all famous people all their lives, and the wives and the widows.

SAFER: For 30 years after Pearl Harbor, Charles Lindbergh was rarely found in the news. When his picture did appear, it was the Gray Eagle, not the Lone Eagle. Lindbergh was nostalgia — the triumph and the tragedy of all our yesterdays. The new Lindbergh, the aging Lindbergh's passions were the environment and primitive people — and, as ever, flying.
Did your husband have any fear in the air?

MRS. LINDBERGH: I don't think so. I used to talk to him about this, and he said, "When one is in action, one doesn't have fear."

SAFER: When he recognized death as the next thing to go forward to, how did he handle that?

MRS. LINDBERGH: With dignity, with a — a great sense of adventure, and with total calm. I never saw him in a panic. He said, "I could have died any time in the last few days. I could have died and it would have been very easy." He said, "It's — it's harder for you watching. It wouldn't be hard for me." I don't think he was afraid of death.

SAFER: In 1974, when he knew he had a few days to live, he made his last flight — home to Maui. Here he gave directions for a simple funeral in the graveyard of this church.

Anne did not always understand Charles, but she saw him whole. Her diaries may reopen old wounds, but as a writer she has done her best to describe the man honestly, uncolored by the rosy haze of his early heroism, or by the warm glow of her abiding love for him. She is at peace again with nature, just like that time long ago when they both soared like eagles.

Dam

AL WASSERMAN, PRODUCER

HARRY REASONER: These last couple of months, Congress has been agonizing over how to cut some $15 billion from the federal budget. But one area Congress seems reluctant to cut is water-resource projects — dam building, navigation projects, harbor dredging, marinas and so on, the kinds of projects that bring federal money into a local area and endear a congressman to his constituents. We decided to take a look at one of those projects — a dam that's been under construction by the Tennessee Valley Authority, the TVA, a dam that was on President Carter's hit list of unnecessary projects.

This is the Columbia Dam on the Duck River, some 40 miles south of Nashville. It's about 30 percent complete, and the cost to finish it would be noticeably more than a hundred million dollars. Right now there's nothing going on here. The dam is bogged down in a battle between opponents, who say it's just another pork barrel project, worse than useless, and supporters, who say that the dam would be even better than Carter's Little Liver Pills for whatever ails the citizens of this part of middle Tennessee.

If you put the dam to a vote in this county, would it win?

JUDGE TAYLOR RAYBURN: Ninety— ninety-nine to one.

REASONER: Ninety-nine to one?

JUDGE RAYBURN: Yes, sir I could gi— assure you on my honor. Ninety-nine to one.

REASONER: Judge Taylor Rayburn is typical of the kind of support the project seems to have in the City of Columbia, just downstream from the dam site. And the enthusiasm extends all the way to Washington. Congressman Robin Beard represents the district in Tennessee where the Columbia Dam is located, and he's all for it.

REPRESENTATIVE ROBIN L. BEARD (R-Tennessee):   I—I see that as a more productive segment of federal spending than I do in our CETA program for New York, or a subway program for Washington, D.C.

REASONER: Beard is completing his fourth term in Congress, and he's a leading spokesman for the dam. We asked him why he thought it was a good idea.

REPRESENTATIVE BEARD: Oh, I think one of the major benefits that I list is the flood control. I've been involved in floods down there almost every year. I've seen young people drown, property damaged. That's probably one of the more emotional areas of supporting my stand.

REASONER: You know, there's a — there's a problem there in our research. We can only find one death in about 25 years of the floods. There was a woman who drove off a bridge.

REPRESENTATIVE BEARD: Yeah, I think that was several years ago. Yes.

REASONER: Right. We can't find any others. Are we looking in the wrong place?

REPRESENTATIVE BEARD: Well, I don't know the exact number. It might have just been one death. But — so let's put a price tag on a death or on potential deaths.

REASONER: We learned later that there were actually four deaths in that one automobile accident. The accident, apparently, was not caused by the floods. There are floods in the City of Columbia. Congressman Beard has described them as "devastating." Well, some older portions of the city are built on the flood plain, a practice that is now discouraged, and over the years they have been flooded periodically. This is some of the flooding this year. The Duck River is not known for flash flooding. The waters rise slowly. As the publisher of the local paper told us, "We have learned to live with the urban floods pretty well." Another reason supporters of the dam claim it's needed is that it would protect 3,700 acres of agricultural land downstream of the dam from flood damage. But a lot of farmers say that seasonal flooding actually helps farm land.

FARRIS JENKINS: Well, it made it better. It settling — settled in and made it richer than what it was before — you know, before it was flooded. I — I liked it. I liked to see it flood every year when I owned it. So, it made a lot better ground.

REASONER: Farris Jenkins is a farmer who used to own some bottom land along the Duck River. The Army Corps of Engineers agrees with Mr. Jenkins. They told us that periodic flooding of bottom land is generally beneficial.

This is what used to be Farris Jenkins' bottom land. He doesn't own it anymore, because it was needed for the dam, along with the rest of his 113-acre farm. He was first approached by TVA back in 1974.

JENKINS: They come back and — and told me that they wanted — that they was going to build a dam here. They didn't ask me if I wanted them to or not. (Reasoner laughs) They just told me they was going to.

REASONER: They didn't give you a vote on that?

JENKINS: No.

REASONER: No.

TVA appraised Jenkins' property and made him an offer to buy — an offer he tried to refuse.

JENKINS: I told them I wouldn't take it, and they kept on. I guess maybe six months later before I finally signed that — signed it.

REASONER: Did they indicate they'd use force?

JENKINS: Yeah.

REASONER: What did they say?

JENKINS: Well, Mr. Bishop told me that if I didn't sign it that day that they could get in— an injunction and condemn it and take it and make me move then.

REASONER: Is that when you signed?

JENKINS: Yeah.

REASONER: As a prime example of the dedication of the local community, you said at one time some 200 people voluntarily left their homes for the public good. These people can never return to their homes, many of which had been in their families for generations. I assume you're talking about the farm families whose land was acquired for the project?

REPRESENTATIVE BEARD: Yes, yes.

REASONER: Well, we spoke to a half dozen or more of those families and they all say the same thing: that they did not cheerfully leave, voluntarily, or leave voluntarily at all. They left because TVA told them that they had to sell their land or they'd be evicted.

REPRESENTATIVE BEARD: They left out of duress.

REASONER: And their feeling is, they couldn't care less about the Columbia Dam.

REPRESENTATIVE BEARD: Exactly. And I think that's a very accurate description.

REASONER: But you had said they left voluntarily?

REPRESENTATIVE BEARD: No, I — well, if I did I certainly didn't mean to, because . . .

REASONER: It's hard to know which Congressman Beard to believe — the one who agrees the farmers couldn't care less about the Columbia Dam, or the one who said at a public hearing that they left voluntarily because of their total commitment to the completion of the dam.

The loss of farm land for the Columbia Dam involves more than a personal loss for Farris Jenkins and the other farmers like him. What's also involved is the loss of twenty-seven-and-a-half thousand acres of land. TVA acknowledges it's some of the most productive agricultural land in the region: more than two-thirds of it crop land, and about 40 percent prime farm land, the best land there is.

The loss of land to the Columbia Dam comes at a time when farm land is an endangered species, disappearing at the rate of over five million acres a year. According to a government study, if that trend continues, we will no longer be a food-exporting country by the year 2000. In exchange for the loss of farm land, what the country would be getting is a dam.

Most dams in the TVA system are designed to generate electricity through hydroelectric power, but the Columbia Dam won't provide any electricity. Another traditional benefit of TVA dams is navigation, opening rivers to cheap transportation of material by barges. Columbia Dam won't do that, either. What the Columbia Dam will provide is another TVA lake behind the dam, and the major benefit of that lake, as well as the single biggest justification for building the Columbia Dam, would be recreation.

Again, according to TVA's cost benefit figures, that is their biggest single justification for going ahead with the project, on the theory that it's something everyone can enjoy, not just the local community or local businessmen. Do you share that feeling?

REPRESENTATIVE BEARD: I share it because that's — that's the way it's been presented to me in the development of the cost benefit ratio. So you have to assume that there will be a great deal of recreational attitudes or recreational opportunities provided by this project.

REASONER: It's true that the reservoirs behind TVA dams are used as lakes that offer a variety of recreation. But TVA has been in the dam-building business for a long time now and, as critics of the Columbia Dam have been pointing out to anyone who would listen, there are already nine recreational reservoirs within 50 miles of the Columbia Dam. Their combined shoreline is 3,000 miles, almost one-third that of all the Great Lakes. This was news to Congressman Beard.

REPRESENTATIVE BEARD: I would think that TVA certainly would have presented this in their presentation in — in defense of the dam or in opposition of the dam, because I'm somewhat confused now as to your statements whether TVA supports the dam or opposes it.

REASONER: Actually, TVA's relationship to the Columbia Dam has been a curious one, and one somehow gets the impression they wouldn't be too unhappy if it just went away. Unlike most projects in the TVA system, this one didn't originate with TVA.

LON MacFARLAND: This was not TVA's idea. It was the four-county ir— idea to develop the project and make a — a — a model project out of it.

REASONER: Lon MacFarland is a lawyer in Columbia, and also heads the local bank.

MacFARLAND: This was developed as a four-county model project to have TVA do with water what they've done with electricity.

REASONER: The chief attraction for the communities involved is that they feel it will prevent a future shortage of water, but TVA has said it can supply enough water for the next 50 years, even without the dam.

MacFARLAND: No, we think that that estimate is not completely accurate; that the growth here and the water use — the water is expanding very — use is expanding very rapidly.

ELMO LUNN: We believe that — that there is adequate water, as far as we know, about future needs to . . .

REASONER: Elmo Lunn is chief of the Division of Water Quality Control of Tennessee's Department of Public Health. We spoke to Mr. Lunn and some of the other staff engineers and biologists. Two of the men are no longer with the division. Last summer, the staff came out with a report that stated the Columbia reservoir would have severe problems with water quality. The technical term for it is "eutrophication."

Is this the process that was so dramatically shown in Lake Erie?

STEVE ANDERSON: Yeah, very similar. Very similar.

REASONER: Which was sort of described as the death of a lake?

ANDERSON: We would anticipate a similar thing here, hopefully not as severe. But yet, we do think that in terms of the uses of the lake — recreation, things such as that — it will not be the type of lake that people would enjoy normally, like they would our other reservoirs around the state.

REASONER: Another fact that might interfere with enjoyment of the reservoir is something called "draw down."

LUNN: They will have to draw it down, or they will draw it down during the winter, in order to —

REASONER: Lower the water level?

LUNN: Lower the water level, in order to provide capacity to retain flood-water runoffs.

REASONER: In the case of the Columbia reservoir, the body of water would become so much smaller that almost two-thirds of the reservoir would be dry land for several months of the year.

JOE ROSSMAN: I can imagine that building a boat dock and having it sit high and dry on a mud flood all winter long could be a little problem for some people.

REASONER: You're aware that they have to change the water level for about five months of the year, leaving about two-thirds of the reservoir as dry land or wet mud, depending on the situation. Is that news to you?

REPRESENTATIVE BEARD: That's news to me.

REASONER: You're being informed by a reporter this morning, at this stage in it, of one major fact that you didn't know before?

REPRESENTATIVE BEARD: Well, if — if what you're — inform me of, I think that it — it's somewhat unique that the leadership of TVA would not have said this before a member of that particular area.

REASONER: Is it possible that might change, or at least affect, your opinion about the dam?

REPRESENTATIVE BEARD: I think that we should do — cer— certainly study it, without any question. I think the whole scenario could be changed.

REASONER: Do you think this part of Tennessee needs another reservoir?

TERRY COTHRAN: In my personal opinion, I wouldn't think so. It's harder in many situations in Tennessee to find a — a free-flowing stream of the size and the length as the Duck River.

ANDERSON: We're not just talking about another reservoir. We're talking about one that over years — 20, 30, 40 years, perhaps — is going to be an undesirable part of the community. There'll be odors associated with it. The ability to use it for a drinking water source will be very remote. It will be very expensive to use it.

REASONER: The staff of the Division of Water Quality Control of — of your state's Department of Health is highly critical of the dam. They say it shouldn't be built. They say it's not going to result in another high-quality Tennessee lake; that there will be severe problems with water quality because of the nature of the dam and the terrain, and they doubt that TVA will be able to deal with those problems successfully.

REPRESENTATIVE BEARD: Once again, I'm confused as to that, because I thought the State Department of Health had come out to — to call for certification. But what was the department's official position?

REASONER: It's true that Tennessee's Commissioner of Public Health, a political appointee, certified that the water released from the dam would be of acceptable quality, but his professional staff agreed unanimously that the reservoir would have severe water-quality problems.

REPRESENTATIVE BEARD: So, in other words, the staff recommended to the commissioner that they — it should not be certified?

REASONER: That's right.

REPRESENTATIVE BEARD: Then I think they should resign in protest.

ANDERSON: This has been really quite difficult for us to go through this analysis, as we said, because we understand the repercussions of it.

ROSSMAN: We've looked at this throughout, from a technical standpoint, however, and I think based on our technical look at it, we can say, or I can say, that the Columbia Dam site is probably one of the worst sites that could have been chosen for a reservoir.

REASONER: Congressman, one of the first expressions you run into in — in a civics class or American History is "pork barrel." It's even in the dictionary. It says: "A — a federal appropriation for some local enterprise that will favorably impress a representative's constituents." As you see it, the Columbia Dam is not pork barrel?

REPRESENTATIVE BEARD: I see it helping my constituents, as had been presented by all the different — the agencies, as to correcting the problems that there were in existence. I see it helping my constituents, and I think as a member of Congress representing that particular area, that's my responsibility.

REASONER: One of your major points has always been to cut down on federal spending. Isn't there a suggestion that you are against federal spending except when it's politically beneficial to you?

REPRESENTATIVE BEARD: Absolutely not. I think that's a — very irresponsible to even suggest.

REASONER: At the risk of seeming perhaps even more irresponsible, we'd like to point out that right now Congress is considering a $4.4-billion bill authorizing a whole new batch of water-resource projects. President Carter has called the bill "very large and wasteful," but the House of Representatives voted overwhelmingly in favor of it. Congressman Robin Beard supported the bill.

Letters

DAN RATHER: In the mail last week was a raft of letters about our story on the Church of Scientology. A lot of them came from viewers who found our report enlightening. Even more, however, came from viewers who found our report: "Irresponsible, unprofessional and prejudiced . . . any mistakes the church has made are infinitesimal compared to the amount of good they are doing."

And there was this: "Do not condemn the barrel because of a few rotten apples."

But another viewer wrote: "Jesus . . . said 'By their fruits you will know them. A good tree does not produce evil fruit.' "

However, a letter from a Scientologist said: "If you really knew what Scientology was about, you would join it in an instant."

About our story on people who buy gems wholesale and then claim the retail price on their tax return when they donate the gems to a museum, a viewer wrote: "The lady who (saved a bundle by giving) her jewels to the Smithsonian said . . . 'People should be happy that I do this.' I would be happier if she paid her taxes . . . and kept her jewels to herself."

And finally, a viewer wrote: "It just goes to show you, no matter how hard we try to disguise it, there's a little bit of Bunky Hunt in all of us."

APRIL 27, 1980

Walking Small in Pitkin County

GREG COOKE, PRODUCER

MORLEY SAFER: What is the stereotype of the western sheriff? Well, certainly he wears a cowboy hat and boots, and certainly he carries a gun slung low on the hip. On his office wall might be some bit of memorabilia from the Old West. And what he does most of all, in the language of the West and law enforcement, is he walks tall — an up-to-date version of Wyatt Earp or Matt Dillon. This story is about a sheriff who does none of the above. Just to give you a hint of his preferences, his office wall is decorated with a peace symbol, and his main opponents these days are not disturbers of the county peace but other police officers who do not like the way he keeps the peace. Before we tell you more about the sheriff of Pitkin County, you should know more about Pitkin County itself.

What Pitkin County is not is typical. What it has is what a good part of America and the world want — peace and quiet and sunshine and air that tastes of nothing but air. So Pitkin County has condominiums with three so-so rooms that sell for half a million dollars. Or old miners' cottages that sell for the same. Or for millions and millions, houses that are spectacularly inside out. What is life without a swimming pool in the living room?

What Pitkin County has above all is Aspen, Colorado. Among the gathering places for the American aristocracy, Aspen ranks near the top. The aristocracy of film stars, and lesser lords — industrialists and hair dressers and other people who get rich in ways you never even think of. And then the great mob of gilded courtiers — affluent, not-so-young, not-so-middle-aged Americans; single, the soon-to-be or recently singled, who like to spend time in an Aspen or a Acapulco. Plus, to be fair, solid citizens who like to prove that to be fifty is not to be finished. And then the permanent residents, comfortably upper middle class, who mainly moved here from elsewhere; almost entirely white and non-Hispanic.

But this is not — forgive that dreadful phrase — one of those "life style stories" about an expensive playground. In fact, it's about law and order. The FBI and the Drug Enforcement Administration say that Pitkin County has become a main drug distribution center, especially for cocaine, the so-called recreational drug of the upper middle class. And they say that the law in Pitkin County not only looks the other way, but actively subverts federal drug enforcement. So what you have here is a collision between the no-nonsense, statistically minded federal enforcers and the sheriff of Pitkin County, a man who sees his duty as a peace officer, well, differently.

SHERIFF DICK KIENAST: The mere fact that we suspected somebody was — was smoking grass or using drugs in his own home would in my mind give us no justification whatsoever to go outside their windows either with binoculars or peeking around the curtains or — or planting hidden microphones in order to hear their conversations.

SAFER: His name is Dick Kienast, age 40, master's degree in theology and philosophy, Notre Dame University. Elected sheriff four years ago. No uniform, no gun. But what truly separates him from much of traditional law enforcement are his views on the rights of privacy. He will not, and will not let his deputies, take part in any kind of undercover work; and more, he will not cooperate with any outside federal agency that wants to work undercover in his territory.

But 200 miles away in Denver, they see things differently. The assistant U.S. attorney, Rodney Snow, who's having a grand jury investigate Dick Kienast.

RODNEY SNOW: The accusations are certainly public at this point, and that is there's some problem perhaps with maybe a local philosophy which is different from the rest of the United States.

SAFER: The regional head of the DEA, Wayne Valentine. He regards Kienast as a threat to drug enforcement.

WAYNE VALENTINE: The need for assistance on a state and local level is very great to DEA. And we receive very great assistance in almost all the areas, with the exception of Aspen; and there, with the exception basically of the sheriff's department.

SAFER: And for the FBI, special agent-in-charge Jack Egnor sees Kienast as a cop gone wrong.

JACK EGNOR: One of our agents received information, while doing another investigation, that some of the members of his department were not only using drugs but possibly involved in selling drugs, and we relayed that information to the sheriff. We also advised, of course, the Drug Enforcement Administration here in Denver, Colorado. And the sheriff gave us the impression that he wasn't going to do very much about it.

SAFER: We'll get to those charges in a moment. But first, it's important to know that Dick Kienast's sheriff's department is like no other — a very relaxed, un-macho atmosphere. No badges of rank, no rank at all. Very much a bean-sprout and friends-of-the-earth look; almost a police commune. The patrol cars are mild-mannered non-threatening Saabs painted a friendly beige. And even the lettering has that "Have a nice day" look about it. But do not be fooled by the laid-back look of this outfit. Kienast is as tough as any redneck sheriff on his deputies in the areas that he feels count. He makes them qualify on the range every three months. If they fail, they're confined to a desk. His rationale is that if they have to use the weapon, he doesn't want any innocent bystanders dead. So in actual enforcement of the law — traffic safety, drunk driving (he's particularly rough on drunk drivers) crimes of violence, robbery, even open drug violations — Kienast would say that he's as vigilant as anyone in enforcing the law. But on questions involving the rights of privacy or undercover police operations, he feels it's his duty as a peace officer to keep his distance.

KIENAST: With all the capabilities, the technological capabilities, we have for invading privacy now, it's time that we really do draw some clear parameters to — to how they can be used and how — how — what individuals should have to themselves in their own lives.

VALENTINE: The use of cameras, the use of electronic surveillance, is an everyday mode with us. We — we use that in Denver. It's not isolated to Aspen. In fact, there's very little technical equipment that's been used up there, compared to what is available to us.

SAFER: Nevertheless, the DEA does use electronic surveillance equipment in Aspen, and it does not tell anyone about it. It especially does not tell Dick Kienast. But in a place like Aspen, secrets are hard to keep.

While we were interviewing Sheriff Kienast, something happened. Something was found in Pitkin County. And here it is. This electronic box was found by these two gentlemen. And what is this — this thing?

MAN: Well, basically it's a — it repeats whatever message is put into it; a coded message, obviously. And it was — it is marked "Owned by DEA."

SAFER: The box was used by undercover DEA agents to communicate with each other on a frequency where they would not be overheard by other law enforcement. The DEA placed the box surreptitiously on a mountaintop on a site owned by a Pitkin County community television company, and plugged into its facilities.

KIENAST: The basic thing that upsets me at the present moment is the fact that it was placed in a private place belonging to Pitkin County at the moment, and — and no permission was granted, as far as I can tell.

SAFER: When it was found and turned over to the sheriff's office, he happily made it public and declared it lost federal property. And the DEA rather sheepishly turned up to claim it.

Are you — are you going to retrieve that magic box of tricks that you — they have here?

JIM ROTH (DEA):   Pardon me. You're —

SAFER: Morley Safer.

ROTH: Morley Safer.

SAFER: You are?

ROTH: Glad to meet you. My name's Jim Roth.

SAFER: Hi, Jim. And you're?

GUS BOWES: Gus Bowes.

SAFER: Hi, Gus.

ROTH: I'm a special agent with the Drug Enforcement Administration.

SAFER: Both of — both of you?

ROTH: No, just myself.

BOWES: I'm a technician.

SAFER: I see.

ROTH: And the reason I came to Aspen was to pick up the equipment which is in the custody of Pitkin County.

SAFER: Uh-huh.

ROTH: I would not refer to it as a "bag of tricks."

SAFER: If that kind of thing isn't enough to cause anger among the Federales, consider this. A couple of years ago when the DEA arranged to have the Mexican marijuana fields sprayed with the herbicide paraquat, a substance that could be dangerous to anyone who smoked the affected weed, the sheriff, as a public service to marijuana users, had an announcement read over a local radio station. Just to give you a better idea of the kind of man Dick Kienast is, we asked the station to read it again, just for us.

WOMAN (in studio, over music):   It's 33 degrees in Aspen at 20 minutes after the hour. If you want to have your marijuana tested for paraquat, contact the Pitkin County Sheriff's Office. They'll provide you with the address of a California laboratory that tests pot samples for a five dollar fee. The Pharm-Chem Foundation says that more than 22 percent of the 2,000 pot samples it's tested from around the country have been contaminated with the herbicide. Health authorities say that smoking marijuana laced with paraquat could result in permanent scarring of the lung tissue. This has been a public service announcement brought to you by the Pitkin County Sheriff's Office.

SAFER: But do you not see how — how an action like that, a community service like that —

KIENAST: Uh-huh.

SAFER: — by Sheriff Kienast could get federal law enforcement people up in arms, the more —

KIENAST: Well, since —

SAFER: — traditional types?

KIENAST: — since they're the ones that sprayed it with paraquat, I would — (laughs) — I would think it might, yeah. (Safer laughs) And I — and I would ask who is truly concerned about the public safety.

SAFER: You are more or less a regular cop here in Aspen. When you worked for the city police, you kicked down the doors, you did all those violent things that policemen sometimes do.

KIENAST: That was a very enlightening experience to me. Here you are, you go and you approach a door, you have five armed police officers, okay, with their guns drawn, one with a shotgun. Okay, you knock on the door and surprise the person and jump in and say, "It's the cops! Everybody hands up!" And you see what — what happens to people. They just, you know, go crazy. I mean, it's like the KGB kicking in the door. And here we were going in and actually producing the possibility of an extremely violent situation. Okay, we were producing that. They didn't produce that. And — and — and scaring the hell out of people, literally. What right do we have to come on with that scale of violence or potential violence for the crime in fact that was committed?

SAFER: Which was?

KIENAST: Which was possession of marijuana.

VALENTINE: The Drug Enforcement Administration feels that there is active heavy trafficking in cocaine in this area.
And I think there's a lot of indications around the states that show this, and I

think we have an obligation to actively pursue all the leads, which are many, to their final conclusion on it.

SAFER: Are there large drug deals going on in Aspen? Big time stuff?

KIENAST: No, I don't think so. First of all, there isn't the population to support that, okay? Second of all, strictly from a marketing point of view, economic point of view, one does not put a distribution point in a remote area of the Rockies.

(Disco music . . . dancing)

SAFER: There is marijuana and cocaine here, of course. Anyplace that celebrates youth, regardless of age, the way this place does, and anyplace that has the affluence that this place has, will have a lot of cocaine. Not to say that anyone you are now watching is a drug user or drug dealer. Whatever use goes on here tends to go on quite privately. And whether it is used more or less than in Fairfield, Connecticut, or St. Louis, Missouri, can only be a guess. The more solid residents of Aspen certainly believe that. And they support their local sheriff. The mayor, Herman Idell, says just because Aspen is Aspen, the federal agencies are carrying a grudge.

MAYOR HERMAN IDELL: This a very glamorous town. There are a lot of people who come here and — quote, "stars," whatever that word means, and they're ignored, they just become another person. It is much more interesting, I think, to investigate that area than where — there's a lovely town down valley about 50 miles. It's called Silt. Silt, Colorado. Now, I don't suggest the DEA is ever going to go into Silt. Yet I assure you there's drugs in Silt.

EGNOR: We in the FBI were not selective in our law enforcement investigations. I think you saw that by the Mi— Miporn case down in Florida, by the Abscam case we had, and by Brilab. We go after anyone and everyone that commits violation of the laws. People talk about Pitkin County, and they're subject to the same laws of the United States as anyone else. Some people think they may have seceded from the Union, but they haven't.

SAFER: You had a deputy here who used cocaine. You got rid of him.

KIENAST: Right. I — I assume he used cocaine. I had —

SAFER: You assume he used cocaine.

KIENAST: — enough information to believe that — (laughs) — that was pretty true, right.

SAFER: Now, are they saying that the fact that you did not prosecute him, arrest him, was more than mere neglect of duty, that it was almost criminal complicity?

KIENAST: Yeah. Well, that's what they're saying. If I had felt I had sufficient evidence, okay, to prosecute him, my responsibility would have been to pursue that, to give that — to pass that on for the DA.

SAFER: Which is the bigger threat here in Aspen: of becoming a major drug center, or having its civil liberties infringed upon?

KIENAST: Absolutely the latter, Morley. I think that the citizens have the rights and grant certain powers to government, as opposed to the reverse, where the government has all the rights and grants certain privileges to its citizens. And if you ask me any choice, any decision, or any of my officers, if they have to make a decision between infringing on somebody's rights and enforcing some other written law, obviously the civil rights come first, because they are the cornerstone, they're the Constitution. And we are to uphold the Constitution as well as the written statutes of our legislators.

SAFER: But in that order?

KIENAST: Ye— absolutely.

SAFER: The federal grand jury in Denver has been dismissed. It did not bring any indictments against Sheriff Kienast. But the FBI is not finished. It says its investigation continues, and that it will ask another grand jury to examine the sheriff. Sheriff Kienast says the FBI is engaged in a vendetta against him, and unless it quits he'll sue for harassment.

"Here's . . . Johnny"

DAVID LOWE, JR., PRODUCER

MIKE WALLACE: Way back last September, at the beginning of the television season just ended, we broadcast a profile of Johnny Carson.* At that moment, Johnny was embroiled in stormy litigation with his employers at NBC. He wanted out of his contract. They said they have him bound legally to do "The Tonight Show" until 1981. Well, now it's seven months later, and the hassle is still going on. Johnny still wants out; NBC is still playing stubborn. And ABC is still casting covetous eyes on Carson. Insiders say the resolution may be nearing, perhaps within the next couple or three weeks. Meantime, the object of all the controversy goes his merry way, lugging his presumed $100,000 to the bank each and every week. We began our profile of Carson almost three years ago, but he backed out after just three days of filming. And then a year ago he relented and said let's try again, and this is the way it went.

Why are you doing this now?

JOHNNY CARSON: Doing what?

WALLACE: This. You walked out on us once before.

CARSON: Didn't walk out —

WALLACE: Well, I —

CARSON: I understood that you're paying me a large amount of money for this.

WALLACE: You're wrong! (Laughs)

CARSON: You — why are you doing this now? I — I'm not running a boiler room operation. I have no phony real estate scam. I'm not taking any kickbacks. I did steal a ring from Woolworth's once when I was 12 years old, and I think that's why you're here.

WALLACE: We're doing this because you're a national treasure. (Carson laughs) That's what they tell me: you're a national treasure.

CARSON: And you know what the dollar is worth nowadays. (Laughter)

---

*This story, originally broadcast on September 23, 1979, is a continuation of an April 29, 1977 interview with Carson.

WALLACE: Carson lives like his peers among the entertainment elite in Bel Air, California, though his two-acre spread could almost be described as modest compared to the more lavish establishments that dot the neighborhood. Nonetheless:

Isn't it over the head, a little bit, of a Nebraska boy?

CARSON: I don't know. Well, look, it's a yard. It's — it's not a big yard.

WALLACE: That's right. It's —

CARSON: It's not a big yard. It's comfortable. It's nice. I like that.

WALLACE: The fact is that he and his wife Joanna are among the more low-key, unaffected residents out there, with none of the flamboyance that Hollywood can sometimes spawn.

Johnny spends most of his time at home alone in his office working, reading newspapers, writing, with his awards and mementos scattered about, his beloved drums close by, and taped jazz always in the background. It was here that we sat down to find out what is Johnny Carson really like.

Well, there's a stereotype of Carson. You know there is.

CARSON: Well, what it — what is it?

WALLACE: It is ice water in his veins —

CARSON: I had that taken out years ago. I went to Denmark and had that done. It's all over now.

WALLACE: — shy, de— defensive —

CARSON: That's probably true. I can remember when I was in high school — if I pulled out my old high school annual book and read some of the things, people might say, "Oh, he's conceited, he's aloof." Actually, that was more shy. See, when I'm in front of an audience, you see, it's a different thing. If I'm in front of an audience, I can feel comfortable.

WALLACE: Why?

CARSON: I'm in control.

WALLACE: That's a key to Carson: control. Professionally, he insists upon it. Socially, he can't demand it, so he retreats. He's uncomfortable. And the fact is that he is shy.

CARSON: There's Carson the performer, and there's Carson the private individual, and I can separate the two.

WALLACE: A day in the professional life of Johnny Carson? The morning is given to reading half a dozen newspapers and magazines, looking for grist for the mill of that evening's monologue. He is a man of habit. And at one o'clock, the family cook, Lisette, gives him lunch in a brown paper bag. Then into the garage and his Mercedes sports car for the 40-minute drive to beautiful downtown Burbank and the NBC factory. No chauffeurs, no entourage.

CARSON (singing):   Some day your prince will come . . .

WALLACE: Five minutes after he arrives, he sits down with Fred De Cordova, "The Tonight Show's" producer and his good friend, to talk about that evening's guests.

FRED DE CORDOVA: She is going to talk to a turtle —

CARSON: Sure she is.

DE CORDOVA: — a bird —

CARSON: Why not.

DE CORDOVA: — a dog and a cat.

CARSON: This is our normal opening —

DE CORDOVA: Normal opening guest, that's right. (Laughter) And that's —

CARSON: She talks to — she thinks they actually talk to her?

DE CORDOVA: Well, she — you can't say mind reader —

CARSON: No.

DE CORDOVA: — but she's an animal analyst.

CARSON: Uh-hmm.

DE CORDOVA: Gets in the mind.

CARSON: Well, she's on the right show. (Laughter)

DE CORDOVA: Yes. Animals, right.

CARSON: After she finishes with the turtle, will you have her go talk to the staff. (Laughter)

ED McMAHON (holding a cat):   Dangerous wild animal.

WALLACE: At about ten past five, his sidekick, Ed McMahon, shows up.

McMAHON (laughing):   Dangerous wild animal.

CARSON: Never like to meet the guest beforehand. (Laughter) What the hell is this for?

McMAHON: That's for the show tonight. We have a lady who's going to analyze these cats.

CARSON: You know I never meet the guest before the show.

McMAHON: I know, it's a mistake. She won't do the show unless she meets you first.

CARSON: Well —

McMAHON (laughing):   Look at that. Okay.

CARSON: Incidentally, these people are from 60 MINUTES, and they want to know about the finances on your house.

McMAHON: Yeah, okay. (Laughter)

WALLACE: Ed, you once said, "Some nights he doesn't have it. Something may have gone wrong in his life. I try to pull him out of it."

McMAHON: Yes.

WALLACE: Explain.

McMAHON: Well, he's had a couple of marital problems along the way, as we all have, and when he bri— carries those with him into the studio, you can feel it. One night we were on the air, and I knew he was particularly upset about a personal problem, really upset. And he didn't want to do the show, he didn't have it. He was like kind of fighting with himself, but he knew he had to go down and perform. So I left him; knew he was in that mood. He got down, and he started — he did the monologue; it was all acceptable. He got to the desk, and now he had a chance to relax and not really get started. And you may have seen nights when it — it looks like he's playing around with things. He doesn't want to bring the first guest out.

WALLACE: Right.

McMAHON: He wants to do something else. So I looked at him, and I said, "Oh, your eyes are really dancing tonight." And he said, "What?" And I said, "Your eyes, they're really — " Of course they weren't dancing, but I got him started. I said, "Oh, they're dancing." He said, "What do you mean, they're dancing?" I said, "Well, look at them." He said, "Well, your eyes are dan— " And that was the whole thing. You know, we did seven minutes on our eyes are dancing. But it changed his mood, and the show was fine.

WALLACE: Do you get sensitive about the fact that people say, "He'll never take a serious controversy?"

CARSON: Well, I have an answer to that. I said, "Now, tell me the last time that Jack Benny, Red Skelton, any comedian, used his show to do serious issues?" That's not what I'm there for. Can't they see that?

WALLACE: But you're not —

CARSON: Why do they think that just because you have a "Tonight Show" that you must deal in serious issues? That's a danger. It's a real danger. Once you start that, you start to get that self-important feeling that what you say has great import. And you know, strangely enough, you could use that show as a forum. You could sway people. And I don't think you should as an entertainer.

"Why do they think that just because you have a 'Tonight Show' that you must deal in serious issues? That's a danger. . . . Once you start that, you start to get that self-important feeling that what you say has great import."

(Carson laughing as he watches tape of "The Tonight Show")

WALLACE: He studies tapes of old shows at home, for Carson is a perfectionist, and a very competitive man.

CARSON: Yeah, there are hazards in that, of course. There are good qualities about it, and there are bad qualities. You know, I mean, being too competitive, I think, sometimes is — is a bad thing. I don't think it's — it's — being competitive in your work is so bad. I think if you get too competitive in other things outside of your work, that can be a hazard, because then you might not enjoy them as much as you should. It's like going out and play tennis. I've found that most celebrities, especially in the public eye, have a far greater opinion of their game than their actual talent. They like to think they play better than they do.

WALLACE: The man speaks the truth.

(Carson and Wallace playing tennis)

CARSON: Nice return.

WALLACE: He's only played the game for four years, and it shows, but he is earnest about it.

CARSON: What are you waiting for, your pacemaker to start? That thing's got to kick in just about when you serve.

WALLACE: He says he uses tennis, which he loves, as a kind of therapy to help get rid of his aggressions. And that goes double for his drums, a gift from Buddy Rich.

(Carson playing the drums to recorded music)

Some people say that it helps you to work out your hostility?

CARSON: Sure.

WALLACE: True?

CARSON: Sure. It's like beating something. (Bangs on drum) That's all it is. You ought to take this up, Mike. You've got a lot of hostilities.

WALLACE: I'd rather beat on you.

If there is one almost universal comment from the guests who have appeared on "The Tonight Show," it is that Johnny is a gentle man, a kind man. And by and large that is true as well with the way he treats people in his nightly monologues.

Are you reluctant, in putting together your monologue, to go hard on a guy?

CARSON: Only when I sense the mood is — and which you can do from an audience, and I'll give you a perfect illustration. When Wilbur Mills had his problem with the famous Fannie Fox and the Tidal Basin and so forth, it was amusing to most people, and you could do jokes about it. I stopped doing jokes immediately as soon as people found out that he was an alcoholic and had emotional problems, and in fact was dependent on alcohol.

Then I think that would be a cheap shot to take, to still do jokes about it. So I immediately ceased doing jokes about that, because it — it was really unfair.

WALLACE: Of course, it takes one to know one.

CARSON: Aah! (Laughs) Cruel. You're cruel.

WALLACE: But there was a time —

CARSON: What?

WALLACE: Come on. There— there was a time when —

CARSON: I used to have a little pop? I sure did.

WALLACE: That's right.

CARSON: I don't handle it well.

WALLACE: You and McMa— really, you don't?

CARSON: I don't handle alcohol well at all, no. Really don't. Oh, Ed and I have had some wonderful times in the past.

WALLACE: You know what Ed told us?

CARSON: What did Ed tell you?

WALLACE (laughing):   He told us that from time to time you were going to take on the whole Russian army, and he — (laughing) and you didn't have the bazookas to do it.

CARSON: That's right. No, that's one reason I found that it's probably best for me to not really entangle with it, because I just found out that I — I did not drink well. And when I did drink, rather than a lot of people who become fun-loving and gregarious and love everybody, I would go the opposite, and it would happen just — (smacks hands) — like that.

JOANNA CARSON: Came to a point in our marriage where when we'd be out I would see this — go out with one person and come home with somebody who was completely different in temperament —

WALLACE: Uh-hmm.

JOANNA: — and it got to be very difficult. And we discussed it, we worked it out, and — I mean, he's just been magnificent; has felt the best because of it. And I think it's something that he's finally said to himself, "Damn it, I'm going to — I'm not going to let that get the better of me or my life or my marriage."

WALLACE: I have never seen you apparently this open. I — I always sense that somehow Carson is on guard, wary.

CARSON: Uh-hmm.

WALLACE: You are?

CARSON: Sure.

WALLACE: Why?

CARSON: I like to keep certain things private. I — I probably do put up a barrier, until I get to know people.

JOANNA: It's very hard for him to express his feelings to — to people; really only those he's — trusts a lot. He doesn't trust very many people. And so, therefore, people who he doesn't trust might find him to be aloof, snobby, stiff: "Don't touch me!"

WALLACE: In *The Rolling Stone* interview recently, they said, "Carson is a man profoundly uncomfortable with his own emotions, and unable to express his pain, insecurity and deep caring without considerable difficulty." That so, Johnny?

CARSON: No, I don't think so. I think I — I'm probably reluctant to do it. I don't find it difficult to do it. I — I'm reluctant to do it with people I don't know well. If I know somebody well, I can sit around.

JOANNA: I have seen John cry deeply only on two occasions in all the years I know him, and that — and I've known him now nine years. He finds that very difficult to do.

WALLACE: May I intrude to ask when, or would you rather I didn't?

JOANNA: I'll tell you just one time, because I don't think he'd mind me telling you that. When Jack Benny died and we came home from the funeral, Johnny wept like a baby. And it was continuous. It was for several hours. I'd — I'd never seen him cry quite like that before.

WALLACE: They were that close?

JOANNA: Oh, I think as a young man growing up, the idol, the — the image, the — everything. Jack was his thing. And, yes, they were close friends.

WALLACE: It's not "The Tonight Show" in Burbank, California; it's The Johnny Carson Show at the Sahara Hotel in Las Vegas, Nevada. He first appeared here way back in 1964 for a mere $40,000 a week. For this three-day engagement, his take is $225,000. And the Johnny Carson you see here in Las Vegas is different from the man you see on NBC.

CARSON: (on stage):   Now, those of us who do comedy have been waiting a long time for a family like the Carters to show up. (Laughter) Oh, yeah, this was sent from heaven. Now, I — (laughter) — this is — this is some kind of family. I — they — they got some weird people there, and I will discuss the — the whole genealogy of the Carter clan, and bring you up to date. I saw a picture of Carter in the paper the other day. You know, if he had a little — what do they call that when your hair stands up? — a little cowlick. If he had a little cowlick, he'd look exactly like Dagwood Bumstead. (Laughter) Oh, yeah. And the way things have been going, he's acting like Dagwood. And now we come — (laughter) — to brother Billy, the — the direct clone of Fred Flintstone. (Laughter)

WALLACE: He can be funnier and meaner and less inhibited on stage than on television.

CARSON (on stage):   Bil — Billy is a real smoothie. He — Billy does not have both oars in the water, I don't think. (Laughter) They got to pump a little more air up in there somewhere. Now, you're all familiar with Billy's wonderful diplomatic little deal he did when the Libyan delegation was here. Now, he was showing the Libyan delegation around Plains, Georgia. And here were these dignified people from the country of Libya, and Billy steps out of the car and relieves himself against the side of a building. (Laughter) That's our President's brother. That's the way you find Billy's house in Plains — you just follow the yellow brick road — (laughter) — right to Billy's house! (Laughter . . . applause) What about Ruth. She's the evangelist. She's the one who is trying to convert Larry Flynt — (laughter) — yes, they're close friends — to religion. Larry Flynt, of course, who produces one of our tastier magazines — (laughter) — Hustler magazine. And Larry Flynt says, "Yes, I've — I've learned a lot of things from Ruth." And if you look at Hustler, it does have religious overtones. I mean, oh, you open it, and you go, "My God!" (Laughter)

WALLACE: You've only had one failure that I know of, professionally.

CARSON: Oh?

WALLACE: Well, isn't that true?

CARSON: Well, what was that?

WALLACE: "The Johnny Carson Show" back in nineteen fifty – whenever it was.

CARSON: Yeah, we were on for 39 weeks, and we went off at the end of 39 weeks.

WALLACE: And Ben Brady –

CARSON: Uh-hmm.

WALLACE: Was he the producer of it, or the –

CARSON: That — that's what I thought.

WALLACE: (reading):   "Carson was trying to be a major comedian in prime time, and he didn't have the power," said Ben Brady. "He is generically not a strong stand-up comedian like Hope, Skelton or Benny. He isn't now and he never can be."

CARSON: Well, I wonder what Mr. Brady would say today.

(Band music)

WALLACE: When we first set out to do this profile a couple of years ago, the only film we'd shot before Johnny called a halt for a while was his appearance to pick up an award as the Hasty Pudding Club's Man of the Year at Harvard University.

CARSON: I suppose it sounds better when you're all awake. (Laughter) You get up just for this?

HARVARD STUDENTS: Yes. Right. Yeah.

CARSON: Okay, back to bed! (Laughter)

WALLACE: I have a hunch that this event meant a good deal to Johnny – a Nebraska boy making good in the Ivy League.
That night, after a long, cold day, the awards ceremony.

(Cheers and applause)

CARSON: This is really lovely, but more important than that, I want to thank the club for letting me and my wife stay in the Master's Residence last night at Elliott House. You really don't know what that means. It's the — (laughter) — it's the first time I've scored with a chick on a college campus since 1949. (Laughter . . . applause)

WALLACE: And finally, a news conference, and a question Johnny pondered for a while.

QUESTION: What would you like your epitaph to be?

CARSON: My epitaph?

QUESTION: Ultimately. (Laughter)

STUDENT: Isn't that premature?

CARSON: Well —

STUDENT: Hasn't seen the show yet.

CARSON: — I'd prefer not to have one at all if — (Laughter) — where it never got to that point. I — I don't know. I think something like, "I'll be right back." (Laughter)

$200 A Week – Tax Free

JIM JACKSON, PRODUCER

HARRY REASONER: This program is completing its twelfth year on the air, which is very old for television programs. One challenge is to stay nervous, as we were in the fall of 1968; because when you are nervous, you also stay fresh and trying. But there's also a kind of comfortable option: to indulge in a little avuncular reminiscing. We propose to do that from time to time this spring and summer by showing you some of the pieces we did in those early years. Our guideline is to show them just as they were, not to freshen or face-lift script or production or correspondent. We'll all see if they've aged nicely, like a good wine, or if they creak a little. One thing you'll notice is that I, and even Morley and Dan, have aged a little. Mike looks just the same.

All right, what you're going to see now is a piece Jim Jackson produced when 60 MINUTES was a year old. You'll see it just as you would have September 30th, 1969. Would have? Maybe you did!

REASONER: Most city dwellers have been approached at one time or another by the skid row panhandler asking for a dime. Those of us who were getting adept at sidestepping this familiar figure may have something more to contend with. There's a new breed of panhandler roaming the streets of our large cities. From New York to San Francisco, there are reports that seemingly healthy and able-bodied young people have taken up this ancient art. And they seem to be doing very well. In fact, some of them have boasted they take home more than $200 a week.

MAN: Excuse me, fair young maiden, could you spare a quarter? I'm trying to get something to eat . . .

MAN: Hey, mister, you got a nickel or a dime? I got to get my bus fare. You know, if you have a few cents.

REASONER: Instead of approaching panhandling as a shameful last resort, they seem to look on it as an easy way to earn a good living.

STEVE: Excuse me, but do you think you could spare 20 cents?

WOMAN: No.

STEVE: Excuse me, could you spare a quarter? I'm trying to get something to eat, please? Thanks.

REASONER: This is Steve, 22 years old, a college graduate, working across from New York's Grand Central Terminal at lunchtime.

STEVE: Excuse me, brother, could you spare a quarter? I'm trying to get something to eat, please?

MAN: I don't have any change. The only thing is I have bills.

STEVE: I'll give you change.

REASONER: One essential ingredient is empathy. Steve always keeps a plaintive quality in his voice.

STEVE: Pardon me, could you please spare a quarter? I'm trying to get carfare back to New Jersey. I don't have any way of getting home. Really appreciate it. Excuse me, sir. Could you spare a quarter?

MAN: Never! Never!

STEVE: Mazeltov.

PRODUCER: How — how much education have you had?

STEVE: I went through college.

PRODUCER: What'd you major in?

STEVE: Psychology.

PRODUCER: Do you think you'll learn anything from this trade?

STEVE: Definitely. A lot. I might do my thesis for my master's in this.

PRODUCER: What do you mean?

STEVE: Well, you have to do a thesis in order — you know, for your master's degree, and I've learned — you know, you come to a lot of psycho— psychological as— aspects through panhandling.

REASONER: A formal education may not seem like the key to successful panhandling, but it sometimes helps.

STEVE: Excuse me, brother, could you spare a quarter? I'm trying to get something to eat, please.

MAN: I — I — I can't — I don't speak very well.

STEVE: Could you spare 25 cents? I'm trying to get some food.

MAN: I — I — I can't — I don't speak very well the English.

STEVE: What language do you speak?

MAN: Spanish.

STEVE: Oh, okay. (Speaks to him in Spanish)

MAN: Oh.

REASONER: Unlike Steve, who deals with a very select clientele, Marty believes in volume business.

MARTY: . . . a nickel or a dime. I need 40 cents. Hey, fella, could you let me have a dime, man? I got to get 80 cents for my bus, you know.

REASONER: That was a favorite pitch, the old bus ticket routine. He's stranded in the city without enough money to get his bus back to the suburbs.

MARTY: Got to get to Jersey, you know. Okay, thanks.
Hey, could you loan me a dime, man? I got to get to Jersey. I got to get 30 cents. Loan me a dime?

REASONER: We asked him how he got started.

MARTY: It was an accident. I went — I was in the Port Authority Bus Terminal one night and I had no money to get home, and I asked a man — I needed 30 cents and I asked a guy for it, and he gave me a dollar. And I said, wow, this is amazing. And I asked somebody else, and they gave me a dollar. And I kept going, and I had about $18 in about an hour. So, I've been doing it ever since, you know. It was an accident.

PRODUCER: Do you live in New York?

MARTY: No, I live in New Jersey. I live in Rutherford.

PRODUCER: Well, how do you get back and forth?

MARTY: Oh, I commute. I take — I take a bus every day to go to work. It's just like working in the city here every day. I try to work during the day. I try to work regular hours. Like, I start around ten in the morning, and I knock off for lunch. And then I — I figure four, five hours a day I'll make $30. I usually average about eight dollars an hour, depending on how long I work.
Hey, pal, you going to lend me a dime, you know, so I can get home? I got to get 80 cents. You got a dime, maybe? A nickel? I got to get 35 more cents, you know. Get some change — good. Thanks.

REASONER: If you have any doubts that a panhandler can make at least eight dollars an hour, watch Marty working at top form.

MARTY: Hey, pal, do you have a dime? I got to get my bus for Jersey. I'm trying to get enough change. I need 30 cents, you know. Can you loan me 30 cents, maybe?

MAN: I'll give you a dime.

MARTY: Do you have another nickel? That would be half of it, maybe. Loan me — okay? A nickel? Ah, okay.

Mister, you have a dime I could have? I'm trying to get to Jersey. I need 60 cents. I need another 60 cents. Do you have a quarter or something? Okay, thanks.

JOHN: Excuse me, ma'am. Do you think you can spare some change for something to eat?

WOMAN: Sorry, but I'm broke.

REASONER: Another successful hustler, John, works near busy shopping districts. He dresses very carefully for the part.

JOHN: Well, I try to dress in a manner that would — to get people to give me the money, you see. So like, this is my panhandling shirt. It has a hole in it over here and it's — it's kind of rundown, and the pants are old, and the hat is floppy, you know. In other words, I look like someone who might need 20 cents to go from here to there on the subway, which is, one of the basic appeals.

Brother, spare 20 cents for the subway?

MAN: I have a dime.

JOHN: That's groovy.

MAN: All I can give you. All right? Sorry.

JOHN: Thank you.

And you know, people just reach into their pockets, you know, without even thinking, some of them. Like the younger ones. That's the line, because, you — it's a quick thing with a younger one. There's — there's very little story involved, you know. I mean, either they're going to give it to you or they're not going to give it to you. And most of them give it to you.

Excuse me, girls. Do you think you can spare some change, girls, so I can get something to eat? Anything at all will help.

REASONER: This is known as the double hit, a much sought after bonus in the trade.

JOHN: Thank you very much.

Sir, think you can spare some change —

MAN: Huh?

JOHN: — something to eat?

MAN: Something to eat? Why don't you take a job, like — like me?

JOHN: Because they won't hire me.

MAN: He — he could use a dishwasher.

JOHN: They won't hire me.

MAN: Huh?

JOHN: They won't hire me.

MAN: Why wouldn't they?

JOHN: Because I spent some time in reform school.

MAN: Huh?

JOHN: Because I spent some time in reform school.

MAN: Oh, yeah?

JOHN: So they won't hire me.

MAN: Well, what are you going to do? Going to starve all the time?

JOHN: Until I can get a job. I've been trying to get a job for like six months now.

MAN: You go down to unemployment, they're looking for people left and right.

JOHN: I know. I'm telling you I went —

MAN: (Indistinct) goddamn thing happened. Like me. See there?

JOHN: I'll tell you what happened. See, I — no, I was in — I was in reform — listen, I was in reform school, right?

MAN: (Indistinct) too goddamn (indistinct).

JOHN: And they taught me carpentry, they taught me a trade. So I went down to the union —

MAN: Umm.

JOHN: — and the union wouldn't hire me because I was in reform school.

MAN: Not the way you look. Got to goddamn look like me.

JOHN: Thank you very much, sir.

MAN: Like a gentleman.

JOHN: Thank you.
       Excuse me, ma'am. Do you think you can spare some change for something to eat?

WOMAN: What? For something to eat? Get a job.

JOHN: I just went through that rap, lady.

REASONER: The trouble with panhandling as a career is that you cannot expand indefinitely, and there are no fringe benefits like hospitalization or a pension. But it has certain advantages for young people: healthful work in the open air, flexible hours, and a chance to meet a lot of interesting people. Some socially conscious observers might say that it is wasteful for qualities like Steve's perception and Marty's aggressiveness to be used in an essentially unproductive line. But our society is notoriously wasteful, and the panhandlers might say that at least they are not a burden on the welfare rolls. It takes, as the man said, all kinds.

MIKE WALLACE: Pardon me, sir, I – I wonder if you could let me have a hundred dollars for lunch at "21?"

REASONER: Why don't you get a decent job, like me!

A Few Minutes
with Andy Rooney

DAN RATHER: It's time now for Andy Rooney, and tonight it's literally that — time for Andy Rooney.

ANDY ROONEY: I guess I've lost my watch. If I haven't lost it, I might as well have, because I haven't been able to find it for about ten days now. I've been thinking about buying a new watch, but it isn't easy. Watches have gotten awfully complicated the last few years. I don't like clever watches. I just want to know how late I am.

I loved the one I lost. It had a face with what I think is a wonderful idea for a watch: it had just two hands, and at the top it had the number twelve, and then it started with number one, two, three, until it got back to twelve again. It was something like this old railroad watch I'm carrying now. This is my idea of a perfect watch face. And it sure runs a lot better than the railroads too. It's too heavy, though; too easy to drop. And I don't like having to dig it out of my pocket all the time.

It's surprising how many old watches most of us have around the house. Look at these I found in drawers around. This is the kind your mother used to have, you know, when you were a kid. She wanted it for dress-up occasions. It had this black strap on it. If she was rich, these were real diamonds.

This is a woman's watch style that was popular for years. It's all case and no face. Remember, they used to advertise watches as having 17 jewels? No one ever knew what that meant, except the more jewels there were, the more it cost. I mean, if I wanted to wear jewels, I'd buy myself a pair of earrings. I don't know why it is. Anytime you take a watch to the jewelers, he always says it needs cleaning for $36. I mean, I never think of myself as getting watches that dirty. This was something I bought for ten dollars four years ago during the Bicentennial celebration. You see the stars going around there?

Here's the exact opposite of this. This must have been somebody's grandmother's watch. This is real good. Make you nervous carrying that around, wouldn't it? Here's a nice woman's watch, but it's one of those watches where the company claims it'll keep time that's accurate to within twelve seconds a year. Then they make a face without any numbers or dots on it, so you have to guess what time it is within about ten minutes. This is a digital quartz watch. Look at this. It tells you more about the time than you want to know. It does everything. It has an alarm. Has a calendar on it. I mean, if you don't know what day it is, how could you care what time it is?

I don't know. Maybe I won't buy a new watch after all. Maybe I'll buy a vest and just keep using this old railroad watch.

Letters

MIKE WALLACE: Most of the mail this week was about our story on Omega 7, the Cuban exile group that has taken credit for several acts of violence in the United States.

One viewer said: "There would be no Omega 7 nor a Cuban refugee problem if the United States had not reneged at the Bay of Pigs. As we sow, so shall we reap."

And there was also this: "(Are you) trying to portray the Cuban exile community as terrorists and . . . murderers? Omega Seven is as much a mystery to (us) as it is to you."

But another viewer, noting that a large number of anti-Castro supporters of Omega 7 lived in New Jersey, wrote: "I think . . . Omega 7 should be renamed Chicken 7 . . . It's kind of like fighting a boxer from row 14. When Castro had a beef against Batista, he didn't fight him from New Jersey."

Followed by this: "It is easy to stand around yelling 'Guerra, guerra' (war, war) when you are safe in a foreign country . . . Perhaps they expect to get rid of Castro by talking him to death."

About our interview with Anne Morrow Lindbergh, in which she talked candidly and not always glowingly about her famed husband, a viewer wrote: "Anne Morrow Lindbergh is a contradiction of the old axiom that behind every success-ful man is a woman. Charles Lindbergh was successful despite (her) and neither you nor (she) can change that fact."

Another viewer said: "What makes first-rate reporters go all soft and squishy at the shrine of super-celebrities? How did you let (her) go free with only an apologia for Charles and none for herself? Or did you forget that she authored *Wave of the Future,* a paean to fascism?"

About Congressman Beard of Tennessee and the federal money being appro-priated for a dam in his district, a viewer wrote from the very place that dam is being built: "I nominate Congressman Beard for a special Emmy — best perform-ance by a politician in a leading role for justifying his support of a wasteful pork barrel water project at the taxpayers' expense in an election year with 18% inflation."

We also heard from a viewer who said of our story: "I now realize the meaning of such terms as biased reporting, hatchet job and out of context."

And finally, there was this from North Dakota: "How dare you expose the (Tennes-see) dam project? Now I have to worry that those funds may be reappropriated toward (an unnecessary dam in my state)."

MAY 4, 1980

The Kissinger-
Shah Connection?

ANDREW LACK, PRODUCER

DAN RATHER: Is there a special relationship between Henry Kissinger and the Shah of Iran? Well, although the exact nature of their relationship has never been spelled out, speculation persists that there is. Kissinger's name came up again recently when the president of Iran told an interviewer that Kissinger had engineered getting the Shah out of Panama and safely into Egypt before the Iranians could get their hands on him for an interrogation. Kissinger was mentioned prominently in connection with the Shah's trip to the United States for medical treatment — the trip that touched off the taking of our embassy and the holding of the hostages.

Whatever the truth of those allegations, they are as of this date unproven. President Carter has denied that Kissinger had a hand in the decision to permit the Shah to come to this country. Kissinger, who one day said he would and the next day said he wouldn't, after many requests finally refused to appear in this story. Recent events aside, there is little doubt that, during the time he was Secretary of State, Kissinger gave the ruler of the Peacock Throne preferential treatment. And the question is why.

In attempting to find that out, people in a position to know pointed us toward a link between Henry Kissinger, the Shah of Iran and the price you're now paying for gasoline.

(Band playing martial music)

This is where it began. October, 1969: the Shah was in Washington for an official visit with President Nixon, and his first real encounter with Henry Kissinger. They talked privately for one hour, it is believed, during which the groundwork was laid for the Nixon Administration's policy toward Iran of continuing military and economic aid to the Shah.

But the policy took on new and extraordinary dimensions when Nixon and Kissinger stopped off in Iran to see the Shah on their way back from the Moscow summit in May, 1972. Nixon and Kissinger saw what they believed was a dangerous situation in and around the Persian Gulf. The British had withdrawn their military presence from the area at the end of 1971. There existed now in the Gulf a power vacuum.

GEORGE BALL: Nixon almost said to him, "You will be our equal. You will do in the Persian Gulf what we do in the rest of the world."

RATHER: When George Ball, a former Undersecretary of State, was brought in by President Carter as a special adviser on Iran, he reviewed the secret national security memoranda covering the Nixon-Kissinger trip.

BALL: Well, in 1972, when Mr. Nixon, and Mr. Kissinger came there to Teheran, they, in effect, said to the Shah, "You are the protector of Western interests in the Persian Gulf." The Shah, in effect, said to them, "All right, if you stay out and you give me what I need, I will undertake this." And what he needed was quite a few things, but principally unlimited access to all of our top military equipment.

Nixon said, in effect, "We'll give you access to our F-14's, our F-15's, our laser-guided bombs, our Phoenix missiles" — whatever. And he instructed the Secretary of Defense, the Secretary of State, not to argue, that if the government of Iran asked for something, they were to get it, and they were to be the judges of what they needed. Even though the technology, the — the — the sophisticated equipment we were giving them, some of it was only on the drawing boards. They were just then being given to our forces in — in Vietnam. The result was that the Shah became a — a megalomaniac.

RATHER: If critics argued the Shah was becoming a megalomaniac as a result of unnecessary American arms sales, it was, in the view of Kissinger's State Department, a small price to pay for protecting our vital oil interests and keeping the Shah and Iran's borders safe from the Iraqis and the Russians.

But across the Gulf in Saudi Arabia, there was a much different view of Kissinger and the Shah. At the OPEC meeting in January, 1974, the Shah led OPEC into a massive increase in oil prices. The Saudis feared this would seriously threaten Western stability and, in turn, their own vast holdings of American dollars, so they urged we intervene with the Shah immediately. We didn't. Our ambassador, James Akins, was warned by Saudi Oil Minister Yamani.

JAMES AKINS: We were talking about Iran, as he frequently did. And he said, "Look," he said, "you're not doing anything in Iran. You're leaving it to me to try to persuade the Shah." He said, "It's very easy for you, Jim Akins. You talk to the king, King Faisal, you talk to me about the necessity of restraining oil prices, and so we listen to you." He said, "We're intelligent, rational human beings, and we restrain oil prices." He said, "Then I have to go by myself and talk to the Shah, and the Shah says, 'God told me oil prices had to go up.' "

RATHER: Akins first cabled the Saudi warning to the State Department in December, '73, before the Shah led OPEC into quadrupling the price of oil. He never got an answer.

AKINS: Well, the Saudis were very disturbed about this, because as Yamani put it to me, he said, "I didn't tell you this for your own delectation. This was because I assumed that you would act on it and the American government would act on it. You did nothing. Why not?" Well, to explain to him that we didn't act because we couldn't get clearances during the Christmas holidays was — was difficult and was never very convincing.

This continued throughout 1974. The Saudis would come to me, and their point was consistently the same: "You must bring the Shah into this. You can do this. He's your friend. He's your ally. He depends on you. You must put pressure on the Shah to cooperate with us on this." And they were never able to understand why we didn't do this.

RATHER: Were you able to understand it?

AKINS: Never.

RATHER: Did you ever have an explanation?

AKINS: Never.

RATHER: The Saudis would say, "You must use your influence, you must do some-thing." You passed it along to Washington. No response. Would it be safe to assume that Dr. Kissinger, yes, probably saw that information?"

AKINS: Oh, I've never assumed anything other than that. How can you?

RATHER: And his response — did you — you — did you receive a response back?

AKINS: No, there was just no response. Generally no response. I was finally told by Joseph Sisco, who was then a high-ranking officer of the State Department, that these reports were annoying the Secretary. This I found really quite puzzling, because there was no question that the reports weren't accurate, no — no suggestion that the analysis was faulty. It was just that I was annoying the Secretary. Well, I wasn't a terribly — terribly alert ambassador, I'm afraid. I — I told Sisco at the time that if they really wanted people to report only things that — that they wanted to hear, then they could get themselves another boy. And they proceeded to do that fairly smartly.

RATHER: Kissinger fired Akins in August of 1975. He never gave him a reason. In fact, after 22 years in the Foreign Service, Jim Akins' career was over with 90 days' notice. Kissinger says now Ambassador Akins' reporting was faulty, his personal-ity was abrasive, and he could not be trusted.

Could we have kept the price of oil down if Dr. Kissinger or anyone had fought the Shah on it?

WILLIAM SIMON: Yes, we could have. And there was great belief, and there is belief still in some circles today, that the State Department — not necessarily Henry Kissinger, but the State Department — was in favor of high oil prices.

RATHER: William Simon was Secretary of the Treasury in the Nixon and Ford Cabinets, serving alongside Henry Kissinger from 1974 to 1977.

SIMON: I feel I had something to do with Jim being appointed ambassador to Saudi Arabia. I was a well-known friend and advocate of Jim Akins, because I re-spected his judgment, his opinion, his ability, his experience. He was a true expert on the subject of the Middle East and oil.

RATHER: That's why the Senate Foreign Relations Committee called Akins to testify under oath during an investigation in May, 1976.

SENATOR FRANK CHURCH (D-Idaho):   Mister Ambassador, since the increase of five or six hundred percent in the price of crude oil, dating from October, 1973, the United States has quadrupled its sales of arms worldwide and particularly in the Persian Gulf area. So we seem to be caught in an escalating cycle of higher oil prices followed by massive U.S. arms sales.

AKINS: Yamani and — and several other Saudi officials were — and I think still are — convinced that the United States is not entirely serious about wanting to bring down world oil prices.

RATHER: Senator Church, who led the investigation, had this to say, quote: "The appetite for sophisticated weapons feeds the need for revenues to pay for the arms. This leads to more pressure for oil price increases, particularly for countries like Iran."

Essentially our policy toward the Shah never changed during the time you were in Washington?

SIMON: No, it did not. And I wasn't looking for a change as much as I was looking for a shift.

RATHER: Why did it not even shift?

SIMON: Because I believe that the State Department and Henry felt that it would put our relationship with the Shah in jeopardy, and they didn't wish to do that.

RATHER: So there was virtually no public debate when the Shah ordered over five and a half billion dollars' worth of military hardware from the Ford and Carter Administrations between October, 1976, and September, 1977. Jim Akins told us —

AKINS: If the oil prices were to go up, then the Iranians would have the money to buy the arms.

RATHER: If we wanted the Shah to have access to our arsenal —

AKINS: Uh-hmm.

RATHER: — then why not just simply give him the arms?

AKINS: Oh, we can't do that. Congress is never going to appropriate the money for the arms. That — that can't be done. He has to have the money for it. We can supply him the arms, but we can't give them to him.

RATHER: So he had to get the money to buy the arms?

AKINS: Had to have the money to buy the arms, and oil, really, was the only way he could get the money for the arms.

RATHER: What do you personally think of the theory that Dr. Kissinger knew full well what he was doing, that he wanted the Iranians and the Shah to have the weapons; in order to get the weapons they had to have the money, and the way they got the money was to raise the oil prices?

SIMON: Well, there could very well be some truth in that, and the fact of the matter is at that time we were heavily involved in Vietnam. We were trying to extricate ourselves. We had a President that was being besieged in the closing days of Watergate. We didn't need any trouble in other parts of the world. And we had to make sure that our allies were in strong positions, so that the Russians could not take advantage of not only our domestic problems but the Vietnam problems and become mischievous, as they're prone to do, in other parts of the world.

RATHER: But if that's true, we paid one hell of a price for arming the Shah.

SIMON: Yeah, and I su— and I suggested it was an unnecessary price to pay, if that were true.

MANSOUR FARHANG: Their relationship was very close.

RATHER: Mansour Farhang is the only Iranian diplomat left in this country now. He is Iran's ambassador to the United Nations.

FARHANG: They complemented one another. For example, if Mr. Kissinger determined that Iran ought to be an outpost of American power, possessing the most sophisticated weapons in the world, the next question is, who is going to pay for it? You can remember in 1970-'71, would it be possible for Nixon and Kissinger to go to Congress, in the midst of the war in Vietnam, to say we want a million dollars or five billion dollars in military grants for Iran? Obviously not. Somebody had to pay for it, and that somebody could not be the United States. Where could the money come from? Where would Iran get the money? Logically, the only way Iran could receive such enormous amount of money was by increasing the price of oil.

RATHER: Do you have any indication, have you ever seen the evidence, that Dr. Kissinger did try to use his influence with — with the Shah to keep the prices down?

BALL: No.

RATHER: I've been told by a number of people that Dr. Kissinger is brilliant, but that his short suit is economics. Would you agree with that assessment?

BALL: Well, I think he would agree with that. I mean, he — he's never made any — any pretenses of knowing anything about economics. And I think his judgment on that is right.

RATHER: Privately you and any — any number of other people have said, "Look, Henry did great work on a number of things, but here's one he blew."

SIMON: Well, obviously I believed at the time terribly strongly, and I think history has proven my position correct, and in that respect perhaps Henry did blow it.

RATHER: You wouldn't want to scratch "perhaps" out of that, would you?

SIMON: Well, I think it's — it's there for everyone to see, just like all my mistakes as Secretary of the Treasury are there for all to see. We don't have any perfection or angels in government. You win some and you lose some.

RATHER: This one, I think you'll agree, though, was a very big one to lose?

SIMON: Yes, it was, and it's becoming bigger every day.

RATHER: Today, this $30 million F-14 is somewhere in Iran — one of 80 we sold the Shah. Shown here in 1976, at the Grumman plant on Long Island, it was a symbol of our close relationship with Iran. The Shah's former son-in-law, Ardeshir Zahedi, was on hand to accept the first shipment.

MAN: Ambassador, I hope you enjoy that airplane. We think it's great.

ARDESHIR ZAHEDI: I'm sure it is.

RATHER: Zahedi was also the Shah's eyes and ears in Washington, his ambassador and closest confidant. From his embassy office, he was in constant touch with the Shah right up until the Iranian revolution began.

Zahedi fled to Switzerland with the contents of that file cabinet. It contained the most sensitive documentation of the Shah's personal dealings in Washington. But upstairs in the telex room were left behind copies of secret cables, dating back to 1973, from Zahedi to the Shah that there apparently had not been time to destroy once the embassy was taken over. Nine months before the Shah personally led OPEC into quadrupling the price of oil, Zahedi sent the following message to the Shah. Translated from the Persian, it reads: "During talks and luncheon with Kissinger today, when the topic of oil came up, Kissinger said in front of all present that sometimes differences have existed between America's views and the Shah's, but the Shah's views have always proven right."*

*Message dated March 10, 1973.

FARHANG: I'm not saying there was a conspiracy. There was a conspiracy of values, a convergence of perceptions, a confluence of interests. So it's a mistake to say who influenced whom and in what direction.

RATHER: But let's consider Dr. Kissinger's argument, then and now, that it was in Iran's best interest, in your country's own best interest, to arm itself against the Soviet Union.

FARHANG: There was nothing new about that. (Laughing) This is — if you — that is Kissinger's typical reasoning for doing anything. But how did militarization of Iran help the Iranian people? In a very perverted and unintended way it did. It perhaps speeded up the development of revolutionary conditions —

RATHER: Speeded it up, not (indistinct) it down?

FARHANG: Sure. Exactly. Speeded it up, yes, because it led to a great deal of corruption and concentration of wealth and dependency on the United States, and therefore mobilized and intensified the — in that sense, God was with us, if Henry Kissinger was not.

AKINS: Had we put pressure on the Shah, would he have listened to us or would he have said, "I'm going my own way?" Can't say. But we didn't try, so we'll never know.

RATHER: Henry Kissinger calls the whole story — quote — "malicious, ridiculous and untrue." He says of former Secretary of Treasury Simon — quote — "We had honest differences over policy . . . but *that* had nothing to do with financing the Shah's weapons with oil price increases." About former Ambassador Akins, Kissinger says — quote — "Akins is lying and engaged in a personal vendetta against me." Kissinger says former Undersecretary of State Ball is — quote — "a partisan political opponent . . . jealous of me . . . and long engaged in a personal campaign to destroy me."

Dr. Kissinger, as we said, refused to appear on this broadcast.

See Letters, May 11, 1980, page 539.

Palm Springs

SUZANNE ST. PIERRE, PRODUCER

HARRY REASONER: Suppose you just bought a house in Beverly Hills for, say, three million dollars. It has a pool and a tennis court and all that. Well, what do you do and where do you go for the weekend? To the Springs, that's where you go. Officially it is Palm Springs, but the Hollywood crowd calls it plain old Springs. It's where the deer and the antelope and the Rolls-Royces roam.

Palm Springs is just one community, about a hundred and ten miles southeast of Los Angeles, but when you say Palm Springs, you're really talking about half a dozen little cities, each one the suburb of the next one, strung out across a desert valley. We're always reading about this, that or the other celebrity or politician or scoundrel who has just bought a place in Palm Springs. So last summer Morley Safer decided to take a look, and we've decided it's worth a second look.*

MORLEY SAFER: If you were Superman, this is the way you'd discover the place. You'd glide over the great emptiness of the desert; then, as you approached the mountains, you'd pull up and over, and there it is before you — not your home planet of Krypton, but Palm Springs, California, the Krypton of the super rich. What Palm Springs is not is your average American community. You're looking at money, old money and new. The swimming pools wink back at you like so many big, blue-eyed, million-dollar babies; more swimming pools here per mortal than anyplace on earth. If someone shouted "Everyone in the pool!" there'd be just five of you in each of them.

No, it's not a country club; it's the country home of Walter Annenberg, owner of *TV Guide,* former Ambassador to Great Britain and crony of Richard Nixon. You measure it not by the square foot but by the hundreds of acres. From the air the Annenberg complex looks like a small country just discovered in the middle of the Gobi Desert.

Palm Springs people are like people in your town and mine, and the house you live in, the search for those four walls that express your personality, is a very important search. We found one for sale. It belongs to Joey Hrudka, the gasket king of Cleveland. It was Mr. and Mrs. Hrudka's dream house until they each married other people, and now it's in the hands of Mrs. Segall.

---

*Originally broadcast on September 16, 1979.

(Commercial for Hrudka house — featuring Zelda Segall of Camel Realty)

Thank you, Mrs. Segall. The price is right, but I'm looking for something with two tennis courts.

For the more simple folk, there are familiar objects like mobile homes, but in Palm Springs a sitting mobile home can cost you $200,000. If you park it elsewhere, presumably the price comes down.

Almost as important in Palm Springs as the house you live in are the wheels you drive on and the wings you fly on. It's best to fly in a manner that does not require the drudgery of schedules and tickets. Lots of people do it in Palm Springs — four times more private landings than public ones.

On the public side, if you need help with your bags you'll likely get it from Jose Ybarra. But only in Palm Springs would the skycap have his own ranch, own five polo ponies, his own playing field and some prime land in Hawaii. If you know that, you just feel silly giving Jose anything less than a $20 tip.

JOSE YBARRA: Thank you very much.

MAN: Very good.

YBARRA: Good to see you.

MAN: You bet.

YBARRA: Thanks.

SAFER: Private planes are a bit ostentatious. And after all, you can't land your Gulf Stream at the Safeway. So twenty-five or sixty or a hundred and twenty thousand dollars for a car in these parts is quite routine. The old saying "Ford and the world Fords with you, Rolls and you Rolls alone" applies to every place but Palm Springs, and in Palm Springs it doesn't even apply on the golf course. (Rolls golf cart)

The golf in Palm Springs, they say, is the best in the world. You have almost 40 courses to choose from, and you never know who you're going to run into. Such old desert rats as Jerry Ford, Telly Savalas, Lawrence Welk, Clint Eastwood, Andy Williams, David Eisenhower, and the sultan of Palm Springs himself, Bob Hope. When the stars grow weary of being gawked at elsewhere, they come to Palm Springs to be gawked at by a better class of people — by, in fact, each other. In Palm Springs almost anything goes — for a price. Take this Korean gentleman. He's selling solid gold golf clubs. Fifty-seven hundred dollars for the putter. Fifty-seven thousand dollars for the set.

MAN: Solid gold. Fifty-seven hundred dollar apiece.

SAFER: You can have your balls in silver or gold only in Palm Springs. But don't get the idea that it's all money and excess. There are spiritual concerns. Mass for the parish of St. Francis of Assisi is held in the Crocker Bank while they're waiting for their church to be built. Nowhere do God and mammon look each other more closely in the eye. Father Ray Bluett was dissuaded by his parishioners from wearing the vestments with the golf motif; instead, he chose the paisley design. Mass on Saturday night in Palm Springs. And polo on Sunday morning.

(Public address announcer calling polo game)

Can anyone think of a better way to spend a weekend? Well, there's always tennis. Over at Mission Hills, you might find some of the more prominent hackers like Jimmy Connors or Bjorn Borg or John McEnroe or Harold Solomon; or for more bizarre tennis, you could visit Dr. J.T. Houk, whose specialty is two-handed tennis. He even wrote a book on it.

If all of the above is just too much for the body, you can always drop in at Palm Springs' most chi-chi restaurant, Melvins. Melvin Haber used to manufacture plastic knickknacks — those cats and dogs that nod at you from the back of other people's cars. Now he sells very expensive room and board.

MELVIN HABER: Palm Springs caters to the creme de la creme of the world. I mean, you will get almost international people of reputation, both the arts, the sciences, industry, whatever, gravitate towards Palm Springs sometime during the course of the year. And my having the in restaurant, so to speak, I get the creme de la creme of the creme de la creme. And there certainly is a big social scene here, primarily because the social strata of every city congregates in the winter in Palm Springs. So you wind up having a strained selection of the social strata of 20 cities all in one city.

SAFER: Your creme — your creme de la creme —

HABER: Absolutely. Same concept — creme de la creme.

SAFER: The concept, as Mr. Haber says, is that the creme de la creme is the lifeblood of Palm Springs; or to put it another way, the big game. These two big-game hunters are Marilyn Visel and Glory Hartley, and they run Palm Springs celebrity safaris. Their equipment: safari suits and hats and Cadillac limos. Their clients are convention wives and the just plain curious.

MARILYN VISEL: Ladies, we're on our way on our Palm Springs safari today, and we're really looking forward to showing you our beautiful city of Palm Springs. Ladies, we're now going to stop by Greta Garbo's house, and this was the famous house that was built for her in 1929 by the very famous John Gilbert. The actress Edna Skinner now resides here, who was the lady that was the neighbor on the Mister Ed — remember the talking horse show? We are having more and more celebrities, personalities, move into Palm Springs, because of our year-around beautiful weather. And I must brag a little bit that Dr. Crick, our leading meteorologist in the whole world, has chosen Palm Springs to live. And he had his choice of any place in the whole world. So I guess he has pretty good taste too. Some people call it God's waiting room, because we do have a lot of senior citizens there.

SAFER: You rarely see an actual star, or for that matter an actual house. You do get a marvelous view of hedges and fences. Of course, it's the safest of all safaris — no danger of being bitten by a Liberace or savaged by a Magda Gabor.

VISEL: I told you that Elvis Presley lived in this area. I was talking with his cousin the other day, and I found out that there are 15 rooms in the house, and there is a television set and a telephone in each room. And here is the home right here, with the iron gate all the way around. The decor in there is a little different, but if you like red and black, you'd love it.

All right, we're going past the new home of Bob Hope. And I know you can't get a very good glimpse of the house, but here's the picture that we took of the house last week. And it's approximately five, six months off from being finished.

SAFER: We went up a few thousand feet to get a full-color view of Bob Hope's eagle's nest, which looks like the TWA terminal at Kennedy Airport. A neighbor of Mr. Hope's further down the mountain is a long-time resident of Palm Springs, a lady with the touch of the old money, Mrs. Liza Gallois.

Is there much glamour?

MRS. LIZA GALLOIS: I don't think there's any glamour at all. That's the point, you see. I think the women that you see at the clubs are either overdressed or the men are underdressed, and there's no style about Palm Springs any more, I don't think. But it depends what you think of glamour, you see. If you want to drive up in a Rolls-Royce and come out dressed in jewels — that's what they like today, I guess. Instead of two chickens in the pot, there's two Rolls in the driveway. But it's fascinating to me where the money really comes from.

SAFER: Where does it come from?

MRS. GALLOIS: I don't know. They speak of buying something for a half a million dollars. Well, that's — it's quite a degree of money, you know.

SAFER: I do — I do know, indeed. But a ha— you don't get much for a half a million dollars in Palm Springs.

MRS. GALLOIS: That's the poi— that's the point.

SAFER: Parties seem to be very important to life here in Palm Springs.

MRS. GALLOIS: Well, I think that's what it is. It's just a string of parties, you see. And they — that's all they do, you see.

SAFER: People troop to parties in Palm Springs the way people elsewhere go to church. It is a kind of religion. Parties and banquets and balls for every conceivable charity in aid of every conceivable disease. Parties to celebrate arrivals and departures. Even parties to unveil face lifts. That's what Jolie, mother of all the Gabors, did. Enough face lifting has gone on in Palm Springs to raise the Titanic.

The newcomers give parties and the natives give parties. Much of that expensive real estate in Palm Springs is the property of the Agua Caliente Indians — at least a hundred million dollars' worth of land. And each land-owning tribesperson collects about $42,000 a year in rent. Plenty of reason, then, to celebrate the presence of those rich white folks who pay big money to flounder around like so many medium-boiled eggs. Of course you need the relaxation, for come sundown you're on again. It could be to meet Count and Countess De Stefano, or the exiled Prince and Princess of Yugoslavia, or just Prince Di Poliolo. But almost certainly you would run into the renowned Jeannine Levitt, widow of one of the builders of Levittown. Mrs. Levitt is an unashamed party giver and party goer. She is very French and very flamboyant, and admits that she works very hard at being both.

Jeannine, you're going to the opera tonight.

MRS. JEANNINE LEVITT: Yes.

SAFER: How on earth can you select what to wear when you've got this many clothes —

MRS. LEVITT: So many clothes.

SAFER: — these many — so many dresses?

MRS. LEVITT: Well, it's very easy. That's upon my mood. If I feel white and want to be pure, I will wear white. If I want to be in beige or skin color very sexy, I will wear something like this. If it gets cold, I will wear the mow— the brown — brow— brown.

SAFER: Gets cold.

MRS. LEVITT: Yes, you don't wear white.

SAFER: That's — that won't keep you warm.

MRS. LEVITT: Well, no, I'd have a mink coat to put on top of it. (Laughs)

SAFER: I see. May I walk through?

MRS. LEVITT: Yes, if you can. You will find very difficult.

SAFER: Two, three, four —

MRS. LEVITT: Whoops-a-daisy.

SAFER: — five, six racks of dresses.

MRS. LEVITT: Well — well, you see, some of them — here of them are short dresses; those one are the more warm dresses; others there are the sporty; some of them are the fur; some of them are the — the velvet — the velvet; and the fur hat, the straw hat.

SAFER: You know, there are very good shops in New York and Paris that do not have this many dresses in them.

Between dressing and the opera, there's just time to shoehorn in one quick party — a small bash for a few friends. Drink some pink champagne and munch on some Iranian caviar.

(Laughter, conversation at party)

We'll do it peasant style, Mrs. Levitt told us; no delicate bits of toast. Instead, you just cram the old sturgeon eggs into a big fat baked potato. Fast food, Palm Springs style.

"Not To My Kid, You Don't!"

BARRY LANDO, PRODUCER

MIKE WALLACE: Tonight, another look back. Nine years ago when we first broadcast the story on busing you're about to see again, some whites in America were dead set against busing and most blacks were all for it.* It's still controversial, but some of your attitudes about it have changed. However, back in '71, 60 MINUTES explored some of the hypocrisy about busing that we found then in our nation's capital. Remember, it was nine years ago, and this is what we said then.

Integration, so the old saw goes, is the wealthy liberal telling the not so wealthy whites to let a black family move in next door. Well, the prickliest integration issue these days is busing — not so much the question of busing black children to white schools, but of white children being bused to black neighborhoods. Now, there are more big-name liberals per square mile around Washington, D.C. than anyplace else in the country, but busing is not much of a local issue there; there just aren't enough white children in the district to bus. The Washington public school system is 95 percent black.

Still, Washington's liberals — its congressmen and journalists and jurists — have been busy advising communities elsewhere that busing is a necessary tool to achieve integration, even if it means busing your child away from your neighborhood school. But what do Washington's liberals do when it comes time to send their own children to school? 60 MINUTES decided to find out.

*This is an edited version of the original broadcast, aired November 14, 1971.

INSTRUCTOR: Number four. Teacher.

STUDENTS (in unison):   Teacher.

INSTRUCTOR: Teacher.

STUDENTS (in unison):   Teacher.

INSTRUCTOR: Right.

WALLACE: W. Bruce Evans Junior High, a public school in Washington, D.C. This is a seventh-grade reading class, but, of 28 students enrolled, only six are able to read at the seventh-grade level. Many can read only at third-grade or second-grade level; some can barely read at all.

INSTRUCTOR: A sore —

STUDENT: A sore — a — and a tooth —

INSTRUCTOR: Sore tooth.

STUDENT: Sore tooth is very servitive.

INSTRUCTOR: Sensitive.

STUDENT: Sensitive to hit —

INSTRUCTOR: Heat.

STUDENT: Heat and —

STUDENTS (in unison):   And cold.

STUDENT: — and cold.

INSTRUCTOR: And — and cold.

STUDENT: And cold.

WALLACE: Who goes to the Washington public schools? Certainly not the children of Washington's liberal establishment. Washington's liberals, for the most part, have managed to find ways to keep their own kids out of schools like this one, and that goes even for prominent black liberals like Walter Fauntroy, the man who represents this city in the United States Congress. He enrolled his son, Marvin, in a Washington private school.

As we were talking, nearby about a hundred fifty representatives of anti-busing groups across the country were protesting in front of the Supreme Court.

After their protest, a group of the ladies — from Texas and Michigan — walked past the Capitol, where Congressman Fauntroy and I were talking.

WALTER FAUNTROY: — going to have to distribute —

WALLACE: May I interrupt you for just a second? Ladies, would you come over here for just a second? We had no idea that you were coming. This is Congressman Fauntroy from the District of Columbia, and we're talking about the very subject of busing. Let me ask you a question, if I may, ladies. What I was just asking Congressman Fauntroy about was this: Senator Kennedy, Senator Muskie, talk a good deal about the necessity for an integrated education, and about the — if not the desirability of busing, at least the fact —

WOMAN: May I ask you a question? Where do their children go to school — private schools or public schools? Elliot Richardson, where does his kids go to school? Kennedy, where does his kids go to school?

WOMAN: Now, you are our leaders and we ask you as our leaders to provide an example. If you truly believe that a — that a child may get a — a quality education in a racially balanced school, we think that you should step forward and say, "Here is my child, and I want to put him in a racially balanced school." That's all we ask.

FAUNTROY: And that's what I have done.

WOMAN: You — you just now put your kid in public school?

FAUNTROY: No, in a — in an integrated school.

WOMAN: No, we want him in public school.

(Indistinct cross-talk)

FAUNTROY: Public school. Well, then I tell you right, because —

WOMAN: You show us the ideal, perfect school.

FAUNTROY: Yeah.

WOMAN: You show — you take one here in Dallas — I mean, in Washington — and set it up as an example for one year. If it works, you won't hear another squawk out of us.

WALLACE: This is the private school where Congressman Fauntroy sends his son: Georgetown Day School. It costs between sixteen hundred and two thousand dollars to send a child here, and the student body is studded with prominent liberal names. Senator Philip Hart, for instance, sends a child here. So does Frank Mankiewicz, Senator McGovern's top strategist, and so does *Washington Post* editor Ben Bradlee.

Many who send their children to Georgetown Day explained it is one of the only truly integrated schools in Washington, public or private. One quarter of the students are black — but they are not ghetto blacks, they are the children of middle- and upper-class blacks who have made it. Justice Thurgood Marshall, the first black appointed to the Supreme Court, sent his two youngsters here. Mayor Walter Washington's daughter went here, and nowadays so does his granddaughter. She is picked up each day by a chauffeur-driven car bearing the mayor's license plates.

Another white liberal with a child at Georgetown Day, Arvonne Fraser. She and her husband, Democratic Congressman Donald Fraser of Minnesota, recently took their daughter, Jeannie, out of a Washington public school and placed her in Georgetown Day, and Jeannie says she likes the change.

JEANNIE FRASER: I think I like it better, because we have sports and because they give you harder things than in the public schools. And in the public schools I was about the head of the class and here I'm about in the middle.

WALLACE: And you like better being in the middle?

JEANNIE: Uh-hmm.

WALLACE: What about — were you the only white girl at your public school?

JEANNIE: I think there was one more white girl in the class.

WALLACE: Do you see any hypocrisy in the journalists, and legislators like your husband, and jurists who talk busing, who talk integration in the schools, but then make darn sure that their kids go to private schools?

MRS. ARVONNE FRASER: Well, no, I guess I really don't, because you've got to say

— your kids only get educated once, and they're your kids and you want a good education. And sometimes you get a choice, you know, and — and the kids, that pers— that particular kid's education may come first.

WALLACE: But they're — they preach —

MRS. FRASER: As a group, I think it's — it's hypocritical, I agree.

WALLACE: As a group you think what's hypocritical?

MRS. FRASER: Well, that every — that the rich have freedom of choice.

INSTRUCTOR: Following your program cards, you will place another card that I have put at each one of your places. It is this. Place that card after your program deck . . .

WALLACE: Probably the most prestigious school where that freedom of choice can be exercised by the rich is St. Albans School for Boys run by the Episcopal Church. (Bells ringing) St. Albans is not only good, it is expensive. It would cost you $2400 a year to send your son here. This is the school where some of Washington's most powerful and persuasive liberal legislators and journalists send their sons. Tom Wicker's son goes here. Wicker writes frequently about subjects like busing on the liberal editorial pages of the *New York Times*. Phil Geyelin has one boy here. He heads up the influential editorial page of the *Washington Post*. And among legislators, two 100-percent ADA liberals — Birch Bayh of Indiana and Senator Ted Kennedy of Massachusetts — each has a boy here. We asked Senator Kennedy to talk to us, but he declined. Where he sends his son to school, he said, is a private matter.

What about some other big-name liberal senators, presidential possibilities? Senator Edmund Muskie says that he doesn't like busing, but that it's a necessary tool, the law of the land. And he goes on, "From time to time we must use uncomfortable means that put us to inconvenience, that impose burdens and create risks and fears." One of his daughters goes to the School of the Holy Child, a private Catholic institution, tuition a thousand dollars a year. Three of the 245 students here are black. Two other Muskie children go to another Catholic school nearby, where none of the 446 children is black. We wanted to talk to the senator about this issue, but his office told us he had no time in his schedule, that he was all booked up until mid-December.

Senator George McGovern is no enthusiast for busing, but earlier this year he blasted President Nixon after the President had said that he opposed compulsory busing for the purpose of achieving racial balance. "The President has encouraged massive evasion of and contempt for the law," said McGovern. "If I were President," he said, "I would not attempt to circumvent the law." Well, the senator and his family moved to the District of Columbia from Maryland suburbs, and before he moved, his daughter went to a private Catholic school. This year she commutes daily out here to the Bethesda Chevy-Chase Public High School. Since the senator doesn't live out here in Maryland anymore, he has to pay tuition charges of $1,450. The number of blacks out here in school? About three percent. Senator McGovern turned down our request for an interview. Where his children go to school, he said, is a private affair between himself and his family.

NICHOLAS VON HOFFMAN: In other words, nobody wants to — to make their children pay for their own social philosophy.

WALLACE: So there is hypocrisy here?

VON HOFFMAN: There's inequality.

WALLACE: I see.

VON HOFFMAN: There's no hypocrisy. I mean, when a rich person buys out, he may try and hide it, but usually he just says, "No, look, I can afford it and I can buy out. I've got the money."

WALLACE: Nicholas Von Hoffman, one of the most outspoken liberal columnists in the country. Like many other Washington newsmen, including several from CBS, Von Hoffman has managed to avoid sending his child to public school. In fact, he pulled his son out of this public junior high school to place him in a private school, where the tuition is about $1,600 a year.

What do you think your liberal friends might say if all of a sudden a law was passed which said a lot of white kids from Virginia and Maryland schools would be bused in to the center city to schools like this one, and a lot of black kids from the center city would be bused out to suburban schools in Virginia and Maryland?

VON HOFFMAN: Well, I think they'd be very unhappy, and I think the reason they would be unhappy is that they would be very scared.

WALLACE: And yet, to listen to them and to read them, you'd never know.

VON HOFFMAN: No, but I think you'd know fast enough if — if a proposition like that came along.

WALLACE: We have not been suggesting that the Washington liberal establishment is racist because they keep their children out of the public schools here. But it is equally false to write off as racist those who object to busing orders handed down by the Supreme Court and other courts across the land. When all is said and done, it seems plain that the main reason Washington's well-to-do liberals — black and white — send their children to private schools is not much different from what prompts less affluent white parents in cities across the country to resist having their children bused away from neighborhood schools. Nor are their desires all that much different from what black parents want for their children: personal safety and a good education. You heard Mrs. Fraser say it: "Your children get educated only once."

A Few Minutes
with Andy Rooney

HARRY REASONER: Breathes there a man with soul so dead who doesn't indulge in a little wishful thinking now and again. Andy Rooney is no exception.

ANDY ROONEY: Every night when I get home, there's a little pile of mail waiting for me. I used to think I'd find something wonderful in the pile, but I never do. I got thinking about the kind of letters I wish I'd received and never did. I had to write these myself.

> Dear Classmate: Just a note to tell you there won't be any annual fund-raising drive this year. Because of the warm winter, the university's fuel bill was less than expected and, by firing some of the dead wood on the faculty, they've been able to stay way under budget and won't need the money. Sincerely, Ham Davis, class secretary.

Here's one from a restaurant I ate in the other night.

> Dear Mr. Rooney: In checking your bill, we noticed that the total was $57.30 for four people, not the $63.40 we charged you. Our check for $6.10 is enclosed.

Here's one I never got from the New York City Police Department.

> Dear Sir or Madame: Please ignore the parking ticket which was placed on the windshield of your vehicle in error. We regret any inconvenience this may have caused you.

Here's one from an insurance company.

> Dear Rooney: You can drop dead as far as the Pilgrim Fathers Life Insurance Company is concerned. We've tried to sell you a policy for the past 20 years. You've never answered one request for information about yourself yet. This is the last letter you'll ever get from us, fella!

Well, I hope so, Pilgrim Fathers.

And here's a letter I'd like to get from a contractor someday.

> Dear Mr. Rooney: Enclosed is the bill for the addition to your house. Our estimate for the job was $6,700, but because of problems we thought we'd have that we didn't run into, we were able to complete it for only $5,100. Martin Construction Company

And after a year of getting letters like those, here's a little note I'd like to find in my mailbox just before Christmas, with a $10 bill attached to it.

> Dear Mr. Rooney: It's been such a pleasure serving you this year that I want you to accept this little token of my appreciation. Signed, your mailman.

Nice?

Letters

MIKE WALLACE: When we do a controversial story like the one last week on the Aspen, Colorado sheriff who refuses to cooperate with federal drug-enforcement officials, we usually get a lot of mail pro and con. Well, this time the mail, for whatever reason, was almost entirely pro. For instance, this letter: "Our Founding Fathers would have been proud of the sheriff. Our country needs a few thousand more like him."

There were, however, in amongst the pro-mail, a few letters like this one: "For 30 years I skied Aspen when it was clean, small and beautiful. I quit 10 years ago when the crazies (took over the slopes). I now see that the crazies have even taken over the law."

Also in the mail were several letters about our retrospective look at panhandlers, circa 1969. One viewer suggested that we should have followed up that story and let you know: "Just how the panhandlers panned out."

Had we followed up, one viewer surmised that we might have found that during the last ten years those panhandlers had: "Shaved off their beards, traded their street garb for three-piece suits, and were now captains of industry — still taking our money."

About our story on Johnny Carson, one of our viewers was incensed that we referred to Johnny as a national treasure, and wrote: "National treasure? He's a dirty old man."

But there was also a letter that said: "Johnny Carson must be getting old. When he was asked what (he wanted on his tombstone) . . . I was dead sure he would have said, 'Here's Johnny!' "

And finally, speaking of getting old, a viewer agreed with something Harry said in introducing last week's story from the past: "You're right, all of you have aged a little . . . with the exception of Mike . . . But (please) explain how he keeps his trench coat looking so young."

MAY 11, 1980

Bonnie

MARION GOLDIN, PRODUCER

MIKE WALLACE: For years the *Reader's Digest* has run a popular feature called "The Most Unforgettable Character" about individuals so uncommon, so out of the ordinary, that their stories just beg to be told. Bonnie is one such – Bonnie Consolo. Watch her a while, especially on this Mother's Day, and we think you'll agree.

(Organ music)

Bonnie Consolo is playing that organ with her feet because 40 years ago she was born with two legs but no arms. First, we would like you to meet Bonnie Consolo the way we first met her, through a film shot a couple of years ago by a young California film maker, Barry Spinella.

BONNIE CONSOLO: There is nothing around my house that I can't do. I'm very independent. If I want something done — you know, if I want someone to help me — then I'll ask. But it — and I say no if somebody asks if I need help. My mother, I give her most of the credit for what I am, because she made me try it. She made me do it. And so that's — I think that's the way that the parents of any handicapped child, no matter what his disability is, to, you know, let him do it, and then if he says that he, you know, asks — asks for help, then — then help him. But if he says "I can't" — no, I don't know those words. I don't un— you know, they're not in my language. (Laughs) I laugh at life. I la— I laugh at myself. My friends that come to the house, and they'll see me, my feet in the sink, and they'll say something about "dishpan hands," and I say "Oh, yeah, I get dishpan feet, too!" (Laughs).

A lot of people notice my ring and they — you know, they — they think it's kind of weird, you know, for me to wear it on my toe. And I just sometimes tell them, "Well, I'm just walking around on my hand." (Laughs) I have thought about, you know, wearing it on a chain around my neck, but then if I do that, then I can't wear, you know, the other necklaces that I have. There was a man once; he walked up to me on the street and he says, "How in the world do you dress yourself?" And I said, "That's none of your damned business." You know? (Laughs) I would have ordinarily said, "Just like you do." You know? But, of course, I — I do do things differently. It's much easier for me to get dressed, I think, than a lot of women. A zipper that zips up the back, I put the dress on backwards, zip it up the front and then turn it around.

Would you believe that I was asked once not to shop in a store? I had been shopping in this store for about two years, and one day I drove up in front, and the manager of the store came out, and he said that certain people had started a petition that they didn't want me shopping in their store, because I touched everything with my feet. And I — the more I looked at that guy, the smaller he got. I just could not believe it. It was the first and the last experience that I have ever had like that.

If I had ever thought that there was any chance at all that my baby would be born as I am, I would never have had children, because I don't feel that I have the right to put anybody through what I went through as a child. Mark and I, we talk about me, and he has often expressed the fact that it — "Wouldn't it be easier for you to do this or that if you had hands?" And I say, "Gee, Mark, I don't know. I never had them, so I wouldn't — I wouldn't know if it would be any easier or not." Even Matt, and he's not even three, he hands me things a little bit lower, you know, than he does his father. I love to see Matt laugh, and he talks to me, and I love to change his diapers, and now, you know, get him dressed and take him for a walk. And I love to be able to just sit quietly and talk with Mark, and he, you know, tells me, in his way of talking, you know, that he's learning in school.

I was a — a breast-fed baby. My mother said that whenever she was nursing me, I would play with her breast; you know, like most babies do with their hands, I would do it with my foot. It was an automatic takeover from hands that weren't there to feet that were. So I would start picking things up with my toes and, you know, putting things in my mouth with my toes, like every other baby does with his hands.

All of our lives, we strive to be different — in what we do, what we look like. And here, you know, it was just handed to me on a silver platter. I'm different. And I know the doctor, the very first doctor that examined me, said that it would be better for me if I didn't live. But I did survive, and I think that I have made my own — my own life.

WALLACE: Well, after seeing that film, we wanted to learn some more about Bonnie Consolo, so we went to her home in a suburb near Columbus, Ohio, where we talked with her, among other places, in the front seat of her car.
Do you swear to me you've never had an accident?

CONSOLO: I never have.

WALLACE: Never one, never close?

CONSOLO: Never. Well, only one time I buckled the fender on my car. But there was not — I don't even call that an accident.

WALLACE: I mean, these are turns and stops and —

CONSOLO: I have driven the freeways in Los Angeles.

WALLACE: Anybody who can do that — (Consolo laughs) — and escape unscathed —

CONSOLO: The only time that an officer asked to see my license was when I had a headlight out. Scared me to death.

WALLACE: I can imagine.

CONSOLO: It did. It really did.

WALLACE: Must have scared him to death, too.

CONSOLO (laughing):   He didn't let on. Would you like me to go faster? (Laughs) You want to be nervous, Mike? You're supposed to be nervous.

WALLACE: I confess that I wasn't nervous, even though her car carried no special equipment, unless you call a CB radio special.

CONSOLO: Guess what my handle is?

WALLACE: What? (Consolo laughs) Armless?

CONSOLO: They call me Venus. (Laughs)

WALLACE: Ah, that's perfect!

You seem to have a remarkable reservoir of composure about — you — you — you — as though you're an utterly normal person. And you'll tell me, "Yes, I am, Mike, an utterly normal person."

CONSOLO: Inside I'm a normal person. I feel about myself probably the way you feel about yourself. And this inside is where the person is, not what they look like.

WALLACE: Her parents and her brothers and sisters are perfectly normal. She was born too long ago to be a thalidomide baby. The fact is Bonnie doesn't really know what caused her armlessness. A virus is the explanation she likes best.

Did you never say to yourself, Bonnie, as a child, "Why did God pick me out for this?"

CONSOLO: Oh, in my prayers at night, Mike, I used to say, "Why me, Lord? Why did this have to happen to me? I don't want it. I can't handle it. Give it to somebody else." And it was a terrible time in my life. I felt very inferior, that I wasn't as good as everybody else. It wasn't because the way anybody treated me. It was within myself.

WALLACE: Uh-hmm.

CONSOLO: Of course, I grew up with people that didn't have handicaps, so I had never really seen anybody, and I thought that I was the only one in the whole world that had a — a gigantic problem.

WALLACE: Well, then what turned you around? You obviously haven't felt that way for years and years and years.

CONSOLO: It was a very slow process of eliminating the fear of people looking at me, and then all of a sudden it began to be funny. I'd walk out of a store, get into my car, and of course there were people lined up on the sidewalk, and they would have a look of pity on their face. I could see it.

WALLACE: Uh-hmm.

CONSOLO: And then they'd see me getting into my car and drive off, and I could almost hear th— hear their chins hitting the cement — you know, like that. They couldn't believe what they were seeing.

WALLACE: In looking at the film and seeing you handle food, and — and when I first see it, it's almost a shock, and then I think, well, now, she walks on the floor and she gets her feet dirty and then she handles the food and — is that as clean as it should be?

CONSOLO: Well, feet are washable, aren't they, Mike? (Laughs)

WALLACE: Yes, I know. (Laughter)

CONSOLO: I probably wash my feet many, many, many more times than most housewives wash their hands.

WALLACE: Bonnie was told by doctors that there was a chance, if she had children, they too might be born without arms.

But you took the chance and went ahead and had children?

CONSOLO: There was no way, Mike, that I would have ended the life of my child, even if I had known that he would have been — had a big problem. No way could I have done that.

WALLACE: And first one and then two.

CONSOLO: Yes. Mark was so beautiful. He was perfect, and — as Matthew is. And I don't think they have any hang-ups. They pretty well have it all together.

WALLACE: Have they ever had any trouble because of you and your armlessness?

CONSOLO: You know, this worried me when they were little, of how they would be able to adjust to me, how they would be able to accept me as just Mom. So as soon as they learned to talk, we talked about me. We laughed about me and we made jokes about me. Never was there a time when I said, "I don't want to talk about it."

WALLACE: Are you aware, Mark, how special your mother is?

MARK CONSOLO: Yeah.

WALLACE: Or does she just seem like anybody else's Mom to you?

MARK: Yeah. She'd look weird with arms to me, because, well, the way I see her, well, it would be just a different way if she had arms. Yeah.

WALLACE: You mean you like her better without?

MARK: Yeah, because she would look very weird with arms.

FRANK CONSOLO: You know, my kids accept this. They don't — (indistinct) — This one here been picking up forks with his feet, you know. He's been do—this one here —

WALLACE: Is that a fact?

FRANK: He does.

MARK: He picked up a cookie and ate it with his foot.

FRANK: And he eats — tries to eat like his mother with a fork between his toes. He's been doing it — he's a comedian, this one here.

WALLACE: Bonnie had corresponded with Frank Consolo — whom she had never met — for more than a year when he asked her to meet him in California. She did, and two and a half months later they were married. That was 13 years ago.

When I saw the film first, Frank, I thought to myself I would very much like to talk to this man who married a woman without arms.

FRANK: She gave me a whole new life. She — I seen the rich philosophy in her.

WALLACE: Bonnie's putting some of that philosophy into her autobiography, elaborating on the simple story she tells as she takes her film around the country. At times, though not for this Easter Seal telethon, she earns a small fee for these appearances, money she needs since her husband lost his job a year ago. You had been married before?

CONSOLO: Yes.

WALLACE: Was he handicapped?

CONSOLO: He was paralyzed from the waist down.

WALLACE: Oh.

CONSOLO: I have told myself that perhaps because I wanted a home and family so much that a handicapped person had to settle for another handicapped person. And, of course, I didn't love him because he was handicapped. I loved him because of the person that he was.

WALLACE: And then, even years later, you said to yourself, "Well, I want children, and this man — God help us both — can't give me children"?

CONSOLO: Right. So we were divorced.

WALLACE: Is there anything, Bonnie, that you desperately want to do that you just can't?

CONSOLO: I want very much to go bike riding with the kids, but I can't. I haven't been able to manage that.

"Is there anything, Bonnie, that you desperately want to do that you just can't?" "I want very much to go bike riding with the kids, but I can't. I haven't been able to manage that."

WALLACE: You mean, truly, that is the only thing that you can think of?

CONSOLO: The only thing that's important to me that I can't do, that I would really like to do.

WALLACE: There are millions and millions of people looking at you right now, and you're saying, in effect, take a look at me.

CONSOLO: Right.

WALLACE: I have no arms, but my life is every bit as good, every bit as fruitful, as fulfilling. I have as much fun.

CONSOLO: This is what I tell everybody. I s— I do want people to look at me. It bothers me when people look at me and then look away when they see me looking at them. But I tell these groups that I talk to, I say, "I, just like you, want somebody to like me or to hate me because of what I am, not for what I look like." A lot of handicapped people stay within four walls because they — they can't handle the stares, the remarks of people. And I would tell these people, "The heck with what people think!" Hopefully people will not refer to me as Bonnie with no arms, but just Bonnie Consolo — a person, a human being, nothing more, nothing less.

Where do you have to go? Which airline?

WALLACE: I'm going to TWA. I'm sure that any one of these doors —

CONSOLO: Okay. People park out here like — like crazy.

WALLACE: My dear, thank you a million.

CONSOLO: Oh, it was my pleasure.

WALLACE: I'm glad. I want — Goodbye.

CONSOLO: Goodbye.

WALLACE: You're a dear.

CONSOLO: Have a good flight.

WALLACE: Thank you. Bye-bye.

CONSOLO: Bye.

WALLACE: Since we filmed that story, Bonnie and Frank Consolo have separated. As Bonnie told us when it happened, armless people get divorced, too.

Highway Robbery

STEVE GLAUBER, PRODUCER

DAN RATHER: It's almost summer vacation time again, and that seems to us a good time to give you another look at a story we did in 1978 about a new breed of highway robber who carried no gun, wore no mask, just the overalls and familiar cap of a service station attendant.* These holdup men dealt in phony auto repairs and worked out of gas stations along freeways and toll roads going north, south, east and west. It didn't matter. Wherever the tourist traffic was the heaviest was where you found them. What's happened to them? Stick around and we'll tell you.

To get to where you want to go on that vacation, you'll probably be driving on an interstate, and what you'll be caring about is getting there quickly and safely. If something goes wrong with your car, you'll be at the trust and mercy of the man running the gas station at the nearest exit. Can you trust him? Listen to one expert who agreed to speak with us only if he remained unidentified. We'll call him John. John used to run gas stations along an interstate in the Southwest. He wasn't the only one who told us that stations like the one he ran pay high rents, don't depend on repeat business, and make their biggest profits, not on gasoline, but on accessories. So, as he once did, some station operators, he says, cheat tourists just to survive.

How widespread is it?

JOHN: Nationwide. It really is.

---

*This segment was previously broadcast September 24, 1978 and May 13, 1979.

RATHER: Is it?

JOHN: Yes. Uh-hmm.

RATHER: It's not confined to just a few interstate highways?

JOHN: No, it happens on all of them. From the Florida coast, Maine out to California, wherever tourists do go.

RATHER: To investigate whether or not tourist rip-offs are widespread, 60 MINUTES took a trip along Georgia's I-75, the interstate northerners must take to reach Florida. Posing as tourists were 60 MINUTES producer Steve Glauber, along with Carol Graves, an employee of the Georgia Consumer Agency, and her son, Matthew.

But first we went to Bob Hawkins, a highly trained certified mechanic, who inspected the car to make sure all parts were in perfect operating condition. We also went for some advice to Rick Matysiak, a Georgia state investigator specializing in auto frauds. He warned us that even experienced investigators have trouble not tipping off unscrupulous operators.

RICK MATYSIAK: Some of the documented cars that we have sent in on different occasions, that — they would pick us apart and actually saying how ignorant we were. Bolts on the license plates were brand new — something that you don't normally think about. Even on the lug nuts, if the tires have been changed recently will put them on notice. Thumb prints on hubcaps. So anything that doesn't look right, they'll stay away from.

RATHER: So Bob Hawkins gave our car the necessary touches.

BOB HAWKINS: We run it through the mud and got mud all underneath. We dirtied up the tires and all, so it would look like it had been on the road. We used out-of-state plates and we dirtied up the plates and everything to make them look like they had been on the road for a lo— good length of time, and you had a bunch of road film and such as that on.

RATHER: The shock absorber trick – how does that work?

HAWKINS: The man will have a plastic bottle in his pocket, either his shirt pocket or in his hip pocket, it's got oil in it. And while he's bending down to check your tires, he'll reach under here and he just squirts oil on the ground, just a small amount. And he'll holler, you know, "Hey, look, you got oil leaking down here. You got a bad shock. Come here and let me show you." And sure enough, you look under there, you got oil on the ground. So you think you got a bad shock and he sells you a set of shocks that you don't even need.

RATHER: Another favorite trick is puncturing tires, better known as honking.

HAWKINS: It's what they call a sticker, and it's a device that's very sharp and efficient and quick. You approach the tire, push it in and pull it out.

RATHER: So we hit the road. The camera crew followed in a motor van out of which they could film. At the first stop, a Gulf, the service was routine. The second stop was at a Shell station.

(Buzzer noise)

STATION ATTENDANT: Fill her up?

STEVE GLAUBER: Could you please fill it up? Also check the oil?

RATHER: A tourist increases his risk if he leaves his car unattended, and that's what we did. What happened next even our cameraman did not catch until we ran the film slow motion. The attendant is taking a bottle from his pocket and will hide it in his rag. In that bottle is oil. Now he is going to the side of the car furthest away from the station house, and when he bends down, he will be hidden from the passengers' view. Now he is squirting oil onto the shock absorbers. By the time he gets up, there will be an oil puddle on the ground. And when Glauber returns from washing up, he will hear some bad news.

ATTENDANT: Not going too far, are you?

GLAUBER: Yes, we are.

ATTENDANT: You've got some brake fluid or something leaking on the front over there.

GLAUBER: Something? What?

ATTENDANT: Leaking.

GLAUBER: Oh, Lord! Yeah, we're going quite a ways. Uh-huh, what's that, do you think?

ATTENDANT: Hydraulic oil. Where you going to? Down to Florida?

GLAUBER: Yes, we are. Down to Miami.

ATTENDANT: Take a minute and we'll raise it up on the boards and see where it's coming from.

GLAUBER: Could you, please?

RATHER: Once in the garage, we were told that one of the shocks was busted and that we needed to replace two of them.

GLAUBER: Well, I saw some dripping, so that means what?

ATTENDANT: That's the fluid from the shock.

GLAUBER: That's the fluid from the shock.

ATTENDANT: Right.

GLAUBER: And that's caused by what?

ATTENDANT: The seal ruptured in there —

GLAUBER: Uh-huh.

ATTENDANT: — where your piston rod works.

GLAUBER: And what could happen if that would have kept going?

ATTENDANT: Well, I'd say it's pretty bad on your front end part —

GLAUBER: Uh-huh.

ATTENDANT: — because that holds your wheel down on the road. And it — it can cause your, you know, car to sway and such as that.

GLAUBER: Uh-huh.

RATHER: We continued on our journey with two new shocks and $50.15 less money, and made our next stop at a station flying the Texaco flag. Once more the passengers left the car and, just like at the last gas station, this attendant seemed to look around to make sure no one was watching, and he too paid special attention to the side of the car hidden from the passengers' view.

Our camera was not in position to see exactly what he did to that right front tire, but what we do know is that by the time our passengers returned to the automobile, that tire was rapidly going flat. The car was driven into the garage and the manager showed us the flat, said that both front tires should be replaced. And then he warned that both back tires were "dangerously worn out."

STATION MANAGER: That thing builds up a little bit of pressure and this wall will come out of it. I'm not trying to scare you or anything, but, I mean, when a tire gets down like that, it should be replaced. But it's just not safe —

GLAUBER: Hm-mmm.

MANAGER: — riding on something like that . . .

RATHER: We didn't take his advice to buy four tires. We bought only two new radials. Price: $154.12. But because we could not positively see what the attendant did to the tire, we went back to expert mechanic Bob Hawkins.
Was there anything wrong with the tire?

HAWKINS: No, sir. The tire had some scuff marks on it where it had been run into the curb, and we went to the extent of checking the tire with water ourself to see if it had any leaks and there was no signs of a leak on the tires that were on the ground.

RATHER: You checked it with water yourself?

HAWKINS: Yes, sir, most certainly did.

RATHER: Now, we drove it approximately 100 miles. He checked it with water, said you definitely need a new tire here. As a matter of fact, recommended that we get four new tires.

HAWKINS: Yes.

RATHER: Professional opinion?

HAWKINS: Probably used an icepick on it, punched a small hole and then put the water with the soap on it and it's going to leak.

RATHER: Back to I-75, and the fourth stop, again a Gulf. Once more, we were told we had problems.

GAS STATION ATTENDANT: I don't know why it's splitting on the side. I don't know why it's doing it, but it's coming apart like a recap. I tell you what we'll do. I'll take one off and break it down and open it up and see what it looks like.

GLAUBER: Okay.

RATHER: This time the attendant showed us one tire with a big gash — a gash that mechanic Hawkins later inspected and found had been made with a sharp tool, probably a knife or razor. And the attendant also told us that another tire was — quote — "separating."

ATTENDANT: You see, it — it don't look bad.

GLAUBER: No, it looks fine.

ATTENDANT: Okay.

GLAUBER: And now you push down the tire?

ATTENDANT: And it's coming apart.

GLAUBER: And see those lines there?

ATTENDANT: That's right. See there?

GLAUBER: Is— isn't that the construction of the tire?

ATTENDANT: Sir?

GLAUBER: It might —

ATTENDANT: I wou— I would say it would be, but it's not supposed to split open. I wouldn't be scared to say to anybody that this tire was coming apart.

RATHER: Tires weren't the only problem. He said one of the shock absorbers was bad and he recommended replacing all four.

GLAUBER: Honey, look at the tires.

CAROL GRAVES: What went wrong with ours?

ATTENDANT: They just wore out. You see, if one goes bad, all four is — is — is bad. You know, going bad, on their way.

GLAUBER: If one goes bad, they all go bad about the same time?

ATTENDANT: It's like buying one shoe and not buying the other one.

GLAUBER: Buy one shoe and not buy the other. (Laughter)

RATHER: We left with two new tires, four new shocks.

Four stations, three hits, a lot of CBS money out of our pockets. First station — nothing happened. Second station — two shock absorbers; $50.15. Third station — two radial tires; keep in mind we did not buy two others that were recommended. But at the third station — two radial tires; price — $154.12. At the fourth station — four shock absorbers and two radial tires; price — $271.98. The grand total — four stations, three hits — the grand total: $476.25.

What do the oil companies say about all this? We spoke with Shell, Texaco and Gulf, who said that, although they don't initiate investigations, they do follow up once they receive enough complaints. As to the extent of the complaints, they agree with Gulf Oil's Southeast Regional Manager, Charles Mattei.

CHARLES MATTEI: The majority of them are honest and ethical. And I don't want — don't want to leave you with the impression, you know, that this is a big problem, a widespread problem. We've got a few bad apples. We don't want any.

RATHER: Now, who are these bad apples who prey on tourists? Surprisingly, they are not just local guys trying to make an extra buck, but skilled professionals who rake in big money. There's even a name for them — fifty percenters. Tim Ryles is administrator of the Georgia Office of Consumer Affairs and he has been trying to catch them for years.

TIM RYLES: Fifty percenters are people who are professionals at ripping tires, selling shop— shock absorbers, alternators, other tires, batteries and accessories. They sign on with a station under the understanding that they will get 50 percent of the proceeds of the sales that they make.

JOHN: The fifty percenter will approach the owner of the service station and tell him that he's been watching his operation for the last hour and a half, two hours, and he likes his flow of traffic, the quality of traffic that's coming through, the states that these people are coming from, and he knows that he could possibly make the owner three or four hundred dollars a day, and himself too.

RYLES: They'll work in Georgia in the winter season generally, which is our heavier season. They will return to the Southwest for the summer months to hit the tourists in that region of the country during that time.

JOHN: They work about, I'd say, six or seven months out of the year and make their fifty or sixty thousand dollars and — tax free, and that's it.

RATHER: Drivers of newer and bigger cars are favorite targets because they're probably bigger spenders. Elderly people are preferred, especially elderly women. Families with children, concerned about safety, are prime targets. Above all, the tourists must be out-of-staters, and the further away the better.

RYLES: We're talking about rip-offs that may range from, oh, sixty or seventy dollars to maybe four or five hundred dollars. When you calculate the costs of coming back to Georgia for a trial, people are going to look at the $500 that they lost and they're just simply going to say it's not worth my expenses to go back to Georgia, or if you're in New York to go to New Mexico, in order to prosecute somebody who does it. So that's the reason for the out-of-state victim. The elderly victim because they just happen to be susceptible.

RATHER: Before leaving Georgia, we revisited the three gas stations in the reverse order of our initial stops to hear what they had to say. First Gulf.

Now the hypothesis put to me is that you saw an automobile pull in here with New York plates on it; that what appeared to be a man, his wife and child looked like the quintessential victim, and that you then conned them — (buzzer sounds) — that you then conned them into doing — (buzzer sounds) — almost $300 worth of repair work.

ATTENDANT: Well, sir, like I said again — (buzzer sounds) — he has the right to say no or yes. I don't hold a gun on him. I didn't scare him into buying. I didn't tell him nothing but, you know, what I thought he needed. I mean, he didn't have to buy. He could have said no.

RATHER: At Texaco we talked to the manager who had sold us the tires.

The hypothesis is — the hypothesis is that somebody worked on the tire while they were down there. Then you put the tire up on the — on the hoist and told him he had tire trouble. Now, that's the allegation. What I'm asking you is, did that happen?

MANAGER: Can you prove that?

RATHER: No, I'm asking, did it happen?

MANAGER: Can you prove that? It don't happen here because we don't do those tactics here.

RATHER: That's what I'm asking.

MANAGER: They might do it down the road. They might do it up the road or somewhere like that.

RATHER (at Shell station):   Have you ever known anybody to do it?

ATTENDANT: No.

RATHER: This is Billy Wagner, our photographer. Well, I'll tell you what — what the problem is for us is that we've been running cars back and forth —

ATTENDANT: Yeah.

RATHER: And —

MANAGER: Hey! I wouldn't talk to them people. Just get the hell out of here!

RATHER: Well, if you hold on just a second I'll tell you what we're about to (cross-talk).

MANAGER: Well, we don't even want to talk to you.

RATHER: Well, the difficulty is that we brought a car in within the last 48 hours in which you did a job on the shock absorbers.

ATTENDANT: Is that right?

RATHER: Yeah. And what I want to know is, who put you up to it?

ATTENDANT: Nobody put me up to it. (Laughs)

RATHER: Uh-huh?

ATTENDANT: No one.

RATHER: You just did it on your own?

ATTENDANT: Well . . .

RATHER: Understand here's what happened. Here's what we have on film. The car pulls in —

MANAGER (in background):   Hey, pal, what the hell are you — (indistinct)?

RATHER: Guy went to the restroom. You go down underneath the car, make the shock absorbers drip grease, and then you tell him you got shock absorber trouble. We had the shock absorber marked, had a master mechanic tell us the shock absorber's fine. Now there's no question it happened.

ATTENDANT: Just his opinion, I guess.

RATHER: No, it's not a matter of opinion. It's a question of who put you up to it, how did it happen.

ATTENDANT: Ain't got any comment.

RATHER: You don't deny that it happened?

ATTENDANT: I — maybe it did, maybe it didn't. I don't know.

RATHER: Well, I'm — you know exactly what he's talking about. You make a commission on it?

ATTENDANT: No, just work here. Part of my job, I guess.

RATHER: Is it part of your job?

ATTENDANT: Whatever you're talking about. All I do is just do my job.

RATHER: Now we filmed along the Georgia interstate. Your opinion we could have found this on other interstate highways?

JOHN: You bet.

RATHER: After we first aired this report in September, 1978, the Georgia Office of Consumer Affairs told us that complaints dropped from 170 before we aired this story to 30 the rest of that year. This year, they've received only three or four complaints. Those Texaco and Gulf stations we saw were closed down, then opened under new management. And that Shell station no longer does repairs, but only sells gas. About the father and son we caught in the act, the Georgia consumer office says they're operating another Shell station now, but no complaints have been received about them. So, at least in Georgia, the lawmen have gotten the drop on the highwaymen.

Fellini

WILLIAM K. McCLURE, PRODUCER

HARRY REASONER: I thought of trying to do this introduction like a disc jockey: "Now 60 MINUTES continues its parade of golden oldies, the pieces that zoomed right off the charts when we first aired them." Doesn't work. So here's another old one. The difference about it is that I have never seen it in final edited form and neither have you. It's a wonderful story that Bill McClure and I did in 1970, when Federico Fellini was filming a show for Italian television called "Clowns." Mr. Fellini and I hit it off — roughly the same age, same physical types. The only major difference: I'm from Iowa, he's from Italy. But before it got on the air, I wandered away to another network, and Morley Safer — younger, different physical type, but also non-Italian — salvaged it. Now you get to see Federico Fellini, maybe the premier film maker of the age, as you would have with me in the winter of 1970, if things had been different.*

(Circus music)

I recently watched Fellini direct his latest film, *The Clowns*. It is a personal and nostalgic look at the world of the circus today and at its past, mixed with his own childhood memories.

FEDERICO FELLINI: It recalled many memories, how I was attracted by these "candy world" figures, pathetic and majestic, with their abstract and strange pantomime.

(Circus music)

When I was about seven years old, my parents took me to the circus. I remember the clowns. They really shocked me. I did not understand what they were, whether they were animals or ghosts. I now realize that I was to be a clown just like them, making pictures, working in the circus of the cinema.

(Music)

Being faithful to the script, which is done beforehand, is absurd. On paper, one can only insinuate what the film will be. But it will always be different. The film's length and breadth will be as unpredictable as any living creature — unpredictable and real. For this reason, the film slowly gives me the impression that it is not me who is directing but the film that is directing me.

(Music)

Faces are the medium with which I express myself, my fantasy, my— my story. Faces are the first real contact with what already exists in my imagination. I look at people — actor or not actors — and their faces say to me, "Look at us. Every one of us is a little bit of your film."

(Music)

It's as if the film already existed. It is just a matter of going around in search of it, to — to recognize it.

(Music)

(Fellini directing)

Every one of my films is a trip. Every trip starts in complete confusion, full of contradictions. (Fellini directing) When the atmosphere is good, everyone

---

*This story was previously broadcast January 5, 1971 and May 4, 1975, with Morley Safer substituting for Harry Reasoner.

embarks on the trip looking for its meaning as the film is being made. It's like the crew of a ship.

(Fellini directing)

Directing an actor, or someone who is not an actor but has a part to play in the film, is the story of a relationship, of a friendship, of likes and dislikes.

(Fellini directing . . . laughter)

I cannot work in a state of sadness. Usually I need around me an atmosphere of gaiety. I'm not the kind of director who likes silence, who has to work alone, without company or curiosity. In that sense, I am really a man of the circus. I need to feel at home, to create a little family. I believe that the film derives richness and strength from the moods and temperaments of all the participants. So I need to have around me people I like, or people I frankly dislike but who have a strong personality. I mean, people who do not correspond to professional labels like cameraman, script girl or assistant director. I mean, people like my wife, Giulietta, or Liana, or Alvero, Gasperino — real people, friends, that I know very well.

(Music)

REASONER: It's difficult to imagine anyone more Roman than Federico Fellini. He refuses to work in a foreign environment. If he made a film in New York, he says, he wouldn't know what sort of shoes or clothes a character would wear. Unlike many other Italian directors, Fellini is not politically oriented, but his vision is very much influenced by the pressures of Italian life, especially those of the Catholic Church.

(Music)

FELLINI: Real religion should be something that liberates men, but churches don't want free men who can think for themselves and find their own divinity within. When a religion becomes organized, it is no longer a religious experience but only superstition and estrangement. Childhood of my generation was conditioned by a sense of duty, by ideals, myths and taboos of the pagan.

(Church bells)

REASONER: Of the great film makers of today, Federico Fellini is truly a magician. His magic expresses his own obsessions, his own fantasies. Remember La Strada, in 1955, his first great film, where he transformed his wife, Giulietta Masina, into the pathetic character of Gelsomina. The Nights of Cabiria, in 1957, with Masina again, as a prostitute with too large a heart. In 1960, La Dolce Vita. Permissiveness became a style and Marcello Mastroianni a star. Now, ten years later, Satyricon, his vision of the decadence of ancient Rome.

But Fellini does not want to be remembered by the films he has already made. He only wants to think about the next one.

FELLINI: I am a very, very, very bad father. When I have — make a picture, the picture has to fend by himself. You know, it's — I don't want to be involved with — too long with a picture. It is always very dangerous to — to live with — long time with your creature, you know. You have to live with your creature just the time that she needs — that it needs you; but when that is finished, you have to try to forget completely, because otherwise you — you run the risk to be eaten from your creature, you know, especially that if your creation is very alive. The more alive, more powerful is the creation of an artist, the more danger there is that this creation try to eat his creator.

REASONER: Federico Fellini's life style still has the conventional facade of Italian middle-class comfort. On Sunday mornings, with Giulietta, he sits on his terrace reading Rome's popular press. Superficially, he is another tired suburban-based husband. But as an artist he is always alone, in the middle of his own work, making his own fantasy. It is only through his subconscious that Fellini the magician appears.

(Music)

FELLINI: What I call magic is the power in each of us to create something. All creators are magicians. And artists are, too, when they work in the dimension of fantasy that they then materialize. An artistic creation is an extremely scientific operation; yet, at the same time, it is irrational, intuitive, emotional. One needs to recognize faces, things, colors, objects, that are part of the film. Sometime, pulling a little tail, one finds an elephant at the other end.

(Music)

I consider myself a lucky man. I only do what I know and can do and no one oblige me to do what I don't want to. All told, my work is not real work but just a long vacation. When I am asked what my hobby is, I never know what to answer because I don't seem to have any; but if I were really sincere, I will say that my hobby is film making and I make films because this seems to be my life.

REASONER: Words of a contented man. Fellini's imagination and vitality seem unlimited. His style and technique have probably affected film making more than that of any other director in the past ten years. Now fifty, how does he feel about aging?

FELLINI: If there is a little wisdom in becoming older and older, I think that it is just to forget to try to know who you are — to try to know who you are in — in terms of moralism, in terms of — of idealism. You know, it's a — that — you lose time. When — when you know that you are exactly So-and-So, so what?

REASONER: You speak in a – a very healthy-minded way, Signor. Don't you have any fears or anxieties or the hang-ups of middle age?

FELLINI: Yes, the physical decadence bother me — to be obliged, for example, don't — to don't do — to don't make love six time a day, like in the past time.

REASONER: Six times a day? (Laughs) That's –

FELLINI: Five. (Laughter)

A Few Minutes
with Andy Rooney

MORLEY SAFER: Recession or no recession, Andy Rooney is thinking about buying a new car. He may not do anything about it, but he is thinking about it. In fact, he's thinking about a lot more than just one new car.

ANDY ROONEY: The people in Detroit are disappointed because more of us aren't buying new cars. One of the problems is deciding which new car to buy – not which brand name so much but which type car. You need a different car to do different things in, that's the trouble. If I was rich, I'd have the right car for every occasion. I'm always carrying furniture around, so I'd want a big, fat American station wagon. This one's a Mercury.

This is one of the greatest inventions since sliced bread. Look at that! This beauty is a Cadillac Seville. It's a diesel. It costs about $21,000. I'd want one of these for days I felt like saving money on gas. I'd want a Volkswagen Rabbit. I wouldn't even mind having an old Volkswagen "bug." I'd certainly want a Rolls-Royce for those special occasions. Of course, a new Rolls would cost you $160,000. This one's ten years old; you could probably pick it up for $70,000.

You ought to have a good, average, everyday American car — you know, just for driving: Pontiac, Ford certainly, good old Buick; you might want a Chevrolet. This is a Honda. I don't really like it all that much, but it gets 40 miles to the gallon. I suppose I ought to have one.

You'd want a beat-up old pickup truck, just for hacking around in, with a plow for winter.

I've always wanted a car with a sun roof. This is an Audi 5000. It's a beautiful car. But $14,000 is a lot to stick your head out the top!

If I had an important lunch, I'd want a chauffeur-driven car. Burger King, please, Valentine.

VALENTINE: Yes, sir.

ROONEY: One of these cars is really mine. Everybody ought to have a little car of his own just to get away in. (Rooney driving off in his car) Now all I need is a 12-car garage.

Letters

MORLEY SAFER: In the mail this week about our story entitled "The Kissinger-Shah Connection?" was a letter from a former Assistant Secretary of the Treasury and Federal Energy Administration official. He called our story: "One of the most unprofessional pieces of reporting I have ever witnessed . . . (Saudi) officials did stress . . . that Iran and others were pushing for higher (oil) prices, but no one said or even suggested that Mr. Kissinger was colluding with the Shah on this issue."

Another viewer said: "We the people are forever on the hook . . . for (our leaders') mistakes. We cannot quietly withdraw and write books . . . Therefore we are entitled to a full and accurate accounting . . . (at least) after the fact if, for security reasons, we cannot be informed . . . ahead of time."

About our look back at a story we did in 1971 that pointed to the discrepancies between the public stand being taken then by people in Washington on the issue of school busing and the private stand they were taking when their own kids were involved, there was this: "I was very interested to see that the outspoken liberals who have pushed this issue are the first not to comment on where their children go to school. Wouldn't it be nice if all people, black and white, were wealthy enough to (send their children) to private schools."

Another viewer asked: "Is it true that after entering his daughter Amy in a Washington public school, a few blocks west of the White House, that (President Carter) recently transferred her to a private school?"

No, that doesn't happen to be true. Amy still attends an integrated public school.

There was also a letter from a viewer who said the students of private schools in and around Washington were not always the children of the rich or the elite. She wrote: "There are legions of ordinary struggling black and white parents sending their kids to private schools — just like the Capitol Hill crowd — to bypass the abysmally inadequate educational system."

Finally, there was this: "I have an idea. If everyone who sent a child to a fancy, expensive private school were required to pay the tuition for a ghetto or barrio child to go with him, we would achieve true integration in a hurry."

MAY 18, 1980

The Establishment vs. Dr. Burton

PHILIP SCHEFFLER, PRODUCER

HARRY REASONER: Research into the cause and cure of cancer is in the hands of a great medical establishment. People who go to each other's meetings are not only published in the same prestigious medical journals, but decide who else is published — learned men and women, who compete in a discreet way for billions of government and charity research dollars. And if these insiders, sizing up an outsider, conclude there's no promise in his theories, he becomes an "unperson." Funds dry up, journals reject his papers; he finds it nearly impossible to get a hearing.

Which brings us to Dr. Lawrence Burton, a prickly, fiercely independent, rejected cancer researcher. Burton ran afoul of the cancer research establishment 15 years ago. He believed immunology offered promise in treating cancer, but the leaders in cancer research were convinced viruses were the answer. Now viruses are out, immunology is in, but Burton is still out, and out of the country. After years of frustration over his inability to get a hearing or support, he finally closed his research lab in New York and moved to the Bahamas.

Dr. Lawrence Burton is a zoologist, not a physician, but he believes that what he has learned from 20 years of studying cancer in mice applies to humans as well. Burton believes, along with a number of other cancer researchers, that most of us probably develop cancers many times in our lives, but that our own natural immune system kills the cancer cells before they spread out of control. The patients who come to be treated at his clinic in Freeport on Grand Bahama Island, he believes, have immune systems which are working poorly. For the most part, these patients have exhausted the kind of orthodox cancer therapy their doctors back home can offer. They must supply complete documentation of their disease: X-rays, body scans, a record of prior treatment and diagnosis. Those who can, pay $2,200 for the first four weeks, $300 a week thereafter. Burton says he has devised a way of measuring, in the patient's blood, how well the immune system is working and how to stimulate the immune system to attack cancer by injecting a serum made up of three natural substances the patient's blood is short of.

DR. LAWRENCE BURTON: I don't think there's a cure. There is no such thing. We'd rather talk about a control. The patient controls their own cancer, because the odds are it will return. But sometimes they won't even recognize it, and they'll control and get rid of it. So they live — it's all — called a symbiotic relationship: the body is living with the cancer.

REASONER: Arden Klar, miraculously, seems to be living with his cancer, a tumor of the brain.

DR. R. J. CLEMENT (medical director, Freeport clinic):   Good. And you — and you're eating well, I hear?

ARDEN KLAR: She's a good cook.

REASONER: Five months ago, his daughter told us, he was given up for dead.

AMIRA KLAR: He was given three days to live. They told us, keep him on codeine, every three hours. Let him pass quietly. Keep him out of pain.

REASONER: Dr. Paul Rosch, a New York internist, remembers seeing Mr. Klar in the hospital.

DR. PAUL ROSCH (president, American Institute of Stress):   Mr. Klar had a grade-four astrocytoma — that's a tumor that does not respond to radiotherapy or any other conventional modality of therapy — and the patient was comatose, moribund when — when I saw him. His overall prognosis was approximately five days to a week; actually, 48 hours, according to his attending physician at a hospital in Connecticut.

DR. BURTON: I tried everything in the world to get out of this one. I figured this was a definite loser. I did everything I could to duck him.

Mr. Klar is good — is a good example of a case which eliminates quite a bit of what has been said about me. I don't think I was a faith healer with may — Mr. Klar. Mr. Klar was started — therapy was started when he was still back in the United States. By the way, his children treated him. No doctor was involved in this.

REASONER: Mr. Klar's children airfreighted samples of his blood daily to Dr. Burton, and they injected their father with Dr. Burton's serum, according to instructions he gave by phone. Mr. Klar lived. In a matter of days, he came out of his coma.

DR. ROSCH: I mean, in three or four weeks he was sitting up in bed watching television, talking on the phone — a most incredible thing. And after, I guess about five or six weeks, was well enough to go to the Bahamas on a conventional aircraft, which is just inconceivable.

DR. BURTON: And I still tell the daughter I can't understand why he came out of the coma and he's starting to function. He has a long way to come back. I don't know if he still will make it.

REASONER: One improvement, even one as dramatic as Mr. Klar's, does not constitute a cure for cancer, nor 20, nor 50. Dr. Burton says a large percentage,especially those with certain tumors, have improved dramatically or stabilized, but the majority have died of the disease.

He freely admits he treats largely by trial and error, that he really cannot state with precision why his theory sometimes works and sometimes doesn't. Still, something is happening down in Freeport.

Dr. R. J. Clement, former head of the Bahamas Medical Association and now medical director of the clinic, says he has seen it.

DR. CLEMENT: Am I convinced something worthwhile is happening? Yes. Yes, I am. I don't think I'd have started unless I had a period of watching the patients working totally outside the clinic, and I saw events happening which were not explainable by anything other than the serum and the treatment they were getting here. And if I hadn't seen that, I don't think I'd have been interested.

REASONER: You do understand what the — the chemistry or the — the medical nature of what he's doing?

DR. CLEMENT: Yes.

REASONER: And it seems reasonable to you and —?

DR. CLEMENT: Yes it does. Yes, completely reasonable.

REASONER: Burton's theories do not seem reasonable to those in the United States who determine the direction of cancer research. For example, Burton is on the American Cancer Society's list of "unproven remedies," a kind of blacklist, which effectively cuts him off from research money and from cooperation from doctors, hospitals and research institutions. The ACS has not itself ever studied Burton or his research, and their objection is largely that he has not published his results, with mice or humans, in a form which can be verified. Burton feels that's a Catch-22.

DR. BURTON: We tried to publish our data. It may be I've been — I hope it isn't: I've not been blackballed. It cou— it's a possibility. It may have gone out that anything that this cluck pu— sends in, don't publish.

REASONER: In 1971, Lawrence Burton tried one last time to get his research published in a medical journal. It was rejected.

DR. BURTON: And with that I decided I will no longer publish. I'm not asking the public for funds. Many scientists publish very rapidly so that they can get grants. It's publish or perish. But no longer did I — was I in that ball game.

RALPH MOSS: He was forced into a corner and reacted as — as he has. And I think, given a sympathetic reception, which he deserves, he would publish and he would bring forward his results.

REASONER: Ralph Moss was assistant public relations director of the Sloan-Kettering Cancer Research Institute for five years. He wrote about Burton in his recent book *The Cancer Syndrome.*

MOSS: So I'd say that the problem is basically in the cancer establishment's attitudes and interests rather than in Lawrence Burton himself. I think there — there's a tendency in the big places to think that they are going to find the cure for cancer, and to resent an upstart, such as a — a man from St. Vincent's Hospital or from the Bahamas, who tells them anything about cancer. The field itself has its own limitations built in, and people who go a — outside the limitations become the heretics and the mavericks, such as Burton.

REASONER: Even if the scientific community has not recognized his work, Burton feels physicians who practice medicine are starting to.

DR. BURTON: Well, we had an individual from California, who — daughter is a nurse for four MD's. He had a metastatic carcinoma of the prostate in the — I think — the pelvis and the spine. And they — when they heard he was coming here, the urologist was aghast. "You're go— they're going to steal your money. They're going to kill you!" Well, we treated him and he went home, and then after six months, well, you're no worse. But you're no better, but you're no worse. I'm a little shocked. He came back here. In another six months, a surprising thing occurred. His scans were much better. Another six months, he had no sign of the disease. And when he arrived here in October, an odd little thing, all four doctors are very interested in him, they are delighted in him, and they had an admission. They wanted him to tell me that if anybody in their family developed a cancer, they would send — or themselves, they would come, but they will not recommend any patients. But they themsel— it's good for them and their family. And this — well, maybe in another six months they may recommend a patient. We're getting there.

REASONER: Dr. William Terry of the National Cancer Institute doesn't think Burton is getting anywhere.

DR. WILLIAM TERRY: There is no evidence that what Dr. Burton is doing with patients has any particular value. To say that he's going in the right direction — he's gone to the Bahamas, perhaps that was in the right direction. I — I — I don't know how to take it beyond that without having more to go on.

REASONER: Dr. Terry had visited Dr. Burton briefly in 1974, when Burton was still in New York.

DR. BURTON: The most antagonistic SOB — and he's an SOB — I've ever met in my life: I, Dr. Terry, co-chairman of — I think — of immunotherapy, come to this — people come to me. And I kept him there for 12 hours just on that, and drove him crazy with that. And I repeated things and I enjoyed myself completely. Well, I made an enemy, and he's been an enemy. And he came here to evaluate.

REASONER: In 1978, Terry went to evaluate the Freeport clinic for the Pan American Health Organization. He had been specifically requested for that review by the Bahamas government chief medical officer.

DR. BURTON: I said, "Pick anybody you want, anybody else but not him. This man has sworn to me he's going to kill me." And this was going to be my reviewer. Dr. Terry came here. He wasn't impressed.

DR. TERRY: The tests made no sense and didn't appear to provide any reasonable basis for determining how you would treat a patient, and the treatment itself made no sense as well. And I think that the most charitable comment that one could make about those charts were shown to us was that there was no evidence that any harm was being done to the patient.

DR. BURTON: I don't know about the cases, but the few minutes I spent with him, he wanted to know about money. "How do you get money?" Who — that's all he talked to me — scientist to scientist — was money. "I want to know all the patients' names. I want to know all of the doctors." Well, he was going to start on a crusade. "Did any doctors ever recommend them here?" We had to fend ourself off. And when he couldn't get that — there was supposed to be a four-day review — Dr. Terry skipped right out. He said, "I've seen enough. Goodbye." So he wasn't impressed. He didn't really care about it.

REASONER: Our information was that you had had a number of conversations with Dr. Charles, the Bahamian health officer, before he asked you, and in — in those conversations you had spoken freely about your au— existing negative feeling about Burton and his work.

DR. TERRY: Yes.

REASONER: Isn't there a suggestion that Dr. Charles, who knew how you felt about Dr. Burton, or your professional opinion of him, was going into that investigation with a stacked deck? Is it possible to get a fair evaluation under circumstances like that?

DR. TERRY: I think it is. Again, I may be unduly kind to myself, but I think that when I went down to Freeport I still had an open mind in the matter.

REASONER: I think you think this man's a phony.

DR. TERRY: I think I don't have enough information to know whether he's a phony or whether he's fooling himself.

REASONER: But you have enough information after a few hours with him to say his test is useless, to say that his — he's — he's pretentious and — and wrong about being an immunologist, to say that his terminology is inexact, and to say that he refuses to cooperate in any way.

DR. TERRY: Uh-huh.

REASONER: I mean, you're — maybe you don't like the word "phony."

DR. TERRY: That doesn't allow me to discriminate between whether he's a phony or whether he's kidding himself.

REASONER: In spite of Dr. Terry's negative report, Bahamian medical authorities left Burton alone. And if the man from the National Cancer Institute didn't see anything worthwhile there, if the American Cancer Society is still waiting for more information, this doctor saw enough to make him want to know a lot more.

DR. PAUL BROWN: So we sent a Ph.D. immunologist down, and we figured he'd be back on the next plane, but he stayed for nine days and his curiosity was piqued enough that he suggested we make an investment and see what Larry really was doing.

REASONER: Dr. Paul Brown, a pathologist, is president of Metpath, the world's largest clinical laboratory. Brown thinks that one of the things Burton is measuring, a certain protein Burton has found in cancer patients' blood, just may turn out to be an accurate diagnostic test for the presence of cancer.

DR. BROWN: Well, what we set out to do was to find out was there really a protein in the blood of patients who have malignant disease, and that's why we sent Dr. Bur— Worthy down to the Bahamas, and that's why we set the lab up.

REASONER: Metpath set up a research lab to see if Dr. Worthy's lab technicians could measure what Dr. Burton said he was measuring.

DR. BROWN: He was able to duplicate it and he was able to find a strange protein in the blood of certain of the specimens. And that was the first phase of our investigation, and that piqued our curiosity a little further, and then we then went on to see if we could do it on a regular basis, and that's where we're at right now.

REASONER: Metpath is now trying to identify that strange protein Dr. Burton thinks is a test for cancer. They will eventually conduct a massive blind test on tens of thousands of blood samples to see if the test can pick out cancer victims, or perhaps even find cancer before it can be measured by any other means. If the end result is a test for cancer, it will be a significant scientific achievement. It will also make Metpath, and Dr. Burton, who will be paid a royalty, a lot of money. But Dr. Brown thinks it will have a side effect of even greater interest to Dr. Burton.

DR. BROWN: There's no question that if the test turns out to be meaningful — whether it be meaningful as a test for cancer for a patient who is — does — not known to have cancer, or is just valuable in confirming a diagnosis — it will indicate that Dr. Burton really has something there, and I don't think there's any question that that will stimulate interest in all of Dr. Burton's work.

REASONER: Dr. Paul Rosch has also become interested in Burton's work. The established establishment New York internist, with the diplomas and memberships in learned societies bearing witness on the walls of his office, is president of the American Institute of Stress, and has written about the relationship of stress and cancer.

DR. ROSCH: One of the intriguing things about Dr. Burton's testing procedure was that it appeared to give an indication or a reflection of how the treated patients were doing, so that, in a sense, he could tell you that, yes, the patient has cancer and, yes, the patient is doing well; his immune system is competent. And that was what was so appealing to me.

REASONER: Rosch asked Dr. Stacy Day, a leading researcher in immunology, recently retired from New York's Sloan-Kettering Institute, to visit Burton and report back. Dr. Day spent ten days at the Freeport clinic.

DR. STACY DAY: I spent 20 hours talking with him, and I think that's a very long time. I think the modalities that he's using, I don't think that they are so brilliant — many of them have been around in the literature for 20 years — but I think he's synthesized a package of ideas, of conventionally good ideas, and is applying them unconventionally. And I — I like the direction. There should be some care and understanding from the conventional side of the establishment to what he's doing. I — I — I think that his language of science isn't perhaps that which is conventionally neat, but I think the direction is the — the — is the — is the right one.

REASONER: Dr. Rosch has raised $250,000 to set up a lab in New York to duplicate Burton's research in a way which would convince the scientific establishment that Burton should be looked at further; to perhaps even convince a major hospital to undertake clinical trials with cancer patients using Burton's methods.

DR. ROSCH: I'm not here to make a judgment as to whether or not Dr. Burton has a cure, or a likely cure, for the treatment of cancer. And I'm not proposing that cancer patients go to Dr. Burton for therapy. Our immediate goal is to find out if he has something. I think there's a lot of evidence, there's a lot of anecdotal evidence, that Lawrence Burton has accumulated. But the scientific community doesn't accept evidence. They want proof, and that's a little bit different. And what we are trying to do is to set up a mechanism whereby we have a protocol that is flawless, and that when we get done with the experiment there will be no question that the thing either A) has a tremendous amount of merit, B) deserves further investigation, or C) is worthless.

Who Killed Georgi Markov?

JEANNE SOLOMON, PRODUCER

DAN RATHER: It's been a little more than a year and a half since Georgi Markov was killed, more than six months since we first presented the story.* And the murder, committed with an umbrella, one of the most bizarre crimes in the files of Scotland Yard, remains unsolved. Markov was a well-known Bulgarian writer, a favorite of the Communist regime, until he fled his homeland in 1969 for political asylum in the West. Living safely — at least he thought he was living safely — in London, he broadcast over the BBC and Radio Free Europe things the Communist government didn't want Bulgarians to hear.

(Excerpt from foreign language BBC broadcast)

Every day, hundreds of immigrants and refugees, many of them from Eastern Europe, come to work here at the headquarters of the BBC World Service in the heart of London. One of them, until his death, was the Bulgarian, Georgi Markov.

Just over a year ago, Markov was contacted by a fellow Bulgarian. To this day, Markov's British wife, Annabel, doesn't know whether that stranger was a Bulgarian agent or a friend trying to warn her husband.

MRS. ANNABEL MARKOV: He told Georgi that they were going to kill him in a way which would make it look as if he'd died naturally; that he would develop a very high fever, but that it would be thought that he'd died of a virus or flu. And he said that the method they've got was untraceable, that they would never be able to find out. Nobody would ever be able to find out how it had been done.

RATHER: Thursday, September 7th, 1978, about two o'clock in the afternoon. Georgi Markov, as he usually did once a week, drove his automobile from home to this car park on the south side of the River Thames under the Waterloo Bridge. He moved from his parked car to these steps, all part of his routine of going to work at the BBC. Anyone standing on the bridge could have easily seen Markov arrive and have watched him as he walked up the steps.

It was raining that afternoon, so Markov, instead of walking across the bridge, as he usually did on the last leg of his trip to work, waited for a bus. Now, get the picture. A woman was standing in front of him, a man behind. Suddenly, Markov felt something hit the back of his thigh. It felt a little like a jab, but then again it

---

*Originally broadcast on October 7, 1979.

stung. As Markov turned around, he saw the man behind him bending down to pick up an umbrella.

Georgi Markov died from that jab, but not until four days later. The hit man with the umbrella disappeared into a sea of umbrellas without a trace. Only ten hours after the attack did Markov complain to his wife of fever and vomiting. Later, in the hospital, doctors were told about the umbrella incident. Though they suspected Markov had been poisoned, they still had no idea how to treat him.

MRS. MARKOV: Georgi didn't want to die. Georgi, more than anybody I've ever met, he loved life. And so I said to him, "You've got to fight. You've got to fight for Sasha and me." And he just said, "Yes, Mama." And then I saw the machine that was monitoring his heart, it just died away. And so, I think if the people who were responsible of — for his death could have seen how bravely he faced death, even they might have experienced shame.

RATHER: Scotland Yard was notified almost immediately, but Markov died before they could question him. The Yard's anti-terrorist squad has been increasingly concerned about London's growing reputation as an assassination capital, a kind of easy city for foreign assassins. So they moved quickly after Markov's death, trying to establish a cause, trying to prove how and why he died. But their own initial investigation, including police pathology, turned up blank.

So they took the unprecedented step of coming here for help — the Defense Ministry's Chemical Defense Establishment at Porton Down. This place was once best known for its research into microbiological warfare, but it is also head-quarters for Britain's leading experts on highly toxic materials. All the experts had to go on were the clinical details of Markov's fatal illness and some skin tissue removed from the place on his thigh where he said he'd been jabbed. But when they began their standard pathology tests, they immediately came across a minuscule metal pellet hidden in the fold of skin tissue. Dr. David Gall, who was in charge of the operation, examined that pellet under a microscope.

DR. DAVID GALL: It was clearly a man-made object, and one which you don't buy across the counter in a shop. Quite clearly, two holes drilled or in some way made across two diameters of the small, nearly spherical pellet.

RATHER: This is it, magnified and photographed next to the head of a pin. So small was the pellet that entered Markov's body that drilling those two holes that must have carried the poison was no small engineering feat. The two holes gave Dr. Gall and his team an important clue about the poison used. It had to be extremely lethal. On that basis, together with the evidence of Markov's symptoms, they eliminated many of the more obvious poisons and, by a combination of deduction and good luck, they came up with a poison called ricin. Ricin is derived from the castor oil plant and, significantly, most of the scientific literature on it has been published in East Europe.

To test their theory, Dr. Gall carried out a laboratory experiment on an animal close in size to a human being.

DR. GALL: We chose a pig, and we injected this with a comparable dose of ricin, and we produced symptoms which were very similar to — to Markov's. In other words, nothing very much happened for some six or more hours, then the animal started developing a fever; was clearly uncomfortable and unwell, off its food; later had a small amount of diarrhea; and shortly before it died it developed gross irregularities of its heart. So, in many respects, although the time course was slightly shorter than Markov's, it was very, very similar indeed.

RATHER: How lethal is ricin?

DR. GALL: Well, perhaps these tubes will give you some idea. On the right here, that tube contains a human lethal dose of cyanide, and on the left we've got a lethal dose of ricin in there.

RATHER: Well, let me be honest with you and tell you I can't see the grain of ricin at all. Oh, there it is.

DR. GALL: It's just in the back of that tube, as you say, almost invisible. And that is (indistinct).

RATHER: But this seems incredible to me. Let me — let me review for a moment. This is the dosage of cyanide it would take to kill the average human?

DR. GALL: That's right, yes.

RATHER: And this is the dosage of ricin it would take to kill someone?

DR. GALL: That's right.

RATHER: No more than that?

DR. GALL: No more than that. So it's a fairly powerful compound.

RATHER: I — that might be an understatement. Any known antidote for ricin?

DR. GALL: None that we know of.

RATHER: Absolutely none?

DR. GALL: Not that we know of, no.

RATHER: In search of a motive for the murder of Georgi Markov, Scotland Yard came here to the headquarters of Radio Free Europe in Munich, Germany. Keep in mind that while Markov read news over the BBC in London, it was with Radio Free Europe that he wrote and spoke his mind. And what he had been saying over Radio Free Europe made him enemies in high places.

In 1971, it was revealed that Radio Free Europe was run by the CIA. Today, the dollars come officially from Congress, and the outfit prefers to forget that Cold War image. The station broadcasts daily in six languages to East Europe, and although the Eastern-bloc countries, including Bulgaria, jam those transmissions, one frequency is left open to allow the Communist authorities to monitor just what is being said.

(Excerpt from foreign language Radio Free Europe broadcast)

On that frequency, Georgi Markov's weekly broadcasts found a very large audience in Bulgaria. Cyril Panov was Markov's boss on the Bulgarian desk at Radio Free Europe. Panov is in no doubt that Markov's criticism of the Bulgarian regime was sufficient motive for his murder.

What was the major thrust of the criticisms?

CYRIL PANOV: The major thrust of the criticism was about the life the establishment, the leadership, was leading, in the sense that they had all the privileges — they could travel abroad, they could get things from the West — while the broad masses did not have the same possibilities.

RATHER: He had great credibility because he'd been there, he'd been in the inner circle. People knew that he knew what he was talking about.

PANOV: Yes, exactly. I mean, any Western politician who would have been criticized in the same way would not have reacted at all. It was in a way a very mild criticism. However, from the Bulgarian point of view, from the totalitarian state point of view, this was really disturbing the Communist regime.

RATHER: The so-called People's Republic of Bulgaria is the second-oldest Communist country in the world. Situated in the heart of the Balkans, it is flanked by the wayward Communist states of Rumania and Yugoslavia to the north and the NATO countries of Greece and Turkey to the south.

But Bulgaria is politically more in the Soviet Union's pocket than any other Eastern European satellite. The real leaders of the country are in Moscow, and these gray-faced individuals keep in power by remembering that fact. They make sure that the rest of the Bulgarian population does the same, with the help of a massive secret police force, the State Security.

Stefan Sverdlov was once a member of that State Security, until he defected in 1971. His job, he claims, included drawing up lists of enemies of the people who were to be eliminated in time of danger. He is now in hiding in Western Europe, an enemy of the people himself, with a death sentence on his head.

Respectfully, but directly, how do I know you were what you say you were? How do I know you weren't a plumber or a newspaperman?

(Stefan Sverdlov answers in Bulgarian)

He showed us an identity card which named him as a colonel in Bulgarian State Security. I asked him who he thought killed Georgi Markov. He replied, "The Bulgarian State Security" — but then added that they are completely subordinate to the Soviet secret police, the KGB. Could Markov have been killed by the Bulgarian secret police without the express approval of the KGB? "Not under any circumstances," he said. "That would mean revolution."

Back in the 1950's, evidence of KGB murder plots was well-documented. Nikolai Khoklov was a KGB staff officer sent to direct an assassination squad in West Germany. The target at that time: a Russian exile. The weapon then: a cigarette case. Khoklov could not go through with it and defected. Nikolai Khoklov today lives in the United States. He is a professor of psychology, but he retains close links with the intelligence community.

Doctor, why would the KGB go to such lengths to assassinate someone such as Georgi Markov?

NIKOLAI KHOKLOV: The strategy was not simply to physically eliminate Markov, but rather to get a message across to the community of dissidents that the times where the dissidents were tolerated, released, forgiven or exiled has passed; that now is the time for judgment and deeds. The aim, the goal, of KGB is still the same: to preserve the power, the ruling elite, by all possible means. Years ago, the KGB did not have to worry about dissident movement inside of the Soviet Union. The Bulgarian intelligence service didn't have to worry about the dissident movement inside of Bulgaria. Today, it has become their main worry.

RATHER: The Bulgarian Embassy in London remains silent. The Bulgarian government's first reaction was — and I quote — "We absolutely reject the fantastic James Bond stories and the groundless slanders and fabrications about the death of Georgi Markov in a campaign aimed against the People's Republic of Bulgaria." But later, when faced with concrete evidence that Georgi Markov had been murdered by poisoned pellets, the Bulgarian reaction shifted to claims that he had been working for Western intelligence and that he had been — again, quote — "taken like a lemon by the CIA, squeezed dry, and then eliminated by them."

MRS. MARKOV: What else are they going to say? Are they going to admit responsibility?

RATHER: You're absolutely certain that he was not involved with Western intelligence?

MRS. MARKOV: Absolutely positive. Absolutely certain. Georgi was an — a writer, an artist. That's what he was interested in. He would have been a rotten person to recruit as a secret agent. For another thing, he — he — he wasn't good at keeping secrets.

RATHER: You think he was or was not an agent?

PANOV: No.

RATHER: You're pretty sure of that?

PANOV: You can never be sure of — of anything. But I didn't see any indications.

RATHER: So there's no doubt in your mind that Soviet officers were actually involved in this assassination of Georgi Markov?

KHOKLOV: Absolutely.

RATHER: Why?

KHOKLOV: Technically, it would be inconceivable for Bulgarian intelligence service to— not only to carry out the design and preparation of such sophisticated weapons, but to get permission to expose such a sophisticated technique. I have a hunch that, in this case, the Soviet bosses of Bulgarian intelligence service wanted such exotic weaponry eventually even to become known. Let the enemies of the Soviet system know what powerful and skillful hand can reach them.

One other aspect, also very important: that the assassination of a political enemy in London during the climate of detente and possible SALT talks cannot be done without the permission of KGB. As a matter of fact, cannot be done without permission of Central Committee of the Soviet Communist Party.

In other words, the sophistication of weaponry, the timing, the territory on which it had to be done, it is absolutely unavoidable to conclude that decision had to be made in Moscow by the Central Committee of the Soviet Communist Party. And I am positive it has been done that way.

MRS. MARKOV: It's as if they were saying to the British government here, "We can come and kill somebody in your — in the streets of London, just like that, and that you're not going to do anything about it." They haven't done anything about it so far, have they?

RATHER: Ten days before Georgi Markov was killed, another Bulgarian, Vladimir Kostov, was attacked in the streets of Paris. He survived, but the pellet which was later removed from his body was found to be identical to the one found in Markov's body. Markov's widow told us a few days ago that Scotland Yard told her they have not given up trying to find out who killed Georgi Markov. The file remains open.

The Rock

JOHN TIFFIN, PRODUCER

MIKE WALLACE: Among our yesterdays on 60 MINUTES is the story of "The Rock" — Gibraltar, one of the last gasps of British colonialism. If Gibraltar has not changed very much in the last couple of hundred years, it has certainly changed even less in the eight years since Morley Safer was there.*

MORLEY SAFER: Her Majesty's Navy and Army have kept the Rock British for almost three centuries, one of the main places from which Britannia ruled the waves. The Spanish want Gibraltar back simply because it's such a clearly visible royal British pain in their backside. The Gibraltarians want to stay British, partly for economic reasons, partly because it seems such a jolly right thing to be. The British want to keep it because — well, because it's there.

Despite insurance-company claims to the contrary, the Rock is not that solid. It's been described as a gigantic Swiss cheese, honeycombed with more miles of military road inside it than paved road around it. It's still secret inside, and guesses about what it contains range from ultra-sensitive listening devices and Polaris submarines to great stockpiles of bully beef, bayonets and gunpowder — and the truth is probably both.

They're a strange lot, these people, descended from Spanish, Portuguese, Genoese, Moors and dallying British seamen who fought with Nelson at Trafalgar. They are both Latinized Englishmen and Anglicized Spaniards. They speak both languages with a curious accent.

MAN 1:   I — I mean, are you proud . . . (continues in Spanish)?

MAN 2:   Oh, yes.

MAN 1:   Are you proud of being British?

MAN 3:   Yes.

MAN 1:   Why?

MAN 3:   Why? Because we have plenty.

RADIO ANNOUNCER: You are tuned to the Gibraltar Broadcasting Corporation. It's exactly 4:30, and that means it's time for the "Sunday Request Show." The first disc has been requested by John Gomez for his fiancee, Maria.

(Music: "The Rain in Spain")

SAFER: On Sunday, among all these two-car families, the thing to do in Gibraltar, just as it is in England, is to go for a Sunday drive. Everybody does it — round and round the Rock. The longest trip you can make without repeating yourself is two and a half miles. One man managed to do 10,000 miles last year.

(Music . . . British Army sergeant shouting commands . . . bugle call . . . more commands . . . fifes and drums)

No changing of the guard at Buckingham Palace ever had a more loyal audience than the regular ceremony in front of the Governor's Palace. Britain keeps 5,000 men in all three services on Gibraltar, not the most difficult duty in the shrinking world of British outposts.

(Fifes and drums)

---

*This is an edited version of broadcasts aired previously on December 31, 1972 and January 4, 1976.

6060606060606060 60 MINUTES/VERBATIM60 MINUTES/VERBATIM 60 MINUTES/VERBATIM   60 MINUTES/VERBATIM   560 MINUTES/VERBATIM   5560 MINUTES/VERBATIM   553

The Garrison Library, it is called in Gibraltar, but it could be the club in Simla, or Poona, or any one of a thousand colonial garrison towns that the British came to and never expected to leave.

WOMAN: Yes, the cake is lovely today. It's delicious.

SAFER: In Gibraltar they stay — the brigadier, the postmaster, the magistrate and librarian. All the caricatures out of a British film comedy are alive and well and living in Gibraltar. Even death does not deprive them of a fourth for bridge. In Gibraltar, there is always another generation ready to slip into the empty chair at the Garrison. And generation after generation, they sit surrounded by volumes recounting an heroic age, looked down upon by admirals and generals and relics of past victories. And every gem in Gibraltarian history, every change in social and political temperature, is recorded by one Dorothy Ellicot.

You never feel claustrophobic?

DOROTHY ELLICOT: We did at the beginning, much more than now. In fact, nowadays, sometimes when you look up and you look out across the bay, you say, "Where is Spain? Oh, there, it's still there!" (Laughs)

SAFER: The place reeks with the eccentric and the absurd that makes up much of the legacy of the British presence anywhere. When the British arrived 268 years ago, they found these Barbary apes up on the Rock, and the British, being what they are, instantly gave them name, rank and serial number.

BRITISH SOLDIER: I am responsible to my commanding officer. I'm the official keeper of the apes. (Indistinct) Tessa! Tessa! Tessa is the one you could see at the top there.

SAFER: Oh, yes.

SOLDIER: She's been injured on the backside, been split up.

Come on! Alley-oop! Come on, that's a good boy! Charlie! Come on up! Come on! Then you have Deirdre.

SAFER: Deirdre?

SOLDIER: Deirdre is one of the oldest females. (Indistinct) The same color.

SAFER: And that — who's that?

SOLDIER: That's Jimmy.

SAFER: Jimmy.

SOLDIER: Now, this is Barbara.

SAFER: Barbara.

SOLDIER: That's another middle-sized ape. She's not had the baby yet. I mean, she's expecting this year.

SAFER: There you go, Barbara. Ahh! (Laughs)

They must be doing something right, these 20,000 fiercely loyal souls. There is no psychiatrist, but there is, of course, a veterinarian. The only demonstration on record was one of loyalty to the Queen. They indulge in such Mediterranean pastimes as darts, and stuff themselves with roast beef and Yorkshire pudding and warm beer. Such gourmets as merchant seamen say that Gibraltar has the world's worst food. British to the core. But even these most understated of all Englishmen do occasionally cut loose.

(Dancing to music . . . applause)

Gibraltar does not stand still. From Europe has come the latest craze: jitter-bugging.

(Jitterbugging to music . . . women shouting in Spanish)

That's Spain over there, just a few paces away. Everyone has relatives in the town of La Linea. It's been a tradition that Gibraltarian men marry Spanish girls. Granny can only see the children from a distance now, unless she wants to fly from Gibraltar to Tangier in Morocco, then over to Spain. The wall has none of the brutality of the Berlin Wall; it's more a lace curtain than an iron one.

(Shouted command . . . march music . . . shouted command . . . bugle call)

No one ever shoots at anyone. They barely flex their muscles. But every evening, there is a confrontation: Who will bring down his flag more ceremoniously? Who will win the battle of spit and polish? The British say it is no contest.

(Shouted command . . . sound of marching feet . . . marching music . . . shouted commands . . . sound of marching feet . . . drums)

And so — as the man used to say — as the sun sinks gently in the west, we say farewell to the friendly peninsula of Gibraltar, where Europe practically meets Africa, where the sun does not quite set on the British Empire, and where the people dash happily headlong backwards into the nineteenth century.

(Bugle call)

WALLACE: We said at the beginning it hasn't changed much in eight years, and it hasn't. But next month, it will change. Britain and Spain have now decided to stop quarreling, and the gate from Spain will swing open once again. The Rock remains true blue, but now Anglo-Spanish.

Letters

MIKE WALLACE: In the mail this week were several letters about the repeat of the story we did back in 1978 on gas stations that rip off tourists by talking them into unnecessary repairs. One of our viewers, a lady from Colorado, offered a solution. She wrote us: "(You left out) the old fan belt trick. (Where) the helpful attendant who checks your oil and water also gives your fan belt a twist and then discovers . . . that the belt is separating . . . Never let an attendant open the hood unless (you're) standing beside him (and) break his arm if he reaches for the fan belt."

About the 1978 story, there was also this: "The most shocking (thing) in your story were the signs (on the pumps) — 56 cents a gallon."

About our story on Bonnie Consolo, the woman with no arms who does everything with her feet, there was a ton of mail, and to nobody's surprise, not an unfriendly letter in the bunch. They were all like this: "After watching (Bonnie) I want her to know (she is) not handicapped. (The handicapped) are those of us who don't have her inspiration."

And finally: "After watching . . . Bonnie . . . I did the only thing that seemed appropriate . . . I took off my shoes and socks and applauded."

MAY 25, 1980

Warning: Living Here May Be Hazardous to Your Health!

ESTHER KARTIGANER, PRODUCER

HARRY REASONER: Just like the warning on a package of cigarettes or a bottle of iodine, the signs were there for everyone to see for many months, but it was a situation where not much seemed to happen until this week. We're talking about the Love Canal.

The Love Canal is an area of Niagara Falls, New York, with a romantic name and an increasingly depressing history. There was a man named Love who wanted to build the canal. He went broke. Then the city and the Hooker Chemical Company used his empty ditch to bury used and dangerous chemicals. When it was full, it was covered up. The city built a school on the site, and a middle-class community grew up around the school.

A couple of years ago, they found the chemicals were seeping out into the air and dirt and affecting people's health. In the past nine days, the canal has been very much back in the news: new studies showing chromosome damage in people living in areas not previously proven dangerous; a decision to evacuate about 700 families temporarily at federal expense. But there's still no agreement on how serious is the problem. As one federal official put it, the only sure thing is that something up there has made some people sick. The thing is, you have to go there to get the feel of it. We went back to the site of the first problems.

The silence here is very loud. Although you get the occasional sound of a plane overhead and kids playing and dogs barking in the street a couple of hundred feet away, what you hear inside the chain-link fence is the silence. It is like Flanders Field, but there are no flowers here, just the wistful evidence that someone tried to grow some once to make a pretty place. You hear the silence and you feel endangered, because this enemy is so pervasive and impersonal. Grown men and women, here only briefly, feel endangered. I don't know who left this ball here, but I know you stop and think a couple of times before you pick it up.

The school is probably the saddest. They say it smells bad inside, and it sits right on top of the dead and choked canal where the danger is buried. It is like those scenes in a horror movie where the suspense of ordinary things builds towards something nameless. The school is probably the saddest, because it reminds you that only a couple of years ago there were unremarkable people here, people who saw only the normal shadows in the dark, people who saw no irony in a routine sign.

What we are looking at tonight is a basic question. There were all kinds of warning signs after the state moved in 1978. In the beginning, there didn't seem to be any doubts.

It was a horror story, and the State of New York treated it like one. They declared a health emergency. At a cost of $10 million, the state bought 239 homes and permanently moved the people out of the first two rings around the vicious ditch. Then they put up a chain-link fence around the area which was to define the limits of the danger. They even printed this fancy brochure — "Love Canal: A Public Health Time Bomb" — explaining proudly how they had handled the health emergency. That was 1978. This is a story of second thoughts. The second thoughts relate to money and to fear. The state quite obviously began to think in terms of precedent and how many millions of dollars might be involved in moving people out of the Love Canal and Lord knows how many other miasmas. The people in the ostensibly "not-unsafe" areas were scared, but until last week they couldn't seem to get anyone's attention.

In the beginning, in the brochure-writing days, the state used that schoolhouse as a kind of command post. They took blood tests and checked everybody in the area for their health history, and, for the time being, decided that the health hazards were serious only for those first two rings of houses.

That was a conclusion the homeowners never bought. Further analysis of the study by the state revealed there was danger outside the first two rings. There were more miscarriages, birth defects and low-birth-weight babies than they had a reason to expect. So when Commissioner of Health Dr. David Axelrod reported these new findings but told them they didn't have any problems unless they were pregnant or under two years old, they reacted rudely.

DR. DAVID AXELROD: We have therefore brought to the governor our recommendation that pregnant women living in the canal area extending from 97th to 103rd Street be removed from the area. We have also brought to the governor our recommendation that children under two years of age be removed from the canal until such time as they are older than two or until such time as extensive — (negative audience reaction) — environmental data — (negative audience reaction.)

REASONER: That, it seems, is when the second thoughts began. It looked, for example, that the state might have to deal with many more high-risk homes. The state gave the impression that it had made its last concession. The homeowners didn't think it was enough, and cancer research scientist Beverly Paigen shares their view.

DR. BEVERLY PAIGEN: You see, looking at human fetus — the baby before birth — is like looking at the miner's canary. You bring the canary down into the mine and, if the canary dies, then you know it's time to get the miners out. They looked at the canary — the human fetus — and when they saw that the human fetus was in danger, they said get the canary out. They didn't say get the miner out.

REASONER: Dr. Beverly Paigen has been the chief — and unpaid expert — working with the Love Canal homeowners — their advocate with state and federal officials.

DR. PAIGEN: Does EPA want to be seen as an agency who's out there doing something? Or is EPA . . .

REASONER: And she helped them design and conduct their own health surveys. More than a year ago, she presented their results to a congressional committee. The homeowners had found more problems with pregnancy and birth than the state had, and they found additional problems the state had not identified: nervous breakdowns, asthma, urinary-tract diseases. Even then, she was calling for drastic action.

DR. PAIGEN: These studies have led me to conclude that a minimum of 140 additional families should be evacuated immediately, and evacuation may need to be extended to as many as 500 more families.

REASONER: Commissioner, I'm sure you're familiar with the Love Canal Homeowners Association.

DR. AXELROD: Oh, yes, I'm very familiar with them.

REASONER: They have conducted a number of studies themselves and follow-up studies and, in effect, they accuse you of minimizing adverse health information that the department has found.

DR. AXELROD: Well, I think that what you have to do is to assume and accept the information that they have as organized subjectivity, because that's the way it was collected. They're not experts. They're not trained in this area.

REASONER: Dr. Paigen, has anyone who might be described as disinterested looked at your information?

DR. PAIGEN: The top-notch panel of epidemiologists spent a day listening to me and my information and they spent a day listening to the Department of Health studies, and they came out and said that my data in— was substantial enough to warrant further studies.

REASONER: The fancy brochure came out in September, 1978, and it was in February, 1979, that Dr. Axelrod told the Love Canal residents they had nothing to worry about unless they were pregnant or very young. But in the many months since then, there's been an ongoing struggle to get the information on which that conclusion was based – the presumably exhaustive and scientifically defensible study of the residents' health story.

They've sealed up that study almost as tightly as they sealed up those homes in the first two rings. They haven't given the homeowners their own health data. They didn't give it to a congressional committee that wanted to see it. And it took a subpoena before they gave it to the Federal Department of Justice, which is suing Hooker Chemical and would like to look at Dr. Axelrod's study. Dr. Axelrod says he's not stonewalling; the only delay is the necessary care in preparing his raw data for release. And because the state is also suing Hooker Chemical, he, like practically everyone else in this horror story, has lawyer trouble.

DR. AXELROD: We are in the process of preparing properly documented scientific publications which will provide the basis for the kinds of recommendations that we have taken, and also provide an opportunity to independently evaluate all of the information that we have gathered. Currently, there is an additional problem that relates to the litigation which is underway, and so that I really do not control the flow of information at this point. My attorneys do, and my attorney in this case is the Attorney General of the State of New York.

REASONER: Dr. Axelrod has been saying that all his recommendations were reviewed by his own blue-ribbon panel. I asked Dr. Paigen why this didn't change her mind.

DR. PAIGEN: If the blue-ribbon panel had been open, if their recommendations had been written, if the blue-ribbon panel had been given tables of data, that would have been fine; then I would have said maybe I'm wrong. But the blue-ribbon panel is secret. The minutes of the meetings are secret. The recommendations are secret.

REASONER: Have you released the names of the blue-ribbon panel?

DR. AXELROD: No, we have not. That still is protected, is considered to be protected by counsel, by the canons of confidentiality under the public health law.

REASONER: We read the public health law and there's nothing in it about protecting the names of any members of Dr. Axelrod's panel.

The President's Commission on Organized Crime — which was certainly subject to a variety of harassment and possible worse — one of the whole points about it was the publication of the names — men of unimpeachable qualifications. This would be almost unique, wouldn't it, Doctor —

DR. AXELROD: Well —

REASONER: — to have a blue-ribbon commission with secret names?

DR. AXELROD: I don't think it would be unique. I believe that there have been panels in the past which have been convened. I can't cite them.

REASONER: And we looked for other examples to cite and we couldn't find them, either.

The people outside the fence, who can't afford to move and are afraid to stay, are unreassured by Dr. Axelrod's unpublished study and his secret panel. They are not even reassured by the $13½ million that has been spent to put a clay cap on the ditch and to install a system so that none of the chemicals could seep out. They are more impressed by statistics the Homeowners Association has assembled. Since the Love Canal story broke, 15 pregnancies occurred in families living outside the first two rings; only two resulted in normal births. Eight of the babies had birth defects, two were stillborn, three were either miscarried or aborted.

Two normal children out of 15 pregnancies would be substantially below what you would expect nationally.

DR. PAIGEN: That's terrible.

REASONER: I mean, I would —

DR. PAIGEN: You don't need statistics, you don't need science. Two normal children out of 15 pregnancies in anybody's book is a disaster.

REASONER: Though Dr. Axelrod admitted concern about pregnancy outcomes, he didn't feel the threat called for more evacuations.

DR. AXELROD: Those individuals who choose to remain there and do become pregnant — either voluntarily or involuntarily, as the case might be — they know what those risks are and they are remaining there with those risks.

REASONER: Aren't you very much thinking of the fact that there are maybe several dozen other potential hazards in Niagara County, several hundred in New York State, many thousand in the United States?

DR. AXELROD: Absolutely. It would be not — it would — it would — it would be facile for me to say otherwise. I think that I'm constantly concerned about it. But that would not change my policy with respect to proceeding to taking the best scientific information and making a recommendation on the basis of that scientific information.

REASONER: I'm not challenging your scientific procedure, but I am suggesting you don't operate in a vacuum. You are appointed by the governor of New York. Do you serve at his pleasure, or is it −?

DR. AXELROD: I certainly do.

REASONER: Serve at his pleasure.

Have you ever had any hint from the governor or anybody in his staff or from anybody in the state that it would be extremely useful to them if it was determined that most of Love Canal was habitable?

DR. AXELROD: I have never had anyone tell me that.

REASONER: Or hint at it?

DR. AXELROD: Or hint at it? Perhaps I'm naive and perhaps there were hints, but that's a subjective evaluation. No one has hinted to me that I should do anything but provide them my best scientific judgment, rather than a political judgment.

REASONER: During the last several months, home appraisers had been working in the neighborhood. Even in the face of the federal government's suit, which claims there is a continuing health hazard and asks for either a total cleanup or a total evacuation of the area, and even in spite of the continuing conflict with the homeowners' studies, the State of New York committed $5 million to a local authority to "revitalize and stabilize" the area. The $5 million could be used to purchase the homes of people who wanted to leave. The appraisals sent to the homeowners totalled $18-million. Niagara Falls Mayor Michael O'Laughlin heads the task force that was working on the "revitalization and stabilization" effort. We asked him if he couldn't get in sudden money trouble.

Let's say half the families decide to move out, which is not impossible, you're out of money then, aren't you? You haven't got enough money to do this job right?

MAYOR MICHAEL O'LAUGHLIN: That — that's a — that's a real problem, and it was so different in the original purchases of the land. There you had a definite amount. You're going to move the houses in those first two rows, the first two rings, and here's the money to do it.

REASONER: One obvious thing in − if you had to buy a lot of homes and ran out of money, would be to sell the homes to somebody else at a bargain or with a tax break. Is that in the cards?

MAYOR O'LAUGHLIN: I would shy away from selling homes at bargain rates. I think they should be pretty much at the market value as appraised here. I would see, however, some kind of arrangement where they would have interest reductions on the mortgage that they would take over over a period of time. I would see that prob— po— possibly having some kind of tax abatement over a period of time.

REASONER: Sir, with all the uncertainties, do you really think that anyone's going to buy a house in that neighborhood?

MAYOR O'LAUGHLIN: I have to say that, under the right circumstances, yes. People smoke, and there are signs on the side of the cigarette package that says it's dangerous. And there are thousands of people in our country and in our city who would be looking for a place or a chance to be a homeowner. This may be one of them.

REASONER: The mayor's opinion may now be moot. Certainly until it's decided how temporary is the current evacuation there aren't going to be any sales to new owners. Some health officials still say the new evacuation is justified only for psychological reasons. There is still no consensus, or apparently the basis for serious discussion to reach one, among the scientists involved. But the other element in the delay and the argument is clearer than ever. More than ever, governments are asking themselves and each other: Who's going to pay for all this and for all the others?

Memory of Vietnam

GREG COOKE, PRODUCER

MIKE WALLACE: Last fall, on Veterans Day, we broadcast a film about three young men who had fought bravely and been severely wounded in the Vietnam War. We had reported on these soldiers first back in 1969, at the hospital they'd come back to in the States. Then three years later, in 1972, we went to see them again to find out how they were making out, how their wounds had healed, how they had adjusted to coming home. And last November, on the tenth anniversary of that first broadcast, we went back again to see them.*

Tomorrow is Memorial Day, an appropriate time, we thought, to take another look at this report on three Vietnam veterans who might have been your son, your father, your husband – or might even have been you.

In 1969, Private Raymond Krings was serving with the Army's First Division – the Big Red One, they called it, their headquarters at Lei Kai, South Vietnam. Now he is back on the land he has always called home, the fertile plains around Lindsey, Nebraska, population 230. But coming back from Vietnam was not easy for Ray Krings 10 years ago. 60 MINUTES was there when he first arrived.

These men have just touched down at Buckley Air Force Base outside Denver, Colorado. They are bound for Fitzsimmons Army Hospital here. Ahead of them lie months or, for some of them, years of healing and rehabilitation and adjustment to a new crippled reality.

In past wars, men wounded as severely as this – multiple amputees, some of them – would have died on some distant battlefield; but in Vietnam, the medivac choppers were able to lift many of them back to medical treatment and to life. A larger number of severely wounded survived the Vietnam War than ever before. But even with the care and surgery, therapy and rehabilitation, no one knew for sure whether many of these men would ever return to a nearly normal life. And during his time in the hospital back in 1969, Private Raymond Krings was bitter about the war.

PRIVATE RAYMOND KRINGS: I — I felt it was just — it's — it's senseless to me, that's the way I feel. Now, it may be because I have lost my legs, but even before that I — the — the feeling I'd never change at all. It's just a —

WALLACE: So you don't really understand what you made this sacrifice for?

KRINGS: That's right.

WALLACE: After his release from the hospital, he returned home to Nebraska, married his high-school sweetheart, Joyce, lived on his disability pension, and did

---

*These first three stories were previously broadcast September 30, 1969, March 19, 1972, and November 11, 1979.

little more with his life than build model ships. Clearly a young man unsure about himself and the future, Ray even detected some animosity toward him among his neighbors.

KRINGS: Oh, I think there's people living in — right in this town and probably right next door that would like to see me go to work. They figure that if I'm drawing money from the government for nothing, free, why can't they.

WALLACE: What would you do if you had your legs back that you can't do now?

KRINGS: I'll be farming.

WALLACE: Well, he found out that a man without legs can be a farmer. He raises chickens now and geese and cows on his farm, along with a sizeable family garden. Ray has no idle time at all. He found out there are all kinds of mechanical equipment he can operate, and easily, and he and Joyce have been raising a family, too.
She Suzanne?

JOYCE KRINGS: Uh-huh.

KRINGS: Suzanne.

WALLACE: She's the youngest, except for the one —

JOYCE: Two months away.

WALLACE: Two months away.

KRINGS (talking to his child):   Ooh, it's hot, huh? Is it hot up there?

WALLACE: Joyce, that's going to be six.

JOYCE: Uh-hmm.

WALLACE: You're going to make this guy work his fingers to the bone.

JOYCE: He's making me work my fingers. (Laughs)

WALLACE: Well, I guess that's true. You do a lot of the work around here with him, don't you?

JOYCE: Right. Keep in shape that way.

WALLACE: There are so many fellows in his position who simply haven't been able to — to put it together the way that Ray apparently has.

JOYCE: Yeah. It — it took time.

KRINGS: It — yeah, it just doesn't happen overnight.

JOYCE: Right.

KRINGS: It — it — it takes some time. The big thing is to — just to get out, you know, to meet new people and — and get new ideas. And —

JOYCE: Live — have to work like everybody else does.

KRINGS: Right. Try to — try to get back in — you know, everybody else has got a job and has to make a living.

WALLACE: And he got himself a job. He is a draftsman at a small manufacturing firm 10 miles from his home. Though his compensation from the government has increased to over $15,000 a year, still he needs the income from his job downtown to support the family life style on their 40-acre farm. With the help of a $25,000 government grant, Ray and Joyce built a wheelchair-conforming home that Ray designed and helped construct. In all, he is a man who has come to terms with his disability.

KRINGS: You have to get used to it, because if you don't you ain't never going to make it. If you don't get used to it and face the fact that that's the way it is, you will not make it.

WALLACE: Ten years ago, he was part of the angry generation. Today, he says he feels nothing for those veterans who are still angry 10 years after Vietnam.

Do you feel any kinship with them at all?

KRINGS: Absolutely not.

WALLACE: None?

KRINGS: No.

WALLACE: How come?

KRINGS: If they want to, they can make it on their own. They can — they're just — they're like everyone else. If they have — they've got the free will, and if they just use their head a little bit and — they can — they make it like everybody else.

WALLACE: You mean, the loss of your legs has not been – it's awful, but it's not been that much of a handicap in the way of your having a fulfilled life?

KRINGS: Not that much.

WALLACE: Larry Kirk came from a military family, and that's the career he wanted for himself. Married, the father of two daughters, Second Lieutenant Larry Kirk volunteered for duty in Vietnam. He was wounded there by a land mine in 1969, and he too wound up in Fitzsimmons Hospital, where, as part of his rehabilitation, he took scuba lessons. Despite his injuries, Larry never seemed to slow down much. And once out of the hospital, he promptly went to work for half a dozen civic causes, including an advocacy of the American role in Vietnam. He joined the Junior Chamber of Commerce. He was a sought-after public speaker, this severely wounded Vietnam veteran. When we went back to see Larry Kirk in 1972, he told us he felt no bitterness about what he had suffered in Vietnam.

LARRY KIRK: I always figured that nothing would happen to me that I couldn't overcome. I didn't realize I was going to have as big a mountain as I got, but I still try to take it in my stride. I just —

WALLACE: You feel that way too, Jackie?

JACKIE KIRK: Uh-hmm. When I married Larry, he was in the service, and we knew that someday he would have to go, and we knew that. I'm just happy he's alive.

WALLACE: When a GI assistance bill was signed into law in '72, Larry Kirk was on hand in the audience, and he got a word with President Nixon. The result? An appointment as staff assistant to the Secretary of HUD, a job Larry stayed with for three years in Washington.

Today Larry Kirk is out of HUD. He chooses not to work, but gives his time instead to local sports programs, a way of life he says he is content with.

He's got a comfortable pension now – $24,000 – but this is a different man somehow from the Larry Kirk we filmed in Indianapolis on a special night a few years ago.

MAN: One of America's ten outstanding young men of 1971 — Larry Kirk.

(Applause, music – as Larry Kirk makes his way to the podium)

KIRK: I think that God had a reason for taking my legs, because I have now entered the third cycle of my life. I will not accept this award — (crying) pardon me — I will not accept this award as a — as a reward for a job well done, but only as an incentive to bigger and better things. And I hope this award means that my countrymen love me as much as I love them. Thank you. (Applause)

WALLACE: I still don't understand what happened to Larry Kirk. The fellow at Indianapolis, he seemed to be on his way.

"Despite his injuries, Larry never seemed to slow down much. And once out of the hospital, he promptly went to work for half a dozen civic causes, including an advocacy of the American role in Vietnam."

KIRK: Maybe I haven't measured up to what Mike Wallace wanted me to be.

WALLACE: Oh, it's not a question of Mike Wallace. Have you measured up to what Larry Kirk wanted to be?

KIRK: I think I had a grandiose opinion of myself: that, you know, I would set the world on fire, and that I would make all these monumental contributions, you know. And I think, through the aging process, I have realized that maybe I won't do that in my lifetime. Sometimes in the early days, I will admit it was hard for me to accept, you know, that I wasn't the stud I used to be. But I know now who I am, and I'm very content with who I am and what I am. And as to what pinnacles I will reach, Woody Allen said, you know, his goal in life was to climb a low mountain, you know. Maybe I've just picked out a low mountain.

WALLACE: Gary Bartlett, a high-school basketball star from Dighton, Kansas, also lost his legs in Vietnam, and he wound up finally at Fitzsimmons Hospital.

("Star-Spangled Banner" playing over intercom)

Tell me something. Here it is five o'clock in the afternoon. They're playing "The Star-Spangled Banner". Does that mean anything special to you, or is it just a record that's playing at this time every afternoon?

GARY BARTLETT: Well, I don't know if it really means anything special. I feel rather proud to be a citizen of the United States, in a sense. I remember standing on the football field; when they played that, I felt about ten feet tall.

WALLACE: Gary was determined to keep his disability from changing his life totally. He married a young woman, Lynn, whom he'd met at Fitzsimmons Hospital. Her brother was a triple amputee from Vietnam. When 60 MINUTES caught up with him in Denver three years later, Gary was trying his hand at rodeo riding.

(Bartlett falling off horse)

BARTLETT: Oh! That was a rough fall.

LYNN: Are you sure you're all right?

BARTLETT: Yeah. Hey, I want to rope again, though, before I lose my confidence.

WALLACE: He doesn't do much riding now. Gary's increasing weight has forced him to seek other pastimes. He decided to come back home to the farming community of Dighton, Kansas. He wanted to work for a living, and eventually he became the town's recreation director. But he left that job when he realized his disability was just too severe. Now he and Lynn spend a good deal of their time out of doors, rock hunting, boating and fishing.

Do you still spend Vietnam nights?

BARTLETT: Oh, yeah. Oh, yeah.

WALLACE: Do you?

BARTLETT: Not real frequent. Sometimes it's one night, sometimes it's two nights.

WALLACE: Fear? Sweating?

BARTLETT: Just recall, but it's there. But I wake up and go out and sit in the front room and stuff; and then go back in and lay down again later. But it's not as bad as it was for a while, though.

(Holding up fish): Yeah, he's a keeper.

LYNN: Oh, he's a keeper.

BARTLETT: He's a keeper.

WALLACE: Gary and Lynn say they are able to live quite comfortably on their $24,000 disability pension, they've begun to raise a family.

MAN: How big is the kid?

BARTLETT: Oh, a little old 19-inch keeper.

MAN: Seen him a while ago, but how many pounds?

BARTLETT: Nineteen— or— let's see: six pounds eight ounces.

MAN: Is that right?

(Baby crying)

WALLACE: That little 19-inch keeper Gary so affectionately boasts about had been a long-awaited joy. While Lynn and Gary can love one another in a normal fashion, his massive injuries left him sterile. Years ago they tried to adopt a child, but they found in cold reality that, because of Gary's disability, the social agencies would not let them. So they turned to artificial insemination.

It's almost as though you were born to the task. I mean, she really knows where she is now. She's with her daddy.

BARTLETT: That's right. (Laughs) I'm sure we're going to have at least one more.

WALLACE: Back in '69, ten years ago, Gary, I asked you:

(1969): Are you proud that you made the sacrifice that you did?

BARTLETT (1969):   Well, I don't know if I'm really proud. I was glad to go to Vietnam and glad to find out what it's about. But the sacrifice happened, therefore I can't really say whether I was happy about it or not. Maybe I'll find out. I've got to think on it for a while. Wait till I get my life started, then I'll pretty well know whether it was worth it or not.

WALLACE: It's 10 years later. Was it worth it or not?

BARTLETT: Well, I don't know if the sacrifice is still worth it, but I know that — that going, for me, was worth it, because I'm more at ease in my mind about — you know, about going. I feel I —

WALLACE: How do you mean?

BARTLETT: — I feel I made the right decision.

WALLACE: Lynn, do you agree? Honest?

LYNN: I feel, you know, it couldn't possibly be worth it, you know, for what they had to sacrifice. But if it eases their mind that they know they did the right thing by going over there, who am I to say?

Hired Gun

JOE DeCOLA, PRODUCER

MORLEY SAFER: Whatever happened to that hired gun who appeared on 60 MINUTES four years ago this month?* Well, the day after his appearance he was arrested in Guatemala and shipped back to the U.S., where he eventually wound up in jail. More about that later.

We first met him in 1976, when the fighting in Angola was at its height and we all began hearing about mercenaries — soldiers of fortune, those international guns for hire who always show up where there is combat; the men novelist Frederick Forsyth called the "Dogs of War." We set out to find an experienced mercenary to discover what kind of people are they, what motivates them. That led us to this man — John Dane. Dane was a 34-year-old Briton who got into the U.S. on a tourist visa in 1967. He volunteered for the Army and served in Vietnam with a unit specializing in sabotage, kidnapping and assassination. He was awarded 12 medals, including a Bronze Star, and was given U.S. citizenship. But at the time Dan Rather met him, he was living south of the border.

DAN RATHER: Mazatlan on the west coast of Mexico, a kind of Mexican Riviera, is the place where he chose to be interviewed. Dane has had several identities and changes passports like most people change clothes. (Shots on shooting range) But we established, to our own satisfaction, at least, that he is what he says he is: a card-carrying member of the international mercenary community.

Let us suppose for a moment that I'm a 17- or 18-year-old young woman in Rhodesia —

JOHN DANE: Uh-hmm.

RATHER: — in the simplest terms, teach me to use this weapon.

DANE: Okay.

RATHER: He began smuggling guns into Spain about 10 years ago, fought in the Congo, worked with the anti-Monarchists underground in Morocco, and traveled widely with guns and explosives through other trouble spots — in Africa, the Middle East, Central and South America.

What are your specialties?

*This story was originally broadcast on May 2, 1976.

DANE: Weapons, explosives, intelligence.

RATHER: Explosives?

DANE: Uh-hmm.

RATHER: What can you do with those?

DANE: Well, you build a bridge, I can bring it down in shorter time than you ever took to build it. (Laughs) Move a mountain for you if you want it.

RATHER: Kidnapping, assassination?

DANE: That usually goes along with a underground organization — yes.

RATHER: Are you qualified to do that?

DANE: I have done it.

RATHER: Competent?

DANE: I've done it, got away with it. Still alive.

RATHER: Was any of this killing, this assassination, done at close range with hand-guns?

DANE: Yes, it was.

RATHER: Did you do any of that?

DANE: Yes.

RATHER: Did the other person have what we would call "a fighting chance"?

DANE: Not if I gave — (laughs) — not if I could help it.

RATHER: Did you enjoy that?

DANE: That's a difficult question. Perhaps I could say I enjoyed the planning, the setting things up, the getting close; the actual end result is an anti-climax. It's — there's nothing there to brag about. It would have been better if there was some other way of doing it — you know, to have instantaneous resurrection. I would probably feel better — put it that way. But there's no such thing. It's a rather terminal operation.

RATHER: You've said that you don't particularly like to kill, that you would prefer that it not have to be done, but that if it must be done that you feel you're the person to do it?

DANE: I'd prefer it be me than somebody else. At least if I am going to do it I'm going to do the job right and I'm not going to mess about. Now some people are so sadistic they'll drag this thing out for ages and ages and torture the poor bugger. There's no — there's no sense in that kind of thing. If you're going to go in and this thing has got to be done, then do the bloody thing and get out. You know, forget about it, you know. But rather than have somebody go and butcher the situation, that's not me.

(Dane shooting at a target)

RATHER: A hole through it and a hole through it. Not bad shooting.

DANE: Not considering it's the first time I've fired this one particular weapon.

RATHER: You picked up this weapon for the first time —

DANE: Just now.

RATHER: — no more than three minutes ago?

DANE: That's right.

RATHER: Mr. Dane's competence as an assassin goes beyond his skill as a marksman; it is based on real experience in this work. The part he would admit to was accumulated while he was in Vietnam.

DANE: These things are the size of a head and we were talking about head shots.

RATHER: So you — you would consider that three head shots right on the button?

DANE: Oh, yes. When you're wearing any kind of flak vest or bullet-proof vest, at least there's no way they can save themselves from this. As I say, very queen — clean, quick dispatch.

RATHER: For whom will you work, for whom will you not work?

DANE: I work only militarily or politically — against military targets or political targets. If it's — if you want your wife knocked off, your grandmother in an accident, or your mother-in-law to be deceased suddenly, that's — you can go down to Los Angeles and get those all you want. That's not my style.

RATHER: I want to play for you a piece of a tape recording, which I don't fully understand. This is a tape recording of a conversation between you and someone else. Let me play it for you first and see if you recall this.

DANE: Hm-hmm.

MALE VOICE (recording):   That they would love it. This — the State of Israel would love to see this man die. Every Jew would love to see this man die. This man is another Adolf Hitler to the Jewish people.

DANE (recording):   Then it would be a — a great saving, then? I mean, there would be a great deal of money saved and effort if this man was — (click of recorder being turned off).

RATHER: Now, do you remember that situation?

DANE: Yes, indeed I do.

RATHER: What was happening in that room when that recording was made?

DANE: I was being contacted to find out whether or not I would be amenable to fulfilling a contract, I think is the term.

RATHER: Killing someone?

DANE: Killing someone.

RATHER: An assassination?

DANE: An assassination.

RATHER: You were contacted in the United States?

DANE: In the United States, yes.

RATHER: Who was the man doing the talking?

DANE: It's a man who said he represented a certain Jewish group.

RATHER: What was that Jewish group?

DANE: The Jewish Defense League.

RATHER: So-called JDL?

DANE: So-called JDL.

IRV RUBIN: In order to save a Jewish life, the question is, how far will you go?

RATHER: Irv Rubin is the West Coast coordinator of the Jewish Defense League. It should be pointed out that major Jewish groups in the United States have gone on record deploring any illegal activities by the JDL, and so has the government of Israel. We interviewed Mr. Rubin in Los Angeles.
Does that include violence?

RUBIN: At some times that might include violence, yes.

RATHER: Murder, kidnapping?

RUBIN: Our commandment says: "Thou shalt not murder." There's a tremendous difference between murdering and killing. Our — our Torah, our Bible, says, "When one comes to slay you, you rise up early in the morning and slay him first."

RATHER: Did you satisfy yourself that he was indeed a representative of the JDL?

DANE: Yes, I did.

RATHER: And what was he proposing?

DANE: He was proposing to have me, in exchange for a substantial sum of money, to go to the Middle East and to kill Yasir Arafat.

RATHER: Yasir Arafat, the head of the Palestine Liberation Organization?

DANE: The same.

RATHER: Let me play you a tape recording, something, and I want to know where this happened and what was being said, what was going down, to use the vernacular of the street.

VOICE (recording):   That they would love it. This — the State of Israel would love to see this man die. Every Jew would love to see this man die. This man is another Adolf Hitler to the Jewish people.

DANE (recording):   Then it would be a — a great saving, then. I mean, there would be a great deal of money saved and effort if this man was put out of — (indistinct) What I'm asking for is a very great deal of money.

VOICE (recording):   No, not when you're considering — not when you consider the target you're going after, which —

RUBIN: I believe it might have been the news conference pertaining to Artukovic. I believe. I'm not certain. There's been many news conferences.

RATHER: No, I think this is a tape recording — I know this is a tape recording — made with a man named John Dane. Do you know Mr. Dane?

RUBIN: I've heard of him.

RATHER: That was your voice on the tape recording, was it not?

RUBIN: I would refuse to comment.

RATHER: Well, I know that that was your voice.

RUBIN: Yeah, okay.

RATHER: You were talking with Mr. John Dane. You were talking about an assassination attempt on Arafat.

RUBIN: We were fantasizing.

RATHER: Did he come to you or did you go to him?

DANE: He came to me.

RATHER: Tell me in brief what his proposition was.

DANE: Just as I've outlined. In exchange for a sum of money, I was to go to the Middle East and assassinate him.

RATHER: Did he care how you assassinated him?

DANE: No, he did not.

RATHER: Can you give me a rough idea of how much money he was offering?

DANE: Two hundred and fifty thousand dollars, American.

RATHER (whistling):   All of it out front?

DANE (laughing):   No. Half in advance, half at the back.

RATHER: Two hundred and fifty thousand dollars for Yasir Arafat's life?

RUBIN: No, there is no way that we could come up with two hundred and fifty thousand dollars. Any person of normal rationality —

RATHER: That's not what you told Mr. Dane.

RUBIN: — could see — could see that we couldn't come up with two hundred and fifty thousand dollars.

RATHER: You told him you could come up with two hundred and fifty thousand dollars.

RUBIN: No, I would beg to differ with you. There's no possible way.

RATHER: Did you seriously consider it as a business proposition?

DANE: Yes, I did

RATHER: Why?

DANE: There's nothing wrong in it.

RATHER: But do you know Yasir Arafat?

DANE: He is a military target.

RATHER: Do you personally have anything against him?

DANE: No, not personally.

RATHER: So you listened seriously to this proposition?

DANE: Yes, I did.

RATHER: How did you leave it with this man that you say was from the Jewish Defense League?

DANE: He was to contact me at a later date to tell me when the funds were to be forwarded and where they were to be deposited, and then I would act from there.

RUBIN: Anybody of their right mind would know that it's impossible to come up with two hundred and fifty thousand dollars.

RATHER: Mr. Rubin, in this conversation —

RUBIN: I would have — as I said to John Dane, "To be perfectly honest with you, you would have to go and contact people in New York. There is no way that we could come up with two hundred and fifty thousand dollars." As a matter of fact, if you played the tape in its entirety, there is no possible way. There is absolutely no possible way.

RATHER: Well, I have the tape in its entirety. First of all, did you know that that conversation was being tape-recorded?

RUBIN: No, I did not know.

RATHER: Who made the original tape recording?

DANE: I did.

RATHER: Why?

DANE: For, again, my own protection. There's no sense in just taking too many chances. There's — there's too many ponderables about the situation. I wasn't going to be caught napping on this one.

RATHER: At that time you believed he could do it?

RUBIN: I didn't believe anything. I couldn't believe —

RATHER: You hoped he could do it?

RUBIN: — I couldn't believe that anybody could kill Yasir Arafat. The — the proof would be in the pudding.

RATHER: You hoped he could do it?

RUBIN: Pardon me?

RATHER: You hoped that he could do it?

RUBIN: Well, yes, I did hope that he could do it, but I didn't think he could do it.

DANE: Well, of course, it would all have to be based upon the latest intelligence synopsis of the area. I'd have to get a lot of information upon his movements, his bases, his likely places of — that he would be at. And, of course, I would have to then calculate the number of men required. I'd have to visit the area, just to have a check-out of the situation to see if there were any other vibrations or anything I could pick up and use. And then, of course, the most important thing is a way of getting in, but more important, getting out.

RATHER: It's the sort of thing that could touch off another war in the Middle East?

DANE: Yes, if it was handled botchily, yes, it would. So it had to be done very, very carefully. There's all kinds of ways. For instance, if he had a known building that he goes to, not necessarily regularly, but at certain intervals anyway, that you can count he's going to go there sometime within a month, say, there's nothing to stop you from going in there — of course, covertly — planting your goodies around the place that would take care of the entire building, rather than just one specific spot.

RATHER: What kind of goodies would you use for this sort of job?

DANE: Anything I could get my hands on.

RATHER: Such as?

DANE: Whether it be dynamite, nitro, plastic explosive — whatever.

RATHER: All right, that would be one way.

DANE: Yes, and then just wait for him to come in before pushing the button.

RATHER: This would be command-detonated explosives?

DANE: Command-detonation, yes.

RATHER: Did you assure him that it could be done?

DANE: Oh, yes.

RATHER: If he came up with the money?

DANE: Absolutely. He was also made to understand that there'd be a lot of people that would be most upset should dear Mr. Arafat be suddenly demised, and that the large sum of money would be required in order to hide from all of his friends and admirers and sponsors — mainly his sponsors.

RATHER: How many times did you talk to John Dane, total?

RUBIN: Might have been twice.

RATHER: Well, we know you talked to him more than twice. You talked to him at the restaurant, the Hollywood restaurant. Right?

RUBIN: No comment.

RATHER: You talked to him in the secret meeting at a private home just outside Los Angeles, right?

RUBIN: No comment.

RATHER: Then you talked to him by telephone, a number of times?

RUBIN: No comment.

RATHER: You talked to him about Claymore Mines?

RUBIN: No comment.

RATHER: Plastique?

RUBIN: No comment.

RATHER: M-16-style rifles?

RUBIN: No comment.

RATHER: Explosives?

RUBIN: No comment.

RATHER: Automatic weapons?

RUBIN: No comment.

RATHER: Hand grenades?

RUBIN: No comment.

RATHER: What in the world could you have been imagining — even fantasizing, to use your word — that you would be doing with Claymore Mines, plastique, hand grenades, M-16 rifles, in the United States of America?

RUBIN: I just couldn't comment.

RATHER: That's a serious matter.

RUBIN: It's deadly serious.

RATHER: Deadly serious. If John Dane had asked you to go along on the plan —

RUBIN: I would never go with John Dane anywhere. (Laughs)

RATHER: Well, John Dane or anyone else, if they'd asked you to go along —

RUBIN: John Dane did not impress me with his professionalism.

RATHER: — to blow up Yasir Arafat, you'd go, wouldn't you?

RUBIN: No. No, I would not go because, again I did not know where John Dane was coming from.

RATHER: Did you get any money from the JDL at all?

DANE: No.

RATHER: They didn't give you a dime?

DANE: No.

RATHER: How soon were they supposed to get back to you?

DANE: Oh, within a matter of weeks.

RATHER: Isn't it a crime to engage in a conspiracy to commit murder in the United States?

DANE: If that person is a resident of the United States, if that person is an alien in the United States and it was to take place in the United States, yes, then that becomes conspiracy to commit murder.

RATHER: Well, it was a conspiracy to commit murder anyway?

DANE: Not in the United States.

RATHER: You mean, not under —

DANE: The man —

RATHER: — United States law?

DANE: Right. The man was not a resident of the United States. It would not take place in the United States. Therefore, it is not a crime.

RATHER: So you were never charged with this?

DANE: Of course not. What are they going to charge me with? Conspiracy to do something which isn't even on the books? Ha!

SAFER: Mr. Dane is correct. Incredible as it may seem, in the case described, neither he nor those with whom he met committed any crime under current U.S. law. But the day after we presented his story, Dane, who had been in jail in the U.S. on a gun-running charge, was arrested again — this time for violating his parole by handling that weapon he fired for us, a weapon that we borrowed from the chief of police in Mazatlan and promptly returned.

After completing his sentence, John Dane today is in Florida, back in jail after being arrested for driving a stolen car with a trunk full of dynamite. Where was he headed? Well, he says he was headed south of the border again — this time to offer his talents to one of the two sides in a dispute on the Caribbean island of Grenada.

Letters

MORLEY SAFER: Most of the letters we received after last week's story on Dr. Lawrence Burton and his fight with the cancer establishment were like this one: "If the American Cancer Society is so eager to find a cure for cancer and collects billions of dollars each year for the cure, why then does it dispute the findings of others? Could it be that they do not want to find a cure?"

And this: "When I walk by the multimillion-dollar American Cancer Society building here in New York, I realize that it is the occupants of that edifice who are truly the victims of a (malignancy) . . . a malignant bureaucracy."

However, there were some letters like this one from a technician at the Sloane-Kettering Cancer Institute: "By presenting (Burton's) work in a sympathetic and favorable light, you are encouraging hundreds of desperate people to risk their lives as well as their life savings on an unproven treatment . . . It is his own ignorance of basic scientific principles that is at the root of his trouble with the establishment."

On a more pleasant note, most of the people who wrote about our story on Gibraltar were fascinated by the way Gibraltarians dance.

(Gibraltarians dancing . . . excerpt from last week's broadcast)

One viewer wrote: "(About that) most delightful dance, can you tell me where I can learn it so I can teach it to senior citizens' groups?"

Followed by this: "Pray tell what was the wonderful little dance? It's nice to know that civilized people still inhabit our planet."

JUNE 1, 1980

A Nuclear Reaction

ESTHER KARTIGANER, PRODUCER

DAN RATHER: Last fall, CBS News reporter George Crile and a crew from the CBS News broadcast MAGAZINE examined a nuclear power plant under construction near Bay City, Texas. They were looking at the quality-control systems — those inspection procedures that are supposed to guarantee that a plant is built so safely that a nuclear accident could not harm the surrounding population. Well, since that story this plant has been at the center of a nuclear controversy

The South Texas Nuclear Project. Original projected cost: $1 billion. When it's completed, it will supply electricity to Houston, Austin and San Antonio. Because of the potential for a nuclear accident at this or any nuclear power plant, every piece of its construction considered safety-related is guided by federal regulation. And at every step in that construction, there is supposed to be an inspector to certify that the work has been done correctly. But does this inspection system, designed to guarantee construction of a safe nuclear plant, actually work?

DAN SWAYZE (Quality Control Inspector, Brown & Root, Inc.):   If they ever got a license to operate, it's — it's — it's criminal, because it's structurally unsound. And I'm not . . .

RATHER: For two years, Dan Swayze was one of the quality-control inspectors at the South Texas Nuclear Project.

SWAYZE: And I had engineers that worked for me, and it is structurally unsound, period.

RATHER: Swayze was one of the men in the gold hard hats, quality-control inspectors, whose job was to watch over the thousands of construction workers laboring around the clock. Inspectors are on the job when reinforcing bars are joined, when concrete is poured; but the problem, as we shall see, is that these inspectors are recruited, trained and on the payroll of the company whose work they're inspecting. And that company, Brown & Root, has already fallen four years behind schedule and gone a billion-and-a-half dollars over the original budget.

The whole inspection process is watched over by federal inspectors from the Nuclear Regulatory Commission. They were at this point on one day we filmed there, but according to a General Accounting Office report, the NRC spends only 16 days a year making on-site inspections. Generally, this is the way NRC inspectors make sure nuclear plants are constructed safely: by inspecting the reports of the Brown & Root inspectors. But some things don't show up in those reports.

Dan Swayze told reporter George Crile what would happen when he spotted violations that could cost his company extra time and money to correct.

SWAYZE: You can go down there in a few hours, and you can cite everything wrong with what they've done in a week. You're immediately surrounded by the superintendent, the general foreman, the foreman and the craft foreman for each ind— individual craft participating in that pour.

CRILE: Well, that's not intimidation, is it?

SWAYZE: Well, when eight of them are huddled around you, and most of them are in pretty good shape, because they've been doing manual labor most of their lives, and they'd — well, what do you want me to say? Exactly what they say?

CRILE: Yes. Yeah.

SWAYZE: Well, say, "You son of a bitch, if you don't sign the bastard at eight o'clock, we're going to kick your ass." Is that what you want? That's what they say.

TOM GAMMON: The public should have high confidence level in the safe construction of the plants.

RATHER: Tom Gammon is chief of Quality Assurance for Brown & Root. Reporter Crile asked him about the conflict between the construction people and the inspectors on the job site.

GAMMON: When one of these groups of people measures the performance of another, there is a natural adversary situation such as a law-abiding citizen might have with a policeman when he's caught for speeding.

CRILE: All right. Now, if you use the analogy of the citizen who's caught speeding, it's hard to sympathize with him if he wants to beat up the policeman.

GAMMON: That — and we don't necessarily sympathize with the construction worker if he wants to beat up the inspector. I think that that is —

CRILE: That's happened, hasn't it?

GAMMON: To extremely limited extent. There have been some cases.

SWAYZE: It went from verbal, continuous harassment, verbal abuse. It finally reached a point in '77, in July, that we attempted to stop a pour for major deficiencies. They threatened to kill me. That night, they assaulted one of my inspectors. The next day —

CRILE: Physically assault a man?

SWAYZE: Physically. Beat the hell out of him. Put him in the hospital for doing his job. The next day we took a vote. It was 100 percent. All the inspectors decided, "Obviously, they want us to do exactly nothing but fill paper out." We took a vote. We started filling paper out, and we did it for five months.

CRILE: Are you saying that for five months you did nothing?

SWAYZE: For five months we did no inspection whatsoever. We sat in our office. We had radios. When they wanted a pour signed off, we went down, the man a— assigned to that area went down, signed the pour card, came back and played cards the rest of the day.

CRILE: All the papers that bear your signature from that time are based on — on fraudulent statements?

SWAYZE: Absolutely nothing. They are based on nothing.

CRILE: How could you have done that?

SWAYZE: When you're hired to do a job, and they threaten to kill you, and they start beating the hell out of the people that work for you, what would you do?

RATHER: Swayze's charges that quality-control inspectors have been intimidated, that parts of the plant have never been inspected at all, were looked into by the Nuclear Regulatory Commission, but they found nothing to be disturbed about. Crile asked the NRC's regional chief, Karl Seyfrit, if his agency had checked out the story with the other inspectors who worked with Swayze.

KARL SEYFRIT: And I am informed that we did not interview the other men that he named, and I understand that some number of those, at least, are no longer at the site.

CRILE: How did you go about deciding whether his allegations were valid or not?

SEYFRIT: There were interviews made with supervisory personnel who would have had some knowledge of these activities, and there was a review of records made, and there was nothing in the records or in the interviews with the other people that would substantiate the allegation that Mr. Swayze made in this regard.

CRILE: (Indistinct) But in this case, the man said he was feeding you documents that were unreliable. They went — now they may have gone on the scene.

SEYFRIT: But I just told you, sir, that we did more than look at records.

CRILE: You talked to supervisors?

SEYFRIT: We did talk to other people, and these are people who would have some knowledge of whether or not these actions have taken place. We couldn't get to all of the inspectors that he named.

CRILE: Well, you didn't get to any of them, apparently.

SEYFRIT: That may be true. I — I am not willing to concede that that is an absolute fact at this point, no.

CRILE: But it's definitely a possibility?

SEYFRIT: Sure, I'll agree to that. It's a possibility that we did not talk to any of them.

RATHER: That reliance on the company's self-evaluations and written reports was criticized by the General Accounting Office. It concluded that the NRC's inspection program cannot independently assure that nuclear power plants are constructed adequately.

Here's an example of how the system can break down. A routine cadwelding operation, a method used to join the reinforcing bars that strengthen concrete walls. Cadwelds, one of which is being tested here, are used only in structures that might be subject to the greatest shocks. Brown & Root was supposed to inspect all of them, but for a period of time, those cadwelds were not inspected on the nighttime shift, and nothing was done about it until a Brown & Root inspector went secretly to the NRC.

Reporter Crile went to Brown & Root's Tom Gammon.

CRILE: What reason do we have to believe that you would have begun inspecting that cadweld operation at night if you hadn't been caught?

GAMMON: It was intended to be done at night, and we had inspectors on the shift to perform the inspections, and —

CRILE: Inspectors who weren't inspecting.

GAMMON: That weren't inspecting cadwelds. It's simply that they chose to do other work that night that they were supposed to do rather than cadwelds.

CRILE: Those — those — those nights?

GAMMON: Those nights.

CRILE: And the— they ultimately began inspecting the cadwelds because the NRC discovered it, embarrassed you?

GAMMON: That's right.

RATHER: A far greater embarrassment for Brown & Root involved this building, the building that will house the nuclear reactor. Its containment wall is the last line of defense in case of a nuclear accident. The pouring of concrete in this containment wall was stopped, because the self-inspection system had failed.

(Sound of instrument tapping containment walls)

That hollow sound indicates air bubbles, known as voids. As in the case of the cadwelds, the voids were discovered and steps taken to correct them only after an inspector went over the head of Brown & Root to report the problem.

CRILE: Don't you see a pattern here?

GAMMON: I see some instances that are disturbing and unfortunate, and we have strived to avoid these things and to encourage our people to work through our own organization.

CRILE: But we've just heard about a — a concrete containment wall which was poured and had voids in it, and your own quality-control inspector, sensing there were voids there, didn't dare go to Brown & Root.

GAMMON: I feel that he could've and should've, and we've tried to encourage them to, and I know of no case —

CRILE: But it means he didn't believe he could, doesn't it?

GAMMON: I don't know what it means. I— it only means that he didn't.

RATHER: Brown & Root was hired by a group of utilities to build this plant, but it is the utlities which must get a license to operate it. They're the ones who must convince the federal government it's safe. Reporter Crile asked the project manager of Houston Light and Power, Dave Barker, if he was concerned about the plant's history of construction problems.

CRILE: Is it safe?

DAVE BARKER: Yes, I can tell you that everything we have done so far to date is safe; that every effort is being made to carry the — the quality standard that we have had so far through to completion.

CRILE: And nothing in the process worries you?

BARKER: Nothing in the process worries me, and it has the top executive-management support of my own company as well as Brown & Root.

RATHER: But how does the process deal with whistle-blowers like Dan Swayze? He says that after looking the other way for five months, he again tried to do his job and reported violations to the Nuclear Regulatory Commission. Brown & Root fired him. They say it was for soliciting bribes. He says it was for doing his job too well. The NRC's Karl Seyfrit agrees there are few protections for nuclear whistle-blowers.

SEYFRIT: We are not able to completely protect identity, and there is nothing in the legal process that permits us to provide the kind of protection that you're suggesting would be nice to have.

CRILE: Don't we need to have some way to protect them?

SEYFRIT: Philosophically, I don't disagree that such protection is desirable, but we simply don't have the authority to provide that kind of protection at the moment. It's not — not there.

CRILE: In your opinion, is the South Texas Nuclear Project any better or worse, in terms of its safety record so far, than other nuclear plants?

SEYFRIT: I don't think that it's significantly different.

CRILE: Like most of the rest of them?

SEYFRIT: Pretty much the same.

RATHER: Well, if they're pretty much the same, the NRC is going to have its hands full, especially the NRC inspectors who have been recently assigned to be full time at each nuclear reactor under construction.

Shortly after that story was broadcast, the NRC launched a full-scale investigation of the quality-assurance program at the South Texas Project. Their conclusion, after their four-month investigation? "Quality-control inspectors have been subjected to production pressures – harassed, intimidated and threatened." The penalties? A fine of $100,000, all that the law allows, and the highest fine ever imposed on a plant under construction. More important, though, the utilities have until the end of July to prove to the NRC why their construction permit shouldn't be suspended. "The deficiencies in the Brown & Root program," the NRC said, "were so extensive that they should have been readily detected." Which prompted one critic to ask, "If they were so extensive, why didn't the NRC detect them long ago?"

One further note: a telex we received from Houston Lighting and Power before we aired this story said, "Mr. Dan Swayze, a fired Brown & Root employee on whose interview (your story) depends, states that the plant is structurally unsound. His opinion, and it is his opinion, is directly refuted by a comprehensive NRC report issued in April, which says — and I quote— 'No major deficiencies were found in any of the construction already completed.' " That's from the Houston Lighting and Power Company telex.

However, the NRC also said — and we quote — "The potential for future problems is great unless corrective action is taken." While Houston Lighting and Power reminded us that they are taking corrective action, the NRC reminded them, "Your past corrective action on the matters have been incomplete or ineffective."

A Man Called L'Amour

JOSEPH WERSHBA, PRODUCER

HARRY REASONER: Who is this country's best-selling novelist? No one knows for sure. The figures are too complicated — hardcover, paperback, and just plain exaggeration. But if you had to give an answer on five fingers, be sure one of those figures counted this man, a man called L'Amour, which happens to be his real name: Louis L'Amour. And you measure L'Amour books not by the copy but by the ton. For his readers, four or five months without a new L'Amour novel is like a year without sunshine. And Louis L'Amour's success, it is fair to say, comes from the fact that he writes only what he knows best, which is the way the West was won, as Morley Safer found out a few years back.

MORLEY SAFER: This is where the great American morality play is performed. It is a part of America that everyone, friends and enemies, understand, even admire. It is the setting for our folklore and our literature. It's even been said that we make foreign policy as if there was still a West out there to be won.

It is, of course, a film set of the Old West. And when we watch a Western movie or television show or read a book, we expect certain things from it, vital ingredients without which we are left dissatisfied. The saloon, for example — this place where good and evil meet to drink — and always close at hand, the dancing girl, the fancy lady with a heart of gold.

(Music . . . saloon scene from *Gunsmoke*)

And the street itself, this avenue of dusty death on which, at opposing ends, good and evil face each other, and the fate of both rests in the quickness of a draw.

(Gunshot . . . street scene from *Gunsmoke*)

And on this street, too, the law-abiding citizenry — good people all — having moved west seeking land and freedom; terror always comes in the form of a ruffian gang of brute killers, who like nothing better than to ride in and shoot up a peaceful town.

(Scene of yelling and shooting cowboys)

And by this door, the sheriff or the marshal sits — a man of strength and silence, a man with an unspoken past who has killed too often and, before the play is over, he knows he must kill again.

(Gunshot)

And over in the hills beyond, the wagon trains move westward ho, making their endless circle, fighting off an endless band of Indians who, with time, have changed from ruthless heathen into noble savage.

Well, what's it all about? Is that the way it was? Is the play a play of fact or is it a Hollywood fantasy? Here's a man who knows.

His name is Louis L'Amour. He's spent a lifetime separating fact from fancy. He is America's most prolific Western writer. Other Western writers – like Zane Grey, who was a New York dentist – may be better known, but no Western writer has sold more books than Louis L'Amour.

LOUIS L'AMOUR: Well, in the first place, let's get back to one thing. The movies have entirely over-dramatized the gunfighter in every sense of the word. The gunfighter was here. He was a natural part of the times, but there were very few men who were known as gunfighters who wanted to be gunfighters. They became so largely by accident. They were men who simply had — had natural skills with guns. And by the time they'd won two or three fights, they were — had the reputation as gunfighters, whether they wanted it or not. And most of them didn't want it. There was always some cheap punk that you hear about in the movies — and there were a few of them, very few — who went around looking for a reputation. But they didn't last long, because the kind of reputation you find there is written on a tombstone. But the gunfighter is completely over-emphasized in the West. There was so much else going on. And actually, usually all that sort of thing took place on the wrong side of the tracks, you might say, on the wrong side of the street. And many of the people in the West never came in contact with it at all.

SAFER: It was a sort of inner-city problem.

L'AMOUR: That's right. That's right. Exactly that. And the prostitutes and the gambling and all that sort of thing went on in one area of town, the red-light district, which actually came from the railroad men hanging their red lanterns in front of the houses when they went in. But the — the gunfighting usually took place over there, you know, and not in the better section of town at all.

SAFER: To his readers, L'Amour is perhaps this country's best known novelist; to book reviewers and the literary establishment, perhaps the least known. And yet, there are nearly 65 million copies of his books in print. He's among the most popular writers this country has ever produced. He's written 66 novels, 400 short stories, and at least 30 of his stories have become movies – movies like *Hondo, Shalako* and *Heller in Pink Tights.*

As a novelist, as a literary man, does it not bother you to not see your books reviewed?

L'AMOUR: Well, they are reviewed. I would like to have them more importantly reviewed than they are. But we have a very queer situation in this country that anything — anything Western is sort of relegated to the ash heap. It's just considered not to be good. Why this is, I don't know, because it — for example, they think it's more important to detail the experiences of somebody in bed, some couple in bed, rather than — than the opening of half a continent. It's — it's un— beyond belief, you know, but it's so.

SAFER: L'Amour is not your tweedy, pipe-smoking, couple-of-hundred-words-a-day kind of writer. He's a man of action, who quickly gets rid of writer's block by punching it out of himself on the heavy bag.

And L'Amour is never far from his roots, from the source of all his wealth and spirit. He takes his summers off, and returns with his wife and children to his own spread near Durango, Colorado.

He's lived the life of a Jack London: soldier of fortune, lumberjack, longshoreman, professional prize-fighter, old China hand, and cowboy. He barely got to high school before he dropped out. He's made a profession of a private passion, the Old West. And you can still see it much the same as it looked when the railways first spanned this country a hundred years ago.

L'Amour is a tenth-generation American with deep roots in the expansion of this country. His great-grandfather fought with the Army against the Indians, and was scalped for his sins. His grandfather fought off Indians while settling a homestead in North Dakota, where Louis was born. When he was very young, he got to meet some old gunfighters, who lit the spark that has made Louis L'Amour a rich and learned man today.

His plots may be fiction, but the details therein are fact. And Louis L'Amour has become our professor emeritus of how the West was won.

L'AMOUR: One of the myths I always like to get away from is the idea that a gunfighter or a group of gunfighters could come in and terrorize a Western town. It just couldn't happen, because, you see, nearly everybody in that town grew up using a gun. They were familiar with it. But the thing was that — that in every town, I would venture to say that two-thirds of the adult men had fought in the Civil War. Well, these men were used to guns. Nobody was going to scare them. No tinhorn was going to come along with a gun and buffalo them at all. So, you can see what happened at Northfield, Minnesota, when the Jesse James and Cole Younger gang tried to rob two banks there. They got shot to pieces by a bunch of farmers and businessmen. And the same thing happened in Coffeyville, Kansas, with the Dalton gang. They got wiped out. The one man who survived had 16 buckshot in him. He lived for a long time, incidentally; became a real estate man.

SAFER: What about the fast draw? Is that an invention of novelists and film makers, or did they really pride themselves on − on − on that?

L'AMOUR: It was very important, because if two men got in a gun battle it — it was important who got off the first shot. But I have talked to at least 30 of the old gunfighters and outlaws, and they all said the same thing. The first one who told me was Bill Tilghman, who taught me how to use a pistol. He said the first — the fast draw is important, but the most important thing is making the first shot count. You may never get another one. And many a man who drew very fast put his first bullet in — in the dust right out in front of him, and didn't — he never got off another one.

SAFER: What about that − the *High Noon* confrontation − two men standing in the main street in town, drawing against each other? True of false?

L'AMOUR: It happened occasionally, but only occasionally. Usually it was a point-blank thing, right at the moment. Sometimes one man wouldn't be armed, and the other fellow would say, "Go get a gun. Go heel yourself and — and you come back." And of course, when he did, then it was open season. I mean, they took a shot at him whenever they saw him.

Another thing that I'd like to — I'd like to get away from is the idea that when a man gets shot he drops. Some people have the idea that a shot always kills a man, and knocks him — it isn't true at all. You take a really tough man, he keeps right on coming. And Colonel Butcher, who made quite a study of gunshot injuries a number of years ago, he decided, after studying very carefully, that unless a man was shot right through the brain, right through the heart or was hit on the big bone, he wasn't going to go down and he was going to keep coming, if he was mad. I mean, if he had adrenalin pumped up in his system.

SAFER: What about the Western saloon — the — the dancing girl with the heart of gold?

L'AMOUR: Well, there were some of those around, there's no question about that, but they — they were very rarely as attractive as they are in the movies, and they weren't dressed the way they were in the movies. They usually wore long dresses, clear down to their ankles. And there weren't many women in saloons. Now, the Long Branch Saloon is famous from a TV series, you know. Actually, there was no women in it at all. It was operated by men, for men, and only men.

SAFER: Well, our perception of the West is that — with the exception of the — the noble sheriff or marshal — was that it was a — a lawless place. Was that true?

L'AMOUR: This — this isn't true. There was — really was a lot of justice, and a lot of very forthright thinking, however. They had very — very little patience. They didn't want justice delayed. They wanted it now. They didn't want long trials. Many of the — many of the lynchings, so-called, of rustlers out in the West happened because some fellow would catch a man stealing his cattle. He'd hang him right on the spot if there was a tree handy, because it was easier than taking him a hundred miles into the courthouse, and jail, leaving him there, riding back home, riding in a hundred miles more to testify, riding back again, leaving his business, leaving all of his work. It was much simpler to hang him on the spot.

SAFER: Was murder — and we get the idea that it wasn't — but was murder a serious crime?

L'AMOUR: Murder was a very serious crime, definitely. You see, when two men shot it out with guns, that was not considered murder. It wasn't considered murder when — when Burr and Hamilton fought back East either, which was not too long before, you know. So you've got to think with perspective. And Thomas Hart Benton, for example, the senator, killed five men in duels. Andrew Jackson killed one, and was involved in over a hundred and two as a second or something. Dueling was a — was a way of settling disputes. It was considered the honorable way. Now, contrary to what you see in the Western movies, there were very few fistfights. There were Irishmen out there, some Irish trackworkers and whatnot, and they fought with their fists. But by and large, the — the Western men did not.

SAFER: Our own perception of ourselves, of the white man settling the West, has changed over the years, and now history writers tell us we were full of duplicity and murder and even genocide, as far as the Indians are concerned.

L'AMOUR: It's — it's not true. It happened. There were cases of murder, there were cases of brutality, there were cases of unnecessary killing — but on both sides. The white man supposedly should have been better, should have been a better person about it. But there was — there was wrong on both sides. And there's no way you can — you can draw the line and say this is all bad. Now, we talk about the treaties; some of them were lived up to, some of them were not. Some of the Indians broke as many as the white man did. This is not — a lot of people don't like to believe this now. They want to put all the blame on the white man, but it wasn't true. And in many cases what the white man paid the Indian for his land, we — he was well paid in the coin of the time. Not today. Of course, they tell the famous story about the Indian selling Manhattan Island for $24. He didn't even own it. That's the — was the first crooked real — real estate deal in America that I know of. The Indian came down out of the hills to go fishing down there, and he didn't even belong on Manhattan Island in that area. And a fellow asked him if he'd sell it — sell him his right to it for this stuff, and he said, "Sure. Why not?" (Laughs) So he sold it. He got his fish and he went back home. But those stories you don't always get.

But the Indian was a terr— fine warrior; in many cases had great wisdom. He had a culture that was perfect for himself, and was changing. All the Indian needed at that time was a Genghis Khan, somebody to come along and weld them into one big group, and we'd have never made it, believe me. They were great fighting men.

SAFER: These days L'Amour is something of a Hollywood cowboy living in some luxury in a Spanish-style villa in Beverly Hills, surrounded by thousands of volumes of books and diaries and maps and explorers' notebooks of the Old West. It's the house that paperbacks built, paperbacks by the scores of millions, in German and French and Spanish and Portuguese and Italian and Serbo-Croatian and, coming soon, Chinese.

He still writes three novels a year; gets the beginning, middle and end in his head before he sits down to a typewriter. And as is the way with such things, Louis L'Amour, after 20 years of success and in his 68th year, is just being discovered. He's becoming a star turn at book fairs, and a noble primitive of literary luncheons.

But here is where he comes to recharge himself, to gather himself together, to see America again as one of Louis L'Amour's own strong silent men might have seen it a hundred years ago.

L'AMOUR: Out here over this country, there were a thousand little Alamos; people who fought and died out there to maintain their homes, to keep themselves, and they were bigger than life because the times demanded it. Right now our times don't. But I'm firmly convinced that it's all still here. The feeling is here, everything. People say that we're greed— they say it's a materialistic society. Society has always been materialistic. Show me a country or a time that wasn't materialistic.

SAFER: Do you think Louis L'Amour was born a hundred years too late?

L'AMOUR: No, I'd — I'd rather be born in this time than any other time. This is an exciting period. Stop and think what's happened in this period. We've put a man on the moon. This is the most dramatic thing since the world began.

People are kind of taking it for granted, but they shouldn't. It's a tremendous thing. This is the first step on — into a new frontier, because we're moving out there where it's all going to happen in the future. And I'm not downbeat about the country at all. I'm very — very optimistic about the whole thing. And there's no reason why not.

If you'll permit me to say so — and you've looked at my library here — I have at my fingertips 6,000 years of man's history, and there have always been times when things were bad. There have always been periods of terrible crime. There's always been te— periods of hardship. But this is the best time that man ever had on the face of this earth, right now — the best time in which to live.

REASONER: We first ran that piece four years ago, so add some new statistics: Louis L'Amour now has 75 books in print, and sometime this summer someone is going to buy the 100-millionth copy of a Louis L'Amour.*

---

*This segment was previously broadcast November 14, 1976 and August 13, 1978.

This Year at Marienbad

WILLIAM K. McCLURE, PRODUCER

MIKE WALLACE: We first broadcast the story you're about to see six long years ago, back in 1974.* The news magazines call it a "back-of-the-book story" — one of those life style features you find around page 72. Well, we don't have a page 72, so we'll run it on page three. From checking up the past couple of weeks, we learned that just about everything now is as it was then — except, of course, the prices for what you're going to see have virtually tripled since '74.

We live in a time of self-indulgence. We give ourselves more to eat, more to drink, more gadgets and more pleasures than anyone in history. Not just Americans, but all of us in the Western world. And at the time, we have a guilty conscience about it, so we do penance: strict regimes of diet, of exercise and self-denial. Well, 60 MINUTES too a look at the mania for physical self-improvement now sweeping Europe.

It is eight o'clock in the morning at Montecatini in Italy, and 10,000 curists are heading for the mineral water fountains.

(Music)

WOMAN: Definitely, if you could come once a year for several weeks you would feel great release of pain and be much freer to move about and enjoy life.

(Music)

MAN: The drinking of the water is the most important form of treatment in Montecatini. We deal with patients that have slow digestion, indigestion, constipation and so on.

(Music)

WOMAN: It's — it's of psychological benefit, obviously, to a lot of troubled people. It's not really a very swinging-type group.

(Music)

MAN: Certainly, it can't do you any harm and it might very well do you a lot of good.

(Music)

WOMAN: It's hot and it doesn't taste so wonderful.

(Singing: "Drink! Drink!")

WALLACE: The labels on these bottles promise surcease from obesity and emaciation, from problems of the liver, the kidneys, the intestines, relief from menopausal symptoms and metabolic malfunctioning. And it will cure your gout. It is big business. Evian turns out a million bottles every day. Each spa — Baden-Baden, Vichy, Perrier, Marienbad — has its own specialty and its own personality.

In Czechoslovakia, Marienbad lures not only the sons and daughters of the proletariat, but travelers from the free West. Their respective states pick up most of the tab. Socialism pays for the Communists. Health insurance does it for the European capitalists.

To be a true curist, it's imperative to go all the way — to bathe in the water as well as drink it — best hot and direct from the springs.

WOMAN: These baths are very powerful, very, very strong, and — and they're —

*This segment was previously broadcast July 14, 1974 and June 22, 1975.

they're apt to — might — to raise your blood pressure if you're not — if you stay in too long.

WOMAN: Oh, I can't have enough of them. (Laughs) It's relaxing, it's soothing. So, I mean, even if you have nothing and just go there and take a swim in this — in this mineral water, it's enjoyable.

(Sound of laughter, splashing . . . sound of gases)

WALLACE: Out of the subterranean springs come gases with the waters — sulphur dioxide. In concentrated form at three feet it is lethal, but at a safer distance and diffuse, it is said to cure impotence. Just one trouble — the gas is most effective at five o'clock in the morning.

MAN: I think that if a man is fitter, then he can perform all of the functions better. He works better. He thinks better. He produces better. He — he, no doubt, makes love better, because he's fitter.

WALLACE: Are your bronchial tubes clogged? Do you have asthma? Marienbad promises relief with this procedure: vaporized mineral water. It is called "nebalisation."

MAN: These people doing their sort of concentration-camp techniques — it cannot be particularly good because they're not happy doing it. I mean, it — it must be hell.

WALLACE: This bathing parlor at Marienbad was designed for England's Edward the Seventh. He nursed his gout here while he waited for Victoria to leave him the throne. Spas were the retreat of the very rich and powerful in Europe for hundreds of years. Emperor Franz Josef found relief from tension at Carlsbad. J. P. Morgan did the same at Aix-les-Bains. But the current client suffers more from simple obesity than from the complexities of state affairs.

(Sounds of exercise equipment)

This is not a torture chamber; this lady is not on the rack. It is mechano therapy at Vichy. The curists seek it out for slipped discs and rheumatism. They find solace in the pain, discomfort and exhaustion it inflicts.

(Sounds of exercise equipment)

For consolation after such an assault upon your body, what else but food. The hoary spas of Europe turn their noses up at the new asceticism of organic diets. They instill the faith of holy water and they turn a blind eye to the sins of calorie consumers. Besides, in Czechoslovakia, where to have cake is to eat it, cream puffs and chocolate cake are luxuries not to be foresworn.

But the new puritans make a cult of self-denial, and more and more of them have lately been turning up at spots like the Bircher-Benner Clinic in Zurich, Switzerland, where your stomach undergoes as strict a discipline as your kidneys get at Carlsbad. This establishment was founded 70 years ago by Dr. Max Bircher-Benner, who believed — long before Adele Davis — that you are what you eat.

Bircher-Benner believed in fresh food, raw food, organically grown. What is cooked is delicately done. Chemical additives are akin to poison here. Accents are added to the food with herbs and ingenuity. The staple of the Bircher-Benner diet is something called muesli, a cold porridge of oat flakes, nuts, yogurt, honey and fresh fruit, tasty enough to have replaced corn flakes on a million European breakfast tables. At the clinic it is served twice daily. Muesli is the gastronomic pinnacle of each day of enforced asceticism. No meat, no fish, no fowl, no cigarettes or alcohol, no coffee — just a bowl of muesli for breakfast along with some whole-wheat bread. For lunch: some fruit, some soup, some leafy vegetables — raw and cooked. They tell you here that too much food can lead to premature old age and illness. Well, at this rate, I shall be healthy for a full 100 years.

If the regime at Bircher-Benner is not a gourmet's delight, its habitués swear by its therapy. Back in 1925, a young patient arrived here with a chronic stomach complaint deemed incurable by her own doctors. In desperation she put herself in the hands of Dr. Bircher-Benner.

And then he persuaded you, obviously, that it worked?

WOMAN 1:   Oh, well, it — he didn't persuade me, I saw it. After about 10 days that I was here, I found out that he was right and I was wrong, because I thought that he was absolutely on the wrong track, but he wasn't.

WALLACE: Yes.

WOMAN 1:   He made me do everything different to what I'd ever done before.

WALLACE: For instance?

WOMAN 1:   All the doctors. Well, I always was told that I had to lie down most of the day, take no raw food at all. Oh, dear me, no! And he made me get up at six in the morning and go out and do gymnastics. So I thought he was mad. But he wasn't. (Laughs)

WALLACE: How old are you now, if I may ask?

WOMAN 1:   84.

WALLACE: You don't look overweight.

WOMAN 2:   No.

WALLACE: And you don't look unhealthy.

WOMAN 2:   I'm not. It's just for relaxing.

WALLACE: You've been here for how long?

WOMAN 2:   One week.

WALLACE: And this —

WOMAN 2:   That's enough. That's enough for me because I'm rather healthy, you know.

WALLACE: Well, you come for what reason, then?

WOMAN 2:   Because I have a lot to do in my life. I have children. I have business. So I come just to — to be quiet for one week, to read a book finally, to write my letters, and to get everything in order again, you know.

WALLACE: The clinic concerns itself not just with what goes into the body but what comes out. The medical staff tries to diagnose and cure such assorted ailments as arteriosclerosis, rheumatism, hypertension. After diagnosis, patients are often ordered to change a lifetime of bad habits.

(People speaking in German)

Daily, everyone takes a siesta. That's the time the doctor comes. Frau Dr. Liechti-von-Brasch is the niece of the clinic's founder.

FRAU DR. LIECHTI-von-BRASCH: How did you sleep?

WALLACE: Superbly.

FRAU DR. LIECHTI-von-BRASCH: Superb?

WALLACE: Yes.

FRAU DR. LIECHTI-von-BRASCH: You dreamed nice dreams?

WALLACE: Yes. (Laughs)

FRAU DR. LIECHTI-von-BRASCH: Do you know, people when they are here, they begin to dream much more, when they change their food, they change their habits — sometimes dreams way back into their childhood.

WALLACE: Why would a change of diet to raw food trigger off dreams – more dreams?

FRAU DR. LIECHTI-von-BRASCH: This is a funny thing, but it's quite true. A change of diet means a change of the whole chemistry of the body, change of the blood compound, change of the circulation — not only in the body, but also in the brain.

WALLACE: You know, when people come here, I get the sense that there's an obstacle course, that they're committing themselves, and that's part of the – part of the cure, no?

FRAU DR. LIECHTI-von-BRASCH: Yes. Yes, they have to have the wish to come — to come from their own will. They want to change something of their life. They want to act themselves because they're asked. It's a challenge. They have to leave away the sweet eating, the alcoholic drinks. They have to — all the irritants and exciting extra food, bits and excitants, are left away. Coffee — no coffee.

MAN: The trick is to cheat a little bit.

WALLACE: How do you mean?

MAN: How do I mean? There's a little restaurant across the street — a very nice little place — that I go to for coffee and tea —

WOMAN: Milk kaffee.

MAN: — milk kaffee, which is steamed — steamed milk with coffee.

WALLACE: You come these thousands of miles from Syracuse to Zurich to cheat?

MAN: That's the only thing I cheat on.

EXERCISE INSTRUCTOR (to music):   And right side, left side, right side, left side, right, left, right, left, hup, hup, hup, hup, hup, hup. And you go forwards — forwards, backwards, forwards, backwards, forwards, backwards . . .

WALLACE: Part of the mystique of Bircher-Benner is masochism – not just in the diet, but in the exercise class; not just in the exercise class, but in the baths.

In a world knee-deep in additives, tensions, pollution and post-nasal drip, there is something therapeutically old-fashioned about places like these – Bircher-Benner, Carlsbad, Evian, Vichy, Montecatini, names that roll off the tongue. All that you need is a general debility and about $500 a week. And it's worth it, if just to tell your friends about the time you took the cure.

By the way, that $500-a-week figure, forget it! Eighteen hundred dollars a week is what you'd need today to get in that tub.

A Few Minutes
with Andy Rooney

HARRY REASONER: Andy Rooney had a little trouble this week getting his act together.

ANDY ROONEY: This week I couldn't decide whether to do something on flowers or political candidates. I decided on flowers.

As much as I like flowers, I've never known much about them. I mean, once I've identified a rose and a pansy, I'm near the end of my horticultural expertise. Over the years I've bought books to identify almost everything — you know, trees, mushrooms and especially flowers. I don't know, nothing in these books I buy ever looks like what I'm seeing when I'm trying to call a flower by name.

No one ever says anything bad about flowers, and I'm not going to either, but flowers make me uneasy. I like them, but they die too soon. Any time I look at a flower, I'm torn between pleasure over how attractive it is and sadness about how little time it has.

I should think you'd have to be pretty hard-hearted to work as a florist. You couldn't let dying flowers get to you every day. You'd have to put them out of your mind when you went home at night, like a veterinarian leaving an animal hospital.

I don't care much for flowers that are too carefully arranged, either. There's no need for the hand of man to try to improve on nature in this case. The best flowers are the ones that grow naturally in the field, arranged only by their own magic. Most arangements make flowers look like a woman who just came from a bad hairdresser. Artificial flowers ought to be illegal. Artificial is exactly what flowers are not.

I don't even like to see flowers in a florist's refrigerator. Flowers ought not be caged, or even fenced.

A lot of American communities that let everything else go to the dogs decorate their towns with flowers in an attractive way. New York City seems like an unlikely place for a display like this. That's where it is, though.

It's touching to see someone trying to brighten an otherwise drab life with flowers, growing them in places that don't come naturally for flowers to grow in. You can look at a living place and never have it occur to you that there is anyone inside with whom you might share a thought or a sentiment, until you see the flowers in the window and you know all of us share everything.

(Music . . . flowers in bloom)

JUNE 8, 1980

Banking on Bahrain

JOHN TIFFIN, PRODUCER

MORLEY SAFER: With the oil nations of the Persian Gulf unstable and threatened by both internal revolution and Soviet expansion, there are few places that the United States and its allies can rely on in the region. One of the places we're banking on is Bahrain — that speck of an island in the Persian Gulf. Not only banking on it, banking in it. Unlike its neighbors, Bahrain is not awash in oil, but it is rich in many other ways. Rich, for example, in the ways of handling the money that comes from its neighbors' oil wells. So a lot of people both in the East and the West are banking on Bahrain staying as stable, neutral and as peaceable a kingdom as it is.

Every Friday, His Highness Sheikh Isa Bin Sulman al-Khalifa, the Amir of Bahrain, turns up at one of his palaces in his 1950 Imperial for the weekly Majlis — a kind of royal sit-in. He is greeted by friends and relatives, prominent merchants and retainers, in the traditional Bedouin way. His most loyal servants, the keepers of the falcons, go wherever the Amir goes. The birds are almost a badge of office, and they're handy if an unfortunate partridge finds itself straying over Bahrain. Otherwise, his kingdom is a peaceable one.

The Majlis is fascinating. These are mostly modern, cosmopolitan technocrats, but they are in touch with their past with an iron grip. Extremely formal people. Everyone, visitors included, waft a wisp of the requisite frankincense on themselves and take the peace offering of coffee before settling down to business.

This may be no democracy, but the Majlis is a kind of open forum. Anyone can petition the Amir. And His Majesty — really a quite gentle soul — on his throne, dappled by one single patch of sunshine, usually goes along with reasonable requests. The Majlis demonstrates how the Bahrainis have come to terms with each other. The Khalifas, second cousins of the Saudis, took over the island 200 years ago. Instead of stomping on the liberal Moslem merchants in the name of militant Islam, they joined the club. Now everyone shares the wealth. When European man was still grunting against the darkness, Bahraini man was happily doing business with the known world. His civilization was ancient when Alexander the Great passed through tossing silver coins around as if they were petrodollars.

It's the site of what some believe to be the Garden of Eden: groves of dates abundant with sweet-water springs; peopled by the most professional traders and

589

seafarers in the world. Most of the world's pearls came from the oyster beds surrounding Bahrain. Then came the bad news in 1930: the Japanese produced cultured pearls. Then came the good news in 1931, when a nice American gentleman dug a hole and came up a gusher. This is the very first oil well in the Persian Gulf.

The rest, you might think, is history. Well, not quite. If you're one of those people who still believes that oil will be here forever, then this granddaddy is proof of what a fool you are, because last year he ran out, gave up. And soon all the oil wells in Bahrain will do the same. Does that mean it's back to pearl-diving and date-farming for all those ancestors of old Mister Bones we saw up front? No, sir.

"Anyone can petition the Amir. And His Majesty—really a quite gentle soul—on his throne, dappled by one single patch of sunshine, usually goes along with reasonable requests."

The Bahrainis were not content to contemplate their Cadillacs — they were making plans. They realized that their little pearl was just inches away on the map from Saudi Arabia and Qatar and Iran and Abu Dhabi and Kuwait — and all that combined oil still being pumped. And what was missing was Switzerland. So they built a Switzerland — an offshore safe house for all that oil money.

(Montage of money traders quoting exchange prices)

And it all zooms through the atmosphere on the world's best telecommunications network. "Offshore" means the banks conform only to the hospitable regulations of Bahrain — a twenty-five- or thirty-billion-dollar nut to be squirreled away each year. And on the horizon, something called a "jumbo bank" — the neutron bomb of banks.

SHEIKH MOHAMED AL-KHALIFA: The development in this part of the world and the progress is happening here is tremendous. There's nothing like it anywhere in the world. I mean, 10 years ago, if you'd come to this part of world — not only to Bahrain, but to the whole area — you can notice the difference which took place in the last 10 years.

SAFER: The foreign minister of Bahrain is Sheikh Mohamed al-Khalifa.

SHEIKH MOHAMED AL-KHALIFA: Well, I think Bahrain is good example of the first country in this part of the world to live the post-oil era. Our oil is depleting, but our economy is booming. So this is an example of a country which (is) preparing itself to live without oil.

SAFER: While everyone around them pumps oil, Bahrain provides the drydocking that the oil tankers need to repair themselves. Other countries in the Gulf wanted this OPEC-financed facility, but somehow the Bahrainis won it. And they got

OPEC to help build an enormous refinery to convert that Saudi oil to gasoline for the growing demands of the Gulf and the Far East. A pipeline funnels it across the 15 miles of strait that separate Bahrain from Saudi Arabia. And against the day when there is no oil, they've built a huge aluminum smelter.

In the Disneyworld of multi-national business, it somehow pays to schlep the raw bauxite from the Far East to Bahrain, smelt it, then send it all the way back to the Far East as aluminum ingots.

All this runs way too smoothly for Bahrain to be a democracy, and nobody here seems wildly in favor of having one. The population is roughly half Shiite Moslem, half Sunni, and whatever differences exist between them have been at least submerged and they share this place without confrontation. (Man praying in mosque)

Even women openly share it. You are looking at scenes that would be perhaps a cause for stoning only 15 miles away in Saudi Arabia. There, a woman is forbidden to drive, forbidden even to enter a taxi alone, forbidden, of course, to show her face. Bahrain sent its girls to school back in the twenties, when most of its neighbors weren't so sure that schools were a good idea for anyone. The idea of women openly flaunting themselves, if you can call this flaunting, is absolutely forbidden elsewhere in the Gulf. The idea of women representing authority would be unthinkable.

WOMAN (answering phone):   Hello? Ward fifty eighty-one.

SAFER: And most unthinkable of all, women as doctors — doctors who treat male patients, in an easy, unself-conscious way that is not even fully accepted in many Western countries.

This does not please Bahrain's new revolutionary neighbors in Iran or its old conservative cousins in Saudi Arabia. (Music) And neither do Bahrain's easygoing laws about alcohol and open displays of flesh. The nightclubs have shows that are only slightly naughty and just a little bit absurd. There is something about a troupe of bare-bottomed Carmen Mirandas fetching up on these coasts that makes you expect the Marx Brothers to pop out of the woodwork any minute. But it's all good, clean fun. They say for a few dollars more it can be a lot more private and a lot more naughty. And they say that many of those conservative Saudi princes hop over for a quiet night out, or just for some relaxed disco dancing.

Bahrain's reputation as a fleshpot is wildly exaggerated. It just seems extraordinary in this part of the world. Bahrainis hate it when foreign journalists make too much of their innocent pleasures — so we won't.

Much of Bahrain is still storybook Arabia — a mood and a people that plays on the mind of anyone who read certain fiction when he was young. It all looks like it's filled with intrigue, and it is — about the price of onions or of spices. And a bit of the real thing, too — smuggling to and fro from India.

What you do not see in Bahrain are the beggars of a Cairo or the con men of a Beirut. Healthy respect for themselves, and for strangers a traditional openness and generosity that you do not necessarily find in other countries in the region. Nor do you see that fascination with everything expensive and excessive that you find elsewhere. The Khalifas and the merchants have built for themselves expensive little palazzos up and down Bahrain, but nothing so outrageous as to send the working people to the barricades. They may strike you as architecturally odd — a mixed bag of design, with such amenities as pipelines in the front garden and gas-storage tanks in the back garden — but that's a matter of taste. It's all merely comfortably upper-middle-class, enough to show who's in charge, not so much as to cause a riot. For working people, public housing that is better than most, at absurdly modest rents that are in truth mortgage payments.

Bahrainis did not accomplish all of this on their own. They contracted a lot of it out to what can best be called "billboard companies" — all those stateless consortia with mailing addresses in every state in the union and every state in Western Europe; hard-hat corporations who think of countries as construction sites, who employ an offshore army of lifelong expatriates.

If it's 1980, it must be Bahrain. Or is it Oman, or Malaysia, or North Slope? The drinks are the same and the jokes are the same, and the young-old faces seeking the tax-free grubstake are the same. And Sally behind the bar sizes them up — a gentle priestess, the English nurse who became part-time barmaid, part-time stringer for a London newspaper and, finally, part-time mortician to the expatriate community. When the sad conviviality is over, she ships them home in boxes — the ones who gin or vodka themselves to a lunchtime death.

Dead or alive, they do not linger long here. When a Bahraini clerk or engineer or computer operator can do the job, the expatriate is expatriated. Again, that canny instinct for the future. They want to become their own homogenous city-state, like Switzerland. To them it means more than simply a healthy respect for money; it means technical savvy and a business environment that welcomes the refugees from other people's heavy fiscal regulation. But most of all, it means an easygoing stability of not getting caught up in the steamroller of other people's passions. The weeks we were here, the Saudis were cutting off the heads of their dissidents, the Iranians were going noisily crazy — but in Bahrain people tended to their business and their pleasures with equal contentment.

On Fridays, the Moslem Sunday, they venture out on a most extraordinary version of the drive in the country. The younger bloods play their familiar games in Bahrain's mini-desert. (Sound of automobile engines) And the more sedate perform a strange, unchoreographed ballet at maybe 12 miles an hour. Round and up and down with a determined aimless purpose they go. There is some socializing car to car, but mainly it is automotive strolling at the pace of a weary camel.

And down in the bazaars they dream the dreams that merchants dream. The market shows its usual manic optimism. The only exception, perhaps, an increased interest in gold, just in case the Russians decide to get even pushier. After all, a pocketful is worth a zillion Japanese stereos, and it's a lot more portable.

(Music)

But otherwise, all the goodies of East and West and places in between still caravan their way through Bahrain, just as they have for five or six thousand years. Their Gulf neighbors went from tending camels to tending fortunes. The Bahrainis simply went from business to business to business, always a half-step ahead of history, and a part of them holding firmly to the past. It is for them an easy marriage. They have no pretentions about being anything more than a corner-store country with very good connections with all the giants, a healthy understanding of their place in the world.

A fatalistic Saudi once remarked, "My father drove a camel, I drive a Cadillac. My son drives a plane, my grandson a supersonic jet. My great-grandson will drive a camel." If that is so, he'll have to go to Bahrain to buy it. Count on it.

God and Mammon

NORMAN GORIN, PRODUCER

MIKE WALLACE: This past week, the issue of church and state once again reached the Supreme Court. It was a case brought to the court by the wealthy Worldwide Church of God, based in Pasadena, California. And what they were asking the Court to do, and what the Court refused to do, was to rule that the California attorney general's investigation of possible misuse of church money violated the church's constitutional guarantees about freedom of religion. The result is that the California attorney general can now continue his investigation into the church's finances.

When we broadcast "God and Mammon" a year ago, we described it as a tale of backbiting and power struggle, of fat expense accounts and disinheritance, in a church whose 100,000 members each year contribute $80 million.* And that is more money than is collected by Billy Graham and Oral Roberts combined. It is the story of Herbert W. Armstrong, founder of the Worldwide Church of God; of his son, Garner Ted, once thought of as the heir apparent, who has now been cast out of the church by his father; and of an unlikely church figure, an accountant, lawyer and businessman, chief adviser to Herbert Armstrong, Stanley Rader. Finally, it is the story of how the State of California is trying to hold the Worldwide Church of God accountable for the tax-exempt money that pours into its Pasadena headquarters. The California attorney general, as we said, wants the church to open its books so they can find out if Herbert Armstrong and Stanley Rader have been siphoning off church money for their own personal use. That is a charge that incenses Herbert W. Armstrong.

HERBERT W. ARMSTRONG: If the state and the judicial system should succeed in this present action, there will be in actual fact no separation of church and state left in the United States of America.

WALLACE: Stanley Rader is equally incensed. It is, says Rader, as though the State of California were to question the integrity of Jesus Christ Himself.

Do you believe him to be an apostle of Jesus Christ?

STANLEY RADER: No question in my mind. He is the most amazing human being that God has ever placed on this earth in 2,000 years. No question.

WALLACE: In other words, he is the equivalent of the men who sat with Jesus Christ at the Last Supper?

RADER: In my opinion, yes.

WALLACE: But Herbert Armstrong's son, Garner Ted, is not so sure.

GARNER TED ARMSTRONG: I certainly do believe that my father is a minister of Jesus Christ, but I don't believe that he is the one and only apostle, no.

WALLACE: Since being cast out by his father, Garner Ted has left Pasadena for his own church in Tyler, Texas, whence he now preaches the gospel over the radio. Garner Ted has misgivings, he says, about the fiscal practices of his father's Worldwide Church of God.

Is there a money scandal of major proportions brewing somewhere under the surface?

---

*Originally broadcast on April 15, 1979.

GARNER TED ARMSTRONG: It depends on how much is brought to light by the current investigation. My own personal apprehensions are that there is (indistinct) —

WALLACE: A scandal, not just spending in the wrong places by the wrong people? It's, in effect, stealing.

GARNER TED ARMSTRONG: I better reserve comment on that. I'm just going to have to wait and see what the legal processes discover in it.

WALLACE: Well, 60 MINUTES set out to find out what it could about the finances of the Worldwide Church of God, but we couldn't talk to Herbert W. Armstrong; Stanley Rader wouldn't let us. Mr. Rader, however, did consent to talk to us; told us he would answer any question that we cared to ask. And first off, he took us on a tour of the church headquarters in Pasadena.

RADER: That auditorium you couldn't reproduce today for $40 million.

WALLACE: These buildings are testimony to the faith and the money the 100,000 followers of Herbert Armstrong have invested in him over the years. Here on 40 green acres sits the spiritual and administrative home of his church. Here too is his Ambassador College that he established nearly 30 years ago to train his followers for "the work," as he calls it.

How much is this whole complex — all of the land, all of the buildings, the entire installation — worth?

RADER: Well, I would say conservatively somewhere between a hundred and twenty and a hundred and fifty million dollars.

WALLACE: All that wealth is administered from this executive suite in Pasadena. This is where Stanley Rader controls the purse strings, for he is treasurer of the church. His office would be the envy of any corporate executive. His job puts a multi-million-dollar jet plane at his disposal to fly him anywhere in the world. And on the ground he is provided with a limousine and chauffeur. The church bought and maintains for him this home in Tucson, Arizona. His other home, near his office in Pasadena, California, is filled with expensive works of art. And he's not at all loath to talk about his salary, which is some $200,000 a year.

RADER: Two hundred thousand plus.

WALLACE: Plus —

RADER: My — my entire employee be— benefit package will bring me closer to three hundred thousand.

WALLACE: And his contract runs to the year 2003. Where do all these tens of millions of dollars come from? They come in response to Herbert Armstrong's interpretation of the Bible, in which Moses says that God commands man to tithe his crop and his herd to the Lord. Thus Herbert Armstrong insists that a member tithe, that is, give one-tenth of his gross income to the church every year. But the giving doesn't stop with the first tithe. There is a second tithe, too; and every third year an extra third tithe, not to mention Mr. Armstrong's pleas to church members for special offerings several times a year. A loyal church member can wind up donating as much as one-third of his gross income to the Worldwide Church of God.

And no steward of God's money within the Worldwide Church of God wields more power than Stanley Rader. Since his modest beginning back in 1957 as the church's accountant, he has managed to climb to the top of the financial ladder of the church; and along the way, he has at times had a financial interest in private firms doing business with the church.

Do you know how much your expenses in the Worldwide Church of God were during 1978?

RADER: I probably incurred expenses for the — for the church probably in the neighborhood of $250,000 or more.

WALLACE: Rader spends that money, he says, to spread the gospel. And a far more lavish expense account was authorized by Rader for a Japanese gentleman who served as advance man for Armstrong and Rader in their worldwide search for converts.

Who is Professor Osamu Gatoh?

RADER: Gotoh. Gotoh. G-O-T-O-H —

WALLACE: Who is he?

RADER: — an acronym for "Go to Heaven."

WALLACE: In a period of about three months in 1975, there's an expenditure of a hundred and seven thousand dollars, all but twelve thousand of it by Gotoh. This is a church organization.

RADER: Yes, Mike, absolutely. He spent on Mr. Armstrong's behalf probably around three-quarters of a million dollars a year, on the average.

WALLACE: To do what?

RADER: To spread the gospel of Jesus Christ.

GARNER TED ARMSTRONG: The only way Gotoh ever spread the word is because some of those dollars say "In God We Trust." He was spending upwards of $813,000 in one year to give away everything from worldwide trips to Japanese senators, which to me is like a miniature Koreagate.

WALLACE: How many converts did your father —

GARNER TED ARMSTRONG: Zero that I know of in Japan.

RADER: No, Mike, our policy was we would make friends wherever we went in order to help us to spread the gospel of Jesus Christ. Mike, if you had a man like Gotoh, you'd be twice as effective as you are today.

WALLACE: We noticed an $8,000 expense item listed to a Dr. Singh.

Why would Gotoh pay for Dr. Singh: $8,000, TWA, a trip Amsterdam-Tokyo-Amsterdam?

RADER: Because he went from Amsterdam to Tokyo to appear — to appear on Mr. Armstrong's behalf, and he went with his wife back and forth. Two round-trip tickets, first-class.

WALLACE: I see.

RADER: He's a member of the International Court of Justice at the Hague.

WALLACE: Do you know something, Mr. Rader? Dr. Singh told us he was too busy; he couldn't make that trip to Tokyo. Never appeared.

RADER: I'm not surprised. I'm not surprised that's what he would say.

WALLACE: You mean he was there?

RADER: Yes, he was.

WALLACE: So he lied to us?

RADER: Yes.

WALLACE: And there were also expenses for gifts that Mr. Armstrong himself carried to foreign dignitaries.
For Steuben Glass, six crystal pillar griffins, $12,000. Gifts.

RADER: Did — did you know, Mike, that Dwight Eisenhower was President of the United States for eight years, and every time he visited a head of state, he gave a piece of Steuben. Did you know that?

WALLACE: But — are you saying —

RADER: Did you know Mr. Armstrong —

WALLACE: Are you suggesting that Herbert Armstrong is a head of state?

RADER: Exactly.

WALLACE: Oh.

RADER: Exactly. You're finally —

WALLACE: And you're the secretary of state?

RADER: You got it. By God, you've got it, Mike. That's it. That's the whole key. This is a state, and we are representatives of God. And I am Mr. Armstrong's secretary of state.

WALLACE: But in truth he is closer to being secretary of the treasury, administrator of a tax-exempt charitable trust. And it was the way he has handled church funds that has prompted some members — dissidents of the church, Rader calls them — to seek out California's special deputy attorney general. Hillel Chodos.

HILLEL CHODOS: They had become concerned, especially in recent months, that church funds were being misused, by Mr. Rader particularly, perhaps Mr. Armstrong. And they had obtained some evidence of that misuse.

WALLACE: The attorney general says the State of California not just has the right, but it has the duty, to protect the assets of a charitable trust.

RADER: He says much more than that, Mike, and I promised the congregation of this church that I'm going to make him eat every one of the words. He has said the property of the church belongs to the state. He has said the church belongs to the state. He has said the church has no rights, the brethren have no rights, the church doesn't even have a right to defend itself. And I promise you, Mike, and I promise your audience, he's going to eat every word, every one of them.

WALLACE: It was not only Stanley Rader and Herbert Armstrong and Professor Gotoh who spent the church's money extravagantly. Garner Ted admits that he did too before he was cast out.

GARNER TED ARMSTRONG: It's awfully hard for me to avoid being painted with the same brush, and I do have a certain degree of culpability in the past because, after all, I was part of it.

WALLACE: You were open enough with Garner Ted Armstrong to offer him what was in effect a $50,000-a-year contract of what seems on the face of it to be hush money —

RADER: Oh, no.

WALLACE: — if he would agree never to release, divulge, disclose, make available or in any other manner make known any such information or documentation in perpetuity which you have within your knowledge, possession —

RADER: Exactly.

WALLACE: — custody or control —

RADER: Exactly.

WALLACE: — et cetera, et cetera.

RADER: Exactly.

WALLACE: Sounds like $50,000 a year worth of hush money.

RADER: Well, you can call it hush money if you want to. I said to keep his bad mouth shut.

GARNER TED ARMSTRONG: I knew the amounts of money going for the overseas trips. I knew the kind of money Gotoh was spending. I knew the kind of money that Rader was spending. I knew about his Beverly Hills home. I knew about the leasing corporation, Gateway Publishing, Worldwide Adverti— on and on and on it went. And practically everywhere you look, if the church has business it is — is performing or bills that it's paying, well, somewhere Rader is involved. How can this be? Why should it be?

WALLACE: And Attorney Chodos would like answers too. For several months he's been trying to get a close-up look at the church's financial records. But Stanley Rader, also an attorney, has resisted by every legal means. He claims that what the State of Calfornia is trying to do violates constitutional guarantees of freedom of religion.
Herbert Armstrong in effect has the right to do with the church what he wants?

RADER: You bet your life. You bet your life, because he is responsible and account-able to God.

WALLACE: As far as you're concerned, there's no constitutional issue involved here, the separation of church and state?

CHODOS: No. Let me explain what I'm talking about. I think people have a constitu-tional right to be stupid, if they want to. They have a right to be generous, if they want to. And they have a right to give money to Herbert Armstrong to light cigars with, if that's what they want to do. And nobody would interfere with them, except for the fact that they have elected to do it with a substantial tax subsidy from the rest of the public on the premise that they are a lawful charitable organization.

WALLACE: Stanley Rader was not a church member until 1975, when Herbert Armstrong baptized him in a hotel bathtub in Hong Kong. And what worries some church members is that Rader sees himself as heir apparent to the leadership of the church. Herbert Armstrong has privately voiced those same concerns.
Just a little while ago you were the bête noire of Herbert Armstrong. Did you know that?

RADER: I? When —

WALLACE: Yes.

RADER: — when was this?

WALLACE: Oh, early January.

RADER: No.

WALLACE: Don't believe it?

RADER: Positive.

WALLACE: Let me quote Herbert Armstrong.

RADER: This is from Mr. Armstrong? To whom?

WALLACE: Herbert Armstrong.

RADER: To whom?

WALLACE: I can't reveal —

RADER: You're sure that's Mr. Armstrong's letter?

WALLACE: He was talking about your attempt to step into the leader's shoes. He said, "He's deliberately trying to put himself there. I don't want to think that anyone in — has their eyes on fifty, sixty, seventy million dollars a year, but that is quite a magnet."

RADER: You really think Mr. Armstrong said that to somebody?

WALLACE: You don't?

RADER: I don't think so.

WALLACE: Next we read a portion of a letter Herbert Armstrong told our source that he was drafting to send to Stanley Rader:
"I have to say candidly, Stan — for we have to face the facts — that very near unanimously, neither the ministry nor the lay members of the church will accept you as their spiritual leader."

RADER: Now, you're saying that that — you have that in a letter from Mr. Armstrong to someone?

WALLACE: You don't believe it?

RADER: Positive.

WALLACE: Positive?

RADER: Positive.

WALLACE: Can we play you his voice saying those things and see what you think?

RADER: Yes, of course.

HERBERT W. ARMSTRONG (audio tape recording):   — that he is deliberately trying to put himself there. I don't know. I — I don't want to think that anyone has their eyes on fifty, sixty, seventy million dollars a year. That is quite a magnet, you know.

WALLACE: The tape we played was a portion of two telephone conversations with Herbert Armstrong which our source had recorded surreptitiously prior to 60 MINUTES beginning its investigation. In this second excerpt, played for Mr. Rader, Herbert Armstrong is reading to our source that letter he's about to send to Stanley Rader, asking Rader to step down from any church posts he holds that might put him in line as successor to Armstrong, but inviting him to stay on as Armstrong's personal adviser.

HERBERT W. ARMSTRONG (audio tape recording): I have just written Stan a letter: "I have to say candidly, Stan — for we have to face the fact — that the — the — that very near unanimously, neither the ministry nor the lay members of the church will accept you as their spiritual leader."

RADER: Now, I say you have acquired this by illegal means. I intend to have my attorneys today not only sue you if you use this — but I mean this, Allan. I want you to go to the district attorney today. That tape is not a complete tape. He — there was a seven-page letter. I'll go to any court in any land and prove to you that the tape is not a complete record. I've already made the letter public to the entirety of the church, and it's been printed.

Mike, look, I think you'd better scrap everything, because you're on my list, okay? You're ne— you're never going to live it down, Mike, I guarantee it. I'll use it as a springboard to show just what the press is, because you're contemptible. I mean this; not for the camera. I'd like you to get out of here, immediately. I hope you got it, and I hope you have the guts to use it.

WALLACE: As we said, Herbert Armstrong did write to Stanley Rader, asking him to step down, and Mr. Rader did publish that communication in a church newsletter. But several weeks later, apparently Mr. Armstrong had a change of heart with Rader, because he defended him passionately before a meeting of the ministers.

HERBERT W. ARMSTRONG: You just don't like him. But I do. And I'm going to keep the man that God gives me, if I want him, and nobody is going to say nay to me.

WALLACE: As we said earlier, we tried to interview Mr. Armstrong, but Mr. Rader would not permit it. Why did Herbert Armstrong apparently change his mind and defend Stanley Rader? Well, another portion of the tape we played for Mr. Rader might offer a clue.

HERBERT W. ARMSTRONG (audio tape recording): Well, I don't know whether Stan will just go along, or whether he's just going to rant and rave and just throw everything overboard. He had made one statement about telling the world what he knows. Now, I don't know what he thinks he knows that could harm the work. Frankly, I don't know of anything that he knows that could do it.

GARNER TED ARMSTRONG: For years these deep-seated jealousies and resentments were just there. Now — boom! — they've all exploded, they've erupted like Vesuvius, and they're out in the open. So, I'm saying that at least some of the people on the top are being a little bit honest for a change.

WALLACE: Do you know what you're describing?

GARNER TED ARMSTRONG: Yes, human nature.

WALLACE: You're also describing a big corporation where everybody is fighting for advantage, for −

GARNER TED ARMSTRONG: Just like any incorporated —

WALLACE: − for salaries −

GARNER TED ARMSTRONG: Sure.

WALLACE: − for perks, for ambition, for power.

GARNER TED ARMSTRONG: Right. Sure.

WALLACE: What in the world is churchly about all that?

GARNER TED ARMSTRONG: Good question. Not one thing.

WALLACE: It seems to me, Mr. Armstrong, that your father and you and Stanley Rader conceivably are giving religion a bad name.

GARNER TED ARMSTRONG: I think that's a good point. I think that over the last few years the Worldwide Church of God, because of its incredible internal difficulties, has tended to give a bad name to religion. I think it's a tragedy.

WALLACE: At the end of our broadcast a year ago, we reported that the IRS was investigating Mr. Rader for tax evasion. Recently, though, the IRS has discontinued that investigation, and has brought no charges against Rader, though the IRS reserves the right to reopen that inquiry. But as we said, the Supreme Court this past week refused to block California's continuing investigation into the alleged misuse of tax-exempt contributions by the church's leaders. Stanley Rader's answer to that Supreme Court ruling? "We will follow God's law, not man's."

Cottage For Sale
WILLIAM K. McCLURE, PRODUCER

HARRY REASONER: Back in 1969, we did a story about a house that was for sale for $1.2 million. These days in some residential areas that would be regarded as a bargain. It's hard to remember that only 11 years ago that price alone was almost enough to justify the story. But there were other reasons, as you'll see as we go back to February 4th, 1969 on 60 MINUTES.

Some kind of cottages are more of a sales problem than others. We heard about one from a real estate agency called Previews, Incorporated, which specializes in unusual property. The unusual property that caught our eye is owned by a handsome and devoted couple in their seventies. It's called Moulin de la Tuilerie, and we thought it would be fun to go to France and let the owners show us around. So we did, and they did.

You start for Le Moulin de la Tuilerie with a 45-minute drive from Paris. You get to the house by turning off on a country lane that is "sans issue," which I judge to mean roughly "dead end." There's a feeling of walking back in history at the old gate, which could have been here when the establishment was a working mill, or before that, when it was a tile factory.

(Knocks on door) Bonjour, madame.

WOMAN: Bonjour, monsieur . . .

REASONER: Inside the gate, what you see is not one house but several, a charming setting for a French historical movie — Cyrano or Roxanne or D'Artagnan would be at home here, as are apparently some small dogs, which you are supposed not to beware of, but considerate of. The French ambience is unmistakable; but the owners, although they've lived here for 15 years, are an Anglo-American expatriate couple, hero and heroine of the most famous and perhaps the most enduring romance of the twentieth century — the Duke and Duchess of Windsor.

Good afternoon, Your Highness.

It is 32 years now since the Duke, then Edward VIII of Great Britain, left his throne to marry Wallis Simpson, the American divorcee.

This is the — what you would call the main house?

DUKE OF WINDSOR: This is the main house, yes, where the Duchess and I live. We have two rooms. There are two staff rooms, and then we've got the big living room upstairs and the dining room.

REASONER: How much land do you have, Your Highness.

DUKE: Twenty-three acres. The mill was renovated in 1773, before the French Revolution.

REASONER: You've done something to it since then, I trust? I mean, you have put in some plumbing, and —

DUKE: We've done a great deal. We've put in four septic tanks, bathrooms for every — every room, and proper electricity.

REASONER: Is it a comfortable place to operate, as a housewife?

DUCHESS: I find it a very easy place to run, because everything's very near. For instance, there's the kitchen window, and there's the dining room. It's only this far. So it's quite an easy house to run. It's a small house.

REASONER: I suppose I should say that I probably don't have the money for the place, but I would like to look at it. It seems very attractive.

DUKE: Glad to show you around.

REASONER: We entered the main building under a marker that established the place was rebuilt before the United States was a nation. I was impressed, even if the dogs were not. This is one of two main salons at the mill, and the one that gets the most wintertime use — for cards and conversation and letter writing. Just next to it is a small room with a television set. There's only one set in the place, but considering French television, that's probably enough.

I'm curious. Why are you selling, Your Highness?

DUCHESS: Now, as we have some ground around us in Paris, it seems foolish to motor 20 minutes. We'd like to go, maybe have a house in the sun somewhere. You know, we're no longer young. We need sun.

REASONER: Why did you buy here, Your Highness? What attracted you to this place?

DUKE: I think the garden especially — I've always been interested in gardening. Gardened in England. I even made over the garden to Government House, Nassau, when I was governor. And I — I had a great yearning to have a garden again.

DUCHESS: And this is quite different from anything the Duke had ever had before. I suppose it's the furthest thing from a palace that one could find.

REASONER: Well, it's a — it's a unique kind of palace, in any event.

DUCHESS: It's a rustic palace.

REASONER: One of the first things the Duke of Windsor did when he and the Duchess settled in France was to establish what the French call an English garden — fonder of growth and rambling than French plantings are. It may or may not be a wistful sign that he misses where he came from.

The room with the reminders of where he came from and who he was is in a building of its own next to the English garden. It is filled with the objects British noblemen of military background cherish. You remember suddenly that this man served four years in World War I, and knew Winston Churchill when they were both in disfavor with the establishment. The Duke has kept almost everything, including copies of the uninspired addresses of welcome heard on countless royal visits and dedications; and other more exotic memorabilia.

DUKE: And that's my great-grandmother Queen Victoria's christening present in 1894. I often wished that she'd given me a more — more useful christening present in the form of a nice cup that one could have used on the table, but it's — it is an interesting piece of Victoriana.

REASONER: Here's a picture of you and your father and —

DUKE: Oh, yes, and my brother.

REASONER: How old were you, then, when you became King?

DUKE: Forty-two.

REASONER: And you were King for —

DUKE: Ten months.

REASONER: Is that long enough to be King?

DUKE: No. (Laughs)

Here's a — here's a medal that was — was struck upon my first visit to America in 1919.

REASONER: That was when you cut — cut a wide swath as probably the world's most eligible bachelor, isn't that so?

DUKE: Yes, or — or in 1924. I remember some — various songs written at that time. Oh!

REASONER: Was that fun?

DUKE: Oh, yes, wonderful.

REASONER: Did you ever meet any American girls at that time that you felt serious about?

DUKE: A great many. I didn't feel too seriously about them, but I met — well, I met a lot.

REASONER: Not until the mid-thirties did one particular American girl make him feel serious. In his private apartment are pictures of Wallis Simpson as she looked then.

I think this picture here of the Duchess, those two, are the first pictures that America saw of her after the news of the romance.

DUKE: They were taken — were taken in 1935 or '36, I guess.

REASONER: Hair styles have changed, but the face looks the same.

DUKE: Yes, the face is the same.

REASONER: I take it that this is not the key to the bathroom or anything, is it?

DUKE (chuckling):   No. It's — that's a souvenir from the top of the Empire State Building.

REASONER: When were you there?

DUKE: It was a thermometer. The first time I went to the top of the Empire State was with Al Smith — Governor Al Smith.

REASONER: What about the mugs that you keep on the shelf?

DUKE: Well, those mugs were made for the — for my coronation in 1937.

REASONER: The coronation that did not take place?

DUKE: That's right. And then, there's one there of Neville Chamberlain when he came back from Munich — "Peace in our time."

REASONER: I remember "Peace in our time." (Duke laughs) That takes me to this game of "if." If you had not abdicated, how would that have changed history, do you think?

DUKE: As — as a constitutional monarch, I don't believe it'd have change— it would have changed it at all. I might have tried to exert some — some — some, say, advice or pressure to try and avoid the Second World War, but it was very unlikely that I should have succeeded.

REASONER: So that the changes in your life and the big decisions have been personal rather than historical?

DUKE: Sure, yes. I — I would say it was entirely personal.

REASONER: No matter who sits on that throne —

DUKE: I said in my book I was very sorry to — to leave. I wanted to stay. I did my best to stay, but — (pause) — it didn't work out.

REASONER: One reason it didn't work out, presumably, was opposition to his marriage from Queen Mary. Ironically, her picture is among the many personal items in the Duchess's private apartment. In this crazy-quilt castle, the Duchess's room is across the hall and up a little flight of stairs from the Duke's. It's full of remembrances, a feminine room: tasteful, warm and luxurious, as his is masculine and almost austere. As he keeps a special picture of her, she keeps one of him. Down a steep stairs from the main salon and the two private apartments is a small dining room.
Is this the room where you have most of your meals, Your Highness?

DUCHESS: No, we hardly ever have anything here. We eat all over the house. We hardly ever do. Occasionally. But it's more fun to have tables in the different rooms.

REASONER: This is a handsome room.

DUCHESS: It's the most convenient room to have food in, but we make it a little more inconvenient by having it in other places.

REASONER: What about the kitchen?

DUCHESS: It's an excellent kitchen. Excellent. Great. We have all the modern things in it. It isn't an old-fashioned kitchen at all.

REASONER: And it will be turned over intact to a purchaser?

DUCHESS: Oh, yes. Absolutely. I wouldn't take anything out of it. It's all made for here you know. It fits in.

REASONER: What about this area of France? Is it — is there good shopping here? Can you get good food?

DUCHESS: You can, because it's grown up so much since we've been here. But we generally bring everything out from Paris. We could get anything in an emergency, because it's — it's grown so, the village, and you see the apartment houses as you come by. And they have a supermarket and all that. But we generally bring things out.

REASONER: Do you keep a pretty close eye on the shopping and the meal planning in your household?

DUCHESS: I do all the meals, but I don't think I can keep an eye on the shopping. That's done differently.

REASONER: How many people — if I bought it, how many people would it take to run it?

DUCHESS: Well, it would —

REASONER: You'd need a staff of, what, a hundred? (Laughter)

DUCHESS: A little exag— where would you find a hundred, firstly? (Laughter) But it would certainly take two gardeners. And then I think it would take from three to four in the house, depending whether you had children that had to be looked after. But I think you could run it easily, I mean very well, with four, and with three comfortably.

REASONER: Would it be a good house for children, Your Highness?

DUCHESS: I think it would be a marvelous house for children, yes, because they'd have so much to do, and the grounds are amusing with the stream all around and so forth.

REASONER: What kind of life do you lead here, as distinct from being in Paris or being in New York? What's different about living out here?

DUCHESS: Rest —

REASONER: Rest.

DUCHESS: — and quiet. I mean, it's very quiet here. You never hear a sound. And then we have our friends out, and we live a very simple life here.

REASONER: Are you going to miss the place?

DUCHESS: Yes, I'll miss it a great deal. But I haven't got the same interest in the garden that the Duke has. I play house here.

REASONER: What about some of the nuts and bolts of it? Are taxes high here?

DUKE: Not so very.

REASONER: Not too bad?

DUKE: Not too bad.

DUCHESS: It's high enough.

REASONER: High enough? Well, they are everywhere.

DUCHESS: Yes.

REASONER: I assume that the statue of Queen Victoria and things like that will go with you, but how much of what's here will stay here?

DUCHESS: Well, quite a bit of the furniture would stay. All the beds and the dressing table and that sort of thing. Certain pieces in this room I would take, but not too many.

REASONER: In other words, I could move in and cook a meal and sleep that night?

DUCHESS: Absolutely, yes. Comfortably, I hope.

REASONER: Well, I suppose, as you say in real estate conversations, I will talk to my wife and let you know, Your Highness. (Laughter)

DUCHESS: Exactly. Exactly.

REASONER: We found out the asking price on the property. It is $1,200,000, most of the furniture and ambience included. In that range, you don't ask how much down.

In the last 11 years, things have changed, of course. The Duke of Windsor is dead; the Duchess is very ill. And the house is again for sale. It will be auctioned later this month. A possibly encouraging anti-inflation note. The expected sale price: still $1.2 million.

Letters

DAN RATHER: Quite a bit of mail came in last week about our story on the inspection procedures at a South Texas nuclear plant under construction by the firm of Brown & Root. One of those we heard from was the president of the Texas Building and Construction Trades Council. He said, "Brown and Root . . . does not have a contract with any building trades union (and that may be) one of the major reasons why there have been so many construction faults on the job."

Another viewer said, "By neglecting to mention the fact that the majority of nuclear powerhouses are being built by union labor you are leading people to believe all nukes are being built as shoddily as the (non-union) one (you showed last week)."

A viewer who said he had been manager of quality engineering at a reactor in the State of Washington wrote, "The (Nuclear Regulatory Commission) has no idea what goes on in those plants. I never talked to a NRC inspector in nine months on the project . . . The falsification of records (and the) intimidation of inspectors (as you reported in your story) will kill the nuclear industry — an industry we need."

But there was also a letter that said, "Once again . . . 60 MINUTES revealed its insane nuclear bias . . . You are pathetic in your ignorance, arrogant in your assertions and hypocritical in your intent. You smugly condemn others for doing shoddy work to make a fast profit while you cynically milk the anti-nuclear hysteria to maintain ratings for the greater glory of CBS."

Finally, about our story on health spas, a story we filmed back in 1974, a viewer wrote, "While you were lavish in your display of feminine flesh bobbing about in the healing waters . . . Mike Wallace (was) covered in soap bubbles . . . I have no doubt that in the current atmosphere of sexual equality, if that episode had been filmed (in 1980) we'd have seen a lot more of Mr. Wallace. Right?"

JUNE 15, 1980

What Johnny Can't Read

NORMAN GORIN, PRODUCER

MIKE WALLACE: Who decides what textbooks Jane and Johnny can read in school? Where do those books come from? Who chooses them? And most crucial of all, who decides what shall be in them? Traditionally, that decision has been left to the education professionals who spend about $700 million a year in tax money to buy public school textbooks. But now the people whose money is being spent want to get into the act; ethnic groups, who want to be represented fairly in what our children read; minorities, who object to racism in textbooks; pressure groups; feminists, who want to get rid of sexual stereotypes.

But there is one woman down in Texas who says that if all these assorted groups can have their say about our textbooks, then she wants the views of the silent majority — her views — represented, too. Her name is Norma Gabler, and she is formidable.

She has been called education's public enemy number one. Who is she? Well, she is simply a housewife, the mother of three sons, and a grandmother, too. And though she has never gone to college, when Norma Gabler speaks, the education establishment of the State of Texas listens.

NORMA GABLER: Every child should not have to sit in the classroom and read profanity and gutter language. You have an opportunity to read the textbooks. Go to Austin and tell them what you don't want in the books. It's your money, it's your children, and you have that right. And the State of Texas . . .

WALLACE: At this parents' meeting in Henderson, Texas, some poems taught in elementary schools were discussed, and Mrs. Gabler found one poem from the inner-city *Mother Goose* especially offensive, for it contained a frequently-used vulgarity.

All right, what's wrong with it?

NORMA: Well, I — you'd better not read page eight. Now you read page eight, but don't read — don't read out loud.

WALLACE: Boys and girls come out to play,
The moon doth shine as bright as day;
Leave your supper and leave your sleep,
And join your playfellows in the street;

> Come with a whoop and come with a call,
> Up (word left out) against the wall.

And you know what word I left out.

MEL GABLER: If you put it in a schoolbook, you're condoning it.

NORMA: I don't want my kid to use gutter language to — to express it.

WOMAN: That's right.

WALLACE: She worries not only about what's going on in Texas, but she and her husband, Mel, have embarked on a kind of crusade, warning parents all across America to watch out for what's in their children's textbooks.

NORMA: Every time they're trying to clean up the television, I said clean up your textbooks first, because your textbooks — your children are a captive audience. They don't have the right to get up and walk out. Your television, you can turn the dial or you can turn it off. You don't turn off a classroom.

Fifteen years ago, parents wouldn't put up with what's going on in the classrooms today.

WALLACE: What does she find intolerable in classrooms today?

NORMA: We found in the writing of today's history they have played up the faults of the great men and played down their great deeds.

WALLACE: And in eight American history books they looked at?

NORMA: We found that Nathan Hale's speech was in none of the eight. And it all goes back, I think, to one thing: is that our children are being denied the right to learn of their own heritage.

WALLACE: And Mrs. Gabler quarrels with how these books teach youngsters good citizenship.

NORMA: To be a better citizen, they decided that you could be that by how — learning how to apply for welfare at the age of 14. Now I've suggested they give them a job application. I did not know that the dirtiest word in English language was W-O-R-K.

WALLACE: Now, just how important are the Gablers?

PROFESSOR EDWARD JENKINSON: They probably have more influence on the use of textbooks in this country than any other two people.

WALLACE: Professor Edward Jenkinson of the University of Indiana heads up the Committee Against Censorship of the National Council of Teachers of English.

PROFESSOR JENKINSON: They've learned very, very well that if a book is not successful in Texas, the publisher will have a very, very hard time selling it elsewhere.

RICHARD CARROLL: In a ten-year period, the last ten years, they've become more and more of a force for publishers to contend with.

WALLACE: Richard Carroll is president of Ginn & Company, one of the largest textbook publishers, who says that to sell his books in the lucrative Texas market he must make them palatable to Mrs. Gabler.

CARROLL: Publishers have come around to almost playing a guessing game with her and trying to anticipate what her — her worst pet peeves are.

THOMAS MURPHY: If we want to sell the book, we are either faced with the dilemma of changing the material or not changing the material and se— and taking the risk of not selling the material.

WALLACE: Tom Murphy is vice president of the textbook division of CBS-owned Holt, Rinehart. Has Murphy's publishing house ever changed material to suit the Gablers?

MURPHY: Yes, we did. Sometimes we do change textbooks. All publishers do.

WALLACE: And these changes, made just to please the Gablers in Texas, will wind up in those textbooks all across the nation, because it's too expensive to put out more than one edition.

MURPHY: We have to find a book that is most acceptable in most places. That's what it boils down to.

PROFESSOR JENKINSON: I don't think that two people should have that power, that degree of influence. I — I'm more concerned about what they don't like than what they like, because what they don't like is legion.

NORMA: Another thing, I'll tell you what — I'll share with you what a — what an English teacher — she was curriculum chairman for one of our large counties in Texas — and she said, "Mrs. Gabler, I would like very much to go back to traditional grammar, but I do not have a single teacher in my entire county that knows how to teach it."

MAN: I asked my child something about the parts of speech that I learned in English, in grammar. He said, "What's that, Daddy?" I said, "I'm talking about nouns and pronouns and adjectives and adverbs and interjections." "Interjections? What's that, Daddy?" And we want somebody to tell us what is it, who is it, or what has been created, to rule out reading, writing and arithmetic?

WOMAN: The children are taught that what the parents say is old-fashioned.

WALLACE: Now, in what part of the country are most of today's textbooks published?

NORMA: I hate to tell you it's from the East — in the Boston, New York area.

WALLACE: Fifteen-hundred miles southwest of the liberal Eastern establishment home of the American textbook publishing business lies the home of Norma and Mel Gabler. This is a fortress of conservatism here on Berry Lane, in Longview, Texas. For 18 years, Norma and Mel Gabler have been fighting the battle of the textbooks. They have been putting American textbooks on trial. And inside that modest ranch house there is a virtual factory of propaganda.

What began as a part-time mission to get rid of objectionable material they found in their young sons' schoolbooks has expanded into a full-time calling, and along the way Mel and Norma Gabler have formed a tax-exempt foundation called "Educational Research Analysts" to carry on their work. They and their assistants examine the products of the textbook industry with a fine-tooth comb, and then the Gablers send reviews of these textbooks to anyone, in return for a nominal, tax-deductible contribution. And when Norma goes on the road to preach her gospel, her expenses are picked up by the group that invited her. They reported a total income last year under $60,000, yet rumors persist that much of their money comes from right-wing sources like the H. L. Hunt Foundation.

NORMA: Now I want you to show me where there's anything from H. L. Hunt. In fact, I have never met the man. I'd love to have all the money that they claim they do. We do with hard work what other people do with money.

WALLACE: In Texas, by state law, any publisher who wants to sell his books to the public schools must make copies available to regional libraries months in advance of state approval hearings, and Norma and Mel Gabler check out these books carefully to see what's in them. It's like studying for a final exam for the Gablers — preparing their objections to these textbooks for the annual hearings of the State Textbook Adoption Committee.

MEL: We see year after year the Defense Department takes a big slice of our budget. Now —

NORMA: Yeah, but where is the balance? After all, now, do the — I — I cannot find anything in the book, in reading it, that it says anything about what they spend on welfare.

WALLACE: Norma and Mel make no secret about their political persuasion: it is conservative.

MEL: We do not want imposed on the students just our viewpoint, but we feel it's totally unfair to have our viewpoint totally censored when at least half of the United States might be considered favorable toward our viewpoint.

NORMA: It doesn't make a difference if it's government or history or literature, where's the balance?

WALLACE: Working with them in their converted kitchen is Sheila Harrelson, a 24-year-old college graduate who screened one of the textbooks on government up for approval this year.

SHEILA HARRELSON: They have a whole column in discussion of the women's rights movement and how women have gotten involved in politics. The whole book is written as if all women agree with this position, and that's simply not true, and so for that reason it is biased.

NORMA: I was appalled when I read, for a first course in American history, for fifth-grade students, ten-year-old or eleven-year-old children, about Marilyn Monroe, a sex symbol, and only mentioned George Washington. I said, "It didn't even tell me about Martha." They forgot her. I said, "After all now, Martha did have some part of George Washington's life." I mean, if you want to have a woman, why don't we put in Martha? But, no, we're going to put in a sex symbol.

WALLACE: After Mrs. Gabler called our attention to this history book — *Search for Freedom*, published by Macmillan Company — we looked at it more closely. And what did we find? Not only does it devote seven pages to Marilyn Monroe, with nothing about Martha Washington, but it contains no mention of Lyndon Johnson or Richard Nixon. Even the assassination of John Kennedy goes unmentioned. We wanted to find out why seven pages for Marilyn Monroe and nothing about Kennedy, Nixon or Johnson. But the Macmillan Company simply refused to talk to us about it on camera.

In Texas, high school students are required to take a course in health. It is usually given in the ninth grade to 14-year-olds.

HARRELSON: In this section of the book they're talking about petting, and they say first, "Petting may be a goal in itself, a pleasurable activity that may result in orgasm."

WALLACE: I think I get the idea. In other words, that — obviously you object to this.

HARRELSON: I think it has no place in a mixed class in high — in high — for ninth-grade students. I think that's the parents' responsibility.

WALLACE: Random House is the publisher of the book, but they withdrew it from consideration in Texas shortly after the Gablers began to examine it. Seibert Adams, Random House editor, told us the book was originally a college text, and was only later introduced into high schools.

You'll sell where it'll go.

SEIBERT ADAMS: Correct.

WALLACE: Okay. That's —

ADAMS: And the reason we do this is because this book takes no moralistic view.

WALLACE: It sure doesn't.

ADAMS: And we're proud of that.

WALLACE: Are the people who choose these books of a different class, a different type? Do they have different values? Do they have different dreams for America's children?

MAN: We — we're not in a position here to judge whether or not they're good people or not. I'm not here to judge whether or not they're good. They may just be lazy. I don't know. But the point is the books are coming through, and that's got to stop.

WALLACE: To capture their share of the annual $30 million Texas market, publishers will often change their textbooks to meet the objections of Mrs. Gabler. And Professor Jenkinson calls that "prior censorship."

PROFESSOR JENKINSON: I think that a teacher must have the right to teach so that students will have the right to know, and I believe that those two rights are guaranteed by the First Amendment.

NORMA: Now, it's — it's strange that if they choose it, it's academic freedom; it's — it's a right of selection. Okay, if we do it, it's censorship. The highest form of censorship is denying a parent a right to be heard, and who is doing that? That's the professionals. And I call that censorship. And if you don't fight, nobody else will. And it's going to have to be the parents. If there's going to be a change, it'll be the parents. It'll not be anybody else.

WALLACE: And Norma Gabler says that too often today's parents still don't know what's in their children's textbooks.

The Foreign Legion

WILLIAM K. McCLURE, PRODUCER

HARRY REASONER: When you were a kid and frustrated, sometimes you'd say, "Nobody loves me, everybody hates me! Guess I'll go eat worms." When you got older and she said, "No way," you said, "I'm going to join the French Foreign Legion." You may be surprised, as we found out last year, that you still can.* The Legion has changed, of course; there may be no real reason for it to exist. But you can still disappear into it from wives and creditors and Social Security numbers.

---

*This segment was originally broadcast on November 18, 1979.

Okay, so we know why a guy would want to join the Legion, but why should the Legion want him?

(Legionnaires singing in French as they march)

Who are the Legionnaires? Well, in a factual way they are 8,000 men, down from 30,000 in the 1950's and '60's. By law, they may not be French, but probably half of them are French. Nobody asks too closely. The other half are of 70 nationalities: British, German, Irish, and so on; very few Americans.

(Legionnaires singing in French as they march)

In a non-factual way, there have always been two views of them. They are romantic men with shrouded pasts, forgetting a lost love or protecting a guilty one. Or they are the dregs of half the world, scum hiding from vengeance. Hollywood created the picture most Americans have of the Legion. The Legionnaire is Gary Cooper and Ray Milland, with just a touch of Brian Donlevy.

(Excerpt from movie *Beau Geste*)

Beau Geste, 1939.

(More from *Beau Geste*)

Since World War II, and particularly since the multiple disasters of Indochina, the glamour of armies has mostly gone out of style. It is hard to get the children of the sixties and the seventies to take them seriously. But while some soldiers in Western Europe were joining unions and while the U.S. Army is letting its men decorate their own barracks, the French Foreign Legion quite unsmilingly marches to commemorate honor and fidelity and a Mexican adventure of 116 years ago.

As in the case of most of its battles, there was some question in that one as to the victor. Sixty or so Legionnaires fought off 2,000 Mexicans, until there were only three of the Legion left alive. Ninety-one years later, in magnified numbers and importance, almost the same thing happened at Dien Bien Phu, where France lost Vietnam.

What this has bred in the Legion is a mystique. From the first days of training, they learn that they have to be tougher than anyone else. No one tells them so, but it is bit into them that this is because they are more tragic. Because they are more tragic, they are more romantic. More romantic, therefore exempt from the trivial headaches of life that the rest of us have. If they can take the training and the discipline and the apartness, the Legion offers them a strange freedom — freedom from everything but the Legion. That means a new identity, a new name, new papers. A lot of these men are hiding from old loves and old errors. It means not being allowed to marry until you are promoted, or not having to marry, depending on your viewpoint. It means not having to make choices. The Legion tells them what to do and when to do it. If they can take it, they have found a home. It's a question of an exchange of values. It's not all racing up hills with 60 pounds on your back. The pay is good for soldiering: $12,000 a year at least, and good food and clean quarters. And if you stay in, it's a career. A career right now for men of something like 70 nationalities.

The Foreign Legion was founded in 1831 to be composed of foreigners with foreign blood to shed, not necessarily to fight on foreign soil. But physical divorcement from the French mainland has always been part of the Legion's mystique. So when their headquarters was driven out of Algeria, they came here to Corsica. Now Corsican resentment and left-wing opinion in France has forced headquarters back to the mainland. But Corsica, with its vaguely foreign feeling, remains the base for the Legion's paratroop units.

The paratroopers are typical of the Legion's small and specialized units. They may be the world's best paratroopers, but in the one time recently when they had to go to Africa to jump, they had to borrow the airplanes from the United States Air Force.

An Englishman stationed in Corsica named Mike McMullin.

What does being a Legionnaire mean to you, Mike?

MIKE McMULLIN: In the Legion we — we, the married people, we put ourselves first for the Legion, and the mar— and the — the wives come afterwards.

REASONER: With no major wars going on and with the French colonial empire almost gone, what's the Legion for? What kind of future do you see for it?

McMULLIN: They'll alway— they'll always need us, because we proved that last year in Kolwezi.

REASONER: Kolwezi was that African trip we mentioned — May, 1978. They went in because of trouble in the south of Zaire, in the old Province of Katanga, now Shaba. They went in fast because invading insurgents were killing European residents. (Gunfire) From the Legion's standpoint, it was a good affair, not only because it was quickly and professionally and economically handled, but because it was a rare chance to practice their highly specialized trade.

In the days when the French were losing Vietnam and Algeria, there were more chances. Simon Murray, now a Hong Kong businessman, wrote a book about those days. He had joined to forget — or maybe to get the attention of — a girl named Jennifer.

SIMON MURRAY: I think the Legion — the legend of the Legion itself creates a mystique. You know, for the last 140 years they've fought in four continents, thirty-odd countries; they've left dead, their dead, all over the place in — in countries and places that you or I have never heard of, for no reason. They haven't even known what they were fighting about sometimes. In fact, it's the very — the mystique of the Legion is almost created by the fact that people know so — so — so little about it.

REASONER: Simon, in your book you talk a good deal about the discipline in the Legion. Was it — was it fair?

MURRAY: There's a certain amount of dislike for the NCO's, particularly in — in basic train— training, where we were subjected to incredible punishments and beatings-up, which at the — the time, and indeed now, seem quite mindless in the degree of brutality that went on. The officers never stepped in and tried to halt it. And the Legion has its traditions; they die hard. Honor, discipline, loyalty to each other, fighting to the last man and those sort of things, and they don't change. And discipline is one of those. There was never hesitation when obeying orders. That may sound robot-like, machine-like or whatever, but if you were the officer and — and trying to get something done, it's very good news to have people obey orders instantly. I mean, if there was one unit I would not have coming at me, it would be — it would be the Foreign Legion. They go to the last man.

(Gunfire . . . singing)

REASONER: The Legionnaires willing to fight to the last man are very definitely divided into two classes. These are the officers. In the first place, they are not Legionnaires; they are French army officers, graduates of St. Cyr, the French West Point, assigned to lead the Legionnaires. They like the duty because their men are professionals and volunteers, and the officers can employ a discipline in the

Legion that regular French draftees would resent and write to their congressmen about.

They can wallow in ceremony. This is a ritualistic dinner in Corsica. The solemn song, we're told, is an old Legion ditty vaguely insulting to the Belgians. It's not quite clear why they want to insult the Belgians, and it isn't quite clear why this officer wears the sombrero to read the menu aloud. The officers are as brave as the men they lead, but it is the bravery of tradition and elan and camaraderie. If you are brave and willing to die for France, the theory is you are entitled to a good life before the event. The officers of the Legion live well — in quarters in Corsica or in the field.

(Bugle call)

In all armies, the enlisted men have a different perspective. To Legionnaires, sacrifice and discipline and possible death are not necessarily glorious but part of the bargain they made. We talked to a deserter who left his post here at Bonifacio in Corsica to avoid a prison sentence. His name is Barry, and his memories of the Legion are somewhat different from Simon Murray's.

When did you first begin to have some doubts about it?

BARRY GALVIN: In my second or third minute in Corsica — about that time.

REASONER (laughs):   Two or three minutes in Corsica and you began to have doubts?

GALVIN: That was about it, yeah.

REASONER: Why?

GALVIN: This attitude towards the recruits changed somewhat. Instead of patting you on the back, they were now patting you on the nose and kicking you around the yard and throwing your kit after you.

REASONER: In the American Army, it's against the rules for an NCO to physically touch a recruit. Is that true in the Legion?

GALVIN: No. In the Legion, it's against the rules not to touch them.

REASONER: How long did you hold your corporal's rank?

GALVIN: On the first occasion for six weeks, and then I went to prison for a month.

REASONER: What'd you go — what'd you go to prison for?

GALVIN: Well, I spent a lot of time in there. Small things. And we sold the captain's wife at one stage. We (indistinct) —

REASONER: You — what — what did you do to the captain's wife?

GALVIN: We sold her.

REASONER (laughs):   You sold her?

GALVIN: Yeah.

REASONER: To whom?

GALVIN: To some sailors.

REASONER: Not with — not with her permission, I expect.

GALVIN: Umm, not altogether, no, no.

REASONER: Not altogether, but it was a — it was a prank, not a — not an assa— not a kidnapping.

GALVIN: No, short of cash.

REASONER: Barry thinks Legion discipline makes tough soldiers, but less from spirit and tradition than from fear and anger.

GALVIN: You've got to have them all angry, you know, all worked up and raring to go. So, you know, the — they start getting like chained dogs. And the day that a war does arrive or they are needed to sort out a combat situation, they're raring to go. You just take them, wind them up, point them in the direction of the enemy, and off they go.

REASONER: Are there enough men like that to keep a Foreign Legion going in the next 50 years?

GALVIN: Certainly. As long as there's a human race, you'll have misfits. So you've got the fuel there.

REASONER: And the Legion is really for misfits?

GALVIN: Oh, yes. Very much so.

(Machine-gun fire)

REASONER: Somewhere between the hyperbole of glory and the cynicism of a deserter there's a more typical ground — the Legionnaires who are soldiers in the way some people are plumbers or doctors. They have ended up in the Legion because it's the freest place around to ply their craft. This Scotsman is 35. He's found a home in a foreign army after a good many years in his own.

SOLDIER: I went to Germany. After Germany, I went to Aden. After Aden, I went to Cyprus. After Cyprus, I went to Borneo. After Borneo, we came back to Aden. After that, we went back to the United Kingdom. I done three tours in Vietnam. I also served in Malaya.

REASONER: He said he's been wounded.

SOLDIER: Yes. Do you want to see where?

REASONER: Yes, we did.

SOLDIER: Yeah? You'd bloody enjoy that, wouldn't you? It went from there to there, up the center of my head, here, here, and on through my foot. I found home, comrades, you know. A place.

REASONER: The Legion needs professionals for its current duties. They guard French interests in the new Republic of Djibouti, below Africa's horn, well aware that across the border in Ethiopia are thousands of Cubans, also now a foreign legion. To the west, they fight for the French-oriented government of Chad in the long guerrilla warfare there. They are stationed in the tiny remnants of empire in the Pacific paradise of Polynesia. And they are very much in French Guyana.

French Guyana is technically a department of mainland France, but it is also the last foreign colony in South America. The Legionnaires patrol the River Oyapock on the border of Brazil. They work the tributaries and the backwaters. They practice a kind of swampy, rotting jungle warfare that is about as far from *Beau Geste* as you can get. And when they aren't practicing, they are busy trying to keep up Legion standards formulated in far more welcoming climates. They keep up the Legion standards off the post, too. That may be easier.

The Legion has always faced the fact that it is a highly masculine organization and that many of its males are there because they had trouble with women. Mostly, they say, that even in the confined male precincts of the barracks homosexuality is not a major problem. If it isn't, it's because the Legion has always admitted that combative, sexist males need the society of women in a particular unromantic way.

MURRAY: Each regiment of the Legion has its own traveling bordello. And when we went on operation looking for the rebels and we would come in for a day or two, relax up, have some hot food instead of the tinned sardines, and the — the bordello, the brothel tent, was there waiting for anybody who wanted to sort of — (laughs) — ease up a bit.

REASONER: Is that a good idea?

MURRAY: Excellent idea.

REASONER: Does the Legion still provide these services?

MURRAY: I don't know. I hope so — (laughs) — for those that are there.

REASONER: Why do the French keep the Legion going? Well, for the Kolwezi that could come along next year. France still feels the need for a force of foreigners that can go anywhere and run any risks. Nobody worries in French politics if a Foreign Legionnaire gets killed. And maybe the world needs the Legion — a last place to run to for both the lovelorn and the rejects, the professionals and the restless.

"Who Gives A Damn?"

JOHN TIFFIN, PRODUCER

MORLEY SAFER: Last December we reported on the American trust territory of Micronesia, and we called it "Who Give A Damn?" We'll remind you why in a moment. Micronesia is a collection of 2,000 islands scattered over 40,000 square miles of the Pacific, wrapped up as a package — a trust territory of the United States, administered by the U.S. Interior Department.

This story examines the results of three and a half decades of American trusteeship. When the former Secretary of the Interior, Walter Hickel, expressed concern about the islands around a decade ago, in the privacy of a cabinet meeting, Hickel told us that Henry Kissinger said, "There are only 90,000 people out there.

Who gives a damn?" Dr. Kissinger denies he said it. But if you visit Micronesia, you might well ask, "Just who does give a damn?"*

This picture represents, perhaps too graphically, what this story is about. A Micronesian who is not employed and has no intention of ever being employed is feeding his favorite pig prime U.S. beef – a gift from the United States. The pig obviously enjoys his Big Mac, and his owner obviously prefers pork. How come this man, and 120,000 other Micronesians, are part of a welfare state he never dreamed of, never wanted, and yet is now hopelessly addicted to? How come? This is how come.

(Sound of rocket taking off)

The Kwajalein missile range in the Marshall Islands is the most important American rocket tracking station in the world. Missiles from Vandenberg Air Force Base in California thunder across the Pacific at 18,000 miles an hour, and splash into Kwajalein lagoon. They are tracked every inch of the way, all part of the missile and anti-missile missile program.

Stated simply, without a Kwajalein we wouldn't know whether our hardware worked or not. A fairly sobering thought, really. But there are other equally sobering thoughts as you stand out here a million miles from nowhere on a stage set for the next war to end all wars. First of all, the relics of the last war to end all wars, these utterly silent memorials to the hundreds of thousands of Americans and Japanese who died here on patches of coral whose names are as American as Gettysburg and Bunker Hill – Saipan, Truk, Yap, Peleliu, Kwajalein itself. Can it be it was only 35 years ago that we used such weapons? From today's missile range, they look like so many bows and arrows. Ancient history. But those lives lost and this missile range have everything to do with that man and his pig that we began with.

Thirty-five years ago, when the United States claimed these islands by conquest and were given them in trust by the United Nations, we became the masters of a people who, one way or another, got along. Small clans living on islands, lagoons teeming with fish; islands of plenty: breadfruit, coconut, pineapples, taro root. A people who seem unable to show meanness or narrowness of spirit. It sounds stupidly nineteenth century to say that Micronesians are by nature happy, easy-going people, but that indeed is what they seem to be.

Through the fifties, the official U.S. policy here was one of benign neglect. The Navy pretty much ran the islands, and they let them be as they were. In the sixties, noises were made at the UN about American colonialism, and the Kennedy Administration decided that the islands were too important strategically to be cast adrift on some passing wave of independence. Micronesia would therefore be brought fully into the American embrace. Policy changed from benign neglect to a kind of malignant generosity. The delicate relationship between the people and their land and their lagoons was finished. A paradise of welfare had begun.

And we swamped these islands with government programs, from Head Start to care for the elderly. Needed or not, they were, by heaven, going to get all the benefits of the New Frontier and the Great Society. This unique, traditional, scattered island society was treated as if it were Inner City, U.S.A. It's not as if there weren't people, thoughtful people, along the way who could sense the danger of what was happening – Micronesians like Tony de Brum.

TONY De BRUM: There were responsibilities. For example, the elderly people were

---

*This story was originally broadcast on December 23, 1979. See Letters, December 30, 1979, page 229, for a reply by Henry Kissinger.

required, under our own custom, to take care of younger people, the — the little children. They babysat, they told them stories, they passed on legends. This is dead now. No one does it any more. The older people go to the old-age center and learn how to make wallets.

SAFER: And the kids?

De BRUM: Kids are left running around as they are. They must now go to Head Start or other federal programs that take care of children.

SAFER: Great machinery for great projects was brought in, but the machinery decayed before anyone was trained to run it. And the plans for the projects lie mildewing on Capitol Hill — Capitol Hill, Saipan, the headquarters of the trust territory government. Of the 17,000 paid jobs in Micronesia, 11,000 are government jobs; and on any given day, a third of the work force does not turn up for work. The government payroll is virtually the only source of income. Government handouts seem to have wiped out any possibility of creating other income. When the U.S. Department of Agriculture started handing out food, food production in Micronesia fell in ten years from 33 million pounds a year to one million pounds. So much food is dumped on these islands that American and Micronesian officials have given up trying to account for it. This is the supermarket of a housewife's dreams. But where there is no price, there may well be no pride. But the food keeps coming in, and the checks keep rolling out — cash into a society that a short time ago had no need or use for it. The cash goes on cars that go from dockside to disaster in months.

These islands are a bitter perversion of an old American ideal: two wrecks in every garage, and a USDA boneless chicken in every pot.

De BRUM: This culturing a dependency that, to use your own example, we find ourselves so hooked on it we can't get weaned. It is indeed a — a generous policy, but it has fostered dependency, a sense of defeatism amongst the people.

SAFER: Micronesia can feed itself and a good part of the world right from its own doorstep. These waters run with great schools of tuna and mackerel. But it's the Japanese fishing fleet that forages here. The Micronesian boats have been pulled up for good. And even when the United States tried to do something about it — get commercial fishing going in the smallest way — it becomes another costly disaster.

All of this does not mean that the Micronesians have given up their taste for fish. You can still buy tuna and mackerel, but it has to go to Japan first, and come back in a can.

De BRUM: We would like to be able to obtain nets and lines and hooks, but the United States would much rather give us USDA food.

SAFER: Even clearly noble enterprises have a nasty habit of becoming abject bureaucratic disasters. A multimillion-dollar hospital for the island of Yap gets built, but someone forgets that there's no sewage system. So it sits, about as useful to Yap as a space program. But someone did bring in cable television, and it works: the *Hollywood Squares* and *Love Boat* and *The Muppets,* complete with Los Angeles commercials.

(Excerpt from Sears TV commercial)

The commercials create a taste for goods they can't afford, yet nevertheless will probably acquire.

(More excerpt from Sears TV commercial)

Yap's gross national product is near zero, yet they spent a million and a half dollars on beer last year; that's $200 per man, woman and child. Beer cans have become such a litter problem that the government is now paying two cents a can for them. Stone disks were the old symbols of wealth; mounds of beer cans are the new symbols.

If someone gets past the temptation to be more than a civil servant, he's usually thwarted. This young man was sent to the University of Florida to study marine biology. He's back as a bellhop in Truk. Meantime, in Truk lagoon, somebody in Washington's bright idea for a maritime program waits to sink, torpedoed by time and indifference.

What's so sad, so hopelessly sad, to anyone who's had anything to do with Micronesia is that we could have done so much more with so much less. Instead of pinpointing the places that needed the food or the money or the help, we atom-bombed these islands with it. Example: a primary school could not get a simple Department of Education grant for the basic tools of teaching; it had to take an audio visual expert, eight assistants, and $150,000 worth of electronics that will break down before the expert's contract is up.

I could give you a list as long as your arm of this kind of Catch-22 aid and assistance. I asked a young American girl – a teacher, who'd just been sent out here as a specialist in special education – what happens to her job if there are no retarded or handicapped children in her district? She said, "Well, I'm part of the package. I'll find some handicapped children. I have to."

Something like $200 million goes into Micronesia every year on near 170 different federal projects, but it's so far provided less than 60 miles of paved road on 2,000 islands. It may be money in the bank for the Japanese auto industry, but what positive difference has our presence made here? That's exactly what an official of the Interior Department wondered as he was taken on a tour of Micronesia. His name is C. Brewster Chapman, and he stood in the dusty and decrepit main street of Ponape, looked at the dead and dying cars and trucks, threw up his hands, and said, "Where, oh where, has all the money gone?" Shortly after that, he was effectively fired by Secretary of State Vance.

Where did all the money go? Well, on Ponape we ran into a man who may be the most frustrated person in these islands – Lee Hoskins, a retired Army intelligence officer who now runs the Micronesian Bureau of Investigation.

LEE HOSKINS: My estimates, based upon the investigations that I have done, would indicate that at least 10 cents on the dollar is perhaps lost through some form of white-collar crime or corruption; that another significant portion of that dollar, perhaps as high as 60 or 70 cents, is not totally wasted but badly abused in mismanagement; and that perhaps the remaining 20 cents or so will pass through to something effective that you can put your finger on as an advancement or a development.

SAFER: Has anyone ever done an audit of the monies that have been spent in these islands?

HOSKINS: The General Accounting Office has the overall responsibility for the government funds that are passed through the Congress for — for audit. They have attempted a number of audits over the years. And if I believe — if I'm in — not incorrect, the last time they attempted that, they declined any further audits, because the management system employed by the government in the trust territory was determined to be inauditable. That the —

SAFER: Inauditable?

HOSKINS:— that the management records and the records — financial records of the government were not in an auditable state, and they declined it.

SAFER: What happens when the word gets back to the Department of Interior, for example? Does an— anything ever come back saying, "Clean up your act out there," or do heads ever roll, or does anything ever happen?

HOSKINS: I have not observed any — any real, serious action having been taken to — to correct the situation.

De BRUM: Too many things fall into place at the given — the right time for it to be just bureaucratic incompetence. I — I — I once thought that perhaps that was the answer, but it seems to me that there is — there is more than that. There is definitely a policy of fostering dependence. There must be.

(Music . . . scene in pool hall)

SAFER: We declared war on Micronesia's backwardness, and we have only casualties to show for the effort. With a good heart and an open hand, we have tried to make over a society and we have botched it. If, on the other hand, we did it with cynicism, determined to keep Micronesia dependent forever, so we will have these islands for strategic reasons forever, then we have succeeded beautifully. As Henry Kissinger said, "There's only 90,000 of them out there. Who gives a damn?"

(Music . . . scene in pool hall)

A Few Minutes
with Andy Rooney

MORLEY SAFER: While the rest of us spend most of our lives on the road, Andy Rooney finds plenty to talk about right at home.

ANDY ROONEY: Because it's easier to bring the camera to the kitchen than the kitchen to the camera, we're going to my kitchen.

Sure collect a lot of stuff over the years, don't you? Some of it's good, some of it I'll never use again. Did you get caught with the big Teflon advertising two years ago? You know, fry an egg without any grease in the pan? Forget it!

Here's a blender — every kitchen should have one. Very good piece of equipment, except the salesman got into this one. A blender should have two speeds — fast and slow. This one has 14 buttons on it — stir, whip, coarse chop, beat, grate, mix, chop, grind, crumb, shake, blend, aerate, puree and liquefy. Who needs it?

Here's a wonderful item. If you want to — you want to slice an egg, you put the egg in here, and then you pull this down on the egg like that. Crumbles it to little bits is what happens.

Here's the most oversold piece of kitchen equipment of the last decade. It was originally made by Cuisinart. This is a fake Cuisinart — probably isn't quite as good, costs half as much. It's one of those things that you gradually move towards the back of the shelf. It's interesting how many of these things have gone out of style. Now, for instance, this bottle opener. You don't take a cap off a bottle much anymore — you know, you twist it open.

And now here's something I'll bet our kids and our grandchildren, 20 years from now they're going to be collecting these for — as antiques. Probably get $35 for that in another 20 years. It's a beer opener, you know. Don't use these anymore.

You have — they have those rings on the beer can and you just pull them out and throw them on somebody else's lawn.

I've been making ice cream for most of my life. They finally came up with a good homemade ice cream freezer. Here it is — it's a revolution. The engine is underneath on this one. And you can make it with just four trays of ice cubes packed around here. You put the mixture in here. Very good.

This is in case you want to make a loaf of round bread. You stuff the dough in here. My son gave this to me for Christmas. Well, it's the thought that counts.

Letters

MORLEY SAFER: The mail last week was mainly about our story on the very rich Worldwide Church of God and the man who controls the church's pursestrings, treasurer Stanley Rader. One viewer, a church member, asked: "What's wrong with Stanley Rader making as much money as he does? If he were doing the same job for someone else he would probably be making more money . . . *We* haven't given religion a bad name. *You* have."

But another viewer wrote: "In the glory of their own self-righteousness . . . they have neatly overlooked the proverb that says: 'It is better to give than to receive.' But I guess it depends which end you're on."

There was also a letter that said: "Your story on the Worldwide Church of God is further evidence of the pro-Catholic bias of CBS . . . You've jumped on Methodists, Mormons, Oral Roberts, Brother Roloff and Coptic marijuana smokers, (but you show) only favorable stories on the Catholics."

From another viewer came this: "Many thanks for your exposure of the Worldwide Church of God. The more we have of this (kind of story) the bigger the church grows. Between your snide remarks and the lies (told about us in the media) the church is growing by leaps and bounds."

About our story on Bahrain, the sheikdom off the coast of Saudi Arabia that is thriving even though they no longer pump oil, a viewer wrote: "It's an eye-opener . . .(because) it's important for us to understand that as the oil runs out we will have a harder time adjusting than they will."

And finally, about that land that started out as the Garden of Eden, there was this: "Instead of wasting time at the Emir's Palace, the Westerners' gathering place and the go-go discotheque, (you) should have been . . . checking out the corruption of the multi-national corporations . . . and . . . the immorality of (their) type of 'modernization' being forced upon Bahrain."

JUNE 22, 1980

Canary
DREW PHILLIPS, PRODUCER

HARRY REASONER: This is a story about a woman who wanted to be a jazz singer and refused to let anything stop her. She started singing at the age of twelve for coins thrown on a dance floor. She just barely made enough money to pay the rent as a band singer — a "canary" — in the forties. She had two bad marriages, and was a heroin addict for fifteen years.

She survived all that to become one of the world's great jazz singers just at the time the world turned its back on jazz and flipped over rock and disco. It's the story of Miss Anita O'Day, who, at 60 is at her peak and is now beginning to get a little recognition and make a little money as the disco fad begins to fade and jazz makes a comeback.

(Anita O'Day singing)

ANITA O'DAY: One time I'm a saxophone, next time I'm a trumpet.

(O'Day singing)

REASONER: We can hear most of you saying, "Anita who?" But among jazz musicians, she is considered one of a handful of great singers. Critic Leonard Feather agrees.

LEONARD FEATHER: I've always felt that there are four basic elements that go into a great jazz vocal performance. One is the singer's tone quality, or time to the individual tone and sound of the voice. Another is the phrasing — the extent to which he or she has a jazz feeling. A third element is the choice of accompanying musicians. Another one is the choice of material.

Well, Billie Holiday, who, to me, was the greatest female jazz singer of all time, had all those elements. Ella Fitzgerald has them. Sarah Vaughn has them. Carmen McRae has them. And Anita O'Day has them.

(O'Day singing)

REASONER: Anita started singing 46 years ago and, right from the start, it was not easy.

O'DAY: Did you ever hear of walkathons?

REASONER: Were they like dance marathons? Or —

O'DAY: Like dance marathons, right.

REASONER: When was the first time you got paid to sing?

O'DAY: It started a walkathon, because a dollar was sent up for the girl, couple number 18, to sing a song. And the emcee says, "Couple number 18, can you sing a song?" You know, I'd been practicing, so I was ready. I think it was "I Can't Give You Anything But Love, Baby." And then the emcee would say, on the microphone, "Now, if anybody out there really liked what this gal did, let's all reach in our pockets and throw a penny or a nickel or a dime." And all this money would be thrown on the floor. And then the contestants would help pick it up and you'd put it in your trunk in the back, and that was yo— kind of your salary, because you'd wa— I walked for three months once.

REASONER: What was your first time, full — full-time singing job? I mean, where you worked at a place and got paid for singing?

O'DAY: Oh, this would be, like after the walkathons, into a tavern in Chicago. Every night from nine to six. (Laughter) Right.

REASONER: Really?

O'DAY: You start at nine. Four o'clock it's an after-hour place. We had a breakfast show at 5:30. I was on at six and then I went home.

REASONER: She met bandleader Gene Krupa at another Chicago tavern, and a year later she became the Krupa band's canary.
(Music)
Canary, some of you will remember, was the pretty girl in the bouffant dress who spent most of the evening sitting on a chair in front of the big band, snapping her fingers and bouncing a little in time to the music.
There you are in the center. That's what you did, you stood around in a bouffant skirt —

O'DAY: I sat in front of the drums and my ears were killing me. I sat in front of the drums for five years.

(O'Day singing)

REASONER: "Thanks for the Boogey Ride" and another song she sang with the Krupa band, "Let Me Off Uptown," were big sellers. Anita's name began appearing on music magazine lists of most popular singers. She had hit the big time and was making all of $40 a week.
Anita moved on to other bands, and then, as the big-band sound lost popularity to small jazz groups, still not making any money to speak of, but learning to make the transition from canary to jazz singer. Then, in 1954, she got hooked on heroin. She stayed on it for 16 years, through several arrests.
Anita has sort of blocked the heroin years out of her mind. She tends to gloss it over, make it seem unimportant. All she remembers is she kept singing.

O'DAY: You think you're really doing something and, in reality, maybe I wasn't moving at all.

REASONER: Uh-hmm.

O'DAY: I don't know. But it was very interesting, and — and I thought, well, you could walk away at any time, you know. Then you try to walk away, ho-ho-ho- — (laughs) — that's another one!

REASONER: And you can't.
(O'Day singing)

One of her most critically acclaimed appearances was at the Newport Jazz Festival in 1959. We showed her a tape of that appearance.

Would you have used drugs that day, or would you wait until afterwards, or — how does that work?

O'DAY: It doesn't go by day, it goes by hours. It's a matter of how many hours —

REASONER: So you certainly would have used something —

O'DAY: — it wears down, and you — then you —

REASONER: You would have used some that day, then?

O'DAY: I would say, yes.

(O'Day singing)

REASONER: Anita insists she was working constantly during the heroin years, but friends and musicians who knew her say she lost a lot of weight and was ill a lot and had serious bouts of depression. During one of those she took a big overdose and was declared dead at a California hospital.

O'DAY: They put the sheet over my head. I was out. I understand this is the story. Some doctor came running out and said, "We'll try this new apparatus." Because he thought I had a heart attack. And evidently it worked, because the heart started pumping.

REASONER: As soon as she got out of the hospital she went to Hawaii and broke the heroin habit.

O'DAY: When I got the chills, "The Man with the Golden Arm" chills —

REASONER: You were doing this without medical advice? Or you were doing it on your own?

O'DAY: Oh, this is just — this is just me.

REASONER: Cold — cold turkey?

O'DAY: Right. Just me. I lived — happened to live just across the street from the beach in the Hawaii hot sun. When I got the chills, the hot sun, just laying in the hot sand would really do it. Then you get the perspirings, because your respiratory system isn't exchanging right, so you jump in the ocean. You do that for about five months, you get pretty straight.

(O'Day singing)

REASONER: She returned from Hawaii singing better than ever; more important, singing jazz better than most women ever have.
(O'Day singing)
But Elvis Presley and the Beatles had changed her world. Rock was in. There were no jazz audiences. So, as usual, there was no money for Anita. There was one big payday, and it sounds like something out of a Doris Day movie. She bought a song for five dollars from a man she met in a bar. She recorded it and it didn't sell too well, but then a major record company called her about it.

O'DAY: Les Paul and Mary Ford were in Duluth, Minnesota, and they heard this rendition on the radio. So Capitol says, "We'd like to buy that song." And I said, "Well, go ahead." Because I really wasn't business-conscious or money-conscious. And one day they gave me a check for $10,000. That's quite a profit.

REASONER: That was the biggest money you'd ever made.

O'DAY: Tha— I would say so. And from five dollars to ten thousand dollars, that's quite a profit. (Sings) "Vaya con Dios" in three-fourths.

(O'Day singing)

REASONER: Now there may be a lot of big paychecks on the horizon. A few weeks ago she sang in Carnegie Hall. She plays Marty's in New York several times a year, and Lulu White's in Boston, and clubs in Chicago and Malibu and Los Angeles, and Japan. She's very popular in Japan. And it's not just nostalgia buffs out there in the audience, the young people are there, too.

O'DAY: There they are, all the youngies. They even say, "My father says hello," and things like that. (Laughter) Okay. But, no they're all right.

REASONER: You haven't gotten to the place where Bob Hope said that he ran into a guy in Vietnam who said, "My dad knew you on Guadalcanal"? You haven't — you haven't gotten that far yet?

O'DAY: Almost. (Laughter)

(O'Day singing)

REASONER: If you're interested in jazz or if we have piqued your interest, consider this: Billie Holiday is dead, and Anita, Sarah Vaughn, Carmen McRae and Ella Fitzgerald are getting on. The real sad thing, according to Leonard Feather, is that there are no young singers coming up to replace them. Jazz takes too much time and discipline, there's not enough money in it.

(O'Day singing)

So that's the story of Miss Anita O'Day. She got hurt and scared and confused along the way and put a kind of laughing lid on her emotions. When she finally got herself off heroin, she says she avoided getting back into trouble this way: when her old drug buddies tempted her, she would walk on by. She walks on by a lot of things, except music. In a way that the old cliche never meant, she lives not only for her music but in it. And if she could do it all over, there's not much she would change.

O'DAY: How many people enjoy going to their job, you know?

REASONER: Yeah.

O'DAY: And that was the main thing I liked about the music, so I — I keep it in that form.

(O'Day singing . . . applause)

Handcuffing the Cops?

STEVE GLAUBER, PRODUCER

DAN RATHER: People continually cry out that crime is on the rise because the courts are handcuffing the police. There are also a lot of people who complain that it's the police that need to be handcuffed. It wasn't too long ago that police routinely broke and entered into homes without legal authority and beat confessions out of suspects. It was routine because police who did this were not penalized and because the illegally seized evidence could still be used legally in court. In hopes of deterring police misconduct and protect constitutional liberties, the United States Supreme Court evolved what is known as the exclusionary rule. And as we first reported in March, what it means is simply this: confessions and evidence obtained in violation of a defendant's constitutional rights are thrown out of court, even if it means that guilty people go free.

JOHN VAN DE KAMP: Do you want to have the guilty go free because a policeman made a minor error? Do you want a robber, do you want a murderer, a rapist, a serious criminal to go free because some technical error has been committed along the line?

RATHER: John Van de Kamp is district attorney of Los Angeles.

VAN DE KAMP: Analogize it to the game of football. If a player goes offsides, what? A five-yard penalty. You don't give the game to the other — other side, do you? And yet, that's what's happening, you see, when you deal with the exclusionary rule.

RATHER: All states must follow the rule, but nowhere is it followed more closely than in California. Here, as elsewhere, police are taught the basics of the rule. They can stop and search only when they have probable cause that a crime has been committed. As for confessions, they are considered − quote − "voluntary" only after suspects are read their so-called Miranda rights: the right to a lawyer and the right to remain silent. If the rule is violated, whatever evidence is obtained cannot be used in trial, no matter how innocent the police mistake or how horrible the crime.

(Cheryl Cole playing the piano)

Take the case of Cheryl Cole. She and her husband, Steven, were accosted as they arrived home by three men who put a bag over his head and tied him up and then repeatedly and brutally raped Cheryl. They were caught and convicted, but because of an arguably irrelevant error, the convictions were overturned.

CHERYL COLE: It changed my life completely, because ever since the crime I've been living wondering if these guys who have gotten off because of this law are looking for me. Are they following me? As I think about these guys, there were something like seven misdemeanors and eight felonies and they're out on the street. Twelve citizens said, yes, they are guilty. But, no, the court system says, well, we'd better let them go because somebody made a mistake.

RATHER: The mistake that led to the overturning of their convictions was made by a probation officer who the court said acted improperly in obtaining a lead from a defendant, a lead which police insist they were about to develop anyway themselves. Under the exclusionary rule, none of the incriminating evidence obtained as a result of the probation officer's lead was admissible, and the three men went free.

STEVEN COLE: As far as I'm concerned, when the guy broke into my house, that ended any right that he might have from there on and my rights should have started from that point on. And it didn't — didn't weigh out that way. I think we got a little short-changed and they got the l— the — the good end of the stick.

RATHER: The three defendants were not retried because there was not enough admissible evidence. While the local district attorney points to the Cole case as an example damning the exclusionary rule, civil libertarians like California criminal lawyer Ephraim Margolin contend that the rule is necessary and the Cole decision fully justified.

What can you say to these victims who went through this terrible experience if they said, "Why do we have to continue to live in fear while these people walk the streets?"

EPHRAIM MARGOLIN: It would be difficult for me to talk to them. I will have to say, in the final account, that that's the price we pay for living in our society. And our society has its bad aspects. Lenin said at one point that it is better to shoot 99 innocent people to make sure that one guilty person is shot, too. Our jurisprudence always took the position that it is better to let 99 guilty people go than to shoot this one innocent person.

RATHER: Law-enforcement officials insist that innocent people are not protected by the exclusionary rule for searches and seizures, because sawed-off shotguns, bags of heroin and the like are indisputable evidence of the existence of some crime. The issue under the exclusionary rule is whether the evidence can be used or not because of what police did to get it. As for judges being worried about back-room justice, police swear that their current professionalism makes such concerns outdated. Others, however, are not so sure, especially poor minorities who have reason to suspect police misconduct, as well as criminal lawyers hired by rich defendants, criminal lawyers like Richard "Racehorse" Haynes of Texas.

RICHARD "RACEHORSE" HAYNES: There are still those who subscribe to the — I guess the — for want of a better terminology — the Ayatollah Khomeini rule, and that is, they feel like everything that they can do they ought to do, and then — in the name of the law. Police officers make innocent mistakes. But librarians traditionally do not make good police officers; ex-Marine Corps people make good police officers. It takes a sort of a take-charge person, it takes an aggressive person, and without the exclusionary rule we would be an Iron Curtain country. We'd be a police state. This would be 1939 Nazi Germany.

RATHER: It would be difficult to find an officer who agreed with that, but it's a snap to find one who insists that the rule has become too complicated to obey. Pasadena, California officer Ron Foss.

RON FOSS: You have a situation: you stop a vehicle, or you stop a person on the street; you've got to make your decision and run through your mind all the court decisions in the last year or the last week that you've heard about; you have to make your — your — your stop and think within a minute. You go to court; they throw it out and say you didn't take your time. They sit there for hours and deliberate the — what you have to do in a minute.

HAYNES: I don't think it's a matter of — of the police not knowing. I think they know exactly where the line is. I think what happens is that the overzealous police officer, because they need the — something on their report card, over-reaches the rules.

RATHER: When it comes to the rules for stopping and searching moving vehicles, it's easy to understand how mistakes can be made. Two uniformed West Covina, California policemen and two plainclothesmen, plus a plainclotheswoman, helped us demonstrate why. Remember as you watch this re-enactment that once a mistake is made all evidence obtained thereafter is unusable, no matter what. Officers see a car go through a red light and speeding. Now everyone knows they can stop it — but is it legal for the officer to have the driver get out?

OFFICER: Will you step to the curb point, please?

RATHER: Yes, because it was a request. But had it been an order, it would not be legal because drivers in California can't be ordered out of their cars on a simple traffic stop, although in some states that would be okay.

OFFICER: Sir, I can let you go on — you ran the red light. I'm going to cite you for the speed and I'm going to run you for a warrant check, okay? It'll just take a second. Want to step over here, please?

RATHER: Is it legal to run a warrant check? Yes.

OFFICER (on police radio): Six-four-one . . .

WOMAN (on police radio): Six-four-one, computers are down, sir.

RATHER: But the computer is down, and if the driver is detained for any time longer than it would take under normal circumstances, a warrant check is not legal.

OFFICER: Here, Mr. Hermanski, you come back with an outstanding warrant for 65-50. I'm going to have to take you in. Could you turn around and put your hands on your head, please?

RATHER: There is an outstanding warrant, so an arrest is legal.

OFFICER: Is this your wallet, sir?

SUSPECT: Yeah, it's my wallet.

OFFICER: This is a — shows identification to a Rosemary Hughes.

RATHER: Can the dropped wallet be examined? If the officer knows that Miss Hughes has reported her wallet stolen, the arrest for stolen property is legal. If not reported? Illegal — maybe. Lawyers are not sure.

OFFICER: Check records also to Rosemary Hughes.

RATHER: Can the checkbook be examined? Not if the officer can easily bend it, as that indicates no weapon is hidden. But if he doesn't try to bend it, then his search might be legal. Assuming the arrest is legal, a search of the car would not be, unless there is consent.

WIFE OF SUSPECT: Excuse me?

OFFICER: Hm-hmm?.

WIFE OF SUSPECT: If you're taking my husband to jail, can I take the car?

OFFICER: This will take several hours. We're going to need to get a search warrant and search the car for other stolen property.

WIFE OF SUSPECT: Well, I haven't got several hours. I got kids to pick up at school. Is there anything that I can do?

OFFICER: No, ma'am. We have to wait for the — the search warrant.

WIFE OF SUSPECT: How about if I give you permission to search it now?

RATHER: Was that consent? Probably so. But if the wife had said her child was ill, indicating she was under duress, then her consent probably would be considered involuntary. If it is okay for the cops to look into the trunk and there they find a woman's purse, a briefcase and a cardboard box, they had better be extra careful, as there are different legal interpretations for each object. If they are wrong, none of the incriminating evidence can be used.

(Siren)

If the exclusionary rule makes it difficult for the police to search a guilty person, it also makes it difficult for police to force an innocent person to confess to a crime he or she didn't commit. In that respect, everyone agrees it's a good law. What many people don't agree with is that the rule sometimes lets a clearly guilty person go free.

Shortly after midnight, August 23rd, 1976, Oakland area sheriff's deputies were called by Barry Braeseke to the home of his parents. There officers found dead Barry Braeseke's mother, father and grandfather. All had multiple gunshot wounds. The house appeared to have been ransacked, but there were no signs of forced entry. And Barry Braeseke's trousers had blood splattered on them.

MICHAEL CARDOZA: I said, "Barry, you've got blood on your pants. We think you're lying to us. We think you did it. We think you're involved." At that time, Barry becomes a suspect. They Mirandize him.

RATHER: The prosecutor was Michael Cardoza.

CARDOZA: At that point he says, "I want an attorney." They tell him at that point, "All right, if you want an attorney, we are not going to question you any more. We can't, under the law as it is. We're going to book you into jail, because we think you did it."

RATHER: The detective who booked him was Bernie Cervi.

BERNIE CERVI: I started asking the questions that are on the form. But where we come down to, "Who's your next of kin?" and he stopped. If I'm — in fact, you can see the wheels turning in his head. But he stopped, and he said, "Can I talk to you alone? Can I talk to you off the record?" And I agreed.

And at that time he asked me, "What if I told you that rifle was somewhere where the kids could find it?" And, in essence, it came down to, "Well, what if it did happen the way you say?"

RATHER: All right, this is in the off-the-record conversation?

CERVI: That's correct. And he says, "Okay." He says, "I'd like to talk to you about it." And it was at this time I said, "Well, okay. Can I take a formal statement? Can we turn on the tape recorder and will you give me a formal statement?" and he said he would.

RATHER: Braeseke then confessed to the three murders. But just before the confession, Cervi did not recite the Miranda warnings completely, as he had done the first time when he had read them off a card. Only six hours after confessing to Cervi, Braeseke repeated his confession to Cardoza, after Cardoza meticulously went through the Miranda warnings again and went over what Cervi had done.

CARDOZA (on tape):   At the time that the sheriff read those rights to you, did you understand those rights?

BRAESEKE (on tape):   Yes.

CARDOZA (on tape):   Did he read them to you as I read them to you?

BRAESEKE (on tape):   Yes.

CARDOZA (on tape):   Did he explain them to you?

BRAESEKE (on tape):   He didn't need to. I understood them.

CARDOZA (on tape):   And there was no confusion in your mind about these rights, was there?

BRAESEKE (on tape):   No.

CARDOZA: From the mouth of Barry Braeseke we have, "I did, too, understand my Miranda rights. He didn't have to explain them to me."

RATHER: Based on his confessions, Braeseke was convicted of three counts of first-degree murder. Then his public defender, Clifton Jeffers, appealed, claiming his client's Miranda rights had been violated, thus making his confessions legally not voluntary.

CLIFTON JEFFERS: He wanted to talk off the record, didn't want to say anything that could be used against him. The police officer made the mistake in that instance of allowing that conversation to continue.

RATHER: But he allowed — when the police officer said, "May I tape-record this?" he said okay.

JEFFERS: But they never would have gotten to that point if they had, in fact, respected his wish not to talk without an attorney being present.

RATHER: But even after the appeal was filed, Braeseke described the crime yet again, this time to Mike Wallace, who was reporting a story about PCP, a drug Braeseke claimed led to his murderous acts.

BRAESEKE: I was in my room and I had my rifle with me, and I came downstairs, and I walked into the family room and the family was watching the TV set with their back to me.

MIKE WALLACE: Hm-hmm.

BRAESEKE: And then I started firing the rifle. I was standing behind my — my dad and I shot him.

WALLACE: Through the head?

BRAESEKE: Yes.

WALLACE: And then right away — ?

BRAESEKE: Almost instantly my mother.

RATHER: More than three years after Braeseke's two confessions to the police and after his confession on 60 MINUTES, the California State Supreme Court sitting here in San Francisco reversed the conviction. The vote was four to three. The majority said that there was not proof beyond a reasonable doubt that Braeseke had waived his right to silence. The minority of the court said — and I quote — "The conduct of the police was irreproachable; therefore the lesson derived from today's decision can only be that this court no longer accepts convictions based on voluntary confessions."

Braeseke is still in jail awaiting a retrial. And neither the prosecution nor the defense yet knows whether that 60 MINUTES interview can be shown to a jury. Even without that film, courthouse observers say Assistant District Attorney Cardoza would have had an open and shut case, except for the way detective Cervi went about getting Braeseke's confession. The case was a snap, they say, even without the confession.

CARDOZA: How would we prove this case? There is no evidence to show that Barry Braeseke committed three — these three murders until he told us he did. We weren't going to find the weapon. That weapon was secreted out in the middle of nowhere. He had to lead us to that weapon. There was no way we were going to prove this case without his confession.

HAYNES: The guilty sometimes are acquitted as a consequence of the application of the exclus— the exclusionary rule, but when that happens, it's the law that permits him freedom.

JEFFERS: If the law calls for the exclusion of a confession where there is a triple murder, it should apply just as it does if it's a second-degree burglary.

HAYNES: If, in fact, the government does not dot all the i's and cross all the t's, then the question of guilt or innocence is not really the — the issue, but one is entitled to be free, period.

RATHER: The two purposes of the rule are to breed respect for law and deter police misconduct. Many studies have been done, but none offers any direct proof that this actually has happened. This may be because a policeman who breaks the law is rarely penalized by his superiors.

When the case was reversed, did your superior say anything to you?

CERVI: Well, they simply told me that it had been reversed.

RATHER: Did they reprimand you?

CERVI: No.

RATHER: Have you been penalized in any way?

CERVI: Oh, no.

RATHER: There are two alternatives most often proposed, both of which would allow illegally seized evidence to be used in court to convict a defendant and then permit the now-guilty defendant to get some satisfaction and money if his rights have been violated. The first way is to set up an independent civil review board to decide whether and, if so, how police should be penalized, and whether a defendant should be paid money out of tax dollars. The other way is to write a law that would allow defendants to sue police officers in regular civil court. Now, while these ideas may sound good, there are many people who believe they simply won't work.

MARGOLIN: The plaintiff is a criminal, a burglar, a very unsavory character. So they beat him up, so what? Can you see the plaintiff winning?

CARDOZA: Because it hasn't worked in the past, does that mean it's not going to work in the future? Why don't we explore other avenues? Why do we have to do it by punishing society? That's the question I ask.

RATHER: I'm sure you've heard the argument that cases such as yours are very tough to swallow, but swallow them we ˈust. It's part of the price we pay for our constitutional and Bill of Rights guarantees. What's your reaction to that?

CHERYL COLE: My reaction is that if — if someone is a thief their hand should be cut off. And I don't think that's cruel, because when you weigh it out the most cruel thing is that this same criminal will come back and an innocent citizen could be victimized because, you know, the laws are the way they are.

RATHER: Only last month, the Supreme Court decided a case much like Braeseke's.* A Rhode Island murder suspect told police interrogators that he wanted a lawyer, and questioning stopped. But the suspect later led police to the murder weapon, not after overt questioning, but after policemen expressed fears that students at a nearby school for the handicapped might stumble across the weapon and hurt themselves.

Voting six to three, the Supreme Court majority upheld the conviction, stating — quote — "Police cannot be held accountable for the unforeseeable results of their words or actions." Unquote. Dissenting, the minority accused the Court of constructing — again, quote — "a trap in which unwary suspects may be caught by police deception."

---

*This story was originally broadcast on March 2, 1980.

Rolls-Royce

JOHN TIFFIN, PRODUCER

MORLEY SAFER: Now another of our so-called "golden oldies." When this story about Rolls-Royce cars was first broadcast nine years ago, we said the cheapest Rolls sold for $24,000, the most expensive for $50,000. Here's what inflation has done: the cheapest is now $85,000 and the most expensive $156,000. But enough talk of money. This story is about quality. And this is the way we began it back in November, 1971.*

Rolls-Royce is the longest lasting and the last of the great handmade cars — Hispano-Suiza, Duesenberg, Packard, Isotta-Fraschini, all of them dead. But Rolls survives, more old ones on the road than new ones — one of the few things in life that is not built for the junkyard.

The statistics bear this out in a remarkable way. In the 67 years since Sir Henry Royce built his first motorcar, only 65,000 have been built. Of those, 30,000 are still on the road in daily use. In its best week, the Rolls plants produce 53 cars; just over 2,000 a year. GM make 21,000 cars in a single day.

It's a difference in philosophy. Henry Ford wanted to put the world on his wheels. Henry Royce wanted to build the world's best car, one at a time.

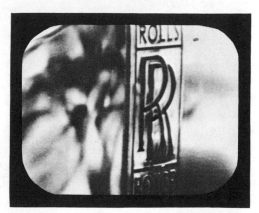

"It's a difference in philosophy. Henry Ford wanted to put the world on his wheels. Henry Royce wanted to build the world's best car, one at a time."

All of us know the frustration of Willy Loman, the tragic hero of Arthur Miller's play *Death of a Salesman.* "Once in my life," he said, "I would like to own something outright before it's broken. I'm always in a race with the junkyard. I just finish paying for the car and it's on its last legs. They time those things. They time them so when you finally pay for them they're used up."

Willy was right, you know, and this will soon be the fate of the car you're driving today. The trouble really is that nothing these days is built to last, and the motorcar best represents the fact that we live most of our lives in a junk society. Our durables are not very durable. But when something is built by hand out of materials given by nature, old-fashioned pride is maintained, a throwback to the principle of "The One-Horse Shay" — the schoolboy poem by Oliver Wendell Holmes.

---

*This story was originally broadcast on November 2, 1971.

> So the Deacon inquired of the village folk
> Where he could find the strongest oak,
> That couldn't be split nor bent nor broke —
> That was for spokes and floors and sills;
> He sent for lancewood to make the thills;
> The crossbars were ash from the straightest trees;
> The panels of white-wood, that cuts like cheese;
> But lasts like iron for things like these;
> Step and prop-iron, bolt and screw,
> Spring, tire, axle, and linchpin, too,
> Steel of the finest, bright and blue;
> Thoroughbrace, bison-skin, thick and wide;
> Boot, top, dasher, from tough old hide
> Found in the pit when the tanner died.
> That was the way he "put her through."
> "There!" said the Deacon, "Now she'll do!"

At the Rolls-Royce factories in London and Crewe, the same philosophy is maintained. The car division of Rolls was saved from the bankruptcy that faced the Rolls-Royce airplane engine complex. So it's built today in the same painstaking way, engineering always taking first place over styling.

The car seems almost too well made. The cheapest car they make costs $24,000, and you can pay as much as $50,000 for one. And you wonder, is it all really necessary, all that care?

The testbeds look more like an incubator ward than a production line. Every hundredth engine is pulled to pieces. A piece of every crankshaft is snipped off and is filed away with the number and pedigree of the car it was built for.

It is the atmosphere of a cottage industry — local craftsmen doing what they know best. The salaries at Rolls are slightly lower than those in the big automotive plants, but the tyranny of machines does not exist here. They say that the car has a personality, and the men who build it have managed to keep their own.

Is this a perfect car?

MAN: Well, I would say it is, yes. Why I say that is I've been at it all my life — 48 years. Naturally it's — it's varied slightly in those period of years. I mean, it used to be all timber at one time and now we're getting the bits of timber and metal.

SAFER: Well, what's the difference between this and a stamped-out car?

MAN: Well, a stamped-out car is just a stamped-out car, isn't it? I mean, anybody can build them.

SAFER: How long does a door like this take to make?

MAN: Well, it comes to me assembled like that, and I have to hang it and lock it and put the frames in — it takes me five days. That's each side. So that's ten days for each — for the complete job, you see.

SAFER: And then once it's all done and you see it drive out the back —

MAN: Well, I feel rather proud at times, naturally.

SAFER: How would you like to work in one of the big auto plants and run a machine that simply punched out one of those doors every ten seconds?

MAN: Well, I think it would bore me within two or three hours, I think. I'd sooner use my hands and make it myself.

SAFER: The youngest of the craftsmen at Rolls is the managing director. David

Plastow was only 38 when Rolls-Royce engines went bankrupt. He has managed to keep the car division out of the hands of the receiver.

What about this car costs $24,000? What makes it cost that much money?

DAVID PLASTOW: The amount of time that we spend making the pieces, after we've selected the very best materials. And in that context, you know, we make a lot of our own nuts and bolts because, in that way, we can check the material before we make the nuts and bolts, probably a very good example. And then we take a lot of time inspecting at the various stages of assembly, and eventually when the car is put together we test it extensively as well. And the whole gestation period is something like three or four months from the time that we issue an instruction to our workshops to build a car. And that's a very expensive process. And to get our cars quite significantly better than these very good American cars costs a great deal of money.

SAFER: Rolls-Royce produced their little red book long before Chairman Mao thought of his, but there is something about the language and the tone of the voice that give the two a great deal in common. The book is the *Rolls Royce Chauffeur's Guide.* Just listen to some of this.

Under deportment: "Never drive with your arm on the windowsill even when alone. You will not have full control of the car in an emergency and it looks untidy."

Under personal appearance: "A chauffeur must always present a smart appearance in full uniform and should wear a white shirt and collar, a black tie and black shoes. Leather gloves must be worn when driving and your cap at all times. When driving members of the royal family, see 'Royalty.' "

Passenger comfort: "It is your duty to ensure your passengers arrive safely and ready to conduct their business in a pleasant state of mind. Let there be no doubt in their opinion that this is the best car in the world."

After completing the course and after a three-year trial period of driving, the chauffeur receives the most coveted prize in Rolls-Roycery — the sterling silver cap badge.

There is something about a Rolls-Royce that is indisputably British. The style of the car changes every 10 years, and all these cars are at least 12 — some of them 15 — years old. But there is nothing dated about them. It's said that owning a Rolls changes the attitude of the owner. He begins to care about how he drives and how the car is looked after, one reason why the Rolls lasts so long. Letting the car down is somehow unpatriotic, and the familiar complaint about depreciation by new-car owners can hardly be applied to the Rolls.

John Gordon, a London used-car dealer:

JOHN GORDON: A very strong possibility with certain cars, already of the postwar era, that they have appreciated — certainly, yeah. We would say that a — a Silver Cloud, one today we are selling for more or less the same sort of price as we were three years ago.

SAFER: How long do you think a Rolls is meant to last when it's built?

GORDON (laughs):   Well, this one's 1934 — so this has lasted for, you know, 36, 37 years, and it's going to last another 36 or 37 years, one — well, you know, one can say without any fear of contradiction.

SAFER: One reason why Mr. Gordon's 37-year-old car will last so long is that Rolls-Royce is a British institution with an almost mythical tradition. In the bowels of the factory, two men who are the very pillars of the institution: Quigley, spare parts; Trimming, records. From Quigley you can get a connecting rod for a 1910 Silver Ghost, and from Trimming the complete engineering history of every car ever built.

Mr. Trimming, we've done a little bit of research of our own and we found that the longest continuous owner of the same Rolls-Royce is a Miss Overend of Dublin, who bought her car in 1926 and the chassis number is GNJ 52. Do you think you could find that for us?

TRIMMING: I have a record of that, yeah. (Indistinct) Miss L. Overend, and it — delivered on the 9th of June, 1927.

SAFER: We went to Dublin and found her. She is named Lutitia Overend. She is 91 and has been driving the car steadily since the day she bought it in 1927. Miss Overend and her mother ventured from Dublin to London to make the purchase. At first they looked at a Bentley, but decided on a Rolls because a Rolls could be started with a crank. Miss Overend would not have a car that could be started by hand. She stopped cranking this one every day when she was 87, on doctor's orders.

Miss Overend, you've had this car for 45 years now.

LUTITIA OVEREND: Yes, 44. Yes.

SAFER: Are you a satisfied customer?

OVEREND: Absolutely. I wouldn't change it for anything.

SAFER: Did you never feel like trading it in on a new one?

OVEREND: I never did, indeed. I wouldn't lose it for anything.

SAFER: What do you think of the new Rolls-Royce or the new Silver Shadow? You're disappointed in the new —

OVEREND: Oh, I — very much. And they — they've lowered the bonnets; it's not half as dignified. And they have the engine, it looks to me as if someone without much knowledge had taken a lot of components and just thrown them together. And you could not maintain it yourself — too complicated.

SAFER: The new Rolls-Royce sent many old Rolls fanciers into shock. They said it looked like nothing more than something out of Detroit in the fifties, with the fins cut off. They felt that Rolls had finally fallen victim to the fickle hands of modernity. Too many gimmicks, they cried.

OVEREND: I think automatic is an excellent thing for people with some disability, but if you have the use of your arms and legs and hands, I don't see what you want. Because the interest of driving is doing these things.

SAFER: You car is almost 45 years old now. How do you service it?

OVEREND: I service it myself — altogether myself. There are about 30 greasers; each of them takes five actions of your hand. I do the greasing; always started up till about four years ago when I got bad flu and the doctor wouldn't let me start it by hand after that, because it was quite bad. I'm all right now, but I start it by the starter. But there's this handle.

SAFER: Crank handle.

OVEREND: For cranking it, yes. And I think it's a wonderful thing. I think you should treat it as you would an animal or a person. Have sympathy with it and understanding of it and help it along. I couldn't imagine a Rolls owner neglecting their car. Now look at that leather. That's the original. It's real leather. Now look at that, that's 44 years there. Never renewed. Isn't that good? You should be proud of being able to have the fruits of man's brain that can produce a thing like this. That's the way I look at it. (Laughs)

SAFER: You've been driving now?

OVEREND: Since 1919. Count that. (Laughs)

SAFER: Fifty —

OVEREND: Two years.

SAFER: — two years.

OVEREND: The first was a Ford, a second-hand Ford, very good. The second was a Hillman, a two-seater, very good. The third was a Talbot.

SAFER: A Talbot.

OVEREND: And then the — this one. And this will see me out.

SAFER: And, indeed, it did. Lutitia Overend died a few years ago. The car, however, is still going strong.

Letters

ANDY ROONEY: The rest of the fellows all went out to play and they've asked me to read the mail.

Most of the mail this week was about our story on Norma and Mel Gabler, the Texas couple who are leading a crusade to get textbook publishers to put more patriotism and less material that the Gablers consider objectionable in school-books. The mail was predictably mixed. We got lots of letters like this one: "Thank God for Mr. and Mrs. Gabler. We need more people like them to protect our children from the wrong type of material that is printed in some of our school-books. This is not censorship. This is protecting the rights of our children."

And this one: "(Your story) on school textbooks makes it quite apparent that the educational bureaucrats are making second-class dummies out of our children, but that's because the textbooks are made up by first-class dummies."

But we also got lots of letters like this one: "As if we didn't already have enough trouble, we are now being plagued by a gang of self-appointed cops bent on dictating the words, actions and deeds of every man, woman and child. (They) look upon themselves as (having) a mandate from God to force us all to conform to their image."

And this one from an officer of the National Council of English Teachers: "The Gablers' scare tactics, half truths, innuendos, distortions and smear techniques are familiar propaganda devices. How low (will) the Gablers . . . stoop to promote their particular brand of taste, purity and Americanism?"

And there was this: ". . . 60 MINUTES incorrectly identified Richard Carroll as president of Ginn and Company. Mr. Carroll is president of (another textbook publisher) Allyn & Bacon. We would appreciate a timely correction."

We stand corrected.

About our story last week on the U.S. trust territory Micronesia, where once self-sufficient people now exist on government handouts, a viewer wrote: "Micronesia (is) a microcosm of the direction (the) entire United States is going . . . a nation in which the citizens are the clients of the government, instead of vice versa. Who is going to . . . pick up the tab when all of us discover the way to welfare paradise?"

And this: "While the . . . Micronesians eat chicken and beef, some people in our country eat dog and cat food. I guess we should all move to Micronesia."

As long as they've left me here alone, there's something I'd like to say about the mail. There are roughly four kinds of letters we get. First, there are the real nice letters from people who write to say they like what you do. You know, people with good taste. Then there are the letters from people who hate what you do. Maybe they have a specific complaint about something you did wrong. We all feel terrible when we get one of these, specially when the person with the complaint is right. I mean, they're the worst kind. You get quite a few letters from bright nuts. You know, they write to warn you about the end of the world or something like that. They are usually 14 pages, single spaced, written on both sides of the paper, and after they seal the letter they remember something they forgot to say, so they write it all around the outside edge of the envelope. I don't read those. Fourth are the letters from old friends. Every so often I'll get a letter from someone I played with in the third grade or someone I knew during the war. I often think how lucky those of us who appear on television are. All of our lives are compartmentalized, but most people lose track of old friends from other compartments, because neither knows where to find the other. If you appear on 60 MINUTES, people know where to find you.

INDEX

A

Abernathy, Ralph, 394
abortion, rights to, 1
Abrams, Robert, 142
Abscam, 384
Acoin, Michael, 191, 192
Adams, Seibert, 610
Adorno, Henry, 85
Aernandez, Keith, 426
aerobic dancing, 135
Afghanistan, 314-17
  and Soviet Union, 384-85, 436-45,
    469, 470
airplane accidents, 219-24
Akins, James, 508-509
Alberta Farms, 177-78
Alfanao, Diana, 458, 459
Al-Khalifa, Mohamed, 589-92
All About Eve, 266
All You Need to Know About the IRS
    (Strassels), 346
American Cancer Society, 573
American Medical Association, 210
Armstrong, Herbert W., 593-600
Anderson, John, 334-39, 361, 382,
    486
anesthesia, hypnosis for, 209
angel dust, 36, 325, 326
Anstalt, 163-64
anti-Semitism, 7-11, 432, 480
Antoniou, Michael, 220, 221, 222
Arafat, Yasir, 9, 200, 203, 204, 302
ARAMCO companies, 201, 216
Armstrong, Scott, 165-70
Armstrong, Ted, 593-600
Army Corps of Engineers, 483
art, tastes in, 359-60
Arthritis Foundation, 452
Ash, Mary Kay, 88-93
assassination, 547-51, 566-72
Associated Press, 179-80
Astroturf, 246, 279

athletics:
  and academics, 296-31, 328, 344,
    403-404
  Bobby Knight, 377-81
  injuries in, 245-50, 279
  salaries in, 426-30
attitudes and health, 172-77
auctions for cars, 124-25
Auletta, Ken, 224-28
Avanti, design of, 77, 80
Aviation Week, 467
Avnari, Uri, 466-67
Axelrod, David, 556-59

B

Baeder, Don, 184-89
Bahrain, Amir of, 589-92, 620
Baker, Howard, 355, 356
Ball, George, 508
"Ballad of Rodger Young, The," 126
Bani-Sadr, 369-70
Banoun, Raymond, 453, 454
Barker, Dave, 578
Barnard, Brain, 180
Bartlett, Gary, 563-65
baseball, salaries in, 426-30
basketball, 377-81
battered family, with children, 143-48
Baum Garn, 177-81 360
Baum, Peggy, 177, 180
Beard, Robin L., 482-87, 506
Beechcraft plane, 219, 221-22, 223
Begin, Menachem, 11, 303, 304, 465
Bell, Griffin, 103
Benn, Anthony Wedgwood, 74
Benny, Jack, 498-99
Benton, Thomas Hart, 572
Berg, David, 149, 150
Bernstein, Jamie, 319
Bernstein, Leonard, 318-23, 344
Berry, Varreece, 401

Berwid, Adam, 420-25, 451
Berwid, Ewa, 420-25
Bessman, Samuel, 133, 135
Beverly Hills Doctors Hospital, 69
bio-feedback, 134, 275
Bircher-Benner Clinic, 585-86
Black, Hugo, 167, 168, 169
Blackmun, Justice, 169
Blake, William, 158, 159
Blecker, Robert, 228
Bleir, Rocky, 250, 279
Blood, Steven W., 393, 395, 396, 397
blood pressure, self-reading of, 131
Blue Angels, 269-71
Blue Eagle, 94
Blue Light, The (Riefenstahl), 433
Boeing, 58, 59
Bond, Langhorne, 219
Boren, Sen., 383
Boston University, 234-39, 262
Bottarini, Tony, 172-77
Bowes, Gus, 490
Bowles, Chuck, 159
Bradshaw, Terry, 245, 246, 248, 279
Brady, Ben, 499, 500
Brady, Ray, 446
Braeseke, Barry, 628, 629
Branca, Ron, 148
Brandeis, Justice, 167
breast examination, self
    administration of, 131
Brennan, Justice, 168, 169, 171
Brethren, The (Woodward and
    Armstrong), 165-70
Brezhnev, 340
Briggs, John, 72
Brookins, H. Hartford, 396
Brown, Bernard, 110, 111
Brown, Cecil, 45, 46
Brown, Gordon, 373, 374
Brown, Harold, 316
Brown, Jerry, 73, 354, 358
Brown, Paul, 545
Brown & Root, 575-79, 605
Brzezinski, Zbigniew, 316
Buckner, Quinn, 379
BU Exposure, 236, 237
Bugatti, Royale, 124

Bulaich, Norm, 245
Bulgaria, 547-51
Bureau of Biologics, 198
Burger, Warren, 165-70
burglary, 399-403
    and insurance, 400
    recoveries from, 401-402
Burnett, Carol, 271, 278
Burton, Lawrence, 541-46, 573
Bush, George, 256-60, 279, 289, 338,
    355, 356, 382
busing, 520
Butler, Fred, 300
BU Women's Yellow Pages, 236
Byrne, Brendan, 160

C

Califano, Joseph, 103
California Department of Health, 71,
    72
California Water Quality Control
    Board, 184, 185
Campbell, Earl, 249
Camp David agreements, 373
cancer, 172-77, 541-46
Cancer Syndrome, The (Moss), 543
Canull, Carl, 350, 351, 352
Cardozo, Justice, 167
Cardoza, Michael, 628, 629, 630
Carmel Ranch Partners, 62
Carnahan, Charles, 184, 185
Carroll, Richard, 607, 635
Carson, Johnny, 38, 493-500, 522-23
cars, 631-35
    antique car clubs, 122
    auctions, 124-25
    maintenance of, 121-25
    shilling for, 124
Carter, Billy, 415, 435, 499
Carter, Jimmy, 13, 16, 23-27, 56, 59,
    74, 82, 94, 128, 129, 130, 203,
    260, 306, 327, 354, 363-64, 383,
    499, 507
Cass, Nancy, 458, 459
Castro, Fidel, 23-27, 471-78

Catholics in Northern Ireland, 27, 28, 31, 33, 48
Cazares, Gabe, 454, 455, 456
CCCP-TV in Moscow, 230-33
Center for Attitudinal Healing, 172-77
Cervi, Bernie, 628-630
Cessna plane, 219-23
Cezanne, 49-55, 82
Chalmers, Laurence, 49-55
Chamberlain, Neville, 345, 603
Chapman, C. Brewster, 618
Chappaquiddick, 217, 218, 358
Charity Fraud Bureau of New York State, 137, 141
Chateau Renaissance Motel, 475-76
Chatterton, Robert, 1-6
Cheevers, Randy, 44, 45
chemotherapy, 175, 176
Cherayavev, 283
Chesterton, G.K., 33
Chiang Kai-shek, 40
Chicago Art Institute, 82
  stolen paintings from, 49-55
children and divorce, 411-15
China Syndrome, 149
Chodos, Hillel, 596, 597
Church, Frank, 509-10
Church of Jesus Christ of the Latter Day Saints. See Mormons
CIA, 27, 66, 257, 258, 362, 366, 367, 369, 439
Cincinnati Enquirer, 96
cinema, 536-38
City of God, 284-89
Civiletti, 367
civil rights movement, 137-42
Clearwater Conspiracy, 453-59
Clement, R.J., 542-43
Clements, Martha, 194
Cleveland Clinic, 134
Clinton Project, 150-52
Clowns, The (Fellini), 536
cocaine, 324, 325, 326, 492
Corcoran, Tommy, 168-69
Cohn, Roy, 224-29
Cole, Cheryl, 625, 630
Collins, Marva, 115-21, 136, 210
Columbia Dam, 482-87

Commodity Credit Corporation, 94
Commonwealth monthly magazine, 236
Congress and business regulation, 308-13
Connally, John, 212-18, 244, 257, 338, 355, 356
Consolo, Bonnie, 524-28, 554
contract, for murder, 143-48, 567
Cook, Bill, 155, 156
Coolidge, Calvin, 93
Cooper, Gary, 123
Cooper, Paulette, 456, 458
CORE, 137-42, 171, 397, 452
Cornelson, Ronald, 2-3, 4
Cornick, Carter, 472
cosmetic company, 88-93
Cottam, Richard, 367, 368
Cowart, Donna, 197
Crile, George, 574-79
crimes:
  burglary, 399-403
  murder, 143-48, 420-25, 572, 582
  and rights of accused, 624-30
  robbery, 529-35
criminal justice system, 189-94
Criswell, W.A., 18, 19
Crout, Richard, 407, 408, 410
Cuba and Castro, 23-27, 471-78
Cuban Nationalist Movement (CNM), 471, 474, 476, 477
Cunningham, Ray, 138, 139, 393, 395, 397, 398
Cunningham, Riggs, 123
Curtiz, Michael, 263, 264

D

Dale, Parker, 463-64
Dalton gang, 571
Dane, John, 565-72
Danforth, John, 310-11
Darrington Prison Farm, 399
Davis, Bette, 263-68, 295
Davis, Cordelia, 349-54
Davis, William, 297-98

Day, Stacy, 546
Dayan, Moshe, 9, 303
DBCP, 186-87
De Brum, Tony, 391, 616-17
De Cordova, Fred, 494, 495
Dedham House of Correction, 189
defense and Middle East, 372-77
Defense Nuclear Agency, 391
DeLuca, Joseph, 14
De Maro, Joseph, 421
Dennison, Mary, 137, 141
Denver Center for the Performing
    Arts, 107
Department of Agriculture, 82
Department of Energy (DOE), 14-17,
    391
Department of Health, Education and
    Welfare, 102, 103
Department of Justice and religious
    group, 453
Department of Labor, 109
Dershowitz, Alan, 191, 193-94
Desautels, Paul, 459-60
design of commercial products,
    77-81
  simplicity in, 78
Deukmejian, George, 188-89
DeVillez, Bernard, 143-48
DeVillez, Joyce, 143-48, 171
Dien Bien Phu, 611
Diggett, Charles, 206
divorce, 411-15
  and taxes, 413
DMSO (dimethyl sulfoxide), 405-11,
    434, 452
Dolce Vita, La (Fellini), 537
Dole, Bob, 355
Donzis, Byron, 248, 249
Dorsett, Tony, 245
Dosa Assessment Team, 391
Doss, Dwight H., 351-52, 353
Douglas, William, 167
Dover, Willard, 460-61
Drug Enforcement Administration,
    489, 490, 491
drugs, 434
  and DMSO, 405-11, 434, 452
  and hypnosis, 208

program for abuse of, 271-78
regulation of, 489-91
and religion, 83-88, 113, 154
risks in, 187
slang for, 36
student use of, 33-38
trade in, 323-27
Duesenberg SSJ, 123
Dunbar, Ethel, 240
Dymally, Mervin, 72

E

"Earn it" program, 189-94
  victims in, 191-92
Eastman Kodak, 448
Echols, Randy, 299, 300, 301
economy, inflation, 384
Edson, Robert, 183, 184, 185
education:
  adult literature for children, 115-21
  integration in, 539, 517-21
  university administration, 234-39
Edwards, Edwin, 13-17
Edwards, Harry, 297-98, 299
Edwards, Mike, 436
Eggspuehler, Jack, 219, 220, 223
Egypt:
  and Israel, 303, 304-305
  and Sadat, 128-29
electrical outlets, 153-54
Ellenberger, Norm, 344
Ellicot, Dorothy, 553
Ellington, Mark, 76, 77
El Paso natural gas case, 168
embargoes and arms, 469
Enewetak, 419
  nuclear problem at, 388-93
Enger, Vladik, 283
Environmental Protection Agency
    (EPA), 556-57
Equal Rights Amendment (ERA), 42,
    177, 336
Esposti, Julie, 134
Ethiopian Orthodox Church, 113

Ethiopian Zion Coptic Church of
    Miami, 82-88, 113, 154
Evans, R.D., 269, 271
Exxon sign, 201, 216
    design of, 77, 80

F

Fall, Dennis, 32
Farhana, Mansour, 510, 511
Farley, John, 156, 157
Farmer, James, 141, 142
Farmers Home Administration
    (FmHA), 60-65
Fauntroy, Walter, 518, 519
FBI, 384, 592-93
    and burglary, 402
    and Cubans, 471, 472, 474, 475,
    477
    and espionage, 281, 282
Featherston, Royce, 399-403
Federal Aviation Authority (FAA), 219,
    222, 223-24
Federal Center for Disease Control
    (CDC), 99, 100, 101
Federal Deposit Insurance
    Corporation, 95
Federal Trade Commission (FTC),
    308-13, 328
Fellini, Federico, 536-38
Feninger, Mario, 458, 459
Ferguson, Tom, 131-36
Ferrell, Milton, 85
first amendment rights, 85, 610
Fitzgerald, Ed, 429
Fitzsimmons Hospital, 560
Fjorback, E.M., 19, 20
Florida Correctional Institution for
    Women, 46
Flynt, Larry, 499
Food and Drug Administration (FDA),
    405, 410
football, 245-48, 279
Ford, Benson, 224
Ford, Gerald, 13, 98, 102, 126, 258,
    355, 357, 382, 383
Ford, Henry, 226, 631

Foss, Ron, 626
Francis, Russ, 245
free agent system, 427, 428-29
French Foreign Legion, 610-15
Fullwood, James, 461

G

Gabler, Mel, 625
Gaiman, David, 456-57, 458
Galante, Carmine, 226
Galil rifles, 466, 467
Gall, David, 548
Gallois, Liza, 515-16
Galvin, Barny, 613, 614
Ganja, 84
Garnett, Wendell, 137
Garrison Library, 553
Garvey, Ed, 246, 250
Gassner, Hans-Peter, 163, 164, 165
gas stations, fraud in, 529-35, 554
Gauguin, Paul, 49
Gabler, Norma, 606-10, 625
General Accounting Office (GAO),
    575, 577, 618
Gent, Peter, 247
Genthner, Wade, 207, 208
Georgetown Day School, 519
Georgia Consumer Agency, 530
Gerstner, Bill, 150, 151, 152
Gibraltar Broadcasting Corporation,
    552
"Gimme Shelter," 459-65
Ginn Company, 607
Give Me That Prime Time Religion
    (Sholes), 286
Glauber, Steve, 530-32, 533
Glenn, Stan, 298-99
Glover, Scott, 206-207
Glover Clinic, 206
Goebbels, Joseph, 431-432
Goering, 479
Goldwater, Barry, 40, 382-85, 404
Gonzalez, Henry B., 213, 215
Goodman, Bob, 259, 260
Gordon, John, 673
Gordon, Keith, 85, 86, 87

Gore, Albert, 188
Gorum Company, 448
Gottlieb, Bob, 124
Graham, Billy, 7-11
Grapes of Wrath (Steinbeck), 60
Graves, Carol, 530, 533
Great Britain and Northern Ireland,
    27-33
Great Depression, 93-95
Great White Brotherhood, 242-43
Green, Joe, 246, 247, 248
Green Book (Qaddafi), 415
Grezlecki, Frank, 448
Griffith, Bill, 447
Griffith, Clark, 427, 428
Gross, Katherine, 131
Grossman, Shary, 54
GRU, 280-84
Gubriel missile, 466, 467
Guidry, Ron, 428, 452
Guillain Barre Syndrome (GBS),
    98-103
Guthrie, D.A., 186, 187

H

Haast, Bill, 195-98
Haber, Melvin, 515
Hackbart, Dale, 247
Hackett, Mims, 155-60
Haig, Alexander, 383
Halberstam, Michael, 132
Halloran, Colonel, 389-90
Hamilton, Carrie, 271, 278
Hammond, Wayne, 412
handicapped as musician, 524-28
Harlan, Justice, 168
Harrelson, Sheila, 609
Harris, Robert, 185-86
Harrison, Ben, 447
Hart, William, 151
Hatch, Orrin, 308-309
Hattwick, Michael, 101
Hauser, Rita, 214
Hauthal, H.G., 408
Havlichek, John, 380
Hawkins, Bob, 530, 532

Hayes, Woody, 403
Haynes, Richard, 626, 629, 630
health care:
    attitude support system for, 172-77
    cancer, 172-77, 541-46
    fraud in, 68-73
    natural baths, 584-87
    self-care in, 131-36
    swine flu, 98-103
health fairs, 132
Hecla Mining Company, 447
Helms, Ambassador, 365
Helping Hand Clinic, 133
Hendler, Joel, 68-73
Hendrix, Charlotte, 145-46
heroin, 208, 324, 325, 326
Hickel, Walter, 229, 615
Hikmatyar, Gulbadin, 443
Hitler, Adolf, 430-31, 433, 479
Hodgson, Voigt, 248
Hollings, Ernest, 310
Holmes, Oliver Wendell, 167, 631-32
homicide, 143-48
Hooker Chemical Co., 183-89, 210,
    555-60
Hooks, Benjamin, 397
Hooley, Joyce, 191, 192
Hoover, Herbert, 93
Hoskins, Lee, 618
hostages in Iran, 127-31
Houston Lighting and Power, 578-79
Hoving, Walter, 448, 449
Hua, Chairman, 340
Hubbard, L. Ron, 453, 454, 455, 457,
    458
human rights, universal, 468
Hunt, Nelson Bunker, 445-46, 449,
    450, 470, 487
hypnosis, 205-209
    and anesthesia, 209
    and drugs, 208

I

Idell, Herman, 492
Illinois Commerce Commission, 151
Illinois Power Company, 149-53, 294

immigration, illegal, 107-12
Immigration and Naturalization
    Service, 108
Imperial Hospital, 69
incest, 144
Indiana State Prison for Women, 143,
    148
Indiana University, 377-81
Industrial Testing Laboratory, 326
infants/fetuses:
    brain damage in, diagnosis of, 1-6
    rights of, 1-6
    Weaver case, 1-6
influenza vaccine, 101
Innis, Doris, 140
Innis, Roy, 137-42, 171, 394
integration in education, 539
Internal revenue service (IRS), 279,
    346-49, 371
    and nonreported income, 251-56
    and religious groups, 453, 600
    and tax shelters, 463-464
International Ladies Garment
    Workers, 111
Iran, 127-31, 362-71, 387, 467, 469
Irish Republican Army (IRA), 27, 29,
    48
Islam:
    and terrorism, 128
    and women, 129
Israel, 9, 10, 302-308
    and arms sales, 465-69
    and oil, 214-15
    and Palestinians, 128-29

J

Jackson, Andrew, 572
Jackson, Jesse, 7-11, 22
Jackson, John, 394, 395
Jackson, Reggie, 429
Jacob, Stanley, 405, 407, 408, 409,
    410, 434
James, Jesse, 571
Jampolsky, Jerry, 173, 174, 175
Jarrett, Jacqueline, 411-14, 435
Jarrett, Walter, 411-15, 435

Jeffers, Clifton, 628-29
Jekinson, Edward, 607, 608, 610
Jenkins, Farris, 483
Jewish Defense League (JDL),
    567-69
Johnson, Lyndon, 25, 167, 213
Johnson, Sterling, 325
Johnson, Tim, 352-53
Jones, Bert, 245
Jordan, Barbara, 213, 214, 215
Journal of the American Medical
    Association, 405, 407
Jushkevitshus, Henrikus, 231
justice and race, 155-60
Justice Department, 103, 453

K

Keiker, Walter, 163, 164
Kennan, George, 314-17, 345
Kennedy, Edward, 72-73, 96, 181-82,
    217, 218, 259, 307, 335, 354,
    357-58, 383, 475, 520
Kennedy, John, 25, 27
Kennedy, Robert, 225
Kfir C-2, 428
KGB, 66, 280-84, 550
Khomeini, Ayatollah, 127-31, 203,
    362, 467, 550, 551, 626
kidnapping, 155-60
Kienast, Dick, 488-93
King, Martin Luther, 213, 214, 393
Kirby, Charles, 121, 122
Kiriakos, Keo, 191
Kirk, Larry, 562
Kirkland, Lane, 58
Kirkpatrick, Curry, 378
Kirschenman, Arnold, 60-65
Kissinger, Henry, 229, 292, 368, 374,
    375, 507-12, 539, 615
Klemow, Marvin, 466, 467
Knight, Bobby, 377-81, 403
Knight, Doug, 146
Kohlhof, Ken, 326
Korea:
    labor in, 111, 112
    wages in, 111

Kostov, Vladimir, 551
Koussevitsky, 318, 319
Koziar, Jim, 269-70
Kramer, Albert, 189, 190, 191, 193,
    194
Kramer vs. Kramer, 411
Krings, Raymond, 560-62
Krupa, Gene, 622
Kruse, Dean, 125
Kruse Auctioneers, 125
Kurtz, Dan, 137, 138, 140, 141
Kurtz, Jerome, 463, 464
Kwajalein missile, 616

L

Lack, Andy, 436
Lady Reeding Government Hospital,
    443
Lambert, Jack, 246
L'Amour, Louis, 579-83
Lando, Barry, 50, 51, 52
Latham, Jim, 269
Leaf, Jesse, 365
Lee, William, 140, 141
Lefkowitz, Louis, 140, 142
Lefler, Ray, 137
Legal Aid Service, 46
Leicht, Wayne, 461
Lenin, 626
Lessiovsky, Victor, 283, 284
Letelier, Orlando, 476, 477
Levitt, Jeanne, 516-17
Lewis, David, 99
Liberia, 239-43, 262
Libya, 415-18, 435
Liechtenstein, 160-165
Lindberg, Arthur, 281, 282, 283
Lindbergh, Anne Morrow, 478-82,
    506
Lindbergh, Charles, 478-82
Llewellyn, Betty, 462
loans, federal, for farmers, 60-65
Loeb, William, 354-59, 371
Loewenwarter, Paul, 149, 150, 152
Loewy, Raymond, 77-81, 97
Losee, Richard, 179

Louv, Brother, 83-88, 113, 154
Love Canal, 183, 555-60
Love Canal Homeowners
    Association, 557, 558
Lowery, Joseph, 394, 395, 396
Lucas, Jerry, 380
Luce, Clare Booth, 39-43, 66-67
Luce, Harry, 39
Lunn, Elmo, 485, 486
Lunsford, Clyde, 178

M

Maayan, Yosef, 465, 467, 468
McBride, Lloyd, 58
McCarthy, Eugene, 337, 338
McCarthy, Joseph, 224, 228
McCarthy, Max, 364
McClure, Bill, 536
Macevily, Charles, 421, 422, 423
McFarland, Lon, 485
McGovern, George, 212, 337, 338,
    475, 520
McGregor, Robert, 45
McGuire, Al, 379, 380
McGuire, Robert, 324, 326
McInerney, Christopher, 191, 192
McKhann, Guy, 198
Mackie, Maitland, 76
McMahon, Ed, 495, 496
Macmillan Company, 609
McMullin, Mike, 612
MacPhal, Lee, 429
McWilliams, Larry, 280, 281, 284
Manchester Union Leader, The, 354,
    355
Maples, Ladell, 131
Maraynes, Allan, 54
Margolin, Ephraim, 625, 626, 630
Marienbad baths, 584-87
marijuana, 33, 83-88, 113, 154, 326,
    491, 492
Markov, Annabel, 547-48
Markov, Georgi, 547-51
Marshall, Thurgood, 167, 168
Martin, D., 408
Martin, William, 17-21

Mary Kay Cosmetics, 88-93
Massachusetts Civil Liberties Union, 234
Mastroianni, Marcello, 537
Mattei, Charles, 533
Matysiak, Rick, 530
Maynis, Ron, 269
Mazur, Don, 16
Meany, George, 58
Medicaid fraud, 96
MediCal Fraud Unit, 68-73
Medical Self-Care, 132
Medicare and fraud, 69
Meehan, Bob, 271-78
mental retardation and attitudes, 120
Mercedes SSK, 123
mercenaries, 565-72
Merrill, Michael, 267
Messelson, Matthew, 331, 332
Messersmith, Andy, 427
Messner, Karen, 195, 196
Mesurado Corporation, 242
Metcalf, Arthur, 235, 238
Metropolitan Opera, 105, 106
Meyer, Jr., Harry M., 198
Meyer, Russ, 221
Micronesia, 615-19, 635-36
Middle East Economic Survey, 216
military arms sales, 465-69
Millard, Vincent, 227
Miller, Marvin, 427, 428, 452
Minton, Michael, 413, 414
Mintz, Lowell, 450
Mirage jet, 468
Mitchell, Ted, 388-89
Mobil, 201, 216
Moffitt, Michael, 476
Monteleagre, Felicia, 319
Moore, Terry Jean, 43-47
Moore, Tom, 72, 73
Mormon Church, 177, 199
Morrow, Charles, 506
Morton Salt Mine, 13
Moses, Harry, 331
Moss, Larry, 156, 158
Moss, Ralph, 543
Mother Goose, 606
Mott, Stewart, 338

Moulin de la Tuilerie, 600-605
mujahadeen, 436, 469
multiple schlerosis (MS), 195-98
Munson, Thurman, 219
murder, 143-48, 420-25, 567, 572
    in old West, 582
    second-degree, 143
Murphy, Thomas, 607-608
Murray, Simon, 612, 615
musicians, jazz singer, 621-24
Muskie, Edmund, 355, 383
MX missiles, 58, 59, 336-37

N

NAACP, 397, 398
Naby, Eden, 437-40
NASA, design in, 80
National Academy of Sciences, 408
National Association of Flight Instructors, 219
National Black Community Fund (NBCF), 397
National Cancer Institute, 186, 544, 545
National Council of English Teachers, 635
National Multiple Schlerosis Society, 198
National Operating Committee on Standards for Athletic Equipment, 248
National Recovery Administration (NRA), 94
National Urban League, 398, 419
NCAA, 296-31, 379, 381
Negrin, Eulalio, 473, 475
Nevins, Edward, 330-33, 360-61
New Deal, 94-95
New Jersey Public Health Lab, 99
Newman, Kenneth, 32, 33
New York Chinatown, 109, 112
New York Hypnosis Center, 208
NFL, 279
    injuries in, 245, 246
    rules in, 247-48

Nicaraguan National Guide, 467
Nicket Enterprises, 62
Nights of Cabiria, The (Fellini), 537
Nixon, Richard, 25, 166, 292, 355, 383, 384, 508
Noel, Tom, 13
Noll, Chuck, 250
North American Rockwell, 223
North Dallas Forty, 247
Northern Ireland, 27-33
Novo, Guillermo, 476, 477
Novocaine, 326
nuclear power, 149-53, 388-93, 574-77, 605
Nuclear Regulatory Commission (NRC), 152, 153, 575, 576, 577, 605
nutrition, 135
    and self-care, 133

O

Occidental Oil, 75, 183-89
O'Connor, Peter, 436
O'Day, Anita, 621-24
Office of Consumer Affairs, 532
Offner, Arnold, 234, 235, 236
oil, 12-17
    Israel, 214-15
    and labor, 72-77
    in Oman, 372-73, 377
    price levels of, 200-204, 510
    profits in, 216-17
    recovery in Middle East, 589-92
    and safety, 15
O'Laughlin, Michael, 559
Olson, Bob, 401, 402
Olympia (Riefenstahl), 430
Olympics, 316, 383, 432
Oman, 372-77, 403
Omega 7, 471-78, 505-506
OPEC, 12, 56, 74, 75, 200, 202, 508, 591
opium, 323
Oral Roberts University, 287
Orange, New Jersey, 155-60
Orsini, Betty, 455, 456

Osborne, A., 185
Overby, Bob, 146
Overend, Lutitia, 634-35
Owens, Brig, 247
Owens, Jesse, 432

P

Packard sedan, 124
Pahlevi, Mohammed Riza. *See* Shah of Iran
Paigen, Beverly, 556-58
Palestine Liberation Organization (PLO), 9, 373, 568
Palestinians, 9, 373, 415, 568
    and Israel, 128-29
    and oil, 202
    and Soviet Union, 203-204
Palmer Drug Abuse Program (PDAP), 271-78, 294-95
Palm Springs, 513-17
Panama Canal, 357, 359
Pan American Games, 377
Panov, Cyril, 549
Pap-smears, self-administration of, 131
Parker, Dave, 426
parole board, 47
Pastorini, Dan, 245, 248, 249
patent rights, 423-24
Patterson, Eugene, 455, 456
Patton, George, 238
Pavarotti, Luciano, 104-107, 126
PCP, 36
Peay, Marvin, 138, 139, 142
Peninsula Counseling Center, 208
Pepper, Claude, 434
Pertschuk, Mike, 308-13, 328
pesticides, waste dumping, 183-89
Petroleum Wives Club, 76
pets, dogs, 434
Pharm-Chem Foundation, 491
Phillips, "Bum," 249
Phillips, Martin, 171
Phoenix House, 34, 35, 36, 323, 325
Phoenix missiles, 508

Pilgrim State , 422, 423
Pinoak Publications, 288-89
Piper plane, 219, 223
Pitkin County, 488-93
Plastow, David, 632-33

Players Association, 452
plutonium wastes, 390
police and rights of society, 624-30
Posner, Volodya, 232
Possert, Frank, 157

Powell, Justice, 169
Powell, Lewis, 165-66, 167
Precht, Henry, 371
President's Council on Environmental
    Quality, 185

prices, 450-51
Procaine, 326
propaganda, 232, 430-33, 480
Propper, Eugene, 476
Protestants in Northern Ireland, 27,
    28, 31, 48

Provos, 29
Pudding Club, 500
PUSH, 394, 395, 397, 398

Q

Qaboos, 376
Qaddafi, Muammar el-, 415-18, 435
Quaalude, 323, 324
Quarles, Williams, 131
Quillen, Jim, 110

R

race relations, 7-11, 137, 155-60,
    517-21
Radcliffe, Steve, 150, 151, 152, 153
Rader, Stanley, 593-600, 620
Radio Free Europe, 549
Raimond, Ralph, 108, 112
Ralston, Ralph, 45, 46
Ramirex, David, 209
Random House, 610

Rather, Dan, 7-17, 56-60, 81, 83-88,
    107-12, 121, 126-36, 153,
    155-60, 189-94, 205-209,
    219-24, 229, 244, 256-60,
    271-78, 289-93, 302, 313-17,
    328-33, 377-81, 399-403,
    430-33, 436-45, 469-70, 487,
    505, 507-12, 529-35, 547-51,
    565-72, 574-79, 605, 624-30
Ray, Roger, 390-93
Rayburn, Taylor, 482
Razmi, Reza, 368, 369
Razo, Joe, 108
Reader's Digest, 524
Reading, 606-10
Reagan, Ronald, 114, 218, 289-93,
    313, 317, 338, 355, 356, 357, 382
Reasoner, Harry, 11, 17-21, 33-38,
    43-47, 73-77, 93-95, 121-25, 136,
    149-53, 170, 177-81, 195-98,
    210-11, 230-33, 245-50, 269-71,
    295, 308-13, 323-27, 344-45,
    349-54, 371, 382-86, 418-19,
    426-30, 445-50, 465, 482-87,
    500-504, 513, 521, 536-38,
    541-46, 555-60, 600-605,
    610-15, 621-24
Reconstruction Finance Corporation,
    94
Reese, Peewee, 428
religion:
    and drugs, 83-88, 113, 154
    financial excesses in, 593-600
    and media, 284-89
    and Northern Ireland conflict, 27-33
    preaching style in, 17-21
    and taxes, 88, 464, 453
    and women's rights, 177
Reshev patrol boats, 467
Retail Merchants Association, 111
Reyes, Andres, 473, 475
Ricin, 548-49
Riefenstahl, Leni, 430-33
Riley, Don, 189, 191, 193
Rio Bravo Tennis Ranch, 64
robbery, 529-35
Roberts, Baden, 285
Roberts, Judy, 98-103

Roberts, Oral, 284-89, 313
Roberts, Vadeen, 285
Rockefeller, David, 355, 356
Rock of Gibraltar, 552-54
Rolls-Royce, 123, 631-35,
   Chauffeur's Guide, 633
Rooney, Andy, 11, 47-48, 66, 81-82,
   95-96, 112-13, 126, 153-54,
   170-71, 199, 261, 278, 294,
   327-28, 343-44, 359-60, 386,
   418-19, 434, 450-51, 505,
   521-22, 538-59, 588, 619-20,
   635-36
Roosevelt, Eleanor, 41
Roosevelt, Franklin, 41, 94, 95, 480
Rosch, Paul, 542, 546
Rose, Teresa, 133, 134
Rosenthal, Mitchel, 34-37, 326
Rossman, Joe, 486, 487
Rowsell, Richard, 448-49
Royal Ulster Constabulary (RUC), 32
Rozelle, Peter, 246, 250
Rubin, Edward, 68-73, 114, 181
Rubin, Irv, 568-69
Rumsey, Tim, 133
Russo, Marty, 311
Ruth, Babe, 428
Ryan, Nolan, 426
Ryles, Tim, 533-34

S

Sadat, Anwar, 128, 303, 304, 305,
   373, 465
Safer, Morley, 21-22, 39-43, 60-65,
   77-81, 88-93, 104-107, 115-21,
   143-48, 160-65, 172-77, 189,
   210, 212, 218, 224-29, 239-43,
   251-56, 261-62, 278, 279,
   284-89, 294, 334-39, 354-59,
   386-93, 513-17, 536, 539-40,
   573, 579-83, 589-92. 615-19,
   620, 631-35
Sahara Hotel, 499
Said, Qaboos bin, 372-77
St. Albans School for Boys, 520
St. Cyr, 612

St. Patrick's Roman Catholic Church,
   20
salaries, in sports, 426-30
Salt II, 58, 59
Samghabadi, Raji, 363, 364, 366
Santana, Armando, 471-74, 477, 478
Santana, Eduardo, 471, 474, 477, 478
Satyricon (Fellini), 537
Sugier, Robert, 51
Savak, 364-67
Scandal of Scientology, The
   (Cooper), 456
Scarborough, Gale, 269
Scherer, Bob, 472, 478
Schmidt, Mike, 429
Schoenfeld, D., 123
School of the Holy Child, 520
Scientific American, 122
Scientology, 453-59, 487
Scotland and oil, 73-77
Scotland Yard, 548
Scripps-Booth touring car, 122
Search for Freedom, 609
Seasons of Shame (Yeager), 250
Seaver, Tom, 427
Secret Service, U.S., 266
Securities and Exchange
   Commission (SEC), 95
Seitz, Peter, 427
Sencer, David, 100-102
Senn, Deborah, 151
Serratia marcescens, 330-33
sexual abuse, 144
Seyfrit, Karl, 576, 577
Shafrir missiles, 467
Shah of Iran, 127-28, 129, 204,
   362-63, 367, 368, 370, 371, 376,
   510-11, 539
Sheppard, Ben, 196, 197
Sherrick, Sandy, 408-10
Shevchenko, Arkady, 280, 281, 282,
   284
shilling for cars, 124
Shipper's Export Declaration, 402
Sholes, Robert, 286-89
Shriver, Paul, 148
Siegfried, Harry, 380
Silber, John, 234-39, 262

silver:
  investment of, 470
  price of, 445-50
  uses of, 449

Silver, Brent, 221
Silver Commodities Exchange, 447
Silver Ghost, 633
Simmons, Irv, 323, 324
Simon, William, 509, 510, 511
Sisco, Joseph, 369
Six Day War, 468
Sloan Kettering Cancer Research
  Institute, 543

Smith, Al, 602
Smith, D.L., 269, 270
Smith, Gary, 179
Smith, Warren, 325-26
smoking and disease, 35
snake venom for MS treatment,
  195-98

Social Security, 95, 112, 252-54
Solomon, Arthur, 413
Somoza, Anastasio, 467
Sotheby's Gallery, 52, 54
South Africa and Israel, 9
Southern Christian Leadership
  Conference (SCLC), 393-98, 419

South Texas Nuclear Project, 574-78
Soviet Union:
  and Afghanistan, 314-17, 384-85,
    436-45, 469, 470
  and Cuba, 23, 24, 26-27
  and Middle East, 589
  and oil, 376-77
  and Palestinians, 203-204
  spies of in U.S., 280-84
  television in, 230-33, 261

Spiegel, Herbert, 205-209
spies, Russian in U.S., 66, 280-84,
  550

Standard Oil, 216
Stanton Hospital, 69, 71, 72
Stargell, Willie, 428
Steinbeck, John, 60
Steinbrenner, George, 429
Stennett, Rennie, 427

Sterns, Gerry, 222, 223
Stevens, John Paul, 168
Stewart, Potter, 166, 169
Stingley, Darryl, 245, 247, 250
Stockholm International Peace
  Research Institute, 468
Strada, La (Fellini), 537
Strassels, Paul, 346-49
strategic oil reserve, 13, 14
stress therapy, 135
strike, projected, 430
Supreme Court justices, 165-70
  competency of, 166
  disability of, 167-68

Swan, Craig, 426
Swayze, Dan, 574, 575, 576
Swedish hospital, 135
swine flu, 98-103

T

Taimur, Said bin, 375
Taiwan, labor in, 112
Tass, 233
Tatum, Jack, 250
taxes, 64, 279
  and charity, 461
  and divorce, 413
  and energy, 347-48
  and illegal immigrants, 112
  and Liechtenstein, 160, 163-64
  and religion, 88, 464, 453
  shelters for, 459-65
  and unreported income, 251-56

Taxpayer Compliance Measurement
  Program (TCMP), 347

Tekben, Erdogan, 422-25
television:
  Johnny Carson, 493-500
  in Soviet Union, 230-33, 261

Templeton, Gary, 426
Tennessee Valley Authority (TVA),
  482-87
Tennessee Water Quality Control,
  485, 486

terrorism, 9
    assassination, 547-51, 566-72
    Cuban group, 471-78
    of mercenaries, 566
    torture, 128, 163-66
Terry, William, 544
Texas Building and Construction
    Trades Council, 605
They Call Me Assassin (Tatum), 250
Thompson, C.T., 286-87
Thompson, Kay, 209
Thorne, David, 30-31, 33
Three Mile Island, 149, 388
Thunderbirds, 295
Tilghman, Bill, 571
Time magazine, 39, 40
Tito, Marshall, 339-43, 361
Tolbert, A.B., 243
Tolbert, Stephanette, 242
Tolbert, William, 240, 241, 242
Toscanini, 318
Toulouse-Lautrec, 49
tourists, rip-offs of, 530
Towers, Bernard, 4, 6
Townley, Michael, 476
Travis, John, 133, 134
Triumph of the Will (Riefenstahl), 431,
    432
Tubman, Shad, 242
Tubman, William, 240
Tweedy, Jim, 75

U

Udall, Mo, 338
Ujiland, 391
unemployment insurance, 95
United Churches of Florida, 454
United Nations:
    and Cuba, 26
    and espionage, 282-84
    and Iran, 362
United States Air Force
    Demonstration Team
    (Thunderbirds), 269
Utah and Mormons, 178-179, 180
Uzi submachine gun, 466

V

Valentine, Wayne, 489,490
Vance, Cyrus, 9, 26, 316, 368
Vanderberg Air Force Base, 616
Van der Kamp, John, 397, 625
Van Hoffman, Nicholas, 520, 521
veterans of Vietnam, 560-65
Veterans Day, 126
Vietnam veterans, 560-65
Volpe, Robert, 52-53
Von Felz-Vein, Edward, 162
Vonnegut, Kurt, 338

W

Waddill, William, 1-6
wages for illegal immigrants, 109-11
Wain, Harold, 209
Waksman, Byron, 198
Walker, Terry, 145
Walker, Wesley, 245
Wallace, Mike, 1-6, 23-24, 47-55,
    66-73, 95-103, 127-31, 137-42,
    165-70, 177, 181-89, 200-204,
    212-18, 234-39, 251, 261,
    263-68, 280-84, 294-95,
    302-308, 318-23, 362-77, 386,
    393-98, 403-11, 419, 434-35,
    451-59, 465-69, 471-78,
    493-500, 505-506, 517-28,
    552-54, 560-65, 584-87,
    593-600, 606-10
Wallenstein, Herbert, 140, 141, 142
Walter Reed Army Hospital, 209
Warren, Earl, 170
Washington-Main Medical Clinic, 68,
    70, 72
Watergate, 166, 383
water quality standards, 485, 486
Watson, Adam, 76
Weaver, Mary, 1-6
Weedman, Charles, 2, 6
Weingarten, Jack, 111
Weizman, Ezer, 302-308, 466-68
Weizman, Shaul, 305
wellness movement, 131-36

West Side Preparatory School,115-21
Whatever Happened to Baby Jane?, 267
Wheat, Richard, 330, 332-33
Whisenant, John, 344
White, Byron, 166
Whitman, Kenneth, 456, 458
Whitmore, Kay, 448
Wicker, Tom, 520
Wilhelm, Bob, 196-97
Wilkenfeld, J., 186, 187
Williams, Clarence, 156, 159
wills and estates, 349-54
Windsor, Duke, 600-605
Winpisinger, William, 56-60
Wolf, Max, 111
Women, The (Luce), 42
women's rights, 129, 177
Woodward, Bob, 165-70
World Baptist Alliance, 241
Worldwide Church of God, 593-600, 620

X

X-rays, 449

Y

Yale Medical School, 132
Yamani, Ahmed Zaki al-, 200-204, 508, 509
Yassini, 438, 439, 440, 436
Yazdi, Ibrahim, 368, 371
Ybarra, Jose, 514
Yeager, Bob, 250
Yockley, Gail, 70
Young, Andrew, 7
Young, Rodger, 126
Youner, Cole, 571
Younger, Irving, 225
Yugoslavia, 339-43, 361

Z

Zagel, James, 254, 255
Zahedi, Ardeshir, 366, 367, 511
Zaire, 612
Zarillo, 156-57
Zinn, Howard, 237
zoning laws, 113
Zorin, Valentin, 232